POLARITY AND
ANALOGY

POLARITY AND ANALOGY

TWO TYPES OF ARGUMENTATION IN

EARLY GREEK THOUGHT

BY

G. E. R. LLOYD

Fellow of King's College, Cambridge

CAMBRIDGE

AT THE UNIVERSITY PRESS

1966

PUBLISHED BY
THE SYNDICS OF THE CAMBRIDGE UNIVERSITY PRESS

Bentley House, 200 Euston Road, London N.W. 1
American Branch: 32 East 57th Street, New York, N.Y. 10022
West African Office: P.M.B. 5181, Ibadan, Nigeria

©

CAMBRIDGE UNIVERSITY PRESS

1966

Printed in Great Britain at the University Printing House, Cambridge
(Brooke Crutchley, University Printer)

LIBRARY OF CONGRESS CATALOGUE
CARD NUMBER: 66–10042

CONTENTS

and began to consider the question of the relation between a theory and the grounds or evidence in its support.

The period of Greek philosophy which we shall be considering is marked by notable advances in both the theory and the practice of logic and scientific method. My main problems concern certain aspects of these developments. The first systematic exposition of a set of rules of argument is found in Aristotle, but a number of questions may be raised concerning the use of argument in earlier Greek writers and the circumstances in which various modes of argument came to be recognised and analysed. Even though modes of argument were not at first identified as such, we may nevertheless consider not only what arguments were commonly used in practice in early Greek literature for the purposes of inference or persuasion, but also how they were used; how far, in particular, is it possible to determine what assumptions were made concerning the cogency of different types of argument in the period before Plato? How far do pre-Platonic thinkers explicitly formulate the principles or assumptions on which their arguments are based? And how far did Plato carry the analysis of different types of argument? If we can detect certain developments in the assessment of certain modes of argument in the period before Aristotle, we may also ask how far these developments influenced the actual arguments which were subsequently used, and whether the analysis of techniques of inference led to any major modification in the methods of argument which the philosophers and others employed.

One topic that invites study is the use and development of modes of argument in the sixth to the fourth century. Another is the related question of the use and development of methods of explanation in the same period. Again it was Aristotle who (in the *Posterior Analytics*) put forward the first fairly complete theory of what may be called 'scientific method', but again certain questions may and should be asked concerning the earlier period. The Presocratic

INTRODUCTION

AIMS AND PROBLEMS

The aims of this study are to describe and analyse two main types of argument and methods of explanation as they are used in early Greek thought from the earliest times down to and including Aristotle, and to consider them, in particular, in relation to the larger problem of the development of logic and scientific method in this period. First I should say why the subject and the period I have chosen seem to me important. It is arguable that natural science, cosmology and formal logic all originate (so far as the West is concerned) in Greek philosophy. But while it is convenient and quite justified to see these disciplines as having a definite historical beginning, in each case the influence of previous thought on those who were primarily responsible for initiating the new inquiry raises an intricate issue. The Presocratic philosophers may be credited with the first systematic attempts to give rational accounts of natural phenomena and of the universe as a whole. But both their scientific and their cosmological theories undoubtedly owe a certain debt to the common stock of pre-philosophical Greek beliefs. Aristotle is generally held to be the founder of formal logic as we know it, and this is evidently true in that it was Aristotle who introduced the use of symbols into logic, for example.[1] But before Aristotle the dialogues of Plato deal with many problems which may reasonably be considered problems of logic, particularly in connection with the method of Dialectic. And we can trace a certain awareness of some logical and methodological issues earlier still, for it was in the pre-Platonic period that philosophers and scientists first debated the respective merits of 'reason' and 'sensation' as sources of knowledge, for example,

---

[1] See, for example, Cornford, 5, p. 264. Aristotle himself claimed originality for his work in logic at *SE* 183b 34 ff.

philosophers and the medical theorists in the Hippocratic Corpus attempt to elucidate a wide variety of natural phenomena. How far is it possible to decide, either from their actual theories and explanations, or from their explicit pronouncements on method, where these exist, what they expected of an 'account' of a natural phenomenon? As in the study of the development of modes of argument, three types of problem present themselves, first to identify the modes of explanation which were most commonly used in practice, second to trace the development of ideas on methodological problems, and third to analyse the interaction between theory and practice (where one may consider how far the ideas expressed by different Greek philosophers and scientists on the subject of method influenced either the types of theories they proposed or the way in which they attempted to establish them).

The immediate purpose of this inquiry is to elucidate the use and development of certain modes of argument and methods of explanation, but I hope thereby to throw some light also on some of the broader issues of the place of informal logic in early Greek thought before the invention or discovery of formal logic. Indeed the broader issues raised by the problem of the nature of 'archaic logic' can, perhaps, only be discussed in terms of such concrete topics as the use of certain types of argument. In a series of works beginning with *Les Fonctions mentales dans les sociétés inférieures* (1910)[1] Lévy-Bruhl developed the hypothesis of a 'pre-logical' mentality, a mentality which is ignorant of the law of contradiction and which is 'utterly mystical', and as this hypothesis had a profound influence on at least one generation of historians of early Greek philosophy, some comments should be made on it here. Cornford, for example, was much influenced by

---

[1] See also *La Mentalité primitive* (1922) and *L'Ame primitive* (1927). One typical passage may be cited from *La Mentalité primitive* (trans. L. A. Clare, 1923, p. 438): the primitive 'will always seek the true cause [i.e. of 'natural phenomena'] in the world of unseen powers, above and beyond what we call Nature, in the "metaphysical" realm, using the word in its literal sense'.

Lévy-Bruhl's theory in *From Religion to Philosophy* (1912), and Brunschvicg,[1] Reymond,[2] Rey,[3] and Schuhl,[4] in turn, provide ample evidence of the stimulus which Lévy-Bruhl's ideas had on classical scholars interested in the problems of the development of logic and science in ancient Greece, even when they challenged certain features of his interpretation. More recently, Snell, in his influential book *Die Entdeckung des Geistes*,[5] still attempted to distinguish between 'mythical' and 'logical' thought, using these two terms because (as he put it) 'they effectively describe two stages of human thought'.[6] The influence which Lévy-Bruhl's hypothesis had is all the more remarkable considering the criticisms to which it was subjected from various quarters. Already in 1912 Durkheim contested the postulate of a 'pre-logical' mentality: 'Ainsi, entre la logique de la pensée religieuse et la logique de la pensée scientifique il n'y a pas un abîme. L'une et l'autre sont faites des mêmes éléments essentiels, mais inégalement et différemment développés. Ce qui paraît surtout caractériser la première, c'est un goût naturel aussi bien pour les confusions intempérantes que pour les contrastes heurtés.... Elle ne connaît pas la mesure et les nuances, elle recherche les extrêmes; elle emploie, par suite,

---

[1] *L'Expérience humaine et la causalité physique* (1st ed., 1922; 3rd ed. Paris, 1949), especially Book 4, chs. 9 and 10.

[2] *Histoire des sciences exactes et naturelles dans l'antiquité gréco-romaine* (1st ed., 1924; 2nd ed., Paris, 1955), pp. 116 ff.

[3] *La Science dans l'antiquité*, vols. 1 and 2 (Paris, 1930, 1933), e.g. vol. 1, pp. 434 ff.

[4] *Essai sur la formation de la pensée grecque* (1st ed., Paris, 1934). In the 2nd edition, 1949, p. xiv and n. 4, Schuhl lists a number of other classical scholars who were influenced by Lévy-Bruhl and also notes that Lévy-Bruhl himself modified his thesis in the *Carnets* (see below, p. 5).

[5] 2nd ed., Hamburg, 1948, trans. T. G. Rosenmeyer, *The Discovery of the Mind* (Oxford, 1953), pp. 223 ff.

[6] Snell went on to note that these two stages or types of human thought do not exclude one another completely, but he then described the difference between them, as he conceived it, in the following vague and seemingly confusing terms (*3*, p. 224): 'Mythical thought requires receptivity; logic cannot exist without activity. Logic does not materialize until man has become cognizant of the energy within him, and the individuality of his mind. Logical thought is unimpaired wakefulness; mythical thinking borders upon the dream, in which images and ideas float by without being controlled by the will.'

les mécanismes logiques avec une sorte de gaucherie, mais elle n'en ignore aucun.'[1] Moreover Lévy-Bruhl himself radically modified his position in his later writings. In a letter to Professor Evans-Pritchard (written in 1934 and published in the *British Journal of Sociology* in 1952) he granted that the term 'pre-logical' was 'rather unfortunate', while in the *Carnets* (no. III, dated 1938, published in 1947 in *Revue philosophique*) we find the following note (p. 258): 'En ce qui concerne le caractère "prélogique" de la mentalité primitive, j'avais déjà mis beaucoup d'eau dans mon vin depuis 25 ans; les résultats auxquels je viens de parvenir touchant ces faits [i.e. beliefs reported from certain African societies] rendent cette évolution définitive, en me faisant abandonner une hypothèse mal fondée, en tout cas, dans les cas de ce genre.'

The hypothesis of a 'pre-logical' mentality has long been discredited,[2] and it was eventually abandoned by its author himself. But some, at least, of the difficulties which that hypothesis was invented to solve remain real difficulties. No doubt it would be unwise to compare the problems facing the student of early Greek thought with those facing the anthropologist too closely[3] (and the methods of the two disciplines

---

[1] *Les Formes élémentaires de la vie religieuse* (Paris, 1912), p. 342.

[2] Writing in 1954, G. Lienhardt, for example, began a discussion of primitive modes of thought with the warning that 'none of us who study savage societies would say, today, that there are modes of thought which are confined to primitive peoples' (in *The Institutions of Primitive Society*, ed. E. E. Evans-Pritchard, Oxford, 1954, p. 95). The most recent full-length study of primitive thought is C. Lévi-Strauss's *La Pensée sauvage* (Paris, 1962), in which Lévi-Strauss shows with a great wealth of documentation how, for example, the members of primitive societies often observe and classify natural species with extraordinary accuracy and minute attention to detail.

[3] The cautious judgements of, among others, Schuhl (pp. 5 ff.) and Guthrie (*4*, pp. 18 ff.) on the subject of the use of comparative anthropology, provide an important corrective to the tendency to assume that material collected by the anthropologists necessarily affords the key to the understanding of ancient Greek beliefs. Yet in two contexts, in particular, it may prove very useful to consult such material: first, for a negative purpose, to counter a suggestion that some Greek belief is simply the result of a hypothetical 'universal tendency of human thought'; and secondly, with a positive aim, to suggest possible lines of inquiry which we may follow in our attempts to elucidate what at first sight may seem incomprehensible beliefs or practices.

differ profoundly since the evidence for ancient Greek thought is almost entirely literary). But dissatisfaction with Lévy-Bruhl's concept of a 'pre-logical' mentality may prompt both the anthropologist and the classical scholar to attempt to give a more adequate account of the informal logic implicit in primitive or archaic thought. Indeed the evidence of early Greek literature, limited though this is, is especially interesting and valuable since it enables us to study not only the nature of the logical principles implicit in archaic beliefs, but also the development of logic itself and the gradual recognition and analysis of those principles. In particular, the evidence for ancient Greek thought in the period down to Aristotle provides us with a unique opportunity to consider how far the invention or discovery of formal logic merely rendered explicit certain rules of argument which were implicitly observed by earlier writers, or to what extent the analysis of various modes of argument involved the modification and correction of earlier assumptions.

METHOD AND EVIDENCE

The broad field of this inquiry is the modes of argument and forms of explanation of early Greek thought down to Aristotle, but the method of approach to this subject which I have adopted should be defined, and some remarks should be made on the nature of the evidence on which this study is based. First on the question of method. In dealing with the types of argument and explanation in early Greek thought two main methods seem to be possible, which might be called for want of better terms the analytic and the synthetic. The first would attempt a full description of the relevant texts, reaching general conclusions only at the end of an exhaustive survey of the evidence: this has the advantage of completeness. The second method would offer preliminary generalisations as working hypotheses, as it were, which may, and indeed probably will, require modification in the light of the particular evidence: this has the advantage of clarity. As my main purpose is to reveal and examine the principal, but not necessarily the only, types of argumentation in early Greek thought, I have preferred the second method. I have, accordingly, chosen to deal with what I have called Polarity and Analogy (though some, at least, of the gaps left after the discussion of these two will be filled in a concluding chapter). Few of those who study early Greek thought can fail to be struck by the recurrent appeal to *pairs of opposites* of various sorts both in general cosmological doctrines and in accounts of particular natural phenomena. The common use of *analogies* in similar contexts is less strange, perhaps, though still, in certain respects, quite remarkable. A considerable part of what follows will, then, be taken up by an analysis of the way in which these two admittedly very general schemata were used in early Greek speculative thought. Some of the theories and explanations in question strike us as either obscure or obviously inadequate or both, and in some cases, where the theory on a particular problem appears to bear no relation whatsoever to any empirical data, we may wonder why it was put forward at all. This will lead us, then, to consider what may be said on the general problem of what the Presocratic philosophers or later writers may have expected of an 'account' of a natural phenomenon, or what their criteria for a good theory or explanation were. How far do any early Greek theorists appear to have recognised the desirability of checking and corroborating their accounts by empirical methods, and how far, indeed, was the verification or falsification of their theories possible, in different fields, with the means of investigation which were at their disposal?

A large number of the theories and explanations which were put forward in early Greek speculative thought may be said to belong to one or other of two simple logical types: the characteristic of the first type is that objects are classified or explained by being related to one or other of a pair of opposite principles, that of the second type that a thing is explained by being likened or assimilated to something else. But apart from the occasions when an assumed opposition or similarity between things was made the basis of theories or explanations (in which the aim of the writer is to account for certain phenomena), we may also consider how the relationships of opposition and similarity were used in explicit arguments, where the writer's purpose was to demonstrate, or to gain assent to, certain conclusions. Both in pre-Platonic texts and in the dialogues of Plato himself we find many arguments in which pairs of opposites of quite different sorts (e.g. being and not-being, one and many, great and small, like and unlike) appear to be treated as mutually exclusive and exhaustive alternatives in whatever sense or in whatever relation they are used. And quite often, too, it seems to have been assumed that when two cases are known to be similar in certain respects, it necessarily follows that what holds true for one holds true also for the other. It may be suggested that in their theories and explanations of natural phenomena early Greek writers sometimes tended to ignore lesser degrees of similarity and difference in stressing the complete correspondences, or the absolute oppositions, between things. But the explicit arguments of the pre-Platonic period provide further and more definite evidence of a certain failure to distinguish sufficiently between 'similarity' and 'identity', or between those modes of opposites that form mutually exclusive and exhaustive alternatives, and those that do not. This will lead us, then, to discuss how the assumptions underlying the use of certain types of argument were revealed and clarified in the fourth century B.C. In particular, we must consider the steps which led to the formulation of the principle of contradiction and the law of excluded middle, to the analysis of analogical argument, and to the recognition and definition of various degrees of similarity and difference. And finally we must ask, in each case, whether an increasing awareness of the complexity of these relationships led to any major change in the way in which they were actually used in argumentation.

8

The evidence to be used in this study is, quite simply, the sum of Greek literature from the period from Homer to Aristotle as it has come down to us, combined with the extant reports of later writers concerning the doctrines of early Greek philosophers and scientists. A caution should be entered here concerning the nature of *all* this evidence. The results obtained from this, as from many other inquiries into early Greek thought, are necessarily based on only a small proportion of the evidence that we should ideally have liked to have. In the absence of the major part of the works of many important philosophers, not to speak of those of many medical theorists and other writers, there is an obvious temptation to oversimplify, to fit the data that are available into clear patterns that may, perhaps, be quite inappropriate. In the present study, where I have often attempted to generalise concerning methods of explanation and modes of argument in early Greek speculative thought, the lack of adequate first-hand evidence for the early Pythagoreans and for the Atomists has been a particular handicap. Once we have expressed these cautions, however, we must go ahead and make the best and fullest use of the evidence that we have. This presents two particular difficulties, those of authenticity and date. As a general rule I have not commented on evidence of which the authenticity is in serious doubt, wherever alternative sources of information are available. Sometimes, however, we have no such alternative sources, and on such occasions it has been necessary to discuss the reliability of the evidence I have used in some detail.[1] As regards the problem of date, the Hippocratic Corpus presents special difficulties which are all the more regrettable since this collection of works deals not merely with strictly medical questions, but with problems ranging over the whole field of biology, and it contains some of our most valuable

---

[1] An excellent general assessment of the doxographical sources for Presocratic philosophy is readily available in Kirk and Raven, *The Presocratic Philosophers* (Cambridge, 1957), pp. 1–7.

evidence for early Greek science. Few of these treatises can be dated absolutely with any degree of precision, and on several the conjectures which have been offered by different scholars have spread over more than a hundred years.[1] Moreover, many of the treatises are composite productions, made up of several independent pieces which are sometimes, it would seem, the work of different hands, and this, of course, makes the problem of dating even more acute. Yet there is fairly general agreement that with few exceptions the extant Hippocratic treatises date from some time between the middle of the fifth and the end of the fourth century B.C., and while I have as a general rule avoided basing any interpretation of developments in Greek scientific thought on conjectures concerning either the absolute or the relative date of these works, I have excluded from this study only those treatises which are indubitably post-Aristotelian productions.[2]

DEBT TO EARLIER WORK

So far as I am aware, this is the first attempt to undertake a general analysis of the types of argument and methods of explanation of Greek thought in the period down to Aristotle, and in particular of the use and development of what I have called Polarity and Analogy. Yet many aspects of the problems which I consider have, of course, been discussed by

---

[1] The most recent general discussion of the date of the Hippocratic treatises is that of L. Bourgey, *1*, pp. 27 ff., but see also, especially, L. Edelstein, *1*, ch. 4, pp. 152 ff. and K. Deichgräber, *1*, pp. 169 ff.

[2] The most important of these treatises are *Precepts*, *Decorum* and *Law*. It should, perhaps, be noted that the main argument that Littré used (*1*, pp. 218 ff., 382 ff.) to date such treatises as *On the Heart*, *On Fleshes* and *On Nutrition* 'not before Aristotle and Praxagoras' is invalid. Littré argued that Aristotle was the first to hold that the heart is the source of the veins (though he noted that the generalisation that all previous writers regarded the head as the starting-point of the veins (*HA* 513a 10 ff.) is inconsistent with the account which Aristotle himself has just given of the theory of Diogenes of Apollonia), and that treatises that contain this view must therefore be posterior to Aristotle's work. Yet quite apart from the doubtful assumption that Aristotle's knowledge of the medical theories of his predecessors was exhaustive, it is quite certain that he was not the first to suggest that the heart is the origin of the veins as this view occurs unmistakably in the *Timaeus* of Plato (70ab).

scholars whether in relation to individual thinkers or to groups of thinkers. I may refer especially to Diller's article entitled 'ὄψις ἀδήλων τὰ φαινόμενα' (*Hermes*, LXVII, 1932, pp. 14–42), to Snell's *The Discovery of the Mind*, to the work of Senn,[1] Regenbogen,[2] Heidel,[3] Bourgey,[4] and Kühn,[5] on the Hippocratic writers, to that of Ranulf,[6] Goldschmidt,[7] and Robinson,[8] among many others, on Plato's arguments and dialectical method, and to the books of Le Blond[9] and Bourgey,[10] on the theory and practice of logic and scientific method in Aristotle. These are some of the works to which my debt is especially great. But in a study that ranges over the whole field of Greek speculative thought from Thales to Aristotle, I am necessarily indebted to innumerable other scholars as well. Yet only the most essential bibliographical references are included in my text. The separate bibliography at the end of the book is more complete, listing the more important works I have consulted, but it is still far from being exhaustive. But if some of my debts must go unacknowledged, I am none the less conscious of those I owe to scholars both in the field of classical studies and in other disciplines. Finally, I should record my very deep sense of personal gratitude for all the help and encouragement I have received from my teachers and colleagues in Cambridge, and especially to Mr G. S. Kirk, to Mr J. E. Raven, and to Mr F. H. Sandbach, each of whom has given me invaluable advice both general and specific on my work at various stages.

[1] 'Über Herkunft und Stil der Beschreibungen von Experimenten im Corpus Hippocraticum', *Archiv f. Gesch. der Medizin*, XXII (1929), pp. 217–89.
[2] *Eine Forschungsmethode antiker Naturwissenschaft*, Quell. und Stud. zur Gesch. der Mathematik, Astronomie und Physik, Abt. B, 1, 2 (1930–1), pp. 131–82.
[3] *Hippocratic Medicine: its spirit and method* (New York, 1941).
[4] *Observation et expérience chez les médecins de la collection hippocratique* (Paris, 1953).
[5] *System- und Methodenprobleme im Corpus Hippocraticum*, Hermes Einzelschriften, 11 (1956).
[6] *Der eleatische Satz vom Widerspruch* (Copenhagen, 1924).
[7] *Le Paradigme dans la dialectique platonicienne* (Paris, 1947).
[8] *Plato's Earlier Dialectic* (2nd ed., Oxford, 1953).
[9] *Logique et méthode chez Aristote* (Paris, 1939).
[10] *Observation et expérience chez Aristote* (Paris, 1955).

INTRODUCTION

EXPLANATION OF TERMS

A brief note of explanation is necessary on some of the terms which I use. As is well known, the translation of certain key Greek terms into English presents certain problems. There is no single English equivalent for the Greek τέχνη, for example, which covers not only what we should call arts, but also crafts and skills, indeed any rational activity of any kind. I have attempted to choose the least inappropriate English term wherever I translate τέχνη or refer to the general field it covers, but where, as often, any English expression tends to be too specific, I put 'arts' or 'skills' in inverted commas, a practice for which I hope I may claim indulgence. Again the terms the Greeks used to refer to various branches of philosophy and natural science often cover slightly different areas from those of their nearest English equivalents. First, it should be remembered that down to the mid-fifth century, at least, 'no line is yet drawn between philosophy, theology, cosmogony and cosmology, astronomy, mathematics, biology and natural science in general'.[1] I use the old-fashioned term 'natural philosophy' to refer to what the Greeks themselves called 'the inquiry about nature' (περὶ φύσεως ἱστορία).[2] As for the main divisions of 'natural philosophy', I should explain that I use the term 'cosmology' of doctrines which refer to the universe as a whole, its origins or the principles of its constitution, while I classify theories which deal with particular natural phenomena very approximately according to the branch of natural science which deals with equivalent subject-matter today: thus I refer to theories dealing with the functions or phenomena of living things as 'physiological' doctrines. However, I retain the term 'meteorology' (in inverted commas) as the equivalent of the

---

[1] Guthrie, *HGP*, ɪ, p. x.
[2] E.g. Plato, *Phaedo* 96a; cf. *On Ancient Medicine*, ch. 20, *CMG* ɪ, ɪ 51 10 f. where the term φιλοσοφίη is explained with the comment καθάπερ Ἐμπεδοκλέης ἢ ἄλλοι οἳ περὶ φύσιος γεγράφασιν. Aristotle, in turn, frequently refers to the Presocratic philosophers as φυσιολόγοι.

Greek μετεωρολογία, which covers not only what is now known as meteorology, but also what is now known as geology (its nearest modern equivalent would be 'geophysics' taken in the largest sense).[1]

TEXTS AND ABBREVIATIONS

Except where otherwise stated, the fragments of the Presocratic philosophers are quoted according to the edition of Diels, revised by Kranz, *Die Fragmente der Vorsokratiker* (6th ed., 1951–2) (referred to as DK), the works of Plato according to Burnet's Oxford text, the treatises of Aristotle according to Bekker's Berlin edition (1831) and the fragments of Aristotle according to the 1886 Leipzig edition of V. Rose. For the Hippocratic treatises I have used Heiberg's edition (*Corpus Medicorum Graecorum*, vol. I, 1 (Leipzig, 1927), referred to as *CMG* I, 1) for those works that he edits, and in default of him, the edition of E. Littré (10 vols., Paris, 1839–61, referred to with the initial L followed by the number of the volume in Roman numerals). I have also used the *Corpus Medicorum Graecorum* edition of later Greek medical writers (Galen, Oribasius), though for those treatises of Galen not yet edited in *CMG* I have referred to the edition of C. G. Kühn (Leipzig, 1821–33). I cite the text of Anonymus Londinensis given by Diels (Supplementum Aristotelicum, III, 1, Berlin, 1893). For the poems of Sappho and Alcaeus I have used the edition of Lobel and Page (*Poetarum Lesbiorum Fragmenta*, Oxford, 1955, referred to as LP), for those of the melic poets, Page's *Poetae Melici Graeci* (Oxford, 1962, referred to as P). Otherwise early Greek lyric poetry is cited according to the third edition of Diehl (vols. 1–3, Leipzig, 1949–52, referred to as D), though for more important texts I also give the reference in the 4th edition of Bergk (Leipzig, 1878–82, referred to as B).

The abbreviations for the Hippocratic treatises, the dia-

---

[1] The scope of μετεωρολογία is defined by Aristotle at *Mete.* 338a 26 ff.: among the phenomena with which it deals are comets, shooting-stars, winds, thunderbolts and earthquakes.

logues of Plato and the treatises of Aristotle are those in Liddell and Scott (9th edition revised by Jones, 1940, itself referred to as LSJ). Thus *On Ancient Medicine* appears as *VM*, Plato's *Symposium* as *Smp.*, Aristotle's *Physics* as *Ph.*, etc. And on other occasions, too, I have used the abbreviations of LSJ where these leave no room for confusion. Full particulars of the books and articles to which I refer will be found in the bibliography. In the text I refer to these works by the name of the author (with initials in cases of doubt) followed, where necessary, by a number in italics corresponding to the number indicated for each work in the bibliography. Thus Cornford, *1*, p. 165 refers to F. M. Cornford, *From Religion to Philosophy* (London, 1912), p. 165. Two exceptions have been made to this rule. I refer to G. S. Kirk and J. E. Raven, *The Presocratic Philosophers* (Cambridge, 1957), as KR, and to W. K. C. Guthrie, *A History of Greek Philosophy*, 1 (Cambridge, 1962), as *HGP*, 1.

PART ONE: POLARITY

CHAPTER I

THEORIES BASED ON OPPOSITES IN EARLY GREEK THOUGHT

PRELIMINARY SURVEY OF SPECULATIVE THEORIES BASED ON OPPOSITES

The frequency, variety and range of theories based on different sorts of opposites are well known to every student of Greek philosophy. Aristotle, indeed, asserted on several occasions that *all* his predecessors adopted opposites as principles. At *Ph.* A 5 188b 27 ff., for example,[1] he says 'πάντες γὰρ τὰ στοιχεῖα καὶ τὰς ὑπ' αὐτῶν καλουμένας ἀρχάς, καίπερ ἄνευ λόγου τιθέντες, ὅμως τἀναντία λέγουσιν, ὥσπερ ὑπ' αὐτῆς τῆς ἀληθείας ἀναγκασθέντες'.[2] Now Aristotle has often been criticised for distorting his predecessors' theories by interpreting them in the light of his own philosophical doctrines, and the judgement I have quoted might seem to be a particularly glaring example of this tendency, since the hot, the cold, the wet and the dry form the basis of Aristotle's own physical theory, and more generally he refers to Form and Privation as opposite principles. Yet Aristotle was well aware of the *variety* of opposites which earlier philosophers had used in their theories, and while his statement at *Ph.* 188b 27 ff. certainly needs qualifying, there is a large body of evidence in the fragments of the Presocratic philosophers themselves which tends to bear it out, at least as a broad generalisation.

The major Presocratic cosmological theories based on

[1] See also *Ph.* 188a 19 ff.; *Metaph.* 1004b 29 ff., 1075a 28, 1087a 29 f.

[2] 'For they all identify the elements, and what they call the principles, with the contraries, although they give no reasons for doing so, but are, as it were, compelled by the truth itself.'

opposites may be summarised quite briefly. The general doctrine that 'most human things go in pairs' (δύο τὰ πολλὰ τῶν ἀνθρωπίνων) is attributed by Aristotle to Alcmaeon, whose theory he compares with the Table of Opposites of the Pythagoreans (Aristotle does not claim to know with whom the theory originated). One group of Pythagoreans apparently referred to ten definite pairs of opposite principles: limit and unlimited, odd and even, one and plurality, right and left, male and female, at rest and moving, straight and curved, light and darkness, good and evil, square and oblong (*Metaph.* A 5 986a 22 ff.). Alcmaeon's theory, on the other hand, was less definite, referring to 'any chance contrarieties', such as 'white and black, sweet and bitter, good and bad, great and small' (*Metaph.* 986a 31 ff.). Opposites are, or are among, the principles or elements on which the cosmological theories of other Presocratic philosophers are based. The one surviving fragment of Anaximander refers to the continuous interaction of opposed factors of some sort ('for they pay the penalty and recompense to one another for their injustice according to the assessment of time') and in his theory of the formation of the world from the Boundless the first things that appear seem to have been a pair of opposed substances, whether 'the hot' and 'the cold' or 'flame' and 'air' or 'mist'.[1] Parmenides' cosmogony in the *Way of Seeming* begins with the two substances *Fire*, or *Light*, and *Night*, which are equal (Fr. 9 4) and opposite (τἀντία Fr. 8 55 and 59). In Empedocles' system, *Love* and *Strife* are opposites, bringing about opposite effects on the four 'roots', earth, air, fire and water (e.g. Fr. 26 5 ff.). Anaxagoras describes in Fr. 4 an original mixture of all things which contains pairs of opposites (e.g. the *wet* and the *dry*, the *hot* and the *cold*, the *bright* and the *dark*) among other things (e.g. earth). These are the best and clearest examples of the

[1] Ps.-Plutarch, *Strom.* 2 (DK 12 A 10), on which see, for example, Hölscher, pp. 265 ff., KR, pp. 131 ff., Kahn, pp. 85 ff., 119 ff., and *HGP*, I, pp. 89 ff. I have discussed the evidence for Anaximander's use of opposites at some length elsewhere (*JHS*, LXXXIV, 1964, pp. 94 ff.).

use of opposites, though our secondary sources refer to other pairs, notably 'the *rare*' and 'the *dense*', in interpreting the cosmological doctrines of other philosophers.[1] Again while Heraclitus' theory was exceptional in that he particularly emphasised the interdependence or 'unity' of opposites, it was typical in so far as he too analysed the data of experience generally into pairs of opposites (such as hot and cold).

Many of the detailed theories which the Presocratic philosophers put forward relating to physical, physiological or psychological phenomena were also based on opposites. We find some remarkable examples among the theories which were offered to account for the differentiation of the sexes.[2] Parmenides probably held that the sex of the child is determined by its place on the *right* or *left* of the mother's womb (right for males, left for females).[3] Empedocles seems to have held that the determining factor is the temperature of the womb when the embryo is conceived (males being formed when the womb is *hotter*, females when it is *colder*).[4] Anaxagoras made a third suggestion, that the determining factor is the side from which the seed of the male parent is secreted (right for male children, left for females, again).[5] On other problems, too, the Presocratics often proposed solutions based on an appeal to a distinction between opposites. In psychology, Heraclitus, for example, attributed various states of the

[1] See in general Aristotle, *Ph.* 188a 22 and *Metaph.* 985b 10 ff., and on Anaximenes in particular, Simplicius, *in Ph.* 24 26 ff. and 149 28 ff. (DK 13 A 5).

[2] On the history of the theories put forward on this subject in antiquity the monograph of E. Lesky should be consulted.

[3] Parmenides Fr. 17 is quoted and explained in this sense by Galen, *in Epid.* vi 48; *CMG* v 10,2,2 119 12 ff.

[4] See Frr. 65 and 67. These are, however, somewhat ambiguous. Galen (*in Epid.* vi 48; *CMG* v 10,2,2 119 16 ff.) took it that Empedocles was referring simply to a difference between hot and cold parts of the womb, not to variations in the temperature of the womb as a whole over the monthly cycle. Contrast Aristotle, *GA* 764a 1 ff.

[5] See Aristotle, *GA* 763b 30 ff. (DK 59 A 107) and cf. Hippolytus *Haer.* 1 8 12 (DK A 42). Aristotle also mentions Democritus' theory, that the sex of the embryo is determined by whichever of the two parents' seed is dominant (*GA* 764a 6 ff.): and a number of similar theories, based on differences between 'strong' and 'weak' or 'male' and 'female' seed, appear in the Hippocratic Corpus, e.g. *Genit.* ch. 6 (L vii 478 1 ff.), *Vict.* i, chs. 28 f. (L vi 500 23 ff.).

'soul', e.g. waking and sleeping, and even wisdom, and drunkenness, to differences in its *wetness* and *dryness*.[1] And in biology, Empedocles apparently explained how animals came to live in the sea by postulating a difference in temperature between water-animals and land-animals: according to this theory, water-animals had originally lived on land, but they had moved to the sea in order to counteract the excessive *heat* of their constitutions.[2]

Although pairs of opposites are by no means the only elements or principles which we find used by the Presocratic philosophers, and although they appear in very different roles in different types of theory,[3] most major philosophers from Anaximander down to, and perhaps including, the Atomists may be said to have referred to opposites in one context or another in their general cosmological doctrines or in their explanations of particular natural phenomena. In many respects the Atomists' theory is exceptional: the atoms differ from each other in shape, arrangement or position alone (Aristotle, *Metaph.* 985b 13 ff.): such opposites as sweet and bitter are not 'real', but exist 'by convention' νόμῳ only (e.g. Fr. 125). Yet it might be suggested (and Aristotle did suggest) that the Atomists too used an opposition of a sort, namely that between the atoms and the void, which Aristotle interpreted as 'the full and the empty' (*Metaph.* 985b 4 ff.), although it should be pointed out that these opposites are unlike any others with which we have been dealing so far, in being a heterogeneous, not a homogeneous, pair. Even the Eleatics, with the possible exception of Zeno for whom we

---

[1] Sleep, waking and death are connected with the fieriness or wateriness of the soul (Frr. 26 and 36 and Sextus, *M.* vii 129 f., DK 22 A 16, on which see KR, pp. 207 ff.). In Fr. 118 'a dry soul' is said to be 'wisest and best', and in Fr. 117 drunkenness is associated with the soul being 'wet'.

[2] Aristotle, *Resp.* 477a 32–b 9 (partly quoted in DK 31 A 73).

[3] Thus in monistic theories opposites were sometimes used to account for the generation of the manifold world from an original undifferentiated unity: see, for example, Diogenes of Apollonia Fr. 5: 'For (air) is multiform, being both hotter and colder and drier and wetter and more stationary and more quickly mobile, and many other differentiations are in it, of taste and colour, an infinite number.'

have comparatively little evidence, still analysed the data of experience into opposites although they denied the existence of change and plurality. As we saw, Parmenides' cosmogony in the *Way of Seeming* starts by postulating a pair of opposite primary substances, Light and Night, and Melissus, too, analysed the apparent changes in the physical world partly in terms of opposites: δοκεῖ δὲ ἡμῖν τό τε θερμὸν ψυχρὸν γίνεσθαι καὶ τὸ ψυχρὸν θερμὸν καὶ τὸ σκληρὸν μαλθακὸν καὶ τὸ μαλθακὸν σκληρόν[1] (Fr. 8).

It was not only the Presocratic philosophers who made extensive use of pairs of opposites in their theories and explanations. The Hippocratic treatises of the late fifth or fourth centuries provide many further examples of theories which have a similar general form. *On the Nature of Man*, for instance, puts forward a cosmological theory based on the *hot*, the *cold*, the *wet* and the *dry*. The writer asserts that generation can only take place when these opposites are correctly balanced, and that, on death, each of the four opposites in the body returns to its like, 'the wet to the wet, the dry to the dry' and so on (ch. 3, L vi 36 17 ff.). *On Regimen* i is one of a number of other works which propose theories about the elements of which our bodies are composed.[2] This writer says

---

[1] 'For the hot appears to us to become cold, and the cold hot, and the hard soft, and the soft hard.'

[2] Cf. also *Carn.* ch. 2; L viii 584 9 ff. Here there are four elements, of which the most important is the hot 'aither'. Of the other three, earth is cold and dry, 'air' is hot and 'wet', and the part which 'is nearest the earth' is 'wettest and densest'. (As Heidel, *6*, p. 19, n. 6, for one, has observed, this schema resembles Aristotle's theory, in *GC* 330 b 3 ff.: yet the agreements between the two are not, in my view, such that we should conclude that the author of *Carn.* is copying Aristotle.) It should also be noted that in the account of Greek medicine preserved in Anonymus Londinensis (which derives in part, at least, from the *Iatrica*, or medical history, of Menon, the pupil of Aristotle) doctrines of opposite elements in the body are ascribed to several medical theorists of the late fifth or the fourth century. See especially the accounts of Philolaus (xviii 8 ff.: our bodies consist originally, i.e. as embryos, of the hot, though on birth we inhale the outside air, which is cold), Petron of Aegina (xx 1 ff.: there are two main elements, the hot with which the dry is associated, and the cold with which the wet is associated) and Philistion (xx 25 ff.: there are four elements, but these have opposite 'powers', fire being hot, air cold, water wet and earth dry).

POLARITY

that all living things are made of *Fire* and *Water*, the former
hot and dry (although 'there is moisture in Fire'), the latter
cold and wet (but 'there is dryness in Water').[1] Even in
On Ancient Medicine, a treatise which attacks the use of
theories based on the hot, the cold, the wet and the dry in
medicine, the body is held to consist of many component
kinds, among which the writer includes such pairs of opposites
as the *sweet* and the *bitter*, the *astringent* (στρυφνόν) and the
insipid (πλαδαρόν) (ch. 14, *CMG* I, I 45 26 ff.).

It was a commonplace of Greek medical theory that health
consists in the balance of certain opposed factors in the body.
Some such doctrine seems to have been held by Alcmaeon, for
Aetius (v 30 1; DK 24 B 4) reports that he held that health
lies in the ἰσονομία or 'equal rights' of certain 'powers' in the
body and that disease arises from the μοναρχία or 'supreme
rule' of one of them: as examples of what he calls the 'powers',
Aetius mentions wet, dry, cold, hot, bitter and sweet. Similar
doctrines of health and disease appear frequently in the
Hippocratic Corpus, as, for example, in *On Ancient Medicine*
(ch. 14, *CMG* I, I 46 I ff.) and *On the Nature of Man* (ch. 4, L
VI 40 2 ff.). Specific diseases are often attributed to the effect
of one of the opposites, such as hot, cold, wet, dry and so on,
as when in *On Diseases* I the condition which the writer
describes as erysipelas in the lung is said to be caused by
dryness (ch. 18, L VI 172 I ff.). One type of general pathological theory is found in *On Affections*: 'in men, all diseases
are caused by bile and phlegm. Bile and phlegm give rise to
diseases when they become too dry or too wet or too hot or
too cold in the body' (ch. 1, L VI 208 7 ff.). Another appears
in *On the Places in Man*: 'pain is caused both by the cold and
by the hot, and both by what is in excess and by what is in
default' (ch. 42, L VI 334 I ff.).[2] The notion that diseases are
caused by states of *repletion* and *depletion* (πλήρωσις and

---

[1] *Vict.* I chs. 3 and 4, L VI 472 12 ff., and 474 8 ff.
[2] Cf. also, for example, *Nat. Hom.* ch. 2, L VI 36 I ff.; *Morb. Sacr.* ch. 14, L VI
388 3 ff. and *Morb.* I ch. 2, L VI 142 15 ff., 19 f.

κένωσις) occurs in several treatises among which is *On Ancient Medicine*,[1] a work which is outspoken in its criticisms of pathological theories based on the hot, the cold, the wet and the dry.

The converse of the theory that disease is caused by one of a pair of opposites is that cures may be effected by counter-balancing the opposites, and this doctrine, too, is extremely widespread in the Hippocratic writers. The principle behind this type of theory is expressed quite clearly at one point in *On Ancient Medicine*: 'for if that which causes a man pain is something hot, or cold, or dry, or wet, then he who would carry out the cure correctly must counteract cold with hot, hot with cold, wet with dry and dry with wet'.[2] *On Breaths* is one of a number of treatises which state the doctrine generally: 'again, depletion cures repletion, and repletion depletion.... *And, in a word, opposites are cures for opposites.*'[3] In conjunction with this type of theory we find many rather crude or over-simplified accounts of the effects of certain treatments. The effects of different foods, for example, are often analysed in terms of simple opposites. 'Pure honey is hot and dry', announces the author of *On Regimen* II (ch. 53, L VI 556 13) and according to *On Affections* (ch. 51, L VI 260 15 f.) 'warm bread and hot meats dry the body when taken on their own'. Similar examples could be multiplied almost indefinitely.[4] But it should be pointed out that the doctrine of seeking a balance between opposites led to many sensible and moderate recommendations as well as to dogmatic pronouncements of the type I have quoted. *On Regimen in Health*, for example, is

---

[1] *VM* chs. 9 and 10; *CMG* I, I 41 17 ff., 42 11 ff. Cf. *Nat. Hom.* ch. 9, L VI 52 4 ff.; *Morb.* IV chs. 32 and 33, L VII 542 11 ff., 18 ff.; *Loc. Hom.* ch. 42, L VI 334 2.

[2] *VM* ch. 13; *CMG* I, I 44 9 ff. The writer denies the relevance of these particular opposites in disease, yet his own theory of 'repletion' and 'depletion' may be said to imply another, more general, scale of opposites with a mean between them.

[3] ἑνὶ δὲ συντόμῳ λόγῳ τὰ ἐναντία τῶν ἐναντίων ἐστὶν ἰήματα, *Flat.* ch. 1; *CMG* I, I 92 6 ff. Cf. also *Nat. Hom.* ch. 9, L VI 52 4 ff.; *Aph.* sec. 2 ch. 22, L IV 476 6 ff.; *Loc. Hom.* ch. 42, L VI 334 8 ff.

[4] Especially in *Vict.* II and III. Contrast, however, the much less dogmatic analyses of diets in *Acut.*

one of several treatises which make reasonable suggestions concerning the way in which diet and exercise should be varied to suit the season of the year.

Some of the more obscure pathological theories which are found in the Hippocratic Corpus should also be mentioned briefly. One common idea is that '*odd*' and '*even*' days (calculated from the first day of the disease) are significant in the course of diseases. *On Diseases* IV states that 'it is on odd days that a man is cured, or dies' (ch. 46, L VII 572 1 ff.) and even such a work as the first book of the *Epidemics*, rightly famed for its cautious, empirical approach to medicine, puts it that 'diseases which have exacerbations on even days, have crises on even days, while those with exacerbations on odd days, have crises on odd days' (sec. 3 ch. 12, L II 678 5 ff.).[1] Sometimes diseases were directly attributed to seasonal factors, which were often analysed into pairs of opposites. The effects of the *North* and *South* winds are referred to particularly frequently in this context.[2] Some theorists, too, held that the course of diseases was determined by the nature of the part of the body affected, and in this connection we find the parts of the body classified as '*strong*' and '*weak*', '*hot*', '*cold*', '*wet*', '*dry*' and so on.[3] On other occasions differences between the *right* and the *left* side of the body are postulated as the explanation of various pathological conditions. In *On the Sacred Disease*, for instance, an imaginary difference between the veins on the right and on the left of the body is cited to account for certain fluxes which are said to be more frequent

---

[1] Jones, *1*, vol. I, Intro. pp. liv f., relates the theory of critical days to the periodicity of malaria. It may also be noted that the theory was not always expressed in a rigid or dogmatic form. The author of *Prog.*, for example, says that the critical periods cannot be calculated exactly in whole days (ch. 20, L II 168 16 ff.).

[2] E.g. *Morb. Sacr.* ch. 13, L V 384 4 ff. (cf. 376 13 ff., 378 17 ff. etc.), *Hum.* ch. 14, L V 496 1 ff.; *Aph.* sec. 3 ch. 5, L IV 488 1 ff. *Aër.* contains a lengthy analysis of the effects of different seasonal factors, mostly seen as pairs of opposites (e.g. chs. 3 and 4 deal with cities facing the hot South, and the cold North, winds respectively, *CMG* I,1 57 11 ff., 58 6 ff.).

[3] See, for example, *Morb.* 1 ch. 1, L VI 142 2 ff.; *Nat. Hom.* ch. 10, L VI 56 13 ff.; and *Loc. Hom.* ch. 1, L VI 276 1 ff.

on the right (ch. 10, L vi 378 10 f.). But it may be mentioned that the differences which were suggested were not always purely imaginary. W. H. S. Jones (*1*, vol. ii, p. 17, n. 1) has pointed out that the passage in *Prognostic* (ch. 7, L ii 126 7 ff.) in which it is remarked that a swelling on the left side of the hypochondrium is less dangerous than one on the right, may well be the first reference in Greek literature to appendicitis.

Cosmological, physiological and pathological theories based on opposites are extremely common both in the Presocratic philosophers and in the Hippocratic writers. Further uses of opposites are found in fourth-century philosophy, in Plato and in Aristotle. In Plato one might mention, first of all, the general antithesis between the world of Being and the world of Becoming, between Forms and particulars. His theory of the relation between these two is, of course, a subtle and a complex one, and it almost certainly underwent considerable modification in the course of the development of his thought. But in some passages, at least, there is a direct opposition between the two types of existing things, between what is, in the terms of the *Phaedo* (80b), 'divine and immortal and intelligible and uniform and indissoluble and ever constant and true to itself' on the one hand, and what is 'human and mortal and manifold and not intelligible and dissoluble and never constant nor true to itself' on the other. Yet this type of antithesis is in one important respect different from the majority of the theories which we have considered so far. Whereas the pairs of opposites which the Presocratic philosophers and Hippocratic writers used in their theories and explanations belong, as a general rule, to the same order of reality (e.g. hot and cold, light and night, odd and even),[1] Plato's Forms and particulars belong to quite different orders of reality. This is, then, a different type of opposition, one between two distinct worlds, not between members of a single

---

[1] An exception may be made of the Atomists' 'atoms and the void' (above, p. 18.) and a closer parallel to Plato's theory may perhaps be seen in the distinction between the *Way of Truth* and the *Way of Seeming* in Parmenides.

world of reality. In other contexts, however, Plato's use of opposites compares more closely with that of earlier writers.[1] It is worth mentioning, in particular, a passage in the *Phaedo* in which he offers what appears to be a general analysis of 'coming-to-be' and 'passing-away'. At *Phaedo* 70 d ff. Socrates first states, and then attempts to establish, as a general law of becoming, that 'opposites come to be out of opposites', e.g. greater from less, less from greater, weaker from stronger, faster from slower, waking from sleeping and so on. As each of these processes may be reciprocal, he concludes, by analogy, that not only does death follow life, but life death (71 d–72 a). The purpose of the passage is to establish or recommend the doctrine of the immortality of the soul, but the particular argument which Plato here puts into the mouth of Socrates is one which is based on the generalisation that coming-to-be as a whole takes place between opposites.[2]

Finally we should consider briefly some of the many theories based on opposites which we find in Aristotle. When in *Physics* A he discusses the problem of the ἀρχαί of change, the first two principles which he postulates (after considering his predecessors' theories) are the opposites *Form* (εἶδος or μορφή) and *Privation* (στέρησις), to which he later adds other principles, the substratum and the moving cause. At *Physics* 188 b 21 ff., for example, he suggests that all coming-to-be and passing-away take place 'from opposites or to opposites and their intermediates',[3] and similarly changes in the categories of quality, quantity and place are also said to

---

[1] There are, of course, several doctrines based on opposites in the *Timaeus*, for example, which are probably modelled directly on those of earlier theorists. Thus at *Ti.* 82a certain diseases are attributed to a state of πλεονεξία or ἔνδεια (cf. the Hippocratic πλήρωσις and κένωσις, 'repletion' and 'depletion'). It should also be noted that Aristotle describes Plato's material principles as the opposites 'the Great' and 'the Small', e.g. *Ph.* 187a 17, 203a 15 f., *Metaph.* 988a 26, though this is not a doctrine we find in Plato's extant writings.

[2] See, for example, *Phaedo* 71a 9 f., 'ἱκανῶς οὖν ... ἔχομεν τοῦτο, ὅτι πάντα οὕτω γίγνεται, ἐξ ἐναντίων τὰ ἐναντία πράγματα;' Some illuminating comments on the passage as a whole will be found in Leach, pp. 130 f.

[3] Cf. also *Cael.* 270a 14 ff.; *GC* 331a 14 ff., 335a 6 ff.; *Metaph.* 1087a 36 ff.

take place between opposites,[1] locomotion in a circle alone being excepted from this analysis, with the result that it alone may be eternal.[2] Then in *GC* B 1–3 he sets out to consider what are the fundamental constituent elements of physical objects and establishes his own doctrine with an argument that is both precise and economical. Coming-to-be and passing-away are impossible without perceptible bodies (*GC* 328 b 32 f.), which in turn cannot exist apart from contrarieties; for a body must be either light or heavy, either cold or hot (329 a 10 ff.). But of the possible sorts of contrarieties, tangible contrarieties alone will be the principles of perceptible body (b 7 ff.). The various tangible contraries are then enumerated, and these are reduced to two pairs, one active, the *hot* and the *cold*, and the other passive, the *wet* and the *dry* (b 24 ff., 330 a 24 ff.). Moreover the possible combinations of these four opposites are four in number,[3] and these four combinations represent the primary bodies: earth is cold and dry, air hot and 'wet',[4] water cold and wet, and fire hot and dry (b 3 ff.).

It is not only in his general physical doctrine, but also in many of his specific theories and explanations, notably in biology, that Aristotle uses the *hot*, the *cold*, the *wet* and the *dry*. Thus generation is said to be effected by heat (whether that imparted by the male parent or, in spontaneous generation, the external heat of the surrounding atmosphere).[5] The principle of life itself is conceived as a special form of heat (e.g. *GA* 736 b 33 ff.), and this leads Aristotle to explain monsters and other abnormalities in terms of an insufficiency or disproportion of heat.[6] His theory of nutrition and growth

---

[1] See especially *Ph.* 200 b 33 ff., 261 a 32 ff.; *Cael.* 310 a 23 ff.; *Metaph.* 1069 b 3 ff.

[2] *Cael.* A 3 and 4.

[3] The combinations 'hot and cold' and 'wet and dry' are, of course, impossible, *GC* 330 a 31 ff.

[4] The Greek term ὑγρόν is wider than our 'wet' or 'moist', being used of both liquids and gases, i.e. of anything that is not solid or firm.

[5] See, for example, *GA* 743 a 26 ff., 32 ff.

[6] See *GA* 743 a 29 ff. (on deformities) and 767 a 13 ff. (on infertility) and cf. 772 a 10 ff. and 775 b 37 ff.

refers to the same four primary opposites,[1] and both respiration and sleep are explained in terms of an interplay of hot and cold in the body.[2] The importance of these four opposites in his biology is clearly expressed at *PA* 648b 4 ff., where he says that 'it seems evident that these [i.e. the four primary opposites] are practically the causes of death and of life, as also of sleep and waking, of maturity and old age, and of disease and health'. Finally it should be added that other opposites, too, besides the hot, the cold, the wet and the dry, figure in various important roles in Aristotle's detailed physical and biological theories: his use of *right* and *left*, *above* and *below*, and *front* and *back* is especially remarkable and will be considered in detail later.

QUESTIONS TO BE INVESTIGATED. SOME MODERN INTERPRETATIONS

The attempt to classify, or otherwise account for, other things in terms of pairs of opposites is a feature of a great many theories and explanations which appear in various branches of early Greek philosophy and medicine, and this fact calls for some discussion or comment, though first we should be clear what it is about the use of opposites in Greek speculative thought that is particularly remarkable or that requires elucidation. The doctrines we have reviewed above are of many different types and refer to opposites of many different sorts, and in each case we must examine and assess the theory that was proposed in relation to the evidence on which it was based and the phenomena which it was supposed to explain.

[1] 'It is by things which are dry or wet or hot or cold that all living beings are nourished' (*de An.* 414b 7 f.). Cf. *PA* 650a 2 ff. (food consists of the wet and the dry which are 'concocted' and changed by the hot) and *GA* 740b 25 ff. (hot and cold are the tools which nature uses to effect growth and nutrition). At *de An.* 414b 11 ff. hunger is said to be a desire for the dry and the hot, thirst a desire for the wet and the cold.

[2] Respiration is, for Aristotle, a process of refrigeration, the cooling of the excessive heat in the region round the heart (*Resp.* 478a 15 ff., 26 ff., *PA* 668b 33 ff.). Sleep is caused by the brain, which is cold, chilling the hot evaporations which rise from the lower regions of the body (*Somn. Vig.* ch. 3, 456a 30 ff., *PA* 653a 10 ff.).

Indeed it is only by investigating these questions in relation to particular doctrines that we can hope to arrive at any general conclusions concerning the use of theories based on opposites in Greek speculative thought. Some of these doctrines have an obvious empirical basis. Thus changes in temperature and humidity are usually observed in connection with most pathological conditions. The question that is worth considering here is why, among the mass of data associated with such complex phenomena as diseases, *pairs of opposites* were so often singled out and assumed to be the causes at work. But granted that many of the theories in question are connected with observed facts, others appear to be much more arbitrary, and some seem to have no foundation in experience whatsoever. Why, for example, was the sex of a child believed to depend on which side of the womb it was conceived on, or on the womb's temperature? In such cases we must clearly ask on what grounds the theory was put forward at all, or what evidence or argument its author or proponents could have adduced in its favour.

In view of the mass of theories and explanations based on opposites which we find in Greek philosophy and medicine, it is surprising how little this recurrent feature of Greek speculative thought has been discussed by scholars and historians of ancient philosophy. One notable exception, however, is Cornford's early book *From Religion to Philosophy* (especially ch. 2, pp. 60 ff.) in which he put forward some suggestions concerning the origins of the doctrines of the elements and the grouping of the elements into pairs of opposites. Cornford's theory is based on several arbitrary assumptions, and it should be remarked that in his later work, e.g. in *Principium Sapientiae*, he made no attempt to develop the line of interpretation which he had used in chs. 1 and 2 of *From Religion to Philosophy*. But some aspects of his earlier treatment of the question are worth recalling. He derived the philosophical conception of the elements from what he called a 'collective representation', that of the departmental ordering of the divine powers by Moira. Influenced by the essay on primitive forms of classification by Durkheim and Mauss,[1] he suggested that the origin of the notion of the divisions of nature is to be found in the social organisation of primitive societies. On the question of the use of opposites in particular, he claimed that 'the prototype of all opposition or contrariety is the contrariety of sex' (*1*, p. 65), and he again referred to his conception of the development of social organisation to support this claim, for he saw sex as the principle of division which underlies the organisation of many primitive tribes into two exogamous phratries, or moieties (*1*, p. 68).

Cornford's attempt to find the origin of the use of opposites in primitive social organisation provoked a brief reply from Burnet in *Early Greek Philosophy*, in which he evidently rejected not only Cornford's conclusions, but also his whole method of approach to the problem. Burnet protested (*3*, p. 8, n. 3) that 'there is no need to derive the doctrine of the "opposites" from a "religious representation"' and he suggested a very different explanation of its origin. 'The cycle of growth and decay is a far more striking phenomenon in Aegean lands than in the North, and takes still more clearly the form of a war of opposites, hot and cold, wet and dry. It is, accordingly, from that point of view the early cosmologists regard the world. The opposition of day and night, summer and winter, with their suggestive parallelism in sleep and waking, birth and death, are the *outstanding features* of the world as they saw it. The changes of the seasons are plainly brought about by the encroachment of one pair of opposites, the cold and the wet, on the other pair, the hot and the dry, which in their turn encroach on the other pair' (*3*, pp. 8 f., my italics).

Now the chief objection to Cornford's reconstruction of the historical origin of the doctrine of opposites in ancient Greece is that it is purely speculative. He admitted, as well he might,

---

[1] See the bibliography under Durkheim–Mauss.

that there is no conclusive evidence that the primitive form of ancient Greek society was 'totemic' (though he does not exclude that possibility, *1*, pp. 55 f.).[1] But in his references to the data from modern primitive societies he evidently presupposed a theory of the evolution of society from an archetypal form (a simple dualist organisation comprising two exogamous phratries).[2] But this, like all evolutionary theories of society, is a mere conjecture. Moreover, Cornford's particular suggestion, if it proves anything, is in danger of proving too much, for if the archetypal form of society provides the key to the origin of Greek theories of opposites, we might ask why similar theories of opposites are not universal.

How far, on the other hand, does Burnet's positivist interpretation take us towards an understanding of the theories based on opposites which we find in early Greek thought? If it were true that the opposites hot, cold, wet and dry 'force themselves on our attention' in Greek lands (Burnet, *3*, p. 8, n. 3), we should, I think, naturally expect a close correspondence between the cosmological doctrines of the Greeks and those of other peoples enjoying a similar Mediterranean climate. Yet while other oppositions and antitheses of various sorts are common enough,[3] there is no evidence that the hot, the cold, the wet and the dry *as such* played an important part in the cosmological beliefs of any of the ancient Greeks' Near Eastern neighbours, for example. Nor is it clear how important these four opposites were in ancient Greece itself before the rise of philosophical speculation.[4] It is obvious that the four primary opposites may be identified with

[1] On the question of so-called totemic societies, anthropological theory has, of course, come a very long way since Durkheim: see especially Lévi-Strauss, *2* and *4*.

[2] This is suggested by such remarks as 'the two contrary phratries *by whose fission* the exogamous grouping of society first came into being' (Cornford, *1*, p. 69, my italics).

[3] Thus the role of certain recurrent antitheses (e.g. between heaven and earth, or on earth between north and south) in ancient Egyptian beliefs has been discussed by Frankfort, *1*, pp. 19 ff. and n. 12 on p. 350 (and see his Index under 'Dualism').

[4] See further below, pp. 43 ff.

seasonal factors, summer heat, winter cold, rain and drought. But we should hesitate before concluding that the circumstances of the Greek climate provide of themselves a sufficient explanation for the development of this type of cosmological theory.

Burnet and Cornford are among the comparatively few scholars who have attempted to elucidate the use of theories based on opposites in Greek philosophy as a whole, but both offered what appear to be much oversimplified accounts of this usage. It is clear that many of the theories that referred to hot, cold, wet, dry and other pairs of opposites are based on certain factual evidence. Yet even when such theories have an empirical basis this is only one of the factors to be taken into account when considering why the theories took the form they did. Moreover, some of the theories in question have no such foundation in experience, and several (as we shall see) are even in apparent contradiction with observed facts. On the other hand it is not useful to attempt to connect the early Greek use of opposites, as Cornford tried to do, with some supposedly archetypal feature of social organisation. But if Burnet's and Cornford's general interpretations both seem rather inadequate, how far can we go towards answering the questions which we propounded earlier concerning the use of theories of this sort in early Greek thought, and in particular the question of the grounds on which such theories were proposed when they were evidently not the outcome of empirical observation? In attempting to understand and elucidate the various types of theories based on opposites which we find in early Greek speculative thought we should, I believe, begin by considering the comparative evidence. The fact is that other societies (whether ancient or modern) provide a great deal of evidence concerning dualist theories and beliefs of different sorts, and some of these theories are strikingly reminiscent of certain ancient Greek doctrines. This fact has received less attention from classical scholars than it deserves. Yet it is only by considering the parallels from other societies that we can hope to distinguish between what is common and general, and what is peculiar and special, in the Greek use of opposites. A review of the comparative evidence is, then, a necessary preliminary to an assessment of the role of theories based on opposites in Greek philosophy and science.

THE COMPARATIVE EVIDENCE

The evidence which relates to the role of opposites in the theories and beliefs of primitive societies is extremely extensive, and the first point that should be noticed is a general one, namely the frequency of dichotomous classifications of reality as a whole. Often such a classification mirrors the apparently dualist organisation of the society itself, the division of the tribe into two exogamous phratries or moieties (the camp or location of the tribe is itself often correspondingly divided into two main areas, for example two semi-circles or two concentric circles). Now Lévi-Strauss[1] has recently argued that the *actual* social structure of many societies which are, or were, normally termed 'dualist' is on close examination a good deal more complex than that label would suggest. But if Lévi-Strauss is correct, it is interesting and significant that in many such cases *the members of the society themselves* describe their own social organisation in terms of a simple dualist structure.[2] If this is the case, it seems that this type of description of social organisation may itself be one example of the tendency to fit complex phenomena into simple dichotomous classifications. Be that as it may, the evidence for comprehensive dichotomous classifications of reality is widespread and relates to societies of many different types in many different parts of the world. Natural substances,

---

[1] See especially two papers entitled 'Les structures sociales dans le Brésil central et oriental' (*Proceedings of the 29th Congress of Americanists*, 1952) and 'Les organisations dualistes existent-elles?' (1956) reprinted as chs. vii and viii in Lévi-Strauss, *1*, pp. 133 ff., 147 ff.

[2] See Lévi-Strauss, *1*, pp. 148 f., where he reproduces the plans of Winnebago villages which P. Radin drew up from the information supplied by the Winnebago themselves.

seasons, colours, winds, species of animals and plants, artificial objects, food and occupations are very often grouped into two opposite classes. The classification may cover not only obvious pairs of contraries (such as white and black, summer and winter), but other things which we do not normally consider members of contrary groups (e.g. species of plants or types of food). Some examples will illustrate the type of classification in question.

C. Nimuendaju[1] is our chief authority for a South American tribe called the Eastern Timbira. In the rainy season this tribe is divided into two groups called '*kamakra*' and '*atukmakra*', that is people (*kra*) of the 'plaza', or central village area (*ka*), and people from without (*atuk*). This division is the occasion of a general dichotomous classification of nature. 'All of nature', Nimuendaju says, 'is antithetically divided between the two groups, as indicated by the following incomplete scheme:

kamakra	*atukmakra*
east	west
sun	moon
day	night
dry season	rainy season
fire	firewood
earth	water
red color	black color

This dichotomy', Nimuendaju goes on, 'does not involve the opposition of the sexes, but extends to animals and plants: all species that are black and show marked black coloring fall into the *atuk* category; all those conspicuously red or white are *ka*. Maize and manioc are *ka*, the sweet potato and cucurbit *atuk*; yams are, according to the species, divided up between the two groups.'

Similar quite comprehensive dualist classifications of reality can be cited from several Indonesian societies.[2] The people of Amboyna provide one example. On Amboyna,

[1] Nimuendaju, pp. 84 ff., cf. Lévi-Strauss, *1*, pp. 163 ff.
[2] See especially J. M. van der Kroef, pp. 852 ff.

according to J. M. van der Kroef, 'the village...is divided into two parts: each part is not only a social unit but a cosmic classification category comprising all objects and events in the world around the villager'. Van der Kroef goes on to give a list of the objects and characteristics which are associated with each of the two divisions:

left	right
female	male
coast or seaside	land or mountainside
below	above
earth	heaven or sky
spiritual	worldly
downwards	upwards
peel	pith
exterior	interior
behind	in front
west	east
younger brother	older brother
new	old

Another comprehensive table of opposites is drawn up by R. Needham in a study of the beliefs of the Meru of Kenya:[1]

left	right
south	north
black clans	white clans
night	day
co-wife	first wife
junior	senior
subordinate age-division	dominant age-division
woman/child	man
inferior	superior
west	east
sunset	sunrise
darkness	light
religious authority	political power
predecessors	successors
younger	older
black man	white man
honey-collecting	cultivation

---

[1] R. Needham, *1*, pp. 25 f. (I have abbreviated Needham's table). See also the schema of Purum symbolic classification in R. Needham, *2*, p. 96.

Yet another society which apparently adopts a general dichotomous classification of reality is the Miwok of North America. An early observer, E. W. Gifford,[1] pointed out that the Miwok themselves are divided into two moieties called '*kikua*' or water-side, and '*tunuka*', land- or dry-side. Gifford went on to report that 'all nature is divided between land and water', adding that in his view the division was carried out 'in a more or less arbitrary manner...as shown by the classing of such animals as the coyote, deer, and quail on the "water" side'.

Even where the classification is more complex and refers to more than two groups, the classes into which things are divided are still very often pairs of opposites. The Zuñis,[2] for example, adopt a sevenfold classification of nature, but these seven groups are the three pairs of opposites, *north* and *south*, *east* and *west*, *zenith* and *nadir*, with the addition of 'the perfect *middle*' as the seventh group. Similarly, the Javanese adopt a fivefold schema, according to van der Kroef,[3] but these five divisions are *east*, *west*, *south*, *north* and *centre*. Under these five divisions are grouped colours, metals, days of the week, characters, professions and other objects, so that 'the whole framework comprises the world of natural phenomena, including man himself'.

These are a few of the dualist classifications of phenomena which can be cited from contemporary societies. But examples of a similar tendency to classify things in terms of opposites can be given from other, ancient societies as well.[4]

---

[1] Gifford, pp. 142 ff.

[2] This example was already used by Durkheim and Mauss in their essay on primitive forms of classification, pp. 34 ff., where they refer to F. H. Cushing's account of Zuñi beliefs (*1* and *2*) as their source.

[3] Van der Kroef, pp. 854 f. He notes that the Javanese are 'also familiar with a division into two, in which the categories of east and south unite and stand opposite west and north', the former comprising the 'underworld', and the latter the 'upper world'.

[4] On the dualism in ancient Iranian religion see, for example, the studies of Duchesne-Guillemin, *1* and *2* (especially pp. 189 ff.), and cf. Frankfort's remarks, *1*, pp. 19 ff., on the role of certain fundamental antitheses in ancient Egyptian beliefs.

The role of opposites in ancient Chinese thought is, of course, well known, particularly the doctrine of Yin and Yang.[1] Originally Yin is the 'shady side' of a hill or house, Yang the 'sunny side'. On the one hand darkness, cold, the female sex, night, moon, earth, west, north, soft, heavy, weak, behind, below, right and death are Yin. On the other light (daylight), warmth, the male sex, day, sun, the heavens, east, south, hard, light (as opposed to heavy), strong, in front, above, left and life are Yang. But this doctrine does not only apply to what we should term natural objects or phenomena: Yang is regarded as noble, Yin as common, so that on the one hand joy, wealth, honour, celebrity, love, profit and so on are considered as belonging to Yang, while on the other such things as sorrow, poverty, misery, bitterness, ignominy, rejection and loss belong to Yin. The notion of the interdependence of Yin and Yang was, moreover, a key doctrine of ancient Chinese speculative thought for many centuries. *I Ching*, or the *Book of Changes*, is a comprehensive pseudo-scientific system based on these opposites, for it consists in a set of symbols, eight trigrams and sixty-four hexagrams, each of which is composed of a different combination of unbroken, or Yang, lines and broken, or Yin, lines.[2] This, in origin probably a system of divination, later developed into what J. Needham calls a 'comprehensive system of symbolism containing in some way all the basic principles of natural phenomena'.[3]

It is clear from the examples which we have considered (and many more could, of course, be cited) that a tendency to classify phenomena into opposite groups is found in a great many societies, ancient and modern, besides that of the ancient Greeks. The variety of the classifications in question

[1] On Yin and Yang in Chinese thought see especially Forke, pp. 163 ff., Granet, *1*, Book 2, ch. 2, pp. 115 ff., and J. Needham, vol. II, pp. 273 ff. As regards the date of the introduction of this theory, Needham estimates that the philosophical use of the terms Yin and Yang began about the beginning of the fourth century B.C.

[2] On I Ching see Granet, *1*, pp. 182 ff., and J. Needham, vol. II, pp. 304 ff.

[3] J. Needham, vol. II, p. 328.

should not be underestimated: no one pair of opposites appears consistently as the principle of the division; the division between the sexes is often part of the classification, but sometimes it is excluded; the correlations which are proposed between different pairs of opposites are by no means always the same; the classification uses sometimes two, sometimes more than two, classes. But notwithstanding this great variety of primitive dualist classifications, it is fairly evident that such notions as Alcmaeon's 'most human things go in pairs', the Pythagorean Table of Opposites, and perhaps even cosmological doctrines based on opposites such as the Light and Night of Parmenides' *Way of Seeming*, may be compared, at least very broadly, with beliefs which are found quite commonly in many other societies. This fact is itself of some interest to the classical scholar, but we may then ask whether there is anything more than just a very general similarity between ancient Greek conceptions such as those I mention and the beliefs reported from other societies. How far does the use of opposites in primitive thought help us to understand these or any other ancient Greek theories based on opposites?

One line of interpretation is suggested by the work of Durkheim, who in his discussion of primitive modes of classification argued that a close correlation existed between dualist classifications of reality and dualist social organisations. Subsequent work has, however, shown that the organisation of so-called 'dualist' societies is often extremely complex, and in many cases their 'dualism' is only apparent or is confined to certain superficial features of their social structure.[1] Today it would be considered hazardous to attempt to set out a general theory connecting dualist classifications of reality directly with a specific type of social organisation, and we might add that even if such a theory were possible, we have so little evidence concerning the original structure of ancient Greek societies that its relevance to our particular problems would be dubious.

We can hardly hope to go far towards elucidating the use

[1] See the two papers of Lévi-Strauss already referred to on p. 31, n. 1.

of opposites in Greek speculative thought along the lines of the simple social interpretation suggested by Durkheim. But anthropologists have drawn attention to one recurrent feature of primitive dualist beliefs which does seem particularly relevant to the understanding of some Greek theories of opposites: this is the use of pairs of opposites to symbolise certain important religious or spiritual distinctions. In this field the pioneering work was done by Robert Hertz,[1] a pupil of Durkheim. Hertz studied the phenomenon of the widespread belief in the superiority of the right hand as opposed to the left, collecting a good deal of remarkable material which shows the *values* or *ideals* with which right and left are very commonly associated. Our own English usage may be taken as one illustration of this, for 'right' the adjective may mean (1) morally good ('do the right thing'), (2) true or correct (the 'right' use of words, the 'right' way of doing something) and (3) sound or sane (in your 'right' mind), while 'right' the substantive stands for a legal entitlement ('right' of way, 'right' to the throne). But in primitive societies there are many beliefs and practices which show how right is generally assumed to be essentially different from, and superior to, left, the former good, honourable, pure, blessed, the latter bad, dishonourable, impure, cursed. Thus Hertz noted that in some societies the left arms of children or youths are bound up and put out of action for long periods so that they will learn the lesson that the left is impure and not to be used.[2] He compared the feelings of a left-handed person in a backward society with those of an uncircumcised man in countries

---

[1] Hertz, pp. 89 ff. Much work has subsequently been done on the subject of right and left in various societies: see a forthcoming handbook edited by R. Needham, entitled *Right and Left*.

[2] Cf. Evans-Pritchard, *3*, pp. 234 ff., who notes this as a custom of the Nuer and describes other practices which illustrate the Nuer belief that the right is the good, the left the evil, side. Thus 'when a fruit or animal is cut in two at sacrifices the left half may be either thrown or given away and only the right half be consumed by the people of the home. It is propitious for a sacrificial ox stabbed with the spear to fall on its right side and unpropitious for it to fall on its left side. A dead man is buried to the left of his hut or windscreen, the side of misfortune' and so on.

where circumcision is law, and said that 'the fact is that right-handedness is not simply accepted, submitted to, like a natural necessity: it is an ideal to which everybody must conform and which society forces us to respect by positive sanctions'.[1] He remarked that certain other oppositions which are apparent in nature, e.g. light and darkness or day and night, sky and earth, male and female, etc., acquire similar symbolic associations, and he went on to relate these oppositions to a 'fundamental' antithesis which 'dominates the spiritual world of primitive men', that between the 'sacred' and the 'profane'. This distinction is, one may say, one of the basic tenets of orthodox Durkheimian anthropology: according to Durkheim himself,[2] sacred objects are those which are protected and isolated by certain interdictions, profane objects those to which those interdictions are applied, and he believed that the distinction between these two is universal, that, as he put it, the sacred and the profane have always and everywhere been conceived by the human mind as two distinct classes, as two worlds between which there is nothing in common.[3]

Whether or not we approve of the Durkheimian terminology in which Hertz formulated his theory, it is clear that he drew attention to a point which is of great importance if we are to understand the significance that some pairs of opposites may have in primitive thought. Certain manifest natural oppositions, such as day and night, male and female, and perhaps especially right and left, are often taken as the symbols or embodiments of fundamental religious or spiritual antitheses ('pure and impure', 'blessed and cursed'). Indeed such concrete oppositions as right and left seem often to provide the chief means for conveying what are (to our way of thinking) highly abstract religious concepts. It should be noted that this may still be true even when the usual symbolic

---

[1] Hertz, p. 93. I am grateful to Dr and Mrs Needham for permission to quote this and other extracts from their translation of Hertz's essay.

[2] See Durkheim, p. 56.   [3] See Durkheim, p. 53.

values are reversed, i.e. when left, for example, is identified with what is pure or 'sacred'. Hertz himself knew that there are some peoples who are predominantly right-handed, but who nevertheless consider the left the nobler side, although he tended to dismiss these cases as 'secondary developments'.[1] Thus among the Zuñi[2] the left and right sides are apparently personified as brother gods, but the left is the elder and wiser of the two, and among the ancient Chinese[3] the left was Yang and therefore superior, the right Yin and inferior. Yet this reversal of the usual associations is itself good evidence of the part played by social, as opposed to physiological, factors in determining the attitude to right and left. The distinction between the two sides of the body, and their symmetry, are, of course, data of experience, and it appears to be generally true that right-handedness is more frequent than left-handedness (though this results, no doubt, not only from anatomical causes, but also from training and habituation).[4] Yet the fact that left is sometimes considered noble, and right ignoble, illustrates the *arbitrary* element in the symbolic associations which these opposites acquire. It seems that righ and left tend to be used as the symbols of opposite spiritual categories *whichever of the two is believed to be the superior.*

Hertz's discussion of the nature of certain beliefs concerning right and left helps to elucidate a recurrent characteristic

[1] See Evans-Pritchard's comment in his introduction to Hertz, p. 22.

[2] As Hertz noted, the fact that the Zuñi are a peaceful agricultural people no doubt contributes to the relative estimation in which they hold the right, or spear, hand and the left, or shield, hand.

[3] See Granet, *1*, pp. 361 ff. and *2*, pp. 263 ff. The Chinese attitude towards this antithesis is complex, for while the left is generally Yang and superior, and the right Yin and inferior, yet in the sphere of what is itself common or inferior, the right in some sense has precedence over the left. Thus the right hand is used for eating (Granet, *1*, p. 364) and the right side is the appropriate side for women (while the left belongs to men, Granet, *1*, p. 368).

[4] On the anatomical factors involved in right-handedness, see Hertz, p. 90, and the translators' note. That there is a functional asymmetry of the brain—the left cerebral hemisphere being more developed, in some respects, than the right—is agreed. Hertz, however, suggested that as the exercise of an organ leads to the greater nourishment and consequent growth of that organ, we might as well say that we are left-brained because we are right-handed, as say that we are right-handed because we are left-brained.

39

of dualist conceptions in primitive thought, namely the tendency to correlate or identify the members of different pairs of opposites. Often, of course, such correlations correspond to certain obvious facts of experience, as when day, light and white appear on one side of a Table of Opposites, and night, darkness and black on the other. Yet we find that pairs of opposites are also correlated even when there is no manifest connection between them, as, for example, when east is identified with right, or evil or female with left. The evidence for this tendency is extensive.[1] Evans-Pritchard, for instance, has noted that in Nuer belief there are two sets of opposites, the one comprising the left side, weakness, femininity and evil, and the other the right side, strength, masculinity and goodness. As often, east and west are associated with life and death respectively, but then east is also identified with right and west with left 'thus bringing into the left-right polarity the polar representations not only of life and death but also of the cardinal points east and west.'[2] If we consider them individually, the different pairs of objects that are included in such Tables of Opposites are often remarkably heterogeneous. The relationship between age-groups (young, old) strikes us as quite different from that between the sexes (male, female) in at least one important respect, in that the young become old in their turn. Alongside east and west we often find daylight and darkness in such classifications. But if we reflect that not only does it get light first in the east, but it also gets dark first in the same quarter, the common identification of west and night may also strike us as being a little arbitrary. Then sun and moon are often correlated with these two pairs, although sun and moon are not contraries at all. According to Hertz's view, the reason why male, old, east, day, sun and right may so easily be correlated is that each of these terms stands to its opposite in a relation of 'sacred' to 'profane'. Whether it holds good of all primitive dualist

[1] See especially the articles of van der Kroef, and R. Needham, *1*.
[2] Evans-Pritchard, *3*, p. 235.

classifications of reality, that the two groups are related to one another as 'sacred' to 'profane', is at least open to doubt. It is often difficult to verify this point in the reports of field-workers who did not examine the system of classification of the society which they studied in relation to its religious beliefs or ideals. Yet the evidence collected by Evans-Pritchard for the Nuer, by Needham for the Meru and by van der Kroef for several Indonesian societies shows that some-times, at least, a whole series of pairs of terms is associated, in primitive beliefs, in an *elaborate Table of Opposites* in which each pair is taken to embody an *analogous symbolic distinction*. The opposed terms may be of many different sorts, and the table may include some terms which are not, strictly speak-ing, contraries at all (e.g. species of plants or animals, occu-pations, foods and so on); but whether or not the pairs of terms are contraries, and whether or not apparent inter-connections exist between all the various pairs, a single com-plex system is built up in which the dominant motif is the *recurrent antithesis* between what is superior, pure and holy, and what is inferior, impure and unholy.

'RELIGIOUS POLARITY' IN EARLY GREEK THOUGHT[1]

The work done by Hertz and other anthropologists on one type of dualist notions in primitive thought opens up the way for an interpretation not only of certain ancient Greek beliefs and practices in general,[2] but also of some of the speculative theories of the philosophers in particular. Many of the oppositions which are apparent in nature were, of course, associated with religious notions in ancient Greece from the earliest times. One such pair of opposites is *sky* and *earth*, for with sky and earth are associated two fundamental religious

---

[1] This section develops the argument of two papers in *JHS*, LXXXII (1962), pp. 56 ff. and LXXXIV (1964), pp. 92 ff., in which I discussed right and left, and the hot, the cold, the dry and the wet in particular.

[2] Hertz himself mentioned a number of Greek beliefs and practices involving the opposites right and left, see for examples notes 36, 44 and 69.

antitheses, (1) the distinction between Olympian and chthonic deities, and (2) the general opposition between gods and men, between the immortal ἐπουράνιοι and the mortal ἐπιχθόνιοι.[1] And I have suggested elsewhere that the three pairs right and left, male and female, and light and darkness have particularly marked symbolic associations for the ancient Greeks. The evidence concerning the attitude towards *right* and *left* is well known and need not be repeated in detail: right is the auspicious, left the inauspicious, side; the right hand is used for such 'sacred' actions as pouring a libation or giving a pledge; the lucky direction from left to right was observed in such activities as the serving of wine round a group of guests; two of the words for left, εὐώνυμος and ἀριστερός, are euphemisms, and a third σκαιός comes to mean 'ill-omened' and 'awkward', like the French 'gauche', the opposite of δεξιός, meaning 'clever', 'skilful'.[2] As regards *male* and *female*, it is not only the case that the Greeks generally considered women inferiors,[3] but the myth of Pandora, for instance, implied that women are the source of all evil: as Hesiod puts it, before Pandora, the first woman, appeared on earth, men lived free from evils, toil and disease.[4] As for *light* and *darkness*, it is worth recalling that 'to live' was often expressed in Greek by such phrases as 'to be in' or 'to see, the light' (e.g. *Iliad* 18 61). φάος or φόως, light, itself, often means safety or deliverance in Homer (e.g. *Iliad* 6 6), and later the words for light, φῶς and φέγγος, are used of such

---

[1] On the importance of these two distinctions in Greek religious thought, see, for example, Guthrie, *4*, especially chs. 3 and 4, and chs. 8 and 9.

[2] References will be found in *JHS*, LXXXII (1962), p. 58.

[3] The idea that women are innately inferior to men recurs, of course, in Greek philosophical texts: in the *Timaeus* 90 e f. Plato suggested that cowardly and unjust men become women in their second incarnation, and Aristotle considered the female sex a deviation from type, a 'natural deformity', e.g. *GA* 767b 6 ff., 775a 14 ff.

[4] Hesiod, *Op.* 60 ff., esp. 90 ff., cf. *Th.* 585 ff. In Semonides, too, womankind is 'the greatest evil that Zeus has made' (7 D, 96 f., 115). One may compare Evans-Pritchard, *3*, p. 234 on the connection between the female principle and evil in Nuer belief, and Hertz (p. 97) noted that according to a Maori proverb 'all evils, misery and death...come from the female element'.

things as good news, joy, fame, marriage, wealth and virtue.[1] Conversely, darkness is associated with, and indeed stands for, death, as in such phrases as στυγερὸς δ' ἄρα μιν σκότος εἶλεν[2] (*Iliad* 5 47). The comparison 'like night' (νυκτὶ ἐοικώς) conveys the terror which a god or hero causes (*Iliad* 1 47, cf. 12 463), and Night herself, one of whose names is the euphemism εὐφρόνη and one of whose epithets is 'deadly', ὀλοή (Hesiod, *Th.* 224), is a personage of whom Zeus himself stands in awe (*Iliad* 14 258 ff.), while the conception of Night as a malignant principle is strongly suggested by the list of her offspring in the *Theogony*, which includes various personifications of death and fate, as well as Misery, Deceit, Old Age and Strife (*Th.* 211 ff.).

The general relevance of Hertz's concept of 'religious polarity' to ancient Greek beliefs will, I think, readily be granted, but two questions are worth considering in particular in relation to the pre-philosophical Greek evidence. First, how extensive was the tendency to use opposites as the symbols of religious or spiritual distinctions? If it is clear that such pairs as right and left, light and darkness, and for that matter white and black, and up and down, possessed or acquired strong symbolic associations for the ancient Greeks, how far is this also true of other pairs of opposites as well, such as hot and cold, or dry and wet? Secondly, to what extent does it appear that such symbolic antitheses formed a single comprehensive system, comparable with the unified dualist schemata which anthropologists have drawn up in reporting the beliefs of various present-day societies? How far do we find correlations proposed between different pairs of opposites or how far is there anything that could be called a Table of Opposites in our pre-philosophical texts?

On the first question I should begin by pointing out that there is no evidence in our extant pre-philosophical texts to

---

[1] See, for example, Aeschylus, *Pers.* 300 f.; *A.* 601 f.; Pindar *P.* 8 96 f.; *O.* 2 53 ff., 10 22 f.; *N.* 3 64, 83 f.; Euripides, *IA* 439. On the use of light as a symbol in Greek literature, see especially the articles of Bultmann and Tarrant.

[2] 'Then hateful darkness seized him.'

suggest that in that period 'the hot', 'the cold', 'the dry' and 'the wet' *as such* were considered either as important ingredients of physical objects or as major cosmological forces.[1] The contrast between the heat and the drought of the Greek summer and the cold and the rain of the Greek winter is, of course, most marked,[2] but no schematic correlation between the four opposites and the four seasons as a whole is found before the fifth century B.C. There is an interesting difference between the description of the seasons in Homer and Hesiod, and in some later theoretical writers. In the Hippocratic treatise *On the Nature of Man*, for instance, the author puts forward a neat schema in which spring is hot and wet, summer hot and dry, autumn cold and dry and winter cold and wet (ch. 7, L vi 46 9 ff.). With this we may compare the quite undogmatic description of the seasons in Homer, who in referring to ὀπώρη, autumn or late summer, for example, mentions now its drying winds (*Iliad* 21 346 f.), now its violent rains (*Iliad* 16 384 ff.). Nevertheless this is not to say that the two pairs, hot and cold, and dry and wet, did not have certain quite important associations for the ancient Greeks already in the pre-philosophical period, although in the case of dry and wet, at least, their associations appear to be somewhat ambivalent. Thus like ourselves, the Greeks connected warmth not only with life itself, but also with such emotions as joy and relief.[3] Conversely cold was associated,

---

[1] The first explicit reference to these four opposites in an extant philosophical text is Heraclitus Fr. 126. But before him certain opposed substances undoubtedly played an important part in Anaximander's theories (both in his general cosmological doctrine and in his theories on such topics as the origin of living creatures), although I should agree with those scholars who have expressed the opinion that the substances in question were more likely to have been, for example, (hot) 'flame' and (cold) 'mist' than 'the hot' and 'the cold' as such. See further *JHS*, LXXXIV (1964), pp. 95 ff.

[2] Hesiod, for instance, has a vivid description of the time of the year when 'Sirius dries the head and knees and the skin is parched by the burning heat' (*Op.* 582 ff., esp. 587 ff.). Compare also his description of the rains and cold of the winter month Lenaeon (*Op.* 504 ff.).

[3] Thus the basic meaning of ἰαίνω seems to be to 'warm' (e.g. *Odyssey* 10 359, cf. 'melt', *Od.* 12 175), but when applied to the θυμός, for example, it comes to mean 'comfort', e.g. *Od.* 15 379; *Il.* 24 119; cf. ἰαίνομαι *Od.* 19 537.

naturally enough, with death, and then also with such emotions as fear.[1] As regards the pair dry and wet, several usages suggest that the Greeks conceived the living as 'wet' and the dead as 'dry'. At *Od.* 6 201, for instance, the expression διερὸς βροτός is used apparently as the equivalent of ζωὸς βροτός (e.g. *Od.* 23 187) to mean 'living mortal', and there seems to be no good reason to suppose that διερός here is anything other than the common Greek adjective which literally means 'wet' (e.g. Hesiod, *Op.* 460).[2] Conversely dead or dying things are 'dry'. This is obviously true of dead wood (e.g. *Iliad* 4 487), and 'dead' parts of the body, such as the nails, are also described as 'dry' (e.g. Hesiod, *Op.* 743). The dead themselves were called ἀλίβαντες (e.g. Plato, *R.* 387c), which was taken to mean 'without moisture',[3] and the old, too, were apparently thought of as 'dry', for when Athena is about to transform Odysseus into an old man at *Od.* 13 397 ff. she says she will 'dry up' his fine skin.[4] These usages are, for the most part, clearly derived from such obvious facts of experience as the dryness of dead wood, the warmth of living animals and the cold of the dead. From this biological point of view, hot and wet are naturally associated together and opposed to cold and dry. Yet as we have already mentioned, from another point of view, namely that of the Greek climate, another correlation naturally suggests itself, the heat and dryness of the Greek summer being opposed to the cold and wet of the Greek winter. Again if the antithesis between

---

[1] Among the objects to which the epithets κρυερός and κρυόεις (cold or chilly) are applied in Homer or Hesiod are Hades (*Op.* 153), fear (*Il.* 9 2), war (*Th.* 936) and γόος (wailing, *Il.* 24 524).

[2] Cf. also *Od.* 9 43, and see Onians, pp. 254 ff., on these passages. Other evidence which suggests that the ancient Greeks also associated sexual love and desire with moisture is discussed by Onians, ch. 6, pp. 200 ff.

[3] Cf. Aesch. Fr. 229 which speaks of the dead in whom there is no moisture (ἱκμάς). In the Orphic Fragment 32 (a) and (b) (in DK as 1 B 17 and 17a) the dead man who speaks describes himself as 'dry', αὖος, and the belief that the dead are thirsty evidently underlies the widespread Greek practice of offering them libations.

[4] κάρψω μὲν χρόα καλόν (*Od.* 13 398, cf. 430). Cf., for example, Soph. *El.* 819 where Electra, foreseeing her old age, says 'I shall dry up my life' (αὐανῶ βίον).

sky and earth is particularly important in early Greek religious beliefs, the hot and the dry are both naturally associated
with the sun and so with the sky. Unlike right and left or
light and darkness, neither hot and cold, nor dry and wet, it
seems, possessed any strong positive or negative values *in
themselves*, though they acquire such values *by association* in
different contexts. But while hot and cold have uniformly
positive and negative associations respectively, the dry and
the wet, on the other hand, appear to have ambivalent
associations. On the one hand the Greeks connected both the
hot and the wet with what is alive, and both the cold and the
dry with the dead, and here wet acquires certain positive
overtones, dry certain negative undertones: but on the other
hand observation of the seasons naturally suggested to them a
different correlation, in which the *dry* and the hot are the
positive terms set over against the negative cold and *wet*.

The second question I raised is how far our sources for the
pre-philosophical period suggest a single comprehensive
system of dualist beliefs. There is a good deal of evidence
which shows that white and up and high, for example, are
each associated, in certain contexts, with the Olympian gods,
and black and down and low with the chthonic deities.[1] Yet
Homer and Hesiod nowhere have occasion to draw attention
explicitly to such correlations, let alone to draw up a complete Table of Opposites. Moreover the evidence we have
just discussed shows that certain pairs of opposites, such as dry
and wet, would probably have to be excluded from any
general schema which we might draw up on the basis of the
information that may be collected from scattered individual
texts. For the most part such correlations as the Greeks
appear to have made between different pairs of opposites

---

[1] Thus it may be that, as a general rule, the colour of a victim sacrificed to an
Olympian deity was white, that of the chthonic gods' sacrificial victims black
(at *Il.* 3 103 a white ram and a black ewe are sacrificed to the sun and to
earth). Other general distinctions between the rites associated with the
Olympians and those of the chthonic deities have been collected by Guthrie, *4*,
pp. 221 f., and several of these reflect the symbolic associations of pairs of
opposites, e.g. up and down, high and low.

reflect obvious empirical data. The association of light and east and white, and sky and up, on the one hand, and of darkness and west and black, and earth and down, on the other, depends, in part at least, on certain facts of experience. Again the common conception of the earth as a mother, and of the sky as a generating father, is evidently based on an obvious analogy between the growth of plants and sexual reproduction.[1] One of the correlations which we find is, however, more arbitrary. To judge from *Iliad* 12 238 ff.,[2] the ancient Greeks, like many other peoples, thought of the *east* as on the *right*, and of the *west* as on the *left*, and this belief goes beyond the immediate data of experience, while it corresponds to the symbolic values of these opposites. To conclude, the evidence clearly does not permit us to speak of any developed or systematic Table of Opposites in Homer or Hesiod. On the other hand the members of different pairs of

[1] See especially Aeschylus, *Danaids* Fr. 44, Euripides Frr. 898 and 839 (where Aither is addressed as 'the father of men and of gods' and Earth 'who receives the moistening drops of rain' is said to be 'rightly considered the mother of all things'). At *GA* 716a 13 ff. Aristotle notes that 'of living creatures, we call male that which generates in another, female that which generates in itself. And so with reference to the world as a whole, men speak of the nature of the earth as female and a mother, and they address the sky and the sun and things of that kind as generators and fathers.' (I read ὀνομάζουσιν in preference to Bekker's νομίζουσιν at a 16.) Both ideas are, no doubt, of great antiquity. See further, for example, Guthrie, 6, chs. 1 and 2.

[2] Hector's words at *Il.* 12 238 ff. are τῶν [sc. οἰωνῶν] οὔ τι μετατρέπομ' οὐδ' ἀλεγίζω, | εἴ τ' ἐπὶ δεξί' ἴωσι πρὸς ἠῶ τ' ἠέλιόν τε, | εἴ τ' ἐπ' ἀριστερὰ τοί γε ποτὶ ζόφον ἠερόεντα ('Nor do I trouble myself or care at all whether the birds of omen fly to the right, towards the dawn and the sun, or to the left, towards the misty west'). This has sometimes been taken to refer to the position of the Trojan lines, which happen to face North, but it is surely much more likely that Hector's words describe the usual method of interpreting omens, in which ἐπὶ δεξιά is identified with πρὸς ἠῶ. The theory (taken up more recently by J. Cuillandre) that right is identified with light because the worshipper faces the rising sun, which then passes to his right on its transit westwards, was rightly dismissed by Hertz (n. 86). A decisive argument against the theory is that we should expect the *opposite* correlation to be made by many peoples in the *southern* hemisphere, for if they face the sun at its rising, it passes, of course, to their left. In fact, this is not found to be the case. For the Maori and primitive societies in Australia, for example, the right is the good side, associated with life and with light, and the left is the bad side, associated with death and darkness, just as they were for the ancient Greeks and are still for the majority of peoples in both hemispheres.

47

opposites were undoubtedly associated together at an early stage in various Greek beliefs and practices, and in some cases the correlations which were made appear to have been determined not so much by what is given in nature, as by the symbolic values which the opposite terms possessed.

'RELIGIOUS POLARITY' IN THE SPECULATIVE THEORIES OF THE PHILOSOPHERS AND OTHERS

So far I have considered the evidence for what Hertz called 'religious polarity' in early Greek thought as a whole and in particular in pre-philosophical beliefs: certain antitheses (immortals/mortals, Olympians/chthonic gods) are fundamental to Greek religion, and many natural oppositions (sky/earth, light/darkness, etc.) had marked symbolic associations for the ancient Greeks at an early period. But we have now to examine more closely the use of different pairs of opposites in the work of the philosophers and medical writers. It is one thing to point out a general similarity between the role of certain antitheses in Greek religion and some of the dualist beliefs which are reported from other societies. But it is quite another to suggest that beliefs and assumptions of the pre-philosophical period may have influenced the theories of philosophers and scientists of the fifth and fourth centuries: and here I refer not only to their religious and moral beliefs, but also, and more especially, to some of the explanations which they put forward to account for various natural phenomena.

First it is clear that the placing of right, male and light on the side of Limit and the good, and of left, female and darkness on the side of the Unlimited and evil, in the Pythagorean Table of Opposites, corresponds to notions which are implicit, to a greater or less extent, in our earliest Greek sources. Moreover, if it is rather doubtful how far the various dualist beliefs which we find referred to in different contexts in earlier writers form a unified system, the Pythagorean Table which

Aristotle gives at *Metaph.* 986a 22 ff. brings ten pairs of opposite terms together in a single comprehensive schema which was evidently held in some way to represent the fundamental principles which underlie all reality. The Table as reported by Aristotle is a remarkable synthesis of new, and very old, beliefs. Several of the pairs mentioned (e.g. odd and even, straight and curved) reflect the particular Pythagorean interest in mathematics and should no doubt be related to their tendency to equate things with numbers.[1] But the antitheses right and left, male and female, light and darkness were considered important enough to be included, and this part of the Table, the arranging of right, male and light on one side, the side of the good, and of their opposites on the side of evil, may be seen as the explicit expression, or rationalisation, in ethical terms, of much older Greek beliefs.[2] It should be added that several of the so-called ἀκούσματα or σύμβολα which are attributed to the Pythagoreans (or rather to one group of them) emphasise the symbolic distinction between certain pairs of opposites, such as right and left, white and black.[3] And elsewhere, too, in Greek philosophy we find various pairs correlated together in passages which have a religious or mystical context. In the eschatological myth in Plato's *Republic* (614c f.), for example, the souls of men are imagined as divided by their judges into two groups: the just travel to the *right, upwards* through the *sky*, carrying tokens of their judgement on their *fronts*, and the unjust go to the *left, downwards* (into the *earth*) bearing their tokens on their *backs*.[4]

In part the Pythagorean Table of Opposites reflects, at the same time as it makes more explicit, much older Greek beliefs concerning the antitheses right/left, male/female and light/

---

[1] See especially Aristotle, *Metaph.* A 5 985b 23 ff.   [2] Cf. Hertz, n. 50.

[3] E.g. 'Putting on your shoes, start with the right foot; washing your feet, start with the left' (Iambl. *Protr.* 21, DK 58 C 6, and cf. *VP* 83, DK C 4); 'do not sacrifice a white cock' (Iambl. *VP* 84, and cf. Diogenes' gloss, VIII 34, DK C 3, that 'white is of the nature of the good, and black of evil').

[4] Cf. also *Laws* 717ab, where 'even' and 'left' are assigned as honours to the chthonic deities, and their superior opposites, 'odd' and 'right', to the Olympians.

darkness. But these opposites figure not only in the comprehensive Pythagorean schema which was apparently held in some obscure way to represent the principles of all things, but also in specific physical and biological theories, and the survival of earlier beliefs and associations of ideas in this context, where the aim of the writer was to give a satisfactory account of certain natural phenomena, is especially remarkable. I may refer first to some of the theories which were put forward to account for the differentiation of the two sexes. Parmenides, as we saw, referred to the position of the embryo on the right or left side of the mother's womb, Anaxagoras to the side from which the seed of the male parent comes,[1] and the Hippocratic treatise *On Superfetation* implies quite specifically that seed from the right testicle produces male children, seed from the left females.[2] Although these writers disagree, for example, about which parent is responsible for the sex of the child, they all assumed that *male* and *right* are connected, and so too *female* and *left*. We have already noted various dualist beliefs, both Greek and non-Greek, which illustrate a tendency to correlate or identify the positive poles of various pairs of opposites on the one hand, and their negative poles on the other. It is interesting, then, that these early Greek explanations of the origin of the two sexes took the form of variations on the theme that male and female derive from right and left respectively. We cannot say what evidence (if any) Parmenides and others may have appealed to, in order to establish their theories,[3] but it seems clear that the

[1] On the theories of Parmenides and Anaxagoras, see above, p. 17. Parmenides' version of the theory also appears in several Hippocratic treatises (*Epid.* II sec. 6 ch. 15, L v 136 5 ff.; *Epid.* VI sec. 2 ch. 25, L v 290 7 f.; *Aph.* sec. 5 ch. 48, L IV 550 1 ff.; cf. *Prorrh.* II ch. 24, L IX 56 19 ff.).

[2] *Superf.* ch. 31, L VIII 500 8 ff.; cf. also the theory attributed to a certain Leophanes and others by Aristotle, *GA* 765a 21 ff. Lesky, pp. 62 ff., has traced the survival of various beliefs in a connection between the right side of the body and male children in much later medical literature, including, for example, Galen (*UP* XIV ch. 7, and Kühn IV 172 ff., especially 175).

[3] A passage in Aristotle, *GA* 765a 21 ff., suggests that evidence was sometimes invented in order to corroborate such theories. The passage in question is discussed below, p. 73.

symbolic associations of these opposites contributed to fortify the belief in a connection between the positive or superior terms, male and right, on the one hand, and between the negative or inferior terms, female and left, on the other. Here one may note that among the ancient Chinese, who held the left to be more honourable than the right, there were theorists who believed that an embryo on the left side of the womb would be a boy, and one on the right a girl, proposing a theory which is the reverse of that of the Greeks, but in keeping with their own associations for left and right.[1]

Several Presocratic philosophers and Hippocratic writers put forward doctrines which consist of attempted correlations between male and right, and female and left. But other theories which also reflect the symbolic values of such pairs of opposites as right and left appear in fourth-century philosophy, in Aristotle himself. Aristotle, it is true, rejected the idea that a difference between right and left in any way determines the sex of the child. He criticises the doctrine that males and females are formed in different parts of the womb in *GA* Δ 1, and where others had been content to assume that males are formed on the right side of the womb and females on the left, for instance, Aristotle refers to the evidence of anatomical dissections to prove that this does not hold true as an absolute rule.[2] Yet if his use of the decisive evidence of dissections in this context clearly marks an important advance on previous theorists, it is far from being the case that Aristotle himself was free from preconceptions on the subject of right and left and other opposites. His use of the three pairs right and left, above and below and front and back is

---

[1] See Granet, *1*, p. 370 and *2*, pp. 273 f.

[2] *GA* 764a 33 ff., 765a 16 ff.; see further below, pp. 73 f. A passage at *HA* 583b 2 ff. should also be noted, however, for it might suggest that at one stage Aristotle may have been rather less critical of the theory that males are on the right, females on the left, of the womb. There it is said that the first movement of male embryos usually takes place on the right about the fortieth day, that of females on the left about the ninetieth day, although this statement is then qualified ('yet it must not be supposed that there is any exactness in these matters') and he notes that there are many exceptions.

particularly striking: the evidence that might be adduced to illustrate this is extensive, but some of it may be briefly noted here.

In Aristotle's view, right and left, above and below, front and back, are not merely relative terms. At *Cael.* 284b 24 ff. right, above and front are said to be the ἀρχαί, the starting-points or principles, not only of the three dimensions, breadth, length and depth, respectively, but also of the three types of change, locomotion, growth and sensation, in living beings. At *IA* 705b 29 ff., for example, he attempts to establish that all locomotion in animals proceeds from the right, although the evidence which he adduces for this is slender, and his interpretation of it rather arbitrary.[1] Then because he assumes that the motion of the heavenly sphere (which he thinks of as alive) must be 'from the right', and 'ἐπὶ τὰ δεξιά', he infers that the northern hemisphere, the one in which we live, is the lower of the two hemispheres.[2] Again because 'upwards' is defined in relation to the place from which food is distributed and from which growth begins (e.g. *IA* 705a 32 f.), the 'upper' portion of plants will be where their roots are, and Aristotle accordingly speaks of plants as 'upside down'.[3] Right, above and front are, then, defined by certain functions. But Aristotle holds that as ἀρχαί they are *more honourable* than their opposites. This is stated explicitly in a number of passages. At *IA* 706b 12 f., for instance, he says that 'the starting-point is honourable, and above is more honourable than below, and front than back, and right than left', and this becomes an important doctrine in anatomy, for Aristotle believes that 'as a whole,

[1] See further below, pp. 72 f.

[2] *Cael.* 285b 22 ff. (cf. also *Cael.* B 5, 287b 22 ff., on why the heavens revolve in one direction rather than in the other). On the complex problem of the meaning of the phrase ἐπὶ τὰ δεξιά as applied to circular motion, and its interpretation in *Cael.* 285b 20, see especially Heath, pp. 231 ff., and Braunlich, pp. 245 ff. Whether ἐπὶ τὰ δεξιά applied to circular motion corresponds to the direction we call 'clockwise' or what we call 'counterclockwise', the association with *right* marks it out as the *more honourable* direction.

[3] E.g. *PA* 686b 31 ff.; *IA* 705b 6; and cf. *PA* 683b 18 ff. on the Testacea.

unless some more important object interferes, that which is better and more honourable tends to be above rather than below, in front rather than behind, on the right rather than on the left' (*PA* 665a 22 ff.). He uses this principle to explain a whole series of facts, such as the relative positions of the windpipe and the oesophagus, those of the two kidneys, and so on.[1] His comments on the position of the heart are particularly interesting. According to Aristotle the heart is the principle of life and the source of all movement and sensation in the animal (*PA* 665a 11 ff.). At *PA* 665b 18 ff. he says that in man the heart 'lies about the middle of the body, but rather in its upper than in its lower half, and more in front than behind. For nature', he goes on, 'has established the more honourable part in the more honourable position, where no greater purpose prevents this.' Faced with the obvious difficulty that the heart lies on the left side of the body in man,[2] and not on the more honourable right, Aristotle argues that this is to 'counterbalance the chilliness of the left side' (*PA* 666b 6 ff.). On this occasion, when he encounters an obvious and important fact which apparently runs counter to his doctrine of the superiority and greater nobility of the right-hand side, he does not abandon that doctrine, but refers to a second arbitrary assumption, the purely imaginary distinction between the temperature of the two sides of the body.[3]

---

[1] *PA* 665a 18 ff., 671b 28 ff. (though in fact Aristotle is mistaken in suggesting that the right kidney is always higher than the left, for in man, for example, the left kidney is usually higher). Cf. also *PA* 667b 34 ff. on the relative position of the 'great blood-vessel' and the aorta, and 672b 19 ff. on the function of the diaphragm, which is conceived as that of separating the nobler, upper parts of the body from the less noble, lower ones. Other passages where Aristotle explains the relative position of organs and other phenomena by referring to the superiority of right, front and above, are given by Ogle, note to *PA* 648a 11.

[2] Aristotle is mistaken in asserting, as he does on several occasions (cf. *HA* 506b 32 ff.), that it is in man alone that the heart inclines towards the left side of the body.

[3] Yet elsewhere the difference in temperature between the two sides of the body is itself said to depend on the heart. It is striking that Aristotle recognises that in man the heart inclines towards the left (and by itself this would naturally lead us to expect him to suggest that the left is the hotter side), but still argues

At *PA* 684a 26 ff. Aristotle first remarks that 'in all the Crawfish (κάραβοι) and the Crabs (καρκίνοι) the right claw is bigger and stronger' (than the left)[1] and then follows this with the generalisation that 'all animals naturally tend to use their right limbs more in their activities'. Yet sometimes he notes exceptions to the general rule that limbs on the right are stronger than those on the left, and it is instructive to consider how he deals with these cases. At *PA* 684a 32 ff., for instance, he remarks that in the lobsters (ἀστακοί) it is a matter of chance whether the right or the left claw is the bigger. But he goes on to say that the reason for this is that lobsters are deformed, and do not use the claw for its natural purpose (prehension) but for locomotion.[2] Again it is clear from such passages as *IA* 714b 8 ff. that he acknowledged that right and left are not clearly distinguished in such classes as the Testacea:[3] but again the reason which he suggests for this lack of differentiation is that the Testacea are a deformed class (*IA* 714b 10 f.). Aristotle carried out extensive observations of many different kinds of animals, and his descriptions of the internal and external organs of many species are remarkably detailed and accurate. Yet his investigations did not lead him to modify his doctrine that right is naturally and essentially superior to left. He believes that this is true in man, and man is the norm by which he judges the rest of the animal kingdom. At *PA* 656a 10 ff., for example, he puts it that in man alone 'the natural parts are in their "natural" positions, and his upper part is turned towards that which is

that the right is the hotter side, giving as the reason for this that the right hand chamber of the heart contains the most, and the hottest, blood (*PA* 666b 35 ff.).

[1] This statement is not true without qualification: contrast the more cautious judgement concerning the Crabs, at least, at *HA* 527b 6 f.

[2] *PA* 684a 35–b 1, cf. *HA* 526b 16 f. It is not true, however, that the chelae of lobsters are used solely for locomotion: indeed at *HA* 526a 24 f. Aristotle himself remarks that they are naturally adapted for prehension.

[3] Yet at *IA* 706a 13 ff. he attempts to establish a 'functional' distinction between right and left in the stromboid Testaceans, saying that they are δεξιά because they do not move in the direction of the spire, but opposite to it. Here he appears to argue that *because* they move in the direction opposite to the spire, *therefore* the spire must be assumed to be 'on the right'; cf. *HA* 528b 8 ff. and D'A. W. Thompson's note *ad loc.*

upper in the universe,'[1] and at *IA* 706a 19 f. he says that man is 'of all the animals, most in accordance with nature (κατά φύσιν). But naturally (φύσει)', he goes on, 'right is better than left and separate from it. And so the right is "most right-sided" in man (διὸ καὶ τὰ δεξιὰ ἐν τοῖς ἀνθρώποις μάλιστα δεξιά ἐστιν)'. Accordingly, the reason that he gives for the absence of any marked distinction between right and left in some species is that they are imperfect or 'deformed' animals.

He believes not only that there is what we might call a physiological distinction between right and left (the right side being hotter than the left), but also that in making this distinction nature fulfils an important purpose. The distinction between right and left is an *ideal*, to which the animal kingdom aspires, but which is most fully exemplified in man.[2] A detailed knowledge of different biological species, in many of which no distinction, or no marked distinction, between right and left is found, did nothing to uproot Aristotle's belief that right is naturally stronger and more honourable than left. On the contrary, that knowledge led him to conclude that the differentiation between right and left is a mark of man's superiority to the animals, and of his greater perfection.[3]

[1] Cf. also *HA* 494a 26 ff.

[2] So too the distinctions between upper and lower, and between front and back, which are connected with growth and sensation respectively, are said to be more fully present in the higher living beings than in the lower (see *IA* chs. 2 ff., e.g. 705b 6 ff. on 'up' and 'down' in plants). Aristotle also holds that it is *better* for the two sexes to be distinguished (e.g. *GA* 731b 20 ff.).

[3] It is remarkable that the notion of the essential superiority of the right side persisted in Greek philosophy even though the social factors which are involved in the greater physical development of the right hand did not pass unnoticed by Greek theorists. Plato, especially, points out that childhood training contributes to the greater usefulness of the right hand at *Laws* 794d f., where he recommends that children should be taught to use both hands equally. He criticises the view that right and left are naturally different in usefulness, observing that this is not the case with the feet or lower limbs. 'But through the folly of nurses and mothers', as he puts it (794d 8 ff.), 'we have all become lame, so to speak, in our hands.' He notes that athletes can become ambidextrous, and says that the Scythians are in fact so. Aristotle, too, recognised that we can become ambidextrous (at *HA* 497b 31 f. he says that this is true of man alone of all the animals), but he holds that the right hand is still *naturally* stronger than the left (*EN* 1134b 33 ff.; cf. *MM* 1194b 31 ff.).

One set of theories which we find in early Greek speculative thought clearly reflects the symbolic values and associations which such opposites as right and left, male and female, light and darkness, up and down, and front and back had for the ancient Greeks. In the Pythagorean Table of Opposites, right, male and light are placed on one side, the side of the good, and their opposites on the other, the side of evil. Parmenides, Anaxagoras and several Hippocratic authors proposed various theories correlating the superior terms male and right, and the inferior terms female and left, although none of their theories can be said to be based on any cogent empirical grounds. Although Aristotle refuted the notion that the difference between the sexes is to be derived from a difference between right and left, he explicitly stated that right, above and front are more honourable than their opposites and he based several of his physical and biological theories on this principle. But the question that we must now discuss is how far the tendency to divide opposites into a positive, and a negative, pole influenced the use of other pairs in early Greek philosophy and medicine. How far are other opposites, besides those which we have already considered, correlated according to preconceived notions of fitness, rather than according to any empirical data? We noted earlier that in pre-philosophical literature such pairs as hot and cold and dry and wet do not appear to have particularly strong symbolic associations, and those of dry and wet, at least, seem to be somewhat ambivalent. These opposites are, of course, the two most prominent pairs of all in early Greek speculative thought, and we must examine how far the philosophers tended to conceive these pairs too as consisting of on the one hand a positive or superior pole, and on the other a negative or inferior one.

Unlike right and left or male and female, the pairs hot and cold and dry and wet do not figure in the Pythagorean Table of Opposites given by Aristotle. Furthermore they appear predominantly in our extant sources in theories in which the relation between them is conceived as a continuous, balanced interaction, and in which there is nothing to suggest that one of each pair is thought of as in any way superior to the other.[1] If we consider the connections that are suggested between these and other pairs, some of these seem to reflect a 'cosmological', others a 'biological' point of view. Anaxagoras Fr. 15, for instance, refers to a separation between, on the one side, cold and wet and dense and dark (which are associated, in all probability, with earth), and on the other side, hot and dry and rare (which are connected with aither), and Parmenides, too, very probably associated hot, as well as rare, with fire and light, and cold, as well as dense and heavy, with night or darkness.[2] On the other hand there is plenty of evidence to show that the popular belief in the connection between life and the hot and the wet continued to find expression in the theories of the philosophers and medical writers.[3]

Sometimes, then, hot and dry are together opposed to cold and wet, sometimes hot and wet are associated together, and as I suggested before, two main sets of observations seem to underlie these two types of correlations, on the one hand such meteorological phenomena as the alternation of summer and winter and day and night, and on the other such biological phenomena as the warmth of living creatures, and the coldness, and in some cases the dryness, of what is dead. But when we turn to some of the more detailed doctrines which

---

[1] See, for example, the cosmological doctrine of *On the Nature of Man* and the pathological theory of Alcmaeon, mentioned above, pp. 19 f.

[2] This is explicitly stated in a scholion reported by Simplicius, *in Ph.* 31 3 ff., and cf. Parmenides' own words in Fr. 8 56 ff.

[3] The idea that living beings originated in the wet when this was acted upon by the sun is attributed to Anaximander at Hippolytus *Haer.* 1 6 6 (DK 12 A 11) and a similar theory appears in the cosmology reported in Diodorus (1 7 3 ff., DK 68 B 5, 1). Again when Aristotle discusses the reasons which may have led Thales to adopt water as the ἀρχή, he mentions the idea that 'the hot itself comes to be from this (i.e. water) and lives by this' (*Metaph.* 983 b 23 f.). In the Hippocratic Corpus, *On Regimen* 1 chs. 32 f. (L vi 506 14 ff.) develops the theory that generation takes place from an interaction between the hot and the wet (or Fire and Water) and *On Fleshes* also points out a connection between humidity and vital heat (ch. 9, L viii 596 9 ff.).

were based on these two pairs of opposites, we find theories which apparently have no basis in empirical evidence at all. It was widely assumed that the difference between the two sexes is in some way to be connected with a difference between hot and cold or one between dry and wet, even though there was no general agreement as to which opposites corresponded to which sex. The view that women are hotter than men is mentioned by Aristotle at *PA* 648a 28 ff., where he ascribes it to Parmenides among others. Moreover the main *grounds* on which this theory was adopted are clear both from Aristotle's report and from the Hippocratic treatise *On the Diseases of Women* I (ch. 1, L VIII 12 17 ff.): menstruation was thought to be due to an abundance of (hot) blood, and was taken, therefore, as a sign of the greater heat of women. But if this was one opinion that was put forward, the contrary view, that men are hotter than women, was maintained, for example, by Empedocles.[1] If we ask why *this* position was adopted, the answer lies not so much in any empirical data that could be adduced in its favour, as in the belief that male and hot are inherently superior to their respective opposites female and cold. True, both the author of *On Regimen* and Aristotle feel it necessary to defend this view with arguments, but on examination their arguments can be seen to consist largely of special pleading. (1) At *On Regimen* I ch. 34 (L VI 512 13 ff.) the writer suggests that males are hotter and drier (*a*) because of their regimen, and (*b*) because females purge the hot from their bodies every month. But (*a*) depends on the writer's schematic, *a priori* analysis of the effects of food and exercise, and (*b*) is clearly a case of special pleading, since if the effect of menstruation is taken to be that females become colder, then by the same reasoning they should also become *drier* on the loss of blood. Yet in the writer's view *males* are hotter and *drier* (conforming to the element Fire) and females are colder and wetter (conforming to the element

[1] See Aristotle, *PA* 648a 31 and cf. Empedocles Frr. 65 and 67, noted above, p. 17.

Water). These opposites are, in fact, arranged according to the writer's notions of fitness (hot, dry, male and fire each being the positive or superior terms), rather than according to his observation of the differences between the two sexes. (2) Aristotle has a similar doctrine, but the arguments which he uses to support it are no more convincing. At *GA* 765b 8 ff. he distinguishes males and females by their ability, or inability, to 'concoct' the blood, assuming that that which becomes the menses in females, becomes semen in males. He notes once again (as at *PA* 648a 28 ff.) that other theorists took menstruation as a sign of the greater heat of the female sex, but he suggests that this view does not take into account the possibility that blood may be more or less pure, more or less concocted, and he argues, or rather asserts, that semen, though smaller in quantity, is purer and more concocted than the menses.[1] While it is interesting that Aristotle refers here to qualitative, rather than to purely quantitative, differences in order to determine what is 'hot', his view that males are hotter than females depends first on the notion that semen and menses are the end-products of strictly comparable processes, and second, and more important, on the quite arbitrary assumption that semen is the *natural* product of the process of concoction, and the menses are an *impure* residue. Aristotle considers the female to be like a deformed male,[2] and it is this conviction, rather than any empirical considerations, that underlies his doctrine that males are hotter than females.

We have considered one clear instance where certain theorists correlated hot and cold and dry and wet and other opposites according to preconceived ideas of fitness and value,

---

[1] There is an obscure comparison with the production of fruit at *GA* 765b 28 ff. ('the nutriment in its first stage is abundant, but the useful product derived from it is small'—Platt). The idea seems to be that as plants turn their food first into leaves, then into fruit, so animals turn theirs first into blood, and then (in males) into semen (see Platt's note *ad loc.*).

[2] E.g. *GA* 737a 27 ff., τὸ γὰρ θῆλυ ὥσπερ ἄρρεν ἐστὶ πεπηρωμένον, καὶ τὰ καταμήνια σπέρμα, οὐ καθαρὸν δέ ('For the female is like a deformed male, and the menses are semen, only not pure').

and other examples could be given from fifth- and fourth-century writers.[1] But the most important evidence concerning the way in which these two pairs were sometimes treated as consisting of a positive and a negative pole undoubtedly comes from Aristotle, whose theories should now be examined in more detail. First we should note how he defines these four terms at *GC* 329b 26 ff. 'Hot' is 'that which combines things of the same kind' (τὸ συγκρῖνον τὰ ὁμογενῆ), 'cold' 'that which brings together and combines homogeneous and heterogeneous things alike' (τὸ συνάγον καὶ συγκρῖνον ὁμοίως τά τε συγγενῆ καὶ τὰ μὴ ὁμόφυλα), 'wet' is 'that which, being readily delimited (i.e. by something else), is not determined by its own boundary' (τὸ ἀόριστον οἰκείῳ ὅρῳ, εὐόριστον ὄν) and 'dry' 'that which, not being readily delimited (i.e. by something else), is determined by its own boundary' (τὸ εὐόριστον μὲν οἰκείῳ ὅρῳ, δυσόριστον δέ). These definitions are quite abstract and certainly convey no hint that these opposites had any positive or negative values for Aristotle. Moreover, elsewhere he points out the ambiguities of these terms in common Greek usage and draws attention to the disagreements that existed between different theorists on the subject of which things are 'hot', which 'cold' and so on.[2] It is all the more surprising, then, that in several places these pairs are clearly conceived as divided into a positive and a negative pole. This is particularly evident in the case of hot and cold. As we have just seen, Aristotle's belief that the male sex is hotter than the female reflects his preconceived notions of the superiority of *male* and *hot* and

---

[1] Thus there is an elaborate schema in which the four ages of man are correlated with pairs of opposites in *Vict.* I ch. 33 (L VI 510 24 ff.), the first age being hot and wet, the second hot and dry, the third cold and dry, and old men cold and wet. But this schema seems dictated in part, at least, by the author's desire to associate the second age, that of the young man, with the male sex and the superior element Fire, and old age with the inferior element Water (cold and wet): in particular his view that the old are *wet* runs counter to the generally accepted Greek notions (see above, p. 45), though it also appears in *Salubr.* ch. 2 (L VI 74 19 ff.).

[2] See especially *PA* B 2 and 3, e.g. 648a 24 ff., 33 ff.

cannot be said to have any verifiable empirical basis. Then he also held that the right-hand side of the body is hotter than the left (suggesting at *PA* 667a 1 f. that this difference depends on a difference in the temperature of the right and left sides of the heart), but this doctrine, too, has no valid basis in fact and derives from certain *a priori* assumptions. Elsewhere he postulates differences in the temperature and purity of the blood between the upper and lower parts of the body,[1] and contrasting man with other animals, he asserts at *PA* 653a 27 ff. that the region round the heart and the lungs is hotter and richer in blood in man than in any other animal, and this is another doubtful generalisation which illustrates his belief in a connection between heat and perfection.

In Aristotle's theory hot is clearly the positive term, cold the privation: indeed this is explicitly stated on several occasions.[2] His attitude towards the pair dry and wet is, however, less clear. At *PA* 670b 18 ff. where he correlates hot and right on the one hand, and cold and left on the other, the inferior left side of the body is said to be both cold and *wet*. Again at *GA* 766b 31 ff. he says that parents who have a 'wetter and more feminine' constitution tend to produce female children, and this suggests that wet is also associated, in his view, with the inferior female sex.[3] On the other hand at *GA* B 1 (732b 15 ff.) he defines the main genera of animals according to their methods of reproduction (which correspond to differences in their constitutions) and here the most perfect animals, the Vivipara, are said to be 'hotter and wetter and less earthy by nature' (732b 31 f.). The second

---

[1] *PA* 648a 11 ff. In the same chapter (648a 2 ff.) he argues that differences in the strength and courage and intelligence of different species of animals are attributable to differences in the temperature and purity of their blood, and he suggests that 'best of all are those animals whose blood is hot and thin and clear: for such animals are favourably constituted both for courage and for intelligence at the same time'.

[2] E.g. *Cael.* 286a 25 f.; *GC* 318b 16 f.; *Metaph.* 1070b 11 f.: contrast, however, *PA* 649a 18 f.

[3] The view that men are dry and hot, and women wet and cold, is also often expressed in the pseudo-Aristotelian *Problemata*, e.g. 879a 33 ff.

group, the ovo-viviparous animals (e.g. cartilaginous fishes)
are cold and wet, the third and the fourth (those oviparous
animals that lay perfect, and those that lay imperfect, eggs)
are hot and dry, and cold and dry respectively, and the fifth
and final group (insects) are 'coldest of all' (733a 1–b 12).
Greater perfection clearly corresponds, in this schema, to a
combination of greater heat and greater 'humidity'. Again
at *Long.* 466a 18 ff. he says that 'we must assume that the
living animal is by nature wet and hot, and life too is such,
while old age is cold and dry, as also is that which is dead: for
this is plain to observation'. Yet he goes on to note that both
the quantity and the *quality* of the 'humidity' of animals
affect their length of life: 'for not only must there be a lot of
the wet, but it must also be hot' (466a 29 ff.). The pair dry
and wet occupies, then, a rather ambivalent position in
Aristotle's system, as indeed it had also done, to some extent,
in earlier Greek speculative thought. On the one hand he
notices a connection between humidity and life, and between
dryness and death (and here he develops a notion which can
be traced back to Homer and Hesiod). Yet this does not
prevent him from suggesting or implying, in other contexts,
that the wet is the inferior, privative term, when he correlates
it with female, left and cold.

Already in Homer and Hesiod, as we saw, certain natural
oppositions are associated with, or used to symbolise,
important religious or spiritual distinctions, and we find some
evidence of a tendency to correlate the positive and the
negative poles of different pairs of opposites respectively, even
when there is no manifest connection between the terms in
question. But where we might have expected these associations to have been soon forgotten or ignored in early Greek
philosophy and medicine, we find, on the contrary, that they
continued to play a part in quite a number of theories and
explanations, and what is more, it was certain philosophers
who first explicitly formulated the distinction in *value* between
the opposite terms of certain pairs, and who extended and

developed this use of opposites into comprehensive systems. The extent to which present-day primitive peoples themselves consciously formulate the system that underlies their dualist beliefs is often difficult to determine from the reports of the anthropologists: neat Tables of Opposites such as those which I have noted above (pp. 32 ff.) generally represent the field-worker's own analysis of a complex series of beliefs and practices, rather than a verbatim report of the notions entertained by a particular member of the society investigated. As regards the ancient Greek evidence, at least, it may not be purely fortuitous that the first such Table for which we have evidence is the work of speculative thinkers, the Pythagoreans. In part, the Pythagorean Table given by Aristotle certainly reflects and follows much earlier beliefs, but it seems possible, or indeed quite probable, that this Table represents the first major attempt to define and systematise such beliefs in a single schema. Other attempts to bring various pairs of opposites into a single system can be traced in other early Greek philosophers. The dualist cosmology of Parmenides' *Way of Seeming* seems to contain one such attempt, and it might also be suggested that the pairs of personifications mentioned in Empedocles Frr. 122 and 123 represent something like a Table of Opposites expressed in mythical terms.[1] But it is

[1] These two fragments from the *Purifications* contain the following list of personifications: 'Chthonie' and 'Heliope', Rivalry and Harmony, Beauty and Ugliness, Swiftness and Loitering, Truth and Obscurity, Birth and Decay, Sleep and Waking, Movement and Immobility, Greatness and Defilement (Φορύη), Silence and Voice. We cannot be certain in what context these personifications were mentioned (KR, n. 1 on p. 353, call Fr. 122 a 'catalogue, in mythical garb, of the opposites that characterize' the 'vale of tears' of Fr. 121—although in Fr. 121, in contrast with Frr. 122–3, only *evil* personifications appear). But the list reads very much like a Table of Opposites. The figures Movement and Immobility (Κινώ, 'Αστεμφής) may be compared with the Pythagorean 'at rest' and 'moving' (ἠρεμοῦν, κινούμενον). Chthonie and Heliope (Earth and Sun) recall, perhaps, Parmenides' Night (which is identified by Aristotle, *Ph.* 188a 20 ff., at least, as Earth: cf. its description as dense and heavy in Parmenides Fr. 8 59) and Light or Fire. The pair Silence and Voice may also have figured in the *Way of Seeming* (cf. Theophrastus' account of Parmenides' theory of perception, *Sens.* 4, DK 28 A 46). Most remarkable of all is the mention of 'Αρμονίη and Δῆρις, for these must, surely, be Love and Strife themselves: 'Αρμονίη is used elsewhere of Love (Fr. 27 3, Fr. 96 4) and Δῆρις seems to stand for Strife in Fr. 27a.

particularly notable that the tendency to try to incorporate pairs of opposites into a single comprehensive schema should survive to the extent that it does in Aristotle, even though he was fully aware of the lack of agreement among Greek theorists on the subject of the hot, the cold, the wet and the dry, for example, and drew attention, on several occasions, to the ambiguities which the use of these terms involved. He never presents his theory in the form of a complete συστοιχία, yet from remarks scattered through the physical treatises we can piece together a Table of Opposites comparable with that of the Pythagoreans (and Aristotle's use of the terms συστοιχία and σύστοιχος to refer to some of his own theories seems to suggest that he recognised a general similarity between his own ideas and those of the Pythagoreans).[1] Thus right, male, above, front, hot and dry would certainly appear on one side, set over against left, female, below, back, cold and wet, and such other pairs as light and heavy, and rare and dense, might also be included in the list, correlated with hot and cold, or dry and wet—the Table as a whole reflecting both empirical and *a priori* considerations.[2] Indeed, although, as we have seen, there appear to be certain inconsistencies in

---

[1] Thus at *PA* 670b 17 ff. Aristotle first explains the 'watery' quality of the spleen in certain animals partly by referring to the generally 'wetter and colder' nature of the left side of the body, and then goes on: διήρηται γὰρ τῶν ἐναντίων ἕκαστον πρὸς τὴν συγγενῆ συστοιχίαν, οἷον δεξιὸν ἐναντίον ἀριστερῷ καὶ θερμὸν ἐναντίον ψυχρῷ· καὶ σύστοιχα γὰρ ἀλλήλοις εἰσὶ τὸν εἰρημένον τρόπον ('Each of the opposites is separated according to the column which is akin to it, as right is opposite left, and hot opposite cold, and they are coordinate with one another in the way described' (i.e. right and hot are in one column, left and cold in the other)) (b 20 ff.).

[2] At *Cael.* 286a 26 ff. 'heavy' is said to be the privation of 'light', and at *Ph.* 217b 17 ff. and *Cael.* 299b 7 ff. 'heavy' and 'dense' are associated together, and so too 'light' and 'rare' (for this reason, perhaps, as well as because of the association between 'thin' and 'clear', the blood of males is said to be 'thinner' than that of females, *PA* 648a 11 ff.). Yet with such a pair as 'soft' and 'hard', we find different types of correlation proposed in different contexts: on the one hand 'hard' is associated with 'dense' (e.g. *Ph.* 217b 17), but on the other it is assimilated to 'dry' (at *GC* B 2 330a 8 ff. in a chapter in which Aristotle reduces various pairs of opposites to 'hot' and 'cold' or 'dry' and 'wet' while at the same time pointing out some of the ambiguities of these terms). From other passages (e.g. *Ph.* 259a 6 ff.) it would appear that like the Pythagoreans Aristotle thought 'one' superior to 'many', and 'limited' to 'unlimited'.

Aristotle's attitude to certain pairs, it is clear from repeated statements in the *Metaphysics*[1] that he believed it to be true of contrary terms as a whole, that one of each pair is a positive term, the other a (mere) privation.

SCHEMA AND VERIFICATION IN THE USE OF THEORIES BASED ON OPPOSITES IN EARLY GREEK THOUGHT

We have considered one group of theories which are evidently influenced by dogmatic assumptions concerning the values of certain pairs of opposite terms, but it is obvious that there are many other theories in which such assumptions play no part, and we must now broaden our inquiry to take these into account. Time and again in attempting to identify the constituent elements of man or of the universe as a whole, to describe the formation of the world, to establish the causes of diseases or to suggest their remedies, Greek speculative theorists proposed doctrines based on a pair or pairs of opposite principles. But one of the problems which faced *any* theorist who attempted to tackle such questions is, one may say, that of reducing the multiplicity of phenomena as far as possible to simple principles, and if we ask why *opposites* are referred to especially frequently in different contexts in such doctrines, one fairly obvious suggestion that we may make is that opposites provide simple and distinct reference points to which other things may be related. This point can be illustrated by considering for a moment some of the many dualist classifications which were put forward by Greek writers outside the fields of cosmology, physics and biology. Aristotle provides several interesting examples of the use of such classifications in ethics, politics and elsewhere. He uses various classifications of political constitutions in the *Politics*, but in one of these he treats all constitutions as varieties of either democracy or oligarchy.[2] At *Pol.* 1290a 13 ff. he notes

---

[1] E.g. *Metaph.* 1004b 27ff., 1011b 18f., 1055b 14.
[2] *Pol.* Δ–Z ('polity' is a mean between the two kinds, 1294a 30 ff.). Elsewhere, however, Aristotle proposes a sixfold schema of constitutions, three being

that this corresponds, in the main, to the popular way of referring to constitutions, and he cites two parallels to this type of classification, first the way in which winds were generally classed as either 'northerly' or 'southerly' (other winds being treated as deviations from, or varieties of, these two kinds), and then also the way in which the modes of music were classified under the two heads 'Dorian' and 'Phrygian'.[1] Again in his account of characters in the second book of the *Rhetoric* (chs. 12–14) he uses a pair of opposite categories, with a mean between them, in a similar fashion, dividing characters into the three groups, those of 'the young', 'the old' and 'men in their prime'.[2]

In cosmology, physics and biology, too, part of the attraction of opposite principles lies, no doubt, in their abstract clarity and their apparent comprehensiveness. Yet unlike attempts to classify political constitutions, for example, when opposite groups may be referred to purely for the sake of a certain convenience in exposition, these speculative theories are intended as true accounts of the causes at work. To refer to a pair or pairs of opposite principles has obvious advantages in terms of clarity and economy, but *we* demand not only that a scientific theory should be simple and intelligible, but also that it should yield predictions which can be submitted to practical tests. This leads us, then, to ask a series of questions concerning Greek doctrines of opposites severally and as a whole: how far were their authors conscious of a need to devise empirical tests which would confirm or refute their theories? What methods did they in fact use to substantiate their doctrines, that is

true constitutions (monarchy, aristocracy and 'polity') and three the 'deviations' (παρεκβάσεις) from these (tyranny, oligarchy, democracy), e.g. *Pol.* Γ 7 and *EN* 1160a 31 ff.

[1] The principle once established that oligarchies and democracies are contraries, Aristotle suggests that inferences can be drawn from one to the other: 'Reasoning from opposites, we should infer each oligarchy by calculating it according to the opposite democracy' (*Pol.* 1320b 18 ff.).

[2] He explicitly states that the character of the old is 'for the most part contrary' to that of the young (*Rh.* 1389b 13 f.). The purpose of the whole passage is to provide the orator with information which will enable him to play on his audience's emotions.

what kinds of evidence or argument did they adduce in their support? And we must consider, too, not only the constructive efforts that were made to establish different theories of this general type, but also the destructive criticisms which such theories evoked from the Greeks themselves. Each new theory on a particular topic involves an implicit correction of alternative doctrines, but we also find writers who explicitly refute their predecessors' views, and such criticisms provide valuable evidence on the general problem of what different Greek theorists may have expected of an 'account' of a natural phenomenon, that is the criteria which, in their view, such theories should fulfil.

Theories based on opposites provide many illustrations of the dogmatic tendencies in early Greek speculative thought, the tendency to construct simple, comprehensive doctrines on the most general, complex problems. But an important sceptical and critical strain is evident in Greek thought from the earliest times. If, for example, the superstitious belief that omens on the right are lucky, those on the left unlucky, was extremely widespread among the ancient Greeks, we should certainly not assume that this belief was *never* denied. In describing their own first-hand experiences among primitive societies many anthropologists have remarked that individuals frequently express considerable scepticism not only about the efficacy of particular magical practices, but also about traditional religious beliefs.[1] Certainly by the time of Homer, at least, such scepticism was not uncommon among the ancient Greeks. The alternative attitudes which might be adopted towards traditional beliefs are clearly illustrated in a well-known passage in the *Iliad* (12 195 ff.) to which I have already referred in another context. An eagle appears on the Trojans' left, and Polydamas duly

---

[1] See, for example, Evans-Pritchard, *1*, p. 193: 'it is important to note that scepticism about witch-doctors is not socially repressed. Absence of formal and coercive doctrines permits Azande to state that many, even most, witch-doctors are frauds'. Cf. also pp. 427, 466 and 475 ff.

interprets this as an evil portent.[1] Hector, on the other hand, rejects its significance, declaring that he does not care at all 'whether the birds of omen fly to the right, towards the dawn and the sun, or to the left, towards the misty west' (238 ff.). Hector does not, of course, *examine* the assumption that right and left are lucky and unlucky respectively, he simply *rejects* it. We may guess that in such contexts the alternative views of the believer and the sceptic often led to an impasse. If the outcome of events happened to bear out the prophecy which had been made, the sceptic would say that this was a pure coincidence. Conversely, when events proved the prophet wrong, *he* might still protest that what was at fault was not the method of interpretation itself, but merely his own application of that method in a particular instance.

When we turn to philosophy, we are dealing not so much with religious beliefs, as with scientific theories which claimed to account for certain phenomena, and we have quite extensive evidence concerning the debates which revolved round some of the doctrines based on opposites which we have been considering, although we find several cases where a writer rejects one particular doctrine only to propose another which follows a broadly similar pattern. The criticisms which various theories based on the hot, the cold, the dry and the wet provoked are especially interesting. It seems likely that the question of the nature of the hot and the cold was raised as early as Anaximenes, for according to a report in Plutarch (*de prim. frig.* 7, 947 f–948 a, DK 13 B 1), Anaximenes argued that the cold and the hot are to be identified with what is dense and what is rare respectively, supporting this suggestion by referring to the apparent difference in the temperature of the breath depending on whether it is exhaled through compressed lips or with the mouth wide open. Anaximenes' method, his reference to this simple test, is noteworthy, although the effect of his criticism was merely to reduce one

---

[1] On the element of analogy in Polydamas' interpretation of this omen, see below, p. 182.

pair of opposites (hot/cold) to another (rare/dense) and to claim priority for the latter. But a much more devastating attack on the theory of the hot, the cold, the dry and the wet, as applied to medicine at least, is contained in *On Ancient Medicine*, and both the form which this attack takes and the nature of the theory which the writer suggests as an alternative are worth careful examination. The writer makes both general and particular criticisms of the theories he attacks. First he protests, in ch. 1, *CMG* 1, 1 36 15 ff., that medicine has no need of a 'hypothesis', 'like obscure and problematic subjects, concerning which anyone who attempts to hold forth at all is forced to use a hypothesis, as for example about things in heaven or things under the earth: for if anyone were to speak and declare the nature of these things, it would not be clear either to the speaker himself or to his audience whether what was said was true or not, since there is no criterion to which one should refer to obtain clear knowledge (οὐ γὰρ ἔστι, πρὸς ὅ τι χρὴ ἀνενέγκαντα εἰδέναι τὸ σαφές) '. This passage makes several extremely important methodological points. Among these is the suggestion that 'hypotheses', that is arbitrary assumptions or postulates, should be banned from medicine, and the passage also comes close to suggesting, as a general rule, that physical theories must be verifiable (at least according to the writer's standards of verifiability), for it implies that where no criterion is available by which they may be judged true or false, theories are quite worthless.

But this writer also has specific criticisms to make concerning the use of the hot, the cold, the dry and the wet in medical theories. In chs. 13 ff. he attacks the notion that any of these opposites could successfully be prescribed as a remedy for a disease. Imagining a case in which a change of diet from raw to cooked food has brought about a cure, he asks: 'What are we to say in such a case? That the patient was suffering from cold, and that it was the taking of these hot things that cured him? Or the opposite? In my opinion this question raises great difficulties for my opponent. For when bread is prepared, is it the heat or the cold or the dryness or the wetness which is abstracted from the wheat?' (ch. 13, *CMG* 1, 1 44 25 ff.). These criticisms illustrate very clearly some of the difficulties which faced those who attempted to apply the theory of the hot, the cold, the dry and the wet to particular problems. But when we turn to consider the author's own theories, it is obvious that he hardly managed to live up to his expressed ideal of excluding all arbitrary assumptions from the study of medicine. True, his physiological doctrine is quite a complex one: he admits the presence, in man, of very many different kinds of things with 'powers' of all sorts (ch. 14), and his theory is stated not in terms of simple physical opposites such as hot and cold, but in terms of such savours as the salty, the bitter and the sweet, the acidic, the astringent and the insipid, and so on. And yet a doctrine which identified these as the component substances in the body is evidently open to objections which are broadly similar to those which the author himself brought so effectively against his opponents. Then again in his pathological theory he recognises the complexity of diseases, and, perhaps more important, he stresses that it is only very rarely that exactness can be attained in medicine.[1] But he suggests, for example, that diseases arise from both 'repletion' and 'depletion' (chs. 9 f.), and while this doctrine is rather more general than the one he criticises, we may hazard a guess that the application of these vague notions to particular problems of diagnosis and cure was scarcely less arbitrary and obscure than that of the theory of the hot, the cold, the dry and the wet itself.

Some of the criticisms which were raised against particular doctrines based on opposites were undoubtedly very damaging, and yet in certain cases a writer rejects one such theory only to propose an alternative doctrine which takes a similar form and is open to roughly similar objections. But we must

---

[1] Ch. 9, *CMG* 1, 1 41 20 ff., and cf. ch. 12, 43 27 ff.

now consider more closely how various types of evidence were brought to bear to support or refute different theories based on opposite principles. We should note, first of all, that at one stage, at least, there were some theorists who considered it permissible to refer to the real or supposed etymologies of words in support of their physical doctrines. One of the controversies that had arisen towards the latter part of the fifth century on the subject of hot and cold, to which Aristotle refers at *PA* 648 a 24 ff., concerned the humours in the body. The usual view[1] was that phlegm is cold, and bile and blood hot, but Philolaus, for one, held that phlegm too is hot, and according to the report in Anonymus Londinensis (xviii 41 ff.) he supported his view by suggesting that φλέγμα is derived from φλέγειν, 'to burn'. Again at *de An.* 405 b 26 ff. Aristotle reports that some people argued that the soul is hot on the grounds that ʒῆν, 'to live', is derived from ʒεῖν, 'to boil', while others thought that it is cold on the grounds of the connection between ψυχή, 'soul', and κατάψυξις, 'cooling'.

More often, it is true, theories involving opposites were supported by more solid evidence, even if that evidence was often quite inconclusive. It is striking that the same piece of evidence, the fact of menstruation, was referred to (but interpreted in different ways) both by those who, like Parmenides, held that women are hotter than men, and by those who, like the author of *On Regimen* I, maintained the opposite view.[2] Yet the fact of menstruation tells us nothing, of course, about the *relative* temperature of males and females. Again the same data seem to have been adduced both by those who said that water-animals are cold (as fish, for example, are to the touch) and by those who, like Empedocles, maintained, on the contrary, that they are hot, arguing that the cold of their environment counterbalances the heat

---

[1] E.g. *Morb.* I ch. 24 (L vi 188 19 ff.). Cf. *Nat. Hom.* ch. 7 (L vi 46 9 ff.), where a neat schema is proposed in which phlegm is cold and wet, blood hot and wet, bile hot and dry, and black bile cold and dry.

[2] See above, p. 58.

of their constitutions.[1] On some occasions, however, the evidence which was brought to support a theory based on opposite principles is more elaborate and extensive. Several of these theories concern topics (notably in biology) on which a great deal of research had already been done by Greek scientists before the end of the fourth century, even though the interpretation which they put upon the evidence they collected was sometimes quite arbitrary. We should certainly not underestimate the extent of the investigations which Aristotle, in particular, carried out in the natural sciences, and yet I have already remarked on his reluctance to abandon certain of his preconceived opinions when the results of his observations appeared to run counter to those opinions (when it was seen that the heart inclines to the left side of the body in man, for instance),[2] and a further example which illustrates how selective his use of evidence in biology sometimes was can be given from *On the Progression of Animals*. This short treatise contains many interesting and quite detailed observations concerning the way in which animals move. But at *IA* 705b 29 ff. Aristotle attempts to establish that all locomotion proceeds from the right. The main evidence for this which he brings is (1) that men carry burdens on their left shoulders, (2) that they step off with the left foot—in both cases, according to Aristotle, the right is the side which initiates the movement—and (3) that men defend themselves with their right limbs.[3] Yet on (2) one may remark that elsewhere (*IA* 712a 25 ff.) he suggests that horses step off with the off fore, and on the principle that the side which initiates the movement is that which itself remains unmoved, this would suggest that in horses, at least, the *left* is the ἀρχὴ κινήσεως. Furthermore, in view of this same principle, that the side which initiates the movement remains

---

[1] Arist. *Resp.* 477a 32 ff.; *PA* 648a 25 ff.

[2] See above, pp. 53 f.

[3] Aristotle also notes (*IA* 705b 33) that it is easier to hop on the left leg, and elsewhere (*PA* 671b 32 ff.) he even says that men raise their right eyebrows more than their left.

unmoved itself, it seems paradoxical that he adduces (3), that men defend themselves with their right limbs, as evidence that it is the *right* that is the ἀρχὴ κινήσεως.

So far I have dealt exclusively with evidence which could be acquired without having recourse to deliberate experimentation. But we must now turn to the passages in our extant texts which indicate that some Greek theorists recognised the possibility of investigating certain of their doctrines which were based on opposite principles by means of simple tests and experiments. The failure to experiment has often been pointed to as the chief shortcoming of ancient science. Yet it is undeniable that the *idea* of conducting simple tests in order to support or refute certain theories had occurred to a number of fifth- and fourth-century writers, even if their execution of such tests was often inexact. Thus at *GA* 765a 21 ff. Aristotle refers to a line of argument which certain theorists had adopted in an attempt to support the doctrine that the sex of the embryo is determined by whether the seed of the male comes from the right or the left testicle. Leophanes is named as one of the theorists who apparently maintained that when males copulated with one or other testicle tied up, they produced offspring of a particular sex. 'And some say', Aristotle goes on, 'that the same happens in the case of male animals who have had one testicle cut out. But this is not true, but starting from what is likely, they guess what will happen, and they presume that it is so, before they see that it is in fact so.' Now it is clear that the *idea* of submitting their doctrine to what would have been a decisive test had certainly occurred to these theorists: yet they evidently assumed the result of such a test to be a foregone conclusion and failed to carry it out in practice. On other occasions, however, simple tests were carried out, and were carried out successfully, in order to refute a theory, as we can see, for example, from Aristotle's own investigation of the doctrine that male and female children are conceived in different parts of the womb. In examining this doctrine he

73

refers to the decisive evidence obtained from anatomical dissections. As he puts it at *GA* 764a 33 ff., 'male and female twins are often found in the same part of the uterus: this we have observed sufficiently by dissection in all the Vivipara, both land-animals and fish'.[1]

The theories which suggested that the differentiation of the sexes depended on which testicle the seed of the male parent came from, or the side of the womb on which the embryo was conceived, were theories which could be submitted to decisive tests quite easily by means of vivisection and dissection. But the fact is, of course, that many more of the theories based on opposites which we find suggested in early Greek speculative thought concern such general physical or biological problems as the constituent elements of man or of the universe as a whole, and here it was difficult, or rather in most cases impossible, to devise crucial experiments that would confirm or refute such doctrines as the Greeks put forward. Nevertheless we find several authors who attempt to establish their schematic theories on these and other similarly comprehensive topics by empirical methods. *On the Nature of Man*, for instance, asserts that the component substances in the body are the four humours, blood, bile, black bile and phlegm (though these are analysed in turn in terms of hot, cold, wet and dry),[2] and also maintains that these predominate in turn in the body in the four seasons, spring, summer, autumn and winter respectively. This theory is typical of many which incorporate various pairs of opposites in a neat, abstract schema. But the writer shows some ingenuity in attempting to devise practical tests which will (as he hopes) confirm his general doctrines. In ch. 5, for example, he refers to a series of tests with drugs

[1] Cf. also *GA* 765a 16 ff. and *HA* 565b 13 ff.

[2] To support his analysis of the four humours in terms of the opposites, hot, cold, wet and dry, the writer appeals to the evidence of touch, e.g. in ch. 7, L VI 46 11 ff. (and cf. also ch. 5, 42 3 ff.). But while it is obvious enough that phlegm, for example, feels cold to the touch, he assumes that this indicates its essential nature or constitution (its φύσις). It is, however, worth noting that even though he has no means of measuring temperatures accurately, he does make use of the only standard he possesses, that of touch.

74

in order to establish that each of the four humours is a separate substance and congenital in the body: 'if you give a man a drug which draws out phlegm, he will vomit phlegm', and similarly with bile and black bile, while blood flows out, of course, when a man is wounded (L vi 42 10 ff.), and he adds that these results always occur, whatever the time of day or night and in whatever season. Then in ch. 7 (50 9 ff.) he says that 'the clearest testimony' (μαρτύριον σαφέστατον) that the humours vary in the body according to the seasons is that 'if you will give the same man the same drug four times in the year, his vomit will be most phlegmatic in winter, most liquid in spring, most bilious in summer and blackest in autumn'. Now it seems hardly likely that the outcome of any such experiment would correspond precisely with the results which he describes: *if* he undertook the test, his observations seem to have been quite superficial and he has certainly schematised and simplified his results, and he may perhaps not have carried *this* test out at all, although there are some quite detailed descriptions of the effects of giving a man certain drugs in chs. 6 and 7 which appear to derive from the author's personal experience. Yet we should note that *even if the tests had produced the results which he describes*, they would not prove what he was attempting to establish. He assumes, what is the point at issue, that the humours which he had observed, or thought he had observed, in a man's vomit, are the congenital constituent substances of the body. His method is exemplary in that he attempts to propose practical tests in order to verify his doctrines. His execution of those tests (assuming that he carried out some at least of those he describes) was clearly haphazard, both by our standards, and also perhaps by the standards of his own age. But at the same time we should recognise that the problem which he was tackling, that of the elementary component substances in the body, is one which, in the absence of modern methods of chemical analysis, could be investigated with only a very limited success.

On the Nature of Man is not unique in attempting to devise practical tests in order to confirm quite general physical or physiological theories which incorporate pairs of opposites in an elaborate schema. The treatise *On Fleshes*, for instance, puts forward a four-element theory, one of these elements being identified as the hot and the others associated with hot, cold, wet, dry and other opposites (ch. 2, L vɪɪɪ 584 9 ff.), but it also gives an account of the formation of the different parts of the body, and here 'the glutinous' and 'the fatty' play the chief roles, the former associated with the cold (and the brain), and the latter with the hot (ch. 4, 588 14 ff.). But as 'clear evidences' (τεκμήρια...σαφέα) of the distinction between these two types of substances in the body, the writer proposes a simple test. He suggests that if anyone were to cook the different parts of the body, he would find that the 'glutinous' and the 'sinewy' parts do not cook easily, while the 'fatty' parts do (ch. 4, 590 1 ff.).

But the most interesting and fullest evidence concerning the use of empirical investigations in connection with schematic general theories of opposites comes from the fourth book of the *Meteorologica*. This work (the authenticity of which has sometimes been doubted, although all would agree that if not by Aristotle himself, it comes from the circle of his closest associates)[1] contains the first detailed description and analysis, in extant Greek literature, of the physical properties of a wide variety of natural substances and their reactions to certain simple tests. We are told, for example, which substances are ductile, which malleable, which fissile, and so on, and the reactions of various substances to fire and to water, to being burned, boiled or dissolved in various types of liquid, are also noted down. Many of the observations which

---

[1] The authenticity of the fourth book of the *Meteorologica* has been called in question, e.g. by Hammer-Jensen (pp. 113 ff.) and by Gottschalk (pp. 67 ff.), although other scholars have argued that there are no good reasons for not accepting the book as a whole, or in the main, as the work of Aristotle; see especially Düring, pp. 17 ff., and Lee, 2, 1st ed., pp. xiii ff., and Preface to 2nd ed., p. vii.

are recorded were, no doubt, common knowledge. Some of the more specialised information comes from an acquaintance with contemporary industrial processes, such as ironmaking.[1] But some of the writer's knowledge seems to derive from deliberate investigations (whether or not it was the writer himself who originally undertook these). Thus he says that salt and soda are soluble in some liquids (such as water) but not in others (he specifies olive oil) (*Mete.* 383b 13 ff.). Among the substances which he says freeze solid with cold are not only urine, vinegar, whey and κονία ('lye', the alkaline solution used for washing), but also ἰχώρ, 'serum' (389a 9 ff.), and he distinguishes between different types of wine according to their combustibility and their readiness to freeze (387b 9 ff., 388a 33 ff.). Considering the period at which this work was written, the range of observations which it contains is impressive. Yet the phenomena are interpreted throughout according to the doctrine of the four elements, each of which is either hot or cold, and either dry or wet. Thus when the action of fig-juice on milk is mentioned at 384a 20 ff., the curdling of milk is described as the separation of 'the earthy part' (τὸ γεῶδες). Most compounds are said to be composed of earth and water and are classified according to whether earth or water predominates in them, those that are solidified by cold and melted by fire being said to have a greater proportion of water, while those that are solidified by fire are said to have a greater proportion of earth. But when exceptions to this general classification occur, as with olive oil, for example, which is solidified neither by cold nor by fire, the writer simply refers to πνεῦμα ('air') as an ingredient.[2] As in *On the Nature of Man* and *On Fleshes*, so too in the fourth book of the *Meteorologica*, simple tests were carried out in connection with a general doctrine of opposites, but once again these tests are quite

[1] See *Mete.* 383a 32 ff. (with Lee's useful note, 2, pp. 324–9) and cf. 383a 24 ff. on the manufacture of pottery, and 383b 7 ff. on that of millstones.
[2] *Mete.* 383b 20 ff., cf. *GA* 735a 29 ff. on semen.

inconclusive. They revealed certain facts concerning the properties and reactions of various substances, but of course they neither proved nor disproved the doctrine of the four simple bodies and the four elementary opposites hot, cold, wet and dry.

I may now attempt to summarise some conclusions concerning the types of evidence used in connection with various theories based on opposites which were put forward in different fields of scientific inquiry. First, the value of careful observation and research was undoubtedly recognised by many Greek investigators. Even so much of the evidence which was in fact cited in connection with theories of opposites (at least) was inconclusive, or indeed quite irrelevant to the theory which it was supposed to establish. Furthermore, the Greeks sometimes showed considerable ingenuity in making evidence fit theories, or in explaining it away if it seemed to contradict preconceived opinions. On some notable occasions, however, the use of observation and experiment did lead to the modification or rejection of certain theories based on opposites. The doctrine that males are hot and females cold corresponded to certain preconceptions which many Greeks entertained concerning these two pairs of opposites, but Parmenides and others suggested that women are the hotter sex, and it seems that they based this conclusion on empirical considerations, inferring it from the fact that women menstruate. And then Aristotle, in particular, is responsible for refuting a number of earlier theories, among which we noted the belief that male and female children are conceived in different parts of the womb. Here was an occasion when the use of empirical methods had *decisive* results. More often, however, the tests which were carried out in attempts to confirm or refute theories of opposites failed in their purpose. On such problems as the nature of the constituent elements of man or of the universe as a whole, the theories which were proposed were, indeed, usually so vague and imprecise in form that they were quite incapable of being falsified by simple experiments.[1] Even when rudimentary tests were performed, as they *were* sometimes performed, in connection with such a theory, they yielded evidence which was of little or no value in corroborating or overthrowing the theory. This is the case, for example, with the series of tests with drugs which the author of *On the Nature of Man* proposed in connection with his theory of the constituent substances in the body. Yet if we put ourselves in the place of the early Greek scientists and ask how they might have begun to investigate this problem empirically, it is very difficult to suggest how they should have proceeded, for there is, of course, no single simple and obvious test which they could have carried out which would have made apparent, for example, the fundamental distinction between organic and inorganic substances in the body. We may criticise them for lack of precision in many of the experiments they conducted or claimed to have conducted. But in judging their apparent failure to make more use of experimental procedures as a whole, we should not forget the complexity of many of the problems which they were attempting to investigate, nor the extremely limited techniques of investigation which were at their disposal. A number of Greek theorists evidently appreciated the desirability of testing their doctrines by empirical methods, and the author of *On Ancient Medicine* criticises theories based on arbitrary assumptions in general, implying that where there is no criterion by which a theory may be judged true or false, speculation is pointless. Yet if this treatise contains some very interesting and important methodological recommendations, it sets up what was, at this stage, a quite unattainable ideal for any theorist who attempted to solve such problems as the nature of the elementary constituents of living things or of physical substances in general, or other similarly intractable questions.

---

[1] This applies, of course, as much to the Atomists' theory, or to Plato's doctrine of the composition of the four primary bodies from the elemental triangles (*Ti.* 53 c ff.), as to Aristotle's theory based on the opposites hot, cold, dry and wet.

Many factors appear to contribute to the remarkable pre-valence of theories based on opposites in so many societies at different stages of technological development. First there is the fact that many prominent phenomena in nature exhibit a certain duality: day alternates with night; the sun rises in one quarter of the sky and sets in the opposite quarter; in most climates the contrast between the seasons (summer and win-ter, or dry season and rainy season) is marked; in the larger animals male and female are distinct, and the bilateral sym-metry of their bodies is obvious. Secondly, the duality of nature often acquires an added significance as the symbolic manifestation of fundamental religious or spiritual categories: the classification of phenomena into opposite groups may reflect, and itself form an important part of, a system of religious beliefs which expresses the ideals of the society, and by which the whole life of the society is regulated. And then a third factor must also be taken into consideration: whether or not the terms are divided into a 'positive' and a 'negative' pole, opposites provide a simple framework of reference by means of which complex phenomena of all sorts may be described or classified. Antithesis is an element in any classi-fication, and the primary form of antithesis, one may say, is division into *two* groups—so that the *simplest* form of classifi-cation, by the same token, is a dualist one.

In considering the series of doctrines based on opposites in early Greek speculative thought, we found, first of all, that a number of these theories are influenced by what are, in origin, pre-philosophical beliefs concerning the values of various pairs of opposites. Indeed it seems probable that it was the philosophers themselves who were the first to formu-late some of the assumptions underlying those beliefs explicitly, and to systematise this use of opposites in com-prehensive schemata. But whether or not the opposite terms have any symbolic associations, one of the obvious merits and attractions which such theories possess is their abstract clarity and simplicity. The tendency to simplify reality, to find order in the disorder of experience, is evident in both non-scientific, and scientific, descriptions of the external world. The scientist seeks, after all, to explain a maximum number of phenomena on a minimum number of hypotheses, although he judges a theory not merely by its simplicity, of course, but also, and primarily, by its usefulness, its ability to yield predictions which can be tested. Very few of the Greek theories of opposites which we have reviewed fulfil this criterion of usefulness. But it is still far from being the case that they are all equally far-fetched, or all equally vague and superficial. Even within the period of Greek speculative thought which we have been considering, physical and cosmological theories tend, as time goes on, to be worked out and applied to particular phenomena in much greater detail. In Fr. 11 of the *Way of Seeming* Parmenides promises an account of how various things, including the earth, the sun and the moon, came to be, but even though most of this part of the poem is lost, it seems unlikely that he showed, or attempted to show, in any great detail, how different physical objects were derived from the two primary substances Light and Night: his theory may not have been much more precise than pre-philosophical myths which derived all things from Sky and Earth, for example. Similarly the idea that living things are in some sense 'earth and water' was, no doubt, a very old belief, and it seems quite improbable that Xenophanes had either a very precise or a very elaborate physical theory in mind when he said that 'all things that come to be and grow are earth and water' (Fr. 29). On the other hand the type of theory which referred to hot and cold and dry and wet as the constituent elements of things has, first of all, an obvious and immediate applicability to reality, in that any physical object may be said to be either 'hot' or 'cold' and either 'dry' or 'wet',[1]

---

[1] The Greeks tended to consider 'hot' and 'cold' not as relative positions on a single temperature scale, so much as separate and distinct substances (as we see from Anaxagoras Fr. 8, for example, where he protests that 'the hot' and 'the cold' are not 'cut off from one another with an axe'), and this tendency was, no doubt, encouraged by the common use of the definite article plus the neuter

and Aristotle, for one, attempted a detailed analysis of various sorts of compound substances in terms of his theory of the four simple bodies and the four primary opposites. Again condensation and rarefaction are descriptive generalisations which have a wide range of application to physical changes (even though some of the examples which were cited in antiquity to illustrate this theory are somewhat fanciful),[1] and we may say the same of Empedocles' doctrine of Love and Strife, which refers to the uniting and separating of the four 'roots'. Such theories may not be hypotheses yielding predictions which can be tested empirically, but quite apart from the absence of references to personal, anthropomorphic divinities, they differ from most myths in another respect, as well, that they are generalisations which are based on obvious facts of experience and which are capable of being applied extensively and in detail to describe observed phenomena.

Moreover, if it is the case that most Greek theories of opposites are stated quite dogmatically, they were often the subject of considerable controversy, and were defended on one side, and attacked on the other, both by means of abstract argument and by appeals to empirical evidence. Some theorists, at least, were aware of the need to verify their doctrines by means of practical tests, and indeed the ideal of banishing unverifiable assumptions from natural science is expressed in *On Ancient Medicine*, in particular connection with the doctrine

adjective as a substantive. It should also be noted that the Greek term ξηρόν which is translated 'dry' is used to refer to what we call solids, and ὑγρόν may refer to both liquids and gases.

[1] Among the examples commonly given to illustrate these two types of change are such phenomena as the evaporation of water as ἀήρ ('air-mist') and the condensation of ἀήρ back again into water. But it is often asserted, rather less plausibly, that 'earth' comes to be from 'water' by condensation (among the texts where this doctrine is mentioned are Melissus Fr. 8 (3), Anaxagoras Fr. 16, Plato, *Ti.* 49 bc and cf. Simplicius, *in Ph.* 24 29 ff. and Hippolytus, *Haer.* 1 7 3, DK 13 A 5 and 7, on Anaximenes' theory): apart from the freezing of water as ice, it may be that some writers had in mind such phenomena as the evaporation of sea water leaving behind a residue of salt, or the silting-up of river estuaries. The notion that earth, in turn, becomes stones on condensation is an inspired guess, but is hardly based on any change we can actually observe taking place.

of hot, cold, dry and wet. Yet at the same time the actual use of experiment in early Greek science met with only a very limited success, partly because of the failure of Greek theorists to carry their experiments out sufficiently carefully, but partly because of the extreme difficulty of devising tests which would elucidate the complex general problems of physics, biology and cosmology which the Greeks attempted to investigate. It is small wonder that abstract argument figures a good deal more largely than appeals to practical tests in the debates which were carried on concerning such problems as the ultimate constituents of physical objects. To judge from the evidence we have considered in connection with doctrines based on opposites, much less attention was paid to the criterion of verifiability than to such considerations as the abstract clarity, simplicity and comprehensiveness of a theory. The predicament of the author of *On Ancient Medicine* is especially revealing, for in spite of the methodological recommendations of his opening chapter, his own physiological and pathological doctrines are only slightly less schematic than those which he attacks and are themselves founded on certain arbitrary assumptions. And that sometimes, in constructing their theories, the Greeks consciously employed what we should term the criterion of *simplicity*, can be seen, for example, from the passage where Aristotle establishes the doctrine of hot, cold, dry and wet in *GC* B 2, for there he considers the *minimum* number of principles which are necessary to account for all tangible contraries, and concludes his discussion (*GC* 330a 24 ff.) by saying that 'it is evident that all the other differences are *reduced* (ἀνάγονται) to these four: and these four cannot be reduced to any lesser number (αὗται δὲ οὐκέτι εἰς ἐλάττους)'.

Many of the problems on which the Greeks proposed theories based on opposite principles did not begin to be satisfactorily resolved until the development of chemistry in the eighteenth century, and some not until the development of biochemistry in the twentieth. It is not irrelevant to note, then, in conclusion, that theories of the general type which we have been considering continue to play an important part in speculative thought long after the Greco-Roman period. In alchemical literature,[1] we meet a theory based on the principles sulphur and mercury, which were generally conceived as opposites: sulphur is the spirit of combustibility, mercury that of fusibility,[2] and they were often identified in alchemical writings as the Male and Female principles and referred to cryptically by such titles as Sol and Luna, King and Queen, Osiris and Isis.[3] The sulphur-mercury theory flourished well into the sixteenth century, but other fanciful theories based on opposites are found in even later cosmological writers. In the seventeenth century, Thomas Fludd, for example, put forward an elaborate schema of opposites: in cosmology, Heat, Movement, Light, Dilatation and Attenuation are together opposed to Cold, Inertia, Darkness, Contraction and Inspissation, and in the microcosm Father, Heart, Right Eye and Sanguis Vitalis are together opposed to Mother, Uterus, Left Eye and Mucus.[4] The continued attraction of this schema is obvious. Yet when Read, for example, commented on the recurrence of doctrines based on opposites in the history of chemical theory, he appears to have stressed the similarity between those theories to the point of ignoring or underestimating their significant differences: 'The Sun-god and Moon-goddess; Yang and Yin; masculine and feminine; sulphur and mercury; positive and negative; proton and electron; truly, it may be said of chemical theory that the more it changes the more it is the same thing.'[5] While each of

[1] See especially Read, *1* and *2* (though the former is a fuller account of the period of the alchemists) and Hopkins.

[2] Some theorists, notably Paracelsus, introduced salt as an intermediate between these two opposites (see e.g. Read, *1*, pp. 27 f.).

[3] This theory is commonly derived from the Islamic school of Geber (or Jabir), but Hopkins (pp. 84 ff., 115 ff.) traces it to earlier, Alexandrian sources, and Read (*1*, pp. 18 and 20 f.) also suggests that it owes something to Aristotle's doctrine of the wet and dry 'exhalation'.

[4] See Pagel, pp. 271 ff.

[5] Read, *1*, p. 21. (It should be noted, in view of the reference to 'proton and electron', that Read was writing in 1936.)

these doctrines (along with many others, of course) is alike in this, that it represents an attempt to reduce a multiplicity of phenomena to a pair of opposite principles, there are important, indeed fundamental, differences (1) in how the theories were applied, or were believed to apply, to the phenomena, and (2) in how their authors might have set about trying to justify or establish them, and if these differences are not noted, the comparison may be quite misleading. As far as the Greek material is concerned, I hope to have indicated not only the common characteristics and recurrent motifs of the various theories of opposites in Greek speculative thought, but also some of the features in which these theories differ from one another, notably in the detail with which they were worked out and the methods which were used to support them. Thus in spite of the important respects in which Aristotle's use of opposites resembles, and indeed is influenced by, earlier notions, his physical doctrine of hot, cold, dry and wet may and should be distinguished both from the hypotheses of modern scientific method *and also* from the vague accounts common in pre-philosophical myths and early philosophical cosmologies: for if this doctrine cannot be said to give rise to predictions which can be tested experimentally, it is, on the other hand, far removed from the myth that derives all things from Sky and Earth or from symbolic dualist classifications of phenomena which deal globally with the entire spectrum of reality.

CHAPTER II

THE ANALYSIS OF DIFFERENT MODES OF OPPOSITION

INTRODUCTION

Opposites form the basis of many of the theories which early Greek philosophers and medical writers put forward in their attempts to account for natural phenomena, and I have already noted, in this context, that one of the general attractions which this type of theory possesses is evidently that opposites provide a simple and apparently comprehensive framework by reference to which other things may be described or classified. The next topic which I wish to discuss concerns the development of logic, namely the evolution of ideas on the nature of opposites *qua* opposites, and in particular the gradual clarification and analysis of the distinctions between different modes of opposition.

The English terms 'opposite' and 'opposition', like the Greek ἀντικείμενον and ἀντικεῖσθαι, are used to refer to many different types of relationship. Take first the relationships between various pairs of propositions. Here, following the traditional schedule which derives from Aristotle,[1] we may distinguish between contradictories, contraries and sub-contraries. (1) 'All *A* is *B*' and 'some *A* is not *B*' are contradictories (as also are 'some *A* is *B*' and 'no *A* is *B*'): one or other proposition must be true, and the one that is not true must be false. (2) 'All *A* is *B*' and 'no *A* is *B*' are contraries: if one proposition is true, the other is false; but if one proposition is known to be false, it does not follow that the other is true (for it may be that neither is true, that is to say that some, but not all, *A* is *B*). (3) 'Some *A* is *B*' and 'some *A* is not *B*' are subcontraries: if one proposition is true,

---

[1] See further below, p. 164.

it does not follow that the other is false (for both may be true); on the other hand if one proposition is known to be false, we may infer that the other is true. The most important distinction, here, is that between contradictories and contraries (1 and 2): if two propositions are contradictories, then to prove the one it is sufficient to refute the other; but if two propositions are contraries (incompatible, but not contradictories), then it is not enough simply to refute the one in order to demonstrate the other (for it may be that neither is true).

But opposition is a term which is not only used to refer to certain relationships between pairs of propositions. Indeed 'opposite' and 'opposition' are more regularly used in connection with pairs of terms. Here again certain important distinctions may be noted. Consider the pairs black and white, and odd and even, for instance. The first pair admits intermediates (grey and other colours), but the second does not. It is not the case that all colours are either black or white, but every whole number is either odd or even. But odd and even may in turn be distinguished from odd and not-odd, i.e. a pair of predicates related as affirmation and negation or as contradictories. It is true of all members of a particular class (whole numbers), but not of other things, that they must be either odd or even; but of *any* given subject we must either affirm or deny any given predicate, that is to say we must assert *either* that it is odd, *or* that it is not odd, for example. We should note, too, on what conditions both members of a pair of contraries may, or may not, be truly predicated of the same subject. Contraries may not both be truly predicated of the same subject at the same *time*, in the same *respect* and in the same *relation*, but the addition of these qualifications may be important to avoid confusion: consider the case where Jones may truly be said to be both tall, in relation to Smith, and short, in relation to Robinson, and so on. Odd and even, black and white, tall and short, are all pairs of contraries. So too are such pairs as straight and crooked, moving and

stationary, healthy and diseased, although here one of the
terms is defined by reference to the other, and the two are in
a one-many relationship (there is one 'straight' line between
any two given points, but these may be joined in an infinite
number of ways which may be called 'crooked'). But we
also use the term 'opposite' more generally, to describe the
relationship between any pair of terms between which we
apprehend or imagine a contrast or antithesis. Though there
are no contraries in the strict sense in the category of substance, two substances may be considered opposites in virtue
of possessing opposite properties, for example. Sun and
moon, for instance, are not contraries, but they are opposites
in this respect that one is our main source of light by day, and
the other our main source of light by night. Similarly sky and
earth may be considered opposites in that, from the point of
view of a man standing on the earth, the sky is up and the
earth down. We should point out here that while a quality
can have only one true contrary, a substance may have more
than one opposite, in the sense that it may be contrasted with
several other objects in different respects: thus king, for
example, is opposed both to queen (as male to female) and to
subjects (as ruler to ruled).

The importance of the distinctions which I have outlined
was certainly recognised by Aristotle. Indeed it was Aristotle
who was responsible for the first thorough analysis of the
logical implications of different modes of opposition. But this
raises the question of how opposites were used by earlier
writers, particularly in drawing inferences, or in establishing
or refuting theses. To what extent do earlier Greek philosophers show an awareness of the distinctions between different types of opposites or opposite statements, or how far
were those distinctions ignored?

To begin with, we should refer once again to the comprehensive dualist classifications of phenomena which anthropologists have reported from various present-day societies,
for here the relationships between the different pairs of

opposites which are included in a single schema often vary considerably. One of the examples of such a classification which I mentioned before (p. 32) is that of the Eastern Timbira. Among the pairs which Nimuendaju mentions to illustrate their division of all nature into two groups are east and west, day and night, dry season and rainy season. But alongside these contraries are *sun* and *moon*, which may, perhaps, be opposed to one another in the sense which we have just noted, as 'the main source of light by day' and 'the main source of light by night', *fire* and *firewood*, which are related as agent to thing acted upon, and *earth* and *water*, which are primarily contrasted, perhaps, as solid to liquid. The principles on which the classification is extended to take in other phenomena are, on the whole, fairly clear. First, an object may be included in one or other group because of its similarity to a member of that group. Thus according to Nimuendaju, all species of animals that are black or that show marked black colouring are classed in the *atuk* category, where we find 'black colour' and 'night' themselves. For the purposes of this classification, at least, the most important characteristic of any species would seem to be its colour, which often no doubt had strong symbolic associations, although the fact that an animal has black markings is, of course, usually of little or no importance in determining its biological species or family. Secondly, some things seem to owe their place in the classification not to a similarity, so much as to an antithesis. In our example, it would appear to be by virtue of the contrast with fire (which is in the *ka* category, as are sun and day) that firewood is placed in the *atuk* class. We may observe that as almost any similarity may be used to associate objects together in the same class, so almost any antithesis may be the motive for placing things in opposite classes. Indeed it would appear that any two objects which form a natural pair tend to be divided up and placed on opposite sides in such Tables. The first point that we should note about such classifications is, then, that while they depend to a large extent on the recognition of antitheses, the form of the schema does not allow different types of antithesis to be distinguished. And because the two groups themselves (e.g. *ka* and *atuk*, land-side and water-side and so on) are generally held to be mutually exclusive, the effect of this may sometimes be to assimilate other modes of contrast to contrary opposition. Furthermore, such classifications are often applied exhaustively, or at any rate very comprehensively, so that of any object, or almost any object, it is possible to ask whether it is *ka* or *atuk* (for example) on the assumption that it is one or the other. It would be rash, and probably quite false, to say that the categories '*both* ka *and* atuk' and '*neither* ka *nor* atuk' are *never* used by the Eastern Timbira. But on the other hand it is evident that the more comprehensively such a classification is applied, the more likely it will be that these two categories will tend to be ignored, and the assumptions generally made that the two classes *ka* and *atuk* are (1) incompatible (not *both* ka *and* atuk) and (2) exhaustive alternatives (*either* ka *or* atuk).

THE USE OF 'POLAR EXPRESSIONS'

It is not until opposites begin to figure quite commonly in explicit arguments, that is to say in the Eleatic philosophers, that we can determine at all precisely what assumptions were made by various Greek thinkers concerning the logical relationships between pairs of opposed terms. But before we discuss the arguments of Parmenides and later philosophers, attention should be drawn to certain earlier usages. First of all it is worth noting a stylistic trait which is common throughout early Greek literature from Homer onwards, namely the use of so-called 'polar expressions',[1] i.e. such

---

[1] Wilamowitz was one of the first to give a list of such expressions from Greek literature in his first edition of Euripides, *Herakles* (note to *v.* 1106, vol. II, pp. 245 ff.). The term 'polar' was used to describe such expressions by such German scholars as E. Kemmer in his monograph on the subject (*Die polare Ausdrucksweise in der griechischen Literatur*, 1903) and has subsequently become common in English too.

couplets as 'mortals and immortals', 'men and women', 'young and old', 'slave and free', 'land and sea', 'openly and secretly' and so on. Such couplets, which include not only contraries, but also such pairs of complementary terms as 'word and deed' and 'by guile and by force', are used in a variety of contexts. Sometimes the second member of such a pair is mentioned simply to achieve a certain emphasis, as for example 'by guile and not by force' (δόλῳ, οὐδὲ βίηφιν) at *Od.* 9 408. But two other uses are more interesting. (1) First, we find couplets often used instead of a single inclusive term *to express a general notion*. The pair 'land and sea', for example, is used to refer to the whole earth, as in Hesiod's πλείη μὲν γὰρ γαῖα κακῶν, πλείη δὲ θάλασσα[1] (*Op.* 101) (and in Homer Hermes' sandals carry him 'over the wet sea and the boundless earth' ἠμὲν ἐφ' ὑγρὴν | ἠδ' ἐπ' ἀπείρονα γαῖαν, e.g. *Iliad* 24 341 f., and cf. other expressions, e.g. *Od.* 10 458 f., 11 399 ff.). Again, the pair 'immortals and mortals' is particularly common for 'all living persons'. In Homer, the dawn brings light 'both to immortals and to mortals' (ἀθανάτοισι . . . ἠδὲ βροτοῖσιν, e.g. *Iliad* 11 1 f.), and 'no one' is sometimes expressed emphatically as 'none of the gods or men' (e.g. *Iliad* 18 404). 'The body of the people' is expressed by different pairs of opposites in different contexts. At *Iliad* 2 789 and *Od.* 2 29, for instance, we find the couplet 'young and old', and in both cases the context is the holding of an assembly (where the older men have certain privileges),[2] and in the context of war and battle we naturally find such pairs as 'brave men and cowards' (e.g. *Iliad* 9 319), 'horsemen and foot-soldiers' (e.g. *Iliad* 2 810) and so on. (2) Secondly, such couplets are sometimes used *to express an alternative*, and in particular to put an *alternative question*. When Odysseus meets Nausicaa, for instance, he addresses her with the flattering inquiry 'are you some goddess, or a mortal?' (θεός νύ τις, ἦ βροτός ἐσσι; *Od.* 6 149). Similarly, when Telemachus arrives

---

[1] 'The earth is full of evils, and so is the sea.'
[2] See *Il.* 9 53 ff., *Od.* 3 24.

at Sparta, Menelaus asks the purpose of his visit and prompts his reply with the question 'are you on public, or on private, business?' (δήμιον, ἦ ἴδιον; *Od.* 4 314).

There is, as I have said, an extensive use of such polar expressions throughout early Greek literature from Homer onwards. Greek writers seem to have had a special fondness for coupling terms in this way, using opposites as points of reference by which to indicate a class as a whole or to mark distinctions within one, and sometimes we find that *both* opposite terms are mentioned when *only one* is strictly relevant. At *Od.* 14 178 f., for instance, Eumaeus says, with reference to Telemachus, τοῦ δέ τις ἀθανάτων βλάψε φρένας...ἠέ τις ἀνθρώπων.[1] Both terms of the common pair immortals/mortals are mentioned here, although it seems that only one is relevant, for as a general rule no *mortal* harms any other man's φρένες.[2] A similar usage is also found with some couplets in which the terms are not contraries, as, for example, 'words and deeds'. Thus at *Od.* 15 374 f., *both* these terms are mentioned: ἐκ δ' ἄρα δεσποίνης οὐ μείλιχον ἔστιν ἀκοῦσαι | οὔτ' ἔπος οὔτε τι ἔργον,[3] yet the verb ἀκοῦσαι is obviously strained when made to govern ἔργον as well as ἔπος.

It should be observed that the categories to which most pairs of opposites refer are quite flexible. There are several different formulations, in Homer, of each of the pairs land/sea, brave/cowards, friends/enemies, secretly/openly, which

---

[1] 'One of the immortals has harmed his mind..., or some man.'

[2] A similar point may be made concerning some of the 'polar expressions' which we find in later writers, including the philosophers. See, for example, Xenophanes Fr. 23, εἷς θεός, ἔν τε θεοῖσι καὶ ἀνθρώποισι μέγιστος, 'One god' (or, alternatively, 'god is one'), 'greatest among gods and men', a fragment which has caused considerable difficulty to those who have attempted to answer the question of whether Xenophanes was a Monotheist or not. Xenophanes himself clearly saw no contradiction between his reference to a supreme god (in the singular) and his reference to gods in the plural both in Fr. 23 and elsewhere (particularly Fr. 34), but whatever we make of the reference to 'gods' in the plural, the reference to '*men*' here adds little but rhetorical emphasis (cf. also Heraclitus Fr. 30). Cf. Burnet, *3*, p. 129, n. 1; Deichgräber, *3*, pp. 25–31; KR, pp. 169 f.; Kahn, p. 156, n. 3; and *HGP*, 1, pp. 374 f.

[3] 'From my lady one cannot hear any pleasant thing, either word or deed.'

convey different nuances of meaning and are not simply alternative metrical expressions of the same identical notion.[1] More important, references are sometimes made to *intermediate terms*. While it is generally the case that two opposites are used by themselves to indicate a class as a whole, there are exceptions to this rule. On occasions the battle-field, for example, is divided into a right, a left and a middle (e.g. *Iliad* 13 308 f.), even though the simpler division into right and left is more often employed. Similarly at *Iliad* 12 269 f. there is a reference to those who are neither particularly brave, nor particularly cowardly, but, as it were, undistinguished in battle (the word used is μεσήεις). And intermediates between opposite pairs are, of course, referred to quite commonly when a course of action is recommended which is a mean between two extremes, as, for example, at *Od.* 15 70 f., where Menelaus remarks that both excessive hospitality and excessive inhospitality are unseemly in a host, and what is fitting, αἴσιμα (that is, by implication, the mean between them), is better.

Finally we should note that while polar pairs are used quite often in Homer and other writers to put an alternative question, this use may, and should, be distinguished from the later, argumentative use of questions which have a similar form, notably in the philosophers. As we shall see, questions which put a choice between a pair of opposite alternatives play an important role in the argumentation of several Greek philosophers, where the aim of the person who puts the question is to gain agreement to one or other of the alternatives which he proposes. In Homer, however, such questions generally have little or no *persuasive* force, but are simply put in order to elicit information, as is the case, for example, with Menelaus' question to Telemachus at *Od.* 4 314, asking whether his business in Sparta is 'public, or private'. Not

---

[1] Compare, for example, *Od.* 14 330 which contrasts 'openly' with 'secretly' (ἢ ἀμφαδὸν ἠὲ κρυφηδόν) with 1 296, which contrasts it with 'by trickery' (ἠὲ δόλῳ ἦ ἀμφαδόν).

infrequently in Homer, as also in the tragedians, for instance, the person who replies to such a question does so in the terms in which the question has been put to him. Polyphemus, asked by the Cyclopes whether someone is overcoming him 'by guile or by force', replies 'by guile, and not by force' (*Od.* 9 406, 408). Yet the person who answers such a question may perfectly well do so in his own terms, without referring directly to the alternatives which the questioner has mentioned, and we find that Telemachus, for instance, answers the question put to him by Menelaus only indirectly in his reply at *Od.* 4 316 ff.

THE PYTHAGOREANS AND HERACLITUS

'Polar expressions' are used quite often in early Greek literature from Homer onwards as a convenient means of referring to a class as a whole or of marking divisions within one: the fondness that many authors had for such expressions is particularly evident on the occasions when both members of a pair are referred to when only one is relevant, but on the other hand the way in which a third, or intermediate, term is sometimes added to such a pair suggests that the divisions which were used in referring to certain classes remained quite flexible. We may now begin the more difficult task of analysing the use of opposites in the philosophers. How far can we determine the logical assumptions which underlie the use of opposites in the earlier Presocratic philosophers? The first two pieces of evidence which we should consider in this connection are the Pythagorean Table of Opposites and the fragments of Heraclitus.

I suggested before that when natural phenomena as a whole are classified into two groups, two general assumptions tend to be made: (1) that the two classes are incompatible (not *both* the one *and* the other), and (2) that they are exhaustive alternatives (*either* the one *or* the other). The Pythagorean Table of Opposites, as reported by Aristotle, differs from most of the dualist classifications of phenomena which the anthropologists have described from present-day societies in at least one important respect: whereas the classes referred to by such societies as the Miwok or the Eastern Timbira have strong local and concrete connotations (land-side and water-side, centre of the village and periphery), the primary principles of the Pythagoreans are remarkably abstract, namely Limit and Unlimited, and Odd and Even. Moreover, if we bear in mind that the Pythagoreans are said to have identified all things with numbers (e.g. Aristotle, *Metaph.* 985 b 26 ff.), we can see how an exhaustive classification of reality may be given in terms of these principles. With respect to the class of whole numbers, the pair odd and even fulfils the two conditions of being mutually exclusive and exhaustive alternatives (no whole number is both odd and even; every whole number is either odd or even).[1] Once the assumption that all things are numbers is granted, the Pythagorean classification into Odd and Even is undeniably comprehensive (although the identification of particular objects with particular numbers[2] was, no doubt, just as arbitrary as the Miwok grouping of natural objects as land- or water-side).

The principles Limit and Unlimited, Odd and Even, are opposites which exclude intermediate terms, and so too are some of the other pairs which appear in the Table (e.g. straight and curved). Yet the Table contains other pairs of opposites of a different logical kind: the pairs right and left, light and darkness, good and evil, do admit intermediates (i.e. 'middle', 'twilight' and 'morally indifferent'). We

---

[1] For some Pythagoreans, the Unit itself seems to have been an exception, for according to a passage in Aristotle's lost work on the Pythagoreans (Fr. 199) preserved by Theo Smyrnaeus (22 5 ff., Hiller, DK 47 A 21), the Unit was identified as 'even-odd', ἀρτιοπέριττον, on the seemingly quite inadequate grounds that when added to an even number it makes it odd, when added to an odd one, even (and this would be impossible if it did not share in the nature of both). Cf. Stob. *Ecl.* 1 21 7c (DK 44 B 5), and see KR, pp. 317 f. and *HGP*, 1, pp. 243 f.

[2] Some examples of such identifications are mentioned and criticised by Aristotle, e.g. *Metaph.* 985 b 29 ff., 990a 22 ff., 1078b 21 ff., and by Alexander, *in Metaph.* 38 10 ff. See KR, pp. 248 ff. and *HGP*, 1, pp. 302 ff.

noted that in dualist classifications, while almost any antithesis may serve as the motive for placing terms in opposite
groups, the schema does not allow different modes of
antithesis to be distinguished within it. So too with the
Pythagorean system, the effect of correlating their ten pairs
of opposite principles in a single Table is, to some extent at
least, to obscure the differences between the logical relationships between different pairs, and in particular to leave out of
account the fact that some of these pairs are not exhaustive
alternatives (like odd and even) but admit intermediates: *for
the purposes of this classification at least*, the relationship between
other pairs of opposites is assimilated to that between the type
pairs Limit and Unlimited, and Odd and Even.

Two features of Heraclitus' philosophy are especially
important for our present discussion: (1) his apprehension of
the analogy between different examples of opposition, and (2)
his alleged violation of the Law of Contradiction.

(1) In the Pythagorean Table of Opposites, the relationships between the various pairs of terms, right/left, male/
female, at rest/moving, straight/curved, etc., are presumably
held to be equivalent or analogous in this, at least, that they
each exemplify the relationship Limit/Unlimited in some
way. Heraclitus' very different conception of the relationship between opposites also seems to depend on recognising
an analogy between widely differing instances of 'opposition'.
The extant fragments contain many examples in which
Heraclitus asserts that a pair of opposites is 'one' or 'one and
the same' or 'common' (ξυνόν).[1] In Fr. 57, for instance, he
says that day and night are one, in Fr. 60 we are told that the

[1] In some fragments we find that *several* pairs of opposites are said to be *the
same thing*. The most notable instance of this is Fr. 67, where God is (not only)
day and night (but also) winter and summer, war and peace, satiety and hunger.
Kirk's comment on Fr. 88 (*1*, p. 143) should be noted: 'it is difficult to avoid the
conclusion that he believed the demonstration of unity in things which were
apparently most opposed to each other...to be almost sufficient proof of an all-
embracing unity: if waking and sleeping are "the same" and hot and cold are
"the same", then surely there will be no lack of essential connexion between
waking and the hot'.

way up and down is one and the same, and in Fr. 103 the beginning and end on the circumference of a circle are said to be 'common'. Heraclitus' purpose in these fragments is almost certainly not simply to make a particular point about the circle, a road and the alternation of day and night. In part, these and other examples of the sameness or unity of opposites seem to be cited as instances of what Heraclitus takes to be a general law. Sometimes, indeed, he refers to the interdependence of opposites in quite general terms. One of the images which he uses in this connection is that of 'war', which in Fr. 80 is said to be 'common' and in Fr. 53 is said to be 'father of all and king of all'. Other images, the bow and the lyre, appear in Fr. 51, where he also expresses the doctrine in general terms: οὐ ξυνιᾶσιν ὅκως διαφερόμενον ἑωυτῷ ὁμολογέει,[1] and other fragments appear to convey similar notions. In Fr. 10 he puts it that συνάψιες ὅλα καὶ οὐχ ὅλα, συμφερόμενον διαφερόμενον, συνᾷδον διᾷδον, καὶ ἐκ πάντων ἓν καὶ ἐξ ἑνὸς πάντα,[2] and in Fr. 8 (DK) τὸ ἀντίξουν ('what is opposed', or 'opposition') is said to be beneficial (συμφέρον).

The doctrine that opposites are 'one' and 'the same' is often recognised as a key feature of Heraclitus' thought.[3] But what is particularly remarkable about this doctrine from the point of view of the present discussion is how *widely* it is applied. First of all there are fragments which refer to such homely illustrations as the road (Fr. 60), or a bow (Fr. 48), or writing (reading γραφέων in Fr. 59), or sea water (Fr. 61), in which Heraclitus points out that the same object in one respect, or seen from one point of view, is one thing, but in another respect, or seen from another point of view, quite the

---

[1] 'They do not understand how, by being at variance, it agrees with itself.' Kirk, *1*, pp. 203 ff., prefers συμφέρεται rather than the usual ὁμολογέει (which is itself an emendation for the MSS ὁμολογέειν), but the sense remains the same.

[2] 'The connections between things' (or reading, with Kirk, συλλάψιες, 'things taken together') 'are wholes and not wholes, something which is at variance and something which is in agreement, in tune and out of tune: and one thing comes from many, and many from one.'

[3] The conception of the unity or interconnection of opposites is almost certainly an important feature of the doctrine of the Logos, if not the whole of that doctrine.

97

opposite. Other fragments refer to general physical or cosmological changes: two (Frr. 57 and 67) have already been mentioned in which Heraclitus refers to pairs of opposites that belong to a single continuous process (day/night, summer/winter), while Fr. 126 points out the reciprocal interactions between hot and cold, and wet and dry. Other fragments again refer to changes that affect living creatures in particular, as for example Fr. 88 where Heraclitus appears to suggest that not only waking and sleeping, but also life and death themselves, and youth and old age, belong to what are in some sense reciprocal processes,[1] or Fr. 111 which refers to disease and health, hunger and satiety, fatigue and rest, and in which the point is made that it is by contrast with their opposites that health, satiety and rest are found good and pleasant. And finally there are many fragments which refer to opposite values, such as pure and impure, just and unjust, in some of which it is stressed that one opposite cannot exist without the other (e.g. Fr. 23), while others refer to the fact that the same action may be judged very differently from different points of view (e.g. Frr. 15 and 102).[2]

These fragments are evidently extremely varied: the subjects to which they refer are drawn from the whole field of nature and human experience, and the ostensible points which they make vary considerably, some fragments merely indicating an unnoticed *connection* between a pair of opposites, others suggesting, more boldly, that two opposites are '*the same thing*' or '*one*', others again drawing attention to the fact that the same object seems quite different considered from different points of view.[3] But what *all* the fragments I have

---

[1] See further below, pp. 100 f.

[2] Compare the analyses which Kirk (*1*, p. 72, KR, pp. 190 f.) and Guthrie (*HGP*, 1, pp. 445 f.) have made of the different kinds of relationships included in Heraclitus' doctrine of the 'unity' or 'interdependence' of opposites.

[3] It is at least arguable that Heraclitus himself was quite well aware of certain important differences between the relationships between different pairs of opposites. But whether or not he recognised the *specific* differences between them, his main purpose in citing these varied examples appears to be to suggest their *generic* similarity, that is that they are all instances of a single general law.

mentioned have in common is that they all refer to *pairs of opposites* of some sort and they all point to *some* connection between them, and it is this that seems to provide the link between these strangely assorted utterances, and between them and those fragments such as 8, 10 and 51 which refer to 'what is at variance' or to 'what is opposed' more generally. Heraclitus' conception of the relationship between opposites is quite different from that of the Pythagoreans in this, that he repeatedly stresses not only the *inter*dependence of opposites (e.g. Frr. 10, 51, 67, 111), but also the constant war or strife between them (Fr. 80).[1] Yet both philosophies have this in common, that they contain general doctrines which depend on the recognition of an *analogy* or *equivalence* between the relationships between pairs of opposites of many different sorts, and in Heraclitus, especially, the range of examples of different types of opposition which are cited to illustrate his general thesis is particularly wide.

(2) We should consider next Heraclitus' alleged violation of the Law of Contradiction. In several passages[2] Aristotle suggests, though with varying degrees of assurance, that Heraclitus broke the Law of Contradiction, but to what extent do the extant fragments provide grounds for such an allegation? Three types of fragments should be examined, (i) those in which contrary attributes are predicated of the same subject, (ii) those in which a pair of contraries are identified or asserted to be 'the same', and (iii) those in which Heraclitus both affirms and denies the same predicate with reference

---

[1] On the differences between Heraclitus' conception of ἁρμονίη (Frr. 51, 54, cf. 8) and that of the Pythagoreans, see, for example, *HGP*, I, pp. 435 ff.

[2] The main passages are *Top.* 159b 30 ff., *Metaph.* 1005b 23 ff., 1012a 24 ff. and 1062a 31 ff. At *Top.* 159b 30 ff. Aristotle ascribes to Heraclitus the doctrine that 'good and bad are the same' with the words 'as Heraclitus says' (though Kirk, *I*, p. 95, has emphasised that this does 'not necessarily mean that an exact quotation or even a particularly accurate paraphrase is involved'). At *Metaph.* 1012a 24 ff. Aristotle gives it as Heraclitus' doctrine that 'all things are and are not', though in *Metaph.* 1005b 23 ff. he qualifies this: '*some think*' that Heraclitus said that the same thing is and is not. Finally at *Metaph.* 1062a 31 ff. he suggests that Heraclitus adopted his opinion without understanding what it involved: see further below, p. 102.

to a particular subject. There are undoubtedly several fragments of each of these three types in which Heraclitus might, at first sight, be thought guilty of self-contradiction. But where the interpretation of the fragment is reasonably clear, we can often see that the self-contradiction it involves is only apparent. (i) Although Heraclitus asserts, for example, that 'sea is the purest and the foulest water' (Fr. 61), he adds by way of explanation that 'for fish it is drinkable and healthy, but for men it is undrinkable and deadly'. Fr. 67 puts it that 'god is day night, winter summer, war peace, satiety hunger', but again we should probably take this in conjunction with what follows: '(god) is altered like (fire), which when it is mixed with spices, is called according to the scent of each'. In these and other examples[1] it is evidently *not* the case that contrary attributes are asserted to belong to the same subject in the same *respect* and at the same *time*. (ii) Fr. 60 is a clear instance of a fragment which appears to identify opposites: 'the way up and down is one and the same'. But the literal meaning of this fragment, referring to the fact that the same road travelled in opposite directions may be considered 'the way up' in one direction, 'the way down' in the other, is perfectly unobjectionable (though I should not deny that the fragment probably has other symbolic meanings for Heraclitus). Fr. 88 is more obscure. The first sentence raises particular difficulties: 'the living and the dead, and waking and sleeping, and young and old, exist as the same thing (in us)'. But once again the meaning is somewhat clarified by what follows (which is generally accepted as a genuine part of the fragment): 'these things, having changed, are those, and those, having changed again,

[1] Fr. 48 ('The bow's name is life'—βίος, cf. βιός 'bow'—'but its work is death', is another example in which Heraclitus predicates contraries of a single subject) but in which his meaning is plain enough. Cf. also Fr. 59. Kirk (*1*, pp. 97 ff.) reading γραφέων translates: 'of letters (or, of writers) the way is straight and crooked. It is one and the same.' He goes on to comment (*1*, p. 104) that 'even if the reading γναφέων or γναφείῳ were right and the reference were to a carding-roller or even a screw-press, the import of the fragment would remain roughly the same'.

are these'. The opposites that have been mentioned seem, then, to be considered as examples of alternating processes: Heraclitus appears to maintain, in fact, that the processes of growing old, and of dying, are in some sense part of an alternating cycle, like the process of going to sleep and waking up again.[1] (iii) Finally, there are some occasions when he seems to affirm and deny the same predicate of the same subject, but here too it is often tolerably clear that his affirmation and his denial are to be taken in different senses, or as applying in different respects. In Fr. 10, for example, he says of 'the connections between things' (or of 'things taken together') that 'they are wholes and not wholes' (ὅλα καὶ οὐχ ὅλα) but this presumably depends on whether we consider them from the point of view of their *connections*, or from the point of view of the *separate* things which are connected.[2]

Many of the apparent contradictions in Heraclitus' sayings may be resolved on a careful examination of his meaning. If we bear in mind that contrary attributes may sometimes both be truly asserted of the same subject—in different respects, for example—and that the principle of contradiction specifies that the same attribute cannot both belong and not belong to the same subject at the same *time*, in the same *respect*, and in the same *relation*, then in the extant fragments (at least) there is, I think, no *certain* violation of this principle. To judge from the fragments which we have considered, a consistent meaning generally underlies the apparent verbal inconsistencies. But this is certainly not to deny that Heraclitus' ideas are often expressed in a very obscure, and even misleading, form. The appearance of self-contradiction which several of the fragments give arises, in the main, because he omits to specify clearly the respect or relation in which a

---

[1] Though I should not profess to understand what the precise meaning of Fr. 62 may be, it perhaps illustrates a similar notion ('Immortals [are] mortals, mortals immortals, living their death and dying their life'). Further examples of reversible processes are mentioned in Fr. 126 ('Cold things become warm, what is warm becomes cool, the wet becomes dry, and the dry wet').

[2] Cf. also Fr. 32, where 'the only wise thing is not, and is, willing to be given the name of Zeus'.

particular attribute is asserted to belong to a particular subject. Many of his studiedly vague pronouncements could be, and indeed in due course were, taken as violations of the Law of Contradiction. Yet it is interesting that Aristotle suggests that 'if someone had questioned Heraclitus..., he might perhaps have compelled him to agree that contradictory statements can never both be true of the same subjects' (*Metaph.* 1062a 31 ff.), as if Aristotle himself recognised, perhaps, that the apparent self-contradictions in Heraclitus' sayings arise more from his obscure expression than from his real intention. Indeed it is evident that Heraclitus could not have intended to deny (though he might unconsciously have violated) the Law of Contradiction for the simple reason that no such law or principle had been formulated at this time. Writing at a period before the nature of contradiction had been explicitly analysed, Heraclitus exploits the paradoxes which result from equivocation to great effect, and his fragments illustrate particularly clearly the confusions which may arise from the use of opposite terms in unqualified and undefined senses. Two remarks in conclusion. Although Heraclitus' own main interest in the fragments which we have considered can hardly be described as purely logical, the expression of such paradoxes undoubtedly contributed to the opening up of a new field of discussion, that of the logical problem of the nature of contradiction (and we find that Heraclitus' 'contradictions' figure frequently in, for example, Aristotle's treatment of this problem).[1] On the other hand, we should note that a satisfactory analysis of the nature of contradiction was not to be given for many years after Heraclitus, and as we shall see, the vague use of pairs of opposite terms, in particular, was often a source of confusion in later philosophers.

---

[1] Aristotle pays particular attention to Heraclitean theses in the chapters of *Metaph.* Γ and K in which he deals with contradiction (e.g. *Metaph.* 1005b 23 ff., 1012a 24 ff., 1063b 24 f.). Cf. also his references to those who defended Heraclitus' reported statements for the sake of argument (*Top.* 159b 30 ff., cf. *Ph.* 185a 5 ff.).

ELEATIC ARGUMENTATION: PARMENIDES,
ZENO AND MELISSUS

Both the Pythagorean Table of Opposites and Heraclitus' conception of the unity or interdependence of opposites depend on recognising an *analogy* between the relationships between pairs of opposites of various sorts: by contrast, the *distinctions* between different modes of opposition tend, to some extent, to be ignored, or at least are not explicitly drawn. But we can study the assumptions which were sometimes made concerning the relationships between different pairs of opposites much better when opposites come to be used in explicit arguments, as they are by Parmenides and the younger Eleatics. Eleatic argumentation is a large, and somewhat neglected, subject.[1] But what concerns us here is the way in which opposites are used in establishing or refuting a thesis, and in particular the way in which they are sometimes treated as mutually exclusive and exhaustive alternatives. We may consider, first, some of the arguments which we find in Parmenides' *Way of Truth*.

In Fr. 2 of the *Way of Truth*, Parmenides says, 'Come now, I shall tell you...the only ways of inquiry that can be thought of: the first, that it is and that it cannot possibly not be, is the path of Persuasion, for it accompanies Truth; the second, that it is not and that it needs must not be, this path, I tell you, is wholly inconceivable. For you could not know that which is not (for that is impossible), nor could you utter it.' The problems of the unexpressed subject of the verb ἔστι in the *Way of Truth*, and the ambiguity of this term, have often been discussed.[2] But modern commentators have devoted less attention to the way in which Parmenides argues his case by putting a choice between alternatives, or to the form which these alternatives take, and it is these features of his

---

[1] A useful monograph in which Eleatic argumentation is discussed along with arguments from some of the early dialogues of Plato is Svend Ranulf's *Der eleatische Satz vom Widerspruch* (Copenhagen, 1924). Cf. also Calogero, 2, and Szabó's articles in *Acta Antiqua Academiae Scientiarum Hungaricae* (*1–4*).

[2] See most recently Owen.

argument which I wish to consider here. It is clear that in this fragment he represents 'it is' and 'it is not' as the *only* alternatives (αἵπερ ὁδοὶ μοῦναι διζήσιός εἰσι νοῆσαι). It is true that elsewhere he also refers to a third way, the *Way of Seeming*. But although 'the opinions of mortals' are mentioned in the Proem, Fr. 1 30 ff., and again in Fr. 6,[1] this does not alter the fact that throughout the *Way of Truth* and most notably in the long fragment 8 Parmenides treats 'what is' and 'what is not' by themselves as mutually exclusive and exhaustive alternatives.[2] We should observe the form in which the choice is put in Fr. 2. There Parmenides states the alternatives as *either* ὅπως ἔστιν τε καὶ ὡς οὐκ ἔστι μὴ εἶναι *or* ὡς οὐκ ἔστιν τε καὶ ὡς χρεών ἐστι μὴ εἶναι, that is *either* 'it is and it cannot possibly not be' *or* 'it is not and it needs must not be'. The choice lies, then, according to Parmenides, between (1) 'it is impossible that it should not be' (i.e. 'it is necessary that it should be'), and (2) 'it is necessary that it should not be'. But we may note that nothing is said here (or elsewhere) of two further alternatives, the respective contradictories of these two propositions, namely (3) 'it is not necessary that it should be' (i.e. 'it is contingent that it should be', or 'it may be') and (4) 'it is not necessary that it should not be' (i.e. 'it is contingent that it should not be', or 'it may not be'). In Fr. 2 Parmenides puts a choice between two alternatives as if these were the only alternatives conceivable. But even if we disregard the vagueness or ambiguity of ἔστι, the 'propositions' which Parmenides expresses are not contradictories (of which one must be true and the other false), but contraries, both of which it is possible to deny simultaneously, and it is clear that from the point of view of strict logic they are not exhaustive alternatives.

---

[1] In Fr. 6 this way is described as that 'on which mortals wander knowing nothing, double-headed. For helplessness directs the wandering thought in their breasts.... Tribes incapable of judgement who think that to be and not to be are the same and again not the same.'

[2] See, for example, Fr. 8 11 ('thus it needs must be either that it is wholly or that it is not') and 15 f. ('the decision about these things lies in this: it is or it is not').

Fr. 8 throws more light on Parmenides' conception of the choice between 'it is' and 'it is not'. The addition of the word πάμπαν in Fr. 8 11 should be noted. What he means by the word 'wholly' in the sentence 'thus it needs must be *either* that it is wholly *or* that it is not' becomes clear when we consider the remainder of Fr. 8 where he argues that 'what is' is ungenerated and indestructible (*vv.* 6–21), immovable and unchangeable.[1] 'What is not', conversely, is said to be inconceivable (8 f., 17, 34 ff.), and we are told that nothing can ever come to be from what is not (7 ff., 12 f.). The two alternatives between which Parmenides wishes a choice to be made might, then, be expressed, in this context, as *unalterable existence* on the one hand, and *unalterable non-existence* on the other. But if this is so, Parmenides' alternatives, stated in the form of propositions, are again a pair of contrary, not contradictory, assertions, for the contradictory of 'it exists unalterably' is 'it does not exist unalterably' *and not* 'it is unalterably non-existent'. By taking 'it is' and 'it is not' in *this* sense[2] as exhaustive alternatives in Fr. 8 11 and again in 16 ('it is or it is not'), Parmenides *forces an issue*. Physical objects, subject to change, cannot be said to 'be' in the sense of 'exist unalterably' which Parmenides evidently demands: but since he allows no other alternative besides unalterable existence and unalterable non-existence, then, according to this argument, physical objects must be said not to exist at all, indeed to be quite inconceivable. We should note that when Parmenides asserts that we must choose between ἔστι and οὐκ ἔστι, this is not a conclusion to which he has come after due consideration of all the alternatives (at no stage, of course, does he examine the senses of 'is' in which it is possible to say *both* that a thing is—in one sense, or respect—*and* that it is not

---

[1] See ἀκίνητον at Fr. 8 26, and the denial of all sorts of change at 38 ff.

[2] Even if we take ἐστι in a predicative, rather than an existential, sense, Parmenides' choice again seems to lie between a pair of contrary assertions, i.e. between 'it is wholly so-and-so' (e.g. black) and 'it is wholly not-so-and-so' (not-black), rather than between contradictories ('it is wholly so-and-so' and 'it is not wholly so-and-so').

—in another sense, or respect). It is, rather, the unquestioned assumption on which his argument is based. When he establishes certain attributes of ἔστι in Fr. 8 (that it is ungenerated, indestructible, 'whole-limbed', immovable, without end, present and continuous), the only alternatives which he considers are 'what is' and 'what is not', each in an unqualified sense. Thus in *vv.* 6 ff., for instance, where he sets out to prove that 'it is ungenerated', he asks from what it might be generated, and the only possibility which he discusses (*v.* 7) is that it might be said to come from μὴ ἐόν, 'what is not' in the unqualified sense of unalterable non-existence. Once this possibility has been rejected it is clear that Parmenides believes that *his argument is complete*. Similarly the proof that 'what is' is 'complete' and 'equally balanced on all sides' in *vv.* 42 ff. proceeds along the same lines: once Parmenides has rejected the possibility that 'what is not' might 'prevent it from reaching its like' (46 f.), he draws the conclusion that he wishes to reach. Where Aristotle, for instance, gives various formulations of the principle of Excluded Middle (e.g. 'it is necessary that affirmations or denials must be either true or false', *Int.* 18 b 4 f.), Parmenides uses what might almost be called a principle of Unqualified Exclusion: either 'it is' (and this is taken in the sense of necessary and unalterable existence) or 'it is not at all' (it is inconceivable).

Much of Parmenides' argument in the *Way of Truth* depends on taking 'it is' and 'it is not' as exhaustive, that is to say the only possible, alternatives. A similar technique of putting a choice between opposites recurs in the argumentation of several later Presocratic philosophers. Both Empedocles and Anaxagoras accepted the Parmenidean dictum that 'nothing can come to be from what is not',[1] but neither seems to have constructed arguments on the assumption of treating such opposites as ἔστι and οὐκ ἔστι as exhaustive alternatives. The later Eleatics, Zeno and Melissus, on the other hand,

---

[1] See Empedocles Fr. 12 (cf. Frr. 11, 13 and 14) and Anaxagoras Fr. 17.

provide some interesting examples of arguments based on certain assumptions concerning various pairs of opposite terms.

Our evidence for Zeno's arguments against plurality is regrettably meagre, but the account of their general purpose which Plato gives in the *Parmenides* is most valuable. At *Prm.* 128 ab Socrates suggests that when Parmenides asserted that all things are one, and when Zeno denied that there are many, they were both 'saying almost the same thing'. Zeno is made to assent to this, in the dialogue, and says (128 cd) that his book 'is, in fact, a defence of Parmenides' argument against those who try to ridicule it by showing that if it is one, many absurd and contradictory consequences arise from this argument. My book refutes those who say there are many... being intended to show that their hypothesis, that there are many, gives rise to still more absurd consequences than the hypothesis that it is one'. The method which Zeno adopted in order to defend Parmenides was evidently to refute those who upheld the contrary thesis. In refuting 'the many', Zeno sought to confirm the hypothesis of 'the one', and it seems probable that (like Melissus after him)[1] he assumed that these were the only alternatives open. Yet from a strictly logical point of view, at least, to refute 'the many' (whatever 'the many' is taken to mean) does not, of course, establish 'the one', for both these contrary 'hypotheses' may simultaneously be false.

The form which Zeno's arguments took is original. He refutes 'the many' by showing, or attempting to show, that mutually incompatible consequences follow from it. The extent to which he succeeded in this purpose can be judged from some of the arguments which Simplicius preserves. In Fr. 3, for instance, Zeno asserted that if there are many, then they are both limited (πεπερασμένα) and unlimited (ἄπειρα). The argument apparently ran as follows: 'If there are many, they must be just as many as they are and neither more nor less than they are. If they are just as many as they are, they

---

[1] See below, p. 109 on one and many in Melissus.

would be limited. (But again) if there are many, the things that are, are unlimited: for there are always other things between the things that are, and again others between those. And so the things that are, are unlimited.' Zeno evidently assumes, here, that by showing that 'the many' are both 'limited' and 'unlimited' he may demolish or discredit that 'hypothesis'. Yet not only is the meaning of 'the many' itself obscure,[1] but the sense or respect in which 'the many' have been shown to be both 'limited' and 'unlimited' also appears to have been left quite indefinite. Yet strictly speaking, until 'the many' have been shown to be both limited and unlimited in the *same* sense or respect, it is quite doubtful whether Zeno has shown that the 'hypothesis' is self-contradictory. Another argument which takes a similar form occurs in Frr. 1 and 2, in which 'the many' are said to be both 'great' and 'small', but here the conclusion may be rather more damaging for 'the many', as the meaning of the contraries is made more specific, 'so great as to be infinite in size', and 'so small as to have no size at all'.[2] Zeno's arguments are inadequate, as I have said, for their constructive purpose, if, as I think may well be the case, he assumed that by refuting 'the many' he necessarily demonstrated 'the one': but we may also note that his arguments are only partly successful in their destructive purpose, in demolishing 'the many', for he appears to have assumed that if *any pair of contraries* can be shown to be predicable, *in any sense*, of 'the many', he has shown that that hypothesis is untenable.

[1] On different interpretations of the meaning of 'the many' in this fragment, see KR, pp. 289 f. It may be, for instance, that points on a line, or that numbers, are meant, but that both these interpretations are tenable indicates the ambiguities of the term. Cf. also Melissus Fr. 8, where, however, 'the many' refers unmistakably to physical objects.

[2] The argument may be paraphrased: on the one hand it cannot be that they have no size, for anything which has no size causes no addition or diminution when it is added to, or taken away from, something else (and so what was added or taken away must have been nothing). But on the other hand *if* they have size, they will be infinite in size: each thing will have size and bulk, and one part of it will be separated from another, and the same will apply to the next part, the part next to it, and so on *ad infinitum* (and so they will be infinite in size)

The arguments of Melissus deal with both pairs of opposites, 'the one' and 'the many' (as in Zeno) and 'what is' and 'what is not' (as in Parmenides). In Fr. 8 (2 ff.), for example, Melissus considers the hypothesis 'that there are many', and rejects it on the grounds that the absurd conclusion follows that 'if there were many, they would have to be such as I say the one is' (2, cf. also 6). But we may remark that he adduced this argument for the constructive purpose of proving that 'there is only one'. He explicitly claims this argument to be one of a series of evidences or proofs that 'there is only one' (see Fr. 8 (1): ἀτὰρ καὶ τάδε σημεῖα) as if he assumed that there were *only* these two alternatives, 'the one' and 'the many', so that to demonstrate the truth of 'the one' it was sufficient to demonstrate the falsity of 'the many'.

The way in which Melissus treats the opposition between 'what is' and 'what is not' is also worth noting. Thus Fr. 7 begins, in the manner of Parmenides' Fr. 8, by stating a number of attributes of 'what is'. 'Thus it is eternal and infinite and one and all alike. And it could not perish, nor become greater, nor be arranged differently, nor does it feel pain or distress.' The assumption on which the argument establishing these points depends becomes clear as he goes on: 'For if any of these things happened to it, *it would no longer be*. For if it is altered, then what is is necessarily not ὁμοῖον ("alike", or here, rather, "the same") but that which was before, perishes, and *that which is not comes into being*.' Change of any sort is rejected on the grounds that 'what is not' would come to be.[1] As in Parmenides, in fact, 'what is' and 'what is not' are treated as exhaustive alternatives, although the former is taken in the sense of unalterable existence, and the latter in the sense of total non-existence. Finally, the argument in Fr. 8 takes a similar form and is particularly interesting because Melissus takes 'the many' to refer to physical objects and explicitly considers some of the changes to which

---

[1] Cf. also Fr. 7 (5): 'Nor could what is whole (ὑγιές) feel pain; for what is whole, and what is, would be destroyed, and what is not would come to be.'

they are subject, such as changes of temperature, the slow erosion which wears away even the hardest substances, and so on (Fr. 8 3). Yet he in no way alters his previous assumptions, stating once again (Fr. 8 6) that 'if it changed, then what is perished and what is not came to be'. All change is interpreted, as before, as a coming to be of 'what is not' from 'what is', and this includes, for example, changes of temperature, in which a hot thing becomes cold or vice versa.[1] As with Parmenides, physical objects cannot be said to 'be', in the sense of 'exist unalterably', and so (the argument runs) they cannot be said to exist at all.

Certain general comments should now be made concerning the arguments which we have considered so far. First, the theories with which they deal are obviously extremely imprecise. This is equally true of the 'hypotheses' which the Eleatics wished to refute (e.g. 'the many') and of those for which they wished to gain acceptance ('the one', 'ἔστι'). Most of their arguments are concerned not with propositions, with clearly defined subjects and predicates, but with vague, general concepts, and yet those arguments were conducted as if those hypotheses were propositions which must be either true or false. Secondly, some of their arguments appear to rely on certain oversimplified, or mistaken, logical assumptions. It might be said that the Eleatics were slowly progressing towards satisfactory principles of Contradiction and Exclusion. Zeno attempted to refute 'the many' by showing that certain pairs of contraries belong to it. Yet to judge from some of his reported arguments, he did not always specify at all clearly in what sense or respect the contraries in question were shown to be predicated of 'the many', and it may be that he was not fully aware that both the contrary terms 'limited' and 'unlimited' (for example) may, in certain circumstances, be predicated of the same subject without self-

---

[1] It is striking that in Fr. 8 (3) Melissus says of things that change that 'what was, and what is now, are *in no respect alike*' (οὐδὲν ὁμοῖον), as if no alternatives were possible apart from complete identity and complete difference. Cf. also the use of ὁμοῖον in Fr. 7 (2).

contradiction (e.g. in different respects). Again whereas by the Law of Excluded Middle it is necessary that either a proposition (*p*) or its contradictory (*not p*) is true, the Eleatics seem to have assumed, in some of their arguments, that a similar principle holds good of contrary propositions, indeed contrary 'hypotheses', as well. Thus Parmenides insisted on a choice between 'it is necessary that it should be' and 'it is necessary that it should not be', and Melissus, too, appears to assume that 'it is' (in the sense of unalterable existence) and 'it is not' (in the sense of unalterable non-existence) are exhaustive alternatives. Again Zeno and Melissus evidently believed that 'the one' and 'the many' are true alternatives, that is that one or other hypothesis must be true. It may be suggested, then, that in their arguments relating to existence and plurality, the Eleatics tended to employ oversimplified principles of Contradiction and Exclusion, to assume (1) that opposites are mutually exclusive in whatever sense or respect they may be predicated of a particular subject, and (2) that they are exhaustive alternatives—that of a pair of contrary, as of contradictory, propositions, either the one, or the other, must be true.

ARGUMENTS BASED ON OPPOSITES IN THE PERIOD OF THE SOPHISTS

The original writings of the sophists are almost entirely lost to us, and the interpretation of many aspects of their thought remains very largely conjectural. Yet we have fairly good information, from Plato and other sources, concerning some of the theses involving pairs of opposite terms which were maintained by various thinkers in the late fifth and early fourth centuries, and in the case of Gorgias' treatise *On What is Not or on Nature* we can reconstruct with some probability the detailed arguments which one sophist used to establish or recommend the paradoxical thesis that 'nothing exists'. We may begin by considering some of the evidence which shows how certain dilemmas involving such pairs of terms as one and many, 'what is' and 'what is not', continued to perplex various thinkers in the period before Plato.

The dilemma of *the one and the many* is, of course, Eleatic in origin, but that other pre-Platonic thinkers found the problems raised by this pair of opposites difficult to circumvent is apparent from passages in both Plato and Aristotle. At *Ph.* 185 b 25 ff. Aristotle reports that some thinkers were puzzled how several predicates may be asserted to belong to a single subject. 'Even the more recent of the ancient thinkers were thrown into confusion', Aristotle says, 'lest the same thing should turn out for them to be both one and many', and he goes on to describe some of the expedients which were used to escape this dilemma. 'So some, like Lycophron, omitted the word "is", while others changed the form of their expression, saying not that "the man is white" (λευκός ἐστιν), but that "he-has-been-whitened" (λελεύκωται)...lest if they add the word "is" they should make the one many', and Aristotle concludes (b 34 ff.): 'On this subject, then, they were already getting into difficulties, and admitting that the one was many, as if it were not possible for the same thing to be both one and many, so long as these (that is "the many") are not opposites.' Then Plato, too, refers to the problem of the one and the many in its simplest form in several passages, notably in *Sophist* 251 a–c.[1] There the Eleatic Stranger remarks that the same thing may be designated by a great variety of names, and adds that this provides 'entertainment for the young and those of their elders who have taken to learning late in life. Anyone can take part in it and protest at once that the many cannot be one nor the one many: and indeed they enjoy forbidding us to say that a man is good, but we must say only that good is good and man is man.' Now Plato mentions this problem here, as elsewhere, only to dismiss it as trivial.[2] Yet it is clear from the attempted solutions to the problem which

---

[1] Cf. *Prm.* 129 cd, *Phlb.* 14 cd.

[2] For Plato, the real problem of 'the one and the many' is that of the relationship between a *single* Form and the *many* particular things in which it is present (e.g. *Phlb.* 15 b).

Aristotle mentions, that some thinkers felt constrained to propose quite far-fetched linguistic expedients to avoid having to call one thing many. But it is only if we assume that 'one' and 'many' may not, *under any circumstances*, both be truly predicated of the same subject, that there is any problem here at all. The history of this dilemma provides, in fact, a striking illustration of the perplexities caused by the use of pairs of contrary predicates before Plato himself clarified the question of the nature of contradiction in the *Phaedo, Republic* and *Sophist*.

The question of how or in what sense '*what is*' can be said to come to be from '*what is not*' is another problem which caused great difficulty long after it was first raised by Parmenides. Two texts are worth considering in this connection. First, there is a report in Sextus Empiricus concerning the theory of one Xeniades of Corinth (*M.* vii 53, DK 81), according to which Xeniades maintained that 'everything which comes to be comes to be from what is not, and everything which is destroyed is destroyed into what is not.' Faced with the dilemma of whether 'what is' comes to be (*a*) from 'what is', or (*b*) from 'what is not', Xeniades apparently chose the alternative which Parmenides had described as inconceivable, that it comes to be from 'what is not'. Yet (if we may assume that Sextus' brief report is not quite misleading) it would seem that Xeniades still did not explicate the problem by analysing the two terms which had been treated as incompatible and exhaustive alternatives and showing in what sense 'what is' may be said to come to be from 'what is not': on the contrary, he evidently stated his own view in the terms in which the choice had been presented by Parmenides, and left the apparent paradox that 'what is' comes to be from 'what is not' quite unexplained. Then a text in Aristotle, *Metaphysics* K 6, suggests that in order to avoid being compelled (as they thought) to say that something (white) came to be from 'what is not' (i.e. not-white), some thinkers claimed, paradoxically, that a thing which became white was *both not-white and white* in the first place (1062 b 26 ff.).[1] Yet like the problem of the one and the many, this problem, too, seems to have arisen largely because the terms ἔστι and οὐκ ἔστι were taken to be incompatible in whatever sense they were predicated of a particular subject.[2]

The problem of *false statement* may be considered a special instance of the dilemma of 'what is' and 'what is not', for in Greek ὄντα and μὴ ὄντα may refer not only to what is and what is not, but also to what is, or is not, true. Once an admission had been obtained that it was impossible to describe or conceive μὴ ὄντα in the sense of what is completely non-existent, the conclusion was sometimes drawn that it was impossible to make false statements. Some passages in Plato illustrate the arguments in question and suggest that at one period, at least, the problem was one which caused quite widespread difficulty. In the *Cratylus* (429d), for instance, Socrates mentions the view that false statement (ψευδῆ λέγειν, equated by Cratylus with μὴ τὰ ὄντα λέγειν) is completely impossible, and says that 'there are many both now and in former times who assert this'. Again in the *Euthydemus* (283e ff.) Plato represents the brother sophists Euthydemus and Dionysodorus arguing that it is impossible to lie or to contradict anyone, and again Socrates says that he has heard such an argument used often and by many people: 'indeed the followers of Protagoras used it a great deal, and others before him' (286bc). Indeed in this dialogue Socrates goes on to turn the tables on his opponents and uses the same argument to compel them to admit not only that false statement, but also that false belief, and ignorance, are impossible,

---

[1] The text is difficult, but the thesis to which Aristotle refers is clear from the concluding remark at 1062 b 29 f.: ὥστε ἐκ μὴ ὄντος γίγνοιτ' ἂν κατ' ἐκείνους, εἰ μὴ ὑπῆρχε λευκὸν τὸ αὐτὸ καὶ μὴ λευκόν (Ross's text) ('so that according to them it would be coming to be from what is not unless the same thing were both white and not-white').

[2] Kerferd, p. 25, has pointed out that the use of the verb 'to be' as a copula continued to engage the interest of certain thinkers long after Plato: he instances Cicero, *Tusc. Disp.* 1 6 13, where when speaking of Crassus when he is dead we are asked to prefer the formula 'Miser M. Crassus' to the formula 'Miser est M. Crassus'.

and further that refutation and making a mistake are empty concepts. Finally, a passage in Aristotle's *Topics* (104b 20 f.) informs us that the Cynic Antisthenes was one of those who held that contradiction is impossible. Even if we should, no doubt, allow for a certain element of exaggeration in Plato's references to this dilemma, it seems clear that the problem of false statement, or saying 'what is not', was a third topic which caused several thinkers quite serious perplexities, at least until Plato himself clarified the nature of false statement in the *Sophist* (240d ff.), and once again the problem evidently arose from the tendency to treat the ambiguous ὄντα and μὴ ὄντα as incompatible and exhaustive alternatives in whatever sense the terms were used.

It is apparent from references in Plato, Aristotle and elsewhere that certain dilemmas involving such pairs of terms as one and many, 'what is' and 'what is not', caused serious difficulties to certain thinkers in the late fifth or early fourth century. But in one case we have extensive texts which purport to contain the original arguments which one sophist propounded on the topic of 'what is' and 'what is not'. We have two quite detailed and apparently independent accounts of the arguments in the work of Gorgias known by the title *On What is Not or on Nature*, namely those in Sextus Empiricus (*M.* VII 65 ff., DK 82 B 3) and in the pseudo-Aristotelian *De Melisso, Xenophane, Gorgia*.[1] The relative value of these two reports is disputed, and both of them have evidently reformulated Gorgias' argument to a greater or lesser degree. On some points, however, there is clear and definite agreement between the two versions, and together they provide some reasonably reliable evidence concerning both the content and the form of the original argument.

Gorgias' thesis is stated in *de MXG* (979a 12 f.) as follows:

[1] 979a 11–980b 21 (from Diels's text, *3*). Widely differing views have been taken by scholars on the purpose of Gorgias' treatise and on the value of the arguments he uses; see especially H. Gomperz, *1*, pp. 1–35; Nestle, *1*, pp. 551 ff.; Calogero, *2*, ch. 4; Gigon, *2*, pp. 186 ff.; Bux, pp. 402 ff.; Kerferd, pp. 3 ff.; and Bröcker, pp. 427 ff.

'he says that nothing exists; but that if it exists, it is unknowable; and that if it exists and is knowable, it still cannot be indicated to others', and Sextus describes the same thesis using rather more technical terminology. What particularly concerns us here, however, is the type of argument used to prove the first part of the thesis, that 'nothing exists', and here, too, our sources agree *in the main* in the form of argument which they attribute to Gorgias. This consists in refuting a thesis by first stating a number of alternatives one of which must be true if the thesis itself is true, and then demolishing each of these alternatives in turn, and the likelihood that Gorgias did indeed use this type of argument in this context is considerably strengthened by the evidence of the *Helen* and the *Defence of Palamedes*, two speeches which are now generally accepted as genuine works of Gorgias, in both of which a similar procedure of argument figures quite prominently.[1] Thus according to *de MXG* 979b 20 ff., Gorgias refutes the thesis that 'it is' by arguing that 'if it is, it is either (A) ungenerated, or (B) generated', and then refuting each of these alternatives in turn. A similar method is applied again at 979b 27 ff. in demolishing one of these two alternatives, namely that it is generated (B), for there both the alternatives, ($B1$) that it is generated from what is, and ($B2$) that it is generated from what is not, are considered and rejected in turn.

The validity of this argument depends on whether the alternatives which are considered are indeed such that one of them must be true if the thesis is true, i.e. on whether the alternatives are exhaustive. Both our sources agree that

---

[1] Thus in the *Helen* (DK 82 B 11) Gorgias takes four alternative explanations of why Helen acted as she did, and then shows that whichever explanation is adopted, Helen should not be held guilty. Similarly at many points in the *Defence of Palamedes* (DK B 11a) Palamedes is imagined as putting before his judges a set of alternatives relating to his case, and then showing his innocence whichever alternative is adopted (see further below, pp. 120 f.). On the general similarity between the argumentation in the speeches and that which is used in *On What is Not*, see especially H. Gomperz, *1*, pp. 22 ff.; Gigon, *2*, pp. 190 f., and most recently, Segal, pp. 99 and 115.

Gorgias referred to such pairs of opposites as 'generated' and 'ungenerated' (or 'eternal'), 'one' and 'many', 'what is' and 'what is not', but the sense in which the last two pairs of terms, particularly, were taken, was generally quite indefinite.[1] Like the Eleatics, in fact, Gorgias appears to have assumed that 'one' and 'many', 'what is' and 'what is not' are incompatible alternatives in *whatever sense or respect* they are taken. Yet while Gorgias' argument clearly owes a good deal to those of the Eleatics, in some features it differs from any of the arguments which we have considered so far. First the form in which the alternatives were presented by Gorgias raises a problem. While both our sources agree that he referred to such pairs as 'generated' and 'ungenerated', Sextus' version sometimes mentions a *third* alternative, which consists of both the opposite terms taken together: thus at Sextus, *M.* vii 66 the alternatives are *either* 'what is' *or* 'what is not' *or* 'both what is and what is not', and in 68 'eternal' *or* 'generated' *or* 'eternal and generated at the same time'. If Sextus' version is correct, it seems to imply a modification of the assumption that a pair of opposites *by themselves* constitutes an exhaustive choice, even if on both occasions the addition of the third alternative in Sextus' version turns out to be simply a formal point. To judge from 75, Gorgias did not consider in what *different* senses or respects 'what is not' (e.g. 'what is not X') and 'what is' might *both* be said to exist: rather he argues that if both what is not and what is exist, then what is not is equivalent to what is, in so far as its being is concerned, and so neither of them will exist. Again no new argument is adduced to refute the third alternative 'eternal and generated at the same time' mentioned in 68 and 72. On the contrary this alternative is demolished simply by asserting that the opposites are incompatible (if it is eternal, it is not generated, and vice versa, 72), and again the introduction

---

[1] The vagueness of the term τὸ ὄν in particular is reflected in the disagreement among scholars as to how it should be interpreted and translated (whether as 'Being' or 'what is'). See, for example, Kerferd, pp. 6 ff.

of a third alternative does not lead to a consideration of the *different* respects in which 'eternal' and 'generated' may both be predicated of 'what is' (that is, of things which we say exist).

Then, too, Gorgias' argument differs from those we considered from the Eleatics in its ostensible purpose. Whereas Zeno and Melissus had set out to refute the hypothesis of 'the many' in order to recommend or establish the Parmenidean 'one', Gorgias used similar arguments to demolish *both* 'the many' *and* 'the one', *both* the hypothesis that 'it is generated' *and* the hypothesis that 'it is ungenerated', in order to establish the essentially negative thesis that 'nothing exists'. The ostensible conclusion of *On What is Not* is clear, but the question of Gorgias' real intentions in this treatise has been much debated, and in particular the view has been put forward that the whole work is merely a rhetorical exercise like the *Helen* or the *Defence of Palamedes*.[1] It seems most probable that the *Helen* is indeed intended primarily as a rhetorical piece: Gorgias himself calls it his παίγνιον or 'trifle' (21). But the subject-matter of *On What is Not* is not that of a forensic speech but a threefold thesis concerning what is, what can be known, and what can be communicated, and this marks it out as a quite different case. On the evidence we have, both internal and external,[2] there seems no reason to doubt that Gorgias intended his treatise to be a serious, even if a primarily destructive, contribution to the discussion of these problems. The conclusion he reaches is paradoxical, but no more paradoxical than that proposed by Parmenides in the *Way of Truth*. And as regards the arguments by which

[1] E.g. H. Gomperz, *1*, pp. 1 ff. and 33 ff., and for a discussion of other views see Untersteiner, p. 163, n. 2. Kerferd, p. 3, has recently argued forcefully for the interpretation that *On What is Not* is a serious philosophical work: 'Its general thesis might conceivably amuse those to whom all attempts at philosophy are inherently absurd, but such persons could hardly be expected to work through the difficult arguments which make up the contents of the work. The view that it was purely a rhetorical exercise is no more plausible.'

[2] Gigon, *2*, pp. 187 f., has pointed out that none of the ancient authorities regarded *On What is Not* as a mere 'trifle'.

Gorgias establishes the first part of his thesis, it is clear, first of all, that he saw the possibility of combining the arguments of the Eleatics with those of their opponents. Indeed the author of *de MXG* draws attention to this himself (979a 13 ff.): 'In proving that nothing exists, he combined what had been said by others who, in speaking about things that are, seemed to assert contrary opinions, some trying to prove that it is one and not many, others again that it is many and not one, and some that the things that are are ungenerated, and others that they are generated.'[1] But although Gorgias evidently realised how he might exploit various arguments which different philosophers had put forward on these topics, there is nothing to suggest that he saw how to escape the dilemmas which those arguments posed. The first part of his treatise deals with problems which had been raised by the Eleatics, and it carries the discussion of those problems a step further in that it shows how Eleatic arguments could be used against Eleatic theses, just as much as against the theses of their opponents.[2] But though Gorgias *explored* the difficulties raised by Eleatic arguments, he did nothing to *resolve* them: indeed it is very doubtful whether he, or any other philosopher of this period, clearly understood the assumptions on which such arguments were based or would have been able to resolve the dilemmas which they presented.

The discussion of philosophical issues revolving round the one and the many, what is and what is not, was not the only context in which the Eleatic techniques of putting a choice

---

[1] At 979a 22 f. *de MXG* refers specifically to Zeno and Melissus: 'some theses he (Gorgias) tries to prove by following Melissus, others by following Zeno'. And even what this writer calls Gorgias' 'own proof' (ἴδιον...ἀπόδειξιν, 979a 23 f.) resembles the arguments of the Eleatics in this, that it too involves the opposite pair 'what is' and 'what is not'.

[2] Bröcker has suggested that Gorgias' arguments are directed specifically against the Eleatic conception of Being and further that by implication they establish 'the opinions of mortals' as against the Eleatic *Way of Truth* (Bröcker, p. 438). But this goes far beyond anything that Gorgias actually says in *On What is Not*. Rather the thesis that 'nothing exists, and if it exists it is unknowable, and if it exists and is knowable, it cannot be communicated' is a quite general ontological and epistemological thesis which does not appear to be directed *solely* against the Eleatics.

between opposite alternatives, and of supporting a thesis by refuting the opposite (usually contrary) thesis, were employed in the period before Plato. Similar techniques were also commonly used in the broader context of rhetorical arguments which aimed at persuasion rather than anything approaching a formal proof, where, of course, they are extremely effective. To put a choice between alternatives that are opposite, but not exhaustive, is *formally* incorrect, and equally the refutation of a thesis does not *necessarily* imply that the contrary thesis is true: yet in the field of rhetorical arguments, where the aim of the speaker is not to give a formal demonstration, but merely to convince an opponent, such techniques have considerable persuasive force. Gorgias' *Defence of Palamedes*, for example, provides many instances of the use of arguments involving opposites in a purely rhetorical context. In his speech of defence, Palamedes is imagined putting a series of alternative questions to his judges, and with each of the alternatives which he mentions, he shows or attempts to show either that the suggestion is quite improbable, or that if it is true he should be considered innocent. He begins with a series of what are quite unexceptionable questions about how the act of treason of which he is accused was supposed to have been committed, asking, for instance, whether the bribe which he was supposed to have received was brought by *many* men, or by *one* (9), by *day* or by *night* (10). Then did he commit the crime *alone*, or *with accomplices* (11 f.)? But to undertake this crime was not the work of one man. Who, then, were his accomplices, *free men* or *slaves*? But if free men, then his judges should know about it themselves, and indeed be implicated with him. On the other hand it is surely incredible that he used slaves as accomplices, for they would denounce him, either *willingly* in the hope of their freedom, or *under compulsion*. So much for one series of alternatives which Palamedes puts: but later with a similar question he is patently guilty of sharp practice. He asks (22 ff.) whether his accuser accuses him from *exact knowledge* or from *supposition* (εἰδὼς ἀκριβῶς ἢ δοξάζων). The first alternative is rejected on the grounds that no first-hand evidence has been brought. But then he argues that mere supposition is insufficient foundation for an accusation. But while in the original question (22), we understand 'suppose' (δοξάζων) to refer to anything short of perfect knowledge, when these two are put as alternatives, yet when he comes to consider the possibility that they accuse him from supposition in 24, 'supposition' is there contrasted not with 'exact knowledge' but with 'knowledge' (unqualified) and it is taken to be quite untrustworthy. Finally, a different type of argument, but one also involving opposites, occurs at 25. There Palamedes says that he is accused both of σοφία (a term which means both wisdom and cleverness, though it is in the latter sense that it is taken here), and of μανία (folly), of σοφία in that he was crafty in carrying out his crime, and of μανία in that he betrayed his country, thereby harming his friends and benefiting his enemies. But these two, he says, are 'most opposite' (ἐναντιώτατα), and it is impossible for the same man to possess both attributes. How then, he asks, should they believe the accusation of someone who 'asserts opposite things about the same subject and before the same men'? Here, quite apart from the evident equivocation in the use of the term σοφία, Palamedes has not, of course, shown that his accusers have formally contradicted themselves: indeed this is not generally the aim of such arguments, which is, rather, merely to suggest, as plausibly as possible, that there is *some* inconsistency in the arguments used by the opposing side. Here, too, then, we find an argument involving opposites used for persuasive, rather than demonstrative, purposes, and there are, of course, many other passages in both philosophical and other writers which illustrate the use of what Aristotle calls the τόπος ἐκ τῶν ἐναντίων both in the pre-Platonic period and later.

Finally, a note should be added on certain other typical controversies which originate in the pre-Platonic period, which were carried on largely as debates between two extreme alternatives, even though (unlike that between 'the one' and 'the many') they do not involve pairs of opposite terms. Two such controversies are worth mentioning particularly, (1) that between Reason and Sensation, and (2) that between Νόμος (Convention) and Φύσις (Nature).[1] In neither case are the two terms contraries, and yet the arguments were sometimes conducted as if the two points of view were mutually exclusive and exhaustive alternatives.

(1) First there is the dispute between the rival claims of reason and sensation to furnish knowledge. We should say, no doubt, *both* of the judgements derived from abstract reasoning *and* of those based on the evidence of the senses, that they may be either true or false: we may make mistakes in mathematical calculations, as in interpreting sense-data, although our method of verifying our judgements and our criteria for accepting them as true vary in either case. But at different stages in Greek thought we find expressions of the two extreme positions, (*a*) that reason *alone* furnishes true knowledge and that αἴσθησις (sense-perception or sensation) not only fails to do so but is *inherently misleading*, and (*b*) that sense-perception alone provides true knowledge. Both views may be illustrated briefly. (*a*) Parmenides Fr. 7, for example, contrasts reason and sensation, but it does much more than this, for Parmenides recommends not only that we should use reason *but also* that we should reject the evidence of the senses.[2] A similar theme is taken up by Melissus, who at the end of his discussion of the evidence of the senses in Fr. 8 puts it that 'it is clear, then, that we did not see correctly' (δῆλον τοίνυν ὅτι οὐκ ὀρθῶς ἑωρῶμεν). Melissus evidently adopts this position because the things we perceive are subject to change,

---

[1] Other important antitheses which also tend to be treated in a similar way in the period before Plato, especially, have been discussed by Heinimann, *1*, under the headings 'Wort und Tat', 'Benennung und Wirklichkeit', 'Schein und Sein'.

[2] 'Do not let habit, born of experience, force you to let wander your heedless eye or echoing ear or tongue along this road, but judge by reason....'

and do not, therefore, fulfil his criteria for 'what is', but we should observe that his conclusion is *not* that we perceive things *imprecisely* (he might have said οὐκ ἀκριβῶς ἑωρῶμεν) but that we perceive them *incorrectly* (οὐκ ὀρθῶς) which seems to imply that sensation is positively misleading. And then too in the sophists we find attributed to Xeniades the view that all φαντασία (including probably both what is perceived and what is imagined) is false (Sextus, *M.* vii 53, DK 81). But (*b*) that sense-perception alone provides true knowledge and is indeed infallible is the position of Protagoras, as reported and interpreted by Plato and Aristotle, at least.[1] Running through early Greek epistemological discussions, then, there is a certain tendency to treat the problem of knowledge as a debate between extreme alternatives, namely that appearances are true, and that they are radically misleading.[2] The two modes of cognition, reason and sense-perception, were often contrasted as alternatives: those who boosted the claims of the one to give knowledge tended to ignore the claims of the other, or even to denounce it as quite fallacious, and, indeed, a similar tendency reappears in some of Plato's discussions of epistemological problems.[3]

---

[1] In the *Theaetetus* 152a ff., for example (when Theaetetus has just suggested equating knowledge with sensation or sense-perception), Socrates cites the dictum of Protagoras that 'man is the measure of all things, both of the things that are, that they are, and of the things that are not, that they are not' and goes on: 'He puts it in some such way, does he not, that each thing is for me such as it appears to me, and is for you such as it appears to you?' He cites the case of two persons one of whom feels cold while the other does not, when the same wind is blowing on both, and he concludes that according to Protagoras' view 'sensation is always of what is, and, as knowledge, is infallible' (αἴσθησις ἄρα τοῦ ὄντος ἀεί ἐστιν καὶ ἀψευδὲς ὡς ἐπιστήμη οὖσα, 152c 5 f.). See also *Cra.* 385e f. and Arist. *Metaph.* 1062b 13 ff.

[2] There are, of course, important exceptions to this general rule. Democritus, for one, acknowledged both reason and sensation as forms of knowledge, the former 'genuine', the latter 'obscure' (Fr. 11: if Fr. 125 is authentic, he also recognised that mind is, to some extent, dependent on the senses).

[3] Cf. the argument in the *Phaedo*, 65a ff., in which it is suggested that sensations are positively misleading. Socrates puts the question 'do sight and hearing have any truth-and-reality for men (ἆρα ἔχει ἀλήθειάν τινα ὄψις τε καὶ ἀκοὴ τοῖς ἀνθρώποις), or, as the poets are always telling us, do we neither hear nor see

(2) Then νόμος and φύσις were also sometimes taken not merely as rival, but as alternative, theories, in various contexts, not only in ethical discussions, but also in epistemological theories, theories of language and accounts of the origin of civilisation.[1] The way in which the two points of view were sometimes contrasted may be illustrated, for example, from Plato's *Cratylus*, where Hermogenes and Cratylus hold a νόμῳ- and a φύσει-theory of language respectively. Cratylus' view is that names are naturally right, i.e. that they are suited to the objects to which they refer, and he also denies that whatever people call a thing by convention is its name (383 ab). Hermogenes, on the other hand, adopts the view that names are right by convention alone: 'It seems to me that whatever name anyone attaches to anything is correct; and if again he changes it for another name ... the second is no less correct than the first was' (384 d 2 ff.). As stated here, the two views are extremes: against the φύσει-theory it might be objected that different names are used in different languages to refer to the same thing (cf. 383 b), but equally against the νόμῳ-theory it might be urged that names are not completely arbitrary, as Hermogenes makes out. True, in the course of this dialogue *both* theories of language are investigated quite thoroughly, and on the main question of how we obtain knowledge, the view expressed by Socrates at the end of the *Cratylus* represents a new departure breaking away from *both* theories which had found *some* 'rightness', whether 'natural' or 'conventional', in *names themselves*.[2] Yet it is striking that the original problem in this dialogue is presented in the form of a *dilemma*. When at 383 a Hermogenes

anything exactly?' (οὔτ' ἀκούομεν ἀκριβὲς οὐδὲν οὔτε ὁρῶμεν) and then suggests that the soul is actually deceived by the body (ἐξαπατᾶται 65 b 11) and lays hold on truth in reasoning (ἐν τῷ λογίζεσθαι) alone.

[1] See the full discussion of the history of νόμος and φύσις and of the various contexts in which this antithesis was used in Heinimann's special study (*1*), and cf. also Pohlenz, *2*.

[2] At the end of the *Cratylus* Socrates argues forcefully that to obtain knowledge we must first study things themselves, not their names: see especially 435 d ff.

invites Socrates to join their discussion, he and Cratylus have reached an impasse: they each maintain quite different views on the 'rightness' of names, and Hermogenes' perplexity (to which he refers at 384a and again at 384c f.) arises, in the main, from the fact that he takes these views to be the only possible alternatives.[1] As with Reason and Sensation, so too with Nature and Convention, one may conclude that (like the arguments of the Eleatics and other philosophers which involved such opposites as 'the one' and 'the many') the debate was often carried on as if *a choice had to be made between* the two terms (and between the two *extreme* points of view they were taken to represent).[2]

I may now recapitulate briefly the main types of arguments involving opposites which we find used in the pre-Platonic period. First there is the putting of a choice between opposite alternatives in order to force an admission (as, for example, in Parmenides and Melissus); second the proof of a thesis by refuting the opposite (usually contrary) thesis (as notably in Zeno and Melissus); third the refutation of a thesis by showing that opposite (again usually contrary) consequences follow from it (Zeno); and fourth the refutation of a thesis by first stating certain alternatives one of which must be true if the thesis is true and then disproving each of

---

[1] This is suggested, for example, by the way in which Hermogenes puts his case at 384d 6 ff.: οὐ γὰρ φύσει ἑκάστῳ πεφυκέναι ὄνομα οὐδὲν οὐδενί, ἀλλὰ νόμῳ καὶ ἔθει τῶν ἐθισάντων τε καὶ καλούντων ('it is not by nature that any name belongs to any thing at all, but by convention and the custom of those who are accustomed to name it').

[2] Additional evidence concerning the way in which the argument between Nature and Convention led to paradoxes and dilemmas comes from Aristotle. At *SE* 173a 7 ff. he describes the use of the two standards of Nature and Convention as 'a most extensive topic for forcing your opponent into paradoxes'. These two, he says, are opposites (ἐναντία) and it is possible to trap your opponent into making paradoxes by countering the statements which he makes from one point of view with statements in which the other point of view is adopted. It is especially interesting that Aristotle should *recommend* the *deliberate* use of the antithesis between Nature and Convention in order to lead an opponent into paradox, but it is apparent that in so doing he is following a common earlier tendency to contrast these two points of view. Indeed Aristotle not only cites an example of the argument from the *Gorgias* (482e f.), but goes on to say that 'all the older writers' supposed that paradoxes resulted in this way (173a 9).

these alternatives in turn (Gorgias). Certain criticisms apply to the majority of the arguments which we have considered. (1) It was generally the case that the terms used in such arguments were quite equivocal, e.g. 'it is', 'the many'. (2) It seems that certain 'hypotheses' were often treated as though, like propositions, they must be either true or false. (3) The relationships between opposites of different sorts were evidently sometimes misconceived or oversimplified. Thus (i) it was sometimes assumed that a 'hypothesis' had been shown to be self-contradictory when it had been shown that contrary attributes belong to the same subject (without regard to the respect or relation in which those attributes were said to belong). Again (ii) a choice was often put between opposites that are not, in fact, exhaustive alternatives.[1] And (iii) it was sometimes too readily inferred from the refutation of a thesis that the contrary is true. In such cases the arguments are formally invalid, although they undoubtedly have some persuasive force (and as we shall see later, similar arguments are not only used, but recommended, by Aristotle, for rhetorical purposes). As yet, however, no explicit analysis of the relationships between different types of opposition had, so far as we know, been undertaken. Even though quite a number of terms are used by different pre-Platonic authors to refer to opposites in general (they include ἀντίος, ἐναντίος, ὑπεναντίος and ἀντίξοος)[2] these terms are

---

[1] We noted, however, that Gorgias may have been aware of some of the formal objections to which the typical Eleatic disjunctive question, putting a choice between a pair of opposite alternatives, is open: at least, if Sextus' version of the arguments in *On What is Not* is correct, he sometimes introduced in his questions a third alternative, consisting of both opposites together.

[2] ἀντίος and ἐναντίος are used already in Homer generally in a local sense, 'face to face' (usually of persons, e.g. of opposing armies as at *Il.* 11 216, but sometimes of things, as of two promontories facing one another across the entrance to a harbour, *Od.* 10 89), but ἀντίος is first used in a cosmological context by Parmenides in the *Way of Seeming* (Fr. 8 55 and 59, referring to Light and Night), and both ἐναντίος and ὑπεναντίος are used by the medical writers in the context of the theory that opposites cure diseases caused by opposites (e.g. *VM* ch. 13, *CMG* I, 1 44 20 and *Flat.* ch. 1, *CMG* I, 1 92 8). ἀντίξοος occurs first in Heraclitus Fr. 8 (see above, p. 97) and thereafter is common in Ionic Greek.

not strictly defined, nor is this richness in vocabulary exploited, at this stage, in order to refer to different *kinds* of opposites. In particular there is no evidence that the important distinction between contrary and contradictory opposites had been explicitly drawn, and indeed many of the paradoxes and dilemmas common in this period arose, as we have seen, from a failure to draw this distinction, and a tendency to treat *all* opposites as incompatible and exhaustive alternatives. What we have to consider next, then, is how far Plato went towards a satisfactory analysis of the different modes of opposition.

PLATO

I have suggested that certain of the arguments put forward by the Eleatics and others in the period before Plato depend on an unquestioned assumption that such pairs of opposites as one and many, being and not-being, are necessarily incompatible and exhaustive alternatives. Plato himself was responsible for drawing certain important distinctions between different types of opposites, for clarifying the problem of contradiction, and, in particular, for showing that apparently contradictory statements in which a thing is asserted both to be (in some sense) and not to be (in some other sense) are not contradictions at all. But before discussing Plato's contributions to the analysis of opposites, we should first draw attention to various passages, particularly from the earlier dialogues, in which we find arguments similar in form to those which we have been considering in connection with earlier Greek philosophers. There are, of course, a great many occasions, in Plato's dialogues, when a speaker puts a question in the form of a choice between a pair of opposite alternatives and the fact that the question takes this form has little or no influence on the discussion of the topic in hand. Often, however, the fact that a questioner puts a choice of this sort *is* an important factor in the discussion, a move which enables him to gain certain admissions or to establish certain conclusions (that is if his opponent is unwary and the fact that a third or further alternatives have been suppressed passes unnoticed). Sometimes the context in which a disjunctive question of this sort occurs is, for instance, an *elenchus*, where the argument has a primarily destructive purpose. On the other hand a similar technique of argument is also used in passages where Plato is advancing his own positive doctrines, e.g. in the context of the theory of Forms, and this raises more interesting problems of interpretation. We may begin by considering an example of the first sort, in which Socrates puts a series of alternative questions when conducting an *elenchus*.

A well-known passage in the *Protagoras* (329c–332a) contains a remarkable discussion between Socrates and Protagoras on the subject of virtue.[1] Protagoras asserts (329d 3 f.) that virtue is a single thing and that justice, temperance, piety and so on are its parts. Socrates then asks (d 4 ff.) *whether* these parts are like the parts of a face *or* like parts of a piece of gold which do not differ from one another except in size. The alternatives, as Socrates puts them, are, one may say, whether the parts of virtue are *identical* or *quite different*. Yet a third alternative is also possible, of course, namely that the parts are neither the same as one another, nor yet quite different, but alike in some respects and different in others, and this alternative is not considered although it is the one which best describes the relationship between different sorts of virtues (which are not identical, but bear, as it were, a family resemblance to one another in so far as they are all virtues). At 329d 8 ff. Protagoras chooses the answer that the parts of virtue are like the parts of a face, and when Socrates puts it to him (330a 4 ff.) that the parts of virtue are, then, unlike one another, he agrees. There then follows a passage which has attracted considerable comment from scholars,[2]

---

[1] The passage has been discussed, for example, by Ranulf, pp. 94 ff. and Sullivan, pp. 13 ff.

[2] See most recently Sullivan, p. 14 (who points out that it is common enough, in ordinary conversation, to do what Socrates does here, use the contradictory ('not just') as the contrary ('unjust')), and Gallop, pp. 91 f.

for in it Socrates seems quite blatantly to confuse a contrary and a contradictory. He asks (330 c 4 ff.) whether justice is just or unjust, and Protagoras accepts the answer which Socrates supplies, namely that it is just (the possibility that justice itself is neither just nor unjust is not mentioned). Following up the previous admission that the parts of virtue are unlike one another, Socrates then puts it (331 a 8 f.) that justice, for example, is not οἷον ὅσιον ἀλλ' οἷον μὴ ὅσιον ('not like what is pious, but like what is not pious') and he *then* suggests (a 9 f.) that piety, in turn, is οἷον μὴ δίκαιον, ἀλλ' ἄδικον ἄρα ('like what is not just, but is, then, unjust'). Here again Protagoras fails to raise any objection, although 'not just' is apparently taken to imply 'unjust', and Socrates is allowed to continue unchecked. At 331 b 3 ff., then, Socrates concludes that his own view of virtue is correct, namely that 'justice is either the same as piety or most like it' (ἤτοι ταὐτόν...ἢ ὅτι ὁμοιότατον). Once again only the extreme alternatives seem to be taken into account. Once the possibility that justice and piety are opposites has been rejected, Socrates asserts that they are 'identical or most alike'. The possibility that they may be alike in some respects, but unlike in others, is not considered. Yet the addition of the words ἢ ὅτι ὁμοιότατον in b 5 is remarkable, for they might have suggested to Protagoras how he might escape the dilemma which Socrates has posed, the choice between 'identical' on the one hand, and 'quite different' or 'opposite' on the other. Protagoras does not, however, exploit the possibility that an important distinction might be drawn between 'identical' (ταὐτόν) and 'most, or very, alike' (ὅτι ὁμοιότατον). Indeed he goes on first by granting that justice resembles piety 'in a way' (τι) (d 1 f.), but then by qualifying this statement with remarks which indicate that he quite fails to appreciate the importance of the relationship of 'similarity' as distinct from both 'identity' on the one hand, and 'opposition' on the other. For he continues (d 2 ff.): 'And indeed anything resembles anything else in some way or

9   129

other (ἀμῇ γέ πῃ). *Even the white resembles the black in a way,*
and the hard the soft, and the rest of those things that seem
most opposite to one another.' He ends (e 3 ff.) with a plea
not to call things that have any point of resemblance 'ὅμοια',
nor things that have any point of difference 'ἀνόμοια'. While
Socrates, on the one hand, appears to insist on a choice
between the two alternatives 'identity' and 'opposition',
Protagoras, too, for his part, tends equally to assimilate the
relationship of similarity to that of identity, and that of dis-
similarity to that of complete difference, or opposition.

This passage in the *Protagoras* contains several examples of
arguments in which a choice is put between a pair of opposite
alternatives that are not, in fact, exhaustive, but of course we
need not suppose that Plato himself was in any way deceived
by the arguments by which he makes Socrates deceive Protagoras. Plato draws the distinction between not having an
attribute, and having the contrary attribute, quite clearly in
several passages in quite early dialogues, for example in the
Symposium,[1] and in the *Protagoras* itself the existence of a category intermediate between a pair of contraries (e.g. 'neither
good nor bad') is twice referred to,[2] and it is, therefore, quite
unlikely that he was unaware of the formal objections which
might be raised against the move that Socrates makes at 331 a
9 f. when he converts 'not just' to 'unjust'. Yet if Plato
deliberately ascribed to Socrates a series of, at best, *ad
hominem* arguments in this passage, it is remarkable that he
represented a sophist of the eminence of Protagoras as being
unable to counter these arguments effectively. Protagoras
does not question the choice between a pair of inexhaustive
alternatives which Socrates puts at 329 d 4 ff., nor again at
330 c 4 ff. (where the alternatives are: is justice just or unjust?)

---

[1] See *Smp.* 202 b 1 f. ('do not compel that which is not beautiful to be ugly,
nor that which is not good to be evil'). Cf., for example, *Men.* 91 c 8–d 1, and
see further below, p. 147, on *R.* 491 d, etc.

[2] At *Prt.* 346 cd Socrates points out that it is absurd to say that 'everything
which has no admixture of black is white', and at 351 cd Protagoras himself
refers to certain painful things which are, he says, neither good nor bad.

nor again at 331 b 1 ff., where Socrates concludes that his own view of virtue is the right one. Nor for that matter does Protagoras object when Socrates converts 'not just' to 'unjust' at 331 a 9 f. In his speech at 331 d 1 ff. he too tends to assimilate the relationship of similarity to that of identity and fails to recognise the potential ambiguity of the Greek word ὅμοιον (which may mean either 'like' or 'the same as'), and the end of the whole discussion leaves him confused and angry.[1] Plato himself may not be deceived by any of the arguments which he puts into Socrates' mouth, but at least he thought it plausible to attribute arguments of this type to Socrates, and to describe Protagoras, in turn, as being perplexed and defeated by them.[2]

There are other passages in the Socratic dialogues in which Socrates puts a choice between a pair of opposite but inexhaustive alternatives to gain an admission from an opponent in the course of conducting an *elenchus*. But it is more important to note how a similar technique of argument is used in passages where Plato's purpose is more constructive, e.g. in recommending theses connected with the theory of Forms. (1) In the *Phaedo*, for instance, Socrates puts a choice between two extreme alternatives in gaining agreement that the world of particulars is, in some sense, quite unstable. First at 78 d 1 ff. it is agreed that Being itself, the Equal itself, the Beautiful itself and so on are always constant and unchanging (ὡσαύτως ἀεὶ ἔχει κατὰ ταὐτά d 2 f.) and then Socrates asks (d 10 ff.), 'What about the many beautiful things, such as men or horses or clothes...? ἆρα κατὰ ταὐτὰ ἔχει, ἢ πᾶν τοὐναντίον ἐκείνοις οὔτε αὐτὰ αὑτοῖς οὔτε ἀλλήλοις

---

[1] Socrates breaks off the discussion at 332 a 2 ff. because, as he says, Protagoras seems to be angry (ἐπειδὴ δυσχερῶς δοκεῖς μοι ἔχειν πρὸς τοῦτο).

[2] Another argument from the *Protagoras* is worth noting as it reveals the variety of uses of the Greek term ἐναντίον, which was sometimes used strictly of contraries, sometimes more loosely of any opposed terms. At 332 a ff. Socrates argues (1) that ἀφροσύνη ('folly') and σοφία ('wisdom') are πᾶν τοὐναντίον (quite opposite), (2) that a thing has only one ἐναντίον (here, strictly, 'contrary') (332 d 2 f.), and further (3) that ἀφροσύνη and σωφροσύνη are ἐναντία, in order to prove (4) that σοφία and σωφροσύνη ('temperance') are identical (333 b 4 ff.).

οὐδέποτε ὡς ἔπος εἰπεῖν οὐδαμῶς κατὰ ταὐτά; [1] One may remark that a third possibility (that the many beautiful or equal objects may be subject to occasional, but not constant, change) is not mentioned here, and the effect of putting the alternatives in the form of the contraries 'always the same' and '*never* the same' (rather than in the form 'always the same' and '*not always* the same') is, clearly, to facilitate the conclusion that the world of particulars is 'so to speak' *quite* *un*stable.

(2) In the passage that immediately follows in the *Phaedo* Socrates again appears to force an issue by putting a choice between opposite alternatives. First at 79a 6 f. he distinguishes two classes of things, the 'visible' and the 'invisible', and then obtains Cebes' agreement that the 'invisible' are always constant, the 'visible' never so (a 9 f.). The body is granted to be 'more like' or 'kin to' (ὁμοιότερον, συγγενέστερον) the 'visible' (b 4 ff.), *but then* at b 7 Socrates asks whether the soul is 'visible or invisible' (ὁρατὸν ἢ ἀιδές). Again the question takes the form of a choice between a pair of opposites. Yet 'visible' and 'invisible' are being used, clearly, in a special sense. An admission that the soul is 'invisible' is taken, in fact, as an admission that it is 'like' or 'kin to' the class of invisible unchanging realities, that is the Forms (d 1 ff., e 2 ff.).

(3) Certain theses concerning the distinction between Forms and particulars, and between soul and body, are recommended, in the *Phaedo*, with the help of questions that put a choice between contrary alternatives. But a similar type of question also occurs elsewhere in Plato when the Forms are being discussed, and notably in a passage in the *Timaeus*, 51 b 7 ff. There Timaeus asks: 'Is there such a thing as Fire "just by itself" (αὐτὸ ἐφ' ἑαυτοῦ) or any of those other things about which we are always saying that they exist "just by themselves"? Or is it only these things which we see or which

---

[1] 'Are they constant or, quite the opposite to these, never, so to speak, identical either with themselves or with one another in any respect?'

we otherwise perceive by means of the body that have such reality, and nothing else, besides these things, has any sort of existence at all?' Timaeus then goes on to suggest (d 3 ff.) that 'if reason and true opinion are two kinds (δύο γένη), then undoubtedly these Forms exist "just by themselves", imperceptible to us, the objects of reason only. But if, as it seems to some people, true opinion does not differ in any respect (τὸ μηδέν) from reason, then we must suppose that everything that is perceived by means of the body is what is most stable'. The grounds which Timaeus then gives for distinguishing reason and true opinion do not concern us here. What we may notice about this passage is the way in which Timaeus twice puts a choice between certain alternatives. At 51 b 7 ff. two alternatives are stated; either nothing at all is real apart from sensible objects, or the Forms themselves are real. The only alternative to the theory of Forms which is explicitly mentioned here is the extreme materialist view. And then in the argument which Timaeus puts forward at d 3 ff. the choice is again one between opposite extremes: are reason and true opinion generically different (δύο γένη) or are they identical, 'differing in nothing'? Yet a third possibility, that what we refer to as 'reason' and 'true opinion' are dissimilar, without being generically different, is not considered. The form in which the alternatives are presented once again forces an issue by suggesting that the choice lies between the two extreme views: *either* reason and true opinion are identical, *or* they differ from each other in such a way that their respective objects must be different in kind, the Forms imperceptible and unchanging, and the particulars perceptible, and generated and destroyed.

The passages we have considered illustrate some of the contexts in which we find a choice is put between opposite, but inexhaustive, alternatives in Plato. The question of how Plato evaluated such arguments is a complex one, but we have seen that he uses them not only for destructive purposes, where Socrates gets the better of an opponent by means of what are

sometimes quite specious arguments, but also for constructive ends, where his aim is to procure acceptance of certain of
his own positive theses (e.g. relating to the Forms), and in this
context he evidently considered his arguments had some persuasive force, even if there is no reason to believe that he
would have claimed that they are demonstrative. But if
Plato was prepared to use this form of argument in various
contexts and for various purposes and to let it pass unchallenged, elsewhere in the dialogues we find that arguments of a
broadly similar form are both parodied and criticised extensively, and we must now consider the nature of the criticisms
which are brought against certain such arguments. How far
did Plato go towards analysing such arguments as a whole
from a logical point of view? The first evidence we should
consider is from the *Euthydemus*. This dialogue is valuable
both for the evidence which it provides concerning the use of
certain types of argument in the period immediately preced-
ing, and contemporary with, Plato, and also for the light it
throws on Plato's own attitude towards, and assessment of,
such arguments. And it is interesting to note how many of the
arguments which he attributes to the brother sophists
Euthydemus and Dionysodorus depend on the Eleatic
technique of putting a choice between a pair of opposite
alternatives.[1]

The brother sophists begin (275d 2 ff.) by putting a
number of questions to which they demand one of two given
opposite alternatives as the answer, and it is their confessed
intention to refute the person who answers *whichever* of the
two alternatives he chooses (e 4 ff., cf. 276d 9 ff.). (1) Thus
at 275d 3 f. they ask, 'Who are they that learn, οἱ σοφοί (the
wise, or the clever) or οἱ ἀμαθεῖς (the foolish)?' When the
answer οἱ σοφοί (the clever) is given, it is pointed out that

---

[1] Sprague, e.g. pp. 5 ff. and 12 ff., classifies the arguments in question as fallacies
of equivocation and *secundum quid*. The particular feature of these arguments to
which I wish to draw attention here is that their plausibility (such as it is)
derives from the fact that they put a choice between opposite alternatives and
the presumption is that one or other alternative should be adopted.

people who learn do not already know what they are about to be taught, and are, therefore, 'foolish' (276a 1–b 5). But the answer 'foolish' is also refuted because in general it is the clever, and not the foolish, who are good, or quick, at learning (c 3–7). The equivocation is obvious: 'wise' and 'foolish' are used in respect of a particular piece of information at 276a 3 ff., but are taken to refer to a general ability at c 4 ff. Yet the sophists take 'wise' and 'foolish' as simple alternatives throughout. (2) The second question takes a similar form, for again the sophists put a choice between opposite alternatives. 'Do those who learn, learn what they know (ἐπίστανται) or what they do not know?' (276d 7 f.). Cleinias replies that they learn what they do not know (e 8 f.), but this answer is refuted because (in a sense) they know the alphabet which is used when they learn other facts (which they do not know) (277a 1 ff.). But then the second alternative is also refuted (b 3 ff.) by an appeal to the obvious fact that what people learn is what they do not yet know. But here Socrates comes to the rescue of Cleinias (d 1 ff.) and points out the equivocation in the word 'learn' in the first question, where it is used first in the sense of acquiring knowledge, and then in the sense of having or applying knowledge (for which he says the more usual word is συνιέναι, understand). The sophists are revealing, he says, that the same word is used of people in opposite states, of knowing (in one sense) and of not knowing (in the other). He describes the sophists' argument as a piece of childish sport (παιδιά 278b 2 f.) and he compares them with practical jokers who pull away the seats from people who are about to sit down. With typical irony he says that they will now, no doubt, be turning to more serious matters (278c 2 ff.): they will now show how they should exhort Cleinias to devote himself to wisdom and virtue (d 1 ff.), and he goes on to give a demonstration of the sort of discussion which he has in mind. The sophists, however, continue in their previous fashion. There then follow two arguments in which the ambiguity of ὄν and μὴ ὄν is exploited. (3) In the first (283 c f.) Dionysodorus concludes that because Socrates wants Cleinias to become wise, that is other than he is now, he wants Cleinias to be dead (μηκέτι εἶναι 'no longer to be', without the qualification 'foolish'). (4) Then at 283 e f. it is suggested that speaking falsely and contradiction are impossible, for one cannot say 'what is not' (see above, p. 114), and Socrates succeeds in turning this argument against the sophists themselves (286 b f.) to make them agree that false opinion and ignorance, too, are impossible, and so also are refutation and making mistakes.

After a further interlude in which Socrates and Cleinias discuss the pursuit of knowledge in a serious vein, the sophists put more questions, this time to Socrates, who answers them more guardedly, qualifying his replies in an attempt to prevent the sophists from drawing apparently contradictory conclusions. (5) He is asked whether he knows anything (293 b 7), to which he replies 'certainly, many things, but unimportant ones'. Asked if he is 'knowing' (ἐπιστήμων c 2) he says 'certainly, in just that respect'. Euthydemus is undeterred by the fact that Socrates qualifies his answer, and says that if Socrates is 'knowing', then he must know everything. Socrates naturally objects to this and says that there are many things which he does not know, whereupon Euthydemus tries to draw the conclusion (c 7–d 1) that Socrates is both 'knowing' and 'not-knowing', and so both is and is not the same man 'in respect of the same things and at the same time', κατὰ ταὐτὰ ἅμα. Socrates pours scorn on this demonstration that he knows everything and turns the tables on the sophists by applying the same line of reasoning to the rest of mankind. He asks 'do all other men know everything, or nothing?' (294 a 5 f.), but Dionysodorus is represented as taking this to be a reasonable question, and he reiterates that they cannot know some things and not others, and so be 'knowing' and 'not-knowing' at the same time. Further arguments of the same sort follow. Like 'knowing' and 'not-knowing', 'brother' and 'not-brother', 'father' and 'not-father', 'mother' and 'not-mother' are used in turn (297e 5 f., 298a 1 ff., d 1 ff.) as if each of these pairs of terms represented incompatible and exhaustive alternatives in whatever respect or relation they are used. A series of absurd conclusions is drawn, not only by the sophists, but also, in mockery, by their opponents, who, as Socrates remarks (303e 4 ff.), quickly become adept at this type of argument.

Our patience with the sophists is exhausted long before the end of the dialogue, and we may well wonder why Plato chose to illustrate and parody this type of argument so extensively. The fact that he does so may be taken to suggest not only that arguments of this sort were, or had been, quite common among certain sophists, but also that at one stage they presented serious difficulties. We should note, however, that while the *Euthydemus* parodies various types of sophistic arguments, it contains no general logical analysis of them. Further, Socrates is represented as rejecting the sophists' arguments more because they are *petty*, than because they are *fallacious*. In the speech which he makes at 277d ff. the chief criticism which is levelled at the sophists is that they spend all their time in debating the most trivial subjects and completely neglect the most serious moral problems. But although the stand-point from which the sophists are criticised in this dialogue is primarily a moral one, several important logical points are made incidentally in the course of the argument. We have already noted that at 277d 1 ff., for example, Socrates expressly points out the ambiguity of the term 'learn' in the sophists' first dilemma. But then the argument at 293b 7 ff. also brings out an important logical lesson. There when Socrates is asked whether he knows anything, he qualifies his answer: 'Certainly, many things, though unimportant ones', and he goes on to remark that there are many things that he does not know. But then Euthydemus tries to suggest that Socrates has admitted that he is both 'knowing' and 'not-knowing', that he both 'is' and 'is not' the same man κατὰ ταὐτὰ ἅμα, 'in regard to the same things and at the same time'. In fact this has certainly *not* been shown by the sophists or admitted by Socrates, that it is in the *same* respect that he is 'knowing' and 'not-knowing' at the same time. But it is made abundantly clear to the *reader* that escape from the sophists' dilemmas depends on *qualifying* the terms that are presented as *simple alternatives*. We saw before (pp. 107 f.) that in attempting to demolish the hypothesis of 'the many' Zeno may have held that the contraries 'limited' and 'unlimited', for example, are necessarily incompatible in whatever relation or respect they may be predicated of a particular subject ('the many'). The sophistic dilemmas concerning the one and the many, and being and not-being, provide further evidence that it was quite often implicitly assumed that to predicate any pair of opposites of the same subject in *any* sense, relation or respect, involves a self-contradiction, and in the *Euthydemus* itself a similar presumption is frequently exploited by Euthydemus and Dionysodorus. The passage at *Euthd*. 293 b 7 ff. is important, then, since it may be the first extant text in which it is implicitly recognised that the factors of *respect* and *time* must be taken into consideration in deciding whether two assertions in which contrary attributes are predicated of a single subject contradict one another.

The *Euthydemus* parodies and criticises certain common types of argument based on opposites, and in the course of the discussion raises a point of great importance for the understanding of the nature of contradiction. But elsewhere, in the *Phaedo, Republic* and *Sophist*,[1] Plato explicitly discusses and clarifies the rules or conditions under which opposites may or may not be said to belong to the same subject, and it is

---

[1] The use which Plato makes of the notion of 'self-contradiction' (αὐτὸς αὑτῷ ἐναντία λέγειν) in the early and middle dialogues has been fully discussed by Robinson, 2, pp. 26–32, and there is no need to repeat his analysis here except to note the important point that this phrase is often used loosely when a person has been refuted by a direct appeal to evidence, and not by any demonstration that his statements are incompatible. *Grg*. 482 bc is a particularly striking passage where Socrates warns Callicles of the effects of 'contradiction' on a person's life: 'it is better that my lyre, or that the chorus I have trained, should be out of tune

these passages which contain his most important contributions to the analysis of different modes of opposition. First in the *Phaedo* (102 d f.) there is a passage which refers to the incompatibility of contraries. Socrates says that 'greatness itself' will never admit 'the small',[1] and states it as a general rule for contraries that 'none of the contraries allows itself, while still being what it is, to become and be its contrary at the same time, but either it departs or it perishes...' (e 7 ff.). It may be remarked that Plato is interested here not so much in the problem of the logical relationships between terms, as in the problem of the relationships between real entities. This passage in the *Phaedo* comes, in fact, as a preliminary to one of the arguments for the immortality of the soul: at 105 c ff. it is argued that life is the concomitant of soul, and that soul cannot therefore receive the contrary of life, namely death.

The *Phaedo* passage simply establishes that contraries exclude one another. In the *Republic* the discussion of the problem of the relationships between opposites is carried much further. At 436 b 8 ff. Socrates puts it that 'it is clear that the same thing will never submit to doing or suffering opposite things, in the same respect, at least, and in the same relation and at the same time'. Two possible objections are raised and countered. First, with regard to a man who stands still but moves his hands and head, it is not correct to say that 'the same man is both at rest and in motion at the same time': rather we should say that 'part of him is at rest and part in motion' (c 9 ff.). Secondly, the case of spinning tops is dealt

and discordant (διαφωνεῖν) or that the majority of men should not agree with me but contradict me, than that I, as one person, should be out of tune with myself and contradict myself (ἕνα ὄντα ἐμὲ ἐμαυτῷ ἀσύμφωνον εἶναι καὶ ἐναντία λέγειν)'. Here 'contradicting oneself' is treated not so much from the point of view of the relationship between propositions asserted, as from the point of view of certain psychological disorders that are set up in the soul.

[1] 'It seems to me not only that Greatness itself will never submit to being at once great and small, but also that the greatness which is present in us (τὸ ἐν ἡμῖν μέγεθος) will never admit the small nor allow itself to be overcome, but one of two things will happen: either it will retreat and depart at the approach of its contrary, the small, or when the small has approached it, the great will perish' (102d 6 ff.).

with (d 4 ff.). We should say that they are at rest in respect of
a straight line (for they do not incline to either side) but in
circular motion in respect of the circumference. Socrates
concludes (e 8 ff.) by reiterating that nothing shall persuade
him that 'the same thing would ever suffer or be or do opposite things at the same time, in the same respect and in the
same relation'. As in the *Phaedo* passage (102 d f.), so too here
the emphasis is on the question of the relationships between
things, not on the logical relationships between terms or propositions. Socrates does refer to what it is or is not correct to
say, in dealing with the objections raised at *R.* 436cd,[1] but
what he is primarily concerned with here is the question of
what a single thing may do, or be, or suffer. We should note
that this passage, which contains what is often pointed to as
the first formulation of the Law of Contradiction, comes at
the beginning of a discussion of the nature of the soul. Plato
goes on to infer that because we discover by experience that
the soul does and suffers 'opposite things', it must contain
separate 'parts', that is the rational, spirited and appetitive
faculties. Nevertheless this passage does, of course, make an
important logical point, in that it expresses as a rule what was
already partly implied in the *Euthydemus*, namely that the
factors of *time*, *respect* and *relation* must be taken into account
in deciding whether two statements in which opposites are
predicated of the same subject are incompatible. It brings to
light the simple but important point, quite often ignored in
earlier Greek writers, that to predicate opposites of the same
subject does not necessarily involve a self-contradiction.

Then a second passage in the *Republic* (453 b ff.) throws
further light on the use of opposites, and in particular of the
pair 'same'/'different', in argument. Socrates imagines a
possible objection which might be raised to his policy of
giving women the same education as men: they have agreed
that different natures (i.e. men with different skills) should
have different pursuits, and further that the natures of men

---

[1] E.g. λέγοι 436c 9, λέγειν d 1, φαῖμεν e 1.

and women are different, and yet now they are maintaining that these different natures should have the same pursuits (453 e). This leads Socrates to consider the 'eristic art'. 'Many seem to fall into this, even against their will...owing to their inability to make distinctions between kinds.... They seem to pursue merely verbal oppositions between terms, practising controversy, not dialectic, on one another' (454 a 4 ff.).[1] So in the present discussion they must consider the kind of 'same' or 'different' natures which are in question. He gives an extreme example of the type of argument which might be used (eristically) against them: someone might ask whether the natures of bald and long-haired men are the same, or whether they are not rather quite opposite, and then declare that if the bald are cobblers, then the long-haired should not be (c 1 ff.). He goes on to point out that they did not use the terms 'same' and 'different' in any sense (πάντως), but had in mind only that kind of difference and similarity which is relevant to the pursuits themselves; thus a man and a woman physician both have the same nature, while a physician and a carpenter have different natures (c 7 ff.). One may observe that the description of the controversialists who pursue purely verbal oppositions admirably fits the sort of sophist typified by Euthydemus and Dionysodorus, and the particular eristic argument given at 454c 1 ff., based on the alternative question 'are the natures of bald and long-haired men the same, or opposite?', is just like many such arguments which we have considered in this chapter, in which a choice is put between a pair of vague or equivocal opposite alternatives.

Finally in the *Sophist* Plato clarifies further many of the confusions which had arisen in connection with being and not-being and other pairs of opposites. The thesis that some Forms combine, but some do not, is established at 251 d ff. by means of an argument which is itself worth noticing briefly,

---

[1] κατ' αὐτὸ τὸ ὄνομα διώκειν τοῦ λεχθέντος τὴν ἐναντίωσιν, ἔριδι, οὐ διαλέκτῳ πρὸς ἀλλήλους χρώμενοι.

as it involves putting a choice between certain alternatives. But the alternatives between which the Eleatic Stranger says they must choose are not two (as was so often the case in the arguments of the Eleatics, for example) but three in number, and these are, in effect, exhaustive alternatives: *either* no Forms combine with other Forms, *or* all Forms combine with all other Forms, *or thirdly* some Forms combine but some do not. The first two alternatives are eliminated, and the Eleatic Stranger concludes that the third proposition must, then, be true (252e 1 ff.). He then selects five 'very important kinds'[1] for special study, τὸ ὄν, στάσις, κίνησις, τὸ ταὐτόν, τὸ θάτερον, that is to say Being, Rest, Motion (or rather, more generally, Change), Sameness (Identity) and Difference (Otherness),[2] and at 254b 7 ff. he considers the relations between these. A long section 255e–258c is mainly devoted to showing how 'what is' (in *some* sense) may be said 'not to be' (in *some other* sense), and again how 'what is not' (in *some* sense) may be said 'to be' (again in *some other* sense). At 255e 11 he begins by establishing a series of pairs of assertions:[3] (1*a*) Change is not Rest (255e 14), but again (1*b*) Change is (it shares in Being, 256a 1). (2*a*) Change is not the Same (it is different from Sameness, 256a 3 ff.), but again (2*b*) Change is the same (as itself: in this sense all things share in Sameness, a 7 f.). (3*a*) Change is different (from Difference, 256c 5 f.), but again (3*b*) Change is not Different (it is not Difference, c 8 f.). (4*a*) Change is not Being (256d 5 f.), but again (4*b*) Change is (it shares in Being, d 9, cf. (1*b*) above) and so on. At 256a 10 ff. the Eleatic Stranger expounds the second pair of assertions more fully: 'We must agree, then, that Change is both the same and not the Same, and not feel qualms about this. For when we said that Change is the same and is not the

---

[1] It should be noted that the view that the 'very important kinds' refer to Forms is not accepted, for example, by Peck (*4* and *5*), but this controversy does not materially affect the present issue.

[2] ταὐτόν means both Sameness and the same, θάτερον both Difference and the different.

[3] Cf. the analysis given by Cornford, *5*, pp. 285 ff.

Same, our meaning altered: when "the same", we called it this by virtue of its sharing in the Same with reference to itself; and when "not the Same", because of its participating, also, in Difference, on account of which, being separated from the Same, it becomes not the Same, but different; so that it is correct to say, again, that Change is not the Same.' And at 256c 8 f. and d 8 f. he states further apparent contradictions: 'so according to our present argument it (Change) is not Different, in a sense, and different', and 'clearly, then, Change really is something that is not (οὐκ ὄν) and something that is (ὄν)'. After a passage in which τὸ μὴ ὄν is dealt with more fully, the Stranger points out at 258cd how their own view differs from that of Parmenides. Parmenides asserted (Fr. 7) that 'never shall this be proved, that things that are not, are', 'but we?', the Stranger goes on, 'have not only shown that things that are not, are, but have also declared the real nature of what is not (τὸ εἶδος ὃ τυγχάνει ὄν τοῦ μὴ ὄντος)'. He sums up his conclusions at 259ab, saying that Difference, Being and all the other kinds, taken severally or all together, both *are* in many respects, and *are not* in many respects (πολλαχῇ μὲν ἔστι, πολλαχῇ δ' οὐκ ἔστιν). And he ends by suggesting (b 8 ff.) that 'if anyone doubts these contradictions, let him consider the question and produce some better account than the one we have given': what is worthwhile, though at the same time difficult, he goes on, is to follow the sense in which what is different is said to be the same, or what is the same is said to be different: 'to declare in some unspecified sense (ἀμῇ γέ πῃ) that the same is different, and that the different is the same, and that the great is small, and that the like is unlike, and to be pleased with always presenting such opposites in argument, this is no genuine refutation...' (259cd).

Few would deny that the *Sophist* marks a turning point in the history of the early development of logic, but it is worth noting, in particular, how far this dialogue goes towards elucidating the problems associated with the use of opposites in argument. The Eleatics had insisted that a choice must be made between 'it is' and 'it is not', although neither the sense of the verb 'to be', nor the subject referred to, was specified. And there was a similar tendency to assume that one and many, great and small, limited and unlimited, and other pairs of opposites are necessarily incompatible and exhaustive alternatives in whatever sense or respect the terms are used. Similar assumptions underlie some of the arguments which Gorgias put forward to establish the negative thesis that nothing exists, and in Plato himself, especially but not exclusively in the *Euthydemus*, we find many examples of arguments which involve putting a choice between opposite alternatives. But then in the *Republic*, 436 b ff., Plato stressed the importance of specifying the factors of respect, relation and time with regard to apparent contradictions, and at 453 b ff. he pointed out how one should guard against eristic arguments based on an equivocal use of the terms 'same' and 'different'. In the *Sophist*, he mentions the dilemma of the one and the many (251 a ff.) only to dismiss the problem in its simplest form as trivial, and he also clarifies the dilemma of false statement by indicating the ambiguity of the Greek phrase λέγειν τὰ μὴ ὄντα, 'speaking what is not' (259 d ff., especially 263 b–d). But even more important, at 254 b ff. he takes the five kinds Being, Rest, Change, Sameness and Difference, and considers the relations between them with particular reference to Parmenides' thesis concerning 'what is' and 'what is not'. His analysis of the relations between the five kinds makes it plain, first of all, that a whole series of apparently contradictory statements, so far from being contradictory, as an Eleatic might well have thought, are consistent and true, secondly that the appearance of contradiction arises, in these cases, from the use of 'is', 'same', 'different' and so on in unspecified senses, and thirdly that while it is easy, but trivial, to discover verbal oppositions involving these terms, the worthwhile, but difficult, inquiry is to discover the true relations between these kinds, that is to determine the different senses in which opposites may be predicated of the same subject without self-contradiction.

Plato certainly removed the major difficulties presented by the dilemmas of being and not-being, the one and the many, and false statement as 'saying what is not', by pointing out that the terms involved are equivocal, and by giving examples where both members of a pair of opposites may be truly predicated of the same subject. But what Plato achieved in the *Sophist* is by no means, of course, a complete logical theory of opposites and opposite statements. The limitations of his account of the relations between the five very important kinds should not be glossed over. Differing opinions have been expressed by various scholars on the question of whether, or how far, Plato distinguished the existential, predicative and identitative uses of the verb 'to be'.[1] But nowhere in the *Sophist* or anywhere else in Plato is there a full explicit analysis of the distinctions between these uses. In the four pairs of statements at 255e 11 ff., for example, which we considered above (p. 142), it is clear that the verb 'to be' is used in two different senses in each pair: but it is also evident that it is not always the *same* two senses of the verb 'to be' that are thus implicitly distinguished on each occasion. Thus in (1*a*) (Change is not Rest) 'is' is identitative, in (1*b*) (Change is) existential; but while in (2*a*) (Change is not the Same) 'is' is again the identity-sign, in (2*b*) (Change is the same, as itself) it is predicative. While the identitative use is isolated and named as a Form (Sameness), the distinction between the predicative and existential uses of ἐστι is not so clearly marked out, and on at least one occasion the two uses appear to be assimilated to each other. At 256e 2 ff. the Stranger says that they would be right to speak of all other things, apart from Being, as things that 'are not' (each of them is different from Being) and again, because they share in Being, as things that 'have being and are' (εἶναί τε καὶ ὄντα), and

---

[1] Besides Cornford, 5, pp. 296 f., see especially Ackrill, pp. 1 ff., and Runciman, 2, pp. 83 ff.

this last sentence is generally thought to refer unequivocally to the existential use of εἶναι. Yet when this statement is agreed to, the Stranger goes on immediately: 'so in the case of each of the Forms, there is much that it is, and an infinite number of things that it is not' (πολὺ μέν ἐστι τὸ ὄν, ἄπειρον δὲ πλήθει τὸ μὴ ὄν, 256e 5 f., more literally: there is an abundance of being and an infinite plurality of not-being) and *here* 'being' should clearly be taken not in an existential, but in a *predicative* sense.[1] In his account of the relations between the five chosen kinds in the *Sophist*, Plato goes as far as is necessary in order to show that various pairs of apparently contradictory statements are not contradictory, but consistent and true, and yet so far from there being an exhaustive analysis, in this dialogue, of the various senses of the verb 'to be', there are signs that certain confusions may remain in Plato's own usage.

In conclusion, we should consider how far Plato may be said to have distinguished explicitly between different kinds of opposites as such. I have already noted that in several passages a distinction is drawn between not having an attribute and having the contrary attribute. Thus at *Smp.* 201e ff. when Diotima remarks that Eros is neither beautiful nor good, Socrates asks, 'What do you mean, Diotima? Is Eros then ugly and evil?' Asked by Diotima whether he believes that whatever is not beautiful is necessarily ugly, he first answers 'certainly' (202a 1), but then Diotima points out to him that between wisdom and folly, for instance, there is an intermediate (true opinion) so that it does not follow that what is not wise is necessarily foolish. In this passage Plato evidently takes considerable trouble to draw a simple but important logical distinction (one may compare the dubious conversion of 'not just' to 'unjust' which Socrates is allowed

---

[1] See Runciman, 2, pp. 84 f., who concludes that throughout the discussion at 256d 12–e 6 'there is an assimilation to each other of the existential and copulative senses' of the verb 'to be'. Runciman goes on to point out, however (p. 86), that Plato 'more accurately distinguishes the negative existential sense from those of negative identity and negative predication'.

to make at *Prt.* 331 ab). And yet Diotima's lesson is confined
to pointing out to Socrates that there are certain intermediates between wisdom and folly, mortals and immortals
and so on, in the *strict* sense of intermediates, namely 'true
opinion' and 'τὸ δαιμόνιον': a further point which is not
clearly brought out (presumably because what they are
chiefly concerned with here is how to describe Eros) is that
'neither wise nor foolish' may be predicated of many other
things, too, namely of everything outside the class of rational
animals. Then in the *Republic* 491 d 4 f. a similar distinction is
made when Socrates says that 'evil is more opposed (ἐναν-
τιώτερον) to the good than to the not-good'. Once again
Plato shows his awareness of the distinction between not
having a quality and having the contrary quality, though the
terminology in which he expresses this idea is quite loose; evil
is not *contrary* to 'not-good' at all, for the not-good includes,
though it is not, of course, coextensive with, evil. It is, however, in the *Sophist* that this distinction is first drawn explicitly
in general terms. At 257 b 3 f. the Stranger says 'when we
use the expression "what is not", we do not refer to the
contrary of what is, but simply to something different from it'.
'So then', he goes on at b 9 ff., 'when it is said that a denial
(ἀπόφασις) signifies a contrary (ἐναντίον), we shall not agree,
but agree to this alone, that the prefix "not" signifies something different from the words that follow, or rather something different from the things designated by the words
spoken after the negative.' I remarked before that no
explicit general distinctions are drawn between different types
of opposites in our extant pre-Platonic texts: rather certain
important distinctions, like that between types of opposites
that do, and those that do not, exclude a middle term, tend
to be ignored. Part of the importance of this passage in the
Sophist lies, then, in this, that it marks a first step towards the
classification of different types of opposites *qua* opposites. At
the same time it is apparent that the scattered passages we
have considered from Plato do not take that classification

very far. He nowhere draws an explicit distinction between different kinds of contraries (those that allow intermediates in the strict sense, and those that do not), nor did he undertake a systematic exposition of different types of opposite statements. Plato was certainly responsible for resolving many of the dilemmas which had troubled earlier thinkers, for clarifying the nature of contradiction, and for drawing an important logical distinction between the negation of a term and the assertion of its contrary: but he nowhere gave, or perhaps we should say he nowhere chose to give, a detailed analysis of the various modes of opposites and opposite statements.

THE METHOD OF DIVISION: PLATO, THE ACADEMY AND ARISTOTLE

In many of the arguments of the Eleatics we find that such pairs of terms as 'what is' and 'what is not', one and many, are treated as incompatible and exhaustive alternatives in whatever sense or respect the terms are applied. While Plato removed many of the difficulties which the use of these terms involved, we saw that in various passages not only in the Socratic dialogues, but also in such works as the *Phaedo* and *Timaeus*,[1] one of the speakers forces an issue by presenting a choice between a pair of opposite but not, strictly speaking, exhaustive alternatives. The putting of a choice between a pair of opposites is also a recurrent feature of a method of argument which figures largely in several late Platonic dialogues, and which was taken up and extended by other philosophers in the Academy, namely the method of Division.

---

[1] Besides the passages discussed above (*Phd.* 78 d 1 ff.; *Ti.* 51 b 7 ff.) there are others in the late dialogues in which the putting of a choice between opposite or extreme alternatives is used as a persuasive device, e.g. *Sph.* 247 b 1 ff.; *Phlb.* 29 c 5 ff., e 5 ff., 44 d 8 ff. On the other hand it is noticeable that on a number of important occasions in the later dialogues a choice is put between three, not just two, alternatives ('*A*' or '*B*' or 'some *A* and some *B*'). One instance has already been noted (*Sph.* 251 d ff., pp. 141 f.), cf. also *Sph.* 261 d 5 f.; *Phlb.* 36 c 6 f.; *Lg.* 893 b 6 ff.; and at *Phlb.* 46 a 11 a choice is put between a pair of alternatives, but in the reply these are *combined*.

That *some* philosophers attempted to use this method as a method of *demonstration* appears from the evidence in Aristotle, who also shows that the validity of this method of argument depends, above all, on the type of opposites presented as alternatives. But we should first consider how the method was employed by Plato himself. What form does Division take in Plato, and what was claimed for the method?

The question of how we should interpret the use of division in the *Sophist* and *Politicus* is much disputed.[1] Certain facts are, however, clear. (1) On a great majority of occasions the form that division takes *in practice* is a dichotomy: a genus is divided into two lower genera or species, very often a pair of contraries, and this process is then repeated.[2] (2) When the correct method of dividing is described, it is stressed that divisions should be made 'according to the natural articulations' of the Forms (*Phdr.* 265 e 1 ff.) and again Plato seems to have dichotomous divisions most often in mind.[3] In the *Politicus*, especially, the Eleatic Stranger says that they should divide 'down the middle', which is the safer, though the longer, course (262 b 6, 265 a 4). Examples of correct divisions are given (of human beings, into men and women, and of number, into odd and even), and these are contrasted with incorrect divisions which do not employ strict contraries (of humans, into Greeks and Barbarians, and of number, into the number ten thousand and other numbers). The right method is to divide 'according to the Forms and in two' (κατ' εἴδη καὶ δίχα, *Plt.* 262 e 3 f.). (3) On the other hand, dichotomous division is certainly not the only type of division which is

---

[1] The most important of the many modern discussions of this problem are Stenzel, *3*, pp. 89 ff.; Cornford, *5*, pp. 171 ff.; Cherniss, *2*, pp. 27 ff.; and Skemp, *2*, pp. 67 ff.

[2] There are many references to dividing *into two* in the *Sophist*, in the illustrative division of the angler (219 a 8, d 4, 9, e 5, 220 a 7, etc.), in the preliminary divisions of the sophist (225 a 4, b 3, 226 c 10, e 1, 227 c 8, d 1, etc.) and perhaps most commonly of all in the final division of the sophist (264 d 10, 265 a 11, b 4, e 5, 8, 266 a 5, 11, c 5, d 2, 5, e 4, 267 a 1, b 4, 268 a 9, b 1). Equally in the *Politicus* dichotomous division is *in practice* the rule.

[3] This is suggested, for example, by the image of the body divided into a right and a left side in the *Phaedrus*, 265 e 4 ff.

used,[1] and at *Plt.* 287c Plato explicitly recognises the need to use a more complex form of division (even though this passage suggests that dichotomy is still considered the *ideal* form of division).[2]

The descriptions of the correct method of division are clear as far as they go, and there are plenty of examples from which to judge how the method was applied in practice. What is not generally agreed, however, is how seriously some of the divisions in the *Sophist* and *Politicus* are intended to be taken. Attention has been drawn to the humorous or satirical passages in the preliminary divisions of the 'sophist' and the 'statesman'. Skemp (*2*, p. 67) interprets these as 'fun made of humanity as such....But it is in particular a gentle satire on the over-enthusiastic use of the method of Division by some of the members of the Academy itself.' He points to the failure of the first attempts to define the 'sophist' and the 'statesman' and remarks (*2*, p. 68) that 'Division, as such, is evidently not infallible. Our real interest in the *Politicus* is in the criticism of Division which is expressed in it.' Stenzel, on the other hand, gave a very different assessment of the method of division, suggesting (*3*, p. 92) that 'the "pedantry" of the entire method, which has aroused so much antipathy to it, is simply a consequence of the resolution not to omit, for the sake of brevity, any single step in Division...but to advance by means of exclusive contraries which will conduct us by necessary stages to the concept which we want'. How far is it possible to decide between these two quite contrasting lines of interpretation, and to determine, in particular, how far Plato intended, in the *Politicus*, to satirise an over-enthusiastic use of division?

In both the *Sophist* (227a f.) and the *Politicus* (265b–266d) the Stranger is made to draw attention to the fact that in

---

[1] See especially *Plt.* 287c ff., and cf. *Phdr.* 265b.

[2] The Stranger says 'let us divide them according to the joints, like a sacrificial victim, *since we are unable to divide in two* (ἐπειδὴ δίχα ἀδυνατοῦμεν)' (*Plt.* 287c 3 f.), and he goes on to add that they should always divide into the fewest divisions possible.

carrying out their divisions they have arrived at results which seem quite comic.[1] Yet it should be noted that on *both* occasions he goes on to warn his audience that in their search for definitions they should not be misled by irrelevant considerations of dignity, such as the relative importance or unimportance of the classes to which they refer.[2] The fact that the particular examples of divisions that have just been given are comic or even absurd does not detract from, and might even be thought to increase, the force of the general methodological point which the Stranger is made to express. Plato may wish to poke fun at military strategists by classing their art alongside the catching of lice, but the repeated general warning, that they should not be deterred by irrelevant questions of dignity in their search for definitions, should surely be taken seriously. One might compare,[3] for example, the digression at *Plt.* 283b–287a, where again an important methodological point is at issue, namely that it is irrelevant whether their exposition is long or short, so long as it leaves the hearer better able to find the Forms.[4] In the *Politicus*, at least, the preliminary unsuccessful attempts to define the statesman are made the occasion for the Stranger to bring out certain important lessons in the use of the method. And in both dialogues we are told that the illustrative definitions of 'angling' and 'weaving' are undertaken in order to give practice in the method which they must use in considering more important objects. Thus at *Sph.* 218cd the Stranger says

---

[1] At *Sph.* 227b military strategy and the catching of lice are equal subdivisions of hunting, and at *Plt.* 265b f. the king is found to be the 'shepherd of the hornless herd'.

[2] At *Plt.* 266d 4 ff. the Stranger refers to the point which had been made in the 'inquiry concerning the sophist', that they should pay no attention to whether a subject is more or less dignified, nor account the petty any less worthy of consideration than the great (cf. *Sph.* 227ab).

[3] Another passage we might, perhaps, compare is *Prm.* 130e, where when Socrates has denied the existence of Forms of hair, mud etc., on the grounds that this would be ridiculous, Parmenides remarks that this is because he is still young and when philosophy has 'laid hold on him' he will not despise such things.

[4] See especially *Plt.* 286e 1 ff. and contrast Socrates' rejection of μακρολογία at *Prt.* 335a–c and at *Grg.* 449bc.

that they must first practise the method which they will use on the sophist on something easier, and at *Plt.* 285 d f. he justifies the illustrative definition of weaving on the grounds that it provides the dialectician with the training which he needs to be able to apprehend the highest realities.[1] One may agree with Cornford and Skemp that the preliminary divisions of the sophist and statesman are light-hearted in tone, and the way in which the younger Socrates more than once concludes, prematurely, that the definition of the states-man has been completed[2] serves as an important warning that it needs a dialectician to judge the results of a division. On the other hand, Plato is evidently serious when he recom-mends the method as providing training in dialectic. More-over, although (unlike the younger Socrates) the Stranger never explicitly claims that they have *demonstrated* a Form by a division, he does suggest that the final division in the *Sophist* will *reveal* the true nature of the sophist himself.[3] And it may be argued that the passages in the *Politicus* which expressly distinguish between correct and incorrect divisions (*Plt.* 262 a–e) are themselves important evidence that Plato continued to have faith in the method of division as a means of revealing the interrelations between the Forms.

As described and practised by Plato in the *Sophist* and *Politicus* the method of division is still quite flexible: the form the division takes is usually, though not always, a dichotomy, and it is evidently only in the hands of a dialectician that the

---

[1] The Stranger says that 'no man of sense would wish to track down the definition of "weaving", at least, for its own sake' (*Plt.* 285 d 8 f.). He then goes on to point out that while for many things there are sensible re-semblances which may easily be indicated when anyone asks for an account of them, yet 'for the greatest and most honourable things' there are no such sensible resemblances. 'Therefore we must practise in order to acquire the ability to give and receive a rational account about each subject. For the incorporeal realities, the finest and greatest realities, are clearly displayed only by a rational account and by no other means, and *it is these realities that are the aim of all our present discussions.* But in every case it is easier to practise on lesser objects than on greater ones' (286 a 4 ff.).

[2] See *Plt.* 265 d, 267 cd and 277 a 1 f.

[3] See ἐπιδείξωμεν, *Sph.* 265 a 1, and cf. *Plt.* 292 ac, where the Stranger takes the results of their earlier divisions of the statesman as established.

method will yield reliable results, for mistakes may be made both in the apprehension of the genus under which a form comes and in the proposal of particular divisions. But we must now consider the evidence which suggests that division, and in particular dichotomous division, was developed in the Academy into a dogmatic method of definition and classification. Here we must refer especially to the evidence in Aristotle. Aristotle discusses the method of 'division' (διαίρεσις) or 'dichotomy' (διχοτομία) at length in a number of passages in the *Organon*, the *Metaphysics* and the biological treatises, but the first problem that arises is to decide whose use of division Aristotle had in mind. At *PA* 642 b 12 he mentions certain 'published Divisions' (cf. 643 a 36), and this has been variously interpreted as referring to a work of Speusippus,[1] or to the *Sophist* and *Politicus* themselves.[2] Elsewhere Aristotle refers to certain 'Divisions' which he specifically attributes to Plato (*GC* 330 b 16),[3] and a book of Divisions is referred to in the *Thirteenth Letter* (360 b 8), whose author, if not Plato himself, was at least someone who appears to be well-informed on the activities of the Academy. It may be, then, that a number of collections of Divisions circulated in the Academy, and the 'published Divisions' of *PA* 642 b 12 may refer to any one of these. Yet an analysis of the divisions cited shows that whoever their author may have been, they were much influenced by the divisions which are actually proposed in Plato's *Sophist* and *Politicus*. It has often, of course, been noticed that prototypes of *some* of the divisions to which Aristotle objects in *PA* A 2–3 can be found in those dialogues. But it has not, perhaps, been sufficiently remarked that this is true of *almost all* the divisions which he criticises both in *PA* and elsewhere, in the *Organon* and *Metaphysics*.

---

[1] See Cherniss, 2, pp. 54 ff., and Skemp, 2, pp. 70 ff. The evidence for Speusippus' work is collected by Stenzel in his PW article, 2, cols. 1638 ff.

[2] See Ogle, note to *PA* 642 b 5.

[3] Various attempts have been made to relate this reference to some passage in the extant dialogues, but such connections are quite uncertain: see, for example, Joachim, 2, note *ad loc.*, who takes it as referring to *Ti.* 35 a ff.

The typical division which he takes when criticising the method in *Metaph*. Z 12 and *APo*. B 5 is the definition of man as a 'living creature, mortal, footed, biped, wingless' (*APo*. 92 a 1, cf. *Metaph*. 1037 b 33, 1038 a 21 f.). But *all* the divisions which are used in this definition may be compared with, and perhaps may eventually derive from, passages in the *Sophist* and *Politicus*. Thus the divisions of 'footed' into 'biped' and 'quadruped', and of 'biped' in turn into 'wingless' and 'winged', are proposed by the Eleatic Stranger when he follows what he calls the 'short way' of arriving at the definition of the statesman (*Plt*. 266 e 4 ff.).[1] Moreover, in *PA* A 2–3 the particular divisions which Aristotle implies were used in the 'published Divisions' are those into 'water-animals' and 'land-animals', into 'walkers' and 'fliers' and into 'tame' and 'wild', and each of these, too, can be paralleled in Plato.[2] Indeed the only dichotomy which Aristotle expressly criticises in *PA* for which no Platonic prototype can be found is that into 'black' and 'white'.[3] This does not necessarily mean, of course, that Aristotle is thinking of the corresponding passage or passages in the *Sophist* and *Politicus* when he criticises these divisions. On the contrary, as Cherniss and others have shown, the context in which the divisions occur in Plato is sometimes quite different from the context in which they are criticised by Aristotle.[4] But what

---

[1] Cf. also the division into 'living' and 'lifeless' which occurs in various contexts in Plato (*Sph*. 219 e 7 ff.; *Plt*. 261 b 7 f., 292 b 12 f.), and which is used by Aristotle as an example when he criticises division at *APo*. 91 b 18.

[2] 'Tame' and 'wild' occur both at *Sph*. 222 b 5 (as subdivisions of land-animals) and at *Plt*. 264 a 1 f. (as divisions of animals as a whole: it is to be noted that this passage comes just after the Stranger has given a number of examples which aim to show how to divide *correctly*, 262 a–e). 'Walkers' and 'fliers' (πορευτικά, πτηνά at Arist. *PA* 643 b 1) correspond roughly to πτηνόν and πεζόν used at *Plt*. 264 e 6 (and 'winged' and 'wingless' mentioned, for example, at *PA* 643 b 2 seem to be used at *Plt*. 266 e 5 ff., cf. also 276 a 4). Finally, a division into 'land-' and 'water-animals' occurs both at *Sph*. 220 a 7 ff. (cf. 221 e 2 f.) and at *Plt*. 264 d 1 ff. (ἔνυδρον, ξηροβατικόν).

[3] *PA* 643 b 21, cf. 643 a 20 f. Outside *PA*, the only division which Aristotle criticises which is quite unrelated to any Platonic archetype seems to be 'commensurate' and 'incommensurate', *APr*. 46 b 30.

[4] See especially Cherniss, 2, pp. 54 f.

the close correspondences between the divisions to which Aristotle objects and those which may be found in the later dialogues of Plato do show, is that even the preliminary divisions in the *Sophist* and *Politicus* had a profound influence in the Academy. Divisions which had been suggested in a variety of different connections in Plato, and which were certainly not originally intended to form the basis of a complete classification of biological species,[1] were later used for just such a purpose. Indeed not only do other members of the Academy seem to have adopted a system of biological classification based on dichotomous divisions, but it may be that at one stage Aristotle himself saw no serious objection to defining the species and genera of animals by contrary differentiae in a similar manner.[2]

Aristotle's criticisms of division indicate what some of its exponents hoped to achieve by this method, and reveal why, in particular, division so often took the form of dichotomy. At several points he reports or implies that division was used as a *method of proof*. Thus at *APr.* 46a 35 ff. he says that those who used the method 'tried to convince people that it was possible to give a demonstration (ἀπόδειξις) of substance and essence'. This comment occurs in a chapter on division (*APr.* A 31) which follows close after Aristotle's detailed exposition of the syllogism. Division is criticised as a 'small part' of the method of the syllogism, and 'as it were, a weak syllogism' (*APr.* 46a 31 ff.), and it is clear that Aristotle considered division as, in some sense, a rival to his own method of the

---

[1] Thus we may contrast *Sph.* 220ab, where animals are divided into 'walking' and 'swimming' and the latter group then subdivided into 'winged' and 'water-animals' in a division which aims to define angling as a species of 'hunting', with the *fourfold* classification of living beings in *Ti.* 39e–40a into 'gods', winged creatures, water-animals and land-animals, and with the more detailed list at *Ti.* 91d f., where the three main groups of animals, other than human beings, are birds, 'wild animals that go on land' (four-footed, many-footed and footless) and 'water-animals' (fish, shell-fish, etc.). Cf. also *Laws* 823b, which implies a *trichotomy* of animals into 'water-animals', 'winged animals' and 'those that go on land'.

[2] I have assembled the evidence for Aristotle in an article in *Phronesis*, VI (1961), pp. 59 ff., especially 61–4, 70–1.

syllogism.[1] He points out, however, that division assumes what it ought to prove, namely the answer to the alternative question put by the person making the division (e.g. 46 a 33 f., b 11, cf. also *APo.* 91 b 14 ff.), and that what division does in fact establish is not the essence of the thing to be defined, so much as a disjunctive proposition of the type 'man must be *either* mortal *or* immortal' or 'man must be *either* footed *or* footless' (46 b 10 f., 17 ff.). Yet if in some chapters of the *Analytics* he is severely critical of division as a method of proof, in others he concedes that the method is useful for the purposes of arriving at a definition, and in this context he makes specific recommendations concerning the type of divisions to be used. First at *APo.* 91 b 28 ff. he suggests that some of the objections to division may be removed if certain conditions are fulfilled, namely if they take only elements in the essence, in the right order, and see that what is divided is all within the division and that nothing is omitted. Division, he repeats, still does not demonstrate its conclusion, although 'it may give knowledge in another way' (b 33 f.). And then at *APo.* 96 b 25 ff. division is positively recommended for the purposes of defining, first in order to ensure that the predicates are taken in the right order (e.g. animal, tame, biped, rather than biped, animal, tame) and second in order to avoid omitting any element of the essence of the thing to be defined. Indeed Aristotle says that to use division is *the only way* to make sure that nothing will be omitted (96 b 35 f., 97 a 4 ff.). But if he advocates the use of this method in defining, he also stipulates the form which the divisions should take. In particular he says that they must ensure that the division exhausts the genus, and that this will be achieved if the division is into

[1] Although Aristotle describes division as a 'small part' of the syllogistic method, this should not be taken to imply that he considered his own method a *development* of the Platonic method of division. The remark should rather be related to his claim in the previous chapter that the syllogistic method is universally applicable (i.e. that other methods of proof may be subsumed under it). On the vexed question of the 'origin' of the syllogism, see Shorey, *1* and *2*, Ross, *3*, Solmsen, *2*, and Mansion, *2*.

opposites which exclude intermediates, ἂν ᾖ ἀντικείμενα ὧν μή ἐστι μεταξύ (97a 19 ff., cf. 35 ff.).[1]

The significance of the recommendation which Aristotle makes in this passage becomes apparent when we consider the assumptions on which the whole method of division seems to be based in both Plato and Aristotle. In the *Sophist* and *Politicus* the Eleatic Stranger presents Theaetetus or the younger Socrates with a series of alternatives. In the first illustrative division of the angler (*Sph.* 219a 4 ff.) these are craftsman/non-craftsman, productive/acquisitive, by exchange/by capture, in the open/stealthily, lifeless things/living creatures and so on. Often the division is put as a question, a choice between a pair of alternatives (as at 219a 5 f.), and one is reminded, I think, of the many other occasions, in Plato and in earlier writers, on which we find an alternative question used as an argumentative technique to force a particular issue. In Plato's divisions, the alternatives which are proposed vary a good deal, some being pairs of contraries, others contradictories, others again not being contraries in the strict sense at all, and sometimes, as we saw, the alternatives are more than two in number. But *on each occasion* it must be assumed that the choice presented is an *exhaustive* one. Sometimes this is clearly brought out, as when, for example, the Stranger remarks that all the members of a genus fall under one or other division (e.g. *Sph.* 219d 1 f. and 221b 2 on the division of 'arts' into productive and acquisitive).[2] Again in the *Politicus* where certain recommendations are made concerning the type of divisions which should be used, the Stranger says that they should divide 'according to the Forms' and '*down the middle*' (262b 6, e 3, 265a 4), and the actual examples of correct divisions which are given are,

---

[1] Cf. also *Metaph.* 1037b 27 ff. where Aristotle again advocates the use of divisions in defining and lays down further conditions concerning the method; e.g. they should divide by the differentia of the differentia (1038a 9 ff.) and they should avoid dividing by accidental qualities (1038a 26 ff.).

[2] This division appears, however, to be modified by the introduction of the 'separative' arts at *Sph.* 226bc.

in fact, divisions which refer to *contraries which exclude an intermediate*, namely odd and even, and male and female (262 de). Plato, however, expresses no *general* rule to the effect that division should use contraries of a particular logical type, but then neither does the Stranger profess to demonstrate, but only to reveal, the nature of the object which they are defining (e.g. *Sph.* 264d–265a). In Aristotle, on the other hand, we hear of exponents of division who made more ambitious claims for it, using it to 'demonstrate' 'the substance and the essence', and Aristotle's comments and recommendations help us to understand how this claim came to be made for the method. At *APr.* 91 b 18 ff. the exponent of the method is imagined proceeding as the Eleatic Stranger often does in the *Sophist* and *Politicus*, that is to say he puts a choice between a pair of opposite alternatives: 'Is man a living creature, or lifeless?' He puts the question and then, as Aristotle says, assumes the answer 'living creature'. It is clear that the divider's claim to have *proved* the definition of man rests on the two assumptions (1) that the choice on each occasion is exhaustive, and (2) that the answer to each question is self-evident. Now Aristotle's main objection to Division is that it assumes what it ought to prove, namely the answer to the question putting a choice between certain alternatives,[1] and he accordingly rejects it as a method of proof. Yet he accepts it, as we saw, as a method which may be used to arrive at a definition, and in this context he specifies the type of opposites which should be used in order to ensure that nothing is omitted from the division. By proposing that they should divide by *opposites which exclude intermediates*, he lays down the condition which ensures that the division will be exhaustive, although it may be noted that this condition is in perfect keeping with the recommendations which Plato himself had made in the *Politicus* (262 a–e).

---

[1] E.g. at *APo.* 92a 1 ff. Aristotle considers the definition of man as 'animal, mortal, footed, biped, wingless' and says that at each step in the division we may ask the question 'why?' But the divider, he goes on, will say, and *will, as he thinks, prove by the division*, that all animals are either mortal or immortal.

While in the *Organon* Aristotle proposes certain rules to ensure the formal validity of Platonic division, the biological treatises show that he soon realised the limitations of this method when applied, in practice, to the classification of animals. It is striking that the great majority of examples which Aristotle considers in the various passages where he discusses the method of division are drawn from the field of zoology. Two of the definitions which appear in *APr.* A 31 have as their conclusion the definition of man as a mortal, footed animal, and at *APo.* B 5 he mentions the complete definition of man as 'animal, mortal, footed, biped, wingless' (92 a 1). Moreover, the examples which he takes when *recommending* the use of division in defining are exclusively zoological. In *APo.* B 13 he gives 'animal, tame, biped' as an instance in which the predicates are taken in the correct order (96 b 31 f.), and he also refers to the division of winged animals into whole-winged and split-winged (b 38 ff.), and in *Metaph.* Z 12 he gives such examples as the division of footed animals into 'cloven-footed' and 'not-cloven-footed' (1038 a 14). It is clear that the method was particularly applied to the problems of zoological classification, and it may even be that Aristotle himself was, at one period, prepared to advocate its use in that field. But when we turn to Aristotle's own biological works, his approach to the problem of the classification of animals is markedly different. At *PA* A 2–3 he once again considers the method of dichotomous division. He repeats several of the points which he had made elsewhere, but now raises important new objections to its use in biology. At *Metaph.* 1038 a 17 f. he had mentioned, incidentally, that the number of infimae species will be the same as the number of differentiae used in the divisions, but this is now used (*PA* 643 a 7 ff.) to show the absurdity of applying the method to the classification of animals, because it can hardly be expected that the number of species will, in fact, be 'four or some other power of two' (a 22 f.). Again the fact that a definition will consist of the genus and the last

differentia, which had been pointed out at *Metaph.* 1038a
19 f., is now used as another objection to the method, Aristotle
now suggesting that each species will require more than one
specific differentia (*PA* 643 b 28–644 a 11). Furthermore, as a
new and quite fundamental criticism of the method, he complains that it splits up the natural groups of animals, such as
birds and fish.[1] In contrast, then, with the passages in *APo.*
B 13 and *Metaph.* Z 12 where he had recommended dichotomous divisions as a useful method of finding definitions, in
PA A 2–3 he totally rejects this method, as applied to zoology
in particular: he ends his discussion by asserting (*PA* 644 b
19 f.) that he has shown how dichotomy is in one respect
impossible, and in another respect futile.[2]

The method of division may be considered the most notable attempt, in the period before Aristotle, to devise a
method of proof. As used by Plato the method is not subject
to strict formal rules and remains quite flexible. But to judge
from some of Aristotle's criticisms, there were exponents of
division who saw it as a method of demonstration, who hoped
that by dividing and subdividing animals, for instance, into
opposite groups, they would arrive by necessary stages at
certain conclusions (the definition of a particular species, or a
complete classification of animals). The method consists, in
most cases, in a technique of putting a choice between a pair
of opposites, and yet at first the question of the logical status
of the opposites which were used as alternatives was not
explicitly considered. The assumptions on which the method
was based were, however, analysed by Aristotle, who pointed
out that to ensure that the division is exhaustive, the opposites
should be of a certain logical type, namely contraries which

[1] *PA* 642 b 10 ff., 643 b 10 ff. Contrast *APo.* 97 a 1 ff., 35 ff., where both the
genus 'animal' and the two groups 'birds' and 'fish' appear to be taken as
possible subjects for dichotomous division.

[2] While the chief objects of Aristotle's attack in *PA* A 2–3 were, no doubt, his
opponents in the Academy, some of the objections which he brings against
division appear to be valid against his own earlier modified acceptance of
that method as a means of finding definitions. See further *Phronesis,* VI
(1961), p. 72.

exclude intermediates. But if the effect of this stipulation was to remove one of the formal objections to the method as it had sometimes been practised, Aristotle also showed that the attempt to apply dichotomy to the problems of zoological classification was misguided, and in the biological works he rejects dichotomy outright in favour of a taxonomy which is a good deal more complex, but which pays closer attention to the natural groups of animals.

ARISTOTLE

Among the more important advances for which Plato was responsible in the field of logic are his clarification of the nature of contradiction and his drawing of the distinction between denying a predicate with respect to a particular subject and asserting the contrary predicate. But Plato nowhere undertook a systematic analysis of the different modes of opposites and opposite statements. For the first such analysis we may turn to Aristotle. At several points in the *Organon* and *Metaphysics*[1] Aristotle distinguishes between four types of opposites: (1) correlative opposites (e.g. double and half), (2) contraries (e.g. good and bad), (3) positive and privative terms (e.g. sight and blindness) and (4) contradictories or affirmations and negations (e.g. 'he sits' and 'he does not sit').[2] One of the striking features of this classification of opposites is that oppositions between propositions (affirma-

---

[1] E.g. *Cat.* ch. 10 (11b 15–13b 35); *Top.* 109b 17 ff., 113b 15 ff., 135b 7 ff.; *Metaph.* 1018a 20 ff., 1054a 23 ff., 1055a 38 ff. At *Metaph.* 1018a 20 ff. he mentions 'the extremes from which and to which generations and destructions occur' besides the usual four types of opposites, but neither here nor elsewhere do these play an important part in Aristotle's analysis (see Ross's note *ad. loc.*).

[2] This is the example given at *Cat.* 11b 23. Elsewhere, e.g. *Metaph.* 1055b 9 f., Aristotle sometimes refers (as we also tend to) to such a pair as 'equal' and 'not equal' as an example of contradictory opposites. But he points out at *Cat.* 13b 10 ff. that this type of opposition, unlike the other three sorts of opposites, is not an opposition of simple terms, but of *combinations of words which may be true or false*, i.e. propositions. (The distinction between a sentence, i.e. a significant combination of words, and a proposition, which alone may be true or false, is pointed out, for example, at *Int.* 17a 1 ff.: a prayer is a sentence but is neither true nor false.)

tions and negations) are dealt with alongside oppositions between terms (contraries, correlative opposites, positive and privative terms). Yet this classification enables Aristotle to bring out certain important distinctions between those opposites that do, and those that do not, admit intermediates. His use of the terms μεταξύ and ἀνὰ μέσον is, it is true, rather loose. Sometimes he refers to what we may call true intermediates (the usual example he gives is that of grey and other colours which are intermediate between white and black),[1] but on the other hand he also uses the terms to refer to what is 'intermediate' between two terms only in the sense that neither of the terms may be truly predicated of it (he gives the example of that which is 'neither man nor horse' at *Metaph.* 1011 b 31 where the two senses of μεταξύ are distinguished). He points out, then, that some pairs of contraries admit of many intermediates in the true or strict sense (as the other colours between white and black, or as unnamed intermediates between good and bad, or just and unjust, which we refer to as 'neither good nor bad', 'neither just nor unjust', *Cat.* 12 a 20 ff.). On the other hand, other pairs of contraries admit of no intermediates in this sense (the examples which he gives at *Cat.* 12 a 4 ff. are odd and even, and health and sickness) but nevertheless admit of 'intermediates' in the second sense, since of some subjects neither the one nor the other contrary may be truly predicated. In this sense positive and privative terms and correlative opposites admit of 'intermediates' too, for it is not true of things other than eyes that they must either have sight or be blind. Aristotle establishes, then, that there is only one class of oppositions which do not admit of 'intermediates' at all, namely the class of contradictories or affirmations and negations. He puts it at *Metaph.* 1011 b 23 f., for example, that 'there cannot be anything intermediate between contradictories; but it

---

[1] E.g. *Cat.* 12 a 17 ff. When Aristotle defines μεταξύ at *Metaph.* 1057 a 18 ff. it is this strict sense of intermediate which he has in mind: he concludes (b 32 ff.) that 'intermediates are all in the same genus, and intermediate between contraries, and all composed of contraries'.

is necessary either to affirm or to deny any one predicate with respect to any one subject',[1] and again at *APo.* 72 a 12 f. the opposition between contradictories is 'an opposition which of its own nature excludes a middle', and on many other occasions, too, he refers to, and uses, this principle, the so-called Law of Excluded Middle.

His analysis of opposites is clear and straightforward. If at first sight it seems a little strange that he should group contradictories alongside oppositions between terms, we see that this allows him to emphasise that it is *only* in the case of contradictories that it is necessary that one of the pair must be true and the other false (*Cat.* 13 b 2 ff., 33 ff.). Time and again in considering the arguments of earlier Greek writers we noted that it appears to have been assumed with regard to opposites of various sorts that one or other of two opposites must be true, and the second false. Aristotle has the credit for revealing the precise conditions under which this assumption holds good. On the one hand it is true of certain contraries, namely those which do not admit of intermediates in the strict sense, that one or other must be true of the subjects of which they are properly predicated. On the other hand, of contradictories alone it is always necessary for one opposite to be true and the other false.

Aristotle was the first philosopher to attempt to classify the different kinds of opposites, but he also carried out a full analysis of different types of opposite statements. First he states the Law of Contradiction in the form 'the same attribute cannot at the same time belong and not belong to the same subject in the same respect' (*Metaph.* 1005 b 19 f., cf. 1061 b 36 f.) and describes this as 'the surest principle of all' (1005 b 17 f., 22 f.), devoting two long passages in the *Metaphysics*, not to demonstrating it (for he grants that this would be impossible), but to refuting those who would deny the

---

[1] At *Int.* 17 a 34 ff. he points out that for two propositions to be contradictory the subject and predicate must be the same in each, and not merely the same in an equivocal sense, and he notes that there are other qualifications which they make to counter the casuistries of sophists, cf. also *SE* 181 a 36 ff.

principle.[1] But then in several important chapters of the *Analytica Priora* and *de Interpretatione* he considers different types of affirmative and negative statements at length. In *APr.* A 46, for example, he draws the distinction between 'not to be so-and-so' and 'to be not-so-and-so': the contradictory of 'to be white' is 'not to be white', and not 'to be not-white' (which has, as its contradictory, 'not to be not-white'). The relations between 'to be A', 'not to be A', 'to be not-A', and 'not to be not-A' are then worked out in detail.[2] Elsewhere he goes further in distinguishing different kinds of opposite premisses. At *APr.* B 15 in particular he considers the four pairs (1) 'all A is B' and 'no A is B', (2) 'all A is B' and 'not all A is B', (3) 'some A is B' and 'no A is B', and (4) 'some A is B' and 'some A is not B', in a passage which lays the foundation for the traditional Square of Opposition. While the premisses in (2) and (3) are contradictories,[3] those in (1) he calls contraries, and those in (4) he says are opposed 'only verbally' (κατὰ τὴν λέξιν...μόνον) (*APr.* 63b 27 f.). And he then points out that while contrary propositions (as in 1) are incompatible, and of contradictories (2 and 3) one must be true and the other false, with subcontraries (such as we have in 4) the two premisses are compatible (cf. also *Int.* 17b 23 ff., 20a 16 ff.).

---

[1] *Metaph.* Γ chs. 3–6 and Κ chs. 5–6.

[2] Taking 'to be good', 'not to be good', 'to be not-good' and 'not to be not-good' as A, B, C, and D respectively, he shows that A and B are contradictories, and so too C and D: that A and C are incompatible (contrary), but B and D compatible: and that A entails, but is not entailed by, D, and that C entails, but is not entailed by, B (*APr.* 51b 36 ff.).

[3] The distinctions which Aristotle draws are clear enough, but the terminology which he uses in referring to different kinds of opposites and opposite statements, fluctuates. Thus the terms ἀντικείμενον, ἀντικεῖσθαι which are used of opposites generally, e.g. *Cat.* 11b 16, are used of contradictories in particular in this passage, *APr.* 63b 30 (cf. *Int.* 20a 30), and of contraries in particular, e.g. at *Metaph.* 1011b 34 f. More often Aristotle uses ἀντίφασις of a pair of contradictories, e.g. *APo.* 72a 12, or of one or other member of such a pair, e.g. *APr.* 34b 29 (cf. also ἀντιφατικῶς used with ἀντικεῖσθαι, *Int.* 17b 16 f.). Again the term ἐναντίον is used not only of contrary terms and contrary propositions (as in *APr.* 63b 28) but also on one occasion, at least (*APr.* 59b 10 f.), to refer to both contrary and subcontrary propositions (i.e. *both* the pair 'all A is B' and 'no A is B', *and* the pair 'some A is B' and 'some A is not B').

Enough has by now been said for it to be evident that Aristotle's was indeed the decisive contribution in the history of the analysis of different modes of opposition. But we should note, in conclusion, where his formal analysis of different types of opposites is relevant to the various methods of argument which he recommends or uses in the *Organon* or elsewhere. First we should consider the method of proof known as *reductio ad impossibile*. This consists of two steps: (1) to prove a proposition (*p*), you first assume its contradictory (*not-p*), combine this with some other, known premiss, and deduce a conclusion. But (2) if the proposition thus deduced is false, and the deduction is valid, and if further one of the premisses is known to be true, then the other premiss, the original assumption (*not-p*), is false, and so its contradictory (*p*) is true.[1] Aristotle gives many examples of this method in his treatment of the various moods of the syllogism.[2] Thus the mood Barbara ('if all *B* is *A* and all *C* is *B*, then all *C* is *A*') may be established *per impossibile* as follows: you first assume the contradictory of the conclusion, namely 'some *C* is not *A*'; then combining this with the given premiss 'all *B* is *A*', one may infer (by the mood Baroco in the second figure) that 'some *C* is not *B*'. But this is false (assuming that it is given that all *C* is *B*). But if the inference is valid, and the proposition inferred is false, then given that one of the premisses ('all *B* is *A*') is true, the other premiss (the original assumption, 'some *C* is not *A*') must be false. And so its contradictory, 'all *C* is *A*', is true, which is the conclusion we set out to prove.[3]

---

[1] See, for example, *APr.* 41 a 23 ff., 61 a 18 ff. *Reductio ad impossibile* is referred to at *APr.* 40 b 25 f. as a part of reasoning by hypothesis, though there is some doubt as to which element Aristotle considers the hypothesis. Ross (*4*, p. 372), relying on *APr.* 41 a 32–4 and 50 a 29–32, thinks that it is the second of the two steps outlined above that is ἐξ ὑποθέσεως: and yet Aristotle seems consistently to refer to the former step as the 'hypothesis' throughout the discussion at *APr.* B 11–14 (e.g. 63 a 19).

[2] He devotes four chapters in *APr.* B (11–14) to working out the valid forms of *reductio ad impossibile*, and he points out that the same conclusions that may be proved ostensively may be proved by this method also (e.g. *APr.* 62 b 38 ff.).

[3] See *APr.* 63 a 25 ff. and cf. 62 a 22 ff. (I have altered Aristotle's symbols and quoted them in the form in which they are generally associated with the mood Barbara).

We have seen how the Eleatics, for example, sometimes attempted to establish such a thesis as 'the One' by refuting its contrary 'the Many'. But while the aim of the Eleatics was to establish their own theses by refuting their opposites, their arguments were open to certain objections. First, the theses in question were often quite vague and undefined, and second, even if 'the Many' (for example) were 'disproved', it would not necessarily follow that the contrary thesis 'the One' is true. It is interesting to note, then, that Aristotle's method of proof *per impossibile* has a similar aim, but that *on more than half a dozen occasions* in the chapters of the *Prior Analytics* in which he deals with the method he points out that for a proposition to be proved *per impossibile*, the proposition which must be assumed and shown to be false is its *contradictory, and not its contrary*.[1] Thus for the proof of *A*, *E*, *I* and *O* conclusions, the corresponding propositions to be assumed and shown to be false are *O*, *I*, *E* and *A* respectively. To prove, for example, that 'all *A* is *B*' *per impossibile*, we must assume 'some *A* is not *B*' and show that this is false: it is not enough to assume that 'no *A* is *B*' and show that *this* is false, for all that this would show is that 'some *A* is *B*'.

Reductio ad impossibile represents an application of the principle of Excluded Middle in a formally demonstrative method of argument. But the presentation of a set of opposite alternatives is a common feature of Aristotle's argumentation in, for example, the physical treatises, and here too interesting comparisons are to be made between him and earlier writers. For *destructive* purposes Aristotle often uses a technique of argument which consists of refuting a thesis by first stating a number of alternatives one of which must be true if the thesis is true, and then demolishing each of the alternatives in turn (and we have already seen a similar mode of argument used by Gorgias in his proof that 'nothing exists'). Thus

[1] See *APr.* 61 b 1 ff., 17 ff., 30 ff., 62a 28 ff., b 8 ff., 25 ff. and especially 62a 11–19 ('it is evident that in all the syllogisms it is not the contrary but the contradictory that must be hypothesised').

at *Ph.* 237b 23 ff. Aristotle shows that it is impossible for a thing to travel a finite distance in an infinite time (assuming that it does not cover the same distance over and over again) by considering and rejecting the two alternatives (*a*) that the movement is uniform, and (*b*) that the movement is not uniform, and we may note that in this example, at least, the alternatives are indeed exhaustive. Again for *constructive* purposes he sometimes sets out a series of alternatives with a view to establishing one of them by elimination, and this too, of course, is a method of argument which can be paralleled in earlier philosophers (notably in Plato).[1] Thus at *Cael.* 305a 14 ff., having established that the elements undergo 'generation', he puts it that they are generated either (*A*) from what is incorporeal, or (*B*) from what is corporeal, and if from the corporeal, either (i) from some other body, or (ii) from each other, and he establishes the second alternative in each case (*B*ii) by showing that the first is impossible.[2] Now for either of these two types of arguments to be valid, the alternatives which are passed under review should be exhaustive. And in point of fact the alternatives which Aristotle proposes often fulfil this condition (as when he refers to the exclusive contraries corporeal and incorporeal at *Cael.* 305a 14 ff., for example). Yet while there can be no doubt that Aristotle was fully aware of the distinction between contraries that do, and those that do not, admit of intermediates in the strict sense, this does not prevent him from sometimes proposing arguments in which the alternatives are not, strictly speaking, exhaustive. Thus at *GC* 326b 6 ff., for instance, he poses a dilemma for the proponents of the theory of invisible pores, suggesting that the pores must be thought of as either full or empty, and arguing that in both cases it is unnecessary to postulate the existence of pores in order to explain how things act on, or are acted upon by, one another. But 'full' is taken

---

[1] One example from Plato, *Sph.* 251d ff., is considered above, pp. 141 f.

[2] See 305a 31 f.: 'since it is not possible for the elements to be generated either from the incorporeal, or from some other body, it remains to believe that they are generated from each other'.

in the sense quite full, and 'empty' again as quite empty, and one of the defences which an opponent might adopt, then, is that the alternatives (quite full: quite empty) are not exhaustive.[1]

In the physical treatises Aristotle sometimes proposes arguments based on opposites to which certain formal objections may be raised. But in the *Organon* he not only describes, but also recommends, for certain purposes, various types of arguments based on opposites which are plausible, but deceptive. Two passages in the *Sophistici Elenchi* are particularly interesting as they show that he was well aware of the common tendency, in argument, to assume that opposites of any sort are incompatible and exhaustive alternatives. At *SE* ch. 5, 166 b 37 ff., dealing with fallacies of *secundum quid* (παρὰ τὸ ἁπλῶς τόδε ἢ πῇ λέγεσθαι καὶ μὴ κυρίως), he notes the difficulties that arise when a pair of contrary attributes belongs to a particular subject (167a 9 ff.). In some cases (he says) it is easy to detect the fallacy (he mentions the case of the Ethiopian with white teeth, 167a 11 ff.). Often, however (he goes on), the fallacy passes undetected, and he notes that this happens especially when both the contrary attributes belong to the subject similarly (i.e. in similar respects): 'for there is general agreement that it must be conceded that either *both* the predicates are used absolutely, or *neither* is: thus if a thing is half white and half black, is it white or black?'[2] But then in a later passage we find that he actually *recommends* using questions which take the form of a choice between a pair of (inexhaustive) contraries as *a*

---

[1] Aristotle himself often evades the dilemmas which had perplexed earlier Greek philosophers by suggesting a modification in the alternatives which had been assumed to be exhaustive and incompatible. Thus at *GC* 315b 24 ff. he considers whether the primary units of bodies are divisible or indivisible, and points out the difficulties which each of these views holds. He attempts to solve this particular ἀπορία, however, by appealing to the distinction between potentiality and actuality, and suggesting that the primary units are 'potentially divisible, but actually indivisible' (316b 19 ff., cf. 317a 2 ff.).

[2] *SE* 167a 18 ff., cf. also *Ph.* 240a 19–29. An argument of a similar kind is mentioned at *SE* 168a 7 f.: some things are good, some not good; the questioner asks 'are all things good, or not good?'

rhetorical device to gain admissions from an opponent. At *SE* 174a
40 ff. he says that 'in order to obtain your premiss, you ought
to contrast it with its contrary in your question. For instance,
if it is necessary to secure the admission that "a man should
obey his father in everything", ask "should a man obey his
parents in everything, or disobey them in everything?" And
to secure that "that which is multiplied many times over is a
large number", ask "should one agree that it is a large number, or a small one?"... For the juxtaposition of contraries
makes things appear big, both relatively and absolutely, and
better and worse, in the eyes of men.'[1] Aristotle was the first
philosopher to undertake a full analysis of the different modes
of opposition: but we may also give him credit for drawing
attention to the common tendency to state a problem in
terms of a choice between opposite extreme alternatives (as
we say in terms of black and white) and for showing how
misleading the statement of a problem in these terms may be.

CONCLUSION

In the history of the analysis of different modes of opposition
the decisive contribution was made by Aristotle, but we may
conclude this chapter with a few comments on the nature and
significance of the advances in logic which we have considered. To begin with, in the pre-Platonic period, explicit distinctions do not seem to have been drawn between different
types of opposition. On the contrary, to judge from the texts
we discussed, there was a certain tendency to assimilate
different types of opposites together, to emphasise their
generic similarity (as opposites) and to ignore the specific
differences between them (between contraries and contradictories, for example, or between contraries that do, and
those that do not, admit intermediates). At this period difficulties and dilemmas arose in two contexts, in particular,

---

[1] παρατιθεμένων γὰρ ἐγγὺς τῶν ἐναντίων, καὶ μείζω καὶ μεγάλα φαίνεται καὶ χείρω καὶ
βελτίω τοῖς ἀνθρώποις.

(1) in dealing with contradictions or apparent contradictions, and (2) in the use of disjunctive arguments (in which a choice is presented between a set of alternatives). We have seen that both types of difficulty were eventually clarified and resolved, although neither of them in the period before Plato. Plato was responsible for, among other things, showing under what circumstances it is, or is not, possible to predicate opposites with respect to the same subject. And then Aristotle undertook a systematic analysis of different types of opposites and opposite statements, revealing, in particular, the precise conditions under which a pair of opposites may constitute mutually exclusive and exhaustive alternatives.

These were undoubtedly important advances in formal logic. But what, one may ask, were the effects of such advances in terms of the actual arguments which were subsequently employed? It is evident that the drawing of certain distinctions between different types of opposites and opposite statements did not prevent the continued use of arguments similar in form to those we find in the Eleatics or in some of the early dialogues of Plato, for example. Indeed even when such arguments were seen not to be demonstrative, they nevertheless often retained a certain persuasive plausibility. True, certain dilemmas became avoidable (even if they were not always thereafter avoided) thanks to the work of Plato and Aristotle. But we saw that Plato himself continued to use arguments which put a choice between what are (strictly speaking) inexhaustive alternatives in connection with the theory of Forms in such a dialogue as the *Timaeus*. And if Aristotle explicitly investigated the logic of the use of opposites, he also threw some light on the psychology of their use, and recognised the plausibility of certain argumentative devices based on opposites which are similar to those we find used in earlier Greek writers. Indeed we saw that in the context of 'rhetorical' arguments he expressly recommends the juxtaposition of contraries as a means of securing admissions from an unwary opponent. We may conclude, then, that important though the analysis of the different modes of opposition was from the point of view of formal logic, the effect of the advances we have considered was not so much to preclude the use of certain types of argument based on opposites, as to enable a dividing line to be drawn between those that have a claim to be demonstrative, and those that are at best persuasive, or at worst frankly misleading.

PART TWO: ANALOGY

CHAPTER III

THE PRE-PHILOSOPHICAL BACKGROUND

INTRODUCTION

The fortunes of analogy as a mode of inference and as a method of discovery have fluctuated in the debates which, since Bacon, have been held on the problems of scientific method: nor has there been general agreement on the definition of analogy or on the important question of the relation between analogy and induction. First it is apparent that our use of any general term depends on the recognition of a similarity between the instances to which it is applied. As Snell (*3*, p. 191), for example, put it, 'our habit of referring to the objects in the world around us by means of concrete nouns is itself based on an act of comparison, on the drawing of a parallel. By attaching the name 'horse' to various animals at different times, I equate them in spite of their many distinguishing marks.' The point was put more generally by Jevons (p. 628) as follows: 'the whole structure of language and the whole utility of signs, marks, symbols, pictures, and representations of various kinds, rest upon analogy'. And then philosophers have also drawn attention to the element of analogy in all reasoning. Hume[1] put it that 'all kinds of reasoning from causes or effects are founded on two particulars, viz. the constant conjunction of any two objects in all past experience, and the resemblance of a present object to any of them.... Without some degree of resemblance, as well as union, it is impossible there can be any reasoning. But as this resemblance admits of many different degrees, the reason-

---

[1] Hume, Book 1, part 3, sec. 12 (I, p. 142).

ing becomes proportionably more or less firm and certain.'
Again Mill,[1] for instance, believed that in its most general
formulation ('two things resemble each other in one or more
respects; a certain proposition is true of the one; therefore it is
true of the other') analogy stands as the type of all reasoning
from experience. Further, in the course of his analysis of the
syllogism, he stated the view[2] that 'in point of fact, when
drawing inferences from our personal experience..., we
much oftener conclude from particulars to particulars
directly, than through the intermediate agency of any general
proposition', and he concluded[3] that 'all inference is from
particulars to particulars; general propositions are merely
registers of such inferences already made, and short formulae
for making more'.

The question of the proper place of analogy in scientific
method, and in particular of its relation to induction, raises
difficult problems which have a long and intricate history
and which are still very actively debated by philosophers of
science at the present day. Those philosophers who, like
Bacon and Mill, rejected the usefulness of 'complete' or
'perfect' induction (*Inductio per enumerationem simplicem*) in
scientific inquiry, generally put in its place methods which
depend on 'analogy', i.e. on the analysis of the resemblances
between instances. In his discussion of Induction and Analogy in *A Treatise on Probability*,[4] Keynes remarked that
both Bacon's own inductive method, based on the use of
'exclusions and rejections', and Mill's Methods of Agreement and Difference, aim at the determination of the resemblances and differences between particular instances, at the
determination of what Keynes called the Positive and Negative Analogies.[5] Yet both Bacon and Mill held that their

---

[1] Mill, Book 3, ch. 20, para. 2 (II, p. 88).
[2] Book 2, ch. 3, para. 3 (I, p. 215).　　[3] Book 2, ch. 3, para. 4 (I, p. 221).
[4] Part 3, pp. 217 ff., especially pp. 265 ff.
[5] Thus in the only example in which Bacon applied his inductive method in
detail (the investigation of the form of heat) he began by setting out a *Tabula
Essentiae et Praesentiae*, a table of all the particular instances in which heat is

inductive methods should, and did, enable conclusions to be drawn that are certain, and both found a particular difficulty in dealing with false or misleading analogies. Bacon, for example, drew attention to the danger of relying on 'fortuitous and apparent' similarities, as opposed to similarities that are 'real', 'substantial' and 'physical'.[1] But the contrast between Mill's attempt to distinguish between good and bad inductions according to the truth or falsity of the conclusions proposed, and Keynes's later treatment of the problem, is particularly revealing. Keynes criticised Mill for the statement 'That all swans are white, cannot have been a good induction, since the conclusion has turned out erroneous', and emphasised that all inductive arguments (including all arguments from analogy) are relative to premises, relative, that is to say, to the evidence. He illustrated this with an example from mathematics. From a consideration of the six numbers 5, 15, 35, 45, 65 and 95 we might conclude that all numbers ending in five are divisible by five without remainder (which is perfectly true). But from a consideration of the six numbers 7, 17, 37, 47, 67 and 97 we might conclude that all numbers are prime, which end in seven (which is false). Yet 'the validity of empirical arguments as the foundation of a probability cannot be affected by the actual truth or falsity of their conclusions. If, on the evidence, the analogy is similar and equal, and if the scope of the generalisation and its conclusion is similar, then the value of the two arguments must be equal also.'[2] Unlike Bacon or Mill, Keynes did not demand of induction that it should establish certain conclusions, only that it should establish probabilities,[3] and he awarded a due place in inductive method both to the pro-

present, followed by a *Tabula Declinationis, sive Absentiae in proximo*, containing instances which correspond to those in the first table but in which, notwithstanding this correspondence, heat is absent. See Bacon, I, pp. 236 ff., and Ellis' Preface, I, p. 33.

[1] Bacon, I, p. 280 (cf. also the doctrine of 'idols', I, p. 163).　[2] Keynes, p. 243.

[3] 'An inductive argument affirms, not that a certain matter of fact is so, but that relative to certain evidence there is a probability in its favour' (Keynes, p. 221).

cedure of the multiplication of instances (which he termed Pure Induction) and to the analysis of the resemblances between instances (Analogy).[1]

A certain confusion of terminology appears to persist in the controversy which has continued, since Keynes, on the relation between 'analogy' and 'induction'. As Stebbing (p. 249) has pointed out, analogy is sometimes taken as a form of induction, sometimes induction is said to be based upon analogy, and sometimes analogy is considered as a process of inference subsidiary to induction. Here I shall take 'analogy' in its broadest sense, to refer not merely to proportional analogy $(a:b::c:d)$ but to any mode of reasoning in which one object or complex of objects is likened or assimilated to another (of the two particular instances between which a resemblance is apprehended or suggested, one is generally unknown or incompletely known, while the other is, or is assumed to be, better known), and I shall adopt Keynes's terms 'positive' and 'negative' analogy to refer to the points of similarity, and the points of difference, between the things which are compared. If one judges analogy as a method of argument, it is clear that a particular resemblance between two things may be a very weak basis for inferring further points of similarity between them: and as a form of implication ('if X is A, and Y is like X, then Y is A') analogy is evidently invalid. On the other hand many philosophers and historians of science have, like Keynes, accepted that the apprehension of resemblances between different objects may form an important part of scientific method, as a source of hypotheses which will then be submitted to test and verification.[2]

[1] Of these two procedures, Keynes seems to consider Analogy the more important in scientific inquiry, when, for example, he says (p. 241) that 'scientific method...is mainly devoted to discovering means of so heightening the known analogy that we may dispense as far as possible with the methods of pure induction'.

[2] E.g. Stebbing, p. 255: 'An unexplained resemblance, too striking to be regarded as accidental, may form the basis of an hypothesis which would account for the resemblance.' Stebbing instances Laplace's Nebular Hypothesis as one

What I term analogy is, of course, an extremely general mode of reasoning, and one common in some form to all peoples at all periods of time. My particular subject is the use of this mode of reasoning in early Greek thought to Aristotle, that is in the period which sees both the rise of natural philosophy and the development of formal logic. Two distinct but interrelated topics are worth investigating here, first the *content* of the analogies that were proposed, and secondly the question of how far the ancient Greeks went towards an analysis of the *logic* of their use of analogies in this period. First we may attempt to illuminate both their general cosmological doctrines, and some of their explanations of particular natural phenomena, by identifying certain recurrent types of imagery and analogy, and examining how their uses vary in different speculative writers. And secondly we may consider how far the Greeks became aware of the logical or methodological problems involved in the use of analogy either as a source of hypotheses or as a method of inference in the period down to Aristotle.

Before we turn to the evidence in our sources for the early Greek philosophers, two further preliminaries are necessary. First we should refer briefly to some of the varied uses of analogy in primitive thought which have been described and commented on by the anthropologists, and second, certain aspects of the use of comparison and imagery in pre-philosophical Greek literature are sufficiently remarkable to be considered in some detail.

SOME COMPARATIVE EVIDENCE

The fact that many magical beliefs and practices depend on the recognition of resemblances is well known, and some anthropologists have made it clear that they consider the use of analogies a specially important feature of primitive

important theory suggested by such an analogy, and other examples are discussed by Arber. The most recent discussion of the place of models and analogies in scientific method is Hesse, 2.

thought. G. Lienhardt,[1] for instance, put it that 'it is in the apprehension of analogies that much non-scientific thought seems to lie—analogies such as, for example, sky is to earth as God is to man, as rain is to crops...and so on', although he went on to say that 'it is only when we take (these analogies) to be other than they are—to assert the identity of rain and God, for example, and not an analogical relationship between them—that we begin to wonder how reasonable beings could come to "believe" them'. For Lienhardt the frequent appeal to analogies is a distinctive feature of non-scientific thought, but at the same time he issues a timely warning that we should be careful not to assume that two objects are being identified, when they are only being compared (or when a comparison is being suggested between the *relationships* between different objects), and this question, the question of whether two objects are being identified or merely compared in certain respects, is one which must be raised repeatedly in connection with the ancient Greek evidence, although it is a question to which we can often give no certain or unequivocal answer.

To illustrate some of the more important uses of analogies which are found in primitive thought (though by no means confined to primitive peoples), I may refer to some of the examples which Evans-Pritchard has given in his account of Zande beliefs. In his discussion of Zande notions about disease,[2] for instance, Evans-Pritchard remarks that the names of diseases are often taken from things in nature to which they bear a resemblance (just as we too refer to 'elephantiasis', for example). He goes on to say (*1*, p. 487) that 'in primitive patterns of thought objects which have a superficial resemblance are often linked up by nomenclature and ritual and are connected in mystical patterns of thought. In Zande therapeutics this mystical connexion is found in notions about cause and cure. Ringworm resembles in appearance fowls' excrement, and fowls' excrement is at the

---

[1] In Evans-Pritchard, *2*, pp. 106 f.   [2] Evans-Pritchard, *1*, pp. 479 ff.

same time both cause and cure of ringworm. Blepharoptosis resembles a hen's egg, and a hen's egg is its cure. Generally the logic of therapeutic treatment consists in the selection of the most prominent external symptoms, the naming of the disease after some object in nature which it resembles, and the utilization of the object as the principal ingredient in the drug administered to cure the disease. The circle may even be completed by belief that the symptoms not only yield to treatment by the object which resembles them but are caused by it as well.' This passage illustrates very clearly three quite distinct functions which an analogy may serve. (1) First an object may be named or described by referring to another object which it resembles. (Here it *need* not be implied that there is a causal connection between the two objects, though it is often the case that some causal connection is, in fact, assumed to exist).[1] (2) Secondly, the recognition of a resemblance between two objects may serve as the basis for an explanation of one of them, that is an account of its cause. In the examples given, certain diseases are assumed to be brought about by certain objects which are like them. (3) Thirdly, the resemblances between things may be thought to form magical links between them and attempts may be made to control or influence certain objects by manipulating other objects which resemble them: the Azande hope to effect cures by using the natural object which resembles the particular disease, and such 'homoeopathic' magical practices are, of course, common in all parts of the world.

We can see from these examples how analogy fulfils two roles in what is now for us largely, though not exclusively, the province of science, namely to provide explanations and to control reality. As regards the second function, the most

[1] Evans-Pritchard (*1*, pp. 486 f.) reports that the Azande claim to cure elephantiasis of the leg by making incisions in it and rubbing into them ashes from a burnt piece of an elephant's leg. On the other hand they call harelip 'porcupine-sickness' (because the porcupine is supposed to have harelip) without, apparently, believing that there is any connection between the porcupine and this condition.

important difference between science and magic may be simply their relative effectiveness. Magic fails in practice. Yet its general aim is similar to that of applied science, to control events, and one of the means whereby it hopes to achieve this is using the links which it believes may be formed between things by their similarities. Further, it should be pointed out that the members of primitive societies are sometimes quite conscious of the element of analogy in their magic, giving the resemblance between certain objects as the *grounds* for the magical procedure. The Azande (to use this instance again) 'say "We use such-and-such a plant because it is like such-and-such a thing", naming the object towards which the rite is directed'.[1] As regards the other main function of analogy, that of providing the basis for explanations, the principle that similar effects proceed from similar causes underpins all causal explanations (and not merely those of primitive or non-scientific thought) to a greater or less extent. In other ways, too, the use of analogies in explanations is common sense, for when faced with an obscure phenomenon or one that is difficult to understand, we generally attempt to compare or relate it to something in more familiar experience. The difference between common-sense and science here seems to be that the one tends to *assume*, without further scrutiny, that the analogies and connections which it apprehends are significant, while the other is able to *demonstrate* the connections between events. As Keynes put it, 'the common sense of the race has been impressed by very weak analogies', although another remark of his, that we tend to depreciate the former probability of beliefs which we no longer hold, is also particularly relevant to our assessment of analogies which appear to us to be quite superficial.[2]

---

[1] Evans-Pritchard, *1*, p. 449. He notes that 'often the similarity between medicine and object, and between rite and desired happening, is indicated in the spell, e.g. the tall grass *bingba* which grows profusely on cultivated ground..., is known to all as medicine for the oil-bearing melon *kpagu*. A man throws the grass like a dart and transfixes the broad leaves of the plant. Before throwing it he says something of this sort: "You are melons, you be very fruitful like *bingba* with much fruit."'   [2] Keynes, p. 247.

These brief examples from primitive thought may serve to indicate both the usefulness of analogies (as a means of describing and explaining things) and at the same time the fact that they may so easily be misleading. Both these features of the use of analogy will be amply illustrated throughout the period of Greek thought which we shall be studying, but we shall consider not merely what types of analogies and images recur in early Greek speculative thought, but also how their use changed and developed as their authors became more conscious of the methodological problems involved, and one of the questions we shall discuss is how far the Greeks ever qualified, or attempted to scrutinise and verify, the analogies they proposed in various contexts. We shall examine the use of analogies first in their general cosmological doctrines, and then in their attempts to account for particular natural phenomena, before turning to discuss the use and analysis of argument from analogy. But first, however, to draw in the background to this development, I should say something concerning certain features of the use of analogies before philosophy, namely the role of the recognition of resemblances in certain superstitious beliefs, and the use of comparison, metaphor and imagery in pre-philosophical literature.

THE EVIDENCE FROM EARLY GREEK LITERATURE

(a) *Homoeopathic magic and the interpretation of omens*

Like many, indeed most, other peoples past or present, the ancient Greeks evidently believed that a relationship of similarity may sometimes constitute a magical bond between two things, so that what happens to one of them may influence what happens to the other, and this fact should be noted, although it need not detain us for long. It is true that when compared with the wealth of material which has been collected from many present-day societies, the extent of the evidence for the practice of homoeopathic magic among the ancient Greeks may not appear very great, but we should bear in mind that our information for this, as for most other ancient Greek customs, is derived almost entirely from literary sources. That many references to the practice of homoeopathic magic can be cited from extant Greek literature of various periods is, in any case, well known.[1] We may note a passage in Homer, for instance, which not only refers to such a practice but also reveals the idea which lies behind it. At *Iliad* 3 259 ff. the Achaean and Trojan leaders make a pact before Menelaus and Paris fight their duel. First Agamemnon swears an oath that the winner of the duel shall have Helen. Then a sacrifice is performed and wine taken from a mixing-bowl and poured out on the ground. As the wine is poured out, the Achaeans and the Trojans are described as praying: 'O Zeus, most honoured and most great, and you other immortal gods; whichever party first violates the oaths, *thus* may their and their children's brains flow out on the ground, *just as this wine*; and may their wives be possessed by other men' (298 ff.). To judge from this prayer the action of the pouring of the wine has, on this occasion, a specific magical intention: it imitates the spilling of the transgressors' brains, and is meant both to symbolise and to ensure this desired result. Many ancient Greek customs and practices no doubt had their origin in the belief in the efficacy of homoeopathic magic,[2] but the present passage is remarkable in that the text describes the thoughts of the participants as they performed one such ritual.

One of the common techniques of interpreting supernatural signs is another good illustration of the importance of analogies in early Greek religious or superstitious beliefs. Like many other peoples, the ancient Greeks assumed that some portents symbolise the future, which can, then, be predicted by interpreting the portents by analogy. Thus at *Iliad*

---

[1] Thus several notable instances occur in comparatively late literature, e.g. Theocritus, *Idyll* 2 (17 ff., 22 ff., 27 ff.).

[2] This seems to be true, for example, of some of the obscure rules of behaviour found in Hesiod's *Works and Days* (e.g. 744 f., 746 f.), as also of some of those associated with the Pythagoreans (as KR note, p. 226).

12 200 ff., for example, an omen appears to the Trojans: an eagle flies across their lines with a snake in its talons, but the snake fights back and compels the eagle to let it fall. At 217 ff. Polydamas interprets this portent in the light of the current situation in the fighting, in which the Trojans have driven the Achaeans back to their ships and are about to assault their wall. He foretells that just as the eagle is cheated of its prey, when it seems to have the snake at its mercy, so too the Trojans will be denied victory, even though this seems certain.[1] This method of interpreting supernatural signs continued, of course, to enjoy great popularity in Greece long after Homer. In the fifth century, for instance, Herodotus contains many examples in which a person interprets an oracle, or a dream, or a portent, by apprehending certain similarities between it and features of his own situation.[2]

Both the practice of homoeopathic magic and the technique of interpreting portents by analogy depend on an assumption that there is a magical or supernatural link between similar cases. The ancient Greek evidence which we have considered is in no way exceptional: rather it could be paralleled from numerous societies. But it shows that like many other peoples they sometimes assumed that the similarities between things could be used on the one hand to control or influence events, and on the other to predict the future. In the context of these two superstitious practices the ancient Greeks at an early stage showed considerable ingenuity in discovering resemblances between disparate objects and a readiness to believe that such resemblances were significant.

[1] The fact that Hector rejects the significance of omens in general, and of this one in particular, in his famous speech at *Iliad* 12 231 ff. ('one omen alone is best—to fight for one's country') does not, of course, invalidate this passage as evidence of one of the orthodox methods of interpreting portents. (I have noted above, p. 67, that in primitive peoples, too, a certain scepticism is sometimes expressed concerning superstitious beliefs.)

[2] E.g. 1 67–8 where Lichas interprets a cryptic oracle concerning the place where Orestes' bones will be found as referring to a smithy: the oracle referred to a place 'where two winds blow...and stroke answers counterstroke, and woe is laid on woe', and the 'two winds' are interpreted as the two bellows, the 'stroke

(b) The use of similes and comparisons in pre-philosophical literature

If the ancient Greek adherence to certain superstitious practices based on the recognition of resemblances calls for little comment, the role of comparisons in early Greek literature, especially in Homer himself, is in some respects particularly remarkable. From the point of view of the later development of the use of analogy in Greek philosophy, the first feature of Homeric simile[1] which is relevant and should be noted is simply this, the frequency with which comparisons are used to describe the essential or significant aspects of a scene. Ajax in retreat and turning from time to time on his pursuers is compared with an ass which boys drive from a field of corn with their sticks, but only after it has eaten its fill (*Iliad* 11 558 ff.). Odysseus, swept ashore on the coast of Phaeacia and clinging to a rock as the waves beat about him, is compared with an octopus (*Od.* 5 432 ff.) : 'as, when an octopus is dragged from its lair, many pebbles stick to its suckers, so the skin was stripped off Odysseus' stalwart hands on to the rocks'. It is well known that similes are particularly common in the battle-scenes in the *Iliad*, and this may suggest to a modern reader that they were deliberately used by the epic poets as a literary device to enliven repetitious descriptions. But if this is true, it is only part of the truth, for similes are by no means confined to the stock scenes in the Homeric poems, and as we shall see, they serve important purposes besides those which may very broadly be termed stylistic.

One general function of similes in Homer is simply to describe the striking features of a scene, but an analysis of some of their more specific uses reveals the fundamental role which comparisons play in conveying certain notions. The

and counterstroke' as the anvil and the hammer, and 'woe laid on woe' as the forged iron. It may be noted that Herodotus himself expresses no doubt about the veracity of Lichas' interpretation.

[1] The best and most complete treatment of Homeric similes is still H. Fränkel's *Die homerischen Gleichnisse* (Göttingen, 1921). Among other studies, I may mention those of Riezler, and Snell, *3*, pp. 199 ff., in particular.

way in which similes are used to describe certain qualities and characteristics, though obvious enough, is significant. In Homer, 'whiteness', for example, is expressed by comparisons with the sun (*Iliad* 14 185) or snow (*Iliad* 10 437) or sawn ivory (*Od.* 18 196)[1] and there are similar stock illustrations for sweetness (honey), hardness (stone, iron or horn) and many other physical and psychological qualities. Though the examples which are used to illustrate different qualities vary from one literature to another, some such usage must surely be universal. But if we are familiar with this type of comparison ourselves, we should not ignore the differences between the ancient Greek usage and our own. It is instructive to consider the beliefs which appear to underlie the early Greek use of animals as the symbols of certain psychological characteristics. In Homer, the lion and the boar represent courage and ferocity, the deer and the dove cowardice, the ass stubbornness and so on, and a long list of animals used in a similar way could be given from the lyric poets.[2] But a notable feature of these comparisons, to which Snell[3] has already drawn attention, is that the lion is *always* ferocious, and the deer *always* cowardly. It seems that the early Greeks held that animals not only symbolised certain characteristics, but *permanently manifested* them, and a passage in Pindar is striking confirmation that this was, in fact, sometimes assumed. At *O.* 11 16 ff. he promises the Muses that when they visit the Western Locrians, they will find them hospitable, noble, wise and good, and he goes on: 'neither the tawny fox nor the

---

[1] Cf. 'whiter than an egg' in Sappho (167 LP) or 'whiter than Parian marble' in Pindar (*N.* 4 81).

[2] E.g. in Archilochus (81 D) the fox is the embodiment of cunning, and in both Phocylides and Semonides various animals are used as the prototypes of different sorts of women, the bitch, bee, sow and mare in Phocylides (2 D) and eight different species (as well as the earth and the sea) in Semonides (7 D). On a similar use of animals as the types of characters in primitive thought, see Lévi-Strauss, *4*.

[3] 'The Homeric lion is always a belligerent beast;...even on retreat he remains ever warlike....And all the other animals in the similes: the impudent dog, the stubborn ass...betray the same constancy of disposition' (Snell, *3*, p. 201).

loud-roaring lions change their inborn character (τὸ ἐμφυὲς ...ἦθος)'. Pindar's immediate point is that the Western Locrians have always had certain qualities and will continue to show them. But it is interesting that he uses animals as the paradigms of constancy of nature and disposition. The species to which he refers are clearly assumed to be the unaltering types of certain characteristics. Such an assumption adds greatly to the force of those comparisons in which animals are used to describe men's characters, and we may believe that it is part of the point of many other animal similes, too, particularly in Homer, that animals are assumed to have permanent characteristics.[1]

The next feature of the role of comparisons we may consider is their use to convey ideas of distance and time. Again Homer's usage is slightly different from our own, for where we should tend to refer to an abstract system of measurement, Homer more often uses a concrete comparison. It is obvious that to measure a length often involves a physical act of comparison (the thing to be measured is set beside a foot-rule, for example), and societies which have no abstract system of units of length no doubt largely make do with measurements based on the human body (foot, pace, 'span', 'cubit', etc.). From references in Homer and Hesiod it appears that the early Greeks used such units of length as the ὄργυια (the length of the arms outstretched), the πῆχυς (cubit: the length of the forearm) and the foot-length, though we do not know at precisely what stage these were combined to form a standardised system of measurement.[2] But such references are

---

[1] It is worth noting that the psychological characteristics of different species of animals are discussed at length in Book I of the *Historia Animalium*, 608a 11 ff. (cf. A I 488b 12 ff., Θ I 588a 16 ff.), although at 588a 20 f. Aristotle remarks that such characteristics are more clearly differentiated in men than in animals.

[2] Passages in Herodotus (e.g. 2 149) tell us the relations which obtained in the fifth century between the πλέθρον (cf. the Homeric πέλεθρον, e.g. *Il.* 21 407) and shorter units of length, the ὄργυια, πῆχυς, πούς and παλαστή (or παλαιστή or παλάμη), but we cannot be sure when these were fixed. Standard units of length no doubt became increasingly important as technology developed, and it is worth noting that already in Hesiod (*Op.* 423 ff.) a passage describing various

quite rare in Homer, who more often expresses distances by means of comparisons which refer to other vaguer standards, as in the common 'as far as the flight of a spear' (e.g. *Iliad* 21 251) or in the obscure phrase 'as far as the range of mules' (*Iliad* 10 351 f., *Od.* 8 124)[1] or 'as far as the range of a discus' (*Iliad* 23 431 f.). Again the use of such similes might strike us as principally a poetical device, and it is true that some of them have been embroidered with what are, strictly speaking, irrelevant additions. Yet when little progress had probably been made towards an abstract, standardised system of measurement, such comparisons clearly played an important part in expressing distances, which they succeed in doing quite vividly, if not with very great precision.

The role of comparisons to express time is in some ways similar. Apart from the day itself, the main divisions of time, the year and the month, were readily fixed, at least approximately, by observations of the sun and moon.[2] Within the day, dawn, sunrise, noon, sunset and twilight mark off distinct periods, and in Homer the night (like the day, cf. *Iliad* 21 111) was divided into three parts (*Iliad* 10 252 f.; *Od.* 14 483: in both passages there is a reference to the movement of the stars). But Homer sometimes indicates the time of day by means of a comparison: 'at the time when the woodcutter prepares a meal in the mountain glens...' (*Iliad* 11 86 ff.), or 'at a time when a man rises from the assembly for his evening meal...' (*Od.* 12 439 ff.). Both these similes are

---

implements is full of references to units of length: he speaks of a 'three-foot' mortar, a 'three-cubit' pestle, a 'seven-foot' axle, a 'three-span' felloe of a wheel and a wagon of 'ten palms'.

[1] This is usually taken to be the breadth of land mules plough in a day (assuming a furrow of a given, constant length).

[2] We have no means of determining how accurate an idea of the true length of the lunar month or the solar year the Greeks of the pre-philosophical period may have had. Herodotus (2 4), reporting that the Egyptians had a year of 365 days, contrasts this favourably with the old Greek calendar, which had an intercalary month every other year. It may be noted, however, that Hesiod already uses quite a detailed 'calendar': the days of the month are numbered (and this had a magical significance, *Op.* 765 ff.) and the solstices, and the rising and setting of constellations, were used to determine the divisions between the main seasons of the year, and other dates of importance.

quite elaborate, and in the first example, especially, the comparison has a dramatic purpose, to underline a contrast: the Achaeans make their great effort to break the Trojan ranks at a time of day when a wood-cutter would be taking a well-earned rest. But the main subject of both similes is simply the time of day. We should remember that Homer had no means of measuring the hours of the day. We should not underestimate, then, the purely practical function of these comparisons, their usefulness in expressing the time of day. Where we may tell the time exactly by referring to the minute hands of watches, the ancient Greeks sometimes indicated the time no less correctly (though less precisely) by means of a comparison which referred to an event associated with a particular part of the day.

It is more difficult to show how comparisons are used in early Greek literature not only to express, but also to grasp or conceive the unknown or what is difficult to comprehend. Among the purposes which H. Fränkel found similes serving in Homer, he noted (*1*, pp. 98 f.) that they were used 'to clothe the invisible in sensible images' and to 'make clearer and more comprehensible what is hard to conceive'. Similes are often used, for example, in connection with the divine or miraculous. As is well known, several similes compare the movements of the gods with the flight of birds, although this evidence is difficult to assess because of the literal belief that birds might be the manifestations or embodiments of gods.[1] But the way in which comparisons are deliberately used to conceive and express the divine may be illustrated by other types of simile as well. At *Iliad* 4 75 ff., for example, Athena suddenly appearing on the battlefield is compared with a 'bright meteor which the son of Cronos dispatches..., from which many sparks are discharged', and at *Iliad* 5 864 ff.

[1] Some passages describe the gods appearing *in the form of* birds (e.g. *Od.* 3 372, cf. 22 239 f.), others merely *compare* the gods with birds (e.g. *Il.* 5 778, 13 62, 15 237; *Od.* 5 51 f.), but it is difficult to know what importance to attach to this distinction, or even whether any sharp distinction was consciously drawn between these two cases.

Ares disappearing from the scene is compared with a 'black haze which appears from the clouds after heat, as a stormy wind is stirred up'. On each occasion, the poet apprehends and describes the miraculous appearance or disappearance of the god with the help of a concrete image. But this is not the only context in which similes are used to grasp what is difficult to comprehend. Thus comparisons are used to describe psychological states. At *Iliad* 14 16 ff. Nestor's hesitation between two courses of action is conveyed by a fine concrete image: 'as when the great sea is darkened by a soundless swell; it forebodes the swift paths of the shrill winds, but it remains unmoved, nor is it rolled forward or to either side until a steady wind comes down from Zeus'. In a more complex example (*Od.* 20 13 ff.), when Odysseus observes the misbehaviour of the maids in his palace, we are told that 'his heart snarled (ὑλάκτει) within him. As a bitch prowling round her young puppies snarls at a man she does not recognise and longs for a fight, so he snarled inwardly, indignant at their evil deeds.' The simile here develops the idea behind the metaphorical use of ὑλάκτει in 20 13, but it is interesting to note how the concrete image enables the poet to convey an impression of an inner psychological state. An even more remarkable, if obscure, simile occurs at *Iliad* 23 597 ff.[1] to describe Menelaus' pleasure when Antilochus concedes that he should have the second prize in the chariot race: τοῖο δὲ θυμὸς | ἰάνθη, ὡς εἴ τε περὶ σταχύεσσιν ἐέρση | ληίου ἀλδήσκοντος, ὅτε φρίσσουσιν ἄρουραι.[2] The sense of ἰαίνω applied to Menelaus' θυμός at 598 (cf. 600) is 'cheer', but the literal meaning of this verb (as is clear, for example, from *Od.* 10 359 and 12 175) is 'warm' or 'melt', and this, rather than the derivative 'cheer', is the sense which predominates when the verb is supplied with ἐέρση in the second clause. The 'cheer-

[1] Cf. Onians, pp. 46 ff. (where he also comments on several other passages in early Greek literature in which psychological phenomena are apparently conceived in concrete terms).

[2] 'His heart was "cheered" as when the dew is (melted) on the ears of corn of a growing crop, when the fields are bristling.'

ing' of Menelaus' θυμός is, then, thought of as like the melting of dew on the ears of corn: again a concrete comparison enables the poet to apprehend an obscure psychological reaction.[1]

The role of comparisons to grasp the unknown can be further illustrated by considering some of the comparisons which occur in the *speeches* in Homer. The speeches enable us to study what happens when a character in the poem is confronted with something strange or new, and often his reaction, in such a situation, is to liken the new person or object to something. E. Fraenkel was the first to draw attention to certain passages in Greek literature in which two or more persons each suggest likenesses for one another in certain social contexts, especially when they first meet.[2] There are several instances of this in Homer. Thus at *Od.* 6 150 ff., when Odysseus meets Nausicaa for the first time, he says 'if you are a goddess..., I liken you most nearly in beauty and size and stature to Artemis...', and Nausicaa replies (187), 'Stranger, since you are not like an evil or a foolish man....' Again during the Phaeacian games Euryalus taunts Odysseus with his refusal to take part: 'Stranger, I liken you not to a man who is experienced in the games...nor are you like an athlete' (*Od.* 8 159 ff.), to which Odysseus replies (166 ff.): 'Stranger, what you have said is not good: you are like a reckless man.' Passages from later authors show that this custom continued to be observed, half seriously, half in jest,

---

[1] That similes may even be used to illustrate obscure *physiological* processes in Homer is shown by one example (*Il.* 5 902 ff.) where the healing of Ares' wound by the drugs administered by Paeon is compared with the curdling of milk by fig-juice. It is true that the main purpose of this simile is to describe the *speed* with which Ares' wound heals. But we may wonder whether the curdling of milk was not thought to illustrate the *manner* in which blood clots also. Though the function of this simile in Homer is descriptive, not explanatory, we may note that it was just such comparisons that were later used by the philosophers and medical writers to help explain complex physiological processes; and the particular illustration of the curdling of milk happens to be one that is often used by later theorists (e.g. Empedocles Fr. 33, *Morb.* IV ch. 52, L VII 590 9 ff., and often in Aristotle, e.g. *GA* 729a 9 ff.).

[2] E. Fraenkel, *1*, pp. 171 ff., and cf. *2*, II, pp. 101 f., III, pp. 575 f., 773 f. Cf. also Rivier, pp. 51 ff.

on various social occasions.[1] But this use of comparisons to describe a new or unfamiliar person or object is not confined to such customary or conventional social interchanges. When Priam asks Helen to identify the Achaean leaders for him at *Iliad* 3 161 ff., he points to one of them (Odysseus) and says (197 f.): 'I liken him to a thick-fleeced ram who goes up and down through a great flock of white sheep.' This seems closely parallel to the *poet's* frequent use of animal similes outside the speeches. As Homer uses such comparisons to express the character of a single individual, or to describe a whole scene, so Priam uses one to give his impression of Odysseus. But Priam uses the comparison with the ram to describe someone of whose exact identity, status and character he is ignorant. Comparisons are a means of describing the known: but they may also be used (as this example shows) *to apprehend the unknown* by likening it to something known or familiar.[2] Homer does not, it is true, use comparisons to provide or suggest explanations of natural phenomena (for this, of course, he never undertakes to give). Yet in certain other contexts, some of which I have tried to indicate, comparisons were used quite regularly, in Homer and elsewhere, to conceive and describe aspects of the 'unknown', that is what is new or strange or difficult to grasp, as, for example, the divine or our inner psychological states and reactions.

I have considered the comparisons in Homer from the point of view of the functions which they may fulfil, but one other aspect of their use should also be mentioned here. It has often been pointed out that some of the more ornate similes in the *Iliad* and *Odyssey* are by no means wholly relevant to the subjects which they are apparently intended to illustrate, and sometimes several details of the comparisons seem not merely irrelevant, but positively misleading. At *Iliad* 17 389 ff., for instance, there is an interesting description of the

---

[1] Plato, *Smp.* 215a f. and *Men.* 80a are worth noting particularly.

[2] Cf. Rivier's discussion (pp. 41 ff., 52 ff.) of the use of the verb εἰκάζω (which means both to 'liken' and to 'guess' or 'conjecture').

early Greek method of curing a hide by stretching it and rubbing it with oil: 'they stretch it standing round at intervals in a circle: then the moisture comes out of it and the oil sinks in, as many men pull it, and it is thoroughly stretched in all directions', but this is hardly a happy illustration of the fight round Patroclus' dead body. On the other hand (and this is what I am concerned to note) on a number of occasions the two parts of a Homeric comparison do correspond closely and in detail. To cite a single example, at *Iliad* 17 61–7, when Menelaus has killed Euphorbus and stripped him of his armour, there is a long comparison with a hunting-scene which mirrors the situation in the fight in almost every detail: 'as when a mountain lion, trusting in his own strength, pounces on the finest heifer in a grazing herd; seizing her with his strong teeth, he first breaks her neck [Euphorbus was, in fact, killed by a stroke with a spear which broke his neck, 17 49, although it should be noted that the phrase referring to the lion killing an ox is a stock one, cf. *Iliad* 11 175], and then he tears and devours her blood and entrails [this is probably meant to correspond to the stripping of Euphorbus' armour, cf. also *Iliad* 11 176]; all around him the hounds and herdsmen make a great din, but keep their distance; they are unwilling to close with the lion, for pale fear has seized hold of them. So of the Trojans, no one dared to close with the glorious Menelaus....' Often the points of resemblance between the two parts of the comparison are emphasised by the repetition of words and phrases (as, in this example, ἀντίον ἐλθέμεναι in 17 67 and 69) and there is little need to mention that there is a certain formal balance in the majority of Homeric similes in that ὡς and ὥς, introducing the 'as...' and 'so...' clauses respectively, often stand each at the beginning of a verse. What is interesting and important here from the point of view of the later history of analogy in Greek philosophy, is the fact that already in Homer we find some quite elaborate comparisons in which the correspondences in form and content between the two parts have clearly been worked out in considerable detail. As we shall see later, detailed points of similarity between the two parts of a comparison are a feature, and an important one, of their use in some Greek philosophers, and these similarities are sometimes stressed, as in Homer, by the repetition of key words and phrases.

(c) Metaphor and imagery in the pre-philosophical world-picture

While there can be little doubt or confusion concerning what is, or what is not, a simile or explicit comparison, it is often hard to determine what is or is not a metaphor. We may have little difficulty in distinguishing between the two uses of the word 'shepherd', for example, one for someone who herds sheep, and the other for a king or a priest who is called the shepherd of his people, but in many cases the boundary between the 'literal' and the 'metaphorical' use of a term is quite vague. Again, how far a particular writer may or may not be aware of any distinction between the 'literal' or 'primary' applications of a word, and 'metaphorical' or 'secondary' uses, is often an extremely delicate question. To take an example from Greek literature, Onians (pp. 303 ff., especially p. 331) has discussed the passages in Homer and elsewhere in which the workings of fate are described in terms of a process of spinning, weaving and binding, and he suggests that fate may have been conceived by the early Greeks as just such a process (and such a belief can be paralleled in other societies). He would deny, then, that the 'binding' of fate was originally understood as a metaphor. But on the other hand, if we say that such terms are used *literally*, there is a danger in pressing this interpretation too, if it is taken to imply (what is far from being certainly the case) that Homer and his audience made *no distinction whatever* between the spinning of a particular old woman (whom they could actually see) and the spinning of the fates (which they could only imagine). The spinning, weaving and binding of the fates is a fiction or a myth in the sense that it is imaginary, even if it was anything but fictitious in the sense of false for the ancient Greeks who were convinced, or assumed, that this was indeed the way in which fate worked. Although we should not talk of any *deliberate* suggestion or proposal of analogies here, we may note that the description of the obscure functionings of fate involves the use of concrete images which are derived from everyday human activities.

There is, of course, no cosmology, in the sense of a coherent body of theory on the constituent elements of the universe and their interrelations, in either Homer or Hesiod. Nevertheless, their accounts of the activities of the gods, their remarks on the role of fate, their descriptions of what we should call natural phenomena, convey vivid intuitions and beliefs about the world and the way it works. Now while it is clear that such beliefs are not, generally, the outcome of deliberate theorising or the conscious construction of analogies on the part of individual poets, it is also evident that they largely consist of images derived from features of early Greek society in particular or of general human experience. (Thus the conception of the Olympian gods was surely not in origin a deliberate construction using man as the model: yet their many human characteristics are obvious.) Much could be written on this topic, but some aspects of it are especially relevant to the subsequent development of Greek philosophy and I shall confine myself to these. Three ideas which are of great importance in the history of Greek cosmological theories are (1) the conception of the cosmic order as (or as like) a social or political order, (2) the conception of the world as (or as like) a living being, and (3) the conception of the world as (or as like) the product of intelligent, designing agencies. None of these ideas occurs as such in pre-philosophical Greek texts: but it is convenient to collect together here the material which will enable us to decide how far certain earlier mythical beliefs may be said to be the forerunners of each of these three types of cosmological notions.

The world of the Homeric hero is in a real sense governed

and controlled by the gods. They often influence physical phenomena, such as the sea, the winds, storms, thunder and lightning, either directly or indirectly, and they have power over men too, affecting their physical strength, their morale, even their thoughts and desires. They may be responsible for what we should call chance occurrences (as when Teucer's bow-string snaps at a critical moment, *Iliad* 15 461 ff.), and most important, they direct the outcome of events as a whole. But if it is obvious that the gods have a special role in Homeric accounts of why things happen as they do, certain aspects of the Homeric conception of the gods call for comment. Not only are the Olympians generally conceived in the form of men, but the whole Homeric description of the gods—of their life, their behaviour and the motives which govern it, even of their rudimentary political organisation—faithfully reflects Homeric society itself. Now this idea that the gods form a society like that of men is, of course, found in a great many peoples besides the ancient Greeks, and indeed in a developed form in some of their nearest neighbours. Thorkild Jacobsen,[1] for example, has discussed the evidence which suggests that in ancient Mesopotamia the universe was conceived as a *state* in which the phenomena of nature, each with a will and character of its own, were seen as citizens, or more precisely as the members of a divine legislative assembly. Indeed the Greeks themselves were probably the first to point out not only that men tend to conceive the gods in their own image, but also that they tend to imagine the modes of life of the gods as like their own. Xenophanes noted (ironically, of course) that the gods of the Ethiopians and the Thracians have the physical characteristics of the Ethiopians and the Thracians (Fr. 16), and Aristotle put it (*Pol.* 1252 b 24 ff.) that 'all men say that the gods have a king, because they themselves either are or were formerly under the rule of a king: for they

---

[1] In Frankfort, *2*, ch. 5, pp. 137 ff. In one text which Jacobsen quotes (p. 147 and n. 12) Fire is conceived as a judge: 'Scorching Fire, warlike son of Heaven, | Thou, the fiercest of thy brethren, | Who like Moon and Sun decidest lawsuits— | Judge thou my case....' Cf. also Kelsen, and Frankfort, *1*.

imagine *not only the forms of the gods, but also their ways of life*, to be like their own '. In imagining the gods as forming a society like that of men, the ancient Greeks were, then, only doing what many other peoples have done. Yet the *extraordinary detail* of the analogy between gods and men in Homer is, or seems to be, quite exceptional.[1] Thus the homes and possessions of the gods are mostly just especially fine specimens of the palaces and typical belongings (chariots, jewels, etc.) of the Homeric hero. The occupations of the gods are the occupations of the various members of Homeric society (not excluding those of women and inferiors).[2] Again the main customs of Homeric society are observed by the Olympians as well as by men. For example, the gods greet their divine visitors in just the same way as men greet their guests: it was customary to offer them a chair and a footstool and to give them something to eat or drink, before questioning them on the purpose of their visit.[3] Indeed, in its detailed complexity,[4] the parallelism between gods and men in Homer already seems to equal the most elaborate analogies which the Greek philosophers were to construct between the microcosm and the macrocosm.

The gods' lives mirror those of the Homeric heroes in many superficial circumstances. But it is more important to note how the interrelations between the gods, and the springs of their actions, are described. Honour (τιμή), glory (κῦδος) and fame (κλέος) are the main motives which underlie the

[1] See especially Guthrie, *4*, ch. 4, pp. 117 ff. and Finley, pp. 142 ff. (who sees the humanisation of the gods, in Homer, as a new development in religion, 'a step of astonishing boldness', p. 146).

[2] Calypso and Circe, for instance, are depicted at work at their looms at *Od.* 5 61 ff. and 10 220 ff. (and we hear of a robe which Athena herself made, *Il.* 14 178 f.). Hephaestus is the gods' smith, and he makes not only their armour, but also such humbler objects as chairs and footstools (*Il.* 14 238 ff.).

[3] See, for example, the descriptions of the way in which Thetis is greeted by the gods at *Il.* 24 97 ff., or Hermes by Calypso at *Od.* 5 85 ff., and cf. the accounts of Menelaus' reception of Telemachus (*Od.* 4 30 ff.) or of Alcinous' reception of Odysseus (*Od.* 7 167 ff.). On the importance of offering food and drink to a newly arrived guest, see Finley, pp. 134 f.

[4] As has often been remarked, the gods, even though immortal, share some of the frailer characteristics of humans: they weep, sleep and sweat (*Il.* 4 27) and they may even be wounded, as Ares is at *Il.* 5 855 ff., crying out in evident physical pain.

gods' actions just as they do those of men.[1] The types of appeal which a god uses when asking a favour from another god are, again, the same as men use in similar circumstances. The gods form, in fact, an extremely close-knit society, and the complex web of mutual obligations created by kinship, or by gifts or services rendered or received, is as powerful a determinant of the gods' actions, as it is of those of the Homeric heroes.[2] Further, the power of the supreme god, Zeus, is conceived as a political power. The two images which are used most often to describe his position and authority are those of father and king: he rules over gods and men (e.g. *Iliad* 2 669). Might and birth are the twin bases of his power (as they are of that of the Homeric king). He is the strongest of the gods, and not infrequently threatens them with physical violence when they are disobedient, or look like being so (e.g. *Iliad* 8 5–27, 402 ff., 450 ff.). Yet in Homer, at least,[3] he also rules by right of primogeniture. Thus when he orders Poseidon to stop helping the Achaeans at *Iliad* 15 158 ff., he gives two reasons why he should be obeyed (165 f.): 'because I claim to be much stronger in might and elder by birth'.

Zeus' power is that of a supreme ruler: yet on occasions,

---

[1] See, for instance, *Il.* 7 451 ff., 15 185 ff., *Od.* 13 128 ff.: three occasions on which Poseidon feels his fame and honour are at stake.

[2] Some passages may be cited to illustrate this. The favouritism of the gods for their own immortal *kin* is seen, for example, at *Il.* 5 875 ff. At *Il.* 1 503 ff. when Thetis begs a favour from Zeus, she refers to the *services* she has done him in the past 'either in word or in deed' and then appeals to him as a suppliant, grasping him by the knees. At *Il.* 14 233 ff. when Hera asks Sleep for his help, she refers to past occasions when Sleep has done her bidding (which illustrates the point that in Homeric society the conferring of a favour was thought to convey an obligation on the benefactor as well as on the beneficiary). She goes on to promise Sleep *gifts*, and when Sleep still hesitates, she increases her offer with the promise of one of the Graces for bride. Again at *Il.* 18 368 ff. when Thetis visits Hephaestus to ask for arms for Achilles, Hephaestus recalls how Thetis rescued him when he was thrown out of heaven and remarks (406 f.) that he is under an obligation to pay Thetis the full ζωάγρια, the price for saving someone alive. (Men, too, of course, try to influence the gods by similar methods. *Od.* 5 101 ff., for example, suggests that the gods are beholden to men for their sacrifices, but it is often recognised that sacrificing to a god does not necessarily ensure the desired result.)

[3] E.g. *Il.* 13 355. In Hesiod (*Th.* 478 f.), however, Zeus, like Cronos his father, is a youngest child.

particularly in the *Iliad*, the other gods rebel against him and succeed, at least temporarily, in reversing the tide of battle contrary to his will. In considering such incidents as the revolt of Hera and Athena at *Iliad* 8 350 ff. and Poseidon's reluctance to obey Zeus at *Iliad* 15 184 ff. we may reflect that in this respect, too, Zeus' position may be compared with that of Homeric kings on earth, in that neither he nor they always commanded unquestioning obedience from their kin and subjects. Achilles, after all, refuses to fight for Agamemnon, the paramount king of the Achaeans. Zeus experiences similar difficulties in procuring the gods' willing support, although, unlike Agamemnon, he eventually has his way because he can enforce his decisions thanks to his superior strength. Although Zeus is supreme, the idea that he should personally control everything that happens throughout the world at all moments of time is utterly foreign to Homer. The other gods continually act on their own accounts, and indeed Zeus is sometimes represented as encouraging them to do so (*Iliad* 7 455 ff.; *Od.* 13 143 ff.). He consults the other gods on many occasions, whether in a formal council (like the Homeric council of elders) or otherwise, and though sometimes the gods are summoned merely to hear the decisions which Zeus has already taken, there are other passages which suggest that it is not a matter of complete indifference to Zeus what the other gods think of his plans. When he considers whether he should spare Sarpedon's life, for example, he is dissuaded by Hera who says that 'not all the other gods will approve' (*Iliad* 16 443, cf. 22 181).[1] In short, the relation between Zeus and the other gods is, in many important respects, a faithful reproduction of the relation between the Homeric chief and the people who owe him allegiance, particularly the inner circle of his family and the council of elders. The difficulties which Zeus sometimes has in controlling the gods (difficulties which he is represented as explicitly recognising

---

[1] Cf. also Zeus' apparent concern when he plans something contrary to Hera's wishes (*Il.* 1 518 ff.) or to those of Poseidon (*Od.* 1 76 ff.).

at *Iliad* 1 518 ff. and 5 893), his concern to obtain their support, his occasional hesitation over a course of action, when he asks for, and accepts, their advice, all tally with this image.

The supreme power of Zeus is a recurrent and dominant theme in both Homer and Hesiod, and yet the relations between the gods are not solely determined by the caprice of Zeus. Though he is represented as an arbitrary and despotic ruler, he is bound by certain obligations in his relations with the gods, and the other gods have certain rights and privileges. At *Iliad* 1 524 ff. he assures Thetis that once his promise has been given it is irrevocable, and it appears from *Iliad* 19 107 ff. that he is bound by the oaths which he has sworn however much he may later regret them. More important is the passage at *Iliad* 15 185 ff. where Poseidon implies that he and Hades are masters in their own kingdoms. The three brothers each rule over an area of the world, sky, sea or underworld (earth and Olympus are common to all three) and Poseidon claims that he is ὁμότιμος and ἰσόμορος with Zeus (186 and 209). This partition of the world-areas is the result not of the fiat of Zeus, but of an impersonal drawing of lots. Fate[1] governs the initial partition of privileges, but

---

[1] The Homeric account of the relationship between Zeus and fate is complex and not without ambiguity. The will of Zeus and fate are sometimes *contrasted*, as in the well-known passage where Zeus debates with himself whether to save Sarpedon when he is fated to die (*Il.* 16 433 ff., cf. 22 168 ff. when Hector is about to die). This passage seems to imply that Zeus could, if he chose, alter a man's destiny (though he does not in fact do so, and we may contrast *Od.* 3 236 ff. where Athena tells Telemachus that not even the gods are able to rescue a man who is dear to them 'when the deadly fate of woeful death seizes him'). On the other hand, there are occasions when fate and the will of Zeus are *equated*, as, for example, at *Il.* 21 82 ff. where Lycaon says to Achilles: 'now again a deadly fate (μοῖρ' ὀλοή) has put me in your hands. I must surely be hated by father Zeus, who has thus given me up to you a second time', and compare those passages which speak of 'the fate of Zeus' (Διὸς αἶσα), *Il.* 17 321, *Od.* 9 52, cf. μοῖρα θεοῦ or θεῶν, *Od.* 11 292, 3 269. Again 'fate' sometimes seems to be an expression of Zeus' will and under his direct control, as at *Il.* 6 357 ff. where Helen says that Zeus 'imposed' (ἐπί...θῆκε) an evil fate (μόρον) on herself and Paris (cf. *Il.* 24 527 ff. where Zeus hands out good and evil gifts (δῶρα) from the two jars on the floor of his palace). 'Fate' and 'the will of Zeus' provide in some sense complementary, in another sense alternative accounts of why things happen as they do. Cf., for example, Onians, part 3, chs. 6–8, where the evidence is discussed at length.

this is then a distribution which all three brothers should respect, like a contract.[1] Then in Hesiod we find an account of how Zeus acquired power, and in this he becomes king by virtue of a victory over the Titans which is only achieved with the help of the other gods. After this victory, the other gods 'on the advice of Earth' 'urged' Zeus to rule and be king, and he then assigned to them their various privileges (*Th.* 881 ff.). In this version of the story, then, it is clear that Zeus acquires his supreme position with the consent of the other gods.

The picture of the society of the gods, ruled over by the supreme king Zeus, is drawn in great detail and with the utmost realism in Homer and Hesiod. But how far can this conception be said to contain the germ of cosmological theories? The subjects of the images which we have discussed are not cosmological elements or primary constituent substances, so much as fully personified deities. Moreover, the notion of the gods forming a *society* follows naturally from the conception of the gods themselves in the form of *men*. Yet having noted this major difference between the notion of the society of the gods in pre-philosophical literature and the use of social images in the Presocratics, we may go on to suggest where the images which we have considered do resemble the later use of the idea of social order in cosmological doctrines. We should not forget the links between some, at least, of the major Olympian gods and what we should call natural phenomena. Though Zeus, Poseidon and Hephaestus cannot be seen as cosmological 'principles', they are intimately connected with the sky, the sea and fire. It is true that the relationship between them and these phenomena is never closely defined, and indeed it seems to vary on different occasions. Mostly the gods are spoken of as the beings which control the phenomena (as when Zeus is described as gathering and

---

[1] Cf. the interesting discussion of the role of Moira, Lachesis and the Great Oath of the gods in Cornford, *1*, ch. 1, though Cornford's interpretation would now, I think, generally be considered too speculative.

scattering the clouds, or Poseidon as stirring up the sea), but in some cases the name of the god is also used to refer to the phenomena themselves as if the two were sometimes identified (as when 'Zeus' stands for heaven, and 'Hephaestus' for fire). But the account of the lottery of the sons of Cronos, for example, may be said to describe, in mythical terms, the arrangement which *regulates the relationships between the powers which inhabit* the sky, the sea and the underworld, even if not the relationships between these *world-areas* themselves. No doubt the notion of the supremacy of Zeus, and the contrasting, though still rudimentary, idea of the contract which governs certain of the relations between the gods, are beliefs which have above all a moral and religious significance in Homer and Hesiod. But in certain contexts the conception of the society of the gods may be said to have a certain quasi-cosmological significance as well, at least in so far as some of the gods are connected, or even identified, with world-areas or with what we should call natural phenomena.

We have considered one set of beliefs—the conception of the gods forming a society—which reflects experience of men's own social organisation. The second set of beliefs which I wish to consider here is ultimately derived from the experience of life itself. It is common knowledge that the ancient Greeks (like most primitive peoples) often referred to what we should call inanimate objects as if they had a life and will of their own: but it is far more difficult to say what such references imply.[1] How far, if at all, did the ancient Greeks distinguish between the animate and the inanimate spheres in the pre-philosophical period? Certain distinctions between different modes of existence have surely always been recognised. No one can fail to recognise the fact of death (the difference between the living and the dead animal) though it may be common to wish to minimise its significance and to believe in an existence after death similar in as many respects as possible to life itself. In Homer, the dead man's body is

---

[1] On the Greek use of personification in general, cf. Webster, *1*.

called at one point (*Iliad* 24 54) 'dumb earth' (κωφὴ γαῖα) though the ghost survives death. The Homeric term for life, ψυχή, is also the term for 'ghost', and it is used in the former sense only of men and of animals (e.g. *Od.* 14 426). But if Homer never uses ψυχή of other objects, neither he nor Hesiod ever has occasion to refer to *inanimate* objects as such, as ἄψυχα. If we take a variety of objects and phenomena, e.g. stones, earth, rivers, the sea, the winds, lightning, and the stars, and ask whether, or in what sense, each of them was considered 'alive', the answers we should give would, I think, vary quite considerably.[1] Many natural phenomena, especially those associated with movement of some sort, are, of course, 'personified' in Homer and Hesiod, but by itself this tells us little about how the object was conceived.[2] We should bear in mind that many other things besides natural phenomena are personified in early Greek literature, as, for example, moral qualities and acts ('Lawlessness', 'Murder', Hes. *Th.* 226 ff.) and even sensations such as Pain and Hunger (Hes. *ibid.*). Nor should we underestimate the degree of conscious allegorising in some personifications, as, for instance, in the elaborate description of Prayers and Infatuation in Phoenix's speech at *Iliad* 9 502 ff.[3] As regards what we call natural phenomena, it would, I suggest, be a mistake to assume that the early Greeks necessarily had a single,

---

[1] Artificial objects raise further problems. Spears are, of course, described as 'longing to taste flesh' (λιλαιομένη χροὸς ἆσαι, e.g. *Il.* 21 168) and bronze is 'pitiless' (*Il.* 3 292) in Homer, but these seem to be stock expressions which have already lost much of their original force: cf. KR, p. 97, n. 1.

[2] The term 'personification' itself may be misleading. Frankfort (2, p. 14) rejected it, at any rate as applied to primitive beliefs: 'Primitive man simply does not know an inanimate world. For this very reason he does not 'personify' inanimate phenomena nor does he fill an empty world with the ghosts of the dead, as 'animism' would have us believe.' I have retained the term, but use it without implying that personification is a *conscious* process of attributing life to the inanimate.

[3] 'Prayers (λιταί) are the daughters of great Zeus: they are halting and wrinkled; they look aside and take care to follow in the steps of Infatuation. Infatuation (ἄτη) is mighty and swift-footed so that she far outruns all the prayers and goes before them all over the earth bringing men to their ruin.' For an interpretation of the details of this allegory, see Leaf's notes to *vv.* 502 and 503.

precisely defined conception of each phenomenon. On the contrary, a single phenomenon is often described in a whole series of what seem, to our way of thinking, incompatible images. Sleep, for example, is personified as the 'all-tamer' who lays hold on people (αἱρεῖ or λαμβάνει), the twin brother of Death (*Iliad* 24 4 f., 16 672, etc.): on the other hand, we also find that sleep may be 'poured over' a person (τῷ δ' ὕπνον...χεύῃ ἐπὶ βλεφάροισιν, *Iliad* 14 164 f.) or that it 'wraps' a person round and 'binds' him (ὕπνου...ὅς μ' ἐπέδησε φίλα βλέφαρ' ἀμφικαλύψας, *Od.* 23 16 f.). None of these can be considered *the* definitive description of sleep. Each image illustrates the phenomenon under a different aspect, though each, if pressed, would seem to imply a slightly different conception of the nature of sleep. But the fact that no difficulty was experienced in reconciling these different images is shown by the way in which they may be combined in a single passage.[1] They should, then, be treated as *complementary*, rather than as *alternative*, conceptions of the same phenomenon.[2] The same is true of the descriptions of other natural phenomena as well: the same phenomenon may be referred to *both* as a living being with a will of its own, *and* as a material object directed or controlled by the will of some other being. Lightning and thunder, for example, are personified as two of the children of Earth at Hes. *Th.* 139 ff.: yet elsewhere they are more often described as the 'shafts' (βέλη or κῆλα) or 'implements' (ὅπλα) of Zeus which he holds in his hands or shoots (e.g. *Th.* 707 f., 853 f.).

One way, but not always the only way, in which many particular natural phenomena were conceived, was as living

---

[1] E.g. *Il.* 23 62 f., and cf. the speech in which the personified Sleep refers to himself as 'poured over' the mind of Zeus (*Il.* 14 252 f.).

[2] Cf. Wilson in Frankfort, *2*, pp. 53 f. Wilson remarks that the ancient Egyptian could view the sky equally well as supported by posts *or* as held up by a god *or* as resting on walls *or* as a cow *or* as a goddess whose arms and feet touch the earth. 'Any one of these pictures would be satisfactory to him, according to his approach, and in a single picture he might show two different supports for the sky: the goddess whose arms and feet reach the earth, and the god who holds up the sky-goddess.' Cf. further Frankfort, *1*, Index under 'Multiplicity of Approaches'.

beings with wills of their own. In Homer, rivers, winds, the sun, Heaven and Earth are among the deities who are called to witness oaths or addressed in prayers as if they had the power to influence events.[1] And besides those passages in which various phenomena are themselves personified, there are others which refer more vaguely to the presence of living beings in the world.[2] Certain obscure or rare phenomena, though not themselves personified, are often attributed to the presence of a god. Thus in a number of passages earthquakes or subterranean shocks are associated with a god, particularly with Poseidon.[3] But if living beings figure prominently in pre-philosophical accounts of what we should call natural phenomena in several different roles, we should observe that neither in Homer nor in Hesiod is there any positive evidence that the world itself was conceived as a living creature. The early Greeks probably assumed that the world is 'alive' only in the sense that it is peopled with living beings, not in the sense that it forms an organic whole: the latter idea, which is implicit in several Presocratic cosmological doctrines, may be a natural extension of the belief that individual phenomena are alive, but so far as we know, this generalisation was not made, in ancient Greece, before the philosophers themselves.

If many natural phenomena were, or could be, conceived as alive, we should also consider the way in which the origins of things were sometimes described in terms of biological generation, for this too is important for our understanding of subsequent cosmological theories. The most extensive pre-philosophical example of this is, of course, Hesiod's *Theogony*. At *Th.* 108 ff. Hesiod invokes the Muses to 'tell how first came into being (γένοντο)[4] the gods and the earth and the

---

[1] E.g. *Il.* 3 276 ff., 15 36 ff., 19 258 ff., 23 194 ff., *Od.* 5 445 ff.

[2] There are, of course, many passages in our early texts which refer to the nymphs who *inhabit* the Ocean, mountains, groves, springs, meadows and caves, e.g. *Il.* 6 420, 18 37 ff., 20 7 ff.; *Od.* 12 318.

[3] E.g. *Il.* 20 57 f. ('then from below Poseidon shook the immense earth and the steep peaks of the mountains'), cf. *Il.* 13 18 f.

[4] Here, as elsewhere in the *Theogony*, γίγνομαι may well retain something of its original connotation 'to be born'.

rivers and the immense sea...and the shining stars and the wide heaven above' and he goes on to give an account of the origin of these and many other things as well. Zeus and the Olympians, the rivers, the winds, the stars, Strife and her children (Pain, Forgetfulness, etc.) are all interrelated in one vast and complex genealogical tree. The repeated references to sexual intercourse leave no doubt that the generation of these various figures is thought of, as a rule, in simple biological images. At 378 ff., for instance, Dawn bears certain winds and stars to Astraios, 'a goddess bedded with a god in love'. κύεσθαι and ὑποκύεσθαι are used of goddesses conceiving (125, 308, 405, 411),[1] γείνασθαι and τίκτειν of their bearing children (e.g. 133, 139)—the latter also of gods begetting children, e.g. 287—and ἐν φιλότητι μιγῆναι (e.g. 375), and other expressions, of the parents uniting in love. Nor are such terms by any means confined to passages dealing with the Olympians or other gods who were generally conceived anthropomorphically. Earth 'bears' the mountains at 129, and Dawn the stars at 381 f. It is true that there are certain passages which have been taken as exceptions to the general rule of sexual reproduction. At 126 ff., Earth produces a number of offspring, including Heaven himself, 'without delightful love' (ἄτερ φιλότητος ἐφιμέρου, 132) and at 211 ff. Night produces Death, Sleep and other children 'without having slept with anyone' (οὔ τινι κοιμηθεῖσα, 213). But the image is only slightly different on these two occasions, and it is still a biological one. Earth and Night both 'bring forth' their offspring, the verb used being τέκε (131 and 213). The picture here seems, in fact, to be one of parthenogenetic reproduction. We may compare the way in which Hera is said to produce Hephaestus at 927 ff., 'not uniting in love' (οὐ φιλότητι μιγεῖσα).[2] It is only at the very

---

[1] Even more strikingly Earth produces the Erinyes and other offspring at 184 from the blood of the emasculated Ouranos περιπλομένων ἐνιαυτῶν, i.e. after a period of gestation.

[2] Cf. also the common myth of the birth of Athena from Zeus (although in Hesiod's version of *this*, *Th.* 886 ff., Prudence, Μῆτις, first conceives Athena by Zeus, but is then swallowed by Zeus as she is about to bear her child).

beginning of the theogonical account, 116–22, where the 'coming-to-be' of Chaos, Earth and Eros is described, that there is some doubt as to whether the image is a biological one: and indeed the sense of this passage is particularly obscure.[1] At 123, however, Erebos and Night 'come to be' from Chaos, and then Night *unites* with Erebos *in love* and *conceives* and *bears* Aither and Day (124 f.) and from that point on the imagery is unmistakably biological. How far, in any given context, Hesiod may have used such terms as 'conceive' and 'bear' as deliberate 'metaphors', or how far they are to be understood 'literally', is a question we can hardly hope to answer. But whether or not Hesiod at times *consciously* adopted a biological model for coming-to-be, this *is* the model on which the whole account of the origin of things in the *Theogony* is based, and as such, the *Theogony*, for all the crudity of its images and the arbitrariness of its mythology, may be considered the first in a long line of Greek texts in which the origins of things are accounted for in largely biological terms.

Besides the frequent and important assumption that

[1] Chaos may be taken to mean 'chasm' or 'yawning gap', but whether it refers specifically to an original separation of sky and earth must be considered doubtful. Such was Cornford's interpretation (*10*, pp. 193 ff.), accepted in the main by KR, pp. 24 ff., but attractive as it is, its difficulties cannot be ignored. (1) Nothing in Hesiod definitely says that Chaos is the gap between heaven and earth. On this view, then, as KR point out (p. 29), we must suppose that the idea that these two were originally one mass was so common that Hesiod could take it for granted. (2) If Chaos is to be understood as the gap between heaven and earth, the reference to Earth 'coming-to-be' after it (*Th.* 116 f.) seems odd, and that to Earth *bearing* Heaven (126 f.) intolerable. Cornford tried to avoid the major difficulty by stressing the epithet which qualifies Heaven in 127, ἀστερόεις, 'starry' ('filled with the visible heavenly bodies', as he put it, *10*, p. 195). Yet this is hardly satisfactory. ἀστερόεις is a stock epithet of heaven (cf. *Il.* 4 44) and when used elsewhere in the *Theogony* (106, 414, 463, 470, 891) carries no special significance. Besides, the generation of the Sun, Moon and Stars is explicitly described at 371 ff., 381 f., and if this passage is, as it seems to be, an integral part of the *Theogony*, it can hardly be reconciled with Cornford's suggestion that the significance of 126 f. lies in its referring to the presence of the heavenly bodies in the sky. Yet if Cornford's interpretation of 'Chaos' is open to certain objections, it must be granted that on any alternative view the meaning of χάος γένετο is quite vague and obscure, though perhaps not more so than many other mythological accounts purporting to describe the ultimate origin of all things.

certain things are, in some sense, alive, we should also consider how some obscure phenomena were conceived in terms of what we should call material objects where there is no apparent implication that the phenomena have wills of their own. I have already remarked that the two rather different types of images may be used of the same phenomenon, as sleep, for example, is not only personified as a being with a will of its own, but also described as something which is 'poured over' a person. But many natural objects and phenomena which were, no doubt, difficult to apprehend, seem to have been conceived partly in terms of familiar material objects. Thus the description of the sky as 'brazen' or 'iron' suggests that it was thought of as a bright, solid object.[1] Often, of course, such images convey some notion of the divine purposes which phenomena may serve. Many objects are imagined as the *instruments* of the gods. One of the most obvious examples is that of lightning and thunder which are explicitly called the 'arms' or 'tools' of Zeus in Hesiod (*Th.* 853), but the conception of disease and death as the 'darts' of Apollo or Artemis is also worth noting. When the plague attacks the Achaean camp at *Iliad* 1 43 ff. there is a vivid description of Apollo coming down from the heights of Olympus 'angry at heart, with his bow and close-covered quiver on his back. The arrows clanged on his shoulders.... Then he sat apart from the ships and let loose an arrow and there was a dreadful clanging from his silver bow. First he attacked the mules and the swift dogs, and then he aimed and shot his piercing missiles at the men themselves. And the innumerable pyres of the dead burned continually.' True, most of the details in this graphic picture have been supplied by the poet's imagination. But the basic image which is used to describe the plague itself is by no means completely fantastic: the image of *darts* conveys both the suddenness of

[1] E.g. χάλκεος, *Il.* 17 425; πολύχαλκος, 5 504; σιδήρεος, *Od.* 15 329. As KR note (p. 10), 'solidity as well as brightness is presumably conveyed by these metallic epithets'. Cf. also the description of Atlas holding up the broad heaven (*Th.* 517 ff.).

the onset of the disease, and the pain it causes (as we too use the metaphor 'darting' pain). Homer leaves no doubt as to the divine origin and purpose of the plague (Apollo wishes to punish the Achaeans for slighting his priest Chryses), but though here, as so often in Homer, the emphasis is on *why* a phenomenon occurs, his description also conveys a conception of the nature of the phenomenon itself:[1] the image of the darts not only fits the notion of the divine purpose of the disease, but also expresses a general idea of what the disease itself is like.[2] Elsewhere in Homer the image of darts is modified when sudden, painless deaths are represented as being caused by the 'gentle arrows' of a god or goddess (e.g. *Od.* 11 172 f.), and we find that death itself is described in a variety of concrete images, as a bond which ties a man, or as a band or wrapping which encloses or covers him.[3] No doubt at this stage such images were never *deliberately* formulated in order to provide a satisfactory picture of the nature of the phenomena concerned, and their actual origin is often difficult to guess. Yet clearly it was generally by means of simple concrete images drawn from familiar experience that the nature of such obscure phenomena as death and diseases was apprehended.

Finally, we may note certain occasions when various things are represented not just as material objects, but more specifically as *artefacts*. Nowhere in Homer or Hesiod do we find the idea that the world itself is an artefact, the creation of a craftsman-god, such as we have in later Greek philosophy. Yet in certain limited contexts this type of imagery is already used in pre-philosophical texts to describe the origins of

---

[1] We should note the realistic detail that the plague attacks the animals in the camp, the mules and dogs, before the men.

[2] Cf. Hes. *Op.* 102 ff. where a different aspect of diseases—their unpredictability—is illustrated: 'they roam αὐτόματοι (at will) bringing evils to men, in silence, for wise Zeus took away their voices'.

[3] One striking image for death occurs at *Il.* 16 502 f.: ὡς ἄρα μιν εἰπόντα τέλος θανάτοιο κάλυψεν | ὀφθαλμοὺς ῥῖνάς θ'. Whatever τέλος means here, it is clearly imagined as something material which 'covers the eyes and nostrils'. On this and other images for death, see Onians, pp. 327 ff., 422 ff.

particular things. Perhaps the most striking instance is the story of Pandora, the first woman, which occurs twice in Hesiod (*Op.* 59 ff.; *Th.* 570 ff.). On both occasions, Pandora is *manufactured* by the craftsman-god Hephaestus. First he mixes water and earth together, and then he 'moulds' the figure: the verbs used, πλάσσειν in *Op.* 70, συμπλάσσειν in *Th.* 571, might suggest such images as that of a potter moulding a clay figure before firing it, or a baker kneading dough. Similar technological images are also sometimes used in describing the origins of certain natural phenomena. At Hes. *Th.* 140 f., for example, the personified Thunder, Lightning and 'Arges' (Bright One) are said to give Zeus the thunder and to make, or rather to forge (τεῦξαν) for him the thunderbolt. In both Homer and Hesiod quite a lively interest is shown in the technology of the day (as many Homeric similes testify). But for reasons which lie partly, no doubt, in the status of the craftsman in early Greek society,[1] the supreme god Zeus is not usually represented as a craftsman himself (it is notable that in the story of Pandora he directs Hephaestus what to do). Yet if it is only quite rarely that phenomena are conceived as artefacts in pre-philosophical literature, the passages we have mentioned may be considered the first examples of a type of imagery which was later to be developed and used extensively in Greek philosophy.

Much has necessarily been omitted from this survey of early Greek representations of the world and of particular natural phenomena, but I have illustrated some of the main types of images which figure in these representations. We have seen how pre-philosophical Greek beliefs and intuitions about the external world are built up from conceptions which are derived (consciously or unconsciously) from different features of their experience, whether of universal human experience, or of the particular circumstances of early Greek society. Like most, if not all, primitive peoples, the ancient Greeks often attributed life, or more particularly the power to influence

[1] See Finley, pp. 71 f.

events, to many objects which we should class as inanimate, and often, too, they represented obscure phenomena in terms of certain more familiar material objects (as we noted in some descriptions of death and diseases, for example). Again the notion that the gods, the supernatural forces which largely control the outcome of events, form a society like that of men, is one which, in different forms, is common to many peoples. But then we may also observe how the *particular circumstances* of early Greek society are mirrored in their beliefs about the world. In Homer, the description of the supreme ruler Zeus tallies closely with that of the autocratic kings on earth. We may note the absence of any notion of democratic, or even true oligarchic, government alike from the Homeric world-picture and from Homeric society itself. Again we are not surprised that the supreme god is no craftsman-creator, considering the low status of the craftsman in Homeric society. On the other hand the Homeric chiefs were skilled in the arts of war, and several phenomena are represented as the weapons or missiles of Zeus and the other gods.

In discussing the role of similes and comparisons in pre-philosophical literature, I noted particularly how these were used to conceive and describe the unknown—what is new or strange or difficult to grasp. Our examination of some early Greek beliefs about the external world provides many further illustrations of the way in which obscure phenomena, and the hidden or underlying relations between things as a whole, were conceived and understood by means of concrete images derived from aspects of familiar experience (whether there was a conscious element of comparison in these images or not). It is against the background of this extensive use of imagery and comparisons in pre-philosophical literature that the use of analogies in the philosophers must now be examined. We shall consider first the use of certain types of metaphor and imagery in their general cosmological doctrines, noting in particular both where these depart from, and where they may be said to follow, the patterns set by pre-philosophical beliefs.

CHAPTER IV

METAPHOR AND IMAGERY IN GREEK COSMOLOGICAL THEORIES

SOCIAL AND POLITICAL IMAGES:
THE COSMOS AS A STATE

The first group of images which I wish to consider consists of those in which the relations between cosmological substances are described in terms drawn from social or political organisation.[1] Now there is, as we saw, an extensive and detailed pre-philosophical use of social imagery in describing the relations between the *gods*. In so far as some of the Olympians are intimately connected with such phenomena as the sky and the sea, to that extent such imagery may be said to be used to describe the relations between the powers which inhabit and control certain world-areas, if not those between the world-areas themselves. On the other hand, these gods were, of course, regularly conceived *anthropomorphically*: the notions of rule, of rights and privileges, of mutual obligations and so on, are applied not to abstract cosmological factors, but to gods conceived in the form of men, and it is, no doubt, because they were conceived in the form of men, that these social and political images were so readily applied to them. In the philosophers, one major development should be noted straight away. As is well known, a devastating attack on the anthropomorphic conception of the gods was made by Xenophanes.[2] And thereafter we find Empedocles, for example, rejecting the attribution of human form to the 'holy, unutterable Mind'

---

[1] Many of the most important images of this type have been discussed in two articles by Vlastos (*2* and *5*), and cf. also Gomperz, *2*.

[2] E.g. Fr. 15 ('If oxen and horses and lions had hands and could draw with their hands and produce works of art like men, horses would draw the forms of the gods like horses, and oxen like oxen, and they would make their bodies such as each of them had themselves'). Cf. also Frr. 14, 16 and 23.

which 'darts with swift thoughts all over the world'.[1] But if the traditional conception of gods in the form of men was rejected either explicitly or implicitly by the philosophers, both the Presocratics and Plato nevertheless used imagery derived from various aspects of social organisation very widely in their cosmological doctrines, and indeed it may be argued that the development of certain important cosmological theories is closely linked with the use of certain types of social and political images. First, then, we may consider what ideas were expressed by means of such images. And then we must also tackle the much more difficult question of the status of these images *qua* images: how far did the philosophers themselves recognise any element of transference in their application of social and political conceptions to cosmological problems? Several commentators have suggested that in certain ancient Near Eastern societies (notably in Mesopotamia and Egypt) not only was Nature understood in terms of Society, but there was simply no conscious distinction drawn between the realm of Nature on the one hand and the realm of Society on the other.[2] In Greece, one distinction that was certainly drawn by the end of the fifth century, at least, was that between what is 'natural' (φύσει) and what is 'customary' or 'conventional' (νόμῳ) and indeed the boundaries between these two categories were very actively debated in a number of different contexts, not only in the purely ethical sphere, but also in connection with theories concerning the origins of civilisation, the origin of language and so on.[3] But the question that concerns us here is whether or in what sense the Presocratics recognised the political and social notions which they used in their cosmologies as *images*. In many cases our evidence hardly permits us to answer this

---

[1] Fr. 134. Cf. Frr. 27–9 on the Sphere, the world under the rule of Love.

[2] This interpretation has been developed by Kelsen, e.g. pp. 40 ff., especially, and cf. also Frankfort, *1*, and *2*, pp. 12 ff.

[3] See especially the monograph of Heinimann, *1*, and Pohlenz's article, *2*. (I have considered above, pp. 124 f., some of the evidence which suggests that these debates were sometimes carried on as if the two views presented an exhaustive choice.)

question with certainty. But some light will be thrown on the problem if we consider the way in which these and other types of images or figurative accounts are used in the extant texts of the Presocratics.

The first instance of a cosmological doctrine expressed in social terms occurs in our earliest extant philosophical text, Fr. 1 of Anaximander. The key sentence (and the main part of the fragment which is fairly certainly authentic)[1] runs: διδόναι γὰρ αὐτὰ δίκην καὶ τίσιν ἀλλήλοις τῆς ἀδικίας κατὰ τὴν τοῦ χρόνου τάξιν[2] (Simp. *in Ph.* 24 19 f.). Although the subject of this sentence is doubtful, it is generally agreed that the fragment has a cosmological significance. The sentence seems to refer to the restoration of an equilibrium between equal opposed factors of some sort (the opposed substances which make up the differentiated world, as KR (p. 118) put it), and not, probably, between the innumerable worlds and the Boundless itself as Theophrastus appears to have thought.[3] But this idea of a restoration of a cosmological equilibrium is expressed entirely in social or legal terminology: when an injustice (ἀδικία) is committed, the penalty (δίκη) and recompense (τίσις) must be paid, according to the assessment or ordering (τάξις) of time. Though it is unclear precisely what cosmological processes Anaximander may have had in mind,[4] the literal meaning of his statement is clear enough. As often in pre-philosophical texts, it is in terms of certain social relations that the relations between other things (here,

---

[1] The extent of the fragment is disputed. The sentence I quote is generally taken to derive from Anaximander himself, although some scholars (e.g. Vlastos) have considered the last five words doubtful. See most recently *HGP*, I, p. 77, n. 1.

[2] 'For they pay the penalty and recompense to one another for their injustice, according to the assessment of time.'

[3] Cf., however, Vlastos, *2*, pp. 170 ff., who suggests (p. 172) that 'reabsorption into the Boundless is only the process which insures full reparation among the opposites themselves; the damages are paid not to the Boundless but to *one another*'.

[4] As Burnet (*3*, pp. 57 f.) and others have noted, the cycle of the seasons probably provides the best example of an interaction of the type which Anaximander's fragment appears to describe.

cosmological factors) are understood. But if there is this general similarity, there are also fundamental differences, between Anaximander's fragment and all the earlier Greek uses of social images which we noted. First and foremost it deals not with supernatural, anthropomorphic deities, but with cosmological forces of some sort, and secondly the specific image is new. Anaximander refers not to the *supreme power* of an autocratic king (such as Zeus is, in Homer and Hesiod), but to the *rule of law*, which regulates the relationships between several factors which are *all of equal status*. And one should observe that the nature of the image used by Anaximander is of far more than incidental importance, since it enables him to express (for the first time, perhaps) the notion of self-regulating cosmological relationships, i.e. an idea of cosmological *order*.[1] The alternating cycle of 'justice' and 'retribution' does not hang on the arbitrary whim of a despotic ruler: it is guaranteed by the rule of law which operates among equals.

The evidence from later philosophers is fuller and more certain, and we may distinguish three different types of political images which convey different conceptions of the relationships between cosmological substances. First, there is the image of Strife or War, secondly, that of Justice or a contract between equals, and thirdly, that of the supreme rule of a single principle. Very roughly speaking, one may say that the first describes the world, or the relationships between certain things in it, in terms of a state of constant aggression, if not one of anarchy, the second in terms of an oligarchy or limited democracy, and the third in terms of a monarchy.

(1) In Anaximander's fragment, the 'penalty' which certain things pay one another is requital for an injustice of which they are guilty, and this already suggests that Anaximander imagined that cosmic forces commit acts of aggression, as it were, against one another. In Empedocles, Strife

---

[1] Cf. especially Vlastos, 2, pp. 168 ff. and 5, pp. 361 ff.

(Νεῖκος) causes disruption among the 'roots' or elements,[1] although its activities are counterbalanced by those of the opposite cosmic principle, Love. But it is Heraclitus who expresses most forcibly the notion of the role of War and Strife in the cosmos. Many fragments state or illustrate the doctrine of the unity of opposites, and in particular the notion of the interaction between them. To mention just two examples, Fr. 126 says that 'cold things become warm, what is warm becomes cool, the wet becomes dry and the dry wet', and Fr. 51 puts it more generally: 'they do not understand how by being at variance it agrees with itself'. But this interaction between opposites is described in the metaphors of War (πόλεμος) and Strife (ἔρις). In Fr. 80 (which may well be a deliberate amendment of Fr. 1 of Anaximander, cf. KR, p. 195) Heraclitus says: 'One must realise that war is common (ξυνόν) and justice (or right, δίκη) is strife, and everything happens through strife and necessity.' And in Fr. 53 the metaphor of War occurs again: 'war is the father of all and the king of all...'.[2]

The teaching of these fragments of Heraclitus is unequivocal: war or strife, that is the interaction between opposites, is universal. But Heraclitus also uses a second set of images which illustrates the doctrine of the interdependence of opposites from a different point of view. Whereas, according to Fr. 80, 'everything happens through strife and necessity', other fragments refer to the role of *justice* and *law* in the world. Fr. 94 puts it that 'the sun will not overstep his limits; otherwise the Erinyes, the servants of Justice (Δίκη), will find him out'. The precise significance of these 'limits', μέτρα, is

---

[1] At the same time, however, Strife may bring different parts of the same element together. Though this is not explicitly stated in Empedocles' extant fragments, Aristotle (*Metaph.* 985a 23 ff.) suggests that Strife and Love each have dual roles (that is, Love unites the different elements, but causes disruption between the parts of the same element).

[2] Cf. also Aristotle, *EE* 1235a 25 ff., DK 22 A 22: 'and Heraclitus rebukes the poet who wrote "may strife perish from among gods and men" [*Il.* 18 107]; for there could be no harmony without high and low notes, nor living beings without male and female which are opposites'.

rather obscure, nor is it certain whether 'the sun' here stands for the heavenly body, or for fire, the cosmological principle, or indeed for both.[1] It is clear, however, that in this fragment Heraclitus uses the term δίκη—justice, or what is right, or more simply, the way things are—to refer to certain norms governing the behaviour of various objects in the physical world. And then Fr. 114 includes this passage: 'All human laws are nourished by the single divine law. For it has as much power as it wishes, and is enough for all, with something to spare.' And it is likely that this refers to the doctrine of the unity of opposites, among other things. Although 'everything happens through strife', the interaction between opposites is, nevertheless, in some sense orderly: and Heraclitus' use of the term κόσμος, 'order'/'world-order', in Fr. 30, seems to bear this out.[2] The phrase in Fr. 80 καὶ δίκην ἔριν (sc. εἰδέναι χρή) may itself be read equally well in two senses, (i) as a correction of Anaximander's doctrine: what Anaximander called 'justice' is, in truth, a strife, a constant interaction between opposites, or (ii) as an assertion of the regularity of the rule of Strife: Strife is what is customary, right, just; and it may well be, of course, that this ambiguity is intentional.[3] Heraclitus' use of social metaphors is, then, a complex one. The metaphors of *War* and *Strife* describe the interaction between opposites which he believes to be general throughout the world: but this interaction is itself normal, and so we hear of *justice* at work in the world, and of a single divine *law*.

(2) 'Justice', 'rule' and 'power' are used very often in Presocratic philosophy as terms to describe the relations

---

[1] Cf. Fr. 30, where the 'world-order' itself is said to be an 'ever-living fire, kindling in measures and going out in measures' (here μέτρα is the term for 'measures').

[2] On the development of the meaning of κόσμος in early Greek philosophy, see especially Kranz, *2* and *3*; Kirk, *1*, pp. 311 ff. and KR, p. 159; Kahn, pp. 219 ff.; *HGP*, I, pp. 206 ff. and 454 f.; and Kerschensteiner, *2*.

[3] See also Fr. 23, and cf. Fr. 102 which rejects mankind's use of the categories of 'just' and 'unjust' things: 'to god all things are beautiful and good and just, but men have thought that some things are unjust, others just'.

between cosmological substances of different sorts, but the conceptions which such terms may be used to convey vary. On the one hand a number of cosmic substances may be imagined as being of equal rank or status (their relationships may be regulated by some sort of contract between them, for example). Or on the other hand a single substance may be imagined as having supreme power (though it may exercise this power benevolently, and may secure 'justice' in the world in the role of supreme judge). The former idea seems to be implicit already in Anaximander's fragment, but it is expressed more clearly first in Parmenides, and then, in rather more detail, in Empedocles.[1]

In the *Way of Truth* Parmenides twice refers to a personified Δίκη[2] though neither passage enables us to define his conception very precisely. In the Proem (Fr. 1 14) he refers to 'avenging Justice' who controls the gates of Night and Day. And in Fr. 8 12 ff. he says: 'Nor will the force of conviction allow that from what is not anything should come to be, besides what is. For this end, Justice does not loosen its fetters or let it come to be or pass away, but holds it fast.' Elsewhere when he expresses his conviction that 'what is' cannot be other than it is, he speaks of Fate (Μοῖρα) and Necessity ('Ανάγκη) 'binding' or 'holding' it (Fr. 8 30 f. and 37), and it would appear, then, that Parmenides believed that

---

[1] Alcmaeon, too, emphasised the importance of equality between opposites, but not, so far as we know, in a cosmological context, only in connection with a medical theory. Aetius (v 30 1, DK 24 B 4) reports that he held that the ἰσονομία (equality of rights) of the different 'powers' in the body (e.g. wet, dry, hot, cold, etc.) maintained health, while the μοναρχία (supreme rule) of one of them caused sickness, and thereafter the idea that disease is caused by what has too much power in the body (e.g. τὸ κρέσσον and cf. also the common use of κρατέειν and δύναμις itself) became a commonplace of Greek pathological theory (e.g. *VM* chs. 14, 19 and 22; *CMG* I, 1 45 18 ff., 50 13 ff., 53 1 ff.). Moreover some of the Hippocratic authors who put forward cosmological theories used political imagery similar to that of the philosophers in this connection. Thus the author of *On Breaths*, for example, says with reference to air that it is 'in all things the greatest overlord (δυνάστης) of all' (*CMG* I, 1 92 21 f.). See further Vlastos, 5, pp. 344 ff., 363 ff.

[2] Again, as in Heraclitus, it is difficult to tell whether by Δίκη Parmenides meant Justice or more simply 'the way things are'.

Necessity, Fate and 'Justice' *combine* to ensure that 'what is' is as it is: that it is not only necessary and fated that 'what is' is ungenerated, indestructible, unchanging and so on, but also that it is just and right that it should be so.

While there is no extant reference to Justice itself in the *Way of Seeming*, Aetius (II 7 1; DK 28 A 37) identified the δαίμων who 'steers' all things (Fr. 12) with Justice and Necessity, and Necessity at least is certainly mentioned at Fr. 10 6 f. Moreover we can see one point at which the notion of justice is particularly relevant in this part of Parmenides' poem if we consider his account of the relationship between the two primary cosmological substances Light and Night. These are described as *equals* in Fr. 9: 'and when all things have been named Light and Night, and things have been assigned to each of them according to their powers (δυνάμεις), everything is full at once of Light and of dark Night, which are both equal, ἴσων ἀμφοτέρων'. Neither of these two has supreme power, and it seems likely that the relationship between them was thought of as a just one in which each respects the rights of the other: it may be that this relationship was conceived as regulated by some sort of contract or agreement undertaken between equals (for example), although so little of the *Way of Seeming* is extant that we cannot confirm that this was, in fact, Parmenides' conception.

The evidence for Empedocles is fuller. His six cosmological principles (earth, air, fire, water, Love and Strife) are all mentioned in Fr. 17 18 ff., and then at 27 ff. he goes on to note their *equality of status* (or that of Love and Strife, at least) :[1]

---

[1] Most scholars follow DK in taking ἴσά τε πάντα in Fr. 17 27 to refer to all six cosmological principles. It should be noted, however, that while *v.* 29 ('in turn they gain the upper hand as the time comes round') clearly applies to Love and Strife, it is doubtful whether it also refers, in any sense, to the four roots. The same verse occurs once again at Fr. 26 1, but here too the subject is not clear: while Fr. 26 3 evidently refers to the roots, 1–2 again seem better taken as referring to Love and Strife alone. But if Fr. 17 29 does *not* refer to the four roots, it may be that *v.* 27, too, refers to Love and Strife alone, and that we should take πάντα in that verse as adverbial (not 'they are all equal' so much as 'they—that is Love and Strife—are equal in every way').

they are 'equal, and of the same age, and each holds a different prerogative (τιμή) and has its own character; and in turn they gain the upper hand as the time comes round'. The image here may put one in mind of the passage in Homer (*Il.* 15 185 ff.) in which the relationship between the three brothers, Zeus, Poseidon and Hades, is described. Yet unlike the three sons of Cronos, Empedocles' cosmological forces Love and Strife are conceived as equals and of the same age. The difference is an important one: there is no single supreme ruler (like Zeus, who rules by virtue of primogeniture and superior force), but rather Love and Strife each take it in turns to predominate in the world.[1] The relationship between these two is further described, in Fr. 30, as being governed by an 'oath': there Strife 'leaped up to claim his prerogatives (τιμάς) as the time came round which was fixed for them alternately by a broad oath'. The extant fragments of the physical poem of Empedocles say no more about this 'broad oath',[2] but it seems to represent some sort of contract between Love and Strife, an agreement which they undertake voluntarily as equals, rather than a rule imposed upon them by any higher authority.[3] Here too, then, the relationship between

[1] Cf. also Fr. 128 in the *Purifications*, which refers to the time when Kupris is 'queen'.

[2] In the *Purifications* (Fr. 115), however, there is a reference to an 'ancient decree of the gods' which was 'sealed by broad oaths', where Empedocles goes on to speak of the penalties which await those δαίμονες who have sinned and become polluted with blood. The 'oath' here clearly refers to a religious rule, and the use of the same epithet 'broad' here and in Fr. 30 suggests the distinct possibility of a deliberate echo between the two passages. It should be noted, however, that while in Fr. 115 the 'decree' which applies to the δαίμονες is imposed on them by the *gods*, in Fr. 30 the 'oath' seems rather to represent an agreement which Love and Strife *themselves* undertake (see next note).

[3] KR (p. 332) reject the interpretation that Love and Strife swore the oath themselves, and suppose that Empedocles was guilty of an undetected confusion, 'at one moment asserting that the four elements and Love and Strife are alone ultimate, at another suggesting that even for them there are laws laid down which they cannot infringe'. But though we may find the image of the 'oath' unsatisfactory as an explanation of the change from the rule of Love to that of Strife, there is no need to suppose that Empedocles is guilty of inconsistency. Love and Strife are nowhere said to be subject to laws *imposed on them from above*. The point of the 'oath' is, surely, that it describes the relations between them

these two cosmological factors is conceived in social terms. Love and Strife, like Parmenides' Light and Night, are equals: moreover their relationship is regulated by an 'oath' or solemn, religious contract, and the importance of this social image in his cosmological account becomes apparent when we reflect that it is by this means that Empedocles describes the alternations between the rule of Love and the rule of Strife.[1]

(3) Political images are also used in connection with a third type of cosmological doctrine, the notion of a single supreme principle which controls and directs all things. The idea that the world is governed by a supreme guiding principle continues, of course, long after the philosophers had abandoned any belief in anthropomorphic gods. Sometimes we find the philosophers describing their cosmological principles in terms which directly recall the traditional titles of Zeus, as for example in Heraclitus Fr. 53, where *War* is said to be 'father of all and king (βασιλεύς) of all', although there may well be an element of conscious irony here. But the attributes of power (both physical force and political authority) and intelligence are often ascribed to cosmological factors. In Xenophanes, for instance, the 'one god' is described as 'swaying' or 'shaking' (κραδαίνει) 'all things by the thought of his mind, without effort' (Fr. 25) and he is 'greatest among gods and men' (Fr. 23), implying, no doubt, that he has both supreme force and supreme authority. Anaxagoras (Fr. 12) and Diogenes of Apollonia (Fr. 8) also emphasise the strength and intelligence of their principles Mind and Air (identified by Diogenes as 'what has intelligence' in Fr. 5), and some of the other terms they use in describing their principles have, or may have, more distinctly political associations. Thus Anaxagoras calls Mind αὐτο-κρατές, 'self-ruled', in Fr. 12, and he says that it 'controls' or 'has power over' (κρατεῖ) 'all things that have life', and that

without referring to any higher authority: their alternations are governed by a contract or treaty which they have made as equal, though opposite, powers.

[1] See further below, p. 228.

it 'controlled the whole rotation, so that it rotated in the beginning'. Diogenes, too, uses the term κρατεῖν, with its dual associations of force and authority, of Air, saying that 'by this all men are steered (κυβερνᾶσθαι) and it has power over all things (πάντων κρατεῖν)' (Fr. 5).

But the most notable metaphors of this type are undoubtedly those found in Plato, who uses them repeatedly in expressing his conviction that a rational guiding principle is at work in the world. In the *Timaeus* (47e f.) the world is said to have come to be from a combination of reason and necessity, and reason is represented as '*controlling* (ἄρχειν) necessity by persuading her to lead the greater part of those things that come to be towards what is best'. And in another context political imagery is used in connection with the Craftsman, who is said, for example, to *issue ordinances* (διαθεσμοθετεῖν, cf. διατάττειν 42 de) which are then carried out by the lesser deities. In the *Philebus*, 28c, Socrates says that 'all the wise men agree... that *reason is king* of heaven and earth' and he goes on to vindicate this belief: a 'wondrous intelligence' 'arranges and steers' the sum of things (28d), 'wisdom and reason' are the names of 'the cause which orders and arranges the years and seasons and months' (30c) and 'in the nature of Zeus', we are told, 'there is a *kingly* soul and a *kingly* reason, because of the power of the cause' (30d). In the *Laws* (896de), too, soul is said to *administer* (διοικεῖν) the heaven, the 'best soul' 'takes care of the whole cosmos and drives it on its course' (ἐπιμελεῖσθαι 897c, cf. ἐγκρατές 897b), and later there is a further brief reference to 'our *king*' who 'takes care of the whole' (904a) and by whom all things are arranged with a view to the preservation and excellence of the whole (903b).[1]

---

[1] A rather different notion is conveyed in the myth of the *Politicus* (268e ff.). There while the god who is described as the 'leader' of the universe (ὁ τῶν κινουμένων...πάντων ἡγούμενος, 269e 5 f.) is said to guide (συμποδηγεῖν, 269c 5, cf. 270a 3) and to rule over (ἄρχειν, 271d 3) the revolutions of the world in the *first* part of the cosmic cycle (the 'reign of Cronos', 269a 7 f.), in the *second* half of that cycle he 'lets it go' and the world revolves in the opposite direction of its own accord (269c 5 ff.), and it is in *this* period that we live now.

The political and social images which we have reviewed are obviously far from being merely vacuous ornaments of style, but we must now attempt to define more precisely the role which they played in the development of Greek cosmological speculation. Many of the images in question may, of course, have an ethical or religious significance. The term κόσμος itself, used for the world, tends to imply, and was certainly often used to convey, a belief that the whole is *well* arranged, and a similar conviction is also expressed, in a different form, both by the notion of a cosmic justice (in Anaximander, for example) and by the idea that the world is controlled by a supreme rational principle (as for instance the Mind of Anaxagoras). Heraclitus, for one, explicitly connected human νόμοι (laws and customs) with the 'one divine νόμος' (Fr. 114), and Plato's belief that the world is governed by Reason is, of course, reflected in a great deal of his moral philosophy.[1] But apart from their ethical or religious implications, the images of law, strife, rule and so on provided the means which enabled the early Greek philosophers to express a variety of cosmological doctrines. Time and again in the Presocratics and Plato, the nature of cosmological factors, or the relationships between them, are understood in terms of a concrete social or political situation. In Anaximander, the image is of wrongdoing and the reparation for wrongdoing; Heraclitus speaks of universal War and Strife; Empedocles' conception was that cosmological principles of equal status come to rule in turn, and Parmenides, too, had described his primary cosmological substances as equals in the *Way of Seeming*. Anaxagoras and Diogenes both held that an intelligent principle has supreme power over all things, and Plato, too, described the rational principle which he believed to be at work in the world in political metaphors, using the title 'king' and the epithet 'kingly' to describe

---

[1] Particularly notable is the doctrine expressed in the *Timaeus* (47 bc) that we should imitate the revolutions of Reason which are apparent in the heaven in order to stabilise the wandering revolutions of our own reasoning.

that which 'takes care of', 'administers' and 'controls' all things.

The cosmological doctrines of each of these philosophers were expressed, in part at least, in terms of a concrete social or political situation, and the first question we might ask is how far the images which each philosopher uses in his cosmology correspond to what we know of his political convictions. Plato's rejection of democracy of the Athenian type, at least, is well known, and his anti-democratic, authoritarian bias is evidently reflected in the image of a supreme (but benevolent) ruler which he uses to describe the role of Reason in the cosmos. But for the political views of the Presocratics our evidence is both scanty and rather unreliable. Our information is fullest for Heraclitus and Empedocles, but in neither case do the cosmological images they use seem to tally *exactly* with what we hear about their political beliefs. Heraclitus is reported to have come from an aristocratic family (D.L. IX 6; DK 22 A 1): his hatred of the ignorant mass of the common people is evident in many of his own statements, and two of his fragments, if they have any political significance, seem frankly monarchical in tone.[1] But it is particularly interesting that in several fragments he stresses the importance of law and custom *among men* (Frr. 44, 114), a doctrine which contrasts strangely, to my mind, with the cosmological notion of the universality of War and Strife (even if, as we saw, he *also* uses the terms δίκη and νόμος to convey the idea of the normalcy of strife, Frr. 80, 114). His cosmological theory might lead one to expect that he would prescribe strife and anarchy for his fellow human beings, and yet insolence (ὕβρις), he says in the striking Fr. 43, should be stamped out 'more than a conflagration'. Again Empedocles, we are told, was a staunch democrat (e.g. D.L. VIII 63 ff. and 72; DK 31 A 1), and yet the image of the successive rule of Love and Strife which he uses in his cosmology is consistent with an

---

[1] Fr. 33 ('it is νόμος, law or custom, to obey the will of one') and Fr. 49 ('one man to me is worth ten thousand, if he be the best').

oligarchic or an aristocratic ideology, and is indeed rather more appropriate to such an ideology than to a democratic one.

It would be rash, then, to attempt to set up an *exact* correlation between the cosmological images, and the political leanings, of individual Presocratic philosophers. On the other hand the images we considered clearly do reflect, in several important respects, the *general* circumstances of Greek political life of the sixth and fifth centuries, especially when we contrast those circumstances with those that obtained in earlier periods. By the time the Homeric poems were assembled the picture of the 'king' or βασιλεύς which they present was, no doubt, largely an idealised one, and in Hesiod the authority of the βασιλεῖς is far from being unquestioned or unassailable. But it is clear from the *Works and Days* that the βασιλεῖς were still the sole repositories of justice, which (to judge from Hesiod's frequent complaints) they were liable to administer in a corrupt and arbitrary fashion. But then the late seventh and early sixth centuries witness some fundamental changes in Greek society. The authority of the traditional ruling families was further undermined, and Athens was far from being the only state in which there was an acute and protracted struggle for power between opposing political factions. On the other hand with the codification of laws and the drawing up of constitutions the administration of justice became a much less arbitrary matter in the city-state than it had been in the days of Hesiod. The poems of Solon, especially, are eloquent testimony of the new political ideals of the early sixth century.[1] These developments have their counterparts in the various types of political images which we find in

[1] In poem 3 D (4 B) for example, Solon insists on the importance of 'good order' (εὐνομία) in the state (and he accuses the leaders of the people of having no respect for Justice). But poem 24 D (36 B) should be noted particularly. There Solon says that 'in the judgement of time' (ἐν δίκη χρόνου, cf. Anaximander's κατὰ τὴν τοῦ χρόνου τάξιν) Earth will bear witness on his behalf, and he mentions among his achievements that he 'wrote ordinances for the commoner and nobleman alike, making justice straight for each man'.

the cosmological theories of the philosophers. The social up-heavals of the late sixth century are, of course, reflected in Heraclitus' conception of the universality of war and strife. But more important is the new idea of Justice in the cosmologies of Anaximander, Parmenides and Empedocles especially. We have in most cases little reliable evidence concerning the precise political views of these philosophers: yet each of them expresses some idea of a cosmic *law*, or *justice*, or *contract*, which is independent of the caprice of individuals. The key political image in the cosmologies of these philosophers is not that of the supreme rule of a despotic monarch (such as Zeus) whose power is based, in the last resort, on his superior force: it is, rather, that of an impersonal justice which regulates the relationships between equals. These relationships are governed not by the arbitrary decisions of a wilful ruler, but by immutable laws or contracts, the 'ordering' of Time in Anaximander, the 'Justice' of Parmenides, and the 'oath' of Empedocles Fr. 30. It is not too much to say, then, that the developments that took place in the attitude towards justice and the rule of law in the period of the rise of the city-state were of cardinal importance in the development of cosmology itself (as opposed to cosmogony or theogony), for it was largely by means of the images of law and justice that the earlier Presocratic philosophers expressed the notion that the changes affecting the primary substances in the universe are regular and governed by rational principles.

If the notion of the equal power and status of several cosmological factors is one that runs through the cosmologies of Anaximander, Parmenides and Empedocles, other philosophers, Anaxagoras, Diogenes of Apollonia[1] and most of all

---

[1] We know nothing at all of the political views of Diogenes of Apollonia and little for certain about those of Anaxagoras. Anaxagoras was, of course, closely associated with Pericles and is reported to have been his teacher (Isoc. xv 235; DK 59 A 15), but in most of the (usually apocryphal) stories which give us biographical information concerning Anaxagoras he is represented as more interested in the inquiry into the natural causes of phenomena than in politics (e.g. Plu. *Pericles* 6; DK A 16; and cf. Plato, *Phdr.* 269e f.; Arist. *EN* 1141 b 3 ff.; *EE* 1216a 10 ff.).

Plato himself, draw far more on monarchical or authoritarian images in their cosmologies. Superficially, at least, these images bear a closer resemblance to the traditional description of the role of Zeus in Homer and Hesiod. Yet the differences are obvious and fundamental. In the philosophers, the images of power and rule are applied not to a divine personage, but to reason itself, the rational principle which is at work in the world—in Anaxagoras to Mind which controls everything, including the rotation of the heavenly bodies, and in Diogenes to Air which is identified with the Intelligence without which (as he puts it in Fr. 3) summer and winter, day and night and everything else would not be disposed, as they now are, in the best possible way. And in Plato, too, the metaphors of controlling, ruling and administering are among those which he uses of the rational principle which is manifest in, for example, the revolutions of the heavenly bodies. The authoritarian metaphors of supreme power in these philosophers are quite different in tone from the Empedoclean conception of a contract between equal cosmological factors, for example: yet they still serve to emphasise, from a different point of view and with different overtones, the elements of order and regularity in cosmological changes.

Social and political images play a most important part in the development of early Greek cosmology, notably in connection with the expression of various ideas of cosmic order. But we must now consider how far we can determine the attitude of the philosophers themselves to what I have described as their social *metaphors* or *images*. When do Greek philosophers begin to acknowledge explicitly an element of transference in their application of social and political ideas in their cosmological doctrines? We may start with Plato, for whom alone we have fairly ample evidence. In several passages, notably in the *Gorgias* and *Laws* x, Plato combats those who opposed νόμος and φύσις, man-made convention and nature, and stresses the connection between order in man himself or in society, and order in the cosmos as a whole.[1] But this does not mean to say, of course, either that Plato simply confused the social and the cosmic order, or that he was unaware of the figurative element in the images he used in this context. On the contrary, the burden of his quarrel with the atheists in *Laws* x is not that they separate νόμος and φύσις (for Plato tacitly acknowledges that these two spheres are distinct) but rather that they *oppose* them and wrongly hold that nature is without order and random (τύχη, 889ab). Moreover, on several occasions he draws a general distinction between an image or a myth (εἰκών, μῦθος) and a non-figurative account or a demonstration (λόγος, ἀπόδειξις) and says that on certain subjects we must be content with the former,[2] and there can be no doubt that he was aware of using εἰκόνες when he refers to the 'king' who 'takes care of' the whole world, just as he is when he speaks of the Craftsman or the Father of all things.[3] At the same time it is his firm conviction that a cosmic order exists, even if we have to speak of it largely in images drawn from the human sphere. The picture he presents is that the human order is part of the divine order, and dependent on it. On the one hand, then, his conception may be distinguished from a crude failure to differentiate at all between the realm of Society and the realm of Nature. On the other hand he also disagrees with those who contrasted νόμος and φύσις in that he holds that the world is in a real sense a κόσμος, a world-order. His language is 'metaphorical' in that he often consciously applies terms beyond their primary sphere of reference (human society), but for Plato clearly these metaphors are not empty figures of speech, for he believes that order

---

[1] E.g. *Grg.* 507e f. where Socrates says that a man of unbridled licence can have no part in any community, and so cannot be beloved of the gods, and he goes on: 'the wise men say, Callicles, that a sense of community and friendship and orderliness (κοσμιότης) and temperance and justice hold together the heaven and the earth and gods and men, and for this reason they call the whole a world-order...and not a disorder...'.

[2] E.g. *R.* 505a ff., 506d ff.; *Phdr.* 246a; *Lg.* 897de.

[3] See further below, pp. 284 f., on *Ti.* 28c.

or justice in the human sphere *is a part of* the wider, cosmic order.

It is much more difficult to define the attitude of the Presocratics on this question. We have simply no other evidence of how Anaximander, for instance, may have otherwise expressed the conception of aggression and retribution for aggression which is conveyed in the 'rather poetic terms' of Fr. 1.[1] Heraclitus, however, *connects* human laws and the 'one divine' law in Fr. 114, and it is clearly not the case that Heraclitus simply confused human society and the cosmic order, even though he suggests, in that fragment, that human laws are in some way dependent on (he says 'nourished by', τρέφονται) the one divine law. But when we turn to Empedocles we have for the first time some fairly definite evidence that he recognised his cosmological principles Love and Strife as abstractions, that is as generalisations, or rather one might almost say as extrapolations, from certain experience. Speaking of Love in Fr. 17 20 ff. he tells Pausanias: 'contemplate her with your mind and do not sit gazing with your eyes; for she is acknowledged as inborn in the limbs of mortals, and by her they have a gentle disposition and achieve works of peace, calling her by the names of Joy and Aphrodite'. It is clear that for Empedocles Love is no mere metaphor, in that the

---

[1] It is, however, worth mentioning that a little earlier than Anaximander Solon has two poems in which natural phenomena are used to illustrate social ones. In poem 1 D (13 B) the certainty and swiftness of the vengeance which Zeus takes on the unrighteous are compared with the sudden scattering of the clouds in spring by the winds, and in poem 10 D (9 B) he says: 'from the cloud comes the might of snow and hail, and thunder comes from bright lightning, and from its great men ruin comes on a city...'. Both poems juxtapose natural, and social, causes and effects, and no doubt Zeus is thought of as, in some sense, responsible for both the natural and the moral order: yet we can hardly say that Solon confounds the two. On the contrary, if we ask why he refers to natural phenomena at all in these poems, it is presumably because unlike the moral order, where he explicitly acknowledges that the workings of Zeus are difficult to fathom (poem 1 63 ff. D), the sequence of events in natural causation is certain and manifest to all. Earlier still in Greek literature the recognition of some distinction between the realm of Nature and the realm of human society can be traced in Hesiod, for example, who in the *Works and Days* (276 ff.) contrasts human beings, who possess νόμος and δίκη ('law' and 'justice'), the gifts of Zeus, with fish and wild beasts and birds, who lack them.

sexual attraction of living creatures to one another in ordinary experience is not simply an analogue or model for, but an actual instance of, the force which he believes to be at work in the cosmos as a whole.[1] But on the other hand he evidently acknowledges that to apply the term Love to the four roots requires, as it were, some explanation, as it involves using the term, if not in a new meaning, at least in a new context.

Although the term εἰκών is used often enough in pre-Platonic literature in various senses (e.g. likeness or representation), it is doubtful whether any general distinction between the literal and the metaphorical use of a term was consciously and explicitly drawn before the fourth century. Nor should the divine 'law' of Heraclitus or the Love and Strife of Empedocles be understood simply as figures of speech. Yet Empedocles Fr. 17 is important because it suggests that already in the fifth century one philosopher, at least, recognised that his cosmological doctrines involved applying certain terms beyond their normal sphere of reference. But a further feature of the role of social and political ideas in Empedocles' cosmology should also be noted. The criticisms which Aristotle raised concerning his account of the change from the rule of Love to that of Strife are illuminating. In Fr. 30 (as we saw) the relationship between Love and Strife is described very briefly as being governed by a 'broad oath', and when Aristotle quotes this fragment at *Metaph.* 1000b 12 ff. he complains that Empedocles gave no reason for the change from the rule of the one to the rule of the other. Unless Aristotle's information is at fault, Empedocles' account of this problem seems to have amounted to no more than the suggestion of the social image of the oath or contract between the two equal cosmological forces. Now in Aristotle's view (and in our own too, no doubt) the image by itself is no *explanation* of the cosmological changes to which it refers. The fact is, however, that in the extant fragments of the Pre-

---

[1] On the biological associations of Empedocles' Love, see below, pp. 242 f.

socratics we repeatedly find theories and accounts of natural phenomena which appear to consist of nothing but an image or a comparison (many more examples will be noted in later sections). This would surely suggest that *as a whole* the Presocratics simply did not anticipate the type of criticism which Aristotle directed, in this and other passages,[1] against the images of Empedocles. To *them* it may have seemed 'explanation' enough of an obscure problem to suggest an image from more familiar experience, e.g. to represent cosmological changes in terms of a concrete social situation. We have no reason to believe that any of the Greek philosophers simply conflated Society and Nature, although many of the Presocratics, and Plato too, conceived the social order as part of a wider, cosmic order and described the latter in terms derived from the former. On the other hand it is often the case that the cosmological doctrines of the Presocratics appear to consist of nothing but a concrete image. So far as we know, it was Plato who first drew an explicit general distinction between an image and a demonstrative account, pointing out that the first falls short of the second, and as we shall see as we continue this study of their images and analogies, it is arguable that the Presocratics not only did not formulate this distinction, but tended in practice rather to ignore it.

We have traced the use of social and political images in the cosmological theories of the Presocratics and of Plato. The political metaphors which Plato used in this context, important though they are, are less striking, or at least less frequent, than either his biological or his technological images (which we shall be considering shortly). In Aristotle, political images have only a minor role in his cosmological doctrines, indeed they are hardly used at all, the most important exception being the last chapter of *Metaphysics* Λ. There, when he considers the question of how the nature of the whole possesses the good (whether as something separate and independent, or in the arrangement of the parts) he uses first the illustration

---

[1] See further below, p. 403.

of the army (to suggest that the whole may possess the good in *both* the ways he mentions, 1075 a 13) and then that of the household (to suggest that different objects share in order to different degrees, 1075 a 19 ff.). And at the end of the same chapter there is the famous passage in which he rejects the notion of a plurality of first principles with the remark that 'things should not be badly governed' (τὰ δὲ ὄντα οὐ βούλεται πολιτεύεσθαι κακῶς) and he quotes Homer with approval: 'the rule of many is not good: let one rule' (οὐκ ἀγαθὸν πολυκοιρανίη· εἷς κοίρανος ἔστω, 1076 a 3 f.). Yet Aristotle's Prime Mover, while alive and divine, does not, like Reason or the best Soul in Plato, control or administer the whole cosmos, and it causes movement not as an efficient, but as a final cause, as the 'object of desire' (1072 b 3 f.).

But if political imagery declines in importance in Aristotle's cosmology, we should not leave this topic without noticing briefly that Greek causal theories as a whole (including that of Aristotle himself) are to some extent coloured by the social and political associations which certain key terms possess. The most obvious and important of these are δύναμις, αἴτιον and ἀρχή. δύναμις, it is true, refers originally either to political power or to physical force: but that it sometimes retains some of its political overtones when the medical writers, for example, use it of the effects of various substances on the living organism, can be seen from the way in which they combine δύναμις with such other terms as δυνάστης and δυναστεύω in which the political connotation clearly predominates,[1] even though such overtones are less in evidence in Aristotle himself and the distinctively Aristotelian sense of δύναμις, 'potentiality' as opposed to 'actuality', is unconnected with the political sense of the term.[2] Then before αἰτία comes to be used generally in the sense of 'cause', it means responsibility or blame: and the meaning of τὸ αἴτιον

---

[1] Besides the passages mentioned above, p. 216, n. 1, cf., for example, *VM* ch. 16, *CMG* I, 1 47 13; and *Flat.* ch. 15, *CMG* I, 1 101 19.

[2] The history of the various uses of this term in early Greek thought was made the subject of a special study by Souilhé, and cf. also Jones, 2, pp. 93 ff.

is equivalent to 'that which is responsible'. And this possible range of reference of the term αἴτιον has some bearing on our understanding of such a passage as *Ti.* 28c, where having observed that everything that comes to be necessarily comes to be ὑπ' αἰτίου τινός, Plato follows this remark up by speaking in the next sentence of 'the maker and father of the whole'.[1] But it is perhaps the term ἀρχή that provides the most interesting evidence of the political associations which Greek terms for causation may possess, and here some of the most striking examples come from Aristotle himself.[2] ἀρχή means, of course, both 'starting-point' and 'seat of authority', among other things, and while Aristotle certainly distinguishes these and other senses in his discussion of the term in *Metaph.* Δ 1, it is significant that he draws attention to the common factor in all the meanings of ἀρχή: 'It is common to all ἀρχαί', he says at 1013a 17 ff., 'that they are the first point from which a thing either is or comes to be or is known.... And so the nature of a thing (φύσις) and the element (στοι-χεῖον), thought (διάνοια) and will (προαίρεσις), substance (οὐσία) and the final cause (οὗ ἕνεκα), are all ἀρχή.' Moreover, it is apparent that some of Aristotle's own ideas about 'principles' are influenced by the connotation 'seat of authority' which the term ἀρχή may have. Thus when he refers to right, above and front as ἀρχαί, he seems to have the notion of authority in mind as well as that of origin (we may recall that in this context the ἀρχή is said to be honourable, *IA* 706b 12 f., see above, pp. 52 f.). And when he says that the heart is the ἀρχή of the animal's growth or nature (e.g.

---

[1] Cf. also *Phlb.* 26e–27a. Both passages are further discussed below, p. 282.

[2] Whether Anaximander already used the term ἀρχή of the Boundless (as some have held on the basis of certain passages in Simplicius, some of which derive from Theophrastus, especially *in Ph.* 150 23 f. and 24 15 f.) is disputed (see KR, pp. 107 f. and contrast *HGP*, I, p. 77 and n. 4). It is certainly rather surprising, in view of the expression τὰς ὑπ' αὐτῶν καλουμένας ἀρχάς ('what they call the principles') which Aristotle uses when referring to his predecessors at *Ph.* 188b 28, that the term ἀρχή is found so rarely in the extant fragments of the Presocratics: indeed if we exclude the probably spurious fragments of Philolaus, it is found hardly at all except in the purely temporal or local sense 'beginning' (but cf. Diogenes Fr. 1).

GA 738b 16 f.), the sense 'seat of control' is again present along with the sense 'origin' (of life and movement). At *GA* 740a 7 ff., for example, he says that there must be an ἀρχή in the body from which all the subsequent arrangement (διακόσμησις) of the body is derived, and at *PA* 670a 24 ff. he says that the heart must be well protected, saying that it is 'as it were the acropolis' of the body. Finally in a more general cosmological context there is the passage we have already noted from *Metaph.* Λ (1076a 3 f.) where he passes from saying that there should not be many ἀρχαί, to saying that 'things should not be badly governed', where again the double sense of ἀρχή is in evidence. It is important to emphasise that we cannot simply say that Aristotle failed to detect the ambiguity of this term, for as we have seen he explicitly distinguished the different senses of ἀρχή in *Metaph.* Δ 1. But it is particularly interesting that while he successfully isolates the different meanings which ἀρχή may have, his view is *not* that the term is in any way equivocal, but rather that it is *appropriate* for the *same* term to have a range of reference extending from 'seat of authority' to 'origin', and that the analogy between these different senses is a valid and a fruitful one.

VITALIST NOTIONS: THE COSMOS AS A LIVING ORGANISM

Many natural objects and phenomena are, on occasions, described in early Greek literature as though they were in some sense alive and had wills of their own—though this need not imply that the objects in question were invariably conceived as living beings. Furthermore, accounts of the origins of things were sometimes given in terms of their birth and reproduction, the most notable example being the vast genealogy of deities, natural phenomena, moral qualities, types of social behaviour and so on in Hesiod's *Theogony*. In the philosophers, what we find is not mythological theogonies (if we exclude Pherecydes of Syros), but a series of rationalistic cosmogonies, in which the origins of things and their inter-relations are explained in biological or vitalist terms. Two themes which recur in Greek philosophy from the Pre-socratic period onwards are the notion that the primary sub-stance of things is in some sense instinct with life, and the idea that the world as a whole is (or at least is like) a living organ-ism. First we must consider in what form these beliefs were held by different thinkers at different periods in the early history of Greek cosmological speculation. And then we should also examine how the use of vitalist conceptions in-fluenced the development of different branches of Greek speculative thought, how the development of cosmological and physical theories was both served, and hindered, in dif-ferent ways, by the assumption that the primary stuff of things, or the world as a whole, is instinct with life.

Our information concerning the Milesians is notoriously fragmentary,[1] and yet it is fairly certain that each of them held that the primary substance of things is alive and divine.[2] We are told by Aristotle (*Ph.* 203 b 13 ff.; DK 12 A 15) that Anaximander believed the Boundless to be 'immortal' and 'indestructible'. And Aetius (1 7 13; DK 13 A 10) reports that Anaximenes held that Air is divine. Two beliefs which are attributed to Thales by Aristotle should be considered in this context, though in both cases their interpretation is rather obscure. These are (1) that 'all things are full of gods' (*de An.* 411 a 8; DK 11 A 22) and (2) that the magnet possesses 'soul', that is life (*de An.* 405 a 19 ff.; DK *ibid.*). It is not immedi-ately apparent whether in attributing life to the magnet Thales took it to be *typical* of other objects (and inferred that they too are alive) or whether he saw in the magnet some-thing of a *special* case (are *other* things also alive which do *not* have the power of attracting objects which is possessed by the

---

[1] D. R. Dicks's assessment of the evidence for Thales seems, however, exces-sively sceptical: contrast KR, pp. 87 ff. and *HGP*, I, pp. 54 ff.

[2] Besides the account in Jaeger, 2, ch. 2, see also especially *HGP*, I, pp. 63 f.

magnet, or amber when rubbed?).[1] But that the former view is more likely seems clear from the first dictum, 'all things are full of gods', although this dictum in turn is open to slightly different interpretations. As KR (pp. 96 f.)[2] have pointed out, 'full' may mean either 'absolutely filled out by' or 'containing a great number of'. If the latter sense is perhaps the more probable one, Thales' conception may not have been very different from what appears to have been the common pre-philosophical Greek view. The importance of his dicta is, nevertheless, undeniable. First, if many pre-philosophical texts imply a belief that certain things (including many we should class as inanimate) are alive, Thales may well have been the first Greek thinker to *state* this idea *in a general form* ('all things are full of gods'). And secondly, and more important, his observation concerning the magnet suggests that he had begun to *rationalise the grounds* on which this belief was based, associating life, in this instance, with the power to cause movement.[3]

Whether Thales conceived the world as a whole as a single living organism is doubtful, but there is good evidence that both Anaximander and Anaximenes held some such belief. Anaximander's theory of the evolution of the world from the Boundless is reported in pseudo-Plutarch, *Strom.* 2 (DK 12 A 10), an account which contains, among other things, an

---

[1] Thus Burnet, *3*, p. 50, suggested that 'to say the magnet and amber are alive is to imply, if anything, that other things are not'. But Burnet rejected—to my mind unnecessarily—the attribution of the other belief, that 'all things are full of gods', to Thales. Contrast *HGP*, 1, p. 66, n. 1.

[2] KR suggest a third possible meaning for the dictum, that the world is a single living organism: but while several of the earlier Presocratics seem to have conceived the world as such, this seems a less likely interpretation of the dictum that 'all things are full of gods' (*gods* being in the plural). It is true that there is another version of the dictum, that all things are 'full of soul', but when Aristotle cites the dictum in this form at *GA* 762a 21 he makes no mention of Thales, and we should regard the *de Anima* version as a more accurate report of his belief.

[3] It should also be noted that according to Aristotle (*Metaph.* 983b 18 ff.) the main reasons that led Thales to choose water as the primary substance were that nourishment is moist, that vital heat is connected with moisture, and that seeds are moist: for Aristotle, as Guthrie puts it, *HGP*, 1, p.61, 'the most likely thoughts to have been in Thales's mind are those which link water with the idea of life'.

interesting comparison with the growth of bark round a tree which may well have been original, and which was (I believe) intended to illustrate several features of his quite complex cosmological system.[1] But whatever the precise significance of the comparison with the tree, the report refers to a separating off of τὸ ἐκ τοῦ ἀιδίου γόνιμον θερμοῦ τε καὶ ψυχροῦ, i.e. of 'that which is productive—or germinative—from the eternal, of hot and cold', and it also speaks of a ball of flame 'growing round' (περιφυῆναι) a central core, and it seems clear from this that Anaximander thought of the evolution of the world as the growth of a living being. Not only is the Boundless itself 'immortal', but Anaximander's whole account of the generation of the world was evidently based on the assumption that the world as a whole is instinct with life.

Then Anaximenes may have been the first philosopher to draw an explicit comparison between the world as a whole and man in particular. Aetius (1 3 4; DK 13 B 2) reports his doctrine as follows, οἷον ἡ ψυχή, φησίν, ἡ ἡμετέρα ἀὴρ οὖσα συγκρατεῖ ἡμᾶς, καὶ ὅλον τὸν κόσμον πνεῦμα καὶ ἀὴρ περιέχει,[2] although both the language and the content of this 'fragment' have been severely criticised.[3] Anaximenes is hardly likely to have used the term συγκρατεῖν, and κόσμος used of the 'world-order' may also be anachronistic.[4] But however much the original conception may have been reworded, it seems clear that Aetius attributes to Anaximenes *some* comparison between the breath-soul in man and air in the world. To this it has been objected that such an explicit comparison between microcosm and macrocosm cannot be paralleled in Greek literature before the second half of the

---

[1] This comparison is considered in detail below, pp. 309 ff.

[2] 'Just as our soul, he says, being air, holds us together, so does wind or air enclose the whole world.'

[3] The case against the fragment has been put most forcefully by Reinhardt, *1*, p. 175, *2*, pp. 209 ff., but many scholars accept at least its general contents. KR, p. 159, put it that 'the degree of re-wording... probably is not very great', and Guthrie, *HGP*, 1, p. 131, says that 'the sentence faithfully communicates [Anaximenes'] doctrine'.

[4] But KR (p. 159) suggest that τὸν κόσμον in Aetius could have replaced e.g. ἅπαντα, 'all things'.

fifth century (e.g. in the Hippocratic treatise *On the Nature of Man*). Yet the extant evidence for earlier periods is so poor that this argument loses some of its force. To judge from what we know of the doctrines of the earlier Milesians, there is nothing implausible in suggesting that Anaximenes thought of 'the world' as alive *either* in the sense that it is *peopled* with living beings (cf. Thales), *or* in the sense that the world *as a whole* is a living creature (cf. Anaximander's conception of its evolution). It seems quite possible that Anaximenes chose to illustrate some aspect or aspects of the role of his primary substance Air in the world by referring to the role of breath in man. But if so, it is surely quite improbable that the point of this comparison was simply that air surrounds things in a purely local sense. There seems little reason to doubt that he thought of air as a *vital* principle in the sense that it animates all things (whether or not he had any clear conception of the world as a single organic whole animated by air) or that he found an *example* of its operation in man.

The evidence for Heraclitus is more certainly authentic, but once again the problem of interpretation is a delicate one. In Fr. 30 he calls this κόσμος, i.e. the world-order itself, an ever-living fire (πῦρ ἀείζωον) which 'kindles in measures and goes out in measures'. Fire is not only eternal, but also, it seems, in some sense alive. That 'ever-living' is not merely a poetic equivalent for 'everlasting' is obvious if we reflect that Heraclitus believed that fire is the substance of which our own souls are composed.[1] But if the world-order is thought of as a living fire, the changes which affect fire and other substances are also sometimes described in terms derived from the sphere of living things. In Fr. 36,[2] for instance, he says: 'For souls, it is death to become water; for water, it is death to

---

[1] Besides Fr. 36 which I deal with in my text, there are other fragments which indicate that Heraclitus believed that character and intelligence depend on the quality of the fire of which our souls are composed, e.g. Frr. 117 and 118.

[2] Cf. the use of the terms ζῆν, θάνατος and γένεσις in the three passages collected in DK as 'Fr.' 76 (though I agree with Kirk, *1*, pp. 341 ff., *contra* Kahn, p. 152, n. 1, and *HGP*, I, p. 453, n. 2, that the reference to ἀήρ in these texts is probably incorrect).

become earth; out of earth, water comes to be; and out of water, soul.' As Kirk (*1*, pp. 340 ff.), for example, has suggested, the comparison between this fragment and Fr. 31 which describes an interchange between *fire*, sea and earth, makes it extremely likely that 'soul' in Fr. 36 stands for fire or an aspect of fire. But if Heraclitus may *mean* fire in Fr. 36, the term he uses is not πῦρ, but ψυχή, which refers primarily to the life-force of living things. He evidently saw no anomaly in referring to the soul-stuff alongside earth and water in a single cycle of changes involving both what *we* should call 'animate' and what *we* should call 'inanimate' objects. Moreover, he uses the same terminology of each of the changes to which he refers. The first time that the word θάνατος is used, with reference to 'souls', some of its literal sense 'death' is clearly retained, but then Heraclitus also describes the transformation of water into earth as the 'death' of the former, using the same term θάνατος. Again we should probably translate the term γίνεται, used with the subject 'water', simply 'comes to be', but when the same verb is supplied in the last clause of the fragment, where the subject is ψυχή, it may well preserve some of the original sense 'to be born'. Yet if we attempted to press the distinction between the different uses of θάνατος and γενέσθαι here, we should be in danger of misrepresenting Heraclitus' thought, for where we tend to require 'animate' and 'inanimate' to be kept carefully distinct, Heraclitus' language, in this fragment, seems rather to emphasise the essential continuity of the changes affecting fire/soul, water and earth (not that it follows, of course, that he drew no distinction at all between the living and the non-living). It is clear that Heraclitus conceived the primary substance Fire as instinct with life, indeed to be the stuff of our own souls: but Fr. 36 also provides good evidence that for him both fire and its (apparently inanimate) transformations, water and earth, form a single unbroken continuum.

The next evidence we should consider is that for the early Pythagoreans, for although authentic fragments are lacking, it is clear from our secondary sources that vitalist notions played an important part in several of their cosmological doctrines. At *Metaph.* 1091 a 15 ff. Aristotle criticises Pythagorean cosmogonical theories: 'for they clearly say that when the one was composed, whether out of planes, or out of surface, or out of seed, or out of things they are unable to describe, the nearest part of the Unlimited immediately began to be drawn in and limited by the Limit'. It is generally agreed that some of the ideas mentioned here are genuine Pythagorean doctrines, and this has been thought particularly likely of the theory that the original 'one' was made out of seed[1] (although Aristotle himself did not know how this was meant to take place). And then the second stage of cosmogony, the 'drawing in' of the Unlimited by the Limit, was sometimes described in a further vitalist image, namely as an 'inhalation'[2]—the picture being that of a new-born animal starting to draw breath. We cannot date either the seed or the inhalation doctrines, let alone assign them to any particular Pythagorean authors, but it has been suggested, with some plausibility, that such ideas are likely to belong to a quite early stage in the development of Pythagorean theories, that is to say before Parmenides. Fragmentary though our evidence is, it is fairly clear that at one stage the Pythagoreans too, like Anaximander and perhaps also Anaximenes, assumed that the world as a whole is alive and described its origin and development partly in terms of those of a living organism.

In spite of the difficulties and uncertainties that face us in commenting on the theories of the earliest Presocratic

---

[1] E.g. Cornford, *8*, p. 19; KR, p. 251.

[2] See Arist. *Ph.* 213 b 22 ff. (the text and interpretation of this passage are fully discussed in KR, pp. 252 f.); Stob. *Ecl.* 1 18 1 c (DK 58 B 30 quoting Aristotle's lost work on the Pythagoreans); Simp. *in Ph.* 651 26 ff.; and Aet. II 9 1. It should be mentioned that Philolaus' embryological theory is *roughly* parallel to the cosmological doctrine of the drawing in of the Unlimited by the Limit: according to Anon. Lond. XVIII 8 ff. he held that our bodies are originally composed of the hot alone, but that on birth we draw in the outside air which is cold (cf. KR, pp. 312 f.; *HGP*, I, pp. 278 f.).

philosophers, it is apparent that the cosmological doctrines of each of the three Milesians, of Heraclitus, and of some, at least, of the Pythagoreans are permeated by vitalist conceptions. Probably all the earlier Presocratic philosophers held that the primary substance of which other things are composed, or from which they originate, is instinct with life (the evidence is particularly clear in the case of Anaximander's Boundless, Anaximenes' Air and Heraclitus' Fire, although in many respects the conceptions that these philosophers had of the roles of these substances are, of course, quite different). And then several of them represented the world itself, either in its growth and development, or in its present differentiated state, as a living being (Anaximander and some of the Pythagoreans, and perhaps also Anaximenes, pictured the world as such, though again their theories differ very considerably in other respects). But at this point we should raise two admittedly rather obscure questions: how far do the vitalist notions which we have considered simply reflect certain unquestioned assumptions common to all thinkers at this period? And how far, in particular, did the earlier Presocratics recognise any distinction between the animate and the inanimate sphere? To take the second question first, it is evident that Thales ascribed life to some objects which we consider inanimate, such as the magnet. But what is not at all certain is whether Thales extended this doctrine to include everything in the inanimate sphere (as we call it) without exception. Aristotle tentatively suggests that he believed that soul is 'mixed' in the whole universe,[1] but did Thales hold that soul is present in *every single* object, or merely that soul *pervades* the whole? He is certainly said to have held that 'all things are full of gods', but as we noted, 'full' here may have meant no more than 'peopled by' (and he would surely have stopped short of

---

[1] See *de An.* 411 a 7 f. ('some thinkers hold that soul is mixed in the whole universe and it is for this reason, perhaps, that Thales too thought that all things are full of gods'). Aristotle and Hippias are, however, interpreted at D.L. 1 24 as ascribing to Thales the *general* belief that inanimate things (as well as living beings) partake of soul.

the paradox of attributing life-soul to the dead bodies of animals and plants, at least). The evidence available to us is hardly such that we can settle this question definitively so far as Thales is concerned (and it may be, of course, that his own ideas on this subject were as vague as our reports concerning them seem ambiguous), but not long after Thales there appears to be at least an implicit recognition of the distinction between the living and the non-living in the Pythagorean doctrine of the transmigration of souls (which goes back to Pythagoras himself), for while this doctrine is applied to members of both the animal and the vegetable kingdoms,[1] there is no evidence that it was ever applied to other things. Thales' category of what is alive was evidently wider than ours, and all the earliest Presocratics probably held that the primary stuff of things is alive and divine: but it may be doubted whether for Thales or for any other philosopher the category of what is alive was *all*-inclusive, and in the case of the Pythagoreans, at least, there is some evidence to the contrary, in the distinction we can observe between the objects to which the doctrine of the transmigration of souls applied, and those to which it did not apply.[2]

Our evidence suggests that the doctrine that the primary substance of things is instinct with life was common ground to the three Milesians, to Heraclitus and to some, at least, of the Pythagoreans. On the other hand it is obvious enough that different philosophers proposed different, and sometimes quite elaborate, versions of the doctrine that the world is a living being. Anaximander apparently used not only some idea of a 'germ' of hot and cold, but also a comparison with

---

[1] See, for example, Empedocles Fr. 117, where he says that he has been a boy, a girl, a bush, a bird and a fish. The Pythagorean doctrine reported, for example, by Porphyry, *VP* 19, DK 14 A 8a, that 'all living things' (πάντα τὰ γινόμενα ἔμψυχα) 'must be considered akin', might also be taken to imply a distinction between living and lifeless things.

[2] The term ἄψυχος appears already in the seventh-century poet Archilochus (104 D), where, however, it is not used to refer to objects which are by nature 'inanimate', but in the sense 'faint' (the poet describes himself as ἄψυχος πόθῳ, 'swooning with desire').

the growth of a tree, in his quite complex account of the evolution of the world. Anaximenes referred, it seems, to man's breath-soul to illustrate some aspect of the role of Air in the world at large. The Pythagoreans thought that the Unlimited was drawn into the Limit by a process which they imagined as an 'inhalation'. Granted, then, that each of these philosophers assumed that the primary stuff is in some sense alive, we should not underestimate the original cosmological speculations which their vitalist notions incorporate, for in their attempts to give an account of the development of the world or its present state they clearly showed considerable ingenuity in proposing variations (as it were) on the theme of the world-living-organism.

Before Parmenides, philosophers had assumed the reality of physical change without question, but one of Parmenides' contributions to the development of Greek thought was to raise the problem of how anything can be said to come to be or change at all. In Fr. 8 38 ff. he rejects the common-sense notions of 'coming-to-be and perishing, being and not-being, change of place and alteration of bright colour', and as one might expect in view of the frequency of vitalist notions in earlier cosmologies, there are several passages where Parmenides' attack seems specifically directed against the supposition that the world may 'grow' or evolve as a living organism. In Fr. 8 3 ff. he says that 'what is' is ungenerated, and then asks (6 f.), τίνα γὰρ γένναν διζήσεαι αὐτοῦ; | πῇ πόθεν αὐξηθέν;[1] and at 9 f. he asks again, τί δ' ἄν μιν καὶ χρέος ὦρσεν | ὕστερον ἢ πρόσθεν, τοῦ μηδενὸς ἀρξάμενον, φῦν;[2] Both Empedocles[3] and Anaxagoras[4] followed Parmenides

[1] 'For what birth will you seek for it? How and whence did it increase?'

[2] 'And what need would have moved it to grow, starting from nothing, later rather than sooner?'

[3] In Fr. 8 Empedocles says there is no φύσις of mortal things (i.e. 'birth' rather than, as Burnet translated, 3, p. 205 and n. 4, 'substance') but only the mixture and separation of things which had been mixed. In Fr. 9 he says that he uses such terms as γενέσθαι in the conventional manner, and indeed we find that γενέσθαι, φθίνειν, φύεσθαι and so on are frequently used of what is described more correctly as the mixing or separating of the elements (e.g. Fr. 17 2 ff., Fr. 26 2 ff. and 7 ff.).   [4] Fr. 17.

in rejecting the idea that a thing may come to be from what is not, though both these philosophers reintroduced the notion of physical change, interpreted now as the mixture and separation of existing things. Yet while many of the key ideas in post-Parmenidean cosmological systems have no specific connection with living things or with organic change, a limited, but by no means unimportant, use of vitalist conceptions does continue. Two ideas which are worth considering especially are (1) the use of the model of sexual attraction to describe the coming-together of different substances, and (2) the notion that the particles of substances consist of, or contain, 'seeds'.

(1) Fr. 13 of Parmenides' *Way of Seeming* refers very briefly to Eros as 'the very first of the gods', but if Eros was undoubtedly responsible for bringing together male and female, we do not know precisely to what extent Parmenides may have used this principle to account for the uniting of other pairs of opposites (and in particular of the primary cosmological substances Light and Night themselves).[1] The nature and role of Love in Empedocles' cosmological theory are more certain. In an important passage which we have noted before (Fr. 17 21 ff.), Empedocles says that Love is 'acknowledged as being inborn in the limbs of mortals, and by her they have a gentle disposition and achieve works of peace, calling her by the names of Joy and Aphrodite'. Empedocles' Φιλία is, then, love in both its psychological and its biological aspects, both the spirit of friendliness, and the force of sexual attraction, and sexual imagery reappears in references to the roots 'being desired' by one another.[2] As desire joins the two sexes (Fr. 64) so it unites the different elements in the world at large. It

---

[1] Arist. *Metaph.* 984b 23 ff., however, grouped Parmenides' Eros with the Eros in Hesiod's *Theogony* (where it is mentioned third in order of generation, after 'chaos' and earth, *Th.* 120) and saw both figures as rudimentary efficient causes. It is also worth noting that some of the terms which Parmenides uses elsewhere in the *Way of Seeming* may perhaps retain certain biological overtones, e.g. φῦναι (lit. 'grow', used of the heavens in Fr. 10 6, cf. φύσις in *vv.* 1 and 5, and ἔφυ and τραφέντα in Fr. 19).

[2] E.g. ποθεῖται, Fr. 21 8, and ἐστέρκται, Fr. 22 5.

is clear that Empedocles' cosmological principle, the force which unites the four roots, is both modelled on, and indeed exemplified in, the biological attraction of the sexes, but it is also apparent, as we noted before, that Empedocles himself recognized his Φιλία as an abstraction: as he puts it, 'contemplate her with your mind, and do not sit gazing with your eyes' (Fr. 17 21).

(2) Of all the problems raised by the interpretation of the fragments of the Presocratic philosophers, perhaps none has been so much disputed as the physical theory of Anaxagoras.[1] The aspect of this theory which concerns us here is his conception of 'seeds', which most modern commentators have agreed has an important part in his physical doctrine, although there are wide differences of opinion on what precisely that part is.

Most of the Presocratics derived what we call 'organic' substances from what we should consider 'inorganic' elements. Empedocles, especially, specifies the proportions of the roots, earth, air, fire and water, which go to make up certain such substances, that is bone, flesh and blood (Frr. 96 and 98). Anaxagoras himself, like Empedocles, accepted the Parmenidean dictum that 'nothing can come to be from nothing'. Fr. 17 of Anaxagoras makes a point similar to that of Frr. 8 and 9 of Empedocles, and all three echo Parmenides' Fr. 8 38 ff. But when Anaxagoras says that 'the Greeks wrongly recognise coming-to-be and passing-away. For nothing comes into being nor passes away, but is rather mixed and separated from existing things', his notion of what 'existing things' are is very different from that of Empedocles. The differences between the two theories stem in part, at least, from Anaxagoras' interest in the problems of growth and nutrition, and in particular in the 'coming-to-be' of *organic* substances (as we should call them). In the important,

---

[1] With the account in KR, pp. 367 ff., 375 ff., cf. the sometimes widely divergent interpretations of Bailey, Appendix 1, pp. 537 ff.; Burnet, *3*, pp. 261 ff.; Cornford, *4*; Peck, *1*; and Vlastos, *3*, especially.

though probably re-worded, Fr. 10, he asks the crucial question: 'How could hair come to be from not-hair, or flesh from not-flesh?' The implication is that 'hair', 'flesh', and so on must exist already in some form in our food. By the same argument, clearly, wood, leaves, the different sorts of fruits and so on must pre-exist in the earth and water which are the nourishment of plants. Indeed Anaxagoras states this doctrine in the most general form: 'in *everything* there is a portion of *everything*'.[1] Then because *at no stage* can hair, for example, come to be from not-hair, it is obvious that hair must have existed from the beginning, that is in the original mixture of all things (and again the same applies, of course, to flesh, bark, leaves and the rest). In the original state of the universe, 'all things were together' (Frr. 1, 4 and 6): to begin with, none of these things was manifest because of their smallness (Fr. 1), but as the process of separating off and mixing progressed,[2] recognisable things appeared, each thing being 'most plainly those things of which it contains the most'.[3]

So much is tolerably clear from some of the main fragments of Anaxagoras. But we have yet to consider his references to the 'seeds'. At the end of Fr. 4 he describes the original mixture: 'Before these things were separated off, when all things were together, no colour, even, was manifest. For the mixture of all things prevented it, of the wet and the dry and the hot and the cold and the bright and the dark, and of much

---

[1] Several commentators have attempted, in one way or another, to restrict the scope of Anaxagoras' repeated statement that 'in everything there is a portion of everything (except Mind)' (Frr. 6, 11 and 12). Burnet wanted this to mean that everything contains a portion of the opposites (alone), and Cornford denied that corn, e.g., would have particles of silver or rubies. But KR (p. 376) and Vlastos (*3*, p. 33) are surely right to insist that Anaxagoras' statement means what it says and is intended to apply to every single thing without exception.

[2] Examples of the process of separating off are found in Frr. 15 and 16. This process, as Anaxagoras several times insists, is never complete: Fr. 8 says that hot and cold are not cut off from one another 'with an axe', Fr. 12 says that 'nothing is completely separated off nor divided one from another except Mind', and cf. Fr. 6.

[3] See the end of Fr. 12, and cf. also Arist. *Ph.* 187b 4 ff. and Simp. *in Ph.* 27 5 ff. ('what appears as gold is that in which there is much gold, although all things are in it').

earth that was in it, and of seeds infinite in number and in no way like each other. For neither is any of the other things like any other.' The earlier part of the same fragment also refers to the seeds, this time to their presence in all the things that are 'combining together': 'we must suppose that there are many things of all sorts in all the things that are combining together and seeds of all things with all sorts of forms and colours and tastes'. The first problem which these passages present is the denotation of the term 'seeds'. Organic natural substances, such as hair or bark, must certainly be included and Aristotle, at any rate, evidently took it that the denotation of Anaxagoras' term 'seeds' corresponded to what he himself called 'homogeneous substances' (τὰ ὁμοιομερῆ), including such inorganic natural substances as gold, iron or stones.[1] *Collectively* the seeds seem to represent all the natural substances, including both organic and inorganic kinds (and possibly not only such substances as gold or stones, but also two at least of what were for Aristotle the 'simple bodies', namely earth and water).[2] But still this leaves the problem of

---

[1] E.g. *Cael.* 302a 31 f. Peck (*1*, pp. 28 ff.), however, argues, mainly from Fr. 16, that for Anaxagoras stones are *not* to be included among the elemental substances. But I do not think it is necessary to suppose that the 'separating off' of stones from earth was, for Anaxagoras, any different from that of hair from wheat (say) or of leaves from earth or water (on the question of the status of earth and water, see note 2 below). Might not Anaxagoras have asked, on the analogy of Fr. 10, 'how could stones come to be from not-stones?' and then have inferred that stones must pre-exist in earth, just as hair must pre-exist in our food although we cannot see it? And the unqualified statement that 'all things were together' (Fr. 1) creates a presumption that he did so reason, and that he thought that stones too (like hair and flesh) must be present in the original mixture.

[2] This is, however, contrary to the testimony of Aristotle. Yet Aristotle may perhaps have slightly distorted Anaxagoras' theory at this point in making it out as the opposite of Empedocles' (*Cael.* 302a 28 ff.; *GC* 314a 24 ff.). For Anaxagoras, the Empedoclean elements are certainly composite (though they are elemental in the sense 'primordial'). But so too, surely, are all the other substances that Aristotle classified as 'homogeneous'. Earth and water are not, it seems, any *more* composite than hair or wheat: at least there is nothing to suggest that a lump of earth, for example, is analysable into other substances *without remainder*. But if this is the case, there seems no conclusive reason to confine the term σπέρμα to such substances as gold or hair, to the exclusion of earth and water. True, earth is mentioned separately in Fr. 4 (although it is not impossible that it is given as an instance of a seed in that passage) but in Fr. 16,

how each *individual* seed is imagined, whether (1) as a single natural substance, e.g. hair or gold, *and that alone*, or (2) as an agglomerate of every kind of substance, but with a single kind predominating in it and giving it its character, or (3) as like the seed of an animal or plant, a germ which contains a variety of substances (flesh, hair, blood) each of which gradually manifests itself as the organism develops.

Now Aristotle often refers to the homogeneous substances, whether alone or together with the opposites, as the 'elements' of Anaxagoras (e.g. *Cael.* 302a 31 f.), but although the seeds were certainly elemental in the sense 'primordial' (they were present in the original mixture) it is highly unlikely that they were elemental in the sense of 'simple' (that is, pure substances). In several passages (Frr. 6, 8, 11, 12) Anaxagoras says that nothing, except Mind, is completely separate, and while the term μοῖρα may perhaps be used of simple portions of substances (portions which never exist independently, however) the term σπέρμα does not appear to have been used either as a synonym for μοῖρα or for the μοῖραι of natural substances.[1] The first alternative, that a seed is a pure natural substance, may in all probability be dismissed. But did Anaxagoras believe that each seed is the nucleus of a *particular* substance (e.g. wood or gold) or that each seed developed into a *variety* of substances (as the apparently homogeneous seed of a tree becomes wood, leaves, fruit, etc.)?[2] The latter interpretation preserves the literal, biological sense of seed, but if (as seems to have been the case) Anaxagoras' seeds refer also to inorganic natural substances, it is difficult to imagine how a single seed could be thought of

at any rate, no distinction is drawn between earth and water and stones. See further Vlastos, *3*, pp. 56 f. and contrast KR, pp. 382 ff.

[1] According to the first part of Fr. 4, the seeds are not *of* all sorts of forms and colours and tastes, they *have* these: as KR (p. 380) point out, then, some at least of the opposites (e.g. bright and dark) are actually ingredients in the seeds.

[2] Our source for Fr. 10 says that Anaxagoras did, in fact, believe that the human seed (the term is γονή in our text) contains all the different parts of man, hair, nails, veins, etc., although they are not visible because of the smallness of their parts (διὰ μικρομέρειαν). But what is not clear is whether Anaxagoras would have considered the human seed as one, or many, σπέρματα.

as the source of a variety of inorganic substances (gold and iron and stones, for example) in the way in which the seed of a tree is the source of several organic ones. It seems more likely that each seed was the nucleus, as it were, of a single substance (though it contains a portion of every other kind). Flesh in our body grows by the addition of 'seeds' of flesh which we cannot see, but whose presence we infer, in our food (and in the sequence of changes described in Fr. 16 we might say, perhaps, that what is separated off from earth, when stones become distinct, is the 'seeds' of stones). But if the term 'seeds' itself suggests things which grow and increase, it also suggests particles which to begin with have few distinct characteristics, but which later give rise to substances with far more definite and diverse properties, and this too may be relevant to Anaxagoras' conception. We may note that on both occasions when he refers to seeds, their existence is *inferred*: the words χρὴ δοκεῖν ἐνεῖναι occur both at the beginning and at the end of Fr. 4. Although they have all sorts of colours, etc., the seeds are not distinct either in the original mixture (where 'no colour, even, was manifest') or in 'all the things that are combining together'. Even if each of Anaxagoras' seeds did not (probably) develop into several substances, the term 'seeds' seems apposite to his theory first in that it conveys the idea of nuclei which have a potentiality for growth, and secondly in that it suggests how a substance may exist in the form of small particles in which its distinctive characteristics are not (as yet) manifest. In spite of the problems of interpretation which Anaxagoras' theory presents, the doctrine of seeds seems to be an important instance of the deliberate application and adaptation of a biological model to a general physical theory.

Like Anaxagoras, and conceivably under his direct influence, the Atomists appear to have used an image of seeds, or rather of a 'seed-mixture', in connection with the primary substance, the atoms themselves, although here our evidence comes entirely from indirect reports. Aristotle, at least, uses the term πανσπερμία on several occasions in describing their physical doctrine. The interpretation of *Cael.* 303 a 14 ff. is disputed,[1] but he would there seem to attribute to the Atomists the notion that the substance (φύσις) of the atoms is a 'sort of seed-mass' (οἷον πανσπερμία) for all the elements (i.e. the Empedoclean elements, air, earth, etc.). At *de An.* 404 a 1 ff. there is a further report that suggests that Leucippus and Democritus conceived the πανσπερμία of the atoms to be the 'elements of the whole of nature', and finally at *Ph.* 203 a 19 ff. we are told that according to Democritus the infinite is compounded of the πανσπερμία of shapes (i.e. of the atoms). As we know from Fr. 125, for example, Democritus held that atoms and the void alone are real, and we hear from Arist. *Metaph.* 985 b 13 ff. that he derived the differences between things from differences in the shape, arrangement and position of the atoms. Yet as in Anaxagoras, perhaps, the image of seeds may have been used to convey the idea of the vast diversity of objects which may arise from an original apparently homogeneous mixture (though in Anaxagoras the mixture is only apparently homogeneous, in the Atomists it is in fact so). Moreover, it seems possible that the notion of a πανσπερμία not only conveys the idea of potential diversity, but is also linked with a theory that the original mass of atoms is in some sense instinct with life, although we cannot be certain of this. Some such idea, that the primary stuff of things is instinct with life, was, of course, generally held by the earlier, pre-Parmenidean philosophers, but the reports concerning the Atomists' doctrine are conflicting.[2] We hear

---

[1] ἀέρα δὲ καὶ ὕδωρ καὶ τἆλλα μεγέθει καὶ μικρότητι διεῖλον, ὡς οὖσαν αὐτῶν τὴν φύσιν οἷον πανσπερμίαν πάντων τῶν στοιχείων. Stocks, *1*, was, I think, right to take αὐτῶν (a 16) to refer to the atoms (the 'simple bodies' mentioned at a 11 f.), not, as one might expect, to 'air, water and the rest' in a 14 f. He translates: 'air, water and the rest they distinguished by the relative size of the atom, assuming that the atomic substance was a sort of master-seed for each and every element'. Cf., however, the interpretation in Guthrie, *3*.

[2] Thus Aet. II 3 1–2 reports that 'all the other philosophers [held that] the world-order is alive (ἔμψυχος) and controlled by providence' but says that the Atomists and Epicurus denied both these doctrines.

from Aristotle (*de An.* 404a 2 ff.) that they identified soul with atoms of a particular shape, that is to say spherical, as atoms of this shape are 'best able to permeate everything...and to move other things, being in movement themselves'. The soul is, then, identified as a material object (as in most earlier philosophers), and the soul-atoms were believed to enter the body as we breathe (*de An.* 404a 10 ff.). But from this it is clear that soul-atoms exist in the air around us, and if, as seems to be the case, the Atomists attributed eternal motion to the atoms, this may be due not only to their perpetual collidings and reboundings, but also to the presence of soul-atoms in the whole.[1] We should observe that elsewhere, too, the Atomists' cosmological theories may have drawn on vitalist conceptions: thus in their accounts of the formation of worlds, that which encloses the world was, it seems, conceived as a sort of 'membrane' (ὑμήν is the word used in the reports of Diogenes Laertius and Aetius, although this is not necessarily original, of course).[2] It might be argued, then, that the doctrine of the 'seed-mixture' of atoms not only suggests the variety of things constituted by the atoms, but may also reflect a belief that the atom-mass is instinct with life, in this sense at least, that it was thought to be permeated by soul-atoms.

As has often been pointed out, the work of Parmenides marks a watershed in Presocratic cosmology, for where earlier philosophers had assumed without question that the world had come to be (often representing its development in terms

---

[1] It is clear from Arist. *Cael.* 300b 8 ff. both that the Atomists held that the atoms are in eternal motion, and also that Aristotle did not know what account (if any) they gave of that motion. Certainly the action and reaction of atoms is usually described in terms of their colliding, intertwining and rebounding and so on (e.g. Arist. *Cael.* 303a 5 ff.; *GC* 325a 31 ff.). Yet Aristotle also expressly reports that Democritus held that the soul-atoms are self-moving (*de An.* 403b 29 ff.) and it seems likely from *de An.* 404a 5 ff. that the soul-atoms do, in fact, permeate everything and move other things by their own motion.

[2] See D.L. ix 32 and Aet. ii 7 2 (DK 67 A 1 and 23). (In the latter passage the term χιτών is also used in the same connection, but if this is original, one wonders whether it had its primary sense 'coat', or whether it too was used to mean 'membrane', a sense it often has in medical literature, e.g. *VM* ch. 19, *CMG* i, 1 49 25.)

of the evolution of a living being), the post-Parmenidean philosophers were forced to consider the problem of how change and coming-to-be can be said to take place at all. They all accepted (tacitly, if not expressly) the doctrine that nothing can come to be from nothing, and reduced 'coming-to-be' to the interactions of existing things. Often they gave what we should call mechanical accounts of those interactions—one example is the doctrine of the whirl (περιχώρησις, δίνη) which plays a particularly important part in the systems of Anaxagoras and Democritus.[1] What is more, we find that the notion of a *separate* controlling principle or efficient cause (as Aristotle would have termed it) begins to emerge in several later Presocratic cosmologies.[2] And we should also note that while there is a certain element of doubt as to how far some earlier philosophers distinguished between animate and inanimate objects (or where they drew the line between the two), we have much more definite evidence that these two spheres were recognised as distinct by such thinkers as Anaxagoras and Democritus.[3] Yet as we have seen, vitalist notions continued to play an important part in the accounts of change which were put forward by several of the post-Parmenidean philosophers. The uniting of male and female personified figures had, of course, been a recurrent feature of pre-philosophical myths and theogonies relating how things came to be. But then, following the lead of Parmenides, perhaps, Empedocles described the abstract cosmological

[1] See Anaxagoras Frr. 9, 12 and 13, and Democritus Fr. 167 (cf. D.L. ix 44; DK 68 A 1; and also D.L. ix 31 f., DK 67 A 1, on Leucippus' theory).

[2] Thus Empedocles often describes the role of Love as that of a craftsman, the four roots being the material upon which she acts (see below, pp. 274 f.), and Anaxagoras says that Mind, which controls everything, is 'mixed with nothing' and 'alone by itself' (ἐφ' ἑαυτοῦ, Fr. 12), although, as is well known, it is still described in corporeal terms, as the 'finest of all things and the purest'. Cf. also Xenophanes Frr. 25–26 and Parmenides Frr. 12–13; and contrast Diogenes' god which is identified with air in Fr. 5.

[3] In Anaxagoras the class of things that are alive (ὅσα ψυχὴν ἔχει) is implicitly contrasted with the class of things which are not (Frr. 4 and 12) and Democritus explicitly distinguished the two classes as ἔμψυχα and ἄψυχα if the report in Sextus (*M.* vii 117, Fr. 164) is to be trusted (cf. Fr. 278). Cf. also Diogenes Fr. 5 which says that the ψυχή of animals is air which is of a certain temperature.

principle which unites the four elements as Love (and explicitly referred to the works of Love among men to illustrate and exemplify this principle). The notion of a seed had probably been used both by Anaximander and by some of the Pythagoreans to describe the first stage in cosmogony. But then Anaxagoras used the term 'seeds' in a new context, that is to say of the nuclei round which natural substances (both organic and inorganic) grow and increase, and this too seems a deliberate application of a biological model to resolve a general physical problem. But apart from these specific biological notions which were adapted to particular purposes in accounts of change, it may be that the belief that the ultimate constituents of things, and the world as a whole, are in some sense alive, while modified, was never quite abandoned by the later Presocratics. Diogenes of Apollonia refers to his primary substance Air as immortal and as god (Frr. 5, 7, 8), in much the same way as many of the earlier Presocratics are reported to have done. But the Atomists, too, may have thought of the atom-mass as instinct with life in that it is permeated by self-moving soul-atoms. And even Empedocles and Anaxagoras, the philosophers in whom the separation of the 'moving cause' is most marked, do not seem to have conceived the primary constituents of things, or the world as a whole, as entirely inert and passive. On the contrary, if in one set of images Empedocles describes Love as a craftsman distinct and separate from the roots which are the material upon which she acts, he also uses another set of images which suggest, rather, that Love is inherent in the roots themselves, as when he refers to the roots being 'desired by one another' (Fr. 21 8) or speaks of Love as being ἔμφυτος in the limbs of mortals (Fr. 17 22). And in Anaxagoras, Mind, at least, is present in the world as a whole, in that it is said to control the cosmic revolution, as well as individual living beings (Fr. 12). Without denying the great variety of the main cosmological theories which were put forward in the post-Parmenidean period, we may say that the assumption that the world-whole is permeated by what is alive recurs, in some form, in each one of them.

Before going on to consider the role of vitalist conceptions in later Greek cosmology, we should first glance briefly at some of the evidence in the Hippocratic Corpus which shows that some quite elaborate versions of the doctrine that the world is a living organism were put forward in the late fifth and fourth centuries. Several medical treatises propose analogies of one sort or another between the microcosm and the macrocosm,[1] but two in particular suggest detailed comparisons between the parts of man and the parts of the world as a whole. *On Regimen* I is probably a work of the fourth century, although it is one which copies or repeats many themes of Presocratic philosophy.[2] In ch. 10 (L VI 484 17 ff.) the writer draws a comparison between the human body and the form of the universe. He says that 'fire arranged everything in the body...as a copy of the whole (ἀπομίμησιν τοῦ ὅλου)' and he then elaborates on this, although many of the details of his theory are obscure. Thus the belly is said to have the 'power' of the sea. Round the belly there is an obscure 'structure of cold and wet water' which is apparently described as an 'imitation of the earth which changes everything that falls into it'. Outside this in turn in the body there are three 'circuits', composed of water and fire (though again these are not identified), which are supposed to correspond to the circles of the moon, the 'middle' circles (those of the planets?) and those of the stars. The writer's knowledge of the internal structure of the body is even more vague and inaccurate than his astronomical theory appears to be: but he attempts nevertheless to set up detailed correspondences between microcosm and macrocosm. A second Hippocratic

---

[1] *On the Nature of Man* is one of the many treatises which construct the human body out of the same elements as the universe as a whole, and it is one of several which suggest that the alternations of the elements in the body (here, the humours) correspond to the cycle of seasons in the world as a whole (ch. 7, L VI 46 9 ff.).

[2] As most commentators have pointed out, the treatise contains many echoes of Heraclitus, Empedocles, Anaxagoras and the doctrines of the Pythagoreans.

treatise in which similarly complex analogies between micro-cosm and macrocosm are suggested is *On Sevens*.[1] Two dif-ferent sets of correspondences are proposed between the world and the human body. In ch. 11 the author suggests that various geographical areas of the earth correspond to the various parts of the body, the Peloponnese to the head, the Thracian Bosphorus to the feet and so on: both earth and body are divided quite arbitrarily into seven parts in accor-dance with the writer's conception of the special significance of that number. And in ch. 6 the various substances in the body are compared with those in the world at large. Here the stony core of the earth corresponds to the bones, its surface to flesh, the 'hot and wet' that exist in the earth to marrow and the brain, the water of rivers to blood in the veins, air to breath and so on.[2] As in *On Regimen* I many of the details of these comparisons are obscure. But what these two works show is that quite early in Greek speculative thought there were some theorists who went far beyond the simple notion that the world is alive in proposing complex (and often fantastic) analogies between microcosm and macrocosm.

[1] Widely divergent opinions have been advanced concerning the date of this work. Roscher, in his edition, pp. 117 ff., concluded that the geographical and cosmological theories expressed in it date from the sixth century B.C., arguing this partly on the grounds of the historical situation which he thought was re-flected in the analogy between the body and the areas of the earth in ch. 11 (cf. Kranz, *2*, pp. 135 ff. and *3*, p. 433, who considers that the cosmological doctrines of chs. 1–11 date from not long after 500 although he puts the pathological theories in the latter part of the work in the mid or late fifth century). But although in ch. 11 the Peloponnese is described as 'home of great souls' and identified with the head, this chapter hardly provides a reliable basis by which to date the work: the text is more than usually corrupt, several place-names cannot be identified and others have probably dropped out. The theory of a sixth-century date is in any case difficult to reconcile with the stylistic evidence: the fragments of the treatise which have survived in the original Greek have been dated on stylistic grounds to the late fifth or even early fourth century (cf. Diels, *4*, cols. 1861 ff., who concludes, cautiously, that the treatise should be dated between 450 and 350 B.C.).

[2] A rather different system of correspondences between the substances in the body and those in the world at large appears in the second part of the treatise at ch. 15. Here the water on the earth, for example, seems to correspond to the humours in the body (not, as in ch. 6, to the blood alone). The discrepancy between the two theories was one of the arguments used by Roscher to suggest that chs. 1–11 and chs. 12 ff. are by different authors.

Plato too considers the world a living creature, although his doctrine is remarkable in several respects. Like many of his cosmological notions, even some of those which are considered most characteristically Platonic, the conception of the world as a living being originated in earlier literature.[1] Yet in Plato this idea takes on a new significance, corresponding to his distinctive conception of the nature of the soul and its relation to the body. The fundamental distinction between the body and the soul is a recurrent theme in many dialogues, and from the *Phaedrus* onwards Plato develops the theory of the soul as the origin of all movement. True, both these ideas owe something to earlier Greek beliefs, especially the former to the doctrine associated particularly with the Pythagoreans that the body is, as it were, the 'tomb' of the transmigrating soul, σῶμα-σῆμα. Yet when the Presocratics represented the world as a living being, the emphasis generally lay not on the *different* natures of the body and the (transmigrating) soul, but rather on the idea that the world as a whole forms a *single* living organism.[2] What seems quite new and exceptional in Plato's references to the world-living-animal is, then, that they incorporate and take into account his conception of the distinction in essence between its visible body and its invisible soul, which is the source of movement, life and intelligence in all things.

The notion of a world-soul is first implied, perhaps, in the passage in the *Phaedrus* (245 c ff.) which contains Plato's first sustained exposition of the doctrine that the soul is that which moves itself. As such, soul is the source of movement not only in man, but in the world as a whole, and he says that it must be both ungenerated and indestructible, for otherwise 'the whole heaven and the whole earth would collapse into one

---

[1] At *Laws* 899 b Plato quotes with approval the dictum that 'all things are full of gods' (without, however, mentioning Thales by name).

[2] Thus while Anaximenes 'Fr.' 2, for example, certainly observes a distinction between breath-soul and complete animal ('just as our soul, being air, holds us together...'), soul is not there *opposed* to body (the term used in Aetius' report is ψυχή, but it is clearly the life-force, rather than what survives after death, that Anaximenes had in mind).

and stand still'.¹ Thereafter explicit references to the world as a living creature occur in several contexts,² most notably in the cosmological account in the *Timaeus*. There the world is described as 'in truth a living creature endowed with soul and with reason' (ζῷον ἔμψυχον ἔννουν τε, 30b). It is a 'visible living creature' which contains us and all other visible creatures, and it is fashioned by the Craftsman on the model of the perfect 'intelligible' living creature,³ a detailed description being given of the construction of the body of the world (31b–34b)⁴ and of its soul (34b–36d), and of the fitting together of these two (36de). Many features of this account are obviously not intended to be taken literally, and indeed throughout the *Timaeus*, as modern commentators have rarely failed to emphasise, we are frequently reminded that the account which is given of the material world—the visible likeness of the intelligible model—is not an exact, but only a probable, one.⁵ Yet the fact that the *Timaeus* presents a probable account of cosmology should not lead us to underestimate the importance, or the seriousness, of some of the doctrines it expresses. Plato undoubtedly held that the universe has not only a visible body, but also an invisible soul which permeates the whole and shares in reason and harmony

---

¹ *Phaedrus* 245d 7 ff., reading γῆν εἰς ἕν with Burnet.

² In the myth of the *Politicus* the universe is described as a 'living creature endowed with reason by him who fitted it together in the beginning' (269d 1 f.). Yet in this myth the period when the world moves by its own impulse (αὐτόματον) is distinguished from the period when it is guided and moved by the god: the natural movement of the world-animal is, indeed, in an opposite direction to that which is imparted to it by the god. By combining the doctrine of a directing god and that of a living animal in this way Plato can describe a two-stage cycle without supposing either that a single supreme god is responsible for two contrary movements, or that two gods move the world each in a different direction (both these ideas are rejected at 269e–270a), but this myth is exceptional in that divine ruler and world soul are not usually contrasted, but supplement one another (as it were) directly.

³ *Ti.* 30c–31b, and cf. also 37d, 39e and especially 92c.

⁴ In a passage which recalls themes of Presocratic philosophy, the world-body is said to be spherical and to lack all organs (*Ti.* 33c f.; cf. Xenophanes Frr. 23–24, Parmenides Fr. 8 42 ff., Empedocles Frr. 29 and 134).

⁵ Especially *Ti.* 29b–d. Yet 30bc suggests, rather, that this world is *in truth* (τῇ ἀληθείᾳ)—not merely probably—a living creature endowed with soul and reason (cf. Cornford, *6*, p. 34, n. 1).

(36d–37a, cf. 34b 3 ff.)—and his conception of the essential differences between these two is reflected in the fact that he gives separate accounts of their origins. And then *both* the doctrine of the intelligent world-soul *and* that of the Craftsman who brings things into order from disorder (e.g. 30a) serve to convey Plato's belief in the prevailing element of design in the universe.[1] At 46cd, in particular, the source of intelligent design in the universe is clearly described as *soul*. Leaving the works of Reason and turning to those of Necessity, Timaeus first stresses that 'necessary' causes (cooling, heating, etc.) are subsidiary and incapable of possessing reason or intelligence for any purpose, and then goes on: 'we must say that the only existing thing which properly possesses intelligence is soul' (46d 5 f., cf. also 30b 3).

The dichotomy between soul and body in the world as a whole is a theme which Plato develops in other late works besides the *Timaeus*. In the course of the discussion of the relative worth of intelligence and pleasure in the *Philebus*, he argues (29e ff.) that just as our body is sustained (τρέφεται) by the body of the universe and receives and possesses all its material elements from it, so, as we possess soul, the body of the universe itself must also be endowed with soul (from which our own is derived). As the Cause provides us with soul, so it cannot have failed to provide the heaven as a whole with 'that which is fairest and most noble' (that is, soul) (30b). Finally in *Laws* x the doctrine of the soul's priority to body appears once again (892a ff., cf. *Ti.* 34bc). There Plato establishes this thesis by analysing the different types of motion and showing that soul, as that which is capable of moving itself, is the primary source of all motion. Moreover, he carries this theory to its logical conclusion when he points out that as the cause of all things, soul is responsible not only for good things, but also for evil, not only for what is just, but also for what is unjust (896d 5 ff.). There are, then, several souls at work in heaven and earth, or at least two, the beneficent

---

[1] On the relation between these two doctrines, see below, pp. 284 f.

soul and that which is capable of bringing about the opposite results (896 e 4 ff.).[1] Then at 898 e f. he considers how the soul of the sun moves its visible body, suggesting three possible alternatives, (1) that it moves its body just as our souls move our bodies, or (2) that as 'some people argue', it procures for itself a body of fire or air and acts as body on the body of the sun, or (3) that being devoid of body, but having other 'surpassingly wonderful powers', it 'conducts' its body. He merely states these alternatives and makes no attempt (here or elsewhere) to settle the issue between them. But the fact that he either cannot or will not attempt an exact account of the relationship between the invisible souls of the sun, moon and stars and their visible bodies in no way alters his conviction that they *have* souls, and that their souls are *somehow* responsible for their movements.

In both the *Philebus* and the *Laws* references are made to soul and body in the macrocosm in passages where Plato is recommending certain ethical or religious theses, that is, the superiority of reason to pleasure, and the existence and power of the gods. In these contexts the *distinction* between soul and body, and the *priority* of soul, are emphasised, rather than any *connection* between them. But while the separation of soul and body corresponded, no doubt, to Plato's deep-felt religious and moral convictions, it is apparent that this doctrine left a problem in his theory of motion which he never satisfactorily resolved, namely how the source of motion is related to that which it moves. It is true that he recognises this *as a problem* at *Laws* 898 e, where he discusses how the soul of the sun moves its body, but there he offers no *better* solution than to refer to the analogy of the relation between our soul and our body.

In his final theory of motion, Aristotle denied the Platonic thesis that the origin of movement is that which moves itself. He argues in *Physics* Θ 4–5, for example, that the ultimate

---

[1] A comparison with 900 e ff. and 906 ab suggests that the soul or souls which bring about evil are those on earth: they are, in any case, certainly not those of the gods (see 900 e 6 ff.). Cf. Grube, pp. 146 f.

source of movement is a mover which is itself unmoved, for motion is the actualisation of a potentiality, and that which actualises what is potential must itself be in a state of complete actuality.[1] In all cases of things which 'move themselves', including living creatures, we can and should distinguish between that which imparts the movement (which is itself, *qua* source of movement, unmoved) and that which is moved (*Ph.* 258a 18 ff., cf. *de An.* A 3). In the sublunary sphere Aristotle generally draws a sharp distinction between animate and inanimate things (e.g. *de An.* A 2), although in his biological works he notes that 'nature proceeds little by little from inanimate things to living creatures in such a way that we are unable, in the continuous sequence, to determine the boundary line' (*HA* 588b 4 ff., and cf. also *PA* 681a 12 ff.). In the *de Anima*, he criticises such beliefs as that soul is intermingled in the whole universe (411a 7 ff.) or that the elements themselves are alive (a 14 ff.), although he makes some attempt to explain the grounds on which such doctrines were held.[2] Yet in spite of his rejection of Plato's notion of a self-moving soul, and his contempt for those who held that air or fire is alive, Aristotle's own theories both of heavenly and of sublunary motion are influenced, to a considerable degree, by vitalist conceptions.[3] First of all we may consider his theory of the motion of the heavenly bodies at the different stages of its development.[4]

The connection between the heavenly regions and divinity is a constant feature of Aristotle's theology. He often refers

[1] The example given at *Ph.* 257b 8 ff. is that that which heats is itself hot.

[2] See *de An.* 411a 16 ff.: 'They seem to suppose that soul is present in them [i.e. fire or air] because the whole is homogeneous with the parts. So if it is by taking in some portion of the surrounding substance that animals come to have soul, they must necessarily affirm that the soul [of the whole] too is homogeneous with its parts.' (But at a 9 ff. Aristotle raises the chief difficulty which such a view involves: 'Why does not the soul which exists in air or fire form an animal?')

[3] The best discussions of this aspect of Aristotle's thought are those in J. M. Le Blond, *1*, pp. 346 f. and *2*, pp. 11 ff.

[4] On the question of the development of Aristotle's theory of motion, besides the discussions in Jaeger, *3*; Ross, *2*, pp. 94 ff.; and Guthrie, *1*, *2*, and *3*, pp. xv ff.; see also the contributions of Merlan, *1*, and *3*, pp. 73 ff. and Wolfson.

to religious beliefs[1] shared, he says, by Greeks and Barbarians alike, according to which the heavenly bodies are gods and the heaven itself (the 'uppermost region') is divine, and while he explicitly rejects the 'mythical', that is anthropomorphic or zoomorphic, elements in these beliefs, he frequently affirms his own conviction that both the stars and the aither itself, the fifth element of which the heavens are composed, are divine.[2] But if Aristotle always ascribed divinity to the stars, it is generally agreed that his theory of how they move underwent certain important developments or modifications. From a report in Cicero (de nat. deor. II 16 44; Fr. 24) it seems likely that in the dialogue περὶ φιλοσοφίας Aristotle ruled out *both* the possibility that the motion of the stars is enforced, *and* the possibility that it is natural, and concluded that it is voluntary, that is due to the fact that they are alive and have wills of their own. This has been taken (rightly, I think) to suggest that at one period Aristotle had not worked out the doctrine of the fifth element which moves naturally in a circle, which is set out in *Cael.* A 2–3 and which thereafter forms the basis of his theory of the heavenly bodies. In the *de Caelo* itself, the picture is a complex one. From one point of view soul is no longer necessary to his theory of how the stars move, since the fifth element is said to move naturally (κατὰ τὴν ἑαυτοῦ φύσιν) in a circle (269a 6 f.).[3] And in *Cael.* B 1, 284a 27 ff., indeed, he expressly refutes the idea that their motion is due to a 'constraining soul' (i.e. probably, as Ross, 2, p. 98, suggested, a soul which 'constrains the heavenly

---

[1] E.g. *Cael.* 270b 5 ff., 284a 2 ff.; *Mete.* 339b 19 ff.; *Metaph.* Λ 1074a 38 ff.

[2] Besides the passages mentioned in the last note, see also *Cael.* 278b 14 f., 292b 31 ff. and cf. περὶ φιλοσοφίας Fr. 23 (Cicero, *de nat. deor.* II 15 42).

[3] The stars are carried round in the circles in which they are embedded and do not move by themselves (*Cael.* B 8–9). At 291a 22 ff. he denies that the stars themselves move either with a motion due to their being alive (ἔμψυχον... φοράν) or with an enforced motion, but (as scholars have pointed out) to deny that they move within their circles in either of these two ways, is not to deny that they are alive. Indeed the argument brought at 290a 29 ff. is only valid on the assumption that the stars are strictly comparable with ordinary animals: for if they had had independent movement, Aristotle says, nature would not have failed to provide them with organs of locomotion, especially as the stars are more precious than (ordinary) animals.

bodies to motion contrary to their natural motion'). It might seem strange, then, to continue to believe that the aither is endowed with soul when its circular motion (like the upward or downward motion of the four sublunary elements) is due simply to its natural tendency. Yet the fact is that not only did Aristotle *not* deny the divinity of the substance of the heavenly bodies in the *de Caelo*, but he even reaffirms that doctrine in the chapters in which he sets out his theory of aither: at 269a 30 ff. he infers the existence of a substance which he describes as 'more divine' than the other four elements, and at 270b 5 ff. he refers to traditional beliefs about the divinity of the uppermost region as evidence *in support of* his conception of a fifth element.[1] The question of whether, at the time of writing the *de Caelo*, Aristotle had formulated his proof of the impossibility of self-motion, is more difficult. However, at 279a 33 ff. he appears to refer to the eternally moving sphere as the highest divinity,[2] and at 286a 9 ff. he says that it belongs to the divine to be in eternal motion,[3] and it seems difficult to reconcile these two passages (at least) with the doctrine of the Unmoved Mover.[4] The contrast with the theory put forward

---

[1] E.g. 270b 10 ff.: 'if there is something divine (as indeed there is) then what we have said about the first bodily substance was well said'. Again in *Cael.* B 1 where he denies that the motion of the sphere is due to a 'constraining soul', he suggests that his own theory corresponds to our 'premonitions' about divinity, 284a 35 ff.

[2] 'There is nothing superior that can move it, for that would be more divine than it.' This seems to refer to the heavenly sphere, for he goes on (b 1), 'it is in unceasing motion, as is reasonable...'. (Yet earlier in this admittedly confused passage, 279a 17 ff., he had referred to certain unnamed objects which exist 'outside the heaven' and which enjoy 'the best and most self-sufficient lives', although it seems hardly possible to take 279a 33 ff. to refer to *these*.)

[3] 'The activity of a god is immortality, that is eternal life. *So that necessarily* eternal motion belongs to the divine [or, reading θεῷ, "to god"]. Since the heaven is of this sort (for it is a divine body), for this reason it has a circular body, which naturally moves for ever in a circle.' Contrast *Metaph.* Λ 1072b 26 ff., where the 'eternal life' of god is one that involves no movement.

[4] See further Guthrie, *3*, pp. xxi ff. on *Cael.* 284a 18 ff., 300b 18 and 309b 17. There are, on the contrary, certain passages in the *de Caelo* which *imply* an Unmoved Mover, but these are generally taken as later additions. Cf. Guthrie, *3*, pp. xxiii f. on *Cael.* B 6 and Δ 3: 'in both these chapters the mentions of the unmoved mover occur as appendages to arguments that have already proved their point without them'.

in *Metaphysics* Λ is striking, for there the highest divinity (and the ultimate source of movement) is, of course, quite unmoved. But though often referred to in the impersonal neuter, the Unmoved Mover is nevertheless unquestionably alive and divine. 'And life belongs to it, for the actuality of mind is life, and god is that actuality, and god's essential actuality is the highest and eternal life' (1072 b 26 ff.). Moreover, not only is the Unmoved Mover alive, but Aristotle's account of its mode of operation rests on the assumption that the heavenly spheres themselves are also alive. The Unmoved Mover is said to move these as the object of *desire*: 'it moves by being loved' (1072 b 3). The Unmoved Mover is remote from the sublunary world, indeed, but that both it and the heavenly spheres it moves are alive is an essential feature of Aristotle's final theory of heavenly motion.

Both in his first account of the motion of the stars, in the περὶ φιλοσοφίας, and in the final version of that theory in *Metaph.* Λ, the idea that the stars (or their spheres) are alive is clearly an essential feature of Aristotle's doctrine. In what seems to be an intermediate period, represented by texts in the *de Caelo*, the divinity of the stars is certainly not denied, but it is not apparent that this doctrine forms a necessary part of his theory of the movement of the heavenly bodies. Yet in two contexts the belief that the stars and the heavenly sphere are alive does form the key assumption on which Aristotle bases his explanations of various celestial phenomena in the *de Caelo*. (1) First in *Cael.* B 2 and 5 he discusses whether the heavenly sphere has a top and bottom, right and left, front and back. He notes that these distinctions are not to be looked for in *every* kind of body, but only in those which have a principle of movement within themselves (284 b 30 ff.). But this is true of the heavenly sphere, which is alive (ἔμψυχος) and has a principle of movement (285 a 29 f.). Even though it is spherical, then, it has upper and lower sides, a right and a left, a front and a back, and he then uses this doctrine in *Cael.* B 5 to suggest a possible solution to the problem of why the

heavens revolve in one direction rather than in the other.[1]
(2) Then in *Cael.* B 12 the doctrine that the stars are alive is
invoked when he raises the two questions of why the planets
have more complex motions than either the outermost sphere
or the sun and moon, and why the outermost sphere carries in
it many stars, while those of the planets, sun and moon, carry
only one body each. Once again (as at 287b 28 ff.) he begins
with a disclaimer, pointing out that on the most obscure problems it is a sign of modesty to be content with little knowledge
(291 b 24 ff.). But he then bases possible solutions to his problems on the assumption that the heavenly bodies partake in
life and action.[2] A complex schema is suggested in which (*a*)
that which is in the best possible state (i.e. the first mover)
possesses the good without taking action at all, (*b*) that which
is nearest to it (the heavenly sphere) achieves the good by
means of little, or a single, action, (*c*) that which is further
away (i.e. the planets) achieves it by more complex actions,
while (*d*) further away still are things (sun, moon and earth)
which cannot attempt to achieve the highest good, but achieve
some lesser end. He illustrates the relationship between these
last two kinds (*c* and *d*) by referring to living creatures on
earth (292b 1 ff.). On earth, men have the most complex
actions (they are, in this, analogous to the planets), while the
lower animals have less variety of actions and plants one mode
of action alone (the sun and moon are analogous to these, and
cf. also 292b 19 ff. on the earth which—like plants—has no
local movement at all).[3]

---

[1] He begins by noting that to try to explain everything without exception
may seem to indicate an excessive simple-mindedness or excessive zeal (287b
28 ff.), but he then tentatively suggests that the heavens revolve in one direction
rather than the other because (1) nature always produces the best results possible, and (2) right and front are superior to their opposites (cf. above, pp. 52 ff.).

[2] 'But we think of the heavenly bodies as mere bodies and units which have
order, but are completely lifeless: but we ought to think of them as enjoying action and life' (292a 18 ff.).

[3] Again at 292b 25 ff., when he considers the problem of why there are many
stars in the outermost sphere, but only one body in each of the spheres of the
sun, moon and planets, the first reason he offers refers to the superior *life* of the
first motion (b 28 f.).

It is more difficult to show how Aristotle's theory of change in the sublunary sphere is also influenced by vitalist conceptions. At one point, however, this is obvious enough. The earth itself is said to be subject to cycles of growth and decay (though not as a whole) like the bodies of animals and plants,[1] and this is a doctrine which (as we shall see later)[2] underlies Aristotle's accounts of various geological phenomena including both earthquakes and the saltness of the sea. But we should also consider his theory of the movements of the four sublunary elements. Aither, as we have seen, was held to be divine. The four sublunary elements, on the other hand, are often explicitly contrasted with living things (animals, plants and their parts). At *Ph.* 255 a 5 ff., for instance, Aristotle discusses how light and heavy objects move, and rejects the supposition that they are moved by themselves (ὑφ' αὐτῶν): 'for that is characteristic of life and peculiar to living things'.[3] Yet it is interesting to examine how he does account for the movements of the four elements. He answers the question why fire rises and earth falls by saying that it is natural for them to do so (e.g. *Ph.* 255b 15: αἴτιον δ' ὅτι πέφυκέ ποι). In *Cael.* Δ he defines heavy and light as potentialities for certain natural motions (307b 31 ff.) and says that for each of these to move towards its proper place (down or up) is for it to move *towards its own form* (εἰς τὸ αὐτοῦ εἶδος, 310a 33 ff.). Air generated from water, for example (311a 1 ff.), moves to the upper

---

[1] At *Mete.* 351a 26 ff., for example, when accounting for the changes in the relations between sea and land over the surface of the globe, he says: 'the principle and cause of these changes is that the interior of the earth, like the bodies of plants and animals, has a prime and an old age (ἀκμὴν ἔχει καὶ γῆρας)'. Characteristically, however, he goes on to note the differences between the two cases: 'except that in the latter (animals and plants) the process does not go on by parts, but each of them necessarily grows and decays *as a whole*: whereas it does go on *by parts* in the case of the earth, due to heat and cold'.

[2] See below (pp. 362 f.) on *Mete.* 358a 16 ff. and 366b 14 ff. And at *GA* 777b 24 ff. when he says that all changes in the sublunary region are dependent on the heavenly bodies, he suggests that winds too have a 'life of a sort and a generation and a decay' (778a 2 f.).

[3] He implies, too, that living beings alone are capable of arresting their movements (*Ph.* 255a 7) and at *Cael.* 284b 33 f. he distinguishes animate from inanimate things by pointing out that in the latter we cannot observe a part from which their movement originates.

region: 'once there, it is light, and it no longer "becomes", but "is" there', and this is described as the *potential* moving towards *actuality* (δυνάμει ὄν, εἰς ἐντελέχειαν ἰόν).[1]

Certain distinctions are drawn, in such passages as *Ph.* 255a 5 ff., between the movements of inanimate and those of animate objects, but the analogy between these two types of motion is an important and striking feature of Aristotle's theory, and it might be suggested that to some extent, at least, he tended to assimilate the upward or downward movement of the four elements to such other 'natural' movements as the growth of living beings. In one passage, where he considers whether movement is eternal or not (and he concludes that it is), we even find Aristotle asking whether κίνησις may not be 'as it were a sort of life' (οἷον ζωή τις) to all natural objects (*Ph.* 250b 11 ff.). And some of his other descriptions of φύσις seem primarily applicable to living things, as when he implies that natural objects have an innate impulse (ὁρμὴν... ἔμφυτον) to change (*Ph.* 192b 18 f.) or when matter is described as desiring and yearning for (ἐφίεσθαι, ὀρέγεσθαι) form (*Ph.* 192a 16 ff.).[2] But it is rather when the four elements are said to actualise certain *potentialities* in progressing towards their proper places, and when those proper places themselves are described as their *forms*, that the influence of ideas derived from his analysis of the development of living beings seems particularly marked. Aristotle's explicit statements show that he did *not* believe that the four sublunary elements are alive, and he clearly recognised that the analogy between their natural movements and those of living things is *only* an analogy. On the other hand at certain points his general theory of change appears to be based on conceptions which apply first and foremost to the sphere of living things, and to other

---

[1] Cf. *Ph.* 255a 28 ff. where the movements of fire or earth are described as natural when they actualise the potentialities which these simple bodies possess.

[2] One of the illustrations which Aristotle gives is that of the female desiring the male. Cf. also the metaphor which he uses at *Cael.* 308a 1 ff. where he says that the heavy and the light have in themselves as it were the 'sparks' of movement (οἷον ζώπυρ' ἄττα κινήσεως).

things only by transference. This is especially true of the distinction between potentiality and actuality, for while this is certainly an extremely complex theory which has many facets,[1] it seems fairly clear that the main or primary sphere in which *both* the distinction between the potential and the actual *and* the possibility of change from the one state to the other, are manifest and obvious, is the biological one, where the seed grows naturally into a mature organism.[2]

We saw earlier how various conceptions of cosmic order were expressed by means of the social and political images of law, justice, rule and so on. Vitalist doctrines are doubly important in the history of Greek speculative thought, since the conception of the world as a living organism not only conveyed an idea of the universe as a single whole (made up of interrelated parts), but also enabled an account to be given of its development in terms of a natural growth or evolution. Most of the pre-Parmenidean philosophers shared some belief that the primary stuff of things is alive or that the world itself is a living being, but while these ideas are undoubtedly connected with the religious belief that the primary stuff is divine, this is not their only, nor their chief, importance, for they form the basis of what were sometimes (as in Anaximander) quite elaborate cosmological doctrines which represented the origin and evolution of the world in organic terms. In the period after Parmenides the problem of coming-to-be

---

[1] At *Metaph.* 1071 a 3 ff., for example, Aristotle himself draws attention to the fact that this distinction applies in different ways in different cases.

[2] Consider the three cases (1) a seed growing into a mature animal or plant, (2) a stone rolling down the side of a mountain, and (3) wood and bricks being made into a house by a builder. In the last case the change from 'potential' to 'actual' is marked by a difference in the *function* and use of the material, but this change is only brought about by *external* intervention, the work of the builder. In the second case no external intervention is necessary (except in so far as somebody or something may remove what prevents the stone from falling), but the change from 'potential' to 'actual' is marked only by a change of *position* (and not by one of function). In the case of living things alone, what changes changes *of its own accord* and at the same time develops and achieves a new *function* or fulfilment. The three cases are different but parallel, but it seems that in certain of its features the doctrine of potentiality and actuality applies *primarily* to the changes affecting living things, and only in a secondary, or transferred, sense to inorganic substances.

was more clearly recognised *as* a problem, but vitalist doctrines (the Love of Empedocles, the seeds of Anaxagoras) continued to provide the basis of some of the accounts of change that were put forward, and even the Atomists, who of all the early Greek philosophers gave the most purely mechanical account of causation, did not, it seems, entirely abandon the notion that the world as a whole is pervaded by what is alive. The continued influence of certain vitalist conceptions is quite marked in Plato and Aristotle, and again the ideas in question are not merely religious or mystical beliefs, but play an important part in the solutions to certain problems in cosmology. Plato particularly emphasised the dualism of soul and body, but at the same time he was the first cosmologist to argue explicitly that soul is the source of all movement in the universe on the grounds that it is, by definition, that which moves itself. Furthermore, the doctrine of the world-living-organism is expressed more clearly in the works of Plato than in any other extant fifth- or fourth-century text: for Plato the universe is a living creature, different from ordinary living creatures in being unique in kind and perfect and ageless (*Ti.* 31 b, 33 a), yet a living creature, compounded of soul and body, none the less. In Aristotle clear distinctions are drawn between (1) artificial objects, (2) natural, but inanimate objects, and (3) living beings, and within the class of living beings, between things which have one, or several, of the faculties of soul (nutritive, locomotive, perceptive and so on). Yet he too considered both the heavenly bodies and the Unmoved Mover to be alive and divine, and while these doctrines correspond to his 'premonitions of divinity', they also form an essential part of his theory of how the heavenly bodies move and how the Unmoved Mover operates. In the sublunary sphere, too, he believed that the earth is subject to cycles of growth and decay, and though he certainly denied that the four sublunary elements are alive, it is arguable that his account of their natural motions is to some extent influenced by a tendency to treat the growth of living beings as the paradigm of all natural change. His analysis of the different modes of being, animate and inanimate, may be said to have clarified certain important distinctions which had not always been fully grasped in earlier periods, and he expressly rejected and ridiculed some of the vitalist assumptions which had been commonly entertained by the Presocratics (such as the doctrine that the primary material constituents of things are themselves alive). But at the same time other vitalist beliefs persist in Aristotle's own cosmological and physical theories, both in his treatment of the motion of the heavenly bodies, and in his account of change in the sublunary sphere.

Biological models enabled a concrete account to be given of the nature of the universe and of its evolution. But the set of vitalist notions which we have been studying had, in the long run especially, unfortunate results in several fields of inquiry. The attempt to set up detailed analogies between microcosm and macrocosm nearly always led to the proposal of crude and grotesque theories on the structure of man and of the universe, and we find some quite early examples of this type of analogy in *On Sevens* and *On Regimen* I.[1] But the influence of vitalist beliefs on the development of Greek astronomy and dynamics raises a more interesting and important issue. So long as it was assumed that the heavenly bodies are alive, their motions, and in particular any apparent irregularities in their courses, *might* be attributed simply to their own volitions. Yet it should be observed that the doctrine that the heavenly bodies are alive and divine, which was upheld by both Plato and Aristotle (although it had been abandoned by several of their predecessors and contemporaries),[2] was *not* used by

[1] The extent of the extant evidence for the use of this type of analogy in ancient Greece is, however, quite small in comparison with the abundant material for later periods which has been collected by such scholars as A. Meyer and G. P. Conger in their special studies of this topic.

[2] For example Anaxagoras' view that the sun is a stone was apparently used against him when he was tried for impiety (e.g. D.L. II 12; DK 59 A 1), and cf. Plato's general reference to those who considered the heavenly bodies (mere) earth and stones in the *Laws*, 886d ff.

them simply as an excuse to abandon the study of astronomy. In Plato it served rather as the basis for his explanation of why the heavenly bodies move at all.[1] In the *Timaeus* (39 d) he certainly speaks, in the conventional manner, of the planets' 'wanderings' (πλάναι) saying that these are 'bewildering in number and of wonderful complexity', but whether this should be taken to suggest that at this stage he considered their motions irregular is, to my mind, quite doubtful. In the *Laws* (821 b–822 a), at any rate, he denied with the strongest possible emphasis that any of the heavenly bodies can be said to 'wander'.[2]

Aristotle's doctrine of the heavenly bodies fixed in spheres which carry them round is a more elaborate, and in many respects a more purely mechanical, account than Plato's,[3] although, as we saw, he appeals to the notion that the heavenly bodies are living beings at several points, as for example when he attempts to explain why there are many bodies in the sphere of the fixed stars, but only one each in those of the sun, moon and planets. But we should examine particularly the arguments by which he arrived at his theory of aither, for Aristotle has, of course, been much criticised by historians of astronomy for putting forward the suggestion that the heavenly bodies are composed of a fifth element unlike the other four in that its natural motion is circular. Starting from the generalisation that the natural movement of the elements on earth is either up or down, he was faced with two alternatives: either (*a*) the heavenly bodies are

---

[1] Presumably Plato would also have explained why the courses of the sun, moon and planets are different on the assumption that they are self-moving. As Cornford, *6*, p. 87, put it: 'it is, presumably, the self-motion of the planets that enables them either to counteract the motion of the Different...or to reinforce it'.

[2] At *Laws* 822a he goes so far as to say that each of the heavenly bodies 'travels on the same path, not many paths, but always one, in a circle'. On the difficulties which this passage raises, see Heath, pp. 181 ff.

[3] It is indeed because Aristotle aimed at a mechanical, rather than a purely mathematical, account of the heavenly motions that he modified the theories of Eudoxus and Callippus by introducing reactive spheres (*Metaph.* Λ 8), see Heath, pp. 217 ff.

composed of one (or more) of these elements—but then in this case their movement cannot be natural, but must be enforced (like that of projectiles); or (*b*) they are composed of an entirely different element which naturally moves in a circle.[1] Aristotle adopts the second view mainly on the apparently quite reasonable grounds that the motions of the heavenly bodies are *unchanging*,[2] and therefore natural. And in the *Meteorologica*, A 3, when he refutes the idea that the space between the earth and the outermost heaven consists of fire or air or of both elements together, one of his arguments (340a 1 ff.) is that the *extent* of this area is so great that if it had been composed of fire (for instance) all the other elements would long ago have disappeared. The drawing of a distinction between celestial and terrestrial motion was a particularly influential error which was to remain uncorrected until Newton. But while Aristotle's doctrine of aither owes something, on his own admission (*Cael.* 270b 5 ff.), to traditional religious beliefs according to which the upper regions are associated with what is divine and immortal, it is clear that he was led to his theory of the fifth element by important empirical considerations as well: he assumed it to be a fact that both the movements of the heavenly bodies and their configurations are absolutely unchanging,[3] and he recognised

[1] It is interesting that circular motion, which in *Cael.* A 2 Aristotle assumed to be *simple*, was analysed into two rectilinear motions already in the Peripatetic treatise *On Mechanics* (chs. 1, 848b 35 ff., and 8, 852a 7 ff., and cf. also Aristotle's own brief suggestion at *Ph.* 244a 2 ff. that 'whirling' is a compound of pulling and pushing), and yet this analysis (as Cohen and Drabkin, p. 201, have noted) was not systematically applied to celestial motion until Newton.

[2] At *Cael.* 270b 13 ff. he says that in the whole of past time, according to the records handed down from one generation to the next, no change appears to have taken place either in the whole of the outermost heaven or in any of its proper parts. (It is clear from *Cael.* 292a 7 ff., for example, that Aristotle drew not only on the records of Greek astronomers, but on those of Babylonian and Egyptian astronomers as well.)

[3] It appears from Ptolemy, *Alm.* VII 1–2 that Hipparchus knew of the precession of the equinoxes, but whether it was known any earlier than the second century B.C. is very doubtful (see Heath, pp. 101 ff., 172 ff., and Neugebauer, *1*, pp. 146 f. and *2*, pp. 68 f.).

that the size of the earth is minute in relation to the extent of the universe as a whole.

Finally, the set of beliefs which we have been studying throws some light on the relative failure of the early Greek philosophers to make much progress in the field of dynamics. The way in which the phenomena of gravity were described is particularly interesting. Both in the Presocratic period and later these phenomena were generally explained on the principle that 'like attracts like', but this was an extremely general doctrine that could be, and often was, applied to a whole range of phenomena involving animate, as well as inanimate, objects, e.g. to the behaviour of men and animals[1] as well as to the upward movement of fire and the downward movement of earth (as in Empedocles Fr. 62 6, and cf. Anaxagoras Fr. 15). The tendency to treat both types of phenomena as instances of the same principle is seen especially clearly in a report on Democritus in Sextus Empiricus.[2] According to Sextus, Democritus illustrated the doctrine of like-to-like with various examples: 'For animals flock together by their kinds, doves with doves and cranes with cranes, and so too with the other irrational animals. And the same happens with inanimate objects, too, as we can see with seeds in a sieve and pebbles on the sea-shore', where (according to Democritus) when the sieve is shaken the different sorts of seeds are separated into their kinds, and similarly pebbles are sorted according to their various shapes by the actions of the waves. We have already had occasion to notice that a general distinction is observed here between animate and inanimate objects (ἔμψυχα and ἄψυχα), but while Democritus recognised these

---

[1] E.g. in the various Greek proverbs expressing the idea that 'birds of a feather flock together', ἀεὶ κολοιὸς παρὰ κολοιόν, ὡς αἰεὶ τὸν ὁμοῖον ἄγει θεὸς ὡς τὸν ὁμοῖον (*Od.* 17 218): other similar expressions are mentioned by Aristotle at *Rh.* 1371 b 15 ff.

[2] *M.* vii 117 f., DK 68 B 164, cf. also Aet. iv 19 3, DK A 128. Sextus is here dealing with Democritus' epistemological theory, but the principle of 'like-to-like' was used by the Atomists not only in this context (cf. Empedocles Fr. 109), but also more generally with reference to the separation of atoms (cf. D.L. ix 31; DK 67 A 1).

two types of objects as distinct, he evidently believed that *both* kinds of phenomena to which he refers may be subsumed under the *same* general law. The development of dynamics as such depended, then, among other things, on isolating its subject-matter from those of biology and psychology, and on recognising that the phenomena of gravity, vortices, and so on, are different in kind from the conscious or instinctive behaviour of animals. Aristotle was, of course, well aware of this distinction, and his dynamics, though often severely criticised by modern scholars,[1] was undoubtedly a great advance on the vague notions of earlier writers. Thus he was the first physicist to attempt to distinguish the various factors which govern the speed of moving objects (suggesting how velocity varies with the density of the medium, the weight of the object and so on, in the two cases of 'natural' and 'forced' motion), and although his general dynamical theories are often erroneous, they are not (as is sometimes thought) utterly at variance with experience, but are, rather, hasty generalisations from superficial observations.[2] However, if he often made good use of the data of ordinary experience in his dynamics, it must be conceded that he did not undertake systematic quantitative investigations of different types of motion, and while a similar failure is also evident in other aspects of his physics and biology, one consideration which may help us to understand why he did not apply quantitative methods to dynamics in particular beyond a certain point, is that he tended to treat all types of natural motion as the actualising of potentialities. It may be suggested that in so far as the natural motion of each of the sublunary elements was conceived as a progression towards its form, it must

[1] See, for example, the discussion in Ross, 2, pp. 26 ff., and contrast the rather more favourable accounts given in Duhem, 1, pp. 192 ff., and Drabkin.

[2] The best-known example is Aristotle's doctrine that the velocity of freely falling objects varies directly with their weight (e.g. *Cael.* 273 b 30 ff.). Yet the error here is not to suggest that there is *some* relation between weight and velocity (for in air, at least—though not in a vacuum—heavier objects do fall faster than lighter ones of the same shape and size), but to suggest that the relation is one of direct proportion.

have seemed irrelevant for the understanding of the essential
nature of those motions to undertake precise quantitative
measurements of the various factors which governed them.[1]

TECHNOLOGICAL IMAGES: THE COSMOS
AS AN ARTEFACT

The passages in Hesiod which describe the making of
Pandora (*Op.* 59 ff.; *Th.* 570 ff.; see above, p. 208) are
obvious examples in pre-philosophical Greek literature
where creation is conceived as manufacture by a craftsman-
god,[2] and on certain other occasions, too, we find that
phenomena of various sorts are referred to not merely as the
instruments of the gods, but as artefacts which they have
made, although there is no evidence that the world as a whole
was considered as such by the ancient Greeks in the period
before philosophy. The Presocratics, and still more Plato and
Aristotle, use a variety of images which suggest that a designing, craftsman-like agency is at work in the world, and it is
the history of these images, and their role in the development
of Greek cosmological theories, that I wish to consider in this
section.

One type of image which recurs frequently in the Presocratic philosophers, is that of steering or piloting (κυβερνᾶν,
οἰακίζειν), and although this conveys no notion of any process
of manufacture, it may sometimes be taken to suggest not
merely the idea of power, but more particularly one of intelligent direction. The image probably occurs first in cosmology
in Anaximander if, as seems likely, Aristotle is referring to
him (among others) when he reports at *Ph.* 203 b 10 ff. that

[1] Cf. Le Blond, *1*, p. 348 and n. 4, who has suggested that the 'negligence' of
Aristotle's account of projectiles may reflect his belief that their motion is not
natural, but enforced, and as such hardly worthy of serious study at all.

[2] Similar myths can, of course, be cited from other ancient literatures and
from modern societies, for example, Wilson in Frankfort, *2*, p. 64, on the
Egyptian myth of the fashioning of mankind by the god Khnum on his potter's
wheel, and Evans-Pritchard, *3*, p. 5, on the Nuer belief that God fashioned
man.

those who do not adopt other causes, such as Mind or Love,
besides the Boundless itself, say that it enfolds all and steers
all. But thereafter it is one of the favourite images of the Presocratics, occurring in Heraclitus (who uses both κυβερνᾶν in
Fr. 41, and οἰακίζειν in Fr. 64), in Parmenides (Fr. 12) and in
Diogenes of Apollonia (Fr. 5).[1] If the literal sense of this
term were pressed, it might be taken to imply that the steering agent (that is, generally speaking, the pilot himself, rather
than the rudder) is distinct from the object which is steered,
the ship, and we might be led to conclude that this image
contains the germ of the notion of a separate moving cause.
But whether the Presocratics themselves intended this term to
suggest a distinction between steersman and what is steered,
must be considered very doubtful. On the majority of occasions when it is used (Anaximander, Heraclitus Fr. 64,
Diogenes Fr. 5) the subject which is said to 'guide' or 'steer'
all things is the primary substance itself of which the universe
is composed or from which it originates.[2] In Heraclitus Fr.
64, for instance, it is fire, or thunderbolt, κεραυνός, that
'steers' all things (and will 'judge' and 'convict' them, Fr.
66), although elsewhere (Fr. 30) the world-order itself is
identified as an 'ever-living fire'.[3] The image of steering (like

---

[1] Cf. also in the Hippocratic treatise *On Regimen* I, ch. 10, L VI 486 10, and
elsewhere in Greek literature generally, e.g. Pi. *P.* 4 274 and 5 122, where it is used
of Zeus. Louis, *I*, p. 171, n. 36, compares the epithet ὑψίζυγος used of Zeus in
Homer (e.g. *Il.* 4 166, and cf. also Hes. *Op.* 18), 'seated high on the benches', i.e.
'throned on high'.

[2] In Parmenides Fr. 12, however, κυβερνᾶν is used of the δαίμων whom Aetius
(II 7 1; DK 28 A 37) identified with Justice and Necessity.

[3] It is striking that in Fr. 30 Heraclitus denies that the world-order is the
product of 'any god or mortal': κόσμον τόνδε ... οὔτε τις θεῶν οὔτε ἀνθρώπων
ἐποίησεν. This is such an explicit denial that it looks as if it is directed against
some specific myth or theory. Yet we have considerable difficulty in identifying
this with any certainty from our available evidence. Various suggestions have
been made. Some have seen the fragment as an attack on Xenophanes, whose
Fr. 25 certainly describes god as 'swaying all things by the thought of his mind',
though whether Xenophanes' god had any *creative* function is not clear. Guthrie
(*HGP*, I, p. 454, n. 3) considers that Heraclitus' denial is 'primarily aimed at the
parcelling out of the world into sky, sea and earth, symbolized by the distribution (δασμός) between the chief gods' (as in *Il.* 15 187 ff. and Hes. *Th.* 74, 885).
This too is certainly a possible interpretation, but we should observe that the

that of ruling with which it is sometimes closely associated, e.g. Diogenes Fr. 5) is evidently used to suggest the overall direction exercised by some cosmological factor, but the nature of that direction is often left quite vague and undefined in our texts,[1] and it seems clear that the use of this image did not necessarily imply that 'moving cause' and that which is moved were conceived as separate and distinct.

The notion of a force that steers all things is found in several of the Presocratics, but one fifth-century cosmologist in particular uses much more varied and elaborate images drawn from the skills and crafts. This is Empedocles, who uses such images both to illustrate the processes by which certain things come to be,[2] and to convey an idea of the creative role of Love. It is notable that he draws on technological images especially in connection with the creation of complex structures such as living beings or their parts. Fr. 73, for instance, refers to some stage in the formation of living creatures: there Kupris is described as taking earth, wetting it with water and then submitting it to fire (like a baker, perhaps, kneading and then baking bread, cf. also Fr. 34). Fr. 96 describes the way in which bones are formed: the earth received certain proportions of the elements in its 'wide melting-pots' (χόανοι: this is the term used elsewhere of the receptacles in which metal was melted, e.g. *Il.* 18 470, Hes. *Th.* 863), and then 'the white bones came into being, marvellously fastened together with the glue of Harmonia'.[3] Then too the creation of organs is described with other technological images. Frr. 86 and 87

idea of a god imposing order on disorder is expressed a good deal more explicitly, and in more general terms, in Heraclitus' denial, than it is in any of the extant texts which relate to the distribution of different areas to different gods by means of a lottery, or to the apportioning of different prerogatives to the gods by Zeus.

[1] For a full discussion of the various possible interpretations of the image in Anaximander, see KR, pp. 115 f.

[2] This will be discussed further below, pp. 334 f. and p. 335 n. 1.

[3] The point of this second sentence may be simply that the mixture of elements is a permanent one, but it is possible that the image is more precise than that. Both ἀραρίσκω and κόλλα may refer to wood-working in particular, and if this is so, the sentence may refer not to the creation of bones, but to their arrangement in the body (as Fr. 87 seems to refer to the fastening of the eyes in the head).

refer to the eyes. Divine Aphrodite 'ἔπηξεν'[1] the eyes from certain elements and then 'fastened them with bolts of love' (that is, in the head, presumably). The importance of these images lies (I believe) in part, at least, in the contrast they imply between Love as divine artisan, and the roots which are the material upon which she works. Of course Empedocles' Philia is itself material. It is said in Fr. 17, for example, to be 'inherent in mortal limbs', and when it brings things together and mixes them, it is almost certainly thought of as present itself as an ingredient in the mixture. Thus Aristotle (*Metaph.* 1075 b 3 f.) interprets Love as a principle both ὡς κινοῦσα (as moving cause) and ὡς ὕλη (as material cause) (because, as he says, 'it is part of the mixture'). Empedocles himself sometimes refers to his six cosmological principles in terms which rather conceal the differences between their roles (e.g. Fr. 17 16 ff.). But if on other occasions those differences are more apparent, this is especially true of some of the technological images which he used. Indeed it may be suggested that it is, above all, in the passages in which Love is described as a craftsman distinct from the roots upon which she acts, that Empedocles came closest to treating Love as a purely efficient cause.

Empedocles evidently believes that Love is responsible for the creation of complex organic substances and the organs in the body in particular, though whether it was his intention to suggest that the activities of Love are purposeful and directed towards a good end, is not fully clear.[2] In Plato both the idea

---

[1] This, one of Empedocles' favourite terms, is very difficult to translate. Basically the verb means to fix or make solid, but it is used on the one hand of liquids turning to solids (cf. also συμπηγνύναι at *Il.* 5 902) and on the other of man-made constructions (e.g. of a ship, *Il.* 2 664). Empedocles uses it of salt which is evaporated by the sun (Fr. 56), of the formation of the eyes (here, Fr. 86) and of that of living creatures as a whole (Frr. 75 and 107). Cf. also Anaxagoras Fr. 16, where συμπήγνυσθαι is used of the earth 'solidifying' from water, and of the formation of stones from earth under the effect of cold, and Fr. 4, where it is used of the creation of men and animals.

[2] Aristotle repeatedly states that Empedocles held that the parts of animals, for example, are mostly due to chance or accident (e.g. *Ph.* 196a 23 f.; *PA* 640a 19 ff.; and cf. Empedocles Frr. 53 and 59), but this seems to contrast, rather,

of a moving cause, and that of a purposeful, designing agent, are clearly expressed in a wealth of imagery drawn from the arts and crafts. Already in the *Republic* there are brief references to the 'craftsman of the heavens' (ὁ τοῦ οὐρανοῦ δημιουργός, 530a 6) and to the 'craftsman of the senses' (ὁ τῶν αἰσθήσεων δημιουργός, 507c 6 f.),[1] and thereafter various craftsman images are used of god in later dialogues. The pilot image, common in earlier Greek literature in general and in the Presocratic philosophers in particular, appears in a vivid passage in the myth of the *Politicus* (272e ff.), and in the same myth the god who directs the world in the first of the two stages in the cosmic cycle is referred to not only as father (273b 2) and as guide (269e 6) but also as craftsman (δημιουργός, 270a 5, 273b 1). In the *Laws* (902c ff.), too, the Athenian Stranger argues that as doctors, pilots, generals, housekeepers, statesmen and even masons all pay attention, in their work, to the small items just as much as to the large, so the gods cannot fail to attend to the smallest detail of human affairs, for 'let us not suppose', he says, 'that god is inferior to mortal craftsmen' (902e 4 f.).[2] But it is, of course, in the *Timaeus*, especially, that the notion of god as craftsman, and of the world as his creation, is developed in the greatest detail, and it is this work which gives us the clearest

with Empedocles' ascription of a positive role to Love in the formation of the eyes, for instance (Frr. 86 and 87), especially if we reflect that Aristotle's suggestion that Love is generally responsible for good things and Strife for bad (e.g. *Metaph.* 985a 4 ff.) is to some extent borne out by the epithets used of these principles in the fragments (e.g. Fr. 35 13 refers to the 'gentle-minded immortal stream of blameless Love' and Fr. 17 19 speaks of Strife as 'accursed'). It is clear, however, that while there may be some idea in Empedocles that Love, the divine artisan, is responsible for certain good creations, it is only later, with Plato's Craftsman and Aristotle's Nature, that we find a systematic use of craftsman images to describe the element of design in creation.

[1] Cf. also *R.* 596a ff. where three types of creation are distinguished, (1) that of the god who, in this passage at least, is said to create (e.g. ἐργάζεσθαι at 597b 6 f.) the unique form of a bed, (2) that of the carpenter who creates a particular bed, and (3) that of a painter who imitates the bed which the carpenter made.

[2] Cf. also the description of the fourth kind of being (Cause) in the *Philebus* (27b 1) as 'what creates all these things' (τὸ πάντα ταῦτα δημιουργοῦν) and the reference to a 'creator god' (θεοῦ δημιουργοῦντος) in the *Sophist* (265c 4).

understanding of the role which images drawn from the crafts and arts played in Plato's cosmological doctrines.

From the earliest times the Greeks occasionally attributed creative activity to such gods as Hephaestus, and of the Presocratic philosophers, Empedocles at least sometimes conceived the role of his cosmic principle Love as that of a craftsman.[1] But the *Timaeus* is the first Greek document in which the fashioning of the world *as a whole* is attributed to a craftsman-deity. The variety of the technological imagery which Plato uses in this work is extraordinary. Sometimes referred to as father or generator (e.g. 37c 7), the supreme god who 'brought the world into order from disorder' (30a) is, of course, more often described as the Craftsman, and the visible world as a whole is said to be the copy which he makes from the eternal, intelligible model (e.g. 28c f.). But not only are his activities, and those of the lesser gods to whom he delegates the responsibility for completing the work of creation, described by such general verbs as μηχανᾶσθαι (devise), ἀπεργάζεσθαι (produce), and τεκταίνεσθαι (construct),[2] but we also find a whole series of images drawn from specific arts or crafts. Carpentry, modelling and weaving provide some of the most vivid examples. The gods are imagined as working on lathes (τορνεύεσθαι, 33b 5; περιτορνεύειν, 69c 6, 73e 7), boring or piercing holes (συντετραίνειν, 91a 6; κατακεντεῖν, 76b 1) and gluing or fastening things together with bolts (κολλᾶν, 75d 2; συγκολλᾶν, 43a 2; γόμφοι, 43a 3). The Craftsman himself is called the 'wax-modeller' (κηρο-πλάστης, 74c 6), and πλάττειν (mould) is used to describe the construction of vertebrae from bone, for example.[3] πλέκειν

---

[1] In view of the role of Philia in Empedocles, Cornford's assertion, *6*, pp. 31 and 34, that in the *Timaeus* Plato is introducing the image of a creator god into philosophy for the first time, should be somewhat modified.

[2] E.g. 34c 1, 30b 6, 28c 6, and cf. δημιουργεῖν ('create') itself used, e.g. at 31a 4 and 69c 4.

[3] 74a 2, cf. 42d 6, 78c 3, 92b 3, and ἀποτυποῦσθαι (stamp), 39e 7, and διασχηματίζεσθαι (shape), 53b 4. Modelling images are also used to describe the Receptacle, the 'nurse of becoming' which receives the imprints of the intelligible Forms, at 50a ff.: it is like the gold out of which the modeller makes many

(plait) and ὑφαίνειν (weave) and their compounds are used to describe the joining together of soul and body (36e 2), the interlacing of the veins (77e 1) and so on.[1] Plato also draws on the techniques of agriculture for some of his images. The gods sow (σπείρειν, e.g. 41c 8), and engraft (ἐμφυτεύειν, 42a 3) different things, and the structure of the veins is compared with a system of irrigation channels (77c ff.). And sometimes he combines images from different skills to describe the creation of a compound substance, as, most notably, in the account of the formation of bone. At 73e f. the Craftsman first sifts earth until it is smooth and pure, and then kneads (φυρᾶν) and moistens (δεύειν) it with marrow: so far the image is one of a baker sifting flour and kneading dough (cf. Empedocles Frr. 34 and 73). But then he is described as placing this stuff in fire, dipping it in water and repeating this process until it cannot be melted either by fire or by water. Here Plato seems to be thinking chiefly of some such process as the hardening of iron by submitting it to heat and cold alternately: iron, of course, remains fusible however often this process is repeated, but Plato imagines that the bone-stuff treated in this way acquires the new property of being insoluble by fire or water—as clay, for example, becomes when it is fired.[2]

Both in its general plan and in many points of detail the cosmology of the *Timaeus* is pervaded by images drawn from the arts and crafts. The resemblances between Plato's Craftsman and his human counterparts are especially striking if we compare the god of the *Timaeus* with the omnipotent Creator

different figures, the 'recipient of impressions', ἐκμαγεῖον, 50c 2, in which things are stamped (τυποῦσθαι, e.g. c 5, cf. ἐκτύπωμα, d 4).

[1] Cf. 41d 1 f. on the joining of the mortal and immortal parts of living beings, and 78b f. on the making of the obscure structure of a 'fish-trap' to which Plato refers in his account of respiration (see below, p. 360).

[2] Cf. also the account of the formation of flesh, 74cd, where flesh seems to be conceived as the result of a process like fermentation. The god takes water, fire and earth, and makes a leaven (ζύμωμα) from acid (ὀξύ) and salt, mixing this with these elements to make flesh (which is described as full of sap, ἔγχυμος, and soft).

of Judaeo-Christian thought,[1] for example: in the most important respects in which they differ, Plato's god is much closer to a human craftsman than is the Judaeo-Christian Creator. The Craftsman in the *Timaeus* does not create the world *ex nihilo*, but like human artisans he works on material which already exists in an unformed or chaotic state. He is not omnipotent, but achieves the best possible results within the limitations imposed by the nature of the material itself (e.g. *Ti.* 48a) and here too his situation (one might almost say his predicament) corresponds to that of his human counterparts. But if the similarities between the craftsman god and a human artisan are evidently very close, we must now raise the question round which the whole interpretation of the *Timaeus* revolves, that is whether, or to what extent, we are to take Plato's Craftsman as a 'mythical' figure. How far, if at all, is the account of the creation of the world intended literally? The problem is a particularly complex one,[2] but I shall confine my discussion here to some brief comments on the principal relevant texts in the *Timaeus*.

The key passage which demands interpretation is *Ti.* 28 bc. At the very beginning of his account, 27c 4 f., Timaeus mentions the two alternatives: either the universe (τὸ πᾶν) came into being (γέγονεν) or it is ungenerated (ἀγενές). And at 28b 4 ff. he repeats the question, asking with respect to the 'world' or 'the whole heaven', πότερον ἦν ἀεί, γενέσεως ἀρχὴν ἔχων οὐδεμίαν, ἢ γέγονεν, ἀπ' ἀρχῆς τινος ἀρξάμενος,[3] and this is immediately answered γέγονεν. If we take γίγνεσθαι in its usual and most obvious sense, 'come to be', this passage seems a definite assertion that the world as a whole came into existence, and of the ancient commentators, Aristotle

---

[1] Cf., for example, Cornford, *6*, pp. 34 ff.

[2] The most important recent discussions, besides those in the commentaries on the *Timaeus* by Taylor and Cornford (*6*), are those in Vlastos, *1*, Skemp, *1*, Cherniss, *2*, especially pp. 423 ff., Herter, and Hackforth's article (published posthumously), *2*.

[3] Cornford translates: 'Has it always been, without any source of becoming; or has it come to be, starting from some beginning?', but he holds that γίγνεσθαι is ambiguous (see next note).

evidently interpreted the passage in this sense (*Cael.* 279b 17 ff.). However, Aristotle also reports at *Cael.* 279b 32 ff. that some thinkers defended their position by saying that 'in speaking of the generation of the world, they are doing as geometers do when they construct figures: they do not imply that the world ever came to be, but for the purposes of instruction, διδασκαλίας χάριν, and to make it easier to understand, they exhibit it, like the geometers' figures, in process of formation', and many authorities, both ancient and modern, have chosen to believe that this represents Plato's own true position too.[1] Now here, as at other points in the *Timaeus*, it may be impossible to settle the issue decisively between the 'literal' and the 'mythical' interpretations, but one feature of the way in which Timaeus introduces his account at 28bc seems to favour the 'literal' interpretation in this instance. At 28b 4 ff. Timaeus does not merely suggest, in the manner of such other passages as 48b 3 ff.,[2] that the world 'came to be', but he also rejects (or appears to reject) what Plato himself, on the 'mythical' interpretation of this passage, was supposed to believe, namely the proposition that the world had no beginning. The alternatives men-

---

[1] Cornford, for example, maintained this, but went even further, interpreting γίγνεσθαι at *Ti.* 28b 4 ff. to mean *not* 'come into existence', but 'be in a process of change', and he supported this view by referring to the distinction which is drawn at 27d 6 ff. between 'that which is always real and has no becoming' and 'that which is always becoming and is never real' (γιγνόμενον μὲν ἀεί, ὂν δὲ οὐδέποτε. Hackforth, 2, p. 19, pointed out, however, that ἀεί in this clause is missing in some MSS and in the quotations of Proclus and Simplicius, e.g. *in Ph.* 135 10 f.). If we apply this distinction to 28b 4 ff., according to Cornford, γίγνεσθαι can only mean 'becomes' in the sense of what is always in a process of change. But even if γέγονεν might, perhaps, be taken in some such sense, it remains difficult, or indeed impossible, to account for the phrase ἀπ' ἀρχῆς τινος ἀρξάμενος (28b 7) on this interpretation. Even if ἀρχή need not necessarily mean 'beginning', but may be translated 'source' or 'principle', the verb ἀρχεσθαι must surely mean 'begin' in this context (Cornford himself translated 'starting'). The subject of the sentence is 'the whole heaven', and we have, I think, no option but to believe that Timaeus states that this had a beginning.

[2] At 48b 3 f. we find the expression 'before the coming-to-be of the world' (πρὸ τῆς οὐρανοῦ γενέσεως), at 37e 2 and 52d 4 'before the world came to be' (πρὶν οὐρανὸν γενέσθαι) and at 53a 7 'before the whole came to be arranged from these things' (i.e. the four kinds shaken together in the Receptacle) (πρὶν καὶ τὸ πᾶν ἐξ αὐτῶν διακοσμηθὲν γενέσθαι).

tioned at 28 b 6 ff. are on the one hand 'that it always existed' (and the meaning of this is specified by the addition of the words γενέσεως ἀρχὴν ἔχων οὐδεμίαν, 'having no source, or origin, of becoming') and on the other 'that it came to be' (which is glossed with the phrase ἀπ' ἀρχῆς τινος ἀρξάμενος, 'starting from some beginning'). In general there is certainly nothing implausible in the suggestion that Plato might provide a historical, rather than a purely abstract, account of coming-to-be 'for the sake of instruction'. But it is not necessary, and it seems intolerably confusing, for Plato to go out of his way to make Timaeus emphatically assert that the world started from a beginning and implicitly deny that it 'always existed, having no source of becoming'. At this point the interpretation that the account of the generation of the world takes the form that it does purely and simply 'for the sake of instruction' and 'to make it easier to understand' (in Aristotle's phrases) seems to me to break down, and we are forced to choose between the two alternatives: either Plato was himself confused, or he did indeed believe that the cosmos came to be.[1]

[1] At 37 c ff. there is another disputed passage which seems to suggest that Plato was in earnest in tackling the problems raised by the question of whether or not the world came to be. There Timaeus deals with time and says that days and nights and months and years did not exist 'before the world came to be' (πρὶν οὐρανὸν γενέσθαι); time, as he puts it at 38 b 6, 'came to be along with the universe'. Taylor took this passage as evidence that Plato did not intend the generation of the world to be taken literally: but its significance is, I believe, rather the reverse. Taylor argued (p. 69) that 'no sane man could be meant to be understood literally in maintaining at once that time and the world began together, and also that there was a state of things, which he proceeds to describe, *before* there was any world'. But the objection to this argument (which has been raised not only by Vlastos and Hackforth, but also by Skemp, who shares Taylor's view that the generation of the world is not to be taken literally) is that, for Plato, time and the cosmos are evidently identified with *orderly* motion. There is no κόσμος, and no χρόνος in the sense of periodic time, so long as the motion of things is irregular. The 'coming-to-be' of both the world-order and time itself, in this sense, does not exclude the possibility of duration before the creation of periodic time. An important distinction is drawn, in this passage, between the *everlasting* existence of the intelligible model of the universe, and the *continual* existence, *through all time*, of the copy, the visible world itself. As Plato puts it at 38 c 1–3, 'while the model is in existence through all eternity (πάντα αἰῶνα), the heaven has been and is and will be continually, through all time (διὰ τέλους τὸν ἅπαντα χρόνον)'. The significance of the passage is not that it shows that Plato's whole treatment of the generation of the world is 'mythical'. On the contrary,

This brings us to the question which is of central importance for our present discussion, the interpretation of the role of the Craftsman. The great majority of scholars, whatever their views on the statement at 28b that the world came to be, would concede that the order in which the creation of different things is described in the *Timaeus* is not meant to correspond in detail with a historical sequence of events. Indeed Timaeus is made to remark on the casual or random element in his account when he describes the formation of the world-soul after that of the world-body.[1] But a comparison between the *Timaeus* and other late dialogues enables us to go some way towards distinguishing the essential features of Plato's doctrine of the Craftsman from the graphic but perhaps inessential imagery in which his conception is expressed. The doctrine that anything that comes to be necessarily comes to be by the agency of some cause (ὑπ' αἰτίου τινὸς or διά τινα αἰτίαν) is a principle which Plato affirms repeatedly in the later dialogues, not only in the *Timaeus* (28a 4 f., c 2 f.) but also in, for example, the *Philebus* (26e 3). Without a cause, as he says in both these works, nothing could possibly come to be (*Ti.* 28a 5 f.; *Phlb.* 26e 5), and the chief Cause is variously described as the Craftsman, or Reason, or King.[2] But that god (however described) is not the only cause at work in the

the passage throws important light on the sense in which, according to Plato, the world 'came to be'. For Plato, the whole visible world is not everlasting (for only the intelligible Forms are such): on the other hand he affirms *both* that the visible world 'came to be' *and* that it 'has been and is and will be continually, through all time'. Both time and the heaven itself are eternal in *this* sense, but both came to be when order was imposed on a pre-existing disorder.

[1] 34b 10 ff. Cherniss, 2, p. 424, took this to imply that 'any temporal sequence in the account must be a falsification', but this is questionable. The passage might equally well be taken as an expression of a belief that there *is* a correct temporal order in coming-to-be at this point. Cherniss says that the order which Plato has chosen to describe the generation of body and soul 'enables him to startle his audience out of the vulgar identification of temporal and ontological priority', but if this is Plato's intention, he goes a very misleading way about fulfilling it, for the passage in which Timaeus refers to the casual element in his account is immediately followed by a statement in which Timaeus is himself guilty of just the identification of which Cherniss complains: 'but the god made soul prior to body and more venerable in birth and in excellence' (καὶ γενέσει καὶ ἀρετῇ προτέραν καὶ πρεσβυτέραν, 34c 4 f., and cf. *Laws* 892a ff.).

[2] Cf. above, pp. 220 and 254 ff.

world is another doctrine which recurs in different forms in late Plato. In the *Philebus* Reason is contrasted with random causation at 28 d 5 ff., for instance, when Socrates asks: 'Should we say that it is the power of the irrational and random (ἡ τοῦ ἀλόγου καὶ εἰκῇ δύναμις) and chance that are in charge of all things... or that it is reason and a marvellous intelligence that arranges and steers them?' In the *Timaeus*, the Craftsman who is described as 'the best of causes' (29 a 5 f.) and who 'desired that all things should be good and that nothing should be imperfect, so far as possible' (30 a) is contrasted with Necessity or the Wandering Cause. The causes which bring about such physical changes as heating and cooling, and which are themselves incapable of possessing plan or purpose, are described as the subsidiary causes (συναίτια) which god uses in perfecting the form of the most good as far as possible (46 cd, cf. 68 e).[1] Rational and irrational causation are again contrasted in the *Politicus*, for when the god who guides the world leaves hold of the tiller, the world revolves on its own 'of necessity' in the opposite direction (269 d 2 f.) and is subject to violent disorders which are caused 'by the bodily part of the mixture, the congenital character of its primeval nature, which was full of disorder before it came into its present order' (273 b 4 ff.). Finally in the *Laws* there is first a contrast between soul, the 'primary cause of all generation and destruction' (891 e 5 f.), and the secondary movements which bring about the combining and separating of bodies and so on (897 ab),[2] and then a further contrast

---

[1] Reason overrules Necessity by persuasion to achieve the best results, for the most part (*Ti.* 48 a, cf. 56 c). Sometimes, however, the physical properties of things are such that Reason has to sacrifice one aim for another, higher one: at 75 a 7 ff. for example it is said that keen perception cannot, of necessity, exist along with dense bone and flesh: the lesser gods accordingly choose to leave the head covered with thin bone for the sake of procuring for men a nobler life, even though this means that they are shorter-lived than they would have been had their heads been protected with a thicker covering of flesh.

[2] As the Craftsman in the *Timaeus* is described as making use of the subsidiary causes (e.g. 46 cd), so in the *Laws* soul is said to use these secondary movements (897 b 1) though here Plato adds that this applies to both the rational and the irrational types of soul.

between the two types of soul, that which is beneficent and intelligent, which controls and cares for 'heaven and earth and the whole revolution', and that which is devoid of intelligence or virtue and which brings about evil (896e–897c).

The opposition between the rational and good type of cause, and irrational, random and evil causation, is a recurrent theme in the late Platonic dialogues, and this provides a link between the various images which we have considered in this and other sections. In a passage which should warn us against pressing any of his cosmological metaphors too far, Plato says that 'to discover the maker and father of the universe is hard indeed, and having discovered him, to declare him to all men is impossible' (*Ti.* 28c). But each of the descriptions which recur in the *Timaeus, Politicus, Philebus* and *Laws*—the King, the Father, the Pilot, the Maker-Creator-Craftsman, the world-living-animal—serves, in a different way, to express an idea of the role of an intelligent, beneficent cause in the universe. On the one hand, then, these images are linked by certain underlying themes, and when we find, for example, that the works of the Craftsman are said to be the works of Reason (e.g. *Ti.* 47e) and that Reason, in turn, is said to exist only in Soul (e.g. *Ti.* 30b 3, 46d 5 f.; *Phlb.* 30c 9 f.), there is an obvious temptation to treat all these images as interchangeable equivalents. But that we should not be too eager to attempt to reduce one type of imagery to another (to interpret references to the Craftsman as references to the world-soul, or vice versa)[1] seems clear if only because each of these descriptions evidently has its own part to play in conveying a slightly different picture of the role of the primary cause and of its relation to other, subsidiary causes. Each of the images we have discussed has different associations. As King, he exercises a benevolent control over all things. As Pilot, he is the intelligent directing

[1] Herter has recently argued that not only are attempts to establish a single logically watertight theory of motion in the late dialogues of Plato unsuccessful, but they may be misconceived, in that they may lead to serious oversimplifications in the interpretation of particular texts.

agent in the world. As Father, he is a benevolent creator. As the Good Craftsman he is a skilful and purposeful creator who achieves the best results that the nature of the material will allow (and this theme is elaborated with a whole series of technological images which are used to describe the formation of different kinds of objects). Finally, when speaking of the world-living-animal, Plato develops two oppositions, that between soul and body, and (within soul) that between rationality and irrationality. It is, then, by this remarkable series of interconnected and overlapping images that Plato conveys his conception of the primary cause which is at work in the universe. Largely traditional, or at least pre-Platonic, in origin, these images play a key role in the expression of some of Plato's most important cosmological doctrines relating to such questions as the purposefulness of creation, the source of movement and change, and the causes of imperfection in the world.

Aristotle's Unmoved Mover is no craftsman. Yet technological imagery evidently plays an important part both in illustrating and in recommending some of his general physical theories.[1] The most obvious examples of this are some of the comparisons and metaphors which he uses to describe the role of φύσις. When Aristotle describes the structure of the bones in the body at *PA* 654b 29 ff., for instance, he compares Nature with a modeller in clay who starts with a framework made of some solid material and moulds his clay figure round this, and in another context, at *GA* 730b 27 ff., Nature is said to resemble modellers, who work directly on their material with their hands, more than carpenters, who work with tools. Again at *GA* 743b 20 ff., when the development of the embryo is described, Nature is compared with a painter who first sketches a figure in outline and afterwards applies the colours, and elsewhere she is likened to a good housekeeper (*GA* 744b 16 ff., cf. *PA* 675b 21) or more simply to an intelli-

---

[1] Once again the best discussion of this aspect of Aristotle's thought is that in Le Blond, *1*, pp. 326 ff.

gent human being (*PA* 687a 10 ff.).[1] Many metaphors, too, suggest the role of Nature as craftsman or artist. She is described as creating (ποιεῖν, δημιουργεῖν), devising (μηχανᾶσθαι) and adorning (ἐπικοσμεῖν) living creatures or their parts.[2] Her purposeful activity is expressed, typically, in the often repeated phrases 'nature does nothing superfluous' or 'in vain',[3] but like Plato's Craftsman she is sometimes unable to achieve her ends because of the material with which she has to work.[4] Like Plato, again, Aristotle often uses images drawn from technology to elucidate the function of different parts of the body, and some of his images seem to have been borrowed direct from the *Timaeus*, unless, indeed, they were commonplaces of Greek anatomical theory. Where Plato compares the vascular system with a system of irrigation channels (*Ti.*77 c ff.) Aristotle uses the same comparison (*PA* 668a 13 ff.),[5] and where Plato suggests that the crisscrossing of the blood-vessels which pass round the head serves to bind the head to the trunk (*Ti.* 77 de), we find that Aristotle similarly compares the interlacing structure of the blood-vessels in the body as a whole with wickerwork and suggests that it helps to fasten the front and the back of the body together (*PA* 668b 24 ff.).[6]

[1] Cf. also *PA* 683a 22 ff. where Nature is said to use each organ for a single purpose only, wherever possible, and in this to be unlike a smith who makes an ὀβελισκολύχνιον, i.e. an article which could serve as either a spit or a lamp-holder.

[2] E.g. *GA* 731a 24; *PA* 652a 31, 658a 32.

[3] See, for example, the references given in Bonitz's Index at 836b 28 ff.

[4] E.g. *GA* 778a 4 ff. Cf. also 749b 7 ff., 777a 16 f. where certain facts are explained on the assumption that Nature has only a limited quantity of material for her work.

[5] Aristotle adds another image, that of the piles of stones laid along the lines of the foundations when a house is built, to illustrate his theory that the blood is the material from which the rest of the body is made (*PA* 668a 16 ff.): and elsewhere (*HA* 515a 34 ff.; *GA* 743a 1 ff.) he compares the blood-vessels with κάναβοι (the framework used by modellers) to suggest that they are like a framework round which the flesh accrues (cf. also *GA* 764b 30 f.).

[6] Cf. also the more obvious comparisons of the stomach with a manger (φάτνη, Plato, *Ti.* 70e 2, Arist. *PA* 650a 19) and of the diaphragm with a partition wall (cf. διοικοδομεῖν, Plato, *Ti.* 69e 6, and παροικοδόμημα, Arist. *PA* 672b 19 f.).

The role of φύσις is often illustrated with comparisons drawn from the field of the τέχναι. But Aristotle several times explicitly compares these two main types of coming-to-be. The distinction between them is drawn at *Metaph.* 1070a 7 f., for example, where he says that 'art is a principle (of change) in something else, while nature is a principle in the thing itself', and similarly at *Ph.* 192b 13 ff. things which exist 'by nature' are said to have within themselves a 'principle of movement and of rest', while other things, in so far as they are the products of art, 'have no innate impulse to change'.[1] On the other hand *both* these types of coming-to-be are, of course, analysed in terms of the four causes, and the *parallelism* between them is often brought out. More than once Aristotle puts it that art imitates nature (*Ph.* 194a 21 f., 199a 16 f., cf. *Mete.* Δ 381b 6), and other texts imply even more clearly that natural products are superior to artificial ones.[2] Yet paradoxically it is the sphere of artificial production which provides Aristotle with the majority of his illustrations when he expounds the theory of the four causes.[3] Thus when the four causes are distinguished, perhaps for the first time in the extant treatises, in *Ph.* B 3, most of the examples to which he refers are drawn from the arts, particularly from sculpture, architecture, and medicine.[4] Again in *Metaph.* Z 7–9 artificial productions—the house, the bronze sphere, health (the product of the medical art)—are considered at length, and when he comes to deal with natural causation

---

[1] Cf. *GA* 734b 34 ff., 735a 2 ff., where the point is made that in 'art' the efficient cause is external to the thing which is produced, while in nature it is located in the thing itself (here the movement is derived from the generating parent).

[2] E.g. *PA* 639b 19 ff., on which see below, p. 289.

[3] Le Blond (*1*, p. 338) has indeed suggested that it is in the domain of 'industry' that the four causes were first distinguished by Aristotle, later to be applied to other things, and other scholars have also drawn particular attention to Aristotle's use of technological analogies in illustrating natural causation in general and the role of the final cause in particular (e.g. Mansion, *1*, pp. 197ff., 227ff.; Hamelin, *2*, pp. 270 ff., 274).

[4] There are, however, some exceptions, e.g. *Ph.* 194b 30 f. and 195a 21, where examples from nature are considered.

(which he had first mentioned quite briefly at ch. 7, 1032 a 12 ff.) he says that 'the case is the same with the things that arise naturally as with these [i.e. the products of art]: for the seed produces things in the same way as things are produced by art' (1034a 33 f.).

In the biological treatises, especially, various theses relating to the doctrine of the four causes are illustrated by examples drawn from the 'arts'. (1) The role of 'conditional necessity' in nature is explained by referring to artificial productions. At PA 639b 23 ff., for instance, he remarks that matter, and matter of a certain sort, is necessary before a house can be built, and he suggests that the same is also true in the case of things that are formed by nature (where the application of this principle is, one would say, far less obvious). Again at PA 642a 9 ff. he says that as an axe, for example, must be hard in order to split wood, and if hard, then made of bronze or iron, so the body must be made of suitable materials if it is to fulfil its purpose—for the body, too, and each of its parts, is a 'tool' (ὄργανον).[1] (2) At PA 646a 24 ff., b 3 ff., he refers again to the example of the building of a house in order to point out that while the bricks and stones come before the house itself chronologically, they are 'for the sake of' it, and not vice versa: so too in nature, while the matter and the process of formation are chronologically prior, the formal and the final causes are prior logically.[2] (3) Then too the importance of studying not only the material cause, but also the composite object, and in particular the formal and final causes, in biology, is several times illustrated by considering how we should describe an artefact. If we were describing a bed or some such object, we should try to define the form rather than the matter, the bronze or the wood (PA 640b

[1] Cf. GA 743a 23 ff. where he again illustrates the role of conditional necessity in nature with a technological analogy, that of the carpenter who 'would not make a chest out of anything but wood'.

[2] Cf. PA 640a 15 ff. where Aristotle again refers to the example of building to illustrate the general doctrine that the process of coming-to-be (γένεσις) is for the sake of the substance (οὐσία) and not vice versa.

23 ff.), and a similar point is made at *PA* 645 a 30 ff., where the example given is that of a house.[1] (4) But even more commonly technological analogies are used to illustrate the role of the final cause in nature. At *PA* 639 b 19 ff. he says that 'the final cause (that "for the sake of which") and the good are more fully present in the works of nature than in those of art',[2] but this follows a passage (b 14 ff.) in which the examples he uses to explain the role of the final cause are drawn from the 'arts' (health, the goal of the physician's art, the house, that of the builder's). He again illustrates the final cause in nature by a comparison with 'art' at 641 b 10 ff. There he says that nature makes everything for the sake of something: 'for it seems that as art is present [i.e. here, as the final cause] in the products of art, so in things themselves there is some such principle or cause which comes to us from the universe as do the hot and the cold [i.e. the matter]'. And he refers to the 'arts' yet again in this context at 645 b 14 ff., taking up other themes which we have already discussed: 'since every instrument (ὄργανον) is for the sake of something, and each of the parts of the body is for the sake of something, that is to say some action, it is clear that the body as a whole arose for the sake of some complex[3] action. Just as the saw came to be for the sake of sawing, and not sawing for the sake of the saw, for sawing is the using of the instrument, so the body exists for the sake of the soul, in a way, and the parts of the body for the sake of the functions which each of them naturally fulfils.'

Finally there are two passages in particular, both in *Physics* B, in which Aristotle uses a comparison with artificial production not merely to illustrate, but also, it seems, to

---

[1] Cf. also a long passage in *GC* B 9 (335 b 7–336 a 14) where he draws comparisons between nature and 'art' to illustrate the role of the efficient cause and to suggest that this, and the form, are superior to the matter.

[2] Cf. *PA* 641 b 18 ff. where Aristotle says that orderliness and definiteness (τὸ τεταγμένον, τὸ ὡρισμένον) are more evident in the heavenly bodies than in ourselves: indeed in the heaven 'there is not the slightest indication of the random or disorderly'.

[3] Reading πολυμεροῦς at *PA* 645 b 17 (Bekker πλήρους).

recommend, certain theses concerning the role of the four causes in nature. In *Ph.* B, as in the biological works, the role of the final cause in nature is several times compared with its role in 'art' (e.g. *Ph.* 199a 15 ff., 200a 34 ff.). But at *Ph.* 199a 33 ff. he deals with the occasions when nature fails to achieve her ends, and here it is on the analogy of the failures which occur in 'art' that he explains, or rather explains away, those which happen in nature (monstrosities and the like). As he puts it, 'faults happen in the products of "art" as well...so that it is clear (ὥστε δῆλον ὅτι) that they may also happen in the works of nature'. Then at 199b 26 ff. there is a second striking passage where again it is the final cause which Aristotle is considering. He says that it is absurd to deny that there is a final cause in nature on the grounds that in nature the efficient cause is not seen to deliberate (i.e. there is no conscious craftsman). 'Art', he suggests, does not deliberate either. 'If ship-building were in the wood itself, it would act in the same way as nature. So that if the final cause is present in art [or perhaps: in the art], it is present also in nature (ὥστ' εἰ ἐν τῇ τέχνῃ ἔνεστι τὸ ἕνεκά του, καὶ ἐν τῇ φύσει). And this is especially clear when someone heals himself, for nature is like this person.' It is particularly notable that Aristotle should point out that the final cause in nature is not the result of conscious deliberation, and in general we should certainly not say that he in any way confused the two spheres of natural and artificial production or blurred the major distinctions between them: but on the other hand, if they are distinct, these two spheres are nevertheless 'analogous', and in his account of change he repeatedly draws attention to the parallelisms between them, referring to the circumstances that obtain in the sphere of artificial productions both to elucidate, and to some extent also to support, his analysis of natural change.

The chief significance of the technological images which we have been considering may be said to lie in the part they played in the development and expression of two important cosmological doctrines, the notion of a separate moving cause, and the conception of the element of rational design in the universe. (1) Craftsman images may sometimes suggest a distinction between the moving cause and the material upon which it acts. In Empedocles, no hard and fast distinction is as yet made between efficient and material causes, for Philia itself still appears to be conceived as an ingredient in the finished products which it creates. In Plato, however, the separation between the moving cause and that which is moved is complete. In discussing the history of vitalist notions in Greek cosmology, we remarked that it is an exceptional feature of Plato's theory that he conceived the invisible soul, the source of movement, as a quite separate entity from the visible body which it moves, but a similar type of distinction is also expressed, and indeed expressed much more clearly, by means of technological images where the Craftsman is distinct from the material which he brings into order from disorder. If in Aristotle's theory of natural generation the efficient cause is located in the thing itself and cannot be separated from it in fact (ἔργῳ), he still distinguishes logically (λόγῳ) between the efficient and the material causes, and he relies, in the main, on comparisons with artificial production to illustrate this distinction.

(2) Technological images have a further important role in Greek cosmological theories in expressing various conceptions of the element of rational design or finality which is manifest in the universe. Already in pre-philosophical literature there are many texts which testify to the belief that the supreme god Zeus controls the destiny of things, although Zeus' will is arbitrary and his control was most often conceived in political, not technological images (see above, pp. 196 ff., 208 f.). But then the image of steering or guiding is used by several Presocratic philosophers in connection with their cosmological principles, and sometimes these images serve to convey not only the notion of power, but more particularly that of intelligent direction. Diogenes of Apollonia, for example,

says that air guides all things (Fr. 5) and he also identifies air with the intelligence which has arranged all things for the best (Fr. 3). In Empedocles we find the first extant Greek philosophical texts in which the role of a cosmological principle is conceived as that of a creative craftsman, although it is more difficult to say to what extent the idea of design is also implicit in his use of such imagery. Both Plato and Aristotle, however, convey their different conceptions of the element of finality in the universe largely with the aid of technological imagery. The metaphors which Plato uses to describe the role of the primary cause are very varied, and it is characteristic of him to express his ideas on this topic in the form of images and myths (the interpretation of which is, however, often the subject of disagreement among scholars). Aristotle, too, uses many craftsman images in connection with his doctrine of Nature, but it is characteristic of *him* that he should state the general theory which underlies and justifies these comparisons explicitly, on the one hand noting the points of difference between natural and artificial productions, and on the other asserting that the four causes are 'analogically' the same in both types of coming-to-be.

Finally, a note should be added on the manifest and striking contrast between the low esteem in which Plato, and indeed Aristotle too, held the life of the craftsman, and their repeated use of craftsman imagery in their cosmological and physical doctrines. First it is apparent that the political status of the craftsman improved very considerably during the centuries which separate Homer from Plato. Certainly by the beginning of the sixth century, at least, craftsmen could be, and often were, full citizens in many city-states: at Athens, Solon, it will be remembered, even invited foreign craftsmen to settle with the offer of citizenship.[1] The Hippocratic

---

[1] Aristotle informs us that 'in some states the craftsmen had, in ancient times, no share in government, until extreme democracies occurred' (*Pol.* 1277 b 1 ff.), and cf. 1278a 6 ff. where he notes that 'in ancient times, in some cases, the artisan class (τὸ βάναυσον) were either slaves or foreigners, and therefore most of them are so to this day' and goes on to suggest that 'the best form of state

treatises *On Ancient Medicine* and *On the Art* testify to the high regard in which the τέχναι as a whole (and not just the 'art' of medicine) were held, in some quarters at any rate, in the late fifth and early fourth centuries.[1] Nevertheless, a marked antipathy persisted between the aristocracy and the lower classes (including those engaged in trade and in the βάναυσοι τέχναι, i.e. the manual workers or artisans, especially), and this is, of course, expressed particularly strongly in the dialogues of Plato himself. There is an undeniable anomaly, then, between, on the one hand, the contempt which Plato expresses for craftsmen in the *Republic*, for example (e.g. 495 de, 522 b, 590 c), and on the other, his description of the creator of the universe as the Craftsman or the Wax-Modeller (*Ti.* 28 a 6, 74 c 6) and his use of images drawn from industry to describe his activity.[2] Similarly Aristotle describes the work of Nature with images drawn not merely from the more gentlemanly or liberal arts, but also from the handicrafts, as when he compares Nature herself with a modeller (*PA* 654 b 29 ff.; *GA* 730 b 27 ff.), and yet he too clearly despised the artisan class and considered the life they led not worthy of a citizen (e.g. *Pol.* 1277 a 37 ff., 1278 a 6 ff., 1328 b 39 f.). It is true that the contempt of both philosophers is directed more against those who practised the arts and crafts for their *livelihood* and to the exclusion of higher things, than against the activities in themselves.[3] But it is still remarkable

will not make artisans citizens' (a 8). Cf. also Plato's injunction, in the *Laws*, 846 d, that no resident citizen shall be a craftsman.

[1] See especially *VM* ch. 1, *CMG* I, 1 36 7 ff. and *de Arte* ch. 1, *CMG* I, 1 9 2 ff., and see Festugière, pp. xv ff., and Heinimann, *2*.

[2] When in Hesiod, e.g. *Op.* 60 ff., Zeus is described as directing Hephaestus to make Pandora, the idea may well be that the menial work of fabrication is beneath the dignity of Zeus himself. It is striking that Plato too uses the device of representing the Craftsman as directing other gods to carry out certain tasks (*Ti.* 41 a ff.), but this is not to save the Craftsman from the humiliation of personal involvement in the business of manufacture, but on the contrary to suggest that those products for which the Craftsman himself is not directly responsible are imperfect.

[3] Thus Aristotle puts it that the good man and the statesman and the good citizen ought not to learn the work of those who are ruled 'except for their own occasional use' (*Pol.* 1277 b 3 ff.), and at *Pol.* 1337 b 17 ff. he points out that it

that they both repeatedly describe the creator-god or Nature herself as a craftsman, in view of the low opinion which they express for those who were merely human craftsmen, and we are left to conclude that it was because the arts and crafts provided such striking models for intelligent, purposeful activity that they used these images in their cosmological theories in spite of a certain prejudice against the chief exponents of those activities in human society.

CONCLUSIONS

The present study does not, of course, profess to be an exhaustive survey of the imagery used in the cosmological theories of the early Greek philosophers. Moreover, it should be noted that because the only really reliable evidence, in such a study, is that of the original quotations from the philosophers themselves, comparatively little has been, or can be, said concerning the Pythagoreans, the Atomists and other philosophers who are particularly poorly represented in our extant sources. Nevertheless, the three sets of images which I have discussed are certainly among the most important to appear in Greek cosmological writings in the period down to Aristotle, and the fact that their use is so widespread provides some safeguard against the distorting effects of the fragmentary nature of our evidence.

I may now review some of the main conclusions which an examination of these images would suggest. First of all they clearly play an important part in the development and expression of certain key cosmological doctrines, indeed some of the doctrines in question seem inseparably bound up with the images in which they were expressed. Time and again the Presocratics convey their conceptions of cosmic order, and especially the idea of a self-regulating relationship between the

makes a difference with what end in view a particular activity is practised: an action done for one's own sake, or for the sake of friends, would not appear illiberal, but the same action, done for the sake of others, would be thought servile. (I am indebted to Mr F. H. Sandbach for drawing my attention to this point.)

primary cosmic substances or forces, by means of a concrete political or social image. Again the conception of the world as a living organism provides a further representation of the universe as a single whole, and it enabled its development to be described in terms of a natural growth or evolution. Thirdly, images drawn from technology were particularly important as a means of expressing two ideas, the notion of a separate 'moving cause', and the conception of the element of design in the universe, and in Plato, at least, the creation of the world as a whole was sometimes represented as the work of a craftsman-god. Ideas derived from the spheres of politics, biology and technology are used repeatedly by the Greek philosophers to describe the roles of particular cosmological principles, in generalising concerning the factors which govern change and coming-to-be in the world, above all in conveying various conceptions of the 'cosmos' itself, i.e. the unity which underlies the plurality of phenomena. And it is worth noting that not only is Greek cosmology much influenced by ideas derived from politics and biology, but the histories of Greek political thought and biology are themselves coloured by a similar frequent use of images drawn from other fields. Not only was the cosmos sometimes represented as a state, or as a living organism, but the state in turn was frequently compared with a living being in Greek political theories, and conversely the living organism is often described in the medical writers as a complex consisting of opposing forces or factions.[1] Again some of the most

[1] Some of the political images which commonly appear in Greek medical theory have already been noted, p. 216, n. 1 and p. 230, n. 1. As for analogies between the state and a living being, one of the most notable examples is, of course, the comparison between the city and the individual in Plato's *Republic* (on which see below, pp. 396 f., in my chapter on arguments from analogy). It is interesting that Aristotle uses this analogy on different occasions from both points of view, comparing the living creature with a well-governed city in the biological works (*MA* 703 a 29 ff.), and describing the constitution as the life, as it were, of the city, in the *Politics* (1295 a 40 f., and compare his distinction between 'true' and 'corrupt' constitutions, the latter deviations, παρεκβάσεις, from the former, e.g. 1279 b 4 ff., the verb παρεκβαίνειν being one used, e.g. at *GA* 771 a 11 ff., of monstrous births).

elaborate comparisons drawn between the macrocosm and the microcosm occur in the Hippocratic treatises, where the writer's aim is partly to suggest certain theories concerning the structure of the cosmos as a whole, but partly also to propound certain views on, for example, the anatomical structure of man.[1] This last example shows particularly clearly that cosmological and biological theories had a profound influence on each other. Not only was the macrocosm apprehended in terms of the microcosm, but the reverse process took place too, and the conception of the individual living being was influenced by theories about the cosmos as a whole. Indeed the cosmological images which have been our subject in this chapter are part of a still more vast complex of analogies in which Greek notions concerning nature and art, the state, the living organism and the world-whole itself are interrelated.

Certain typical cosmological doctrines which were developed in the Presocratic period or later were regularly expressed by means of concrete political, biological or technological images. But how far is it correct to suggest that these doctrines follow the pattern of beliefs which can already be traced in earlier, that is pre-philosophical, texts? First a very general point: in considering both the pre-philosophical world-picture (if one may call it such) and early Greek cosmological theories we have traced the predominant role of ideas derived from three main fields of human experience, society, living creatures, and industry. No doubt *all* cosmological doctrines may be said to reflect the experience of their authors to a greater or lesser degree, taking experience in the broadest sense to include their total awareness of their environment. But early Greek cosmology seems particularly dependent on ideas which derive specifically from man's own experience of his fellow beings: this applies especially, of course, to their social, political and technological images, but also, to a lesser extent, to their vitalist notions, in so far as some philosophers

---

[1] See above, pp. 252 f., on *Vict.* I, ch. 10, L VI 484 17 ff. especially.

considered man himself as the type or model of a living creature. If early Greek religion is largely anthropomorphic, one might say that early Greek cosmology is still, in emphasis, largely anthropocentric. Secondly, in some cases there are more specific similarities between the images which the philosophers used and those which occur in pre-philosophical beliefs and myths. This is obvious enough in the case of the traditional conception of Zeus as a supreme ruler: the titles King and Father are used both by Heraclitus (with a certain irony, perhaps) of War, and by Plato of the Craftsman and the cosmic Reason. But it may also be suggested that the creative agents which are described with such a variety of technological imagery in Empedocles, Plato and Aristotle, have a mythical prototype in the figure of the craftsman-god Hephaestus. And in considering the role of Eros and Philia in Parmenides and Empedocles we can appreciate that Aristotle had good reason to suggest a comparison with the earlier use of Eros in Hesiod, for already in the *Theogony* sexual imagery was used extensively to describe the generation of personified figures representing many different types of phenomena.

At the same time, however, the respects in which the philosophers' cosmological theories differ from the pre-philosophical myths and beliefs which we have considered, are obvious and important. First the philosophers' doctrines are, for the first time, *cosmological* theories. There is no evidence in our extant pre-philosophical Greek texts that *the world as a whole* was conceived as a state or as a single living being, let alone as an artefact. Rather it was, in all probability, the philosophers themselves who were responsible for the first clear expression of these three different conceptions of the cosmos as a unity. Secondly, where the pre-philosophical myths which we discussed are generally personal and particular, the images of the philosophers usually refer to abstractions and generalities. Homer and Hesiod have an extremely vivid and detailed conception of the society of the gods, but social imagery is applied by the philosophers not to personal deities, but to abstract cosmological principles. In Homer and Hesiod Zeus is supreme ruler, and his rule is largely (though not entirely) capricious, but in such philosophers as Anaxagoras, Diogenes of Apollonia and Plato the metaphor of supreme rule is applied not to any arbitrary deity but to the principle of order and rationality in things itself (Mind, Air-Intelligence, the cosmic Reason). When we find natural phenomena personified in early Greek texts, it is usually implied that the phenomena have wills of their own, and we find some explicit references to the randomness and unpredictability of their behaviour (as when Hesiod speaks of the personified diseases roaming 'at will' among men, *Op.* 102 ff., see above, p. 207, n. 2). Again the contrast with the philosophers' use of biological notions is marked, for although both Plato and Aristotle continued to believe that the stars are living beings, we argued (pp. 267 f.) that this was in no way connected with any idea that their movements are random: on the contrary, both philosophers reiterate that the movements of the heavenly bodies are supremely orderly. Similarly, technological images are used in Hesiod to describe the creation of Pandora, but the motive for this creation is said to be Zeus' desire for revenge, while in the philosophers craftsman images are used in connection with a generalised conception of a creative force, the Philia of Empedocles, Plato's creator-god, and Aristotle's Nature. We see, then, that while there is a strong element of *randomness* implicit in those pre-philosophical myths and images which involve references to personal deities or personified figures of some sort, in the philosophers images which are often of a broadly similar type are used, above all, to express the notions of *order* and *rationality* themselves, and to convey a conception of the cosmos as a single, unified whole. Finally, the philosophers' images are marked out from their pre-philosophical counterparts not only in being the product of reflection on cosmological problems, but also in that they are the subject of rational debate and criticism. It is true that the notion that the primary stuff of things is alive and divine is common to all the earlier Greek philosophers, but we noted how different cosmologists proposed quite different variations on the theme of the world-living-organism in their attempts to give an account of the evolution of the world or of its present state. And in the case of social and political images, not only do we find three distinct types of models used by different theorists, but in one instance (Heraclitus Fr. 80) we have fairly clear evidence of a Presocratic philosopher deliberately correcting and modifying the image which one of his predecessors had suggested.

We have considered certain respects in which early Greek cosmology seems to follow, and others in which it clearly departs from, the patterns of earlier beliefs and myths. But within the period of Greek philosophy which we have been studying we can trace certain important modifications in the role of images in cosmology and in the attitude towards their use. As Greek philosophy developed, there is an increasing awareness of the distinctions between different categories of objects (e.g. animate and inanimate) or between different areas of reality (e.g. Society and Nature). True, our evidence for the earliest period is such that it is often impossible to be certain what views the Milesians or the earliest Pythagoreans may have entertained on such topics. But it seems clear that Democritus had a truer appreciation of the boundary line between animate and inanimate things than had Thales, and we can trace a definite and marked increase in interest in the distinction between φύσις and νόμος, nature and man-made convention, towards the end of the fifth century. But not only do we find later philosophers drawing certain distinctions which appear to have been blurred, if not completely ignored, by some earlier writers, but we should also, I think, be justified in seeing a general development in the philosophers' awareness of the nature and status of their cosmological images. Empedocles Fr. 17 provides the first clear evidence of a Presocratic philosopher recognising that in his cosmological theory he was applying certain concepts in a new context, and we may conjecture that Anaxagoras was equally conscious of applying the term 'seeds' beyond its normal sphere of reference in his physical theory. And yet the difference in outlook between Empedocles and Aristotle (for example) on the subject of the use of images in cosmology becomes evident when we consider the latter's criticisms of the metaphor of the oath in Fr. 30. Aristotle complained (as we might too) that Empedocles had failed to give any reason for the change from the rule of Love to that of Strife. Yet it may be (I suggested) that Empedocles himself did not anticipate this type of criticism at all: to him the image of the oath may have seemed 'explanation' enough of the change in question. Like many of the cosmological images of the Presocratics, the oath or contract of Empedocles Fr. 30 offers a concrete social model which is quite clear in itself: its inadequacies as an account of *why* the change from Love to Strife takes place only become apparent when we interrogate the metaphor and seek to translate it into physical terms.

Several of the later Presocratic philosophers probably recognised that they were applying familiar conceptions in a new context when they used them in their cosmological or physical doctrines. But it was Plato who first drew a general distinction between images and 'myths' on the one hand, and reasoned accounts and demonstrations on the other. Yet on such subjects as the nature of the Maker and Father of the universe, and the nature of the movement of Reason, Plato explicitly disclaimed being able to give a non-figurative account (*Ti.* 28c; *Laws* 897de), and it is clear that he believed that images are necessary for the expression of some of the highest truths. Many of the metaphors which he uses to convey his cosmological doctrines can be paralleled quite closely in earlier writers, and his use of imagery may be said to have this, too, in common with that of such philosophers as

Heraclitus or Empedocles, that in all three we find a series of contrasting, even conflicting, images describing the role of cosmological principles. In Heraclitus, as we saw, the world-order is identified with an ever-living fire in Fr. 30, but in other fragments (64, 66) fire, in a different role, 'guides all things' and 'will judge and convict them' (and again else-where, Fr. 90, 'all things' are said to be 'an exchange for fire and fire for all things'). In Empedocles the principle which unites the four roots appears (we might say) to be immanent in them when it is described as the force of sexual attraction or friendship (e.g. Fr. 17): but elsewhere (Frr. 73, 75, etc.) Kupris acts as a craftsman and the four roots are her material, and these images, if pressed, might be taken to suggest that Love is, in some sense, a transcendent force. In Plato this tendency reaches, perhaps, its fullest development, for he describes the primary Cause which is at work in the world in a set of overlapping images (as King, Father, Pilot, Craftsman and the good soul) each of which has slightly different associa-tions, and each of which conveys the nature of this cause, and its relationships to other factors in coming-to-be, under a dif-ferent aspect. In each case a modern interpreter, honouring above all else the principle of consistency, might feel tempted to select one image (or group of images) as the philosopher's true and definitive conception, although such an attempt would surely be misguided. Rather, in each case, to under-stand the original thought in all its complexity, we should treat these images (much in the same way as we saw that many pre-philosophical images should be treated, pp. 201 ff.) not as alternative, but as cumulative and complementary accounts, each adding to, but none, as it were, restricting, the writer's conception.

Aristotle was by no means fully emancipated from the influence of vitalist notions such as are found to recur in Greek cosmology, affirming, for example, that the heavenly bodies are endowed with life, and that the earth, too, is subject to cycles of growth and decay. But in general his cosmological theories are notably less dependent on metaphor and imagery than those of most earlier writers. His account of the principles of change and coming-to-be is a case in point. Where Empedocles and Anaxagoras and Plato too had expressed their ideas on coming-to-be mainly with the help of concrete images or models drawn from certain aspects of familiar experience, Aristotle gives an explicit general account of the principles of change in the doctrine of the four causes. The four causes are the same τῷ ἀνάλογον: they apply, that is, in different ways in the different spheres of coming-to-be, and he gives separate analyses of change in nature and in 'art'. The doctrine of the four causes is not based on images, then, so much as on a deliberate analogy: it is not the outcome of a conscious or unconscious assimilation of the unknown to something in familiar experience (for neither nature nor 'art' is intrinsically better known than the other), so much as the result of an explicit comparison between two spheres of coming-to-be which are recognised and kept distinct. Like any general theory of change, this doctrine is, of course, an attempt to suggest certain significant similarities between different areas of reality, but now the different areas of reality in question are analysed separately, and not only their similarities, but also some of their differences, are pointed out.[1] Plato's attitude to the use of images in cosmology is marked out from that of his predecessors in this, that he was fully aware (as they probably were not) of the distinction between a (mere) image and a demonstrative account. But a further, and a greater, difference separates Plato and Aristotle at this point, for while Plato, like most of the Presocratics (and, for that matter, many later philosophers), largely relies on images to express his cosmological doctrines,

[1] Thus he remarks that in nature the efficient cause is located in the thing itself, while in 'art' it is external to the thing produced, and he also observes that while craftsmen consciously deliberate, the same is not true of nature, even if at other points (e.g. when applying the doctrine of potentiality and actuality to the natural movements of the elements) he appears to underestimate or even to ignore the differences which separate the various modes of coming-to-be, natural and artificial.

Aristotle expressly rejects the use of metaphor in reasoning as a whole,[1] and in practice the account which he gives of the general principles of sublunary change (at least) is an explicit, non-figurative one, based on separate analyses of the circumstances that apply in different areas of reality.

[1] See below, pp. 404 f.

CHAPTER V

THE ROLE OF COMPARISONS IN PARTICULAR ACCOUNTS

We may draw a broad distinction between two overlapping strands in Greek speculative thought, the attempt to construct comprehensive cosmological theories, and the attempt to explain specific natural objects or phenomena. I have tried to show the part played by certain types of images in the general cosmological doctrines put forward by Greek philosophers, but we must now consider the role of comparisons in their inquiries into the nature and causes of particular phenomena.

The inquiries of the Presocratic philosophers range over a wide variety of topics. Indeed it is one of their most striking achievements that they opened up so many fields of investigation and were the first to treat *as problems* such questions as the nature of the heavenly bodies, the causes of such natural phenomena as earthquakes, eclipses, thunder and lightning, the origin of living creatures in general and of man in particular, the nature of sensation and so on. It is not until late in the fifth century that we begin to find definite views propounded on the question of the criteria which a scientific theory should fulfil (for example in the Hippocratic treatise *On Ancient Medicine*). But from the very first, if we consider the practice of Greek philosophers in the actual theories and explanations which they proposed, we may observe certain recurrent features in their accounts of natural phenomena. Certainly the absence of references to the supernatural helps to define the nature of their accounts negatively, but one of the most striking *positive* characteristics of the explanations which they put forward is the frequent appeal to analogies. Many of the theories which are attributed to the Presocratics or which appear in their extant fragments involve, or even consist of, an attempt to liken the phenomenon to be explained to some other, generally more familiar, object (whether or not there is any discernible similarity between the two). Now to compare some unfamiliar object with one that is better known is, as I have said, a matter of common sense, and we have considered a number of contexts in Homer where when someone is faced with a new or strange person or thing his reaction is to compare it with some familiar object. But what I wish to consider here is the way in which a similar procedure was employed and adapted by the philosophers and medical writers in the context of their explanations of natural phenomena. To consider what a thing is like is an obvious possible preliminary step towards achieving a greater understanding of its nature, and as we shall see, comparisons have a specially important and fruitful role in early Greek thought as the source of theories concerning phenomena which could not, in the nature of things, be investigated directly. At the same time we must consider how far the earliest Greek investigators went beyond the mere suggestion of a possible analogy in their theories. How strong are the analogies which they proposed, and how critically do they appear to have assessed them? Again how far was it possible, and how far did they attempt, to submit the theories which they suggested on the basis of analogies to test and verification? The role of comparisons in the early stages of Greek science is a complex one, for they were used extensively not merely as the source of theories and explanations, but also as the grounds for recommending them, and in the latter context we find a number of particularly complex analogies proposed, some of which involve the undertaking of specially designed investigations. Moreover, if we consider the rare passages in pre-Platonic writers which formulate views or express recommendations on the subject of the method to be adopted in the inquiry into nature, we shall see that in several notable instances these relate to the use of analogy.

THE MILESIAN PHILOSOPHERS

The first evidence we should consider concerns the Milesian philosophers.[1] Here the reports on which we depend are all second-hand, and many of them late and untrustworthy, so that we are obliged to assess the evidence for each comparison with special care. Yet in one respect the accounts of their explanations of particular phenomena are often more reliable than those which relate to their general cosmological theories, in that the former are less likely to presuppose any knowledge of sophisticated philosophical distinctions (such as that between matter and moving cause). Several of the numerous comparisons which are contained in our secondary sources are striking and apposite, and in some cases it seems much more probable that the image derives from the Milesians themselves than that it is the invention of a commentator. I shall consider some particularly interesting examples from each of the Milesians in turn.

(a) Thales. The earth floats on water

Aristotle twice attributes to Thales the doctrine that the earth floats on water. At *Metaph.* 983 b 21 f. (DK 11 A 12) he says that Thales 'declared that the earth rests on water', though at *Cael.* 294 a 28 ff. (DK A 14) he is more guarded in his ascription of this idea to Thales: 'this is the most ancient account [i.e. of why the earth is at rest] which has come down to us, which they say Thales the Milesian gave, namely that the earth rests because it is afloat, like a piece of wood or something similar'. Already in antiquity[2] it had been suggested that Thales derived this theory (as also the idea that

---

[1] Kranz, *1*, contains a collection of the Presocratics' similes and metaphors (with little interpretative comment). Rather more important contributions to the study of the role of comparisons in the period before Aristotle are the articles of Diller (*1*, dealing particularly with the period from Empedocles to Democritus) and Regenbogen (dealing especially with the Hippocratic treatises *On Generation, On the Nature of the Child* and *On Diseases* iv), and cf. also Snell, *3*, ch. 9.

[2] See Simp. *in Cael.* 522 16 ff., DK A 14, and cf. Plu. *de Is. et Osir.* 34, 364 d, DK A 11.

water is the origin of all things) from Egypt, and the fact is that in one Egyptian myth[1] the earth (Geb) was imagined as floating on Nun, the primordial waters. But whatever value we attach to this suggestion, the point has often been made that Thales' theory should be distinguished from the Egyptian or any other myth in this, that it referred not to personal gods, but to the familiar substances earth and water. It is true that he may well have continued to consider these in some sense divine,[2] but in no other respect do they resemble the anthropomorphic or zoomorphic gods of Greek or Egyptian religion whose genealogies and whose exploits were the subjects of numerous myths.[3]

At *Cael.* 294a 30 ff. the example of 'a piece of wood or something similar' and the explanatory statement which follows 'for none of these things rests naturally on air though they do on water' seem to be Aristotle's own illustration and comment. But if we accept Aristotle's account at all (and there seems no good reason not to do so) Thales evidently thought that the earth is afloat, whether or not he specifically compared it with a piece of wood. If we ask why he held this idea, it may be (as Aristotle suggests) that he intended to explain why the earth does not 'fall': alternatively (or in addition) he may have wished to relate earth to his primary substance water and to suggest the priority of the latter. In either case the notion that the earth floats is open to obvious objections. Aristotle noted that the question of what supports the water on which the earth rests, was not dealt with, and he also pointed out that in fact pieces of earth (unlike bits of wood) do *not* float on water (*Cael.* 294a 32 ff., b 3 ff.). Yet Thales' idea should rather be judged in relation first to the obscurity of the problem (as it must have seemed to him) and

[1] See Wilson, in Frankfort, 2, pp. 54 ff., 59 ff. For various possible Egyptian and Near Eastern parallels for the idea that water is the origin of things, see KR, pp. 90 ff.

[2] The possible implications of the dictum attributed to Thales that 'all things are full of gods' are discussed above, pp. 233 f.

[3] We may note, for instance, that in Egyptian mythology Nun and Geb each have consorts, Naunet, the counterheaven, and Nut, the sky-goddess.

secondly to previous conceptions of the physical connection between different world-masses.[1] We might compare it, for example, with the myth of Atlas holding up the heavens (Hes. *Th.* 517 ff.). Thales' idea, by contrast, is a rational account, a λόγος, first in that it omits any reference to anthropomorphic gods or the supernatural, and secondly in that it is based on a certain positive analogy between the effect to be explained (why the earth is 'held up') and an effect that is observed elsewhere (solid objects being 'held up' when they float). It is true that Thales appears to have ignored the negative analogy (the differences between the behaviour of pieces of earth and wood in water), but rather than dismiss his idea out of hand, it would be more to the point to agree with Aristotle's moderate judgement on those who first tackled the problem of why the earth is apparently at rest: 'they seem to have investigated the difficulty up to a certain point, but not as far as they might have done' (*Cael.* 294b 6 f.).

We should go on to note that Thales may have based a suggestion concerning the nature of earthquakes on his idea that the earth floats on water. According to Seneca (*Quaest. Nat.* III 14, DK A 15) at least,[2] he held that 'the earth is supported on water and is borne like a ship, and when it is said to "quake" it is tossed about by the motion of the water'. This notion, too, bears a superficial resemblance to an earlier mythical conception, for earthquakes were often attributed to the sea-god Poseidon, the earth-shaker, Ἐννοσίγαιος,

---

[1] Homer and Hesiod are more interested in the horrendous aspects of the underworld regions (which are the abode of the dead, the prison of fallen gods, etc.) than in their geography, of which they give a confused picture. Some passages (e.g. *Il.* 8 14) refer to the gulf beneath the earth (through which offending gods are hurled by Zeus). But we also hear of the 'roots' of the earth, which at Hes. *Th.* 726 ff. are said to grow from above Tartaros. Cf. also *Th.* 736 ff. and see KR, pp. 10 f., and most recently Stokes, *1* and *2*.

[2] Seneca is, of course, a late authority, and it should be noted that Aristotle does not mention this theory in his quite full survey of earlier accounts of earthquakes in *Mete.* B 7. But Seneca's report may derive indirectly from Theophrastus, and there seems no need to reject it unless we adopt the extreme pessimistic view recently expressed by Dicks (pp. 294 ff., especially pp. 298 f., 308 f.) that by Aristotle's time little or no genuine information concerning Thales' theories was available.

Ἐνοσίχθων, Σεισίχθων.[1] Yet once again, of course, Thales' theory (if such it was) evidently made no reference to any such deity. A ship rocking on the waves seems to have served as a simple but familiar model for what happens in an earthquake, which is imagined as the effect of the movement of the water on which the earth rests (although nothing is said, in our source at least, about why the water should sometimes be set in motion). It seems possible, then, that Thales used the idea that the earth floats on water not only to suggest how the earth is held up, but also to elucidate the nature of earthquakes. His investigations of these problems (both of which no doubt seemed highly obscure) remained quite superficial. Yet whatever the limitations of his idea of a floating earth, we may perhaps claim for it that it has a certain *economy*, in that it was used in two distinct contexts to deal with two separate problems.

(b) Anaximander. The flame which forms the heavenly bodies grows round the air surrounding the earth like bark round a tree

The account of Anaximander's cosmogony in pseudo-Plutarch, *Stromateis* (2, DK 12 A 10) contains this much-discussed passage: 'he says that that which produces hot and cold from the eternal is separated off at the coming-to-be of this world and that from this a sphere of flame grew round the air surrounding the earth, like bark round a tree. When this [i.e. the flame] was broken off and shut up in certain circles, the sun and the moon and the stars were formed.' Most scholars agree that some, at least, of the conceptions contained in this account derive from Anaximander himself. Other sources confirm, for example, that the heavenly bodies were thought of as circles of flame which are enclosed in mist.[2] But if, as we have already seen, the world is evidently conceived as growing like a living organism, the precise image which Anaximander used, and its exact relevance to his account of the

---

[1] E.g. *Il.* 20 57 f., cf. above, p. 203.
[2] The evidence is discussed below, pp. 312 ff.

heavenly bodies, are somewhat obscure. Was the image primarily a botanical, or an embryological one? Baldry (pp. 29 ff.) drew attention to the fact that several of the terms used in this report, i.e. γόνιμον, ἀποκρίνεσθαι, ἀπορρή-γνυσθαι and φλοιός, have technical senses in the context of embryology (though this does not mean that the author of *Stromateis* necessarily used them here in their special embryological senses).[1] Baldry suggested, then, that the original image is an embryological one, and he argued from the reference to a *sphere* of flame (which suggests an egg-shaped structure) that the words which refer to a tree are unimportant or a later addition. Heidel, on the other hand (*4*, pp. 686 ff.), came to a quite different conclusion. He accepted the comparison with the bark of a tree and argued that the term σφαῖρα is inaccurate. He referred (p. 687) to 'the uncritical habit among later authors of attributing Eudoxian notions to earlier cosmologists', and elsewhere in the doxographical reports on Anaximander we find another instance where a reference to spheres is almost certainly out of place.[2] If, as seems most likely, Anaximander thought that the stars, like the sun and moon, appear at openings in *rings* (not in a sphere or spheres),[3] the idea of a sphere of flame growing round the air surrounding the earth is unnecessary and uneconomical.

[1] It is clear from the addition of the words ὡς τῷ δένδρῳ that the writer of *Stromateis*, at least, is using the word φλοιός in its normal sense 'bark' and not in its embryological sense 'caul' (the membrane enclosing the foetus). KR (note to p. 133) point out that none of the terms used has an exclusively embryological sense: 'they are common terms (except φλοιός, which most frequently means "bark") which would naturally be applied to both embryology and cosmogony'.

[2] At Aet. II 16 5, DK A 18, it is reported that the stars are borne round 'by their circles and spheres' (ὑπὸ τῶν κύκλων καὶ τῶν σφαιρῶν) but the addition of the words καὶ τῶν σφαιρῶν is almost certainly incorrect. The reference to *both* circles *and* spheres involves serious difficulties (on which see KR, pp. 136 f.: and why Anaximander should have thought more than *one* sphere is necessary is quite obscure), but apart from these, there is clear evidence both in Hippol. *Haer.* 16 4 f., DK A 11, and in the present passage, *Strom.* 2, that Anaximander referred to circles for the *stars*, as well as for the sun and moon.

[3] Hippol. *Haer.* 16 4 f., DK A 11; and Ps.-Plu. *Strom.* 2, DK A 10. On Aet. II 16 5, see my last note.

The notion of an egg-shaped structure may or may not have been present in Anaximander's original theory. But when we examine the comparison with a tree, this seems to meet Anaximander's conception of the present state of the world in several important features. Hippolytus (*Haer.* 1 6 3, DK A 11), Aetius (III 10 2, DK A 25) and the author of the *Stromateis* himself agree in attributing to Anaximander the theory that the earth is cylindrical—it is compared with a stone column, for example. When, in the present passage, it is implicitly compared with the trunk of a tree, this seems appropriate enough.[1] Then the heavenly bodies sun, moon and stars, form a series of concentric circles round this cylindrical core, and it is tempting to suggest that here may be a further point at which the tree comparison fits his astronomical theory, in that the regular growth of a tree in concentric rings is meant to illustrate the growth of the different circles of the heavenly bodies, which are also at uniform distances from the centre. But if so, how did he conceive the 'breaking-off' of the flame? There are several species of tree which Anaximander might have known which shed their bark naturally.[2] It is, I suggest, not impossible that some such phenomenon may have recommended itself to him as a model for the breaking-off of the flame which forms the heavenly bodies, though it is true that one of the difficulties which would remain in this interpretation would be to decide whether his idea was that different layers of bark break off one by one, or that a single dense mass of bark breaks off and then separates into its distinct rings.[3]

[1] According to Ps.-Plutarch the breadth of the earth is three times its depth. Both the comparison with a tree-trunk and that with a stone pillar express Anaximander's idea of the cylindrical shape of the earth, though neither, by itself, conveys his conception of its actual dimensions.

[2] Theophrastus, *HP* 1 5 2, mentions ἀνδράχλη, μηλέα and κόμαρος (which Hort classifies as Arbutus Andrachne, Pyrus Malus (apple) and Arbutus Unedo respectively) as common species of trees or shrubs whose bark splits off naturally, and presumably some or all of these may have been known also to Anaximander.

[3] The former suggestion might seem more natural, but the account in *Strom.* seems to refer to a single 'breaking-off'. The reference to the subsequent 'shutting-up' of the flame into circles (the word used is ἀποκλεισθείσης) is obscure on

The interpretation of the account of Anaximander's cosmogony in the *Stromateis* is doubtful at certain points, but it seems very likely that the reference to the growth of bark round a tree is original. This comparison has several remarkable features. First there is the complexity of the analogy, which was clearly a good deal more elaborate than, for example, Thales' suggestion that the earth floats on water. The tree-trunk corresponds to the cylindrical-shaped earth. Round the central core, but as yet not separate from it, grows the flame which will become the heavenly bodies, and here it seems that the concentric rings of growth in a tree may correspond to the eventual configuration of the heavenly bodies in a series of concentric circles round the earth. It is possible, too, that Anaximander imagined the breaking-off of the flame as like the shedding of bark in some species of trees. The points of similarity between the growth of a tree and that of the world seem, then, to have been worked out in some detail by Anaximander. But we should also remark that at some points this model needs to be modified in order to fit his cosmological theory. As already noted (p. 311, n. 1), the tree-trunk suggests the cylindrical shape of the earth, but not its precise dimensions. And the obliquity of the circles of the sun and moon to the axis of the earth (Aet. 11 25 1, DK A 22) is another point at which his model fails to fit his cosmological theory exactly. Anaximander's is an ambitious attempt to describe the formation of the different parts of the world, and we see that the analogy of the tree forms only a part of a more elaborate total theory which expands and to some extent corrects it.

(c) Anaximander. The heavenly bodies are wheels of fire enclosed in mist which have certain openings through which they are visible

Hippolytus and Aetius agree, in the main, in their accounts of Anaximander's theory of the heavenly bodies. Hippol. *Haer.* 1 6 4, DK A 11, reports that 'the heavenly bodies come into

any interpretation, but if, as Heidel suggested, the term σφαῖρα is inaccurate in the first place, some of the difficulties here may have arisen from the apparent need to convert the 'sphere' into circles.

being as a circle of fire...enclosed by mist. And there are vents, certain pipe-like passages, through which the heavenly bodies appear.' Aetius II 20 I, DK A 21, says that the sun 'is a circle...like a chariot-wheel, having a hollow felloe [i.e. tyre], full of fire, at a certain point showing the fire through an aperture as through the nozzle of a bellows', and similar accounts are given of Anaximander's theory of the moon (II 25 I, DK A 22) and of the stars (II 13 7, DK A 18). These reports are late, and in several minor details they are difficult to interpret. The main features of the theory they describe are, however, clear. The heavenly bodies are regarded as wheels or circles of fire which are pierced with openings through which the sun, the moon and the stars appear. The wheels themselves are not visible because they are surrounded by mist. The openings in the wheels are variously described. ἐκπνοαί, which appears in both our sources (Hippol. *Haer.* 1 6 4; Aet. II 21 1, 24 2, 25 1), means, simply, 'vents' or 'breathing-holes'. Hippolytus uses the phrase πόροι τινὲς αὐλώδεις, 'pipe- or tube-like passages'. Aetius uses the term στόμιον, 'mouth', most often (II 13 7, 20 1, 24 2, 29 1) but also on two occasions the expression πρηστῆρος αὐλός (II 20 1 and 25 1). It was Diels (*1*, pp. 25 ff.) who first suggested that πρηστήρ here refers not to some meteorological phenomenon (as it usually does),[1] but to a bellows, and this interpretation has

---

[1] The precise meaning of πρηστήρ when used of meteorological phenomena is often difficult to determine. Derived from the verbal root πρηθ, it seems to share both the senses which that root develops, 'burn' and 'blow'. It appears first at Hes. *Th.* 844 ff. where it is associated with lightning, thunder, winds and thunderbolts. The meaning in Heraclitus Fr. 31 is obscure, but it may well be, as Kirk, *1*, pp. 330 f., has suggested, that it stands for a form of fire (which Heraclitus elsewhere, Fr. 64, calls κεραυνός, 'thunderbolt'). On other occasions we find πρηστῆρες mentioned in association with thunder (Hdt. 7 42), with whirlwind (Ar. *Lys.* 974) and with thunderbolts (Thphr. *Ign.* 1). In Xenophon, *HG* 1 3 1 a πρηστήρ falling on a temple sets it on fire, and at Thphr. *Vent.* 53 πρηστῆρες sink some ships. The fullest description of the πρηστήρ is in Arist. *Mete.* Γ 1 where two types of whirlwind which may be formed by a hurricane (ἐκνεφίας) are distinguished, the τυφῶν which is colourless (371 a 1 ff.) and the πρηστήρ which occurs when the 'exhalation' is 'thinner' and the hurricane 'burns as it is drawn down' (a 15 ff.). The word is evidently used of a number of different phenomena, and may refer either to whirlwinds or to lightning ('thunderbolt') or perhaps to a combination of both. Cf. *HGP*, 1, p. 463, n. 3.

been generally accepted (Burnet, *3*, p. 68, n. 2; KR, p. 136; *HGP*, I, p. 93) although we should not underestimate the difficulties which it presents.[1] But while we cannot be certain of the terms in which Anaximander may have described the openings in the wheels of fire, the substance of his theory is not in doubt.

Burnet (*3*, p. 68) suggested that the Milky Way may have been the original inspiration of the theory of the wheels. But if Anaximander's theory may, perhaps, have originated in some such observation, he evidently developed his conception in some detail and applied it to the heavenly bodies as a whole. His model of the wheels with the apertures in them served not only to describe some of the apparent movements of the heavenly bodies, but also to explain other celestial phenomena. Hippolytus *Haer.* I 6 5 reports that the waxing and waning of the moon were held to be due to the opening and closing of the aperture through which it is seen, and our sources[2] also attribute to Anaximander a theory of the

---

[1] The normal Greek word for bellows, from Homer onwards (e.g. *Il.* 18 468), is φῦσα, usually in the plural φῦσαι, and it should be noted that the *only* parallel which can be cited for πρηστήρ in the sense 'bellows' is a passage in Apollonius Rhodius (4 777) where, moreover, it may be that the word still means 'whirlwinds' and is only used poetically and metaphorically to refer to the bellows of Hephaestus. Diels's suggestion, that πρηστήρ is an archaic word which Anaximander himself employed, must be considered unlikely (though it may be granted that it is difficult to see why Aetius used this word to refer to a bellows, when φῦσαι would have been both more normal and less ambiguous). There are difficulties, too, in the image which is conveyed, if πρηστῆρος αὐλός is to be interpreted as the nozzle of a bellows, for where Anaximander's theory requires *flame* to be shot out through the openings in the wheels, the nozzle of a bellows emits blasts of *air*. It might seem better to retain a meteorological sense for πρηστήρ, then, e.g. whirlwinds or lightning, especially as the word occurs in some such sense in a report in Achilles, *Intr. Arat.* 19, p. 46 Maass, DK 12 A 21, which is generally taken to refer to the astronomical theory of Anaximander. Yet Achilles' evidence is of little value: Diels has shown that he seriously misinterpreted the nature of Anaximander's theory at other points. Furthermore, if πρηστήρ is taken in a meteorological sense in Aet. II 20 I and 25 I, it seems impossible to interpret the term αὐλός which is twice used in connection with it, for this must surely refer to some sort of pipe or tube and this seems quite inappropriate to such phenomena as lightning or whirlwinds. We must admit, then, that the interpretation of πρηστῆρος αὐλός in Aetius is obscure, but 'bellows' is at least etymologically possible as a meaning for πρηστήρ, and this appears to give the best sense for this difficult phrase.

[2] Hippol. *Haer.* I 6 5, Aet. II 24 2, 25 I, DK A 11, 21 and 22.

eclipses of the sun and moon which again refers to the blocking of the apertures in the wheels (though what causes the apertures to be blocked and so brings about these phenomena, we are not told). Of course the theory of the rings leaves many problems unresolved: we might ask, for example, how the sun and moon can be seen through the opaque rings of the stars (which according to Anaximander are nearer to the earth).[1] But the importance of his theory lies in this, that it is the first attempt to construct a *mechanical model* by which to describe the movements of the heavenly bodies and a variety of other celestial phenomena. We may note, too, that this model does not simply involve a direct assimilation of one object to another with which we are already familiar (as Thales' suggestion that the earth floats on water might be said to do), but is a quite elaborate, artificial construction, combining and adapting two disconnected images, the wheels and the pipe-like apertures.

(*d*) *Anaximenes. Lightning compared with the flash made by an oar in water*

At III 3 I (DK 12 A 23) Aetius reports Anaximander's theory of lightning, thunder, whirlwinds and other meteorological phenomena: 'he says that all these happen as the result of wind: for when, having been enclosed in a dense cloud, it bursts out violently owing to its fineness and lightness, then the tearing (ῥῆξις) makes the noise [i.e. thunder] and the rift (διαστολή) brings about the lightning-flash against the blackness of the cloud'. Aetius then goes on to say (III 3 2, DK 13 A 17) that Anaximenes' theory was the same, though 'he added what happens with regard to the sea, which flashes when cleft by oars'. This image should be mentioned because, if it is authentic,[2] it is an interesting

---

[1] See Heath, pp. 31 ff., on this and other points at which Anaximander's theory is obscure.

[2] 'Aetius' alone is not a strong authority, and of our two sources for the *Placita*, one, the *Epitome* of pseudo-Plutarch, omits this particular report. Moreover, Aristotle mentions neither Anaximenes nor Anaximander in the

example of the use of a comparison not to suggest a theory, so much as to support one that had already been formulated (in this case, by another philosopher).

How close an analogy for the lightning-flash does the flash made by an oar in water provide? In one case the medium is water, in the other a cloud (water vapour), and in one instance the effect is produced by an oar, in the other by wind (as it was believed). The main point of similarity between the two cases is in the two effects, the appearance of a flash of light, and it was largely on the basis of this similarity, such as it is, that Anaximenes argued that their causes are similar, that in both cases the phenomenon is the result of a cleaving process. But if the positive analogy is not very strong, the role of the comparison to corroborate the meteorological theory is interesting and should be noted. If we can trust the report in Aetius, the illustration was used to support a theory which had already been put forward by Anaximander. It is not often that there is any evidence that the Presocratics tested their physical theories directly: indeed this was generally impracticable, whether because of the obscurity of the phenomena which they were attempting to explain, or because of the vagueness of the theories which were proposed to explain them. But this example illustrates an alternative method which was quite often used in an attempt to recommend a theory dealing with an obscure meteorological or astronomical problem. The ancient Greeks could not, for obvious reasons, investigate the lightning-flash directly. But Anaximenes attempted to lend support to Anaximander's theory that lightning is caused by the wind cleaving the

chapter of *Mete.* (B 9) in which he discusses previous theories about lightning (although at 370a 10 ff. he does report that a certain Cleidemus, among others, used the illustration of the flashing of the sea when struck by sticks *at night* in connection with a theory that lightning is nothing but an *appearance*). It is always possible that the ascription of this image to Anaximenes is a pure conjecture on the part of Aetius or his immediate source. On the other hand Aetius refers to the image to distinguish, at this point, between Anaximander and Anaximenes, and this seems to suggest that he had particular grounds for attributing the image to the latter.

clouds by citing an analogy where a similar phenomenon is manifestly produced by a similar cleaving process.

(e) Anaximenes. The earth and certain of the heavenly bodies are held up by air, e.g. like leaves

Aristotle (*Cael.* 294b 13 ff., DK 13 A 20) groups Anaximenes with Anaxagoras and Democritus as philosophers who held that the reason why the earth is (apparently) at rest is that it is flat: 'for it does not cleave the air which is underneath, but settles on it like a lid, as flat bodies evidently do'. Hippol. *Haer.* 1 7 4, DK A 7, reports that a similar reason was given to explain what supports the sun and moon and all the other stars (καὶ τὰ ἄλλα ἄστρα πάντα).[1] Our sources add a number of illustrations in connection with this theory. In Aet. III 10 3 (DK A 20), for instance, the earth is 'table-shaped',[2] and at II 22 1 (DK A 15) the sun is 'flat as a leaf'. The specific images of a table, a leaf or a lid (the last being suggested by the verb ἐπιπωματίζειν in Arist. *Cael.* 294b 15) may or may not be original, but it is clear that the theory as a whole is based on an analogy with flat objects of some sort. Just as Thales seems to have based his account of the earth on the

---

[1] Aetius, however, reports at II 14 3 f., DK A 14, that 'Anaximenes says that the stars are fixed in the crystalline like studs' (or perhaps, as Guthrie suggests, *HGP*, I, pp. 136 f., we might take τὸ κρυσταλλοειδές to refer to a membrane, and ἧλοι to wart-like spots on it) 'but some say they are fiery leaves like paintings'. The second sentence here agrees with the theory attributed to Anaximenes in other passages, while the first sentence appears to contradict the evidence of Hippolytus, for the *same* heavenly bodies can hardly ride freely on the air *and* be fixed in the crystalline. Heath, pp. 41 ff., suggested that the discrepancy may be resolved if we take Hippol. *Haer.* 1 7 4 to refer to the *planets* alone, and the first part of Aetius' report, II 14 3, to refer to the *fixed stars*. Taking Aet. II 23 1, DK A 15, also to refer to the planets, Heath concluded that Anaximenes 'was the first to distinguish the planets from the fixed stars in respect of their irregular movements'. This is an ingenious interpretation, but it is perhaps more likely that the report in Aet. II 14 3 f. is simply confused—that the second sentence gives Anaximenes' general theory of the heavenly bodies (as does Hippol. *Haer.* 1 7 4) while the first erroneously attributes to him the notion of the stars being fixed in the crystalline (cf. KR, p. 155, where it is suggested that the first sentence may contain an Empedoclean theory which has been mistakenly transferred to Anaximenes).

[2] Cf. Plato, *Phaedo* 99b 8 where an unnamed earlier philosopher is said to prop up the earth like a flat kneading-trough on air as a base.

knowledge that certain solid objects float in water, so Anaximenes makes use of another familiar phenomenon, that of the resistance which air offers to flat objects, to explain why the earth and certain heavenly bodies do not 'fall' in space. His account of the movements of the heavenly bodies is also based, in part at least, on the assumption that they are supported by air. At Aet. II 23 1, DK A 15, τὰ ἄστρα are said to 'execute their turnings, τροπάς, through being pushed out by condensed and opposing air'. Whether this should be taken to refer to the courses of the planets alone (Heath), or also the movements of the sun in the ecliptic and of the moon in declination (KR, p. 155), it is clear that the notion that air supports the heavenly bodies was the starting-point for Anaximenes' explanation of some of the apparent irregularities in their movements, and here again we may compare the way in which Thales (according to Seneca, at least) used the theory that the earth floats on water in his account of earthquakes.

One further image which Anaximenes may have used in his account of the movement of the heavenly bodies must also be mentioned. Hippol. *Haer.* 1 7 6,[1] reports that 'he says that the heavenly bodies do not move under the earth, as others have supposed, but round it, just as the cap (τὸ πιλίον) turns round our head'. The comparison with the cap is a striking one and may, perhaps, be original. The πιλίον is usually taken to be a close-fitting felt cap, roughly hemispherical in shape (like the visible heavens) and the turning of the cap seems to represent the rotation of the heavenly bodies about an axis through the Pole Star. If this is the correct interpretation, the point of the comparison lies not so much in the nature of the cap itself,[2] as in the movement which it would describe if turned on a man's head. The cap serves,

---

[1] Cf. *Mete.* 354a 27 ff., DK A 14, where Aristotle says that 'many of the ancient astronomers believed that the sun was not carried under the earth, but round it', but does not mention Anaximenes by name.

[2] The πιλίον might suggest that the heavens are a *solid* hemispherical shell, but it is less likely that Anaximenes thought of the stars as fixed to a solid outer shell than that he imagined them as floating free on air (see above, p. 317, n. 1).

then, as a model for the visible heavens, but the model is particularly remarkable in this, that it has to be *put to work* for its significance to be fully understood.[1]

(f) General contribution of the Milesians

The Milesians may reasonably be credited with the first systematic attempts to give rational explanations of a wide variety of natural phenomena. Some idea of the nature of lightning or thunder or disease is, of course, implicit in pre-philosophical writers, though we should stress the word *implicit*. Homer is not interested in discussing the nature of such phenomena or the general circumstances governing their occurrence, so much as in telling us why a particular phenomenon occurred at a particular juncture, and what we might call the proximate causes of many such phenomena are regularly found on the divine or supernatural plane, in the fiat of the gods. The Milesians focused their attention not on this or that particular flash of lightning, but on the nature of the lightning-flash itself, and they eliminated from their accounts references to the wills or motives of the gods. At the same time the 'explanations' which they put forward are often quite rudimentary. Many of their theories appear to have consisted mainly or entirely of some suggestion that a particular phenomenon is like some more familiar object, and once an analogy of some kind had been put forward, their inquiry often seems to have ended. Thus Thales and Anaximenes apparently based their explanations of why the earth does

---

[1] It should, however, be mentioned that some scholars have found this image so artificial that they have sought to interpret it differently. Guthrie (*5*, p. 43, n. 1, and *HGP*, I, p. 138, n. 1) and Webster (*3*, p. 89) have suggested that the πιλίον may be not a felt skull-cap, so much as a *turban*, which is not turned so much as *wound* round the head. But this seems a quite vague illustration of the movement of the heavenly bodies (unless, indeed, what it illustrates is that the heavenly bodies rise and set at slightly different points on the horizon each day). I think it more likely, then, that the πιλίον is, as it is usually thought to be, some sort of skull-cap. It is worth adding that a text in Sextus Empiricus (*M.* IX 37) relates a story that the Dioscuri were crowned with πῖλοι which were decorated with stars and which stood as symbols of the heavens (and here the πῖλοι are undoubtedly hemispherical caps, not turbans).

not 'fall' on the two common observations, that certain solid objects float in water, and that flat objects tend to be buoyed up by air, but both philosophers appear to have ignored the *negative* analogy: neither seems seriously to have examined the question of how their analogies could in fact apply to the *earth*.

The shortcomings of the Milesians' analogies when judged as scientific hypotheses are obvious and do not need stressing: indeed they should hardly be considered hypotheses at all, as they did not serve as the source of testable predictions. But it is more fruitful to take note of the positive aspects of their use of comparisons. In each of the examples which we have discussed an attempt is made to transcend the limits of what could be investigated directly. Obscure natural phenomena such as eclipses, lightning and earthquakes, or what is remote in space or time—the stars, the formation of the cosmos— were apprehended by means of comparisons with things which could be observed directly, and several of the analogies which were proposed were used with a certain *economy*, a single model serving as the starting-point for explanations of a number of different phenomena. Then Anaximenes probably referred to the illustration of the flash of an oar in water not to suggest, so much as to support, a theory concerning the lightning-flash, and here we see the beginnings of what was to become an important practice, the attempt to employ analogies to recommend and establish theories concerning obscure phenomena. But it is Anaximander's use of analogies that is especially bold and striking at this period. Both the model of the growth of bark round a tree and the model of the wheels with their apertures are complex and illustrate several different features of quite elaborate theories concerning the formation of the world and the nature of the heavenly bodies, and the latter example is particularly remarkable in that it is not simply a direct comparison with a single object familiar from everyday experience, but an artificial construction, the first mechanical model of the heavenly bodies deliberately designed to account for a variety of celestial phenomena.

LATER PRESOCRATIC PHILOSOPHERS

To a large extent the astronomical and meteorological theories of later Presocratic philosophers follow the patterns of those which we have already considered from the Milesians, and now we can sometimes, though still all too rarely, refer to the original words of the philosophers themselves to assess their accounts of natural phenomena. Fr. 32 of Xenophanes, for example, which says that 'what men call Iris, this too is a cloud, purple and scarlet and yellow to behold', is worth noting first because it implies that references to personal gods (such as Iris) should be eliminated from accounts of natural phenomena, and secondly because of the nature of the account which Xenophanes himself suggests: he identifies the rainbow as a coloured cloud, assimilating a rare phenomenon to one that is more common, just as the Milesians had often done. Elsewhere too his theories often take a similar form, being based on implicit or explicit comparisons with familiar objects, as, for example, his reported doctrine that the stars are ignited clouds which are kindled and extinguished like coals when they appear by night and disappear by day.[1] Turning to Heraclitus and Parmenides, we find that the models that they suggested for the heavenly bodies are again quite similar in kind to those put forward by Anaximander or Anaximenes. Heraclitus' extant fragments unfortunately contain little information about his detailed astronomical theories, but according to Diogenes Laertius IX 9 f.[2] he imagined the heavenly bodies to be bowls or basins (σκάφαι) with their hollow sides turned towards us. Like Thales' account of the earth, this idea has been compared with an earlier popular myth, that the sun is carried round the earth in a golden

---

[1] Aet. II 13 14, DK 21 A 38. He is also said to have held that the sun is caused by ignited clouds, or by a concentration of fiery particles (e.g. Aet. II 20 3, DK A 40) and to have suggested that lightning, comets and the phenomenon we call St Elmo's fire are all caused by clouds ignited by motion (Aet. III 3 6, 2 11 and II 18 1, DK A 45, 44 and 39).

[2] DK 22 A 1: cf. the passages in Aetius collected in DK A 12.

cup,[1] and this in turn may, perhaps, reflect an Egyptian myth which depicted the sun moving in a *boat* on the waters above the earth by day, and on the waters below the earth by night.[2] But Heraclitus' conception is simply an attempt to visualise the heavenly bodies in concrete terms, and he apparently used his model (as Anaximander had used *his*) in his account of the eclipses of the sun and moon and of the phases of the latter, all of which he imagined to be due to the twisting of their bowls (though we are not told what brings this about). Then in the *Way of Seeing* Parmenides promises to explain 'how the earth and the sun and the moon and the sky...and the Milky Way and the outermost Olympus and the hot might of the stars began to come to be' (Fr. 11, cf. also Fr. 10), and according to Aet. II 7 1, DK 28 A 37, he pictured the heavens as a complex system of intertwined bands or wreaths (στεφάναι περιπεπλεγμέναι, in Aetius' phrase). The details of his account are obscure, but this much is clear, that like Anaximander before him (and perhaps under his direct influence) Parmenides attempted to construct a theory of the heavenly bodies with the help of homely images.[3]

In astronomy and meteorology Xenophanes, Heraclitus and Parmenides propose theories that are similar in type to those which we already find in the Milesians. In biology, the work of Alcmaeon marks a notable advance on that of his predecessors both in the scope of the topics he investigated and in his use of new techniques to investigate them. While Anaximander, especially, had made several striking, if rather obscure, suggestions about the origin of living things and of

---

[1] The earliest reference to this idea in extant Greek literature is in Stesichorus, 185 P, but cf. Mimnermus 10 D (12 B) which speaks of a golden *bed*, hollow and winged.

[2] See Wilson, in Frankfort, *2*, pp. 57 f., where other ancient Egyptian ideas about how the sun moves are also mentioned. It should also be noted that the Egyptians sometimes imagined eclipses of the sun to be caused by a serpent attacking and swallowing it in its boat.

[3] With Diels's interpretation, given in a note to Fr. 12 in DK, compare Heath, pp. 66 ff. and more recently, Morrison, *1*.

man in particular,[1] Alcmaeon investigated the nature of sense-perception and raised such problems as the nutrition of the embryo in the womb and the physiological changes which bring about sleep, besides putting forward a general theory of disease.[2] Furthermore, according to one source, at least (Chalcidius, *in Ti.* pp. 256 f., Waszink DK 24 A 10), he was the first investigator to undertake anatomical dissections, doing so in connection with his theory of the passages which link the eye to the brain.

Alcmaeon's biological researches are, for his day, quite impressive, but what concerns us is the nature of the theories which he put forward, and I should point out how often these rely on simple analogies with familiar phenomena. (1) Thus Aristotle (*HA* 581 a 14 ff., DK A 15) reports that he compared the growth of pubic hair in adolescence with the flowering of plants before they bear seed. The metaphor ἥβης ἄνθος, 'the flower of youth', was, of course, a commonplace of Greek literature as early as Homer (e.g. *Iliad* 13 484), but Alcmaeon's comparison seems to mark the first attempt by a natural philosopher to suggest a more precise correlation between the growth of animals and that of plants. This is the first in a long series of comparisons between animals and plants which occur in Greek biological treatises and which were particularly important in the development of Greek embryological theories. (2) Alcmaeon himself put forward

---

[1] According to Aet. v 19 4, DK 12 A 30, he suggested that living creatures came to be 'enclosed in thorny barks' in 'the wet' (an idea which was no doubt partly based on a belief that animals are spontaneously generated in mud or in the sea). He also seems to have suggested that human beings cannot originally have been born in their present form (with the human child requiring so long to become self-sufficient) but that they first came to be inside some sort of fish (Ps.-Plu. *Strom.* 2, Plu. *Quaest. Conv.* VIII 8 4, 730ef, Censorinus, *de die nat.* 4, 7, DK A 10 and A 30, and cf. Hippol. *Haer.* 1 6 6, DK A 11). RK (n. 1 to p. 142) doubt whether he knew about the embryology of sharks, but if he knew of *no* viviparous sea-animals, it is difficult to see what factual basis his theory could have had (see *HGP*, 1, p. 104, n. 2).

[2] See Thphr. *Sens.* 25 f., DK 24 A 5 (which gives Alcmaeon's theory of the senses), Aet. v 16 3, 24 1, 30 1, DK A 17, A 18, B 4. That Alcmaeon extended his investigations to animals may, perhaps, be inferred from the report at Arist. *HA* 492a 14 f., DK A 7, that he held that goats can breathe in through their ears.

an embryological doctrine which consists of an analogy of another interesting type. According to Aet. v 16 3, DK A 17,[1] he held that the (mammalian) embryo takes in food through its whole body like a sponge. He was clearly unaware of the true function of the umbilical cord. Yet the general principle which underlies his attempt to solve the problem of how the embryo is nourished is far from being unreasonable, for the mammalian embryo, in its different stages of development, may indeed be compared with lower species of animals (as, in Alcmaeon's theory, with a sponge). Once again we should note that the discovery and examination of analogies of this general type was to prove an extremely fruitful method both in later Greek, and in modern, embryological studies. (3) And yet another attempt of Alcmaeon's to found a biological theory on an analogy is reported by Aristotle at *GA* 752 b 22 ff., DK A 16, where he specifically attributes to Alcmaeon the idea that the white of an egg (τὸ λευκόν) is its 'milk' (while he also notes that this was a popular belief). Again it seems that Alcmaeon tried to suggest a correlation between the circumstances attending the development of different kinds of animals, and he evidently appreciated that part of the egg must act as food for the developing embryo, although the fact that *both* yolk *and* white serve for nutrition (the chick developing from a speck on the surface of the yolk—the 'blastoderm') eluded both Alcmaeon and Aristotle (who was one of those who suggested the contrary theory, namely that the yolk, alone, serves as food).

A brief survey of some of the accounts of natural phenomena which were proposed by the thinkers who immediately followed the Milesians shows that analogies continued to form a rich source of astronomical and 'meteorological'

---

[1] Rufus (in Oribasius, III 156, *CMG* VI, 2, 2 136 28 ff., DK A 17) attributes a different theory on this problem to Alcmaeon, namely that the embryo already takes food in through its mouth while still in the womb. Such a view occurs in the Hippocratic Corpus (*Carn.* ch. 6, L VIII 592 11 ff.) and is noted by Aristotle, *GA* 746a 19 ff., without mention of its author. Aet. v 16 1 ascribes it to Democritus and to Epicurus, and Censorinus (*de die nat.* 6, 3, DK 38 A 17) to Diogenes and to Hippo.

doctrines, and that they also figure prominently in the theories which Alcmaeon suggested on some of the new problems which he raised in biology. But by far the most important evidence for the use of analogy in Presocratic philosophy comes from Empedocles. Some of his images have already been discussed in connection with his account of the general cosmological role of Love and other principles. But we may now deal with the more elaborate analogies which he suggested in his explanations of particular phenomena. Our evidence comes not only from brief fragments and second-hand reports, but also from his own detailed statements which enable us to judge both the content of his comparisons and the manner in which they are presented. I may begin by examining the two major analogies of the lantern and the clepsydra.

(a) Empedocles. The eye compared with a lantern

'As when a man who intends to go out on a stormy night makes ready a lantern, a flame of blazing fire, fitting to it panes to screen it from every wind,[1] and these scatter the breath of the winds that blow, while the light leaping out—as much of it as is finer—shines across the threshold with unfailing beams: so then did the primal fire,[2] enclosed in membranes, trap the round pupil in delicate tissues,[3] which are pierced through with marvellous passages and which keep back the deep surrounding water while they let through the fire—as much of it as is finer' (Fr. 84, from Arist. Sens. 437b 26 ff.). The language of this fragment is highly poetical and it contains several terms whose precise meaning is doubtful. Empedocles' theory is, however, clear in the main. That there

[1] I follow the usual rendering of the phrase ἅψας παντοίων ἀνέμων λαμπτῆρας ἀμοργούς, taking λαμπτῆρας to refer to panes of some sort, and ἀμοργούς to mean 'screening', but Taillardat's recent suggestion that ἀμοργούς refers to a tunic or tissues of linen which was made on the island of Amorgos is ingenious and offers another possible interpretation of this obscure verse.

[2] Burnet (3, p. 217) and others have supplied Love as a subject for λοχάζετο ('pupil' being then taken in apposition to 'fire'), but this hardly seems necessary. Ross (5) adopted A. Förster's emendation λοχεύσατο ('gave birth') for λοχάζετο which picks up the pun in κούρην ('pupil' or 'daughter').

[3] I omit (with Mugnier, 2, et al.) the τ' which Diels added in v. 8.

is 'fire' of some sort in the eye was probably a very old belief,[1] and Empedocles evidently assumed that the eye contains both 'fire' and 'water'.[2] But the main point of the comparison with the lantern is to illustrate the function of the membranous tissues which surround the pupil. The panes of the lantern serve to illustrate how, thanks to their 'marvellous passages', these membranes fulfil a double role, *both* allowing through the finer parts of the fire (i.e. the 'visual ray' itself, conceived here as coming from the pupil) *and* at the same time keeping back the fluid in the eye. Yet we should observe that the role of the transparent screen is not exactly the same in these two cases. While the panes in the lantern *protect* the fire inside from the wind which is outside, the membranes in the eye do not *separate* the fire from the water, but enclose both of them, allowing the one, but not the other, to pass through.[3]

Certain comments may now be made on Empedocles' theory and on the role of the comparison with the lantern. First the way in which the analogy is developed is remarkable.[4] The similarities between the eye and the lantern are underlined and emphasised by the formal structure of the fragment and the repetition of certain phrases. The description of the lantern begins 'ὡς δ' ὅτε' and that of the eye 'ὡς δὲ τότ'', and the lines referring to the panes in the lantern are closely echoed in the second half of the comparison.[5] There are, of

---

[1] Some such belief may, perhaps, be implied by such Homeric expressions as πυρὶ δ' ὄσσε δεδήει ('his eyes blazed with fire'), e.g. *Il.* 12 466 (though elsewhere, e.g. *Il.* 1 104, the eyes are merely *compared* with fire). As was already suggested by Aristotle, *Sens.* 437a 22 ff., the origin of this belief may have been the phenomenon we know as 'seeing stars' (when the eye is rubbed).

[2] According to Theophrastus (*Sens.* 7, DK A 86) Empedocles thought that light things are perceived by fire, dark things by water.

[3] Ross (5), however, seems to take it that the membranes separate the fire from the water in the eye, translating 'they kept out the deep water that surrounded the pupil, but let the fire through'.

[4] Cf. the observations of Regenbogen, pp. 180 ff., Diller, *1*, pp. 14 ff., Kranz, *1*, p. 106, and Snell, *3*, pp. 213 ff.

[5] *vv.* 4 f. οἵ τ' ἀνέμων μὲν πνεῦμα διασκιδνᾶσιν ἀέντων,
φῶς δ' ἔξω διαθρῷσκον, ὅσον ταναώτερον ἦεν...
vv. 10 f. αἳ δ' ὕδατος μὲν βένθος ἀπέστεγον ἀμφιναέντος,
πῦρ δ' ἔξω δίεσκον, ὅσον ταναώτερον ἦεν.

course, many quite elaborate similes in Homer which are introduced in just this way, and in which key words and phrases are repeated (as here the phrase ὅσον τανυώτερον ἦεν in *vv.* 5 and 11). But Empedocles uses this style of comparison in a new context, in an explanation of an extremely obscure and complex phenomenon. His problem is to give an account of how the eye functions. The illustration of the lantern may, of course, have suggested to Empedocles certain features of his theory in the first place. But this comparison evidently has a further role to play, being used not merely to convey a conception of how the membranes in the eye work, but also, it seems, to recommend that conception. The fragment contains what purports to be a definitive account of the eye, not a hypothesis which awaited confirmation through fresh investigations. There is no suggestion that Empedocles had undertaken, or intended to undertake, a dissection of the eye (though Alcmaeon may well have done so already). But here it should be remarked that while dissections would certainly have thrown light on the basic structure of the eye and its main component parts, it is very doubtful how far dissections alone would have enabled Empedocles to determine the solution to his main problem, namely how the eye functions in the living animal. This was a problem on which the evidence available from simple visual inspection is quite inconclusive. What Empedocles has done in Fr. 84 is to cite an analogy for his theory of the eye. He refers to a familiar object outside the body where the double effect of the transparent screen is evident. But what is more he is at pains to point out and underline the similarities between the lantern and the eye, attempting to recommend and justify his theory not, it is true, by a method of verification, but rather (one would say) by appealing to the extent of the *positive analogy* between the cases he compares.

(b) *Empedocles. Respiration compared with the action of a clepsydra*[1]

'This is how all things breathe in and out: they all have bloodless tubes of flesh which stretch out to the innermost parts of the body, and at the mouths of these tubes the furthest ends of the nostrils are pierced right through with numerous holes in such a way that the blood is kept inside, while a free passage is cut for the air to pass through. Now when the tenuous blood rushes away from these holes, the bubbling air rushes in with a violent surge; and when the blood leaps back, the air is breathed out again, just as when a girl plays with a clepsydra of bright brass. When she puts her shapely hand on the vent of the tube and dips the clepsydra in the tenuous mass of silvery water, not a drop of liquid enters the vessel, but the bulk of the air within pressing upon the numerous perforations [i.e. at the bottom of the vessel] keeps the water out until she unblocks the dense stream [of air]; then as the air gives place, the water enters in equal measure. In just the same way when water occupies the depths of the brazen vessel, and the passage of the vent is blocked by the girl's hand, the air outside, striving to get in, holds the water back, pressing upon its surface at the gates of the ill-sounding strainer, until she takes away her hand, and then again—the opposite of what happened before—as the air enters, the water rushes out in equal measure. Just so when the tenuous blood, surging through the limbs, rushes backwards and inwards, a stream of air immediately enters, rushing in with a surge, but when the blood leaps back, the air is breathed out again in equal measure' (Fr. 100, from Arist. *Resp.* 473b 9 ff.). The interpretation of this fragment poses several problems and has been the subject of much scholarly discussion.[2]

[1] The clepsydra was a metal vessel used for transferring liquids from one container to another. The top of the vessel had a single narrow opening which could be blocked with the hand: the base was perforated in the form of a strainer. Various vessels of this sort are illustrated by Last, p. 170, and Guthrie, *3*, p. 228.

[2] See especially the recent articles of Furley, Timpanaro Cardini and Booth.

The first main point of dispute concerns the type of respiration which Empedocles is describing: does he refer to breathing through the nose, or to breathing through pores in the skin, or to both? There can be no doubt that when Aristotle quoted the fragment, he took Empedocles to be describing breathing through the nose alone (*Resp.* 473 a 17 ff., 474 a 17 ff.). Yet Diels suggested that Aristotle was misled by the word ῥινῶν in *v.* 4, which he mistakenly took to be the genitive of ῥίς, 'nose', instead of (as Diels thought) the genitive of ῥινός, 'skin'. Diels took *vv.* 1–4 to refer to tubes of flesh stretched out over the surface of the body (this was the sense he gave πύματον κατὰ σῶμα in *v.* 2), and he interpreted the fragment as describing respiration through the pores in the body alone. Diels has been followed by most other commentators, but Furley has raised a number of objections to this interpretation, suggesting, in particular (p. 32), that it is absurd to suppose that Empedocles failed to take breathing through the nose into account at all, whatever he may have believed about breathing through the skin. Furley's own interpretation is more complex, namely that the fragment refers to both types of breathing: 'Empedocles' theory', he says, 'was that breathing in through the nose was simultaneous with breathing out through the pores, and vice versa.' This is ingenious, yet in point of fact Empedocles simply does not refer to any such two-way process either in *vv.* 6–8 or in *vv.* 22–5.[1] Booth in turn challenged Diels's translation of the key phrases πύματον κατὰ σῶμα and ῥινῶν ἔσχατα τέρθρα. He pointed out that πύματον need not necessarily mean 'outermost'—it often means 'hindmost'—and he translated *v.* 2 'tubes of flesh...are stretched out *deep inside* the body'. But if this verse need not imply breathing through the skin, no more need ῥινῶν ἔσχατα τέρθρα, which may, of course, refer to the nostrils.[2] To my mind, then,

---

[1] Furley's tentative suggestion of τούτερον for αἰθέρος in *v.* 24 does little to remove this difficulty.

[2] Booth (p. 11) interprets 'the utmost ends of the nostrils, i.e. their innermost ends', but it is also possible that the phrase means the *outermost* ends of the nostrils.

Booth has successfully vindicated Aristotle's interpretation according to which the whole fragment refers to breathing through the nose.[1]

The second main problem concerns the interpretation of the comparison with the clepsydra. Furley's suggestion, that the vent of the clepsydra corresponds to the nose, and the perforated strainer to the pores of the skin, is neat, but quite unlikely if, as I believe to be the case, we have no good reason for supposing that Empedocles held that we breathe both through the nose and through the skin. But does air in the clepsydra correspond to air, or to blood, in the process of respiration? Empedocles' repeated description of breathing is clear enough and refers to two processes: (1) the blood rushes backwards and inwards, and the air enters (*vv.* 6–7, 23–4); (2) the blood leaps back, and the air is breathed out (*vv.* 8, 25). What happens in the clepsydra is more complex: (*a*) the clepsydra is held in water with the vent covered, so no water comes in, *vv.* 10–13; (*b*) when the vent is uncovered, the air leaves and the water enters, *vv.* 14–15; (*c*) the clepsydra is held up full of water with the vent covered, so the water is held in, *vv.* 16–19; finally (*d*) when the vent is uncovered, the air enters as the water runs out, *vv.* 20–1. Several commentators have started from the assumption that air in the clepsydra must correspond to the air we breathe, but if we consider the changes that Empedocles describes and what brings these about, this seems unlikely. In respiration, it is the removal of the blood which causes the breath to be inhaled in (1), and it is again the movement of the blood which causes the breath to be exhaled in (2). But in the clepsydra it is not the water which determines the movements of the air, but rather the opposite: it is the pressure of the air upon the strainer, as in (*a*) and (*c*), or the release of that pressure, as in (*b*) and (*d*), which determine the behaviour of the water. It seems more likely, then, that it is the water entering and leaving the clepsydra which corresponds to the air we breathe in and

[1] This is also the conclusion reached, independently, by Timpanaro Cardini.

out.[1] The main point which is illustrated by the comparison seems to be that the entry and departure of one substance through a perforated strainer may depend on the variations of pressure exerted upon it by another substance. It is true that on this interpretation (which follows Booth's) there are several details of the description of the clepsydra which have no parallel in the account of breathing. As Booth notes, there is nothing in that account to correspond to the plugging and unplugging of the vent of the clepsydra, nor indeed is there anything in the body that corresponds to the vent itself. Yet this is not so damaging as might at first sight appear. That the analogy does not hold in every respect, even Furley has to admit,[2] and at one point this is fairly obvious: Empedocles states (vv. 4–5) that the perforations of the nostrils are such that they allow air, but not blood, to pass through them, although it is clear that the strainer of the clepsydra does not possess a similar property, but allows both air and water to enter and escape. The lantern analogy in Fr. 84 should serve as a warning to us, for there we found that in spite of Empedocles' evident emphasis on the similarities between the lantern and the eye, the two cases are not *exactly* parallel (p. 326). The apparent lack of correspondence between certain features of the clepsydra and Empedocles' theory of breathing should not be held as an objection to the interpretation suggested: rather the conclusion we should draw is simply that the original analogy was, in certain details, inexact.

If the interpretation of this fragment has been much disputed, widely differing opinions have also been expressed concerning the value and significance of Empedocles' observations of the clepsydra (to which he referred not only in connection with his theory of respiration, but also to prove the

---

[1] Cf. Booth, pp. 12 f., who shows that the parallelism of sentence structure in the fragment favours the same conclusion.

[2] Furley, p. 33, notes that even on his own interpretation 'the analogy is still not wholly exact. Section I of the simile [i.e. vv. 20–1] seems to suggest blood streaming from the pores as one breathes in through the nose.'

corporeality of air).[1] Burnet (*3*, p. 27) called this fragment 'the first recorded experiment of a modern type', and he is not the only scholar to describe Empedocles' investigations with the clepsydra as experiments.[2] This provoked a sharp, and not altogether fair, response from Cornford (*10*, pp. 5 f.): 'all Empedocles did was to draw the explicit inference: "the vessel cannot be simply empty: the air in it cannot be nothing at all". He did not invent the *clepsydra* in a laboratory with a view to testing the hypothesis that air has some substance, and then abiding by the unforeseen result of his experiments.' Unfortunately this discussion was vitiated both by what I believe to be misinterpretations of the theory of respiration which Empedocles was putting forward, and by a failure to examine the exact relevance of the comparison to that theory. Burnet (*3*, p. 245) said that 'the cause of the alternate inspiration and expiration of breath was the movement of the blood from the heart to the surface of the body and back again, which was explained by the *klepsydra*', but how or in what sense this was 'explained' by the simile he omitted to say. Cornford's famous objection (*10*, p. 6) that the theory 'could have been tested by anyone who would sit in a bath up to his neck in water and observe whether any air bubbles passed through the water into, or out of, his chest as he breathed', is simply not valid against what I take to be the correct interpretation of the fragment, namely that it refers to breathing through the nose. More recently Furley and Booth have agreed that the fragment does not contain an experiment in the proper sense of the word, and this we should surely grant.[3] This should not, however, lead us to overlook the genuine merits of the method which Empedocles

[1] Arist. *Ph.* 213a 22 ff. (which refers, however, primarily to Anaxagoras).

[2] E.g. Farrington, *2*, p. 58 ('by these experiments he demonstrated the fact that the invisible air was something that could occupy space and exert power').

[3] Furley, p. 34, comments that 'the whole business lacks certain essential features of the experimental method—the attempt to control the conditions exactly and to find answers to precise questions, and the readiness to let conclusions wait upon results'. He calls the clepsydra a 'persuasive analogy', a description with which Booth, p. 15, agrees.

adopted in an attempt to establish his theory of respiration. We should consider, first, the nature of the problem which he faced. Like the problem tackled in Fr. 84 (the functioning of the eye) this concerns the internal functioning of the living animal, and must, then, have appeared to Empedocles particularly obscure and difficult to investigate. Some of the details of his theory are stated in Fr. 100 with no apparent attempt to justify them on empirical grounds, and the theory as expressed is manifestly incomplete: nothing is said, in this fragment at least, about *why* the blood moves up and down in the body. But his attempt to resolve the difficult problem of what controls the inhalation and exhalation of breath is based on his observation of what he took to be a similar case outside the body. The suggestion that it is the variation in the pressure of the blood which controls the air entering and leaving the body, *is* an idea which Empedocles tried to recommend and justify not, it is true, by investigating the problem directly,[1] but by appealing to the analogy of the clepsydra where we can *observe* how variations in the pressure of the air on the perforated strainer determine the movement of water into, and out of, the vessel.

(c) Other comparisons in Empedocles

In the lantern and clepsydra fragments Empedocles draws two quite elaborate comparisons to suggest theories concerning certain familiar, but obscure, vital functions, and in each case he attempts to justify his theory by underlining the parallelisms between the things he compares in the formal structure and phrasing of the fragments. But in our evidence for Empedocles there are many shorter comparisons which

---

[1] Dissections would have revealed to Empedocles the general structure of the lungs and the air-ducts communicating with it. But what was, perhaps, even more important for a better understanding of how breath is drawn into the body was some knowledge of the dynamic function of the intercostal muscles and the diaphragm, and their function would hardly be immediately apparent from a cursory visual inspection. It may be doubted whether greater knowledge simply of the general disposition of the organs in the thorax would have persuaded Empedocles to abandon his theory based on the movement of the blood.

show that he applied a similar method of arguing from the known to the unknown by analogy in many different branches of inquiry. Thus (1) according to Aristotle (*Cael.* 295a 16 ff., DK 31 A 67) he suggested that the reason why the earth does not fall in space is the swiftness of the movement of the heaven in a circle round it. Aristotle goes on to refer to the example of water in a cup: the water does not fall out of the cup when the cup is swung quickly round in a circle above the head (when centrifugal force temporarily overcomes the attraction of gravity), and it seems probable that some such observation provided the starting-point of Empedocles' theory. Here too, then, it seems that his theory on an obscure astronomical problem, like those he suggested on respiration and the functioning of the eye, was based on an analogy with more readily observable phenomena. (2) Then Aristotle (*Mete.* 357a 24 ff., DK B 55) reports that Empedocles called the sea the 'sweat of the earth', and it is unlikely that this was merely a poetic metaphor. The idea that the universe as a whole is a living organism was common in early Greek philosophy, and the notion that the earth in particular is subject to cycles of growth and decay is one which Aristotle himself adopted (*Mete.* 351a 26 ff., see above, p. 263). Empedocles probably believed that it is no mere coincidence that the sea and sweat are both salty, and it seems likely that he intended to explain the salt of the sea as an excretion of the earth (though whether he attempted to explain, in turn, why sweat is salty, is doubtful). (3) Yet another analogy is cited by Aristotle (*GA* 747a 34 ff., DK B 92) in connection with Empedocles' obscure explanation of the sterility of mules. Empedocles apparently thought that the seeds of both the parent animals are by nature 'soft' (i.e. fertile), but that they become 'hard' (i.e. infertile) when they unite, the 'densities' of the one fitting into the 'hollows' of the other. But this theory was illustrated, and may perhaps originally have been suggested, by a technological analogy, for he compared the biological phenomenon with what happens when two soft metals, copper and tin, combine to form a harder metal, bronze.[1] Finally, I may mention some of the analogies which he proposed between different things in the organic sphere. (4) Fr. 68, for instance, contains a play on words, but one which Empedocles no doubt took to be significant. The first milk (beestings, the Greek term for which is πυός with a long υ) is referred to as 'white pus' (πύον, short υ), and it seems that Empedocles' theory was that milk is blood which has been subject to a process of putrefaction (see Arist. *GA* 777a 7 ff.).[2] Then (5) both Aristotle (*GA* 731a 4 ff.) and Theophrastus (*CP* 1 7 1) quote with approval the fragment in which he suggests an analogy between the fruit of large trees, in particular of the olive, and eggs (Fr. 79). (6) And even more striking is the well-known Fr. 82: 'hair and leaves and the thick feathers of birds and scales...are the same things'. The fragment is quoted at *Mete.* Δ 387b 1 ff. to illustrate the writer's own theory of one class of homogeneous substances, namely 'woody bodies', including, for example, bone and hair, which are composed of earth and water but in which earth predominates, and it seems, then, that Empedocles probably meant that each of the things he mentions consists of the same primary element or combination of elements. But it is possible that Empedocles had a further point in mind as well, and that he saw a similarity in the *functions* of the things he mentions, in that

[1] In other fragments, too, Empedocles referred to technological examples to describe the way in which different substances arise from the four elements. In Fr. 23, for instance, there is the well-known comparison with painters who mix pigments in different proportions to represent different objects, and this seems to illustrate how a great variety of substances can be derived from a small number of simple 'roots'. Elsewhere the illustrations he uses refer to more complex processes. At Fr. 33 there is a brief comparison with the way in which fig-juice curdles milk, and the use of the term χόανοι, 'melting-pots', in Fr. 73 suggests that in that fragment the model he has in mind for the uniting of the elements is a metallurgical one. It is interesting to note that the illustrations he uses in this context refer to what *we* should call chemical combinations, as well as to mechanical mixtures—although we should not, of course, suppose that Empedocles himself distinguished between these two.

[2] Cf. Fr. 81, which contains the cryptic suggestion that 'wine is water from the bark which is putrefied in the wood'. Plutarch (*Quaest. Nat.* 2 912c), at least, took this to mean that πέψις (here, 'fermentation') is akin to putrefaction.

each of them acts as the protective covering of the animal or plant concerned, and if that is the case, the fragment may be said to contain the first attempt to use something resembling the modern principle of homology to relate the parts of different species of living beings.

The search for likenesses between different objects, phenomena or processes is a recurrent feature of Empedocles' physical and biological inquiries. Occasionally he constructed elaborate analogies in his attempts to throw light on obscure natural phenomena. But many of his metaphors too seem to have a similar underlying purpose, to suggest an essential similarity between an obscure or unfamiliar phenomenon or object and one that was, or seemed to be, better known. He was often, of course, quite mistaken when he suggested that two things between which he detected a certain similarity, such as milk and pus, or the salt of the sea and sweat, have similar origins. And yet as a method of investigation his search for likenesses was clearly of great positive value. This was especially true in biology, where the recognition and examination of similarities between different species of animals, and between animals and plants, was to lead to important discoveries. But it is also true more generally. The Milesians and others had already constructed various models to account for certain astronomical and 'meteorological' phenomena, and Alcmaeon had put forward some striking analogies in biology. But Empedocles' more extensive and more elaborate use of analogies suggested even more forcefully how observations of familiar phenomena might provide the starting-point for theories on problems which were difficult, or indeed quite impossible, to investigate directly (especially where it might be argued that the parallelism between the cases compared was a close and detailed one), and Empedocles himself applied this method in dealing with a wide variety of obscure astronomical, physical and physiological problems.

(*d*) The contribution of other late Presocratic philosophers

Other late Presocratic philosophers besides Empedocles also used analogies to suggest or support theories on various obscure problems, although in their extant fragments, at least, we find no such elaborate comparisons as the lantern and the clepsydra.[1] But at this point it is more important to consider the evidence that suggests that some of the later Presocratic philosophers had begun to be aware of problems of method in the inquiry into nature. We have seen that on many occasions and in many different branches of inquiry Empedocles had put forward analogies between the known and the unknown. Yet there is no concrete evidence that he *explicitly* recognised the procedure he uses so extensively *as such*, as a method of investigating obscure phenomena. The idea of the weakness of human knowledge is a commonplace of early Greek philosophy (indeed of early Greek literature in general). Xenophanes, for example, says that 'there never was a man, nor will there ever be, who knows the certain truth about the gods and all the other things about which I speak' (Fr. 34), and both Heraclitus and Empedocles, too, express their notions of the value, but also of the limitations, of the senses as a source of knowledge.[2] But while these philo-

---

[1] Two typical instances of the use of analogy in the later Presocratics may be mentioned briefly. According to Seneca (*Quaest. Nat.* IV a 2 28 ff., DK 64 A 18) Diogenes of Apollonia based his explanation of the much-discussed problem of why the Nile floods in summer on an analogy with a lamp: as in a lamp the oil is drawn up the wick as the wick burns, so the lands around the Nile attract water from other parts of the earth as they grow hotter in summer. Then there is a good example of the use of comparisons in biology in Democritus Fr. 148, where he uses two images to convey his idea of the function of the umbilical cord. He likens it first to the stern-cable of a ship (he evidently thinks of the umbilical cord as 'anchoring' the embryo to the womb), and then he also suggests that it is the first part of the embryo to develop, and here he likens it to a cutting (κλῆμα) from which a plant may grow.

[2] Cf. Heraclitus Fr. 55 ('things which can be seen, heard, learned, these are what I prefer') with Fr. 107 ('eyes and ears are bad witnesses for men if they have souls that cannot understand their language'). Again cf. Empedocles Fr. 3 9 ff., which suggests that we should not reject any 'path of understanding' (e.g. sight, hearing, etc.), with Fr. 2 where he points out how each man is deceived into thinking he has found the whole truth: 'so difficult is it for men to see these things or hear them or grasp them with their minds'.

sophers make general pronouncements on the roles of reason and the senses in obtaining knowledge, none of them offers any clear, positive suggestion about how the limitations of the senses might be overcome.[1] Nor can Parmenides be considered an exception to this rule, for while he stressed the role of reason (and developed a deductive method of argument), he *opposed* reason to the senses and entirely rejected the latter as a means of arriving at the truth. When we turn to Anaxagoras and Democritus, however, not only is the idea of the limitations of sense-perception repeated,[2] but now—for the first time in extant Greek philosophy—we find explicit recommendations concerning how those limitations may be surmounted. The obscure, but highly important, dictum ὄψις τῶν ἀδήλων τὰ φαινόμενα is attributed to Anaxagoras by Sextus Empiricus (*M.* VII 140, DK 59 B 21a), who also reports that Democritus commended Anaxagoras for his saying. The statement that 'things that are apparent are the vision of things that are unclear' is, of course, vague and ambiguous. What are the 'unclear things', and what are the 'phenomena' which provide a 'vision' of them? Sextus does not help us to determine the original meaning and application of the dictum, but some light may be thrown on this by considering its possible relevance to the actual theories and explanations of Anaxagoras and Democritus.[3]

It is tempting to suppose that for Anaxagoras typical 'ἄδηλα' are the 'portions' and the 'seeds' which play such an important part in his complex physical theory, and both of which are imperceptible entities.[4] Yet it is hard to see how 'phenomena' provided a 'vision' of these, except, perhaps, in so far as the qualities of the minute 'seeds' of a particular substance are manifest in the recognisable pieces of that sub-

---

[1] Xenophanes does, however, suggest that 'by seeking men find out better in time' (Fr. 18), though this recommendation is very imprecise. Cf. also Heraclitus' cryptic pronouncement 'I sought myself' (Fr. 101).

[2] E.g. Anaxagoras Fr. 21 and Democritus Fr. 11.

[3] On the history of this doctrine and its various applications, see especially the articles of Regenbogen, and Diller, *1*.

[4] On Anaxagoras' doctrine of 'seeds', see above, pp. 243 ff.

stance. The doctrine that 'in everything there is a portion of everything' is the outcome of Anaxagoras' application of the Parmenidean dictum that 'nothing can come to be out of nothing', rather than of any appeal to phenomena which we can observe. It is perhaps more likely, then, that in Anaxagoras ὄψις τῶν ἀδήλων τὰ φαινόμενα referred rather to certain of the theories which he put forward concerning particular natural phenomena. His reported doctrine that the moon is made of earth and has plains and valleys is one instance where his conjectures concerning what is unclear are, in part, based on a comparison with known phenomena,[1] though the dictum may equally well refer to conclusions that involve no such element of comparison, as when he used the clepsydra and inflated wine-skins to demonstrate the resistance of air,[2] or when he inferred (presumably from a knowledge of meteorites) that there are invisible bodies which are carried round in the aither underneath the sun and moon.[3]

In the case of Democritus, however, it seems easier to judge in what way 'phenomena' provided the basis for conjectures concerning what is 'unclear'. The dictum applies fairly obviously to several important aspects of the atomic theory. When, for example, the Atomists referred to differences in the shapes of the atoms to account for some of the secondary qualities of their compounds, their ideas were clearly based on their knowledge and experience of larger bodies. Thus the atoms combine or rebound from one another according to whether they are 'irregular' (σκαληνά), 'barbed' (ἀγκιστρώδη), 'concave' (κοῖλα) or 'convex' (κυρτά),[4] and Theophrastus reports how different humours or flavours were held to derive from atoms of different shapes: an acid (ὀξύ)

[1] E.g. Hippol. *Haer.* I 8 10, DK 59 A 42. Cf. also, perhaps, his reference to the existence of life and human civilisations on other parts of the earth, or on other worlds, in Fr. 4.
[2] Arist. *Ph.* 213a 22 ff., DK A 68; cf. Ps.-Arist. *Problemata* 914b 9 ff., DK A 69.
[3] Hippol. *Haer.* I 8 6, DK A 42. Cf. also Fr. 19 which remarks that the rainbow is a 'sign' of storm (χειμῶνος σύμβολον) for here too appearances seem to give a vision of the unclear.
[4] E.g. Simp. *in Cael.* 295 16 ff., DK 68 A 37.

22-2

flavour, for instance, was ascribed to atoms that are 'angular' (γωνοειδής, cf. πολυκαμπής), small and thin.[1] Other important principles that were applied to the atoms were also inferred from visible phenomena. We have already considered in other contexts the fragment in which Democritus cites certain examples to illustrate the principle that like moves towards its like, namely the behaviour of certain gregarious species of animals and that of seeds in a sieve and of pebbles on the seashore (Fr. 164, see above, pp. 270 f.). But I may remark here that these *visible* phenomena act as the grounds for the general theory which Democritus then applies to the *invisible* atoms. And a report in Seneca (*Quaest. Nat.* v 2, DK 68 A 93 a) provides a further example in which Democritus supported an idea concerning the behaviour of the atoms by referring to a familiar phenomenon in ordinary experience, for according to Seneca he illustrated his theory of winds by drawing a comparison with a crowded market-place, his theory of winds being that they are caused by a whole multitude of atoms jostling together in a confined space.[2]

In each of the examples we have considered, Democritus used visible phenomena to provide a 'vision', that is an understanding, of things that are, by nature, invisible. But on each occasion his theory depends on an explicit or implicit analogy. He suggests or assumes that similar laws or principles apply both to the observable phenomena which he cites and to the objects which we cannot perceive, *both* to the behaviour of certain animals, for example, *and* to the atoms, or again, *both* to sharp or angular things in the world of ordinary objects, *and* to sharp or angular atoms. ὄψις τῶν ἀδήλων τὰ φαινόμενα is an extremely general formula which

---

[1] Thphr. *Sens.* 65 ff., DK 68 A 135; cf. *CP* vi 1 6, DK A 129.

[2] It was, of course, not only in connection with the atomic theory that Democritus used 'phenomena' as the 'vision' of 'what is unclear'. Thus a report in Aristotle (*PA* 665a 30 ff.) suggests that having observed that the larger 'sanguineous' animals have viscera, he may have conjectured that 'bloodless' animals too have viscera which are too small to be seen, and Fr. 148 contains other analogies which he used to suggest the function of the umbilical cord in the developing embryo (see above, p. 337, n. 1).

can be applied to other types of inference besides those which are based on an analogy. But it would certainly seem to *include* arguments from analogy of the type which we have seen used by Democritus. The dictum formulated by Anaxagoras and approved by Democritus is important because it marks the first *explicit* recognition of the possibility of conjecturing the unknown from known phenomena: but while the method which Anaxagoras apparently means to recommend is not defined at all precisely, his general formula may be taken to relate particularly to the common practice of basing theories and explanations concerning obscure natural phenomena on analogies with more familiar, or more readily observable, objects.

HERODOTUS AND THE HIPPOCRATIC WRITERS

Many other instances of the use of analogies are found in fifth- and fourth-century writers who were not primarily cosmologists, and this evidence is particularly important for two reasons. First there are several texts which contain echoes of the Anaxagorean dictum ὄψις τῶν ἀδήλων τὰ φαινόμενα where the context clearly shows that the method which the writer wishes to recommend is based on analogy. And secondly we find that some of the illustrations which are cited to support certain theories do not simply refer to one or more familiar objects or phenomena, but involve the deliberate undertaking of a piece of research. In this context, where the illustration involves carrying out a test of some sort and it is cited in an attempt to establish a theory or explanation, the question we must consider is how far the appeal to such analogies resembles, or falls short of, the use of an experimental method.

As a historian, Herodotus often bases inferences on analogies (naturally enough) when, for instance, he attempts to reconstruct the past from present data.[1] But it is his more

---

[1] E.g. 1 145 (where he concludes that originally the Ionians were divided into twelve groups, as the Achaeans still were in his own day). Thucydides, too,

surprising use of comparisons in geography and geology that I wish to examine here. A passage in 2 10 is one example which illustrates how useful analogies may be in this context. There he draws a comparison between the Nile Delta and certain other areas, the country round Ilion, Teuthrania near the mouth of the Caicus, Ephesus and the plain of the Maeander, noting that he is 'comparing these small things with great', ὡς γε εἶναι σμικρὰ ταῦτα μεγάλοισι συμβαλεῖν. συμβαλεῖν here means no more than 'compare' (though the verb can also mean 'infer' or 'conjecture'), but the purpose of the comparison is to suggest that each of the areas mentioned is the result of a similar geological process. Herodotus suggests, in fact, that the entire Nile Delta is an alluvial deposit like the other river valleys he mentions, which he cites, no doubt, because in their case the silting up is more rapid and obvious, though less in extent.

On some other occasions the analogies which Herodotus proposes to support his theories are bolder, but less happy. At one point (4 36, cf. 42) he ridicules geographers who introduced a fictitious element of symmetry into their maps of the world, depicting the world as round as if it were drawn with compasses and making Asia and Europe of equal size. Yet he too makes a similar assumption of symmetry when he discusses the question of the course of the Nile at 2 33 f.[1] He says that Etearchus had found a big river on his expedition across Africa and guessed (συνεβάλλετο) that this was the Nile. 'And reason', Herodotus continues, 'endorses this. For the Nile flows from Africa and divides that country down the middle, καὶ ὡς ἐγὼ συμβάλλομαι τοῖσι ἐμφανέσι τὰ μὴ

---

sometimes uses a similar method of inference (e.g. 1 6, where he refers to the customs of contemporary barbarian societies to support conclusions concerning the former customs of the Greeks themselves) although at one point he rejects an argument of a similar type as unreliable (1 10, where he suggests that it would be wrong to infer the extent of the power of ancient Mycenae from the present ruins of the town, and remarks prophetically on how misleading an impression of the real power of Sparta and of Athens would be obtained from the ruins of those two cities, if they were some day destroyed).

[1] Cf. the discussion of this text in Diller, *1*, pp. 16 ff.

γινωσκόμενα τεκμαιρόμενος, τῷ Ἴστρῳ ἐκ τῶν ἴσων μέτρων ὁρμᾶται.'[1] The Danube's course, he says, is known to many, since it flows through inhabited country. It rises in the land of the Celts at the westernmost end of Europe (*sic*), and flows across that continent to its mouth at Istria on the Euxine. 'Concerning the sources of the Nile, however, none can speak, since Africa, through which it runs, is uninhabited and desert. But as much as could be learned from inquiry (ἱστορεῦντα) has been reported already.' However he then goes on to suggest that the mouth of the Nile is opposite (i.e. due south of) Istria. Egypt lies opposite the mountains of Cilicia, from which it is five days' journey to Sinope on the Euxine, and Sinope lies opposite the mouth of the Danube. 'Thus I suppose that the Nile in its course right across Africa matches (ἐξισοῦσθαι) the Danube' (2 34).

Several features of the method which Herodotus uses in tackling the problem of the course of the Nile in this passage are worth noting. First he claims to use research as far as this will take him. But then when this fails, he has recourse to inference. He distinguishes carefully, however, between what he knows (or thinks he knows) and the inferences which he draws concerning what is unknown, which are of the nature of conjectures (συμβάλλομαι, 2 33; δοκέω, 2 34). The phrase ὡς ἐγὼ συμβάλλομαι τοῖσι ἐμφανέσι τὰ μὴ γινωσκόμενα τεκμαιρόμενος, which bears an obvious similarity to Anaxagoras' ὄψις τῶν ἀδήλων τὰ φαινόμενα, is, like that dictum, vague and general. But the way in which Herodotus applies the rule of 'inferring things that are not known from things that are plain' in this passage, is perfectly clear. He makes some effort to establish one point of similarity between the Nile and the Danube, namely that their mouths are opposite one another (though his methods of determining this are quite imprecise), and he apparently believed that so far as it was known the course of the Nile roughly corresponded

---

[1] 'And as I conjecture, inferring things that are not known from things that are plain, it rises at the same distance [i.e. from its mouth] as the Danube.'

343

to that of the Danube. But on the basis of these 'known' similarities, he goes on to infer that *in other respects too* the two rivers are alike, that the length of the Nile is equivalent to that of the Danube (this seems to be what is meant by ἐκ τῶν ἴσων μέτρων ὁρμᾶται, 2 33) and that their courses across their respective continents correspond to one another as a whole (ἐξισοῦσθαι, 2 34). The phrase 'inferring things that are not known from things that are plain' may be quite imprecise, then, but the inference which Herodotus actually draws is evidently based on an analogy. Moreover, the elements of his argument are displayed a good deal more plainly than the elements of the analogies which appear in the extant fragments of the Presocratic philosophers. In Frr. 84 and 100, for example, Empedocles does not explicitly distinguish between the points of similarity which are (as he assumes) given or obvious, and those which he suggests or infers. In Herodotus, on the other hand, there is a clear distinction between the 'known', and the inferred, points of correspondence between the Nile and the Danube. Compared with Empedocles and other Presocratic philosophers (in so far as we can judge their use of analogy from the extant evidence) Herodotus is, in this passage, both more explicit in his formulation of his argument, and more reserved in the claims which he makes for his conclusions. The inference which he draws is, in fact, untrue.[1] But it is worth remarking, in conclusion, that it is not always unjustified to assume a certain symmetry between different areas of the world. Indeed an instance where it was not incorrect to assume such a symmetry can be cited from Aristotle, who at *Mete.* 362 b 30 ff.[2] reaches certain quite true conclusions concerning the origins and dispositions of the winds on the assumption that those in the southern hemisphere correspond, in general, to those in the northern,

---

[1] It is striking that elsewhere (4 50) Herodotus remarked on at least one important point of difference between the Nile and the Danube—the one floods regularly, the other does not—but still did not doubt that their courses are symmetrical in their respective continents.

[2] See below, p. 362.

his argument being similar in kind to that which led Herodotus to the (false) inference that the Nile rises in West Africa.

The Hippocratic Corpus contains extensive texts which illustrate the role of analogy not only in early Greek pathological and therapeutic doctrines, but also in such fields as anatomy, physiology and embryology.[1] Some of the more commonsensical applications of analogy need not detain us long. Thus Greek medical practitioners realised at a quite early stage that study of the man in health is of great value in determining facts about the sick, not only for the purposes of diagnosing diseases, but also in order to discover and predict the effects of certain treatments, but it is interesting that several treatises explicitly recommend the use of this type of comparison in such contexts.[2] But what concerns us here is, rather, the use of analogies in the theories which were put forward on such subjects as the structure and function of different parts of the body, the development of the embryo, the nature of various complex physiological processes, and the origin of certain diseases. On these and other biological and medical problems the Hippocratic writers, like the Presocratic philosophers, attempted to elucidate what eluded their comprehension by means of comparisons with more familiar objects or phenomena which could be observed directly. We may begin by noting briefly some of the more simple examples where homely illustrations are used to throw light on various obscure phenomena.

(1) The author of *On Breaths*, for example, draws a comparison with the steam driven off cauldrons of boiling water when he explains what causes a patient to yawn at the onset of a fever (ch. 8, *CMG* I, 1 96 5 ff.). Just as, when the water

---

[1] Besides the articles of Regenbogen, and Diller, *1*, cf. also Senn, *1*, and Heidel, *5*, pp. 146 ff., and *6*, pp. 75 ff.

[2] E.g. *VM* ch. 10 (*CMG* I, 1 42 11 ff.), where the author says we should learn the effects of 'depletion' and 'repletion' by 'referring to men in health' (ἐπαναφέροντας ἐπὶ τοὺς ὑγιαίνοντας). Cf. also *VM* ch. 8 (40 24 ff.); *Prog.* ch. 2, L II 112 13 ff.; *Acut.* ch. 9, L II 280 8 ff., and *Mul.* I ch. 6, L VIII 30 8 f.

boils, steam is driven off it in great quantities, so as the patient's temperature rises, the air inside the body, he suggests, is forcibly driven upwards through the mouth. (2) The same writer then goes on to explain the sweating that occurs in a fever on the analogy of the drops of water formed by the condensation of steam when it strikes such an object as the lid of a cauldron (ch. 8, 96 15 ff.). Sweating, he suggests, is caused when the air in the body condenses on striking certain pores through which it passes to reach the surface of the body. Many similar comparisons can be cited from other works. In the embryological treatises, for example, we find a series of ingenious analogies with common technological processes. (3) In *On the Nature of the Child* (ch. 12, L VII 488 13 ff.) the formation of a membrane round the seed in the womb is compared with the formation of a crust on bread as it is cooked, though the writer goes no further in attempting to suggest why the membrane and the crust are formed than to say that they occur when the particular substance (the seed and the bread) is heated and then 'distended by air' (φυσώμενος). *On Diseases* IV is particularly rich in such analogies. (4) In ch. 51 (L VII 584 13 ff.) the writer says that when the body is heated, the humours are stirred up and separated out, and here he compares what happens when butter is made. When the milk is churned, the butter comes to the top, the buttermilk comes next and the heavy part of the milk that is used to make cheese sinks to the bottom. So, he suggests, when the humours are stirred up, they separate out: the bile rises to the top, the blood comes next, then phlegm and finally water, which he says is the heaviest of the humours. (5) In the next chapter (590 9 ff.) he considers the effects of the cold on the body and here he refers to what happens when fig-juice is added to milk (for he believes that the curdling of milk is caused by 'cooling'). Similarly, he suggests, when an unwholesome cold affects the body, the humours congeal and thicken. Two more analogies appear in his account of the formation of stones in the bladder. (6) First he refers to the way in which a sediment forms when dirty water is left to stand in a cup or vessel, and he says that a sediment forms in the same way in the bladder when the urine is impure (ch. 55, 600 21 ff.). (7) And then he suggests how a stone is formed from part of this sediment by referring to the smelting of iron from iron ore: while the stone remains and hardens in the bladder under the influence (he believes) of phlegm, the equivalent of the dross is passed out with the urine (602 6 ff.).

Observation of common industrial processes undoubtedly provided a rich source of inspiration for the Hippocratic writers in their attempts to account for various complex changes that take place in the body. Their extensive use of analogies between animals and plants should also be particularly noted and again these are (as we might expect) especially common in the embryological treatises, although not confined to them. (1) Thus *On Diseases* IV draws a comparison between the process of nutrition in animals and that of plants (chs. 33 and 34, L VII 544 17 ff.): as each humour in a plant draws towards itself the humour in the earth which is akin to it (as it was believed), so each of the humours in the body attracts to itself the like humour from the food and drink in the stomach. (2) A similar comparison is used in *On the Nature of Man* (ch. 6, L VI 44 21 ff.) to illustrate the action of drugs in the body. This writer, too, held that seeds draw to themselves from the earth those substances that are like their own nature, and he says that drugs behave similarly in the body, each drug drawing to itself from the body the humours to which it is akin. The growth of embryos is compared with that of plants in several treatises. (3) *On the Seven Month Child* (ch. 1, L VII 436 8 ff.), for instance, compares the way the foetus ruptures the membranes which enclose it at birth with the bursting of ears of corn when they are ripe. (4) In *On the Eight Month Child* (ch. 12, L VII 458 2 ff.) the writer draws a comparison between the umbilical cord and the stalk of a fruit. He suggests that when the foetus is fully developed the umbilical cord becomes thinner and dries up, and he compares the way in which ripe fruit break off at the join of the stalk and the branch. (5) The writer of *On Generation* suggests that the size and shape of the embryo are determined by the womb in which it is formed, in the same way that the size and shape of plants may be affected by their being grown in certain containers (he gives an instance of gourds grown in vessels of different sizes, ch. 9, L VII 482 14 ff.). (6) In ch. 10 (484 9 ff.) he pursues the same analogy, suggesting that just as a tree may become deformed when there is insufficient room for it to grow and its development is obstructed by a stone or some such object, so too one reason why the embryo may become deformed may be the physical deformity of the mother's womb. But the boldest and most detailed analogies between the growth of an embryo and that of plants occur in *On the Nature of the Child*. First (7) there are two brief comparisons between the way an embryo develops limbs and the way a tree grows branches (ch. 17, L VII 498 3 ff.; ch. 19, 506 6 ff.), and then (8) at ch. 22, 514 6 ff., the writer begins a long digression (to ch. 27, 528 25) in which he discusses the growth of plants in detail, at the end of which he concludes that the relation of the embryo to its mother is similar to that of plants to the earth (528 18 ff.) and asserts that 'if anyone wishes to consider from beginning to end what I have said on this subject, he will find an exact parallelism between the growth of things produced in the earth and that of things produced in human beings (εὑρήσει τὴν φύσιν πᾶσαν παραπλησίην ἐοῦσαν τῶν τε ἐκ τῆς γῆς φυομένων καὶ τῶν ἐξ ἀνθρώπων)' (528 22 ff.).[1]

The examples I have given illustrate how a number of Hippocratic writers referred to things outside the body in an attempt to throw light on obscure medical or biological problems.[2] These texts demonstrate a keen interest in plant

[1] Cf. Regenbogen, pp. 165 ff.

[2] Sometimes such comparisons are used even when the phenomenon cited to illustrate the medical or biological problem is itself (we should say) quite obscure. In *On the Sacred Disease* (ch. 13, L VI 384 22 ff.) there is a reference to the effect which the South wind is alleged to have on wine or other liquids stored

life, in the processes of technology and so on, but they refer, generally speaking, to observations which could be made without undertaking any special investigation or research. On other occasions, however, the Hippocratic authors draw comparisons with phenomena which could only be observed by doing a deliberate piece of research, sometimes, indeed, one involving the use of special apparatus. (1) A good example of the type of procedure which we find used in several treatises occurs in *On the Diseases of Women* I. In ch. 1 (L VIII 12 5 ff.) the writer suggests that the reason why women menstruate is that their flesh is softer and more porous than that of men and so attracts more fluid from the stomach than theirs does. 'For in fact if someone were to place over water, or somewhere damp, for two days and two nights, on the one hand some clean wool, and on the other a clean close-woven garment of exactly the same weight as the wool, then on taking and weighing them he will find that the wool is much heavier than the woven garment.' The writer's contention is that the flesh of men and that of women differ in a similar way, and this remains, of course, a pure assumption. Yet the absorbency of flesh, after all, is something which he could hardly have investigated directly. What his test does show quite clearly is that two objects made of the same substance but of different textures may absorb water in different degrees. While this does not confirm his theory about men and women, it may be said to provide certain evidence for the general physical principle (of the relation between absorbency and texture) which he applies in his biological doctrine. And it is particularly notable that in carrying out his test the writer refers to the use of a pair of scales to check the quantities of water absorbed by weight.

in rooms or underground, when the writer suggests that the effect of this wind is to relax and make flabby the brain and loosen the veins. And in *On the Nature of the Child* (ch. 12, L VII 486 13 ff.) the writer refers to analogies with wood, leaves, foods and drinks which (he claims) emit and attract πνεῦμα (air) when heated a great deal or burned, when he argues that the seed in the womb both emits and draws to itself πνεῦμα (here probably breath) as it grows hot.

349

Other Hippocratic writers, too, undertake investigations of the behaviour of substances outside the body in connection with the theories which they put forward to explain complex physiological processes. (2) The writer of *On the Nature of the Child* believes that it is the pressure of the unborn child on the stomach that causes milk to be exuded at the breasts, but to illustrate and support this theory he refers to a simple test (ch. 21, L vii 512 7 ff.): if a hide is allowed to imbibe a lot of oil, and then squeezed, the oil is exuded. (3) Another test is described in *On Generation* to illustrate a theory that the proportion of 'strong' and 'weak' seeds determines the sex of the child. If different quantities of wax and fat are melted together, then so long as the mixture remains liquid, the predominant substance is not apparent, but it becomes visible when the mixture solidifies (ch. 6, L vii 478 11 ff.).[1] (4) *On Diseases* iv refers to a further investigation in connection with a theory that in fever the bilious humour remains in the body while the watery humour is evaporated. If water and oil are put in a vessel and heated for a long time, the writer says, it will be found that the water evaporates much more than the oil (ch. 49, L vii 580 7 ff.).[2] And even more remarkable are the occasions when the writer describes observations which require the use of special apparatus. Thus (5) in *On Diseases* iv the writer wishes to illustrate how the humours travel between the different 'sources' in the body (stomach, heart, head, spleen and liver), and how in particular when the stomach is full of food and drink, these are absorbed by other parts of the body, and conversely, when the stomach is empty, humours flow back into it from the other parts through the

---

[1] Cf. the simpler observations of the effects of adding cold water to boiling water, and of throwing wine on a flame, in the discussion of the physical changes accompanying sexual intercourse (*Genit.* ch. 4, L vii 474 22 ff., 476 1 ff.).

[2] The writer also twice uses observations of the way in which fluids are retained in narrow-necked vessels when the vessels are turned upside down quickly, first to illustrate a theory of how bleeding is stopped by the flesh holding back the blood (*Morb.* iv ch. 51, 588 17 ff.), and then in connection with a theory of how dropsy may sometimes be confined to one particular part of the body (ch. 57, 612 6 ff.).

veins spread out all over the body. In ch. 39, 556 17 ff., he describes setting up an arrangement of three or more vessels on a piece of level ground (this point is stressed): the vessels are pierced with holes and provided with communicating pipes fitted in the holes. He remarks that if water is poured into one of the vessels, it finds its way into each of the others, and conversely, if one of the vessels is emptied, water flows into it from the others: to fill or empty all the vessels, in fact, it is enough to fill or empty one of them. Finally (6) *On the Nature of the Child* also describes a test which requires the use of certain simple apparatus. The writer argues that the various parts of the body are formed by the breath (πνεῦμα), which causes like to come to like, and the test is a physical investigation which he has apparently attempted to adapt to illustrate his theory (ch. 17, L VII 498 17 ff.). A bladder is prepared with a pipe let down into it. Earth and sand and lead scrapings are put into it and water poured on top of them. Then if you blow through the pipe, first of all the solid substances become mixed with the water, but then after a while (the writer claims) the lead, the sand and the earth each collect together, and if you let them dry and open the bladder, you will find that like has come to like.[1]

Unlike Empedocles' description of the girl playing with the clepsydra, for example, or the frequent comparisons the Hippocratic writers themselves drew with technological processes or plant life, the texts which we have just considered do not refer to observations which are part of common experience, but imply the deliberate undertaking of a piece of research, and in this they satisfy one of the criteria of an experiment. Many of the passages in question are, in fact,

---

[1] Senn (*1*, pp. 242 ff.) suggests that the test was, in origin, a 'Sedimentierungsversuch' designed to show how the three solid substances become transposed in the bladder; when they are put in, earth is at the bottom, then sand, and then lead, but when blown on (or, Senn suggests, when the bladder is shaken) the lead with its greater specific gravity falls to the bottom, then comes the sand, and the earth comes to the top. Senn concludes that the author of *Nat. Puer.* did not carry out this test himself.

classed by Senn (*1*) as 'wissenschaftliche Experimente', indeed as 'einwandfrei beschriebene Experimente', but this is a judgement which cannot be accepted without reservations. None of the investigations which we have described provides anything like decisive evidence to establish or refute the theory in connection with which it is adduced. In each case the theory concerns the properties, origins or interactions of complex substances in the body, but the tests refer not to these substances, but to other, generally simpler, ones outside the body, that is not to flesh but to wool, not to seeds of different sorts but to wax and fat, not to bilious and watery humours but to oil and water. These tests can hardly be called experiments in the full sense for the obvious reason that the substances investigated are quite different from those to which the theory relates.[1] What these investigations did was, rather, to provide knowledge of 'visible things' (the behaviour of various substances outside the body) *which was then used* to suggest or illustrate theories concerning 'what is obscure', that is vital processes that take place inside the living organism. For the most part these models share the merits and defects which are noticeable in other early Greek analogies. On the one hand, these Hippocratic authors deserve credit for attempting to bring the evidence of observed phenomena to bear on difficult and complex physiological and pathological problems: but on the other, the theories which they

---

[1] Other Hippocratic texts, however, to which Senn also refers, describe investigations made directly on organic bodies themselves: e.g. *Nat. Puer.* ch. 20, L vii 508 15 ff., and several passages which refer to the results of dissections or vivisections, e.g. *Cord.* chs. 2 (L ix 80 13 ff.), 8 (86 4 ff.) and 10 (88 3 ff.), and cf. the detailed investigations of the development of the hen's egg in *Nat. Puer.* ch. 29, 530 10 ff. (which the writer uses to support his theory of the development of the human embryo). Two further passages are worth noting from *Carn.* as they refer to tests carried out on blood. In ch. 8 (L viii 594 14 ff.) it is observed that blood taken from sacrificial victims does not coagulate so long as it is warm, or if it is beaten, but it does so when allowed to cool (this is then taken to support a theory that the liver is formed from the blood 'when the cold defeats the warm'). And in ch. 9 (596 9 ff.) it is noted that on coagulating the blood forms a skin, and that as often as the 'skin' is removed, another is formed (this is then taken to show that the skin of the body is formed from the blood under the effects of the cold and the winds, πνεύματα).

put forward often depend on vague and arbitrary assumptions, and in their comparisons they often appear to underestimate or ignore the points of difference between the illustration and the thing illustrated.

Comparisons such as we have been considering appear little or not at all in such treatises as the books of the *Epidemics* or in other mainly descriptive works in the Hippocratic Corpus. But most of the theoretical treatises, and especially the embryological works, use comparisons extensively in their biological and medical doctrines. Furthermore, there are several works which explicitly refer to, and recommend, methods of apprehending 'what is obscure' from observed phenomena. The dictum of Anaxagoras ὄψις τῶν ἀδήλων τὰ φαινόμενα seems to be echoed in various forms and in different contexts in a number of Hippocratic works. *On Breaths* (ch. 3, *CMG* I, I 93 5), for instance, says that air is 'invisible to the sight, but apparent to reason', and suggests that the power of air may be inferred from its visible manifestations, such as uprooted trees, and here the inference is a direct one, involving no element of comparison.[1] But when the writer of *On Regimen* I states more generally that 'men do not know how to perceive things which are obscure from things which are apparent' (ch. 11, L VI 486 12 f.), the context makes it clear that the method which he has in mind depends largely on the apprehension of analogies. 'I will show how the visible "arts" are like both the visible and the invisible affections of man', he says (488 1 f.),[2] and he proceeds to devote thirteen chapters (12–24, 488 1–496 19) to suggesting various likenesses between arts, crafts or professions on the one hand, and natural processes on the other. Thus in ch. 12 he announces that divination 'imitates' the

---

[1] Cf. also *de Arte*, which draws a distinction between the sight of the eyes and that of the mind (ch. 11, *CMG* I, I 16 17 f.) and suggests that nature may be made to yield symptoms from which the unknown affections of the body may be inferred (ch. 12, 18 14 ff.).

[2] ἐγὼ δὲ δηλώσω τέχνας φανερὰς ἀνθρώπου παθήμασιν ὁμοίας ἐούσας καὶ φανεροῖσι καὶ ἀφανέσι.

nature and life of man: as the seer infers what is invisible (the future) from what is visible (present signs), so when a man and a woman come together to make a child, they too get knowledge of the invisible (in this case, the child that will be born) from the present. His other suggestions are no less fantastic: his knowledge of the natural processes which affect the living organism is quite superficial, and the analogies he suggests all consist of vague generalities. Yet it is remarkable not only that he should pursue this line of argument at such length,[1] but also that he should confidently present it as a *general method* of 'perceiving the obscure'.

On Ancient Medicine is another and more important work which expressly recommends the use of analogies in medicine. As several commentators have noticed,[2] this writer uses analogies of various types extensively. I have already noted that in ch. 10, for example, he says that in order to discover the effects of 'depletion' and 'repletion' on the sick, we should refer to their effects on men in health. And in ch. 15 (47 5 ff.) there is an obscure but striking passage where he refers to objects outside the body in order to support a theory concerning what happens in the body itself. He argues that different combinations of powers, e.g. the hot and the astringent, and the hot and the insipid, have very different effects on the body. Indeed, he says, they have different effects 'not only in man, but in leather and wood and in many other things which are less sensitive than man'. But then in his discussion of the affections which arise from 'structures' (σχήματα) in chs. 22 f. (53 1 ff.) and again in ch. 24 he *recommends the use of this method explicitly.* In ch. 22 he lists the different structures or forms of the parts of the body: some are hollow and tapering, some 'spread out', some hard and round, some broad and drawn out, some stretched, some

---

[1] He considers the τέχναι of metal-working, fulling, cobbling, carpentry, building, music, cooking, currying, basket-making, gold-working, sculpting, potting, writing and gymnastic training in turn, and concludes that 'all the "arts" participate in the nature of man' (ch. 24, 496 18 f.).

[2] E.g. Festugière, n. 56 on p. 54.

long, some dense, some loose and swollen, some spongy and
porous. He then asks which type of 'structure' is best adapted
to draw fluid to itself, for example, and he suggests that it is
the hollow and tapering one: 'one should learn these things',
he goes on, 'outside the body from objects that are plain to
see' (καταμανθάνειν δὲ δεῖ ταῦτα ἔξωθεν ἐκ τῶν φανερῶν, 53
12 f.). One of the observations he makes is that cupping
instruments (which are hollow and tapering) attract fluid
easily, and he also refers to the fact that it is more difficult to
draw fluid into the mouth when the mouth is wide open, than
if one compresses the lips and inserts a tube into the mouth.
He already knows that of the parts of the body the bladder,
the head and the womb are of this shape, 'hollow and tapering', but he refers to the evidence of objects of similar shape
outside the body in order to confirm that the form of these
parts of the body is adapted to a particular function, that of
attracting fluids. Finally in ch. 24 (55 4 ff.) he considers
more briefly the changes to which the humours are subject,
and once again he recommends a similar method of inquiry.
He asks what a humour which is sweet, for instance, will
become 'if it changes to another kind, not as a result of
admixture, but by departing from its original nature—αὐτὸς
ἐξιστάμενος'. He suggests that it will become acid (we might
conjecture that he is thinking of the way in which sweet wine
may turn sour and vinegary, for example), and he goes on:
'thus if a man were able to conduct his inquiries successfully
on things outside the body (εἴ τις δύναιτο 3ητέων ἔξωθεν
ἐπιτυγχάνειν), he would always be able to choose the best
course of treatment' (55 11 ff.). Many Hippocratic treatises,
as we have seen, appeal extensively to analogies with things
outside the body to explain the hidden changes which take
place within the body, the origin and progress of diseases, the
development of the embryo, the processes of nutrition and so
on. In several cases, particularly in the embryological
treatises *On Generation, On the Nature of the Child* and *On Diseases*
IV, this is such a common method of procedure that we may

suspect that the author may have *consciously adopted it as such*, and this seems particularly likely where tests were made on things outside the body in conjunction with attempts to explain obscure physiological or pathological processes. But in *On Ancient Medicine* we can be sure that this was so, for here the writer explicitly recommends this method of procedure in two different contexts, in discovering the functions of the different 'structures' in the body, and in determining the changes which take place in the 'powers of the humours'.

At this stage we may look back briefly and take stock of the evidence we have considered so far concerning the role of comparisons in the theories and explanations of early Greek science. Whether the problem was to account for the movements of the heavenly bodies, or the nature of lightning, or how the earth was 'held up', or why the sea is salt, or again to explain the functioning of the eye, or the nature of the process of respiration, or how the embryo is nourished in the womb and the different parts of the body develop, early Greek philosophers and medical theorists repeatedly based their suggestions on a comparison between the phenomenon to be explained and some other more readily observable object. Many of their theories are based on quite simple comparisons with familiar objects or phenomena, as, for example, the illustration of the flash of an oar in water used, perhaps, by Anaximenes in his account of lightning, or that of the steam from a boiling kettle which appears in *On Breaths* when the writer explains what he thinks happens to a patient suffering from a fever. On the other hand many of the analogies which we find suggested are a good deal more ingenious and elaborate. Several philosophers, beginning with Anaximander, produced mechanical models by means of which they tried to describe not only the movements of the heavenly bodies, but also such other phenomena as the eclipses of the sun and moon and the phases of the latter. Empedocles, especially, suggested two particularly complex analogies in which he drew a comparison not between one *object* and another, so much as between the *relationships* which obtain between several objects inside the body and between several other objects outside the body, between, for instance, on the one hand the fire and water in the eye and its membranes, and on the other the wind, the fire and the screen of a lantern. And in the Hippocratic Corpus, above all, we find many intricate models, the two most remarkable being the system of inter-communicating vessels by which the passage of the humours between different parts of the body is illustrated and explained in *On Diseases* IV, and the test with the bladder which is referred to in *On the Nature of the Child* to suggest how the various parts of the body are formed.

The early Greek scientists are extremely inventive in suggesting analogies between obscure natural phenomena and more familiar objects. And yet many, perhaps most, of the analogies they proposed were, as it turns out, rather misleading. Keynes remarked that 'the common sense of the race has been impressed by very weak analogies',[1] and this might stand as a comment on many of the earliest Greek attempts to give rational accounts of natural phenomena. We remarked before that neither Thales nor Anaximenes seems to have tackled the problem of how, if certain solid objects float on water or are buoyed up on air, either of these suggestions can be true of the earth itself. And similarly in biology the Hippocratic writers often do not appear to have asked themselves how their physical or technological models can apply to changes that take place within the body (as when *On Diseases* IV concludes that stones in the bladder are the end-product of a process similar to smelting, or suggests that a two-way process of absorption and secretion takes place between the stomach and the other 'sources' in the body). And not only do we find many quite weak analogies cited in early Greek science, but their authors often appear to claim too much for them. The discovery of similarities between two phenomena may well serve as the source of a hypothesis concerning the

[1] Keynes, p. 247, cf. above, p. 179.

357

nature or cause of one of them. But as a general rule[1] the early Greek theorists presented their accounts not as tentative hypotheses, but as definitive solutions to their problems. The Hippocratic writers, in particular, often state their conclusions most emphatically, the ὥσπερ or ὡς of the 'as...' clause of the illustration being followed by a strong οὕτω καί or οὕτω δή introducing the 'so...' clause,[2] and the authors of several treatises refer to their comparisons in terms which indicate that they considered them to be conclusive evidence or proof of the theories they advanced. Thus in *On the Nature of the Child*, to mention a single instance, the writer refers to such examples as those of burning wood and burning leaves as the compelling grounds which he has given (ἀνάγκαι προηγμέναι, L vii 488 8 f.) for his conclusion that the seed, too, emits and draws to itself 'breath' in the womb.[3]

Ideally, no doubt, the theories suggested by the recognition of resemblances should be not only presented as hypotheses, but also tested experimentally. We should not, however, overestimate the occasions on which this was practicable for the ancient Greeks. There are, indeed, certain instances when it was open to a theorist to undertake direct investigations on a topic to which his analogies relate, and he apparently failed to do so. Empedocles, for example, did not, it seems, attempt to dissect the eye, and one may wonder how extensive were the anatomical researches of the Hippocratic writer who compared the organs in the body with a system of inter-communicating vessels. But in many or even in most cases, the analogies which we have considered concern problems

---

[1] Herodotus 2 33 (where he uses the word συμβάλλομαι, conjecture, of his inferences concerning the Nile) is, however, an exception to this rule.

[2] E.g. *Flat.* ch. 8, *CMG* i, i 96 8; *Oct.* ch. 12, L vii 458 6; *Mul.* i ch. i, L viii 12 17; *Genit.* ch. 10, L vii 484 11; *Nat. Puer.* ch. 17, 498 24, ch. 21, 512 10; *Morb.* iv ch. 39, 558 2, ch. 49, 580 13, ch. 51, 584 19 and 588 22 f., ch. 52, 590 12.

[3] Cf. *Morb. Sacr.* ch. 13 where observations concerning the supposed effect of the South wind on wine, etc., are said to show that it necessarily (ἀνάγκη) loosens the brain (L vi 386 7), and *Carn.* ch. 9 (L viii 596 9 ff.) where the writer first cites the fact that blood forms a 'skin' when exposed to the air, and then claims that he has proved (*N.B.* ἀποδείκνυμι in 596 16) that the skin of the body is necessarily (ἀναγκαίως) formed in the same way by the action of the cold.

where it was difficult or impossible for the Greeks (at least) to check the theories they proposed by direct experimental methods. This is obviously true of the analogies which they put forward on such 'meteorological' topics as the nature of thunder and lightning, or on the question of why the sea is salt. But it is also true with regard to such problems as the processes of nutrition and growth, the development of the human embryo, the cause of congenital deformities, or the origin of such conditions as stones in the bladder. Rather, on such questions, the appeal to an analogy with more familiar phenomena was itself the mark of an attempt to investigate the problem empirically. And this technique is carried to its furthest point where the illustration cited to suggest or support a theory about how the body functions involves the undertaking of tests on objects outside the body. It is apparent that Greek theorists often neglected certain obvious points of difference between their illustrations and the things they were intended to illustrate. But the complaint that they failed to carry out experiments to verify the theories they proposed is relevant less often to the examples which we have been considering. Indeed, in some cases, so far from this criticism being relevant, it would tend to obscure the important point that the appeal to analogies constituted a most valuable method by which the Greeks were able to bring empirical data to bear on many seemingly intractable problems.

Towards the end of the fifth century several writers (Anaxagoras, Democritus, Herodotus, the authors of *On Ancient Medicine* and *On Breaths*) express certain views on the problems of method in the inquiry into nature, and though their recommendations are imprecise, the context sometimes shows that the method they have in mind is based on the apprehension of analogies. This seems to provide certain confirmatory evidence of the importance of analogy as a method of discovery and explanation at this stage in the development of Greek science, but the question we must now raise is how far the use of analogy in explanations is modified in later periods. The *theories* which Plato and Aristotle express on the subject of the status of analogical argument will be discussed in my next chapter. But what we must consider here is how far in *practice* the way in which they used analogies in their physical and biological doctrines resembles or departs from earlier uses.

PLATO AND ARISTOTLE

Before turning to Aristotle, who will be our chief concern in this section, we should first consider briefly the role of certain types of analogies in the physical and biological theories of the *Timaeus*. Like many earlier writers Plato constructs certain quite complex models in such contexts as his explanations of certain vital functions. One particularly elaborate example is the model of the weel or fish-trap which he uses in his account of respiration (*Ti.* 78b f.). Here he describes a woven object (πλέγμα) like a weel (κύρτος) which has ἐγκύρτια (funnels) at its entrance, and this apparently represents a network composed of air and fire inside the body. Both the model and the theory it illustrates are, at certain points, obscure,[1] but Plato's purpose in referring to the weel is clear: like many of the analogies which we considered from the Hippocratic authors, the weel is a visible model by which Plato attempts to elucidate an obscure physiological process. More striking are the analogies which underlie his theory of the ultimate particles of matter, but here too Plato may be said to be following the precedent set by earlier (even if only slightly earlier) theorists, namely the Atomists. In Plato's theory the ultimate particles of matter are triangles, the two primary sorts of triangles, isosceles and scalene, going to make up the four regular figures pyramid, octahedron, icosahedron and cube (53c ff.). At 55d ff. he assigns these four figures to the

---

[1] Galen, followed, for example, by Archer-Hind, interpreted the ἐγκύρτια as smaller weels or baskets inside the main weel. But Cornford, rightly I think, took ἐγκύρτια to refer to the conical funnels at the entrance of the weel (κατὰ τὴν εἴσοδον, 78b 4 f.), that is to the essential feature which differentiates the weel from other baskets.

four primary bodies, earth, air, fire and water: the cube, for instance, is assigned to earth, since this is the 'most stable' (ἀκινητότατος) of all the primary bodies, and the cube is the figure whose 'bases are most sure' (τὸ τὰς βάσεις ἀσφαλεστάτας ἔχον). Again the pyramid is assigned to fire on the grounds that fire is the 'most mobile' of the primary bodies, and the pyramid is the 'sharpest' and 'keenest', and so most mobile, figure. Then at 61 c ff. he considers the various tactile qualities of things, heat, cold, hardness, softness, roughness, smoothness and so on, and he again associates these with certain shapes. Hard things, for example, he defines (62 b) as those to which the flesh yields, soft, those which yield to the flesh, but he suggests that a thing is yielding when it has a small base, while the figure which has square bases is most resistant. In such examples Plato's ideas concerning the *special* properties of the *invisible* ultimate particles of matter are clearly derived from observation of the properties which may be associated with certain shapes in *recognisable* objects, and we may compare the way in which Democritus based inferences concerning the behaviour of the invisible atoms on observation of that of visible agglomerations (pp. 339 f.).[1]

Plato's contributions to Greek physics and biology are largely confined to a single work, the *Timaeus*. Aristotle's inquiries in natural philosophy probably range over a greater area than those of any other writer in antiquity, certainly than those of any earlier writer. In the *Organon* and *Rhetoric* (as we shall see later) he condemns the use of metaphor in reasoning and compares analogical argument (the 'paradigm') unfavourably with the syllogism. It is all the more surprising, then, that he should use analogies so extensively in many different contexts in his theories and explanations of natural phenomena. To illustrate the types of

---

[1] Theophrastus, *Sens.* 60 f., in fact contrasts the explanations which Democritus and Plato gave of the sensible qualities of things: see Cornford's notes (*6*, pp. 260 f.), where he also refers to an attempt by a seventeenth-century atomist (Lémery) to explain sensible qualities in a similar way, in terms of the shapes of the atoms.

analogies he uses and the way in which he uses them I shall take examples from each of these three main groups of treatises in turn, (1) physical and 'meteorological', (2) biological and (3) psychological (including the *Parva Naturalia*).

(1) In his discussion of celestial and terrestrial phenomena Aristotle often conjectures a fact or a cause (the ὅτι or the διότι) on the basis of analogies where no direct evidence is available, and the first point that should be made is that sometimes the analogy to which he refers is a *strong* one: there is a close resemblance between the cases compared. Thus at *Mete.* 362 b 30 ff., for example, he suggests that the disposition of the winds in the southern hemisphere corresponds to their disposition in the northern hemisphere, and he infers, for example, that the South wind which blows in the northern temperate zone comes from the equatorial regions rather than from the southern tropic (Capricorn) on the grounds that no northerly wind is observed to blow from the northern tropic (Cancer). Elsewhere, however, Aristotle's analogies are less happy. At *Mete.* 349 b 19 ff. he gives an account of the origin of rivers which is partly based on an argument from analogy. Just as cold condenses ἀήρ (air or water vapour) into rain above the earth, so, he suggests, water is produced by a corresponding condensation of ἀήρ by the cold within the earth. We find, too, several remarkable analogies between terrestrial phenomena and what happens in living organisms (analogies which reflect his belief that the earth itself is subject to cycles of growth and decay). Earthquakes, for example, are compared with the tremblings or spasms which affect the human body (*Mete.* 366 b 14 ff.): spasms are caused by 'the enclosed force of the πνεῦμα (breath or wind) in us', while earthquakes occur when 'the πνεῦμα within the earth produces similar effects', and he later appeals to this analogy again when he considers why severe earthquake shocks are intermittent and do not cease abruptly.[1]

---

[1] 'Just as throbbings in the body do not stop immediately or quickly, but gradually as the affection dies away, so clearly the cause which produces the

He uses a similar type of analogy in his long discussion of why the sea is salt (*Mete.* B 3 356b 4 ff.), a passage which is particularly interesting as in it he criticises the images which earlier theorists had used in connection with this problem. His own theory (358a 3 ff.) is that the salt of the sea is due to an admixture of an 'earthy residue', namely the 'dry exhalation'. He observes that the residues of the body, sweat and urine, are salty (a 5 ff.). Moreover, the residue of the process of combustion is ash, and water strained through ashes is said to take on a salty flavour (a 13 ff., 359a 35 ff.). At 358a 16 ff. he says that 'just as in these examples, so too in the world as a whole' everything that grows and comes to be by a natural process always leaves behind it an earthy residue (and it is this that makes the sea salty). In his own view the salt in the sea is the result of a process similar to that which makes sweat, urine and ashes salty, and yet he criticises other theorists who had referred to *these very examples* before him. The nature of his objections should be noted as they throw light on how he thought analogies should or should not be used in accounts of natural phenomena. First (357a 24 ff.) Empedocles' description of the sea as the 'sweat of the earth' is criticised as a metaphor which, while it may be suitable for a poem, does not clarify the problem at all (for it is not clear why sweat is salty either).[1] And then he offers a further criticism of those who had cited the example of things which had been burned. 'And so some say that the sea is made of burnt earth. To speak in this way is absurd (ἄτοπον), but to say that it comes from something like burnt earth (ἐκ τοιαύτης) is true' (358a 14 ff.). In this instance, then, Aristotle's own theory is illustrated by analogies, but it seems that he would have distinguished his own use from that of earlier writers in two

exhalation and the source of the wind do not use up all at once the whole of the material which makes the wind which we call an earthquake. So...shocks will continue, though more gently, until there is too little exhalation to cause any noticeable movement' (368a 6 ff.).

[1] πρὸς ποίησιν μὲν γὰρ οὕτως εἰπὼν ἴσως εἴρηκεν ἱκανῶς (ἡ γὰρ μεταφορὰ ποιητικόν), πρὸς δὲ τὸ γνῶναι τὴν φύσιν οὐχ ἱκανῶς.

respects. First he stresses the difference between identifying two things ('sea' is *made of* 'burnt earth') and merely suggesting a similarity between them (sea is made of *something like* burnt earth). And secondly he would, no doubt, have claimed that his own theory, unlike that of Empedocles, is based on an analysis of the causes at work in each case. Simply to compare the sea and sweat does not help to clarify the problem of why the sea is salt unless we are able to give the causes of each phenomenon (both are due to residues from processes involving heat).

Elsewhere we find other instances where Aristotle either proposes an analogy quite tentatively or qualifies it by drawing attention to the differences between the cases he compares. At *Mete.* 341 b 35 ff., for example, he considers the nature of shooting stars and one suggestion he makes is that the spurt of flame which we see may be like the flame which leaps from a lamp to ignite another lamp placed below it. But he also mentions a second possibility, that the shooting star is in fact (and not merely in appearance) a solid body which is projected downwards by force (e.g. like fruit stones squeezed from between the fingers), and he concludes that both cases probably occur (342 a 8). On other occasions after drawing an analogy Aristotle explicitly qualifies it by pointing out where the things he compares are dissimilar. There is a good example of this at *Cael.* 289 a 19 ff. where he suggests that the light and heat emitted by the heavenly bodies are caused by the friction which their movements set up in the air. He compares the case of projectiles which he believes catch fire in flight, but he goes on to point out that unlike projectiles, the heavenly bodies, being carried round in their spheres, do not themselves catch fire: it is rather, he suggests, the air which lies beneath the sphere of the revolving body which is heated by the motion (although this does not remove all the difficulties which his theory presents).[1] And then we find a further

---

[1] The main problem lies in the fact that the element which comes immediately beneath the heavenly bodies is not air, but fire, although it has been suggested

instance where he qualifies an analogy in a similar way at *Mete.* 344b 1 ff. There he draws a comparison between the tails of comets and the haloes which appear round the sun and moon, but then goes on to say that in the latter case the effect is due to a reflection of light, whereas the comet's tail (he believes) is really coloured.

(2) The similarities and differences between the various species of animals are a constant theme of Aristotle's biological works, and in this context he draws certain important distinctions between different degrees of similarity and difference. At *PA* 645b 26 ff. he makes a threefold classification of common attributes, 'specific', 'generic' and 'analogical', after he has given examples which illustrate the distinctions between them. Feathers, for instance, are common to the genus of birds. One species' feathers differ from another's by 'the more and the less', as he puts it: that is, some are longer, others shorter and so on (644a 16 ff.). The feathers of a bird and the scales of a fish, however, correspond only 'by analogy', as also do blood and 'that which has the same function' (δύναμις) as blood in the bloodless animals (645b 8 ff.). Empedocles had, of course, already suggested that the feathers of a bird and the scales of a fish and hair and leaves are all 'the same' (Fr. 82, see above, p. 335), but now Aristotle analyses the nature of the similarity between them, and distinguishes between the different senses of 'the same' in saying (*a*) that the feathers of a pigeon and those of a sparrow are 'the same', and (*b*) that feathers and scales are 'the same'.[1]

The analogies between the parts of different species of animals are a recurrent topic in the biological treatises, but the subject which I wish to consider here is not Aristotle's search for, and analysis of, the likenesses between different

that it is the fire which is ignited by the movement of the spheres and that this in turn ignites the air (see the notes of Stocks, *1*, and Guthrie, *3*, and Heath, p. 242).

[1] For further examples of things which Aristotle considered analogically the same, see Bonitz, 48a 31 ff.

groups of animals, so much as his use of comparisons between animals and other things. Such comparisons play an important role in, for example, his interpretations of the functions of different parts of the body. Many instances can be cited where his theory of the *function* of a part or organ in the body is influenced by his observation of a similarity of *form* between it and some object outside the body. One striking example is the comparison between the testicles and the stone weights attached to looms which occurs in a number of passages in *GA*. At *GA* 717a 34 ff., for instance, Aristotle argues that the function of the testicles is to keep the seminal passages taut (though in his view they form no integral part of the passages), and that when the testicles are removed, the animal is unable to generate because the seminal ducts are 'drawn up' internally. He returns to the same analogy at *GA* 787b 19 ff., 788a 3 ff., where he discusses the changes which take place in an animal that has been castrated, especially the change in voice (which he says becomes similar to that of females). He explains these changes by referring again to the idea that the removal of the testicles is like the removal of weights from a string of a musical instrument or from the warp of a loom: the effect is to 'slacken' the seminal passages which he believes to be attached to the blood-vessel 'which originates in the heart near the part which sets the voice in motion'.[1] Elsewhere the analogies which he uses in describing the blood-vessels, for example, not only suggest the craftsman-like activities of Nature, but also convey an idea of their function in the body. We have already noted (p. 286) that, following the use of a similar image in Plato, he compares the network of blood-vessels in the body first with wickerwork (to suggest that they serve to bind the front and the back of the body together, *PA* 668b 24 ff.), and then with the frameworks used by modellers (when he suggests that the blood-vessels provide

---

[1] Platt (note to *GA* 787b 28) says that 'this amazing theory assumes *inter alia* that the removal of the weight will make the note of the string higher! Possibly A. confused the tension of a string with the length.'

a similar framework round which the other parts of the body grow, e.g. *GA* 743 a 1 ff.). And then we also find the lower viscera compared with anchors and studs when he suggests that they too serve to fasten the main blood-vessels to the sides of the body (*PA* 670a 10 ff.). It is, of course, rarely possible to derive any accurate idea of the function of the vital organs of the body from a consideration of their superficial characteristics, and the similarities which Aristotle noted in this context are mostly rather misleading.[1] Yet there is more often some correspondence between the function and the superficial aspect of the external parts of the body, and here some of the images which Aristotle uses are more relevant and illuminating, as when he compares the disposition of the thumb and fingers in the hand with a clamp (*PA* 687 b 15 ff.) or suggests that in winged animals the tail acts as a rudder (*IA* 710a 1 ff.).

Another context in which Aristotle draws some remarkable comparisons is his accounts of various vital processes. The formation of different parts of the body, for example, is often apprehended by means of an analogy. At *PA* 647b 2 ff. he compares the formation of the viscera in sanguineous animals with the formation of deposits of mud in streams. All the viscera except the heart are, he believes, deposits formed by the blood-stream. At *PA* 672a 5 ff. there is an obscure analogy between the natural formation of fat round the kidneys and the residues left after solid substances are burned. He suggests that just as when solids are burned some heat gets left behind in the ash, so when liquids are 'concocted' heat is left behind, and in the case of blood this goes to form fat (which he considers the result of the complete concoction of blood). Then at *GA* 743b 5 ff. he compares the formation of the skin with that of scum on certain liquids when they are

---

[1] Cf., however, his comparison between the blood-vessels and unbaked earthenware, when he makes the acute suggestion that the blood-vessels allow the nourishment, τροφή, to percolate through them to the different parts of the body (*GA* 743 a 8 ff.: a similar comparison is used of the stomach in *Hum.*, ch. 11, L v 492 4 ff.).

boiled, suggesting that the skin is formed as the flesh 'dries up'. In both instances the effect, he says, is the result of the non-evaporation of 'the glutinous part' (τὸ γλίσχρον). And at GA 755 a 17 ff. he compares the growth of fishes' eggs with the swelling of yeast, and again he states the causes at work: in animals it is the 'soul-heat' which brings about the growth, while in the case of yeast it is the heat of the χυμός (humour, juice) mingled with it.

In several of these examples Aristotle draws a comparison between the action of the 'vital heat' in the organic body, and the action of heat elsewhere, outside the body, and this is an analogy to which he refers repeatedly in his account of generation in GA. At 743 a 26 ff., for instance, he says that the embryo may become deformed through an excess or deficiency of heat (the heat residing in the semen), and he compares the way in which in cooking too much or too little heat spoils the food. At 767 a 17 ff. he uses the same illustration from cooking when he suggests that the reason why certain couples are unable to produce children may be that the heat of the male is not 'proportional' to the female: too much fire burns the meat, while too little does not cook it. At 772 a 10 ff. when he explains why a greater quantity of semen does not produce a bigger embryo, but on the contrary 'dries it up and destroys it' (as he believed), he refers to what happens when you boil water: heating water beyond a certain point does not raise its temperature, but merely evaporates it. And the cooking illustration appears yet again at 775 b 37 ff. when he explains the formation of certain abnormal growths in the womb and suggests that the same thing happens to the embryo in the womb as to meat which is undercooked: the abnormality is due not to the heat, but rather to the weakness of the heat. The parallelism between the action of vital heat and that of physical heat applied to objects outside the body is clearly of great importance in Aristotle's theory of generation. We should, however, observe that in one passage, at least, he draws attention to a point where the two cases differ. At

743 a 32 ff. he notes that in cooking it is *we* who apply the heat in the right measure to get the right results, while in nature it is the male parent that does so, or, in the case of animals spontaneously generated, 'the movement and heat imparted by the climate'.

Yet another striking analogy which recurs in Aristotle's account of generation is that between the action of semen and that of fig-juice (ὀπός) or rennet (πυτία, πυετία) in curdling milk, and this too provides important evidence concerning the way in which he employs analogies. This analogy is first introduced at *GA* 729 a 9 ff. There he suggests that as, in the curdling of milk, the milk is the material, and the fig-juice or rennet provides the principle which causes it to curdle, so in generation the female provides the material (the menses), while the male provides the form and the efficient cause. Then at 737 a 12 ff. he refers to the same illustration when he explains why (as he believes) the material part of the semen cannot be detected either leaving the female, or as a part of the embryo: no more, he suggests, would you expect to be able to trace the fig-juice once it has curdled the milk. The curdling of milk is, of course, a particularly striking case where two substances come together and produce a quite new substance. But as *GA* 739 b 20 ff. shows, Aristotle clearly believed that it provides a close analogy to the process of generation. That 'vital heat' is, as it were, the active constituent of semen is suggested in a number of passages (e.g. *GA* 736 b 33 ff.). But rennet, as he says at 739 b 22 f., is 'milk that has vital heat' (γάλα... θερμότητα ζωτικὴν ἔχον).[1] Moreover, he affirms that 'the nature of milk and of menses is the same'.[2] The similarity between the curdling of milk by

---

[1] Rennet alone is considered in this passage, but it seems likely that Aristotle believed that fig-juice, too, is 'hot'. At *Mete.* Δ 389 b 9 ff., at least, it is mentioned, along with blood, semen and marrow, as a substance which is naturally hot.

[2] Both milk and menses are, for Aristotle, 'residues of useful nourishment'. Semen is described at *GA* 726 b 9 ff. as the residue of the nourishment which has been formed into blood, and this description also applies to menses, which are analogous, in females, to the semen in males (727 a 3 f.), though in females the

rennet and the 'setting' of menses by semen is, Aristotle would have said, not merely a superficial and fortuitous one, since the substances in each case have similar essential natures. Nevertheless, he goes on to note, in a later passage, where these two processes differ. At 771b 18 ff. he mentions the analogy between the action of semen and that of fig-juice again when he tackles the problem of why some species of animals produce many offspring at a single birth. He asks why the semen of some animals should produce several embryos, where in the analogous case of fig-juice the curds are never so differentiated. This depends, he suggests, on the limiting size of the embryo of each species, and he notes that in this respect the two processes are dissimilar, for while that which is produced in the process of curdling varies in quantity alone, that which is formed by the semen varies not only quantitatively, but also qualitatively.[1]

Some of the many other remarkable comparisons which figure in Aristotle's biological theories may be mentioned more briefly. Like many of the Hippocratic writers he suggests many analogies between animals and plants, and while some of these are quite vague and general,[2] several of them mark an advance on earlier beliefs.[3] And among other notable comparisons which he draws are those between redundant embryonic growths and eddies in a river (*GA* 772b

residue is greater in quantity and less concocted (726b 30 ff.). The nature of milk is described in *GA* Δ 8, and it too is said to be 'concocted blood' (777a 7 f.). Thus Aristotle explains why women do not menstruate during the period when they suckle their babies on the grounds that milk and menses have the same essential nature (777a 12 ff.).

[1] *GA* 772a 22 ff. Peck suspects that this passage is a parenthesis which has come from a marginal annotation, but its contents seem to represent the view that Aristotle probably held.

[2] He several times states that the stomach fulfils the same role for animals as the earth does for plants, and that the blood-vessels in animals correspond to the roots of plants (e.g. *PA* 650a 20 ff., and 678a 6 ff. where he refers to this analogy when he suggests why animals need blood-vessels).

[3] Thus he draws a comparison between the umbilical cord and the root of a plant (e.g. *GA* 740a 24 ff., b 8 ff.), although he goes on to suggest that one of the first things that happens in the development of the embryo is that it 'sends off' the umbilical cord like a root to the womb (745b 22 ff.).

18 ff.),[1] between catarrhs in the head and rain (*PA* 652b
33 ff.), between eggs going rotten and wine turning sour (*GA*
753a 23 ff.), between the grey hairs of old age and mould or
hoar-frost (*GA* 784b 8 ff.), and between the movements of
animals and those of automatic puppets or toy chariots (*MA*
701b 1 ff., cf. *GA* 734b 9 f., 741b 7 ff.). The way in which
these analogies are used conforms to Aristotle's general
practice elsewhere. Even when the analogy seems to have
been suggested by observation of a superficial similarity
between two effects, Aristotle gives an account of the causes
at work in each case, and shows, or at least asserts, that these
are the same or similar in both the instances which he compares. Thus the reason why eggs go rotten and why wine
becomes sour is, in both cases, that what he calls 'the
earthy part' (τὸ γεῶδες: the yolk of the egg, the sediment of
the wine) is heated and stirred up. Again catarrhs are formed,
in his view, from the 'residue' of nourishment which is
exhaled upwards through the veins and which condenses to
form phlegm and serum in the brain when the brain is
abnormally cold (just as rain is formed when the vapour
exhaled from the earth is condensed by the cold in the upper
air). As for the comparison between greyness, mould and
hoar-frost, he puts it that hoar-frost is generically the same as
greyness (for both are vapour, ἀτμίς), and mould is specifically
the same as it (for both are not only vapour, but vapour that
has 'putrefied', *GA* 784b 21 ff.). When he sets up such a
schema, he evidently acknowledges that the things he compares differ in certain respects, and this is a feature of many of
his analogies. When at *GA* 783b 8 ff. he compares the bald-
ness of humans and other animals with the shedding of leaves
in plants, he first asserts that the cause of both conditions is the
deficiency of 'hot moisture', but then goes on to note that

---

[1] The abnormal reduplication of parts in an embryo is compared with the
splitting in two of an eddy when obstructed. Platt notes that J. A. Thomson,
p. 270, used a similar metaphor: 'those particularly constant forms of whirlpool
which we call the germ-cells, which repeat themselves and propagate themselves'.

while plants lose their leaves, and some hibernating animals their hair, according to the seasons of the year, men become bald according to the 'seasons of life' (i.e. in old age, the 'winter' of life). Again we find that the models of the automatic puppets and the toy chariot which he uses to illustrate the movements of animals are qualified in an important respect. Both models illustrate how a series of complex movements may be initiated by a single simple motion, but Aristotle points out that in neither does any alteration (ἀλλοίωσις) take place, as there does in a living organism where the parts may change their size and form, expanding through heat or contracting through cold (*MA* 701 b 10 ff.).

(3) Finally, we should consider the 'psychological' treatises, the *de Anima* and the *Parva Naturalia*, for these provide some particularly good examples which illustrate how analogies served Aristotle as the source of provisional or tentative suggestions in his discussions of obscure phenomena. These treatises deal not only with strictly psychological, but also with physiological, questions, and they contain several analogies which can be paralleled in the biological works.[1] One such analogy which plays a particularly important part in the discussion of the causes of life and death in the *de Juventute* and the *de Respiratione* is that between the role of heat within the body and outside it.[2] Aristotle is led by this analogy to distinguish two possible causes of death.[3] As a fire may be put out either by being quenched by its opposite (σβέσις) or by being exhausted by an excess of heat (μάρανσις: this takes place when the fire is deprived of air), so living things, he suggests, may die either because the cold extin-

---

[1] The frequent comparisons between animals and plants are a feature of the 'psychological', as of the purely biological, treatises (e.g. *de An.* 412 b 1 ff.; *Long.* 467 a 18 ff.; *Juv.* 468 a 4 ff.).

[2] Cf. also *Sens.* 442 a 6 ff.; *Long.* 465 b 23 ff., 466 b 30 ff. It is worth noting that at *Resp.* 479 b 26 ff. the beating of the heart is compared with an abscess (though the two phenomena are said to differ in that the latter is accompanied by pain) and this in turn is compared with boiling (though again a difference is noted: the liquid thickens in an abscess if there is no evaporation).

[3] *Juv.* 469 b 21 ff.; *Resp.* 474 b 13 ff., 479 a 7 ff.

guishes the vital heat (e.g. in old age) or because of an excess of heat (e.g. in suffocation). It is interesting that while Aristotle appreciates that air is necessary both for combustion and, in many species of animals, for life, he believes that the effect of air, in each case, is one of *cooling*: he holds that in those animals which do not respire (which include fish, in his view) the necessary 'refrigeration' of the 'vital heat' is effected by the medium in which they live, by water, in the case of fish, or by air, in the case of insects.[1]

His discussion of another physiological problem, the causes of sleep, provides a good example where Aristotle appeals to a series of different analogies in considering alternative solutions to his problem. At *Somn. Vig.* 457b 6 ff. he raises the difficulty of how sleep, which he takes to be a cooling, can be brought about by things which are themselves hot (e.g. certain foods and drinks). The first suggestion he makes is that the brain may be cooled by the *movements* set up by the evaporation which arises from the stomach. Alternatively he suggests an analogy with the *shiver* of cold felt by those who have hot water poured over them (here too the effect of something hot is counteracted). Or again the case may, he says, be like what happens to a *fire* which is cooled (temporarily) when fresh fuel is put on it. He goes on to say (b 26 ff.) that while these solutions may be possible, the chief explanation lies in the nature of the brain itself, which is the coldest part of the body: it is this which effects the refrigeration which causes sleep, even though the evaporation which rises from the lower regions of the body is extremely hot. And here he appeals to an illustration which we also find used, in a different context, at *PA* 652b 33 ff., that of the formation of *rain* from the vapour which is raised from the earth by the heat of the sun and is then condensed by the cold upper air. This illustration he now adapts to serve as a model not only

---

[1] E.g. *Resp.* 474b 25 ff., 478a 28 ff. Two pieces of evidence which Aristotle cites for his conception of respiration as a process of refrigeration are (1) that we breathe more quickly when the weather is hot, and (2) that the breath we exhale is warm, *Resp.* 472a 31 ff., b 33 ff.

for the formation of catarrhs in the head (which he here suggests are produced by the 'residual' evaporation), but also for
the formation of the substance which, descending on the
heart, brings about sleep (this is produced by the condensation of the 'wholesome' part of the evaporation).

A complex series of images appears in his account of
memory and dreams. At *Mem.* 450a 27 ff. he picks up (without explicit acknowledgement) the suggestion which had
already been made in Plato's *Theaetetus* (191c ff.) that the act
of perception involves the stamping of an impression, as it
were, upon the percipient organ (cf. also *de An.* 424a 17 ff.),
and he goes on to explain why some people have bad
memories by suggesting different ways in which the texture
of the percipient organ may be defective. Thus he says that
those who are emotionally disturbed, the very young and the
very old are all in a state of flux: in them the part that
receives the impression is like running water (*Mem.* 450b 2 f.),
in others the receiving surface is worn away, like the walls of
dilapidated houses (b 4), and in yet others it is either too hard
to receive the impression, or too soft to retain it (b 9 ff.).
A similar theory of sensation is presupposed in his discussion
of the nature of dreams (*Insomn.* 459a 23 ff.), but here he
introduces a number of new conceptions which modify the
model of the stamping of an impression on a wax tablet. His
theory here depends on the idea that the movement or
affection occasioned by the objects we perceive continues in
our sense-organs even when the external objects of perception are no longer present. He draws a comparison with
projectiles (a 29 ff.) to illustrate how a movement may continue even when the thing that is moved is no longer in con-
tact with what moved it, and he says that the same thing
happens in the case of qualitative changes too: an object
which has been heated, heats the next thing in turn and so
on. And he cites evidence to show that something similar
happens in perception. If, for example, we look at the sun or
some other bright object and then shut our eyes, we imagine

that we see it still (b 13 ff.), and similarly after hearing loud noises we are, for a time, quite deaf (b 20 f.). Even when the external object is no longer there, then, the sensations it has caused may persist and be themselves the objects of perception (460 a 32 ff.). He suggests that this happens both by day and by night (b 28 ff.), but that in daytime, when the senses and mind are active, the movements so caused are blotted out (just as a large fire blots out a smaller one, or as great pains or pleasures blot out small ones, 461 a 1 ff.). At night, however, these movements cause what we call dreams, and here he suggests a further image to account for the differences which we experience in the clarity of our dreams. He compares the movements which cause our dreams with the eddies formed in rivers (a 8 ff.): often they persist in their original shape, but often, when obstructed, they are broken up and change their form. And he adapts this image to suggest why dreams do not occur after meals or to the very young (as he believes to be the case), for here, he says, the movement is too great, and he compares what happens when water is stirred violently— either no reflection at all occurs, or one that is highly distorted (a 14 ff.). In his account of these complex psychological phenomena, sensation, memory and dreams, Aristotle uses a series of physical images, each of which illustrates some aspect of his theory: the image of the stamping of an impression on something like a wax tablet serves to suggest that the faculty of memory depends on the quality of the percipient organ; the reference to projectiles and the transmission of heat suggests how the impressions we receive may persist even when what originally caused them is no longer present; and the image of the eddies that occur in rivers suggests first how these impressions may become disrupted by objects that obstruct them, and secondly how they may become confused when the movements causing them are too violent.

We have seen how Aristotle builds up an account of memory and dreams with the help of a number of images which are complementary to one another. But another passage in the psychological treatises where the models he suggests are not complementary, but alternative, to one another, occurs in his discussion of colour.[1] At *Sens.* 439 b 18 ff. he asks how other colours can come to be from white and black, and he considers three possible answers. The first suggestion he discusses is that white and black are juxtaposed (παρ' ἄλληλα τιθέμενα) in such small particles that neither of them is apparent. Alternatively (440 a 7 ff.) white and black may be superposed on one another (τὸ φαίνεσθαι δι' ἀλλήλων) and he cites two concrete examples which illustrate how superposition might bring about different colours: he refers to the effects produced by painters when they apply one colour over another, and to the way in which the sun, which is 'white', takes on a reddish colour when seen through mist or smoke. And then he makes a third suggestion (a 31 ff.), that the other colours are the result of a 'complete mixture' of white and black, and here he distinguishes between the juxtaposition of minimal parts (e.g. seeds) in what we should term a mechanical mixture, and the 'complete mixture' of things (τῷ πάντη μεμῖχθαι, b 11), a conception which he illustrates elsewhere by such examples as the blending of wine and water, or the combination of tin and copper to form bronze.[2] It is true that his discussion of the problem of intermediate colours starts from the incorrect assumption that they are produced by white and black being conjoined in some way. But the feature of his treatment to which I should call attention is that the three models which he puts forward are in the nature of preliminary hypotheses, which he sets out and then examines before choosing between them. The relationship is *either* one of juxtaposition, like the mixture of different sorts of grains, *or* one of superposition, like paints overlaid on one another, *or* one of total interpenetration, as of two liquids, and having

---

[1] Cf. also the discussion of flavours in *Sens.* 441 a 3 ff., which takes a similar form.

[2] *GC* A 10, 327 a 30 ff., especially 328 a 5 ff. (This seems to be the discussion which he has in mind when he refers at *Sens.* 440 b 3 f. and 13 to 'what has been said in the works on mixture'.)

rejected the first two suggestions as inadequate to account for all the phenomena, he adopts the third hypothesis. Finally, it is worth noting that an element in each of the theories he suggests is that every colour is thought to consist of a different *proportion* of white and black. Here, indeed, he borrows an idea from music and suggests that like the concords, the agreeable colours, such as violet and crimson, are those in which white and black are joined in a simple numerical ratio (as 3:2 or 3:4), while in other colours the ratio between them is not determinate.[1]

The examples which we have considered from the physical, biological and psychological treatises will, I hope, have shown how extensively, in each of these three main divisions of his natural philosophy, Aristotle uses comparisons to elucidate obscure phenomena, whether to infer facts or to suggest or support explanations of causes. Moreover, many of the analogies he put forward are as bold as any which we find in the Presocratic philosophers or in the Hippocratic Corpus, as for example when he compares earthquakes with the shaking which affects the body in spasms, or the action of semen with that of fig-juice or rennet curdling milk, or the role of vital heat in generation with that of physical heat in cooking, or the formation of skin with that of scum on certain liquids as they boil. But if in general Aristotle's use of 'phenomena', that is what can readily be observed, as a 'vision' of the obscure or the unknown is very similar to that of many earlier writers, it may be suggested that at certain points his practice differs from their general usage. (1) There are a number of occasions when he qualifies an analogy either by drawing attention to the differences between the

---

[1] *Sens.* 439 b 25 ff., cf. 440 a 13 ff., b 18 ff. Aristotle's recognition of analogies between the five senses is a constant theme in *de An.* and *Sens.* Thus he suggests that touch and taste, like sight, hearing and smell, are mediated, and that flesh is, then, the medium, not the organ, of touch (*de An.* 419 a 30 ff. and B 11, 422 b 17 ff.). Yet of course he also recognises, and draws attention to, differences between the senses: thus at *de An.* 422 a 10 ff. he says that the object of taste, exceptionally, must be in suspension in a fluid, and it is notable that he insists (wrongly) that while sounds and smells travel, light does not (*de An.* 418 b 20 ff.; *Sens.* 446 a 20 ff.).

cases he compares, or by suggesting that they are similar rather than identical (as he does, for example, in citing the case of burnt earth in his account of the saltiness of the sea in *Mete.* B 3), and this happens a good deal more rarely in the extant texts of earlier writers. Again (2) Aristotle quite often suggests an analogy tentatively, as one of a number of possible accounts which might be given of the phenomena (as happens in his discussion of shooting stars, for instance), and this too contrasts with the dogmatic way in which analogies were almost always presented not only in the fragments of the Presocratic philosophers, but also in the Hippocratic treatises. (3) But what is probably most important from the point of view of Aristotle's *theory* of analogical argument, is that he often follows the proposal of an analogy with an attempted analysis of the causes at work in the cases he compares. While he often criticises the analogies to which earlier theorists had referred, he would probably have justified his own on the grounds that he did not merely draw attention to a similarity between two effects, but went on to show that the cases he compared are indeed instances of the same general laws. Thus both earthquakes and spasms are, he believes, effects produced by air in confined spaces; the 'setting' of the menses and the curdling of milk are parallel because the substances in each case have the same essential natures; the formation of skin is in fact like that of scum as both are due to the non-evaporation of a 'glutinous' substance; grey hair and mould are specifically the same because both are vapour that has undergone putrefaction, and so on. On such occasions *Aristotle's* formal defence of his analogy might be that the particular cases compared have been shown to be instances of the same general laws. Yet *we* might still object that often the causes to which he refers are extremely vague, and that so far from showing that they apply in each case, as a general rule he merely asserts that this is so.

On many occasions Aristotle follows up the proposal of an analogy by stating the causes which he believes to be responsible for the phenomena he compares, and yet this did not, of course, prevent him from being misled by many quite superficial similarities. Once again, however, we should assess his analogies not only according to their strength or weakness as they appear to us, but also, and more particularly, in relation to the type of problem which he was attempting to resolve. As in the Presocratics and Hippocratic authors, so too in Aristotle analogies are used especially often in connection with phenomena whose nature and causes could not be investigated directly. This is obviously the case with such 'meteorological' phenomena as earthquakes or shooting stars or comets. But Aristotle also proposed models in trying to elucidate the physical changes that accompany such psychological phenomena as memory and dreams, for example. Again in biology, even though thanks to an extensive use of anatomical dissections he was able to investigate many problems which had hitherto been matters of pure speculation, there were still many questions which could not be resolved by such simple methods. Thus observations such as Aristotle was able to carry out could not have revealed to him the nature of the vital processes involved in the generation of animals, the fertilisation of the ovum, and so on.[1] In such contexts, the appeal to analogies provided an important means of investigating what must have appeared to be quite intractable problems empirically. *Within* a particular field (such as embryology or psychology or physics) he proposed many suggestive analogies between, for example, the early development of the embryos of different species of animals, between the different senses, and between the phenomena in the upper regions of the sky and those that could be observed on earth. And *between* disciplines some of the bolder analogies he put forward involve a remarkable attempt to *simplify* a complex problem, as when he tried to elucidate psychological

---

[1] It should be noted that like the author of *On the Nature of the Child* (ch. 29) Aristotle undertook quite detailed and quite successful investigations of the growth of the embryo chick by examining eggs at different stages in their development (*HA* Z 3, 561 a 4 ff.; *GA* Γ 2, 752 a 10 ff.).

phenomena by means of physical models (comparing the κινήσεις in the mind with the eddies in rivers, for instance), or when he suggested comparisons between physiological processes and physical changes (e.g. between generation and boiling).

CONCLUSIONS

In the Homeric poems, when a person is confronted with something new or strange or difficult to comprehend, he often likens it to some familiar object. The material we have considered in this chapter shows how far the early Greek natural philosophers expanded and developed this essentially common-sense use of comparisons. The comparisons they draw are generally used to convey an idea not of a unique event or a single instance of a phenomenon, but of the nature of a particular phenomenon itself. And the examples we have discussed include not only simple comparisons in which the phenomenon to be explained is likened to, or identified with, some other object, but also several instances where different images are combined in a complex, artificial model, and others in which the illustration involves the undertaking of a practical test or a piece of research. Here the use of analogy still falls short of experimentation in the strict sense in that the substances which are the subject of the test are often quite different from those to which the theory relates, but it is clear that such analogies offered an alternative method of bringing empirical data to bear on certain problems, and indeed on many problems, for example in biology, it is fair to say that this was the only method open to the Greeks (just as, in certain cases, even today scientists are unable to reproduce exactly, or even very closely, in a laboratory, the circumstances or conditions of the changes which they wish to investigate).

Many of the theories which the Greek scientists proposed on the basis of the similarities which they apprehended between different phenomena are inexact. But even though a large proportion of their analogies might seem, to a later age, rather far-fetched, we should bear in mind that many of them are based on what must have seemed *at the time* quite reasonable presuppositions. In some cases, indeed, the conjectures that were made in antiquity have been vindicated in the light of subsequent advances in knowledge. Anaxagoras, for example, was not far from the truth, when he suggested that the moon has ravines and plains like the earth, and in his discussion of the disposition of the winds Aristotle reached certain quite correct conclusions on the assumption that the winds in the southern hemisphere correspond to those in the northern. Analogies between different types of animals, and between animals and plants, were especially fruitful. In tackling the problem of the development of the human embryo it was natural to consider not only the direct evidence which could be derived from aborted foetuses, but also the development of other species of animals, and for this purpose intensive investigations of the development of the hen's egg were already carried out in antiquity. Plants, too, served the early Greek scientists as useful examples where the conditions accompanying growth and nutrition could be studied, and here too it is not implausible to argue by analogy from plants to other living beings. No doubt it seems much more rash, to our way of thinking, to propose analogies between sterility and the formation of an alloy from two metals (as Empedocles did), or between sweating and the boiling of a kettle (*On Breaths*), or between the action of semen and the curdling of milk (Aristotle). Yet each of these analogies, too, represents an attempt to throw light on what must have seemed quite elusive problems. In dealing with physiological changes the true causes of which were far beyond their comprehension, the Greeks tried to relate them to more or less similar effects which they observed elsewhere, and many of their analogies are surprisingly ingenious, even if in the light of later knowledge they have proved inexact. And it should be noted that the Greeks sometimes came much closer to a true conception of a phenomenon when they cited a concrete analogy than when they formulated a more abstract account. A case in point is the analogy which Aristotle observed between respiration and combustion, although he thought that the effect of air in each case is one of cooling. And while the notions of chemical combination and mechanical mixture were not clearly defined until the seventeenth century, such concrete models as the production of bronze from copper and tin and the juxtaposition of seeds of different sorts already enabled the Greeks to draw certain important, if rough-and-ready, distinctions between different modes of 'coming-together'.

Analogies were a most fruitful source of hypotheses in early Greek science. Yet we found that they were generally treated as not so much a source of preliminary hypotheses, as the basis and justification of definitive accounts. Many Greek investigators may be said to have been rather uncritical in their use of analogies, whether because they claimed too much for them, or because they ignored too readily the negative analogy between the things they compared (although these failings are, of course, by no means confined to early Greek science), and some writers confidently recommended the search for likenesses as a method of tackling various obscure topics without remarking (and without perhaps consciously recognising) that similarities are often deceptive. A more cautious attitude towards the use of analogies in this context is, however, found in Aristotle. Certainly he frequently criticised those which his predecessors had suggested, and he often proposed his own analogies quite tentatively or qualified them by pointing out certain differences between the things he compared. Yet his formal justification of many of his analogies would, it seems, have been that he had shown that the causes at work are the same or similar in each of the cases he compared, and here we should say that his actual analysis of causes is as a general rule quite vague, so that in practice the differences between his own use of analogies and that of earlier writers, while important enough, are less than he appears to claim. The major role of analogy continued to be to provide a source of possible explanations in a wide variety of fields of inquiry, but one of the questions that remain to be considered in my next chapter is how far Aristotle, or any other early Greek writer, progressed towards an understanding of the methodological issues involved in this heuristic function of analogy.

CHAPTER VI

THE ANALYSIS OF ARGUMENT
FROM ANALOGY

SOME PRE-PLATONIC TEXTS

We have discussed in turn the use of images and comparisons in the general cosmological doctrines, and in the accounts which were put forward concerning particular natural phenomena, in Greek thought down to Aristotle, and in both contexts we have considered how the theory and practice of the use of images and comparisons develops in the fifth and fourth centuries. It now remains to examine the use of explicit analogical argument and the steps by which the logical status of such arguments was revealed and analysed.

To infer that something that is true of a particular case is true also of a similar case is certainly one of the main forms of reasoning from experience, indeed Mill would have said the type of all such reasoning. Just as there are many early Greek texts in which this mode of reasoning is implicit, so too there are many explicit arguments which have this general form which occur in Greek literature from the earliest period. First of all, then, we should consider briefly how these arguments are used in pre-philosophical literature, the fields in which they are applied, and the purposes which the arguments serve. Granted that forms of argument as such were not differentiated in the pre-philosophical period, we may nevertheless consider how individual arguments from analogy were used and what assumptions appear to have been made concerning their cogency.

In our earliest texts the use of analogical argument is, as we might expect, largely confined to occasions when questions of human conduct and morality are at issue. Thus in Homer a person often decides on a course of action (for instance) by

384

referring either to his own past experiences or to the experiences described in legends and myths. At *Iliad* 14 233 ff., for example, when Hera asks Sleep for his assistance in the Deception of Zeus, Sleep replies that he would willingly put any other god to sleep, but not Zeus. He speaks of the last occasion when he put Zeus to sleep at Hera's request (when Hera sent a storm to drive Heracles off course on his return from the sack of Troy). Zeus was furious when he awoke, and Sleep would have been hurled into the sea, had not Night come to his rescue. 'Now again', Sleep concludes (262), 'you are asking me to perform an impossible task.' Sleep naturally argues that he will suffer the same unpleasant consequences if he sends Zeus to sleep again. But what is interesting about this example is that Sleep's argument is forthwith challenged by Hera. Hera protests (264 ff.) that the present case is quite different: Zeus will not be so ready to protect the Trojans (against whom Hera's present move is aimed) as he had been to help his own son Heracles. In this instance, Hera adopts the most obvious and effective method of countering an argument from analogy, that is to assert that the analogy does not hold and that there is a significant difference between the two cases which have been compared.

In the text just quoted the person who cites the analogy draws an inference concerning what his own course of action should be. But analogies are also used, of course, to persuade another person to adopt or reject a course of action. A counsel of caution often takes this form, as we see from *Iliad* 1 586 ff., for example, where Hephaestus, advising Hera not to cross the will of Zeus, tells her how he himself was once thrown out of heaven for venturing to oppose him. Or the analogy may be used to induce acceptance of a positive course of action as at *Iliad* 24 599 ff., where Achilles tries to persuade Priam to take food with him by referring to the story of Niobe who ate even when she had lost all her twelve children. Further examples of analogies used for the purpose of persuasion occur in the Embassy to Achilles in *Iliad*, Book 9.

Odysseus, Phoenix and Ajax try various appeals, playing on Achilles' pity, his sense of duty, his desire for glory, and especially his self-interest. But analogies are also cited in an attempt to win him round. At 496 ff. Phoenix uses an argument *a fortiori*:[1] even the gods may be persuaded by sacrifices and prayers, and their excellence and honour and strength are even greater than those of Achilles (who should, then, be more amenable to persuasion than they). Then at 524 ff. he goes on: 'So we have always heard the stories of past heroes, when violent anger came on any one of them, they were to be won round with gifts and persuasion.' Having referred in this way quite generally to the precedents set by heroes in the past, Phoenix cites a specific instance. This is the story of Meleager (527–599) who refused to fight for the Aetolians even when they and his own father begged him to do so with gifts: it was not until their enemies had already breached the town that he changed his mind, and then, since it was his wife who finally persuaded him, he received none of the gifts which the Aetolians had originally offered. The whole story is told at length partly, no doubt, for its own sake, but it is, of course, an elaborate analogical argument designed to persuade Achilles to fight again, and it suggests this additional moral, that he would be wise to accept the conciliatory gifts which he is offered while he still has the chance. We should note, however, that in this example (as in many others) the argument from analogy may seem plausible to the speaker, but it proves quite ineffective: Achilles is completely unmoved by this or any other appeal.

In Homer, analogical arguments are mainly drawn either

---

[1] Arguments *a fortiori* might be described as those in which it is inferred that a proposition which is true in one case is true also in another case which is similar to the first in some respects, unlike it in others, some of the differences between the two cases being such that the probability of the conclusion is strengthened rather than weakened. Another example occurs in the speech of Ajax (*Il.* 9 632 ff.) where he points out that even when a murder has been committed, the injured party accepts compensation (the insult which Achilles has suffered is far less grave: all the more reason, then, for him to accept the compensation which is offered).

from first-hand experience (as in *Iliad* 14 243 ff., 1 586 ff.) or from the store of precedents contained in legends, fables and myths (e.g. *Iliad* 9 527 ff., 24 599 ff.), and the contexts in which such arguments are usually adduced are when a person either decides on a course of action for himself, or attempts to influence someone else in his decision. In both contexts this type of argument is very frequent, but it is of course recognised that, used as a means of persuasion, analogical arguments are often unsuccessful in their purpose (in convincing an Achilles, for example). Furthermore, we find passages where a person is represented as responding to such an argument not merely by rejecting or ignoring the conclusion, but by criticising the analogy, as in our first example, *Iliad* 14 264 ff., where Hera protests that the two cases which Sleep has compared are quite different from one another.

It we turn now to texts of a somewhat later period, the main context in which explicit analogical arguments are adduced continues to be the discussion of questions of conduct and morality, where, indeed, they are used extensively both in such poets as Pindar and the tragedians, and in fifth-century prose writers such as Herodotus. At Herodotus 7 10, for example, there is a typical instance of an argument from past experience when Artabanus is represented as trying to dissuade Xerxes from bridging the Hellespont and invading Greece by means of an argument in which he refers to the dangers which attended Darius' expedition against the Scythians, when Darius had bridged the Danube and left behind him a precarious line of communication. Legends and myths, too, continue to be a frequent source of analogical arguments,[1] but analogies drawn from other fields as well begin to be more prominent. Already in Homer (*Iliad* 23 313 ff.) there is a passage in which Nestor refers to the role of

---

[1] We may note, however, that the Greeks were quick to recognise that their myths provided contradictory precedents for behaviour. In Aeschylus, *Eu.* 640 ff., for example, the Eumenides counter Apollo's claim that Zeus is the upholder of parental rights by pointing out that Zeus himself put his own father in chains.

skill (μῆτις) in wood-cutting and in piloting a ship to bring home to Antilochus the importance of skill, as opposed to brute force, in chariot-racing. But in later writers analogies drawn from various arts or crafts are used increasingly frequently to support moral theses or lessons applied to human conduct. Navigation is referred to especially often in this connection. Thus in Sophocles, *Ant.* 715 ff., for example,[1] when Haemon tries to persuade Creon to relent and spare Antigone, he refers to the way in which sailors must slacken sail in a storm, for otherwise their ship will be overturned. After Homer, again, analogies with animals and plants,[2] and with various natural phenomena,[3] also come to be used more frequently in a similar context.

In discussions of questions of conduct the fields from which the analogies are drawn broaden in the sixth and fifth centuries, but the ways in which they are used remain much the same as they had been in Homer. They are used extensively as a method of persuasion or inference, but the conclusions of individual analogical arguments were, of course, often rejected (for example in the altercations between several persons in the tragedians), and sometimes the analogy itself was specifically challenged. There is, however, no evidence to suggest that in the period before Plato, at least, the validity of analogical argument *as a whole* had been called into question, either in the context of ethical debates, or in connection with the analogies which were used in natural philosophy. Rather, in the latter context we noted several passages in which a

[1] Cf., for example, Solon 10 D; Pindar, *P.* 1 91 f., *O.* 6 100 f.; Aeschylus, *Th.* 208 ff.; Euripides, *Andr.* 479 ff.

[2] E.g. Hes. *Op.* 203 ff. (the fable of the hawk and the nightingale), Sophocles, *Ant.* 712 ff. (a moral is drawn from the fact that those trees that do not bend before a river in flood are uprooted, while those that do, survive) and *El.* 1058 ff. (the behaviour of young birds towards their parents is cited to suggest the desirability of filial piety).

[3] Thus the fact that lightning strikes prominent objects, the tallest trees or buildings, for instance, is used as an argument to recommend moderation in the speech of Artabanus in Herodotus 7 10. And we have already noted several comparisons which Solon (1 D and 10 D) draws between political events and natural ones (above, p. 227, n. 1).

writer, in attempting to establish an account of a natural phenomenon, not only appears to assume, but explicitly claims, that he has demonstrated his conclusion when all that he has done is to cite a persuasive analogy.[1] Our next problem, then, is to determine how far Plato himself progressed towards an analysis of analogical argument as such.

PLATO

In his chapter on Analogy in *Plato's Earlier Dialectic*, Robinson has pointed out that while the hypothetical method is much discussed in the middle dialogues of Plato, it is little used, but that analogy and imagery, on the other hand, are much used but little discussed. 'What the middle dialogues really rely upon, in order to persuade us and apparently also in order to intuit the truth, is analogy and imagery' (*2*, pp. 204 f.), and indeed this is true not merely of the dialogues of the middle period, but of the whole Platonic Corpus. First, then, we should consider the actual use which is made of analogical argument in the dialogues. How far is it possible to assess Plato's own attitude towards the arguments of this sort which he puts into the mouth of Socrates or other persons in the dialogues? And then, too, we must examine the scattered statements in Plato which bear on various aspects of the use of analogical argument, and especially the passages in which he discusses the role of the paradigm or illustrative example, or in which he refers more generally to the deceptiveness of resemblances. How far do these statements appear to be consistent with Plato's actual use of analogical argument? How far can Plato be said to have undertaken a critical analysis of argument from analogy as a whole?

We may begin with some examples of analogical arguments from the early dialogues, and here the general problems of interpretation have been noted before. We are not entitled to assume that the position that Socrates adopts in any of these

---

[1] See above, p. 358 and n. 3.

dialogues, or the judgements he expresses concerning the cogency of the arguments he adduces, necessarily represent Plato's own considered beliefs. All that we can do is to observe what types of argument Plato puts into the mouth of Socrates or other persons in the discussion, what claims are made for these arguments by their proponents, and how other speakers react to these arguments and to the claims made for them. In the *Crito* (47a ff.) there is a typical text in which we find one of the most common types of analogies in Plato, that between the knowledge or skill of the craftsman or artist, and the knowledge which (it is suggested) should be the basis for decisions on ethical and political questions.[1] Socrates asks whether a man who practised gymnastic exercises would pay attention to the opinions of anyone, or to those of his doctor or trainer alone, and Crito says the latter. Socrates then asks a question of a similar form on the subject of 'what is just and unjust and ugly and beautiful and good and evil': 'should we follow the opinion of the many...or that of the one man, if there is an expert (τῇ τοῦ ἑνός [δόξῃ], εἴ τίς ἐστιν ἐπαΐων, 47d 1f.)?' Crito agrees with Socrates here too, and Socrates develops the analogy further and then concludes (48a 5 ff.): 'we must not, therefore,...have regard for what the many tell us, but for what the expert on justice and injustice tells us, this one man and the truth herself?' Here it might be objected that though 'knowledge' of a sort is involved in both cases, in gymnastics and in moral judgements, in one important respect the analogy does not hold. In gymnastics there is general agreement about ends (namely health) and the trainer's decisions relate to the means towards those ends, not to the ends themselves. But in questions of right and wrong, on the other hand, the ends themselves are often in dispute, and the politician's decisions concern *both* means *and ends* (both how the ship of state should be sailed, and in which direction it should point).[2] We should note, however, that Socrates

---

[1] There is a most useful discussion of analogies of this type in Bambrough, pp. 98 ff.　　　[2] Cf. Bambrough, pp. 105 f.

does not explicitly claim, in this passage, to have proved his case. He uses the analogy to recommend the thesis that on the subject of justice and injustice (as on questions of gymnastic training) we should disregard the opinions of the many and value the view of the 'expert' alone, but this conclusion depends on a series of admissions on the part of Crito, and no claim is made that it has been demonstrated.

Elsewhere, however, we do find that a claim is sometimes made that the conclusion of an argument from analogy has been proved. The analogy between health in the body and justice in the soul is particularly prominent in the *Republic* and *Gorgias*,[1] and in one passage in the *Gorgias* Socrates appears to claim that he has proved, by its means, that it is better for a wrongdoer to be punished than to escape punishment. At 477 bc Socrates says that there are three πονηρίαι which affect money, the body and the soul respectively, namely poverty, illness and injustice. He goes on to suggest that just as the art of money-making rids one of poverty, and medicine rids one of disease, so 'justice' (that is, paying the penalty) rids one of the third type of evil, intemperance and injustice (477e ff.). When this has been granted, he has little difficulty in reaching the conclusion that it is better for the wrongdoer to be punished than to escape punishment, for punishment 'cures' the soul of injustice just as medical treatment cures the body of disease, and it is better in each case to undergo the cure even though the treatment itself may be painful. He then asks Polus whether he has proved his view to be true: οὐκοῦν ἀποδέδεικται ὅτι ἀληθῆ ἐλέγετο; and Polus assents: φαίνεται (479e 8 f.). At this point, then, Plato represents Socrates as claiming to have demonstrated his case. Polus is made to accept this: yet Callicles, we should note, clearly does not, for he intervenes shortly afterwards (481 b) and protests at the paradoxical conclusions which Socrates has drawn from Polus' admissions. Yet Callicles himself is defeated by a similar argument, for

[1] Robinson, 2, pp. 205 f., lists and discusses several instances of this analogy.

when at 504b–505c Socrates once again uses the analogy between health in the body and justice in the soul in order to suggest that it is better to suppress the desires of the soul than to be self-indulgent, Callicles in turn is nonplussed and refuses to answer the questions put to him.

In the majority of instances in which analogical arguments are used by Socrates in the earlier dialogues, the analogies go unchallenged. It does, however, sometimes happen that Socrates' respondents object to the analogies he suggests, and though it is quite often the case that their objections are then overruled by Socrates himself, these passages are important for the evidence they afford of Plato's awareness of possible objections to certain of the analogical arguments which he ascribes to Socrates and others. (1) In a well-known passage in the *Gorgias*, 490e–491a, Callicles protests that Socrates is for ever speaking of cobblers and fullers and cooks and doctors who have nothing to do with the subject in hand. But here Callicles merely resorts to abuse, and while he is made to register a general protest against some of Socrates' favourite analogies in this way, he does not attempt to point out where or in what respects the particular argument that Socrates uses may be inexact. (2) In the *Charmides*, however, Critias twice explicitly objects that Socrates has erroneously taken dissimilars to be alike. At 165b ff. Socrates examines Critias' proposed definition of 'temperance' (σωφροσύνη) that it is 'knowing oneself', showing first of all that this means that it is a 'science' (ἐπιστήμη). He points out that medicine produces health, and the art of building produces houses, and so on, and then asks what 'temperance' produces, if this too is a 'science'. But Critias replies (e 3 ff.): 'But Socrates, you are not carrying out the inquiry correctly. For in its nature temperance is not the same as the other sciences, nor are they the same as one another. But you are conducting your investigation as if they were the same.' He points out that the arts of reckoning and geometry do not produce anything either in the way in which the art of building produces a house. But Socrates then says that he can at least indicate the subject-matter of these sciences, that of which they are the science (namely, in the case of reckoning, the odd and the even), and he challenges Critias to tell him what the subject-matter of 'temperance' is, that of which it is the 'science'. But once again Critias raises an objection (166b 7 ff.): 'your inquiry has reached the point at which temperance differs from all the sciences, but you are looking for some similarity between it and the others'. And he suggests that 'temperance' alone is the 'science of the other sciences and of itself'. (3) Similarly in the *Meno* (72d f.) when Socrates has obtained Meno's agreement that health and size and strength are 'the same' whether the object that is healthy or large or strong is a man, for example, or a woman, and then asks whether 'virtue' too is not 'the same' both for men and for women, Meno replies (73a 4 f.) that 'somehow it seems to me, Socrates, that this is not the same as the other cases', although the doubts which he has on this score are subsequently overruled. (4) Lastly we should mention a passage in the *Euthydemus*. This dialogue contains (as we saw) several arguments which depend on putting a choice between opposite, but not exhaustive, alternatives, but it sometimes happens that when the conclusion to which the argument leads is particularly outrageous or paradoxical, the sophists lend it some support by appealing to what by implication they suggest to be similar cases. But on one occasion, at least, this move is countered. At 298bc they argue that a 'father' must be 'father' to all men, since he cannot be 'not-father', and Euthydemus continues: 'for you do not think that what is gold is not-gold, or what is man is not-man?' But to this Ctesippus objects with the remark: 'perhaps, as they say, you are joining flax and not-flax together' (298c 5 f.), a proverb which is ideally suited, one might say, to the rejection of false analogies.

The examples we have considered illustrate how certain specific analogies are challenged in various early dialogues.

But then in works from the *Phaedo* onwards we also find texts which deal in more general terms with various aspects of the use of analogy, whether as a method of persuasion, or as a means of discovering the truth. First there are certain passages in which the use of images is criticised, or in which the dangers of relying on similarities in argument are pointed out. (1) The first of these occurs in the *Phaedo*. At 85 e f. Simmias suggests that the soul may be an attunement (ἁρμονία), and Plato clearly refers to this conception as an image when Cebes comes to raise his own doubts about the immortality of the soul, for there he says that he too, like Simmias, is in need of an image (εἰκών, 87 b 3). But then at 92 cd Simmias refers to his attunement-theory in the following terms: ὅδε μὲν γάρ [*sc.* ὁ λόγος] μοι γέγονεν ἄνευ ἀποδείξεως μετὰ εἰκότος τινὸς καὶ εὐπρεπείας, ὅθεν καὶ τοῖς πολλοῖς δοκεῖ ἀνθρώποις· ἐγὼ δὲ τοῖς διὰ τῶν εἰκότων τὰς ἀποδείξεις ποιουμένοις λόγοις σύνοιδα οὖσιν ἀλαζόσιν, καὶ ἄν τις αὐτοὺς μὴ φυλάττηται, εὖ μάλα ἐξαπατῶσι, καὶ ἐν γεωμετρίᾳ καὶ ἐν τοῖς ἄλλοις ἅπασιν.[1] Simmias draws a quite general distinction, here, between proofs and probable arguments. But his general warning about the unreliability of arguments that fall short of being proofs is clearly meant to apply in particular to his own image of the soul as an attunement. (2) A passage in the *Theaetetus* draws a similar distinction between a probable argument and a demonstration. Protagoras' doctrine was that 'man is the measure', but when Socrates criticises this idea at 161 c f., he asks why one should not take 'pig' or 'baboon' to be the measure.[2] At 162 e f., however, Protagoras is made to defend himself against this objection: ἀπόδειξιν δὲ καὶ ἀνάγκην οὐδ' ἡντινοῦν λέγετε ἀλλὰ τῷ εἰκότι

---

[1] 'I put forward this theory without proof, but with a certain probability and speciousness, which is why most men accept it. But I am well aware that theories which base their proofs on what is probable are impostors; unless one is on one's guard against them, they deceive one very badly, in both geometry and everything else.'

[2] Goldschmidt, *1*, pp. 24 ff., 38 ff. has discussed a number of similar passages in Plato in which persuasive or emotive images are used in an attempt to reduce an opponent's theory to absurdity.

χρῆσθε...σκοπεῖτε οὖν σύ τε καὶ Θεόδωρος εἰ ἀποδέξεσθε
πιθανολογίᾳ τε καὶ εἰκόσι περὶ τηλικούτων λεγομένους
λόγους.[1] Once again a merely probable argument is distinguished from a demonstration, and Socrates' emotive
images of the pig and the baboon are evidently included in
the former class. Then in two passages in the *Phaedrus* and
Sophist Plato calls attention to the fact that likenesses
(ὁμοιότητες) may be deceptive. (3) In the *Phaedrus* (262 a–c)
Socrates is made to refer to the deliberate use of likenesses in
order to deceive, and here he notes that the person who wishes
to deceive another, but not be taken in himself, must know
the likenesses and unlikenesses of things accurately.[2] But, he
goes on, only he who knows what each thing really is will be
skilled, as he puts it, in 'proceeding little by little by means of
likenesses from "what is" to its opposite on each occasion'
(262 b 5 ff.). (4) And in the *Sophist*, when, at one point,
Theaetetus thinks that they have found 'what looks like' the
sophist, the Eleatic Stranger is made to remark (231 a): 'so
too a wolf looks like a dog, the one a most fierce, the other a
most tame animal. But a careful person should always be on
his guard against resemblances above all, for they are a most
slippery tribe.'[3]

These texts leave no doubt that Plato was well aware that
likenesses are often deceptive. But elsewhere in the middle or
late dialogues there are other passages, which we must now
consider, in which the use of analogies is *recommended* in
certain contexts, whether for didactic purposes, i.e. in order
to instruct a pupil, or, indeed, in order to intuit or reveal the
truth.[4] The first such text is the passage which introduces the

---

[1] 'You give not a single demonstration or proof, but rely on what is probable.
But do you and Theodorus consider whether on such subjects you will allow
arguments which are founded on speciousness and probabilities.'

[2] δεῖ ἄρα τὸν μέλλοντα ἀπατήσειν μὲν ἄλλον, αὐτὸν δὲ μὴ ἀπατήσεσθαι, τὴν ὁμοιότητα
τῶν ὄντων καὶ ἀνομοιότητα ἀκριβῶς διειδέναι (262 a 5 ff.).

[3] τὸν δὲ ἀσφαλῆ δεῖ πάντων μάλιστα περὶ τὰς ὁμοιότητας ἀεὶ ποιεῖσθαι τὴν φυλακήν·
ὀλισθηρότατον γὰρ τὸ γένος.

[4] See further Goldschmidt's monograph on the paradigm (*1*), and Robinson,
2, pp. 210 ff.

analogy between the individual and the city in the *Republic*. Having pointed out how difficult the inquiry into justice in the individual is, Socrates suggests that they conduct their search in the following way: 'if, not having very good eyesight, we were told to read small letters at a distance, and then someone spotted that these same letters occurred larger elsewhere and on a larger surface, we should think it a godsend, I suppose, to read the larger letters first and then examine the smaller ones, to see if they happen to be the same' (368d). He proposes, then, to consider justice 'writ large' in an entire city. Now it is obvious that it is one of Plato's main purposes in writing the *Republic* to describe his ideal city. Yet it is interesting that this topic should be introduced, ostensibly at least, as a means of discovering justice in the individual. Moreover, there is some doubt as to whether Socrates means to describe the formation of *actual* cities, or of an *ideal* city. He begins with an account of what he calls the 'healthy' city, and when he modifies this and says they must consider how a 'luxurious' city comes to be (372e), this would seem to be in order to make his city conform to the normal type. But from 374a ff. on, where he takes up the idea (mentioned at 369e–370b) that no man should have more than one occupation, he is clearly constructing an ideal city, as indeed he admits,[1] although this account of the ideal would seem to some extent to presuppose the very definition of justice which it is the ostensible aim of the analogy with the city to discover.[2] The illusion of a search for justice is, however, kept up,[3] and at 434e f. he turns back to the problem of

---

[1] E.g. 434e where he says that they have founded the best city they could.

[2] Thus at 392a ff., for instance, Socrates must presumably have some quite definite idea of justice in order to be able to reject the poets for giving a false account of it. Robinson expresses the difficulty well (2, pp. 211 f.): 'to get ideas by analogy about the actual human soul, it seems that he ought to look at actual cities.... No doubt he might beg the question in deciding which actual cities were just; but he begs it far more definitively in constructing his own.'

[3] E.g. at 394d Socrates professes his own ignorance: he will follow wherever the argument leads; at 427e he appeals to Glaucon to help him; at 432d he 'discovers' justice with the cry 'ἰοὺ ἰού, and at 450e, searching for justice in the individual, Socrates once again describes himself as ἀπιστοῦντα...καὶ ζητοῦντα.

justice in the individual and says: 'so then we must transfer back to the individual what it seemed to us to be there [i.e. in the city], and if it corresponds, all well and good. But if it seems to be something else in the individual, we will return again to the city and test it there, and then looking at them side by side and rubbing them together we may perhaps make justice flash forth as from fire-sticks; and when it is revealed, we shall confirm it among ourselves.' We should note that both here and at 368 d f. when the analogy is first introduced, mention is made of the need to *verify* the points of resemblance between the two cases, the city and the individual.[1] Consideration of the just city will enable them to make certain suggestions about the nature of the just man—for both, after all, in Plato's view, contain the Form of Justice—but then these suggestions have to be checked. And yet (as Robinson, 2, p. 215, has remarked) although Plato insists, in these passages, that they cannot transfer conclusions from the city to the individual without first verifying them, in practice he omits this further scrutiny on several occasions, as, for example, at 577 c ff., where he describes the nature of the 'tyrannised' soul after considering the 'tyrannised' city. The analogy is developed extensively (equivalences being suggested between the five types of political constitution and the five types of man, between the three classes in the state and the three parts of the soul, and so on), but Plato sometimes appears simply to assume, without further examination, that the conclusions which he intuits on the basis of the analogy are correct.[2]

Further light is thrown on both the heuristic and the didactic functions of analogy in Plato by passages in later

---

[1] At 368 d, in the illustration of reading letters, Socrates says they will 'examine the smaller [letters] to see if they happen to be the same'; cf. 369 a, they will 'then consider justice in each individual, looking for the likeness of the greater in the form of the less'.

[2] On the role of the analogy as a whole, Robinson (2, p. 205) says that 'introduced merely as a likely way of suggesting hypotheses about the individual, it gradually comes to profess not merely to suggest such hypotheses but also to prove them true, and in the process it produces a wealth of political philosophy'.

dialogues, particularly those in which the use of the paradigm is discussed. In the *Sophist*, the Eleatic Stranger, noting that the sophist is a difficult species to investigate, remarks (218 cd) that on important subjects 'it has long been universally accepted that there should be some preliminary practice on lesser and easier topics, before one turns to the major subjects themselves'. 'So now', he continues, 'I recommend this course for us, Theaetetus. Considering that the tribe of the sophist is a difficult one and hard to track down, we should practise the method first on something easier.' They then select the example (παράδειγμα) of the 'angler', who is 'familiar to everyone and of little importance', and they conduct a preliminary inquiry on him. So far the paradigm seems to be thought of merely as providing useful practice for the method of inquiry (division) which will be used on the sophist. But it then appears that the example of the angler has *particular* relevance for their inquiry, for when they turn to consider the sophist, the Stranger exclaims (221 d 8 f.) 'by heavens, have we overlooked the fact that these two men are kin?', and at this stage both the angler and the sophist are considered as types of 'hunters'.

Paradigms are employed again in the *Politicus*, and this dialogue contains a fuller account of their use. At 277d 1 f. the Eleatic Stranger states quite generally that 'it is difficult to make clear anything of importance adequately without the use of paradigms'.[1] This is not immediately understood by the younger Socrates, and so the Stranger gives 'a paradigm of paradigm'. He takes the case of children who are learning to read. When they have learned to distinguish each of the letters in the shortest and easiest syllables, but cannot identify them in other, more difficult, combinations, then the best and easiest way of teaching them is 'to lead them first to those syllables in which they judged these letters correctly, and then to set them in front of the syllables which they do not yet know; then, putting them side by side [i.e. the known, and

---

[1] χαλεπόν... μὴ παραδείγμασι χρώμενον ἱκανῶς ἐνδείκνυσθαί τι τῶν μειζόνων.

the unknown, syllables], to point to the same likeness and nature existing in both combinations' (278a 8 ff.). The known syllables act, then, as the paradigms, and eventually the child will be able to identify the letters correctly wherever they occur. We see from this illustration first of all that the paradigm has a *didactic* function; it is a means of teaching a person by leading him from something he knows to something which he does not yet know but which is similar to what he knows. And at 286a and b the idea is expressed that the paradigm provides *practice in method* (as was pointed out also in the *Sophist*). But to these functions of practice and instruction we must, it seems, add a third function, that of *discovery*. The method of the paradigm is represented as one which will help them in their *search* for the 'kingly art'. At 277d the Stranger compares their state with that of knowing all things in a dream (οἷον ὄναρ εἰδὼς ἅπαντα) and he says that they will try, by means of a paradigm, to comprehend the nature of 'tendance' (θεραπεία) in political matters, so that they can transform their dream into a waking vision (ἵνα ὕπαρ ἀντ' ὀνείρατος ἡμῖν γίγνηται, 278e). While in the illustration of the children who are learning to read the instructor himself clearly knows the letters in each of the combinations in which they occur (and knows too that the letters are the same in each case), in the problem in hand they are not being taught the definition of the kingly art by someone who already knows it—they are attempting to discover it for themselves. When the Stranger asks what paradigm they should select so that they will discover what they are looking for, he suggests 'weaving' almost, it seems, as a *faute de mieux*, 'if there is nothing else to hand' (εἰ μή τι πρόχειρον ἕτερον ἔχομεν, 279b 1 f.). Yet as in the *Sophist*, the paradigm which is chosen *turns out to be* particularly relevant to what they are trying to define: there are important resemblances between the art of weaving and that of the statesman which are described at some length at 308d ff. To some extent, no doubt, Plato has emphasised the element of search and discovery in defining the sophist and the statesman simply for dramatic or literary purposes. And yet in the passage in the *Politicus* in which the nature of the paradigm is discussed he conveys what is, surely, an important and entirely serious lesson in method. Paradigms not only provide useful practice in the method to be used on more difficult subjects: they also provide a means whereby we can extend our knowledge from simpler to more complex subjects. Quite simple objects bear resemblances to more complex and important ones, and Plato seems to suggest that by apprehending these resemblances we shall be able to convert our 'dreamlike' acquaintance with the more important realities into a clearer vision.

We should now ask how far these and other passages give a coherent assessment of analogy or one that is consistent with Plato's actual usage. On the one hand he stresses that the conclusions suggested by certain analogies cannot be accepted without verification (*R.* 368 d f., 434 e f.);[1] he distinguishes between merely probable arguments (including, for example, emotive images) and demonstrations (*Phd.* 92 cd; *Tht.* 162 e),[2] and he draws attention to the potentially deceptive nature of likenesses as a whole (*Phdr.* 262 a–c, *Sph.* 231 a). Yet on the other hand (1) analogical arguments continue to be used extensively to recommend, if not to prove, various political and ethical theses, not only in the *Gorgias* and *Republic*, but also in such later works as the *Politicus* and *Laws*;[3] (2) it is

---

[1] Cf. *R.* 489 a, where, however, the verification of the image is said not to be necessary, and cf. also, in a different context, Plato's insistence that the products of the 'Maieutic Art' must be checked (*Tht.* 150 bc).

[2] Cf. also the texts which throw light on the status of 'myths', particularly the eschatological myths, which show that while he himself *believes* them to represent the truth, he does not claim to have *demonstrated* them: e.g. *Phdr.* 252 c, τούτοις δὴ ἔξεστι μὲν πείθεσθαι, ἔξεστιν δὲ μή, *Grg.* 524 ab, ταῦτ᾽ ἔστιν...ἃ ἐγὼ ἀκηκοὼς πιστεύω ἀληθῆ εἶναι, and cf. also *Phd.* 114 d, *R.* 621 bc.

[3] Analogies between the statesman on the one hand, and such skilled 'craftsmen' as the doctor, the pilot, the general and the shipbuilder on the other, are especially common, e.g. *Plt.* 295 b ff. (to recommend the thesis that a good ruler should not be bound by the laws), *Laws* 691 c ff. (to suggest that a statesman should observe the 'due measure', τὸ μέτριον), and cf. 709 a ff., 720 a ff., 961 d ff. And analogies with animals and plants are also used in the *Laws* to emphasise the

far from being the case that he always verifies his analogies in practice, in the sense of establishing his conclusions on grounds independent of the analogy, and (3) when Socrates and the Athenian Stranger tackle such subjects as the Form of the good in the *Republic* (506d ff.), or the nature of the soul in the *Phaedrus* (246a ff.) or the movement of Reason in the *Laws* (897d ff.), they have recourse to images which indicate not what these various objects are, but what they are like, excusing themselves by suggesting that this is the 'safer', the 'easier', or the 'shorter' course.[1] In practice, Plato often seems to ignore the recommendations and warnings which appear in many of the passages in which he discusses the use of images and likenesses. Having pointed out, in connection with the long and complex analogy between the city and the individual in the *Republic*, that the conclusions suggested by the analogy must be checked before they are accepted as true, he often, in fact, dispenses with this step with regard to the many less ambitious analogies he uses in recommending political or ethical theses. Simmias is made to admit, in the *Phaedo*, that his image of the soul is untrustworthy, being based on a mere probability: yet elsewhere Plato uses images extensively to convey his own conception on some of the most important subjects, such as the Form of the good, although formally, of course, there is nothing to distinguish the images of a Socrates from those of a Simmias or a Cebes. The Eleatic Stranger tells us in the *Sophist* that resemblances are a 'most slippery tribe': but they (necessarily) continue to play a most

importance of the early stages of education, for instance (765e ff.), or to recommend the thesis that partners in marriage should be faithful to one another (840de).

[1] Imagery plays an important role in Plato's accounts of many of the highest realities (the Form of the good, the movement of Reason). And yet in both the *Republic* and *Timaeus* he appears to demand a stable and perfect knowledge of that which is itself stable and perfect. In the *Republic* (511a ff.) the highest form of knowledge, νόησις, uses no objects of sense at all, but the Forms alone. And in the *Timaeus* (29bc) he contrasts an account of that which is itself stable and unchangeable (which must, as far as possible, be incontrovertible) with an account of that which is itself a mere likeness (which will be a merely probable one).

important part in Plato's dialectical method, both in the form of paradigms and in the process of Collection.[1] Simmias' false image of the soul in the *Phaedo*, and the Eleatic Stranger's explicit general warning in the *Sophist*, show that Plato was aware of how misleading superficial similarities may be. Yet he evidently held that analogies provided an important means not merely of instructing a pupil, but also of discovering and intuiting the truth, where, to begin with, the dialectician himself knows only dimly what it is he is looking for. Thus the paradigms which the dialectician chooses for the purpose of practice, before tackling difficult inquiries, turn out, in fact, to yield true and significant analogies with the actual subjects under discussion: this is not a mere coincidence, but rather, it seems, the result of a sort of divine guidance.[2]

The appeal to analogies is a recurrent feature of Plato's argumentation from the early Socratic dialogues to the *Laws*. In general, analogies are used as an effective technique of *persuasion*, particularly in recommending various political and ethical doctrines, although it is true that Plato sometimes allows Socrates to claim to have *demonstrated* his conclusions by this means. Already in the Socratic dialogues, however, there are several passages where specific analogies are challenged, and from the *Phaedo* onwards we find a number of texts which comment critically on the use of images and likenesses in argument. In these texts Plato made certain important (and largely original) logical and methodological points, (1) in suggesting the need to verify the conclusions of particular analogical arguments (though elsewhere he often omitted to

---

[1] E.g. *Sph.* 253 b–e; *Plt.* 285 ab; cf. further below, pp. 432 f. In connection with the theory of Anamnesis, too, we are told that Recollection is prompted by similars and by dissimilars (*Phd.* 74 a, cf. *Phdr.* 250 a) though it is emphasised that the similarity between particulars and Forms is quite defective (*Phd.* 74 a, e; *Phdr.* 250 b 3 ff.).

[2] Thus in connection with the analogy between the city and the individual in the *Republic* Socrates remarks (443 bc) that they have 'by the favour of some god (κατὰ θεόν τινα) chanced to hit upon the principle and as it were the type of justice'.

carry this out), (2) in drawing a clear and explicit general distinction between probable arguments (including, for example, emotive images) and demonstrations, and (3) in drawing attention to the potentially misleading nature of resemblances, although at the same time he continued both to use and to recommend the apprehension of analogies (in the form of paradigms) not only as a didactic, but also, it seems, as a heuristic, method. To conclude: Plato certainly made several important contributions to the understanding of the logic of argument from analogy. Yet while we find many scattered remarks in the dialogues that bear on the use of imagery and likenesses and reflect judgements concerning the cogency of specific analogical arguments, it is evident that he did not carry out a formal analysis of argument from analogy as such. For the first such analysis we must, then, turn to Aristotle.

ARISTOTLE

In reviewing earlier theories on various problems, as he so often does before proposing his own doctrines, Aristotle is quick to draw attention to, and to criticise, the use of an image or analogy. One striking example which has already been mentioned is *Mete.* 357a 24 ff. where he says that Empedocles' description of the sea as the sweat of the earth is 'adequate, perhaps, for poetic purposes', but 'inadequate for the purposes of understanding the nature of the thing' (see above, pp. 363 f.). Elsewhere he attacks other images used by Empedocles either on the grounds that the illustration given is itself obscure,[1] or because the things compared are quite different,[2] and he rejects other Presocratic notions as crude or in need of qualification.[3] Plato, too, is criticised on

---

[1] E.g. *GA* 747a 34 ff., referring to Empedocles' use of the illustration of the mixture of tin and copper in his account of the sterility of mules (see p. 334).

[2] E.g. *GA* 777a 8 ff.; *Top.* 127a 17 ff. At *Sens.* 437b 9 ff. he also attacks the belief that there is 'fire' in the eye, a theory which occurs in different versions in Empedocles (Fr. 84) and in Plato (*Ti.* 45b ff.).

[3] E.g. *PA* 652b 7 ff., where he rejects the belief that the soul of an animal *is* fire or some such substance and says that it might be better to say that the soul *subsists in some such* substance.

similar lines. In the *Metaphysics*, as is well known, the theory of Forms itself is attacked on the grounds that 'to say that they [the Forms] are models (παραδείγματα) and other things [particulars] share in them is to speak nonsense and to use poetic metaphors',[1] and in the *Politics*, too, he rejects some of the analogies which Plato had used in the *Republic* and the *Laws* in advancing various political doctrines.[2] There is no need to multiply examples where he objects to the analogies used by his predecessors, but it is perhaps particularly remarkable that Aristotle should sometimes comment directly on their having been misled by superficial similarities. On one occasion he suggests that the reason why Alcmaeon and others had thought that the white of the egg is the 'milk' or nourishment of the embryo is, as he puts it, 'the similarity of colour' (that is, presumably, when the egg is cooked) (*GA* 752 b 25 ff., cf. above, p. 324). And in *Metaph.* N 6 when he criticises some of the connections which had been found between different things on the basis of number (e.g. between the seven vowels, the seven notes of the scale, the seven Pleiades and so on), he compares those who proposed such theories with the old Homeric scholars who 'observe trivial resemblances, but overlook major ones' (μικρὰς ὁμοιότητας ὁρῶσι, μεγάλας δὲ παρορῶσιν, 1093 a 26 ff.).

We may now turn to the passages where Aristotle assesses imagery and analogy in general, and first we may note that he condemns the use of metaphor in reasoning and particularly in giving definitions.[3] At *APo.* 97 b 37 f. he says εἰ δὲ μὴ

---

[1] *Metaph.* 991 a 20 ff., 1079 b 24 ff. At 997 b 8 ff. he compares the belief in an eternal Form of man with the belief in gods who are like men but are eternal: the anthropomorphic gods were simply eternal men, and the Forms are simply eternal sensible objects.

[2] E.g. at *Pol.* 1264 b 4 ff. he criticises the analogy of the hounds in the *Republic* (451 d ff.) and at *Pol.* 1265 b 18 ff. he suggests that the image of the warp and woof used at *Laws* 734 e f. is an inadequate account of the relationship between the rulers and the ruled.

[3] Cf. his frequent concern with the different meanings of words and with the detection of ambiguities in the *Topics*, the *Metaphysics* and the *Nicomachean Ethics* especially.

διαλέγεσθαι δεῖ μεταφοραῖς, δῆλον ὅτι οὐδ᾽ ὁρίζεσθαι οὔτε μεταφοραῖς οὔτε ὅσα λέγεται μεταφοραῖς,¹ and in the *Topics* (139b 32 ff.) he again criticises definitions which contain metaphors, giving as one example the definition of the earth as a 'nurse' (cf. Plato, *Ti.* 40b) and concluding that 'every metaphorical expression is obscure'.² It is true that elsewhere when he discusses *style* he approves of certain types of metaphor, especially those which express a proportion,³ and at *Top.* 140a 6 ff. we find him contrasting metaphor with what is (even) worse than metaphor, namely expressions that are quite unclear, and pointing out that 'in some sense metaphor does make its meaning clear, because of the similarity [on which it is based]'. But it is obvious that Aristotle's approval of metaphor is confined to its use as an ornament of style, while he condemns its use in reasoning altogether.

The main texts in which Aristotle deals with explicit analogical argument are those in which he describes and analyses the paradigm. The fullest description of the paradigm is *Rh.* B 20 (1393a 22–1394a 18). Having dealt with the special modes of rhetorical proof, Aristotle turns to consider the general ones, the κοιναὶ πίστεις, of which there are two sorts, the 'enthymeme'⁴ and the paradigm. Paradigms are then subdivided into three groups. The first consists in the appeal to historical parallels: in the example given a speaker argues that the Greeks should not let the Great King seize Egypt on the grounds that when Darius and Xerxes had captured Egypt each of them followed up his victory with an assault on Europe. παραβολαί form the second group, and here Aristotle refers to τὰ Σωκρατικά and instances the way in

---

¹ 'But if metaphors should not be used in reasoning, it is clear that one should not use metaphors in giving definitions, nor should one define metaphorical expressions.'

² πᾶν γὰρ ἀσαφὲς τὸ κατὰ μεταφορὰν λεγόμενον. Cf. *SE* 176b 24 f.; *Top.* 123a 33 ff., 158b 8 ff.

³ E.g. *Rh.* 1405a 8 ff., 1407a 14 ff., 1410b 36–1411b 23.

⁴ 'Enthymeme' is described, e.g. at *Rh.* 1356a 35ff., 1357a 16, cf. *APr.* 70a 10 ff., as a rhetorical syllogism, drawn from probable premises, in which it may happen that not all the premises are expressed.

which someone might argue that public officials should not be chosen by lot on the grounds that men are not selected as athletes or as pilots by lot. Thirdly, there are fables (λόγοι), and here one of the examples which he gives is an animal fable from Aesop. He goes on to note (1394 a 2 ff.) that fables are suitable for addressing popular assemblies and they have this advantage, that while it is generally difficult to find a parallel from actual historical events, it is easy to invent your own fable. On the other hand historical parallels are more useful for the purposes of deliberation, since 'as a general rule, the future will be like the past' (a 8 f.). He also points out that if no 'rhetorical syllogisms' are available, then we must try to prove our points with paradigms; but if we have enthymemes, then paradigms should be used as supporting evidence. But then the paradigms should not be put before the enthymemes (for in that position they would resemble an induction, and induction is usually inappropriate in rhetorical speeches), but after them, in the role of evidence.

The paradigm clearly represents what we should call argument from analogy. Under the three heads, τὸ λέγειν πράγματα προγεγενημένα, παραβολαί and λόγοι, Aristotle refers, in effect, to three of the most common types of analogical argument which are to be found in early Greek literature, first the citation of historical parallels (such as the argument we noted above, p. 387, which Herodotus, 7 10, puts into the mouth of Artabanus, and compare the arguments from past experience noted from Homer, p. 385), second comparisons drawn from such fields as the arts and skills (see above, pp. 387 f., 390 ff.) and third fables, particularly animal fables (e.g. Hes. *Op.* 203 ff.). Each of these three sorts of analogies is included under the genus 'paradigm', and Aristotle goes on to assess this mode of reasoning. The paradigm is a rhetorical argument, i.e. persuasive rather than demonstrative, but in rhetoric (at least) paradigms have a useful role as supporting evidence, and in the absence of rhetorical syllogisms they are the means whereby we should try to establish our points. And Aristotle points out the different psychological effects produced by putting the paradigms before, or after, the enthymeme. 'If they stand before, you must use many of them' (for there they look like an induction); 'but if put afterwards, one alone is sufficient, for even a single witness will serve, if he is a reliable one' (1394a 14 ff.).

The description of the paradigm in *Rh.* B 20 is confirmed and supplemented in several other texts. Generally, while the enthymeme is called a rhetorical syllogism, the paradigm is the equivalent, in rhetoric, of an induction, although Aristotle's classification of different rhetorical arguments sometimes varies slightly.[1] The popular, or persuasive, nature of the paradigm is often mentioned,[2] and he discusses the procedure to be adopted in order to refute a paradigm used by an opponent in argument.[3] But in the *Organon* (*APr.* B 24, 68b 38 ff.) the paradigm is criticised from the point of view of syllogistic reasoning, in what is the first formal analysis of analogical argument in Greek philosophy. 'Paradigm', Aristotle says, 'is when the major term is shown to belong to the middle term by means of a term which is like the minor term.' This obscure remark is clarified by an example. If we want to show that it is wrong for the Athenians to wage war against the Thebans, we must first know the universal proposition, that 'making war against neighbours is evil'. Evidence of this is obtained from similar cases, e.g. the war between the Thebans and the Phocians. Once the universal proposition has been established, the argument can be put in the form of

---

[1] Thus at *Top.* 157a 14 ff. παραβολαί seem to be co-ordinate with, not subordinate to, παραδείγματα. Again at *Rh.* 1402b 12 ff. enthymemes are said to be *based on* paradigms (for example). This was one of the passages used by Solmsen, *1*, pp. 13 ff., esp. 23, when he suggested that Aristotle's theory of the enthymeme underwent certain developments. Be this as it may, the description of the paradigm itself remained fairly constant (see *Rh.* 1402b 16 ff., the enthymeme based on paradigms is where one assumes the universal proposition on the basis of an 'induction' from one or more like cases, and then argues to a particular).

[2] E.g. *Rh.* 1356b 22 f., 1417b 38 ff., cf. 1368a 29 ff.

[3] E.g. *Rh.* 1403a 5 ff., cf. *Rh. Al.* 1430a 8 ff.

a syllogism: 'since war against neighbours is evil, and the war against the Thebans is a war against neighbours, then it is clear that the war against the Thebans is evil' (69a 5 ff.). Aristotle describes the paradigm as an argument which proceeds 'not from part to whole, nor from whole to part, but from part to part' (ὡς μέρος πρὸς μέρος), when both particulars fall under the same general class and one of them is known (a 13 ff.).[1] And he then goes on to differentiate it from ἐπαγωγή (here, 'complete' or 'perfect' induction). (1) Paradigm is not based on an examination of *all* the particulars (οὐκ ἐξ ἁπάντων, sc. τῶν ἀτόμων), and (2) it applies the general law to a further particular case. The example of the argument which is given (that concerning war against the Thebans) shows that what is discussed here is the same type of paradigm as that described in *Rh.* B 20: according to the classification given there, this example is an 'argument from a historical parallel'. But the purpose of the present passage is to analyse the paradigm from the point of view of the syllogism. Its shortcomings, from this point of view, are made clear: though the argument proceeds from a particular to a particular, it can be analysed into first an inductive, and then a deductive, step. But for the conclusion formally to be valid the induction must be perfect, whereas in the paradigm the universal proposition is taken to have been established on an incomplete induction, i.e. on a consideration of some, but not all, of the particular instances.

In his various discussions of the paradigm Aristotle reveals the weakness of analogical argument from the point of view of demonstrative, i.e. deductive, reasoning, while at the same time granting that it may have a certain usefulness in the field of rhetoric, as supporting evidence, or even as 'proof', in default of rhetorical syllogisms. But some of the passages in which he discusses the use of 'likenesses' (ὁμοιότητες) are also relevant to the question of the role of analogy in reasoning, and in particular to the problem of the relation between

---

[1] A similar analysis is given at *Rh.* 1357b 26 ff.

induction and analogy in Aristotle's logical system. In several passages in the *Topics* and *Sophistici Elenchi*[1] he describes how a dialectician may exploit similarities in order to deceive an opponent (one may compare Plato's general remarks on this subject at *Phaedrus* 262 a–c, see above, p. 395). But at *Top.* A 17 and 18 the consideration of similarities is discussed at some length, and, it would seem, in a more serious spirit. First at *Top.* A 13 105 a 21 ff. 'the investigation of likeness' (ἡ τοῦ ὁμοίου σκέψις) is mentioned as one of the ὄργανα or means by which we may become well supplied with 'syllogisms and inductions'. This is discussed more fully first at 108 a 7 ff. and then again at 108 b 7 ff. In the first passage Aristotle simply notes that we should look for likenesses both between things in the same genus, and between things in different genera, four-term proportional analogies of the type 'as sight is to the eye, so is reason to the soul' being mentioned in particular. But in the second passage (108 b 7 ff.) he gives more explicit reasons for recommending the study of likenesses. 'The examination of likeness is useful for inductive arguments, for syllogisms based on a hypothesis, and for the rendering of definitions.' Each of these uses is then described in more detail. 'For inductive arguments (1), because by means of the induction of particulars in like cases we claim to bring into evidence (ἐπάγειν) the universal. For it is not easy to make an induction without knowing the similar cases. Then (2) for syllogisms based on a hypothesis, because it is generally admitted that among similars what holds true for one, holds true also for the rest.... And (3) for rendering definitions, because if we are able to recognise (συνορᾶν) what is the same in each case, we shall have no difficulty, when defining, in determining the genus into which we should put the object under discussion.'[2]

[1] See especially *Top.* 156 b 10 ff.: cf. *Top.* 114 b 25 ff., 124 a 15 ff., 136 b 33 ff., 138 a 30 ff.; *SE* 174 a 33 ff., 37 ff.

[2] He goes on to note the usefulness of considering similarities between terms that are far apart, and four-term proportional analogies are again mentioned (108 b 23 ff.).

It is fairly clear that what we have in this chapter of the *Topics* is a number of notes briefly jotted down under the general heading 'the examination of likeness', and we should beware of attaching too much importance to the passage since the *Topics* as a whole deal primarily with 'dialectical' as opposed to 'apodeictic' reasoning, i.e. reasoning from generally accepted premisses, rather than from premisses which are true and primary (see 100a 27 ff.). The second use of 'the study of likeness', at least, is clearly 'dialectical' in character: the hypothetical syllogism referred to does give proof (see τὴν ἀπόδειξιν πεποιήμεθα, 108b 19) but this depends on a preliminary admission that among similars what holds true for one holds true also for the rest (b 13 ff.). But the other two uses of the study of likeness raise interesting issues. Aristotle notes that the recognition of likenesses is useful in giving definitions, to determine the genus, and both the notion and the term συνορᾶν which he uses at 108b 20 are, one may say, reminiscent of Plato's theory of Collection (cf., for example, *Phdr.* 265d 3). And then likenesses are also said to be useful for 'inductive arguments', and this raises an important problem. Aristotle's estimate of the importance of ἐπαγωγή is not in any doubt. At *APr.* 68b 13 f. he says that ἐπαγωγή and syllogism are the two sources of conviction (cf. *APo.* 81a 39 f.). But it is not always clear what he means by the term which is generally translated 'induction'. It is true that when ἐπαγωγή is analysed in *APr.* B 23, 68b 15 ff., it is clearly stated that it depends on a review of *all* the particular instances (i.e. 'complete' induction), and this view is also expressed elsewhere (e.g. *APr.* 69a 16ff.). Yet Ross (*4*, pp. 49f.), for example, has suggested—plausibly, I think—that the main reason why this analysis of ἐπαγωγή is given in *APr.* B 23 is that Aristotle is there trying to reduce all other modes of argument to the syllogism in order to show the more fundamental nature of that form of reasoning. Further, if we consider the *actual instances* of what are called 'inductive arguments' in Aristotle, we find that it is extremely difficult to point to a single clear instance where he carries out in practice a complete enumeration of particulars, as recommended at *APr.* 68b 27 ff.,[1] although there are, of course, many examples where he *asserts* that what applies in a few particular cases, which he actually cites, applies also 'in all' or 'in the rest'.[2] Indeed sometimes no particular instance is mentioned at all.[3] When induction is judged from the point of view of the syllogism, the enumeration of particulars is clearly of key importance, for only if the induction is 'perfect' is the conclusion formally valid. Yet much more often in practice ἐπαγωγή depends not on a complete enumeration of particulars, but simply on the apprehension of what is common to an (incomplete) set of similars. We may remember that the paradigm, an argument proceeding from particular to particular, is often compared with ἐπαγωγή, and in some passages it is actually said to be a kind of ἐπαγωγή:[4] and at *Top.* 108b 7 ff., at least, there is an explicit recognition of the role of 'the examination of likeness' (or, as one might say, the analysis of the positive analogy) in 'inductive arguments'.

We noted that Plato was responsible for drawing a general

---

[1] Ross (*4*, p. 48, n. 4) gives *APr.* 68b 20 f. and *Metaph.* 1055a 5 ff. as instances of inductions where Aristotle 'passes under review all (or what he takes to be all) the species of the genus'. But neither passage seems to me to be a good example of this. (1) *APr.* 68b 20 f. occurs, of course, in the chapter of *APr.* in which induction is analysed in terms of the syllogism, where Aristotle certainly asserts (b 27 ff.) that all the particulars should be taken into consideration. Yet in proving that 'all bile-less animals are long-lived', he gives 'man, horse, mule' as examples of 'bile-less animals', although it is apparent from *PA* 676b 25 ff., for instance, that the class of 'bile-less animals' is wider than this. We are, of course, to understand that all the species have been enumerated, yet Aristotle does not, in fact, carry this out here. (2) Nor is *Metaph.* 1055a 5 ff. a good example of a complete enumeration of particulars in the induction of a general conclusion. The thesis that 'contrariety is the greatest difference' is established not by any collection of particulars, but rather by an argument that shows (*a*) that things differing in genus cannot pass into one another, and so cannot be compared with one another at all, and (*b*) that of things that differ in species, contraries are the extremes.

[2] E.g. *Cat.* 13b 36 ff.; *Top.* 103b 3 ff.; *EE* 1219a 1 ff., 1248b 25 ff.

[3] E.g. *Ph.* 185a 13 f.; *Cael.* 276a 14 f.; passages which refer, simply, to general experience.

[4] E.g. *Rh.* 1356b 2 ff., 1357b 25 ff., cf. 1393a 25 ff.

distinction between mere images and proofs and that he issued a warning about the unreliability of resemblances as a whole, and yet the apprehension of analogies continued to play an important part in his dialectic, both in the paradigms which the dialectician uses in his search for the highest essences, and in the process of Collection. In both these contexts Plato appears to assume that the analogies intuited by the dialectician, unlike those of a Simmias or a Cebes, are trustworthy, though he does not go into the problems which this assumption raises. How far did Aristotle give a coherent assessment of analogy, and how far does his practice tally with his theory? Certainly he not only frequently criticised his predecessors' images and analogies and condemned the use of metaphor in reasoning as a whole, but he also gave the first formal analysis of analogical argument in the form of the paradigm. In the *Rhetoric* he treats the paradigm as a persuasive, rather than demonstrative, argument and when he discusses this type of argument in the *Prior Analytics* he analyses it into an inductive and a deductive step and points out where its weakness lies, namely in that the induction is incomplete. It is a feature of his treatment of both analogy and induction in the *Organon* that as a rule he judges these modes of argument from the point of view of the syllogism, and from this point of view he insists that induction should be perfect, that is based on a review of all the particulars, although in practice the arguments which he labels 'inductive' rarely, if ever, fulfil this criterion. Yet if in the *Organon* analogy is compared very unfavourably with the syllogism, in the physical, biological and psychological treatises Aristotle uses analogies far more often than syllogistic arguments both in order to infer facts, and as a means of establishing his theories and explanations. True, we noted that in some respects he appears to be rather more cautious in his use of analogies than most earlier writers had been, and on many occasions he follows the proposal of an analogy with a reference to the causes which he believes to be at work in each case. But if this suggests how Aristotle might have attempted to justify many of his analogies, namely on the grounds that the cases he compares are each instances of the same general laws, the fact remains that the form which his reasoning takes, on these occasions, does not conform to what the theory of *APr.* B 24 would seem to demand. It does not consist of (1) a careful induction to establish the general rule, and (2) a deduction applying the rule to a further particular case, but rather of a direct comparison between one particular case and another. And if in practice it is often as preliminary hypotheses that Aristotle uses analogies (notably in the psychological treatises), what is missing in the *Organon* is due recognition of *this* role of analogy, not as a method of demonstration, but as a source of tentative suggestions which await criticism and confirmation. He sometimes refers quite generally to 'induction', along with the syllogism, as a means of acquiring knowledge (*APo.* 81 a 39 f., cf. 100 b 3 ff.). But with the exception of the passage in the *Topics* (A 18, 108 b 7 ff.) in which he recommends the 'study of likeness' for various purposes, the heuristic function of analogy is hardly explicitly considered at all, and in that passage he merely draws attention to the usefulness of the examination of likenesses in such contexts as the search for definitions, and he does not discuss how such likenesses should be scrutinised or appraised, or even state clearly that this is necessary.

In the *Organon* Aristotle is preoccupied with the method of the syllogism and the attainment of certainty in reasoning, and assessing the paradigm from this point of view he rejects it and all forms of induction other than the complete enumeration of particulars. Like his clarification of the different modes of opposition, this examination of analogy certainly marked a notable advance in logic: in this case Aristotle clearly revealed the weakness of analogical argument as a mode of inference. Yet his discussion of analogy is, one may say, still incomplete, for while he analyses it successfully from the point of view of demonstration, he devotes far less attention, in the *Organon*, to the heuristic function of analogy and to the question of its role in scientific method as a source of preliminary hypotheses, although in practice analogies figure prominently in this role both in Aristotle himself and throughout early Greek natural science.

CONCLUSIONS

In various contexts and in a number of forms the use of analogy is, as we have seen, extremely widespread in early Greek speculative thought, but the question we must now ask, in conclusion, is how far it is correct to talk of any major changes or developments in either the theory or the practice of analogy in the light of the material which we have considered. We may review the evidence that we have collected concerning each of the three main uses of analogy, in general cosmological theories, in accounts of particular natural phenomena, and in explicit analogical arguments in such fields as that of ethical debate.

Before philosophy, whether we consult Greek or ancient Near Eastern texts, the myths and beliefs that were expressed concerning the origins of things, the operations of fate and so on, do not constitute cosmological doctrines in the strict sense, but may be said to add up to a view of the world and the way it works, and it is obvious that the ideas that are expressed on these topics in the earliest Greek literature are very largely derived from, and reflect, certain main areas of human experience, that is the experience of social relations, of living creatures and (to a lesser extent) of industry. As a very broad generalisation this also applies to a quite marked degree to the cosmological speculations which we find in Greek philosophy, especially, though by no means exclusively, to those of the earlier, Presocratic period, and in some cases certain cosmological notions bear a more specific resemblance to earlier myths (in so far as the craftsman-god Hephaestus, for instance, may be said to stand as a mythical prototype for later philosophical conceptions of the craftsman-like force at work in the cosmos). At the same time, however, we noted where the cosmological doctrines of the philosophers mark a very definite break away from earlier thought. They are for the first time *cosmological* theories, presenting conceptions of the cosmos as a unity: they are subject to rational criticism and debate: and where pre-philosophical myths tend to refer to arbitrary personal deities, the philosophers adapted their political, biological and technological images to express the notions of order and rationality themselves. If we may say that the *types* of images in the philosophers broadly resemble those which can be found in earlier beliefs and myths, these images now become the vehicle for the expression of original and important theories about the nature of the cosmos.

Certain less clearly defined developments which affected the use of images in cosmology take place within the period from the sixth to the fourth century. We remarked that certain classes of things which had previously not been clearly differentiated came to be explicitly distinguished (for example the two classes of animate, and inanimate, beings and the realm of Nature and that of Society). And we suggested that this period is also marked by a gradual increase in the understanding of the use of images in cosmology. Empedocles already seems aware that his cosmic Philia is an abstraction or, as I called it, an extrapolation from ordinary experience, when he refers to 'Joy' and 'Aphrodite' to illustrate and exemplify the principle which he believes to be at work in the world at large. But a general distinction between a figurative and a non-figurative account does not seem to have been drawn before Plato. Yet Plato's recognition of this distinction obviously did not prevent him or any other later philosopher from continuing to employ images extensively to express cosmological doctrines. Aristotle, it is true, uses metaphor a good deal less than most of his predecessors in this context: in his general theory of change the four causes are the same 'analogically' in the different spheres of coming-to-be, and he draws explicit comparisons between nature and 'art' in which both the similarities and some of the differences between them are pointed out. Yet leaving aside the evidence that shows that Aristotle himself was profoundly influenced by traditional vitalist doctrines, for example, we may note that images which are similar in type to those of the Presocratics or Plato continue to figure prominently in Greek cosmology long after Aristotle. The Stoics, in particular, often represented the cosmos as a living creature, and they also thought of the world as governed by divine law and compared it with a state or household.[1] It may be suggested, then, that during the fifth and early fourth centuries B.C. the distinctions between certain categories of things came to be grasped more firmly, and both Plato and Aristotle threw a good deal of light on the role of images in cosmology: and yet it is apparent that neither the fact that Plato drew attention to the differences between 'myths' and demonstrations, nor for that matter Aristotle's more radical criticisms of the use of metaphor, led in practice to any general decline in the use of figurative accounts in cosmological doctrines, let alone to a complete abandonment of their use in that context.

The history of the use of analogy in accounts of particular natural phenomena in some respects follows a similar pattern. In their accounts of meteorological and astronomical phenomena the first philosophers relied heavily on analogies (indeed often once an analogy had been suggested, their

---

[1] Indeed each of the three ideas (1) that the cosmos is a living creature, (2) that it is governed by providence and divine law like a well-administered state or household, and (3) that nature has a craftsman-like, purposeful activity, is an orthodox Stoic doctrine. For (1) see, for example, Sextus, *M.* IX 104 and 107 for Zeno; Hermias, *Irris. Gent. Phil.* 14 (Arnim, I, p. 111) for Cleanthes; D.L. VII 142 f. for Chrysippus. For (2) see Arius Didymus in Eusebius, *PE* XV 15, 817d, Aristocles in Eusebius, *PE* XV 15, 817 a, and the passages collected in Arnim, II, pp. 327 f. (and cf. the reference to the κοινὸν νόμον of Zeus in Cleanthes' Hymn to Zeus, which Guthrie, *HGP*, I, p. 425, n. 5, suggests may recall Heraclitus Fr. 114). And for (3) see D.L. VII 134 and 137 and the evidences collected in Arnim, II, pp. 328 ff.

inquiry seems to have ended), and while we can cite many instances from earlier Greek literature which illustrate a similar use of comparisons to apprehend and describe aspects of the unknown, we noted that the philosophers used this common-sense procedure in what is a quite new context, not to convey an idea of an individual event, such as the appearance of a shooting star, but to explain the nature and causes of shooting stars (for example) as a whole. As a method of elucidating obscure phenomena, analogy has always been a most useful tool of science (if one that should be used with caution), and the early Greek scientists applied it extensively not only in astronomy and 'meteorology', but in each of the new fields of inquiry that they opened up. And if in practice analogies occur very commonly in most early Greek investigators, there are signs that some writers had begun to recognise their usefulness at a quite early stage, for we find several pre-Platonic texts which appear to recommend analogies either as a method of discovery (as in *On Ancient Medicine* chs. 22 and 24) or as a mode of inference (as in Herodotus 2 33). Most of the doctrines which the early Greek theorists proposed on the basis of analogies are, of course, wide of the mark, though there is no need to repeat that the tendency to be misled by superficial similarities is far from being confined to early Greek science. What is, however, more remarkable is that while analogy was successfully analysed as a mode of inference, comparatively little progress was made in exploring the problems raised by its use as a source of hypotheses in the context of scientific method. In comparison with most earlier theorists Aristotle seems rather more guarded in his actual use of analogies in natural science: he suggests many of his analogies quite tentatively, or points out that the things he compares are similar, not identical, to one another. Yet in his theoretical discussion of analogy he is more interested in bringing it into the framework of his theory of the syllogism than in evaluating its role as a source of hypotheses. As regards the heuristic function of analogy, neither Aristotle nor indeed any other Greek writer can be said to have formulated a satisfactory conception of its role in the context of the method to be used in the inquiry into nature, although we noted that the idea that the conclusions suggested by an analogy should be checked before they are accepted as true does occur, in the context of an ethical and political discussion, in passages in the *Republic* which relate to the analogy between the city and the individual. Yet in practice, even though analogies were often used rather uncritically, we have seen that they were the source of many extremely fruitful suggestions in Greek natural science, and this is true not only of the comparisons drawn between things that are similar in kind (as in such fields as comparative anatomy or comparative embryology) but also where the objects which were compared are more disparate and heterogeneous, as in some of the bolder analogies in which the Hippocratic theorists and Aristotle attempted to reduce physiological, pathological and psychological phenomena to those of physics.

Finally, we may consider the theory and practice of explicit analogical argument, and here there can be no doubt as to the progress made, in the period under consideration, in the understanding of the logic of this type of argument. First Plato distinguished merely probable arguments (including images) from proofs and drew attention to the unreliability of likenesses as a whole in the context of dialectic (while continuing, of course, to use analogical arguments extensively, for example to recommend political or moral doctrines). And then Aristotle classified analogical argument (the paradigm) as a rhetorical, that is persuasive, mode of argument, and analysed it from the point of view of the syllogism, where he divided this argument into first an inductive, and then a deductive, step and suggested that the weakness of analogy lies in the fact that the induction is incomplete. The importance of this becomes clear when we reflect that earlier writers had often tended to assume the validity of their analogical arguments without question and sometimes explicitly claimed that a conclusion which had been recommended by an analogy had been demonstrated (as happens for instance, in some passages in Plato, e.g. *Grg.* 479 e, and also in the context of natural philosophy, see above, p. 358). After Aristotle's analysis of the paradigm there was, one may say, little excuse for later writers to claim that the conclusion of an argument that proceeded direct from a particular case to a particular case had been demonstrated, and yet in practice, of course, later writers are found to make mistakes similar to those which were committed before Aristotle wrote. While definite advances were made in the understanding of the logic of analogical arguments, there is little need to emphasise that this did not mean an end to the incorrect use of such arguments.

To sum up: the various uses of analogy in early Greek speculative thought may, in most respects, be considered extensions and developments of common-sense uses examples of which can readily be given from the earliest extant Greek literature. The particular importance of analogy in pre-Platonic thought derives from the frequency and the success with which the first philosophers and scientists adapted analogies to express conceptions of the cosmos as a whole and to suggest accounts of obscure natural phenomena. As Greek philosophy developed, some of the problems involved in the use of analogies come to be discussed: a clearer idea of the status of cosmological images was achieved, and analogy was explicitly analysed as a mode of inference. But while the advances in the knowledge of the logic of analogy are clear-cut and decisive, in practice these did not lead to the abandonment of any particular use of analogy, only to a slightly more cautious application of analogies on the part of certain specific writers. Explicit analogical arguments continue to be both used and misused long after it was first pointed out that they are at best persuasive. While Plato acknowledged that figurative accounts are inferior to demonstrations, he and many others continued to use metaphors extensively in expressing cosmological conceptions. Finally, while Aristotle is, in certain respects, more critical in his use of analogies in natural science than most of his predecessors, analogy remained an extremely important, indeed an indispensable, method of elucidating obscure phenomena in many fields of inquiry long after the fourth century.

PART THREE: CONCLUSION

CHAPTER VII

THE DEVELOPMENT OF LOGIC AND METHODOLOGY IN EARLY GREEK THOUGHT

Under the two heads of polarity and analogy I have dealt with the arguments and explanations of two general types which appear in early Greek thought. But I must now fill in some of the gaps which the study of these two modes of reasoning has left, and we may then consider what conclusions may be suggested, on the basis of the evidence we have collected, concerning the general question of the development of logic and 'scientific method' in early Greek thought.

That certain other types of argument are used in early Greek literature besides arguments from analogy, and disjunctive 'polar' arguments, goes without saying. While myths and fables, for instance, are often cited in arguments which proceed from particular case direct to particular case, they are also sometimes referred to in arguments that draw general conclusions. Pindar, especially, often draws a general moral from a myth that relates to a particular case, using what is an 'inductive' rather than a strictly 'analogical' procedure.[1] Moreover, other arguments which appear in the poets or in prose writers have a 'deductive' form in which the starting-point or premiss is a universal dictum from which an inference is drawn to a particular case,[2] and we also find

---

[1] E.g. *P.* 2 21–48, where the myth of Ixion is told and two general morals are drawn, that one should requite one's benefactors, and observe the mean.

[2] E.g. Hdt. 7 237, where Xerxes argues that Demaratus' advice to him is well intentioned on the grounds that while citizens are jealous of the prosperity of fellow-citizens, strangers are well intentioned towards other strangers when they prosper (and Demaratus is, of course, a stranger).

what may be called 'hypothetical' arguments such as those which take the general form 'if *A*, then *B*; but not *B*; and so not *A*'.[1]

A variety of different forms of argument can be exemplified in pre-Platonic texts, and alongside this we should note the development of various ideas relating to the use of argument in the same period, particularly (1) the idea of logical necessity, (2) that of logical impossibility, and (3) the concept of probability. (1) To begin with, the words ἀνάγκη, χρή and δεῖ are only used in such contexts as those of fate, physical compulsion and moral obligation. But beginning with Parmenides, perhaps, these terms acquire a new use in the context of logic, that is to describe conclusions that follow 'necessarily' from certain premises (whether these conclusions are true or false). It is true that the type of 'necessity' that Parmenides had in mind when he uses these terms is not at all easy to define precisely. When he says at Fr. 8 16 ff., for example, that the decision has been made 'ὥσπερ ἀνάγκη' (as is necessary) between the two ways, to leave the one as unthinkable and nameless and to accept the other as real, we may interpret Parmenides as believing that it is logically necessary that what is is, and logically impossible for it not to be, but it seems likely that he also conceived this necessity as a matter of the real physical conditions of Being, and when he describes 'Ανάγκη as 'holding' what is 'in bonds' (e.g. Fr. 8 30 f.) this may be no mere poetic metaphor.[2] The logical use of 'necessity' appears rather more distinctly in Zeno. In Fr. 1, for instance, he concludes that 'if there are many, then

---

[1] E.g. Hdt. 4 118, where the Scythians attempt to persuade their neighbours that the Persian expedition is directed against them as well as against the Scythians themselves with the argument that 'if the Persians were attacking us alone...then necessarily (χρῆν) they would have left everyone else alone and come straight against us....But in fact (νῦν δέ) ever since they crossed to this continent, they have been subduing everyone they met.' The application of arguments of this type in law-suits to establish guilt or innocence is obvious.

[2] The same ambivalence is seen in some of the passages where the terms χρεών and χρή are used, e.g. Fr. 2 5, Fr. 6 1, though in Fr. 8 11 the logical sense seems to be uppermost: 'it needs must be (χρεών) either that it is wholly or that it is not' (cf. above, pp. 104 f.).

necessarily (ἀνάγκη) they are both small and great', and when he refers to necessity here, he evidently believes that this conclusion (which he holds to be absurd) follows logically from certain considerations that he has adduced.[1] Similarly, when Melissus says that 'if there were many, they would have to be (χρή) as I say the one is' (Fr. 8 2), he too no doubt considered that this (absurd) conclusion necessarily follows from his argument in Fr. 8.[2] It seems likely, then, that the Eleatics were the first to develop and use the notion of logical necessity, although they do not, of course, explicitly define this use. By the time of Plato, both the idea of logical necessity and that of 'proof' (ἀπόδειξις) are used quite freely,[3] though it remained for Aristotle to define 'proof' and to analyse the logical sense of 'necessity' in the context of his theory of the syllogism.[4]

(2) The idea of logical impossibility is the converse of that of logical necessity. Again it is not until Aristotle that what is logically possible or impossible is clearly distinguished from what is possible or impossible as a matter of fact, but again certain Presocratic texts are worth noting. Parmenides provides certain passages in which both senses of 'impossible' seem to be present, as for example Fr. 2, where he says that 'it is not possible for it not to be' (οὐκ ἔστι μὴ εἶναι) and goes on to suggest that 'you could not know what is not, at least, for that is impossible (οὐ γὰρ ἀνυστόν), nor could you describe it'. A similar usage occurs in Melissus (οὐκ ἀνυστόν in Fr. 7 8, cf. Fr. 2) and perhaps also in Empedocles Fr. 12 ('it is impossible, ἀμήχανον, for anything to come to be from what

---

[1] Cf. also Fr. 3, where again ἀνάγκη seems to be used primarily of logical necessity: 'if they are many, they are necessarily as many as they are and neither more nor less than they are'.

[2] Cf. Fr. 7 10: 'it must then necessarily (ἀνάγκη) be full, if it is not empty'.

[3] Before Plato the word ἀπόδειξις is used more regularly of factual proofs, 'proofs' carried out through deeds, than of demonstrations effected by means of appeals to evidence or argument (e.g. Hdt. 8 101), though the verb is used in the latter sense in Hdt. 2 15. ἀνάγκη itself is used of proof in this sense, e.g. in Hdt. 2 22 and in some of the Hippocratic treatises (e.g. *Morb. Sacr.* ch. 13, L vi 386 7).

[4] E.g. *APr.* 25b 30 f.; *APo.* 71b 17 ff.; *Metaph.* 1006b 30 ff., 1015a 20 ff., b 6 ff., 1064b 33 f.

is not at all'). But then one of the earliest texts in which the notion of logical impossibility occurs more distinctly is Anaxagoras Fr. 5, for it seems to be primarily for logical, rather than physical reasons that he says that 'it is impossible, οὐ γὰρ ἀνυστόν, for there to be more than all things', when he notes, in that fragment, that 'all things are neither less nor more than themselves', and that 'everything is always equal'.

(3) Thirdly, we may consider the development of the notion of probability. Some idea of what is probable is usually implicit in any argument from experience, and we can cite examples of arguments which tacitly assume a standard of probability from our earliest texts. Thus in Homer some such notion is implicit when someone weighs up the possibility that supernatural forces have been or are at work. Achilles, for instance, infers at *Iliad* 24 563 ff. that a god had conducted Priam to the Achaeans' ships: 'for you, a mere mortal, would not have dared to come to the camp, even had you been in the prime of life: you would not have got past the guards without being noticed, nor would you have pushed back the bolts of our doors easily'. Thereafter the term τὸ εἰκός becomes common in the fifth century to refer to what is probable. Herodotus makes an explicit appeal to what is probable at 7 239, for example, when he suggests that Demaratus, being an exile from the Spartans, was motivated by feelings of hostility towards them, 'as I think and probability bears me out' (ὡς ἐγὼ δοκέω καὶ τὸ οἰκὸς ἐμοὶ συμμάχεται). And in Thucydides we find the Corinthians at one point (1 121) listing the reasons why it is probable (εἰκός) that they will be victorious in the war, that is to say their superiority in numbers and military skill, their obedience to orders and so on. But apart from these instances where εἰκός describes conclusions arrived at after some appeal to 'what is probable', we also find occasions in early Greek literature when a distinction is drawn between merely probable, and certain, conclusions. We have already noted that there are some important passages in Plato in which 'probability' is distinguished from

'proof' (especially *Phd.* 92 cd and *Tht.* 162 e), but various types of distinctions are already drawn before Plato. A distinction between clear knowledge based on the senses and mere guesswork is already made in Homer (*Od.* 16 470–475). But then the Presocratic philosophers commonly distinguish between knowledge and mere opinion (e.g. Xenophanes Frr. 34 and 35 and Parmenides Frr. 1 28 ff. and 8 50 ff.) and here we should note that the former is generally associated with reason and intuition, the latter with sensation, and the difference is a difference in kind between two types of cognition. With this idea we may contrast that of the historians, for example, when they point out that the evidence available to them on a particular question does not allow certain conclusions to be drawn (e.g. Hdt. 1 57 and Th. 1 1) for here the difference between certain and merely probable conclusions is clearly only one of degree. In this context, a probability could become a certainty given additional evidence, whereas for Parmenides no amount of additional empirical data would allow an opinion about what is likely (ἐοικότα, Fr. 8 60) to be converted into a conviction which is true (πίστις ἀληθής, Fr. 1 30; πιστὸν λόγον . . . ἀμφὶς ἀληθείης, Fr. 8 50 f.).

From the topic of probability we may turn next to the question of the development of the use of evidence. Already in Homer we find frequent explicit appeals to the evidence or grounds for an assertion. When at *Iliad* 13 68 ff. Ajax the son of Oileus infers that what looked like Calchas was in fact a god he points to certain distinguishing marks (his footprints) by which he says he recognised the god. And at *Iliad* 11 613 f., when Achilles sees someone driving Nestor out of the battle he says 'from behind it looked just like Machaon', though he goes on 'but I did not see the man's face'. No one would expect problems of epistemology to be tackled in an epic poem, but Homer has occasion to distinguish between first-hand evidence and evidence from hearsay (e.g. *Od.* 3 93 f., 4 323 f., 8 491), to note that falsehood may look like the truth (*Od.* 19 203; cf. Hes. *Th.* 27 f.) and to remark on certain limitations to human knowledge (*Iliad* 2 485 f.; cf. *Od.* 1 215 f., 10 190 ff.). There is, however, no word in Homer apart from σῆμα to refer to the facts used as evidence,[1] and σῆμα itself is used in this sense only in the *Odyssey* and then with the exception of *Od.* 11 126 (= 23 273) exclusively in passages that describe Odysseus' recognition on his return. This lack of terms referring to evidence and its use in Homer contrasts with the rich vocabulary which was developed in the sixth and fifth centuries. In the philosophers we find μάρτυς used metaphorically of the evidence of the senses (Heraclitus Frr. 101a, 107, cf. ἐπιμάρτυρα in Empedocles Fr. 21 1), τεκμαίρεσθαι for 'infer' (Alcmaeon Fr. 1) and σῆμα and σημεῖον of the evidences or proofs which Parmenides (Fr. 8 2) and Melissus (Fr. 8) bring for their theses concerning 'what is'. And in the historians too the words τεκμήριον, σημεῖον and μαρτύριον for 'evidence', τεκμαίρεσθαι and σταθμᾶσθαι for 'infer', and δηλοῦν and μαρτυρεῖν for 'to be evidence of' are used with great frequency.[2] Technical definitions for most of these terms do not appear until Aristotle,[3] but the extent of their use in the fifth century can be judged from their frequent appearances not only in the prose writers, but in the poets as well. Pindar, for instance, has the verb τεκμαίρεσθαι in middle or active four times,[4] and each of the tragedians provides several examples of exchanges between different persons in which the evidence for an assertion is demanded and given.[5]

[1] The word μάρτυς is used exclusively in the primary sense 'witness' in Homer, and μαρτύριον does not appear. The only other word that comes near to meaning 'evidence' is τέκμωρ and this in one passage alone (*Il.* 1 526), its normal Homeric meaning being 'goal' or 'fixed end'. The vocabulary for terms for evidence is also quite restricted in Hesiod, the Homeric hymns and the early lyric poets.

[2] To give some figures: τεκμήριον, seven times in Herodotus, and eleven in Thucydides; τεκμαίρεσθαι, five and three (also τεκμηριοῦν three times and τέκμαρσις once in T.); μαρτύριον, ten in H. and six in T.; σημεῖον, in the sense 'evidence', seven in T.; and σταθμᾶσθαι, in the sense 'judge by', nine in H.

[3] See *APr.* 70a 3 ff., b 1 ff., *Rh.* 1357b 1 ff., 1402b 14 ff: τεκμήριον is a demonstrative sign, σημεῖον is used either (specifically) of fallible signs or (generally) of signs as a whole (including τεκμήρια).

[4] *O.* 6 73, 8 3; *N.* 6 8; Fr. 152 (OCT).

[5] E.g. Aesch. *A.* 272 ff.; Soph. *El.* 774 ff.; Eur. *Rh.* 94 ff.

The development of a rich vocabulary of terms to refer to the use of evidence is matched by corresponding developments in the variety of different types of evidence which are exploited, and in the methods of research used to obtain evidence. The gnomon, which may have been introduced into Greece by Anaximander,[1] appears to have been the only artificial aid to observation which was available to the Milesians. But as the range of the inquiries of the Greek philosophers, scientists and historians grows, we find new types of evidence referred to and new techniques of research developed. Xenophanes, for instance, was probably the first investigator to attempt to exploit the evidence of fossils in proposing a theory concerning the past history of the earth (Hippol. *Hear.* I 14 5, DK 21 A 33). In their attempts to reconstruct the past, the historians appeal to a wide range of evidence, and this includes both literary[2] and archaeological evidence. Thus Herodotus often refers to the monuments and offerings which he had seen at Delphi and elsewhere when these have some bearing on past events (e.g. I 50), and Thucydides sometimes makes telling use of archaeological evidence, as, for example, when he infers from the character of the remains found in the tombs on Delos that the majority of its ancient inhabitants were Carians (I 8).[3] But by far the most important technique of research in natural science, at any rate, was dissection, a method which can be traced back as far as Alcmaeon, and which included not only the dissection of dead animals, but also, as time went on, the dissection of embryos and vivisection, although there is no evidence that either Aristotle or any of the Hippocratic writers had dissected the human body itself.[4] Finally, we should note the

[1] E.g. D.L. II 1, DK 12 A 1; and see KR, p. 102 and *HGP*, I, pp. 74 f.

[2] E.g. Hdt 2 116, 4 29. The criticisms which Herodotus made of the Homeric account of the Trojan war (2 120) are echoed by Thucydides in the form of a more explicit caution on the use of Homer as evidence (I 9 and 10 and cf. 2 41).

[3] Cf. I 93, where he points to the types of stones to be found in the Long Walls as evidence that they were built hurriedly, and 2 15, where the position of the ancient temples is used as evidence of the original site of the town of Athens.

[4] On the subject as a whole, see Edelstein, *2* and *3*.

extent of the tests and experiments which were conducted before the end of the fourth century B.C.[1] We have already mentioned a number of examples from the Hippocratic Corpus where tests were carried out either directly on the animal body or on substances taken from it (such as blood in the example from *On Fleshes* chs. 8 and 9), or, as happens more often, on other simpler substances outside the body, from the behaviour of which conclusions were drawn, by analogy, concerning the behaviour of more complex substances within the body itself.[2] But the use of experiment was not confined to the investigation of problems in the biological sciences. In such fields as acoustics and pneumatics, for instance, there is evidence that certain simple tests had already begun to be carried out in the Presocratic period, and here one may refer not only to the (largely fictitious) stories which relate to Pythagoras' discovery of the numerical relations between the musical intervals of the octave, fifth and fourth,[3] but also to Plato's criticisms of those who employed empirical methods in such objects as acoustics, whom he describes as 'measuring the harmonies and sounds they hear against one another' (*R.* 531 a–c).[4]

Finally, we should consider how far ideas on the subject of the correct use of evidence developed in the fifth century, and again we may supplement the material which we have already discussed in relation to theories based on opposites and analogies. Already in certain contexts in Homer we find a person withholding judgement where he has insufficient or inconclusive evidence, whether on such a question as the

[1] On this topic, see especially the articles of Blüh, Edelstein, *5*, Farrington, *4*, and Zubov, as well as the important work of Senn, *1*.

[2] See above, pp. 74 ff., 349 ff. and 352 n. 1.

[3] The evidence is collected and assessed by Guthrie, *HGP*, I, pp. 220 ff., especially 223 ff., who notes that if this discovery was Pythagoras' it was no doubt on the monochord that he carried out his experiments. That other Pythagoreans also attempted to carry out experiments in acoustics is suggested by Archytas Fr. 1, for example (on which see Senn, *1*, pp. 271 ff.).

[4] I have discussed some other examples of early Greek experiments in a paper read to the Cambridge Philological Society (*Proceedings*, 190, NS, 10, 1964, pp. 50–72).

identity of someone whom he has just glimpsed (e.g. *Iliad* 11 613 f.) or on such a matter as who one's own father is (*Od.* 1 215 f.) where in the nature of things certainty may be unattainable. If we turn to later Greek literature, we can trace various ideas which relate to the correct use of evidence, as, for example, that the evidence must be checked, that it must be consistent, and that conflicting accounts must be weighed against one another. These ideas have an obvious relevance in a legal context, where witnesses were, of course, not merely cross-examined, but subjected to torture in efforts to procure the truth. But another context in which such notions are relevant is historical research. Herodotus repeatedly gives more than one account of an event or of the motives which may have activated the participants, and he often passes judgement on the reliability of the stories which he has heard (e.g. 1 95 and 214), though this did not prevent him, of course, from accepting many such reports rather uncritically. Again Thucydides notes the ease with which inexact accounts of past events gain credence (1 20) and says that in his own account he has been at pains to test the often conflicting reports which he had received from eyewitnesses (1 22). In historical research quite strict rules of evidence had already begun to be applied by the end of the fifth century, and in certain other contexts, too, a similarly cautious attitude is sometimes, though more rarely, adopted towards theories or assertions which seemed to have insufficient evidence in their support. To take another example from the historians, Herodotus at one point remarks (2 23) that the notion that there is a river running right round the world, and that the Nile floods in summer because it is connected with it, is quite obscure and cannot be tested (this appears to be the sense of οὐκ ἔχει ἔλεγχον). In medicine, too, several of the Hippocratic writers describe in detail the evidence which the physician should take into account in diagnosing,[1] and some of them note the difficulty of interpreting pathological symp-

---

[1] E.g. *Epid.* 1 sec. 3, ch. 10, L 11 668 14 ff.; *Prog.* ch. 2, L 11 112 12 ff.

toms and concede that the same symptoms may arise from different causes.[1] And yet if we take the sphere of natural science as a whole, the most considerable pre-Platonic text which criticises futile speculation on topics where there is no evidence or standard by which the theory may be judged true or false is the passage in *On Ancient Medicine* (ch. 1) which we have already discussed (pp. 69 and 79).

These brief notes have, I hope, been sufficient to indicate some of the developments which take place on certain topics relating to the use of argument and evidence by the end of the fifth century or shortly afterwards. (1) The ideas of necessity and impossibility acquire new senses in the context of logic. (2) The notion of probability and the distinction between certain and probable judgements are both used and referred to quite commonly in fifth-century writers. (3) The fifth century also sees certain important developments not only in the use of evidence and in the techniques employed to obtain it in different areas of research, but also in the awareness of some of the problems connected with its use. Such methodological points as the need to check evidence, to examine its consistency, and to withhold judgement when no reliable evidence is available, are clearly recognised at a quite early stage in a number of fields of inquiry, particularly in law and in historical research. In each of these contexts, then, we can trace certain definite, if gradual, advances in logic and methodology in the period before Plato, and if we include the dialogues of Plato himself, these bring out many important logical points, as, for example, when he analyses a statement (λόγος) into a combination of ὀνόματα (nouns/subjects) and ῥήματα (verbs/predicates) (*Cra.* 425a; *Sph.* 262a ff.), or when he distinguishes between οὐσία (substance) and πάθος (attribute),[2] or when, as happens several times in the early dialogues, it is pointed out that universal affirmative state-

---

[1] See *Aph.* ch. 1, L IV 458 1 ff.; *Prog.* ch. 12, L II 142 12 ff.; and *Acut.* ch. 11, L II 314 12 ff.

[2] *Euthphr.* 11a, cf. *Tht.* 182a where the term ποιότης, quality, is introduced into Greek for the first time.

ments are not simply convertible,[1] or when he distinguishes cause from necessary precondition or *sine qua non* (*Phd.* 99 a), and many other examples might be mentioned. But a general point may be made about such advances in logic and methodology as we have considered, and that is that even when they imply the resolution of a particular logical difficulty, they do not involve the deliberate correction of explicit (but fallacious) logical rules so much as the clarification of quite vague and indefinite assumptions. Thus while mistakes in conversion of the type to which Plato draws attention at *Euthphr.* 11 e must often have been made, there is nothing in our evidence to show (and indeed it is obviously quite improbable) that anyone had explicitly suggested, as a general rule, that universal affirmative statements *are* convertible. But how far is this general point endorsed or contradicted by the history of the development of ideas on the relationships of opposition and similarity? We may now turn back to the evidence we collected under the headings of polarity and analogy to consider what light this material throws on the broader issues of the development of logic and methodology in early Greek thought.

First it should be repeated that it is manifestly not the case that all the arguments and explanations that appear in early Greek thought are of the two types I have discussed. It is, however, undeniable that these two admittedly very general modes of reasoning are particularly common in early Greek thought. Their importance in the period down to Plato can be judged not only from the extent of the actual examples of such arguments and theories which we find, but also from the texts in which the philosophers and others come close to formulating the principles or assumptions on which their reasoning is based. Not only do the Eleatics and others use disjunctive 'polar' arguments a good deal, but both Parmenides (Fr. 8 11 and 15 f.) and Melissus (Fr. 7 9) ex-

---

[1] E.g. *Euthphr.* 11 e f.: if all that is holy is just, this does not imply that all that is just is holy.

pressly refer to the fact that a *choice* must be made between certain pairs of terms. Again not only do we find analogies used extensively, in practice, as a means of elucidating obscure natural phenomena, but in some, at least, of the texts which recommend 'things that are apparent' as the 'vision' of 'things that are unclear', the method which the writer has in mind is evidently based on analogy. Moreover, when we turn to Plato, the recognition of similarities and differences is, one may say, the central problem of the method of dialectic. Already in the *Phaedo* (74a), when he speaks of the theory of Recollection, he says that this proceeds 'sometimes from similars, sometimes from dissimilars': that is, Recollection is prompted by perceiving where the particulars resemble, and where they differ from, the Forms (cf. *Phdr.* 249d ff.). And then in Plato's developed dialectic, when he considers the problem of the relations between the Forms themselves rather more than the question of their relation to particulars, a preoccupation with similarities and differences may be said to persist in the two methods of Collection and Division. The nature and aims of Division (in which a choice is put between certain alternatives, usually a pair of contraries) have already been discussed at length (pp. 148 ff.). But Division is preceded in theory, if not always, it seems, in practice, by a Collection, in which the dialectician apprehends the similarities between things and sees that they partake in a common Form.[1] The job of the dialectician, then, is described in the *Phaedrus* (265de) as first 'to collect the things that are everywhere scattered about under one Form...' and then 'to be able to divide them up again according to their Forms, according to the natural articulations'.[2] Elsewhere in the

---

[1] It is difficult to say whether Collection refers only to the collection of Forms under a more general Form, or whether under this heading Plato also included the collection of particulars under a single Form, but Hackforth, *1*, pp. 142 f., decided, rightly I believe, in favour of the latter alternative.

[2] Cf. also *Phdr.* 273de: the person who knows the truth will be best at recognising the similarities between things, and the true art of speaking is said to involve dividing things up into their kinds and enclosing each thing in a single Form.

late dialogues a similar account of dialectic is given. In the *Sophist* the aim of dialectic is said to be to show 'what kinds agree with what others, and what kinds do not admit one another' (253 bc) and then the dialectician is described as the man who can discern 'clearly *one* Form everywhere extended throughout many, where each one lies apart, and *many* Forms, different from one another, embraced from without by one Form; and again *one* Form connected in a unity through many wholes, and *many* Forms, entirely marked off apart' (253 d).[1] Finally, in the *Politicus* the method is again described in similar terms: it is necessary 'first to perceive the *community* existing between the many, and then not to desist before seeing in it all the *differences* that there are among the Forms; and then having seen the manifold *dissimilarities* in the groups of many, not to be put out of countenance or stop until, bringing all the common features within a single *likeness*, one encloses them in the essence of a Form' (285 ab).

The idea that the central task of dialectic is to distinguish the essential similarities and again the essential differences between things is a point to which Plato returns again and again. Plato's main interest, we should note, is in the *material* problem of which Forms 'agree with' or 'share in' which others, rather than in the *formal* question of the relationships of similarity and difference themselves, and although in various passages he does draw attention to such points as the difference between 'similarity' and 'identity'[2] and to the distinction between the denial of a term and the assertion of its contrary (*Sph.* 257 bc), it is not until Aristotle that we find

---

[1] Translation from Cornford, 5. Whether this passage refers to two or to four procedures, and whether it refers to Forms alone (as Cornford thought) or whether the 'many' referred to in the first phrase at 253 d 6 are particulars (e.g. Runciman, 2, p. 62) are both disputed issues, but neither affects my present point, which is that the task of the dialectician is seen as that of apprehending the differences and unities between things.

[2] E.g. *R.* 476 c where the state of 'dreaming' is said to be that in which a person (whether awake or asleep) 'takes what is like something (τὸ ὅμοιόν τῳ) to be not like it, but the same (αὐτό) as what it is like', i.e. mistakes resemblance for identity.

a full exposition of the relationships of opposition and similarity.[1] The nature and significance of the contributions made by Plato and Aristotle in this department of logic have, of course, to be judged in relation to earlier uses and assumptions, but on this topic (unlike many others where we are in considerable doubt concerning the assumptions on which the logic of the Presocratic period is based) we have quite extensive evidence in the form of the theories and arguments which we reviewed and discussed earlier. Long before Aristotle the Greek language possessed quite a wide variety of terms covering the relationships of sameness, similarity, otherness, opposition and so on, although the meaning and application of some of these terms are imprecise,[2] and the richness of vocabulary referring to opposites, in particular, was not exploited to distinguish between different *modes* of opposition. But not only is there obviously no developed technical vocabulary to refer to different categories of similarity and opposition before Aristotle himself,[3] but in practice we found that the distinctions between certain categories tend to be ignored. Two types of category oversimplification seem to be particularly common in early Greek argumentation. (1) Opposites of any type tend to be taken as mutually exclusive and exhaustive alternatives: a choice is put in the form *either A or B*, when it may be that logically the possibilities *both A and B*, and *neither A nor B*, are open. (2) The relationship of similarity tends to be assimilated to that of complete identity: analogical arguments were often claimed or assumed to be demonstrative, and the possibility that two cases that are known to be alike in certain respects may be alike in *only* those

[1] See, for example, the distinction which is drawn between the different senses in which the term 'one' is used, that is of things which are one (1) 'numerically', (2) in species, (3) in genus, or (4) 'analogically' (*Metaph.* 1016b 31 ff., cf. Δ 9 and 1054a 32 ff. on 'the same' and 'like').

[2] The use of the term ὅμοιος (which may mean either 'like' or 'one and the same', e.g. *Il.* 18 329) is particularly imprecise. Cf. above, pp. 109 f. on Melissus Fr. 7 2 and Fr. 8 3 and pp. 129 ff. on Plato, *Prt.* 329 c ff.

[3] Aristotle gives technical definitions of ἀντικείμενον, ἐναντίον and ἀντίφασις but I noted above (p. 164 n. 3) the extent to which his own use of these terms departs from these technical senses.

respects is generally ignored. In both cases Aristotle pointed out where these assumptions are mistaken, showing both (*a*) under what conditions pairs of opposites of different types are, or are not, mutually exclusive and exhaustive alternatives, and (*b*) where the weakness of analogy as a mode of inference lies. But while it is obviously formally incorrect to assume that all opposites present a mutually exclusive and exhaustive choice, the difference between a contrary and a contradictory opposition is often immaterial in the context of a particular discussion, and to ignore the alternatives 'neither *A* nor *B*' and 'both *A* and *B*' may be of no practical consequence. Again while 'like' (in certain respects) clearly does not *imply* 'the same as' or 'like in other respects', experience teaches us that we may reasonably expect that things that are known to be similar at some points may well be similar at others. The effect of Aristotle's work here, then, was to show that certain modes of argument are not demonstrative: but at the same time the fact that the arguments in question are persuasive is one that he himself recognised and drew attention to, for he points out the usefulness of analogical arguments in 'rhetoric' and what is more he suggests that to put a simple choice between a pair of (inexhaustive) contraries is an effective means of securing admissions from an opponent (*SE* 174a 40 ff.).

In logic the explicit analysis of the relationships of 'same', 'like', 'other', 'different', 'contrary' and 'contradictory' that Aristotle carried out (following, in several cases, distinctions already drawn by Plato) brought to light the complexity of the relationships of 'similarity' and 'opposition' and removed some of the difficulties which had been encountered in their use in argument. But it is, of course, not only in explicit arguments that we find a certain tendency, in early Greek thought, to operate with simple, or indeed oversimplified, logical categories; a similar tendency is a striking feature of early Greek cosmological and scientific theories, for we saw how often these take one or other of two basic forms, either (1) relating or reducing phenomena to a pair or pairs of opposite principles, or (2) assimilating or likening one (unknown) object to another that was or seemed to be better known. Theories of these two general types are of course not confined to the period from the sixth to the fourth century B.C.: on the contrary, they occur very commonly not only in later Greek speculative thought, but also in Medieval and post-Renaissance philosophy and science (not excluding those of the present day). What marks out their role in Greek thought in the period down to Aristotle is, if anything, merely their relative predominance and the degree to which the earliest Greek scientists and cosmologists both used, and placed their confidence in, these two basic modes of explanation. It is clear that in the history of these two modes of explanation the work of Aristotle himself does not mark a distinct watershed, as it may be said to do in the history of logical theory. Yet we noted that certain aspects of the use of these two types of theories do come to be recognised and commented on in the course of the fifth and fourth centuries, and this is reflected in a rather more cautious, certainly a more self-conscious, use of such theories on the part of some writers at least. We described the growing awareness of the status of images in cosmological doctrines, for instance, where we remarked how Greek cosmologists became more conscious of the element of transference in their application of political or social or biological terms to the cosmos as a whole and came to appreciate that while a concrete image conveys an intuition of cosmological changes, it does not demonstrate them. Again in the history of theories based on opposites we noted that Aristotle not only calls attention to the general tendency, in his predecessors, to refer to opposites as principles, but in his own physical theory, based on the hot, the cold, the dry and the wet, he selects his opposite principles with an eye both to their *relevance* to the particular problem (tangible contraries are chosen as the principles of tangible body) and to their *economy* (four such principles are enough, but not less than four).

In conclusion we may summarise the main points at which the study of polarity and analogy throws some light on the development of logic and the nature of 'scientific method' in early Greek thought. The discovery or development of formal logic (comprising the study of propositional forms, their constituents and the relations of inference between them) is a complex question which involves a number of intricate issues. Attention is, of course, generally focused, and rightly so, on Aristotle's invention of the method of the syllogism and his detailed study of its modes in the *Prior Analytics*. But Aristotle was also responsible for clarifying and analysing certain logical relationships, particularly those of similarity and identity and the different modes of opposition, and the importance of *this* aspect of his work in logic may be judged from the material which we have considered (though it should be noted that at this point Aristotle's work is by no means entirely original, but owes a good deal to Plato especially). Here, then, is one of the branches of logic in which the fourth century sees a clear-cut advance in knowledge: but at the same time it is worth emphasising that in so far as we can determine the assumptions which underlie the use of the relationships of similarity and opposition in earlier writers, these are oversimplified rather than totally false, and the development of logic is marked, at this point, not so much by the direct denial of earlier views, as by a recognition of the need to qualify them and a greater awareness of the complexity of the problems.

No similarly clear-cut development takes place in the period we have considered in either the theory or the practice of methods of explanation. The history of the use of theories based on opposites or on analogies provides, however, a certain insight into what the early Greek theorists expected of an 'explanation' or an 'account' in science and cosmology, and once again we find that these views become more explicit in some fourth-century writers. Judged as abstract schemata, the two main types of theories which we find to be particularly common in early Greek speculative thought both have obvious

437

merits in terms of their intelligibility, their simplicity and (in the case of those based on opposites, particularly) their apparent comprehensiveness. While it is quite often the case that their theories were put forward on purely *a priori* grounds, I have been at pains to point out the empirical elements in early Greek science and the attention which many philosophers and medical writers paid to the question of the evidence supporting their accounts of natural phenomena. The appeal to an analogy with easily observable phenomena was itself often the mark of an attempt to bring empirical evidence to bear on a problem which could not be resolved by direct investigation. Several early Greek writers show their awareness of the desirability of carrying out tests in conjunction with their theories, and in practice they took some at least of the opportunities that presented themselves to carry out research and to conduct simple experiments (even if the experiments they did perform were often inconclusive). What is, however, generally lacking in science at this period, and indeed for many centuries to come, is the present-day conception of the close and special relation between theory and empirical data. This is not to say that this idea was totally foreign to Greek scientists: on the contrary the notion of banishing theories based on arbitrary assumptions from the study of medicine is clearly stated in at least one important text, in *On Ancient Medicine*. And yet I suggested that the ideal expressed in this treatise was largely impracticable, at this stage, on the majority of the topics which the early Greek scientists were investigating (such subjects as the constituent elements of man or of physical bodies as a whole, or the general causes of diseases). Thus in the Hippocratic Corpus the differences between the pathological doctrines of *On Ancient Medicine* itself and the type of theory which it attacks are less striking than their common features, and the only treatises which do not appeal to one or other schematic theory of diseases are those (like the *Epidemics*) in which no general pathological doctrine is expounded at all.

In raising the question of the nature of things, the Greeks initiated both cosmological and scientific inquiry. At different periods in the history of thought, the view has been taken that the key to progress in natural science lies in the painstaking accumulation of factual knowledge, and cosmology, by contrast, is often dismissed as so much worthless conjecture (the ancestor of the latter view, at least, is the author of *On Ancient Medicine*). But whatever the merits or defects of this type of inductivist thesis so far as twentieth-century science is concerned, a study of the origins of science among the Greeks reveals the predominant, and one may say necessary, role of abstract, schematic speculation. The Greeks asked simple-seeming, but fundamental questions about the nature, origins and constitutions of things, and the theories they proposed are, as a whole, obviously more remarkable for their abstract clarity than for the closeness of the link between theory and empirical data. But one may reflect that had the Greeks confined their attention to those problems where specific issues could be settled definitively by observation and experiment, what we know as Greek natural science would simply never have been brought into being. So far from inhibiting the growth and development of scientific thought, the two general modes of explanation we have been considering provided essential vehicles for the expression of ideas in the debates that were conducted on fundamental problems in each of the physical and biological sciences. We have outlined some of the achievements of Greek science in the period from the sixth to the fourth century: great advances were made both in the understanding of the nature of particular problems, and in the amassing of factual knowledge, and the end of the fourth century sees the beginnings of quite extensive research not only in zoology and botany, but also in some branches of what we now call physics and chemistry. But the construction of neat, comprehensive schemata remained as much a feature of fourth century science as it had been of that of the earlier period. The aims and ideals of the fourth-century scientists and philosophers were, in essentials, similar to those of the earlier theorists, while they became rather more explicit. In particular, the demand for demonstrability, a recurrent feature of much Greek speculative thought, is illustrated and expressed most vividly in Aristotle. We saw, for instance, that in his discussion of analogy in the *Organon* he was more interested in considering it from the point of view of deductive, syllogistic reasoning, than in assessing its heuristic function, its role as a source of preliminary hypotheses, and indeed throughout the *Posterior Analytics* the emphasis is on the attainment of unshakeable knowledge which rests on necessary basic truths (*APo.* 74 b 5 ff.) and demonstrates essential connections (75 b 21 ff.). And while this idea is in evident contrast with the cautious ideal of verifiability expressed in *On Ancient Medicine*, it is Aristotle who represents more closely the actual apparent aims of the majority of early Greek speculative theorists, whether philosophers or medical writers, and whether of the sixth or of the fourth century.

BIBLIOGRAPHY

The editions for the classical texts and the abbreviations used in connection with them are given in the Introduction, pp. 13f.

ACKRILL, J. L. 'Plato and the Copula: *Sophist* 251–259', *Journal of Hellenic Studies*, LXXVII, part 1 (1957), 1–6.

ANTON, J. P. *Aristotle's Theory of Contrariety* (London, 1957).

ARBER, A. 'Analogy in the History of Science', *Studies and Essays in the History of Science and Learning*, offered to G. Sarton (New York, 1947), pp. 221–33.

ARNIM, H. VON. *Stoicorum Veterum Fragmenta*, 4 vols. (Leipzig, 1905–24).

BACON, F. *Works*, collected and edited by J. Spedding, R. L. Ellis and D. D. Heath, 14 vols. (London, 1858–74).

BAILEY, C. *The Greek Atomists and Epicurus* (Oxford, 1928).

BALDRY, H. C. 'Embryological Analogies in Pre-Socratic Cosmogony', *Classical Quarterly*, XXVI (1932), 27–34.

BALME, D. M. (*1*). 'Greek Science and Mechanism. I. Aristotle on Nature and Chance', *Classical Quarterly*, XXXIII (1939), 129–38.

BALME, D. M. (*2*). 'Greek Science and Mechanism. II. The Atomists', *Classical Quarterly*, XXXV (1941), 23–8.

BALME, D. M. (*3*). 'Aristotle's Use of Differentiae in Zoology', *Aristote et les problèmes de méthode*, communications présentées au Symposium Aristotelicum 1960 (Louvain–Paris, 1961), pp. 195–212.

BALME, D. M. (*4*). 'γένος and εἶδος in Aristotle's Biology', *Classical Quarterly*, NS, XII (1962), 81–98.

BAMBROUGH, J. R. 'Plato's Political Analogies', *Philosophy, Politics and Society*, ed. P. Laslett (Oxford, 1956), pp. 98–115.

BEARE, J. I. *Greek Theories of Elementary Cognition from Alcmaeon to Aristotle* (Oxford, 1906).

BERG, G. O. *Metaphor and Comparison in the Dialogues of Plato* (Berlin, 1904).

BERGER, H. *Geschichte der wissenschaftlichen Erdkunde der Griechen*, 2nd ed. (Leipzig, 1903).

BERTHELOT, M. *Les Origines de l'alchimie* (Paris, 1885).

BEST, E. (*1*). 'The lore of the *Whare-Kohanga*. I', *Journal of the Polynesian Society*, XIV (1905), 205–15.

441

BEST, E. (2). 'The lore of the *Whare-Kohanga*. II, III, IV', *Journal of the Polynesian Society*, xv (1906), 1–26, 147–62, and 183–92.

BIGNONE, E. *L'Aristotele perduto e la formazione filosofica di Epicuro*, 2 vols. (Florence, 1936).

BLÜH, O. 'Did the Greeks Perform Experiments?', *American Journal of Physics*, xvii (1949), 384–8.

BLÜMNER, H. *Technologie und Terminologie der Gewerbe und Künste bei Griechen und Römern*, 4 vols. (Leipzig, 1875–87).

BOCHENSKI, I. M. *Ancient Formal Logic* (Amsterdam, 1951).

BONITZ, H. *Index Aristotelicus* in Bekker's Berlin edition of Aristotle, vol. v (Berlin, 1870).

BOOTH, N. B. 'Empedocles' Account of Breathing', *Journal of Hellenic Studies*, LXXX (1960), 10–15.

BOURGEY, L. (1). *Observation et expérience chez les médecins de la collection hippocratique* (Paris, 1953).

BOURGEY, L. (2). *Observation et expérience chez Aristote* (Paris, 1955).

BRAUNLICH, A. F. '"To the Right" in Homer and Attic Greek', *American Journal of Philology*, LVII (1936), 245–60.

BRÖCKER, W. 'Gorgias contra Parmenides', *Hermes*, LXXXVI (1958), 425–40.

BRUNET, P. and MIELI, A. *Histoire des sciences: Antiquité* (Paris, 1935).

BRUNSCHVICG, L. *L'Expérience humaine et la causalité physique* (1st ed. 1922), 3rd ed. (Paris, 1949).

BULTMANN, R. 'Zur Geschichte der Lichtsymbolik im Altertum', *Philologus*, XCVII (1948), 1–36.

BURNET, J. (1). *Plato's Phaedo*, edited with introduction and notes (Oxford, 1911).

BURNET, J. (2). *Essays and Addresses* (London, 1929).

BURNET, J. (3). *Early Greek Philosophy* (1st ed. 1892), 4th ed. (London, 1948).

BUX, E. 'Gorgias und Parmenides', *Hermes*, LXXVI (1941), 393–407.

CALOGERO, G. (1). *I fondamenti della logica aristotelica* (Florence, 1927).

CALOGERO, G. (2). *Studi sull'eleatismo* (Rome, 1932).

CASSIRER, E. *Logos, Dike, Kosmos in der Entwicklung der griechischen Philosophie* (Göteborg, 1941).

CHERNISS, H. (1). *Aristotle's Criticism of Presocratic Philosophy* (Baltimore, 1935).

CHERNISS, H. (2). *Aristotle's Criticism of Plato and the Academy*, vol. I (Baltimore, 1944).

CHERNISS, H. (3). 'The Characteristics and Effects of Presocratic Philosophy', *Journal of the History of Ideas*, XII (1951), 319–45.

CLAGETT, M. *Greek Science in Antiquity* (London, 1957).

COHEN, M. H. 'The Aporias in Plato's Early Dialogues', *Journal of the History of Ideas*, XXIII (1962), 163–74.

COHEN, M. R. and DRABKIN, I. E. *A Source Book in Greek Science* (1st ed. 1948), 2nd ed. (Harvard University Press, 1958).

CONGER, G. P. *Theories of Macrocosms and Microcosms in the History of Philosophy* (New York, 1922).

CORNFORD, F. M. (1). *From Religion to Philosophy* (London, 1912).

CORNFORD, F. M. (2). 'Mysticism and Science in the Pythagorean Tradition. I', *Classical Quarterly*, XVI (1922), 137–50.

CORNFORD, F. M. (3). 'Mysticism and Science in the Pythagorean Tradition. II', *Classical Quarterly*, XVII (1923), 1–12.

CORNFORD, F. M. (4). 'Anaxagoras' Theory of Matter', *Classical Quarterly*, XXIV (1930), 14–30 and 83–95.

CORNFORD, F. M. (5). *Plato's Theory of Knowledge* (London, 1935).

CORNFORD, F. M. (6). *Plato's Cosmology* (London, 1937).

CORNFORD, F. M. (7). 'Greek Natural Philosophy and Modern Science', *Background to Modern Science*, ed. J. Needham and W. Pagel (Cambridge, 1938), pp. 3–22.

CORNFORD, F. M. (8). *Plato and Parmenides* (London, 1939).

CORNFORD, F. M. (9). *The Unwritten Philosophy and Other Essays* (Cambridge, 1950).

CORNFORD, F. M. (10). *Principium Sapientiae* (Cambridge, 1952).

CUILLANDRE, J. *La Droite et la gauche dans les poèmes homériques* (Rennes, 1943).

CUSHING, F. H. (1). 'Zuñi fetiches', *2nd Annual Report of the Bureau of American Ethnology* (1880–1), 1883, pp. 3–45.

CUSHING, F. H. (2). 'Outlines of Zuñi Creation Myths', *13th Annual Report of the Bureau of American Ethnology* (1891–2), 1896, pp. 321–447.

DEICHGRÄBER, K. (1). *Die Epidemien und das Corpus Hippocraticum* (phil.-hist. Abh. Akad. Berlin, 1933).

DEICHGRÄBER, K. (2). *Hippokrates, Über Entstehung und Aufbau des menschlichen Körpers* (περὶ σαρκῶν) (Leipzig, 1935).

DEICHGRÄBER, K. (3). 'Xenophanes περὶ φύσεως', *Rheinisches Museum*, LXXXVII (1938), 1–31.

DEICHGRÄBER, K. (4). 'Die Stellung des griechischen Arztes zur Natur', *die Antike*, XV (1939), 116–38.

DICKS, D. R. 'Thales', *Classical Quarterly*, NS, IX (1959), 294–309.

DIELS, H. (1). *Doxographi Graeci* (Berlin, 1879).

BIBLIOGRAPHY

DIELS, H. (2). *Anonymi Londinensis ex Aristotelis Iatricis Menoniis et aliis medicis Eclogae*, Suppl. Aristotelicum III, 1 (Berlin, 1893).

DIELS, H. (3). *Aristotelis qui fertur de Melisso Xenophane Gorgia libellus* (phil.-hist. Abh. Akad. Berlin, 1900).

DIELS, H. (4). 'Die vermeintliche Entdeckung einer Inkunabel der griechischen Philosophie', *Deutsche Literaturzeitung*, XXXII (1911), cols. 1861–6.

DIÈS, A. *Autour de Platon*, 2 vols. (Paris, 1927).

DILLER, H. (1). 'ὄψις ἀδήλων τὰ φαινόμενα', *Hermes*, LXVII (1932), 14–42.

DILLER, H. (2). *Wanderarzt und Aitiologe* (Philologus Suppl. 26, 3, Leipzig, 1934).

DILLER, H. (3). 'Der vorphilosophische Gebrauch von κόσμος und κοσμεῖν', *Festschrift B. Snell* (Munich, 1956), pp. 47–60.

DODDS, E. R. *The Greeks and the Irrational* (University of California Press, Berkeley–Los Angeles, 1951).

DRABKIN, I. E. 'Notes on the Laws of Motion in Aristotle', *Americian Journal of Philology*, LIX (1938), 60–84.

DUCHESNE-GUILLEMIN, J. (1). *Ormazd et Ahriman, l'aventure dualiste dans l'antiquité* (Paris, 1953).

DUCHESNE-GUILLEMIN, J. (2). *La Religion de l'Iran ancien* (Paris, 1962).

DUHEM, P. *Le Système du monde: Histoire des doctrines cosmologiques de Platon à Copernic*, vols. I and II, 2nd ed. (Paris, 1954).

DÜRING, I. *Aristotle's Chemical Treatise, Meteorologica Book IV* (Göteborg, 1944).

DURKHEIM, E. *Les Formes elémentaires de la vie religieuse* (Paris, 1912).

DURKHEIM, E. and MAUSS, M. 'De quelques formes primitives de classification', *L'Année sociologique*, VI (1901–2), 1–72.

DÜRR, K. 'Moderne Darstellung der platonischen Logik', *Museum Helveticum*, II (1945), 166–94.

EDELSTEIN, L. (1). περὶ ἀέρων *und die Sammlung der hippokratischen Schriften* (Problemata, 4, Berlin, 1931).

EDELSTEIN, L. (2). 'Die Geschichte der Sektion in der Antike', *Quellen und Studien zur Geschichte der Naturwissenschaften und der Medizin*, III, 2 (1932–3), 50–106.

EDELSTEIN, L. (3). 'The Development of Greek Anatomy', *Bulletin of the Institute of the History of Medicine*, III (1935), 235–48.

EDELSTEIN, L. (4). 'The Relation of Ancient Philosophy to Medicine', *Bulletin of the History of Medicine*, XXVI (1952), 299–316.

EDELSTEIN, L. (5). 'Recent Trends in the Interpretation of Ancient Science', *Journal of the History of Ideas*, XIII (1952), 573–604.

EUCKEN, R. *Die Methode der aristotelischen Forschung* (Berlin, 1872).

EVANS-PRITCHARD, E. E. (*1*). *Witchcraft, Oracles and Magic among the Azande* (Oxford, 1937).

EVANS-PRITCHARD, E. E. (ed.) (*2*). *The Institutions of Primitive Society* (Oxford, 1954).

EVANS-PRITCHARD, E. E. (*3*). *Nuer Religion* (Oxford, 1956).

FARRINGTON, B. (*1*). *Science and Politics in the Ancient World* (London, 1939).

FARRINGTON, B. (*2*). *Greek Science* (1st ed. 2 vols. 1944–9), 2nd ed. (London, 1953).

FARRINGTON, B. (*3*). 'The Rise of Abstract Science among the Greeks', *Centaurus*, III (1953), 32–9.

FARRINGTON, B. (*4*). 'The Greeks and the Experimental Method', *Discovery*, XVIII (1957), 68–9.

FESTUGIÈRE, A. J. *Hippocrate, L'Ancienne médecine* (Études et commentaires, 4, Paris, 1948).

FINLEY, M. I. *The World of Odysseus* (New York, 1954).

FORKE, A. *The World-Conception of the Chinese* (London, 1925).

FRAENKEL, E. (*1*). *Plautinisches im Plautus* (Philol. Untersuch. 28, Berlin, 1922).

FRAENKEL, E. (*2*). *Aeschylus, Agamemnon*, 3 vols. (Oxford, 1950).

FRANK, E. *Plato und die sogenannten Pythagoreer* (Halle, 1923).

FRÄNKEL, H. (*1*). *Die homerischen Gleichnisse* (Göttingen, 1921).

FRÄNKEL, H. (*2*). 'A Thought Pattern in Heraclitus', *American Journal of Philology*, LIX (1938), 309–37.

FRÄNKEL, H. (*3*). *Wege und Formen frühgriechischen Denkens* (1st ed. 1955), 2nd ed. (Munich, 1960).

FRÄNKEL, H. (*4*). *Dichtung und Philosophie des frühen Griechentums* (1st ed. New York, 1951), 2nd ed. (Munich, 1962).

FRANKFORT, H. (*1*). *Kingship and the Gods: A Study of Ancient Near Eastern Religion as the Integration of Society and Nature* (Chicago, 1948).

FRANKFORT, H. (ed.) (*2*). *Before Philosophy* (1st ed. *The Intellectual Adventure of Ancient Man*, Chicago, 1946), 2nd ed. (London, 1949).

FREDRICH, C. *Hippokratische Untersuchungen* (Philol. Untersuch. 15) (Berlin, 1899).

FRITZ, K. VON (*1*). 'νόος and νοεῖν in the Homeric Poems', *Classical Philology*, XXXVIII (1943), 79–93.

FRITZ, K. VON (*2*). 'νοῦς, νοεῖν and their Derivatives in Pre-Socratic Philosophy (excluding Anaxagoras). I', *Classical Philology*, XL (1945), 223–42.

445

FRITZ, K. VON (*3*). 'νοῦς, νοεῖν and their Derivatives in Pre-Socratic Philosophy (excluding Anaxagoras). II', *Classical Philology*, XLI (1946), 12–34.

FRUTIGER, P. *Les Mythes de Platon* (Paris, 1930).

FURLEY, D. J. 'Empedocles and the Clepsydra', *Journal of Hellenic Studies*, LXXVII, part 1 (1957), 31–4.

GALLOP, D. 'Justice and Holiness in Plato's *Protagoras*', *Phronesis*, VI (1961), 86–93.

GIFFORD, E. W. *Miwok Moieties* (University of California Publications in American Archaeology and Ethnology, 12, 4, Berkeley, California, 1916), pp. 139–94.

GIGON, O. (*1*). *Untersuchungen zu Heraklit* (Leipzig, 1935).

GIGON, O. (*2*). 'Gorgias "Über das Nichtsein"', *Hermes*, LXXI (1936), 186–213.

GIGON, O. (*3*). *Der Ursprung der griechischen Philosophie* (Basle, 1945).

GILBERT, O. (*1*). *Die meteorologischen Theorien des griechischen Altertums* (Leipzig, 1907).

GILBERT, O. (*2*). 'Spekulation und Volksglaube in der ionischen Philosophie', *Archiv für Religionswissenschaft*, XIII (1910), 306–32.

GOHLKE, P. *Die Entstehung der aristotelischen Logik* (Berlin, 1936).

GOLDSCHMIDT, V. (*1*). *Le Paradigme dans la dialectique platonicienne* (Paris, 1947).

GOLDSCHMIDT, V. (*2*). *Les Dialogues de Platon: structure et méthode dialectique* (Paris, 1947).

GOMPERZ, H. (*1*). *Sophistik und Rhetorik* (Leipzig, 1912).

GOMPERZ, H. (*2*). 'Problems and Methods of Early Greek Science', *Journal of the History of Ideas*, IV (1943), 161–76.

GOTTSCHALK, H. B. 'The Authorship of *Meteorologica*, Book IV', *Classical Quarterly*, NS, XI (1961), 67–79.

GRANET, M. (*1*). *La Pensée chinoise* (Paris, 1934).

GRANET, M. (*2*). 'La Droite et la gauche en Chine', *Études sociologiques sur la Chine* (Paris, 1953), pp. 263–78.

GRENE, M. *A Portrait of Aristotle* (London, 1963).

GRENET, P. *Les Origines de l'analogie philosophique dans les dialogues de Platon* (Paris, 1948).

GRUBE, G. M. A. *Plato's Thought* (London, 1935).

GUTHRIE, W. K. C. (*1*). 'The Development of Aristotle's Theology. I', *Classical Quarterly*, XXVII (1933), 162–71.

GUTHRIE, W. K. C. (*2*). 'The Development of Aristotle's Theology. II', *Classical Quarterly*, XXVIII (1934), 90–8.

GUTHRIE, W. K. C. (*3*). *Aristotle, On the Heavens*, Loeb trans. (London, 1939).

GUTHRIE, W. K. C. (*4*). *The Greeks and their Gods* (London, 1950).

GUTHRIE, W. K. C. (5). 'Anaximenes and τὸ κρυσταλλοειδές', *Classical Quarterly*, NS, VI (1956), 40–4.

GUTHRIE, W. K. C. (6). *In the Beginning: Some Greek views on the origins of life and the early state of man* (London, 1957).

GUTHRIE, W. K. C. (7). 'Aristotle as a Historian of Philosophy: some Preliminaries', *Journal of Hellenic Studies*, LXXVII, part I (1957), 35–41.

GUTHRIE, W. K. C. (8). *A History of Greek Philosophy*, vol. I (Cambridge, 1962) (= '*HGP*, I').

HACKFORTH, R. (1). *Plato's Examination of Pleasure* (Cambridge, 1945).

HACKFORTH, R. (2). 'Plato's Cosmogony (*Timaeus* 27d ff.)', *Classical Quarterly*, NS, IX (1959), 17–22.

HAMELIN, O. (1). *Essai sur les éléments principaux de la représentation* (Paris, 1907).

HAMELIN, O. (2). *Le Système d'Aristote* (1st ed. 1920), 2nd ed. (Paris, 1931).

HAMMER-JENSEN, I. 'Das sogenannte IV. Buch der *Meteorologie* des Aristoteles', *Hermes*, L (1915), 113–36.

HEATH, T. L. *Aristarchus of Samos, the Ancient Copernicus* (Oxford, 1913).

HEIBERG, I. L. *Geschichte der Mathematik und Naturwissenschaften im Altertum* (Munich, 1925).

HEIDEL, W. A. (1). 'The Logic of the Pre-Socratic Philosophy', *Studies in Logical Theory*, ed. J. Dewey (Chicago, 1903), pp. 203–26.

HEIDEL, W. A. (2). 'Qualitative Change in Pre-Socratic Philosophy', *Archiv für Geschichte der Philosophie*, 19, NF 12 (1906), 333–79.

HEIDEL, W. A. (3). 'περὶ φύσεως: A Study of the Conception of Nature among the Pre-Socratics', *Proceedings of the American Academy of Arts and Sciences*, XLV (1909–10), 77–133.

HEIDEL, W. A. (4). 'On Certain Fragments of the Pre-Socratics: Critical Notes and Elucidations', *Proceedings of the American Academy of Arts and Sciences*, XLVIII (1912–13), 679–734.

HEIDEL, W. A. (5). *The Heroic Age of Science* (Baltimore, 1933).

HEIDEL, W. A. (6). *Hippocratic Medicine: its spirit and method* (New York, 1941).

HEINIMANN, F. (1). *Nomos und Physis, Herkunft und Bedeutung einer Antithese im griechischen Denken des 5. Jahrhunderts* (Basle, 1945).

HEINIMANN, F. (2). 'Eine vorplatonische Theorie von der τέχνη', *Museum Helveticum*, XVIII (1961), 105–30.

447

HERTER, H. 'Bewegung der Materie bei Platon', *Rheinisches Museum*, C (1957), 327–47.

HERTZ, R. 'La Prééminence de la main droite: étude sur la polarité religieuse' (originally published in *Revue philosophique*, LXVIII, 1909, 553–80), trans. R. and C. Needham in *Death and the Right Hand* (London, 1960), pp. 89–113 and 155–60.

HESSE, M. B. (*1*). *Forces and Fields: The concept of Action at a Distance in the history of physics* (London, 1961).

HESSE, M. B. (*2*). *Models and Analogies in Science* (London–New York, 1963).

HIRZEL, R. *Themis, Dike und Verwandtes* (Leipzig, 1907).

HÖFFDING, H. (*1*). 'On Analogy and its Philosophical Importance', *Mind*, NS, XIV (1905), 199–209.

HÖFFDING, H. (*2*). *Der Begriff der Analogie* (Leipzig, 1924).

HOFFMANN, E. *Die Sprache und die archaische Logik* (Tübingen, 1925).

HÖLSCHER, U. 'Anaximander und die Anfänge der Philosophie', *Hermes*, LXXXI (1953), 257–77 and 385–418.

HOPKINS, A. J. *Alchemy, Child of Greek Philosophy* (New York, 1934).

HORT, A. *Theophrastus, Enquiry into Plants*, Loeb trans. 2 vols. (London, 1916).

HUME, D. *A Treatise of Human Nature*, ed. A. D. Lindsay, Everyman Library, 2 vols. (London, 1911).

JACOBSEN, T. 'Mesopotamia', *Before Philosophy* (H. Frankfort, *2*), pp. 137–234.

JAEGER, W. (*1*). *Paideia: the Ideals of Greek Culture*, trans. G. Highet, 3 vols. (Oxford, 1939–45).

JAEGER, W. (*2*). *The Theology of the Early Greek Philosophers* (Gifford Lectures 1936), trans. E. S. Robinson (Oxford, 1947).

JAEGER, W. (*3*). *Aristotle: Fundamentals of the History of his Development*, trans. R. Robinson, 2nd ed. (Oxford, 1948).

JEVONS, W. S. *The Principles of Science*, 2nd ed. (London, 1877).

JOACHIM, H. H. (*1*). 'Aristotle's Conception of Chemical Combination', *Journal of Philology*, XXIX (1904), 72–86.

JOACHIM, H. H. (*2*). *Aristotle, On Coming-to-be and Passing-away*, a revised text with introduction and commentary (Oxford, 1922).

JONES, W. H. S. (*1*). *Hippocrates*, Loeb trans., 4 vols. (vol. III with E. T. Withington) (London, 1923–31).

JONES, W. H. S. (*2*). *Philosophy and Medicine in Ancient Greece* (Suppl. 8 to the Bulletin of the History of Medicine, Baltimore, 1946).

JONES, W. H. S. (*3*). *The Medical Writings of Anonymus Londinensis* (Cambridge, 1947).

KAHN, C. H. *Anaximander and the Origins of Greek Cosmology* (New York, 1960).

KAPP, E. *Greek Foundations of Traditional Logic* (New York, 1942).

KELSEN, H. *Society and Nature*, 2nd ed. (London, 1946).

KEMMER, E. *Die polare Ausdrucksweise in der griechischen Literatur* (Würzburg, 1903).

KERFERD, G. B. 'Gorgias On Nature or that which is not', *Phronesis*, I (1955), 3–25.

KERSCHENSTEINER, J. (*1*). *Platon und der Orient* (Stuttgart, 1945).

KERSCHENSTEINER, J. (*2*). *Kosmos: quellenkritische Untersuchungen zu den Vorsokratikern* (Zetemata 30, Munich, 1962).

KEYNES, J. M. *A Treatise on Probability* (London, 1921).

KIRK, G. S. (*1*). *Heraclitus: the Cosmic Fragments* (Cambridge, 1954).

KIRK, G. S. (*2*). 'Some Problems in Anaximander', *Classical Quarterly*, NS, V (1955), 21–38.

KIRK, G. S. (*3*). 'Men and Opposites in Heraclitus', *Museum Helveticum*, XIV (1957), 155–63.

KIRK, G. S. (*4*). 'Popper on Science and the Presocratics', *Mind*, NS, LXIX (1960), 318–39.

KIRK, G. S. (*5*). 'Sense and Common-Sense in the Development of Greek Philosophy', *Journal of Hellenic Studies*, LXXXI (1961), 105–17.

KIRK, G. S. and RAVEN, J. E. *The Presocratic Philosophers* (Cambridge, 1957) (= 'KR').

KNEALE, W. and KNEALE, M. *The Development of Logic* (Oxford, 1962).

KRANZ, W. (*1*). 'Gleichnis und Vergleich in der frühgriechischen Philosophie', *Hermes*, LXXIII (1938), 99–122.

KRANZ, W. (*2*). 'Kosmos und Mensch in der Vorstellung frühen Griechentums', *Nachrichten von der Gesellschaft der Wissenschaften zu Göttingen* (phil.-hist. Kl. 1, 2, 1938), pp. 121–61.

KRANZ, W. (*3*). 'Kosmos als philosophischer Begriff frühgriechischer Zeit', *Philologus*, XCIII (1938–9), 430–48.

KROEF, J. M. VAN DER. 'Dualism and Symbolic Antithesis in Indonesian Society', *American Anthropologist*, LVI (1954), 847–62.

KUCHARSKI, P. *Les Chemins du savoir dans les derniers dialogues de Platon* (Paris, 1949).

KÜHN, J.-H. *System- und Methodenprobleme im Corpus Hippocraticum* (Hermes Einzelschriften, 11, 1956).

LACEY, A. R. 'Plato's *Sophist* and the Forms', *Classical Quarterly*, NS, IX (1959), 43–52.

LANG, P. *De Speusippi Academici Scriptis* (Bonn, 1911).

LAST, H. 'Empedokles and his Klepsydra Again', *Classical Quarterly*, XVIII (1924), 169–73.

LEACH, E. R. *Rethinking Anthropology* (London, 1961).

LEAF, W. *Homer, Iliad*, 2 vols., 2nd ed. (London, 1900–2).

LE BLOND, J. M. (*1*). *Logique et méthode chez Aristote* (Paris, 1939).

LE BLOND, J. M. (*2*). *Aristote, Philosophe de la vie* (Paris, 1945).

LEE, H. D. P. (*1*). *Zeno of Elea* (Cambridge, 1936).

LEE, H. D. P. (*2*). *Aristotle, Meteorologica*, Loeb trans. (1st ed. 1952), 2nd ed. (1962).

LESKY, E. *Die Zeugungs- und Vererbungslehren der Antike und ihr Nachwirken* (Wiesbaden, 1951).

LÉVI-STRAUSS, C. (*1*). *Anthropologie structurale* (Paris, 1958).

LÉVI-STRAUSS, C. (*2*). *Le Totémisme aujourd'hui* (Paris, 1962).

LÉVI-STRAUSS, C. (*3*). *La Pensée sauvage* (Paris, 1962).

LÉVI-STRAUSS, C. (*4*). 'The Bear and the Barber', Henry Myers Memorial Lecture 1962.

LÉVY-BRUHL, L. (*1*). *How Natives Think* (*Les Fonctions mentales dans les sociétés inférieures*, Paris, 1910), trans. L. A. Clare (London, 1926).

LÉVY-BRUHL, L. (*2*). *Primitive Mentality* (*La Mentalité primitive*, Paris, 1922), trans. L. A. Clare (London, 1923).

LÉVY-BRUHL, L. (*3*). *The 'Soul' of the Primitive* (*L'Ame primitive*, Paris, 1927), trans. L. A. Clare (London, 1928).

LÉVY-BRUHL, L. (*4*). 'Les *Carnets* de Lucien Lévy-Bruhl', *Revue philosophique*, CXXXVII (1947), 257–81.

LÉVY-BRUHL, L. (*5*). 'A letter to E. E. Evans-Pritchard', *British Journal of Sociology*, III (1952), 117–23.

LIENHARDT, G. 'Modes of Thought', *The Institutions of Primitive Society* (E. E. Evans-Pritchard, *2*), pp. 95–107.

LITTRÉ, E. *Œuvres complètes d'Hippocrate*, 10 vols. (Paris, 1839–61).

LLOYD, A. C. 'Plato's Description of Division', *Classical Quarterly*, NS, II (1952), 105–12.

LOUIS, P. (*1*). *Les Métaphores de Platon* (Paris, 1945).

LOUIS, P. (*2*). 'Remarques sur la classification des animaux chez Aristote', *Autour d'Aristote*, recueil d'études...offert à M. A. Mansion (Louvain, 1955), pp. 297–304.

LUKAS, F. *Die Grundbegriffe in den Kosmogonien der alten Völker* (Leipzig, 1893).

LUKASIEWICZ, J. *Aristotle's Syllogistic from the standpoint of modern formal logic* (1st ed. 1951), 2nd ed. (Oxford, 1957).

McDiarmid, J. B. 'Theophrastus on the Presocratic Causes', *Harvard Studies in Classical Philology*, LXI (1953), 85–156.

McKeon, R. 'Aristotle's Conception of the Development and the Nature of Scientific Method', *Journal of the History of Ideas*, VIII (1947), 3–44.

Manquat, M. *Aristote naturaliste* (Paris, 1932).

Mansion, A. (*1*). *Introduction à la physique aristotélicienne* (1st ed. 1913), 2nd ed. (Louvain, 1946).

Mansion, A. (*2*). 'L'origine du syllogisme et la théorie de la science chez Aristote', *Aristote et les problèmes de méthode*, communications présentées au Symposium Aristotelicum 1960 (Louvain–Paris, 1961), pp. 57–81.

Marignac, A. de. *Imagination et dialectique* (Paris, 1951).

Masson-Oursel, P. 'La Sophistique: étude de philosophie comparée', *Revue de métaphysique et de morale*, XXIII (1916), 343–62.

Merlan, P. (*1*). 'Aristotle's Unmoved Movers', *Traditio*, IV (1946), 1–30.

Merlan, P. (*2*). 'Ambiguity in Heraclitus', *Proceedings of the 11th International Congress of Philosophy* (Brussels, 1953), vol. XII (Louvain–Amsterdam, 1953), 56–60.

Merlan, P. (*3*). *Studies in Epicurus and Aristotle* (Wiesbaden, 1960).

Meyer, A. *Wesen und Geschichte der Theorie vom Mikro- und Makrokosmos* (Berner Studien zur Philosophie und ihrer Geschichte, 25, 1900).

Meyer, J.-B. *Aristoteles Thierkunde: ein Beitrag zur Geschichte der Zoologie, Physiologie und alten Philosophie* (Berlin, 1855).

Mill, J. S. *A System of Logic*, 9th ed. (London, 1875).

Miller, H. W. '*Dynamis* and *Physis* in *On Ancient Medicine*', *Transactions and Proceedings of the American Philological Association*, LXXXIII (1952), 184–97.

Mondolfo, R. (*1*). *Problemi del pensiero antico* (Bologna, 1936).

Mondolfo, R. (*2*). *L'Infinito nel pensiero dell'antichità classica* (1st ed. *L'Infinito nel pensiero dei Greci*, 1934), 2nd ed. (Florence, 1956).

Morrison, J. S. (*1*). 'Parmenides and Er', *Journal of Hellenic Studies*, LXXV (1955), 59–68.

Morrison, J. S. (*2*). 'Pythagoras of Samos', *Classical Quarterly*, NS, VI (1956), 135–56.

Mugnier, R. (*1*). *La Théorie du premier moteur et l'évolution de la pensée aristotélicienne* (Paris, 1930).

Mugnier, R. (*2*). *Aristote, Petits traités d'histoire naturelle*, Coll. Budé (Paris, 1953).

Needham, J. *Science and Civilisation in China* (in progress) (Cambridge, 1954–).

NEEDHAM, R. (*1*). 'The Left Hand of the Mugwe', *Africa*, xxx (1960), 20–33.

NEEDHAM, R. (*2*). *Structure and Sentiment: a Test Case in Social Anthropology* (Chicago, 1962).

NESTLE, W. (*1*). 'Die Schrift des Gorgias "über die Natur oder über das Nichtseiende"', *Hermes*, LVII (1922), 551–62.

NESTLE, W. (*2*). *Vom Mythos zum Logos*, 2nd ed. (Stuttgart, 1942).

NEUBURGER, A. *The Technical Arts and Sciences of the Ancients* (*Die Technik des Altertums*), trans. H. L. Brose (London, 1930).

NEUGEBAUER, O. (*1*). 'A Table of Solstices from Uruk', *Journal of Cuneiform Studies*, I (1947), 143–8.

NEUGEBAUER, O. (*2*). *The Exact Sciences in Antiquity* (1st ed. 1952), 2nd ed. (Providence, R.I., 1957).

NILSSON, M. P. *Geschichte der griechischen Religion*, vol. I (1st ed. 1941), 2nd ed. (Munich, 1955).

NIMUENDAJU, C. *The Eastern Timbira*, translated and edited by R. H. Lowie (University of California Publications in American Archaeology and Ethnology, 41, Berkeley, California, 1946).

NUYENS, F. *L'Evolution de la psychologie d'Aristote* (Ontwikkelings-momenten in de Zielkunde van Aristoteles), trans. A. Mansion (Louvain–Paris–The Hague, 1948).

OGLE, W. *Aristotle, De Partibus Animalium*, Oxford trans. (1911).

ONIANS, R. B. *The Origins of European Thought* (Cambridge, 1951).

OWEN, G. E. L. 'Eleatic Questions', *Classical Quarterly*, NS, x (1960), 84–102.

PAGEL, W. 'Religious Motives in the Medical Biology of the XVIIth Century', *Bulletin of the Institute of the History of Medicine*, III (1935), 97–128, 213–31 and 265–312.

PATZIG, G. (*1*). Review of E. W. Platzeck, *Gnomon*, XXVII (1955), 499–507.

PATZIG, G. (*2*). *Die aristotelische Syllogistik* (phil.-hist Abh. Akad. Göttingen, 1959).

PECK, A. L. (*1*). 'Anaxagoras: predication as a problem in physics', *Classical Quarterly*, XXV (1931), 27–37 and 112–20.

PECK, A. L. (*2*). *Aristotle, Parts of Animals*, Loeb trans. (London, 1937).

PECK, A. L. (*3*). *Aristotle, Generation of Animals*, Loeb trans. (London, 1943).

PECK, A. L. (*4*). 'Plato and the ΜΕΓΙΣΤΑ ΓΕΝΗ of the *Sophist*: A Reinterpretation', *Classical Quarterly*, NS, II (1952), 32–56.

PECK, A. L. (*5*). 'Plato's *Sophist*: the συμπλοκή τῶν εἰδῶν', *Phronesis*, VII (1962), 46–66.

PIAGET, J. (*1*). *The Child's Conception of the World* (*La Représentation du monde chez l'enfant*), trans. J. and A. Tomlinson (London, 1929).

PIAGET, J. (*2*). *The Child's Conception of Physical Causality* (*La Causalité physique chez l'enfant*), trans. M. Gabain (London, 1930).

PIAGET, J. (*3*). *The Language and Thought of the Child*, trans. M. Gabain, revised ed. (London, 1959).

PICARD, J. 'Les trois modes du raisonnement analogique', *Revue Philosophique*, CIV (1927), 242–82.

PLATT, A. *Aristotle, De Generatione Animalium*, Oxford trans. (1910).

PLATZECK, E. W. *Von der Analogie zum Syllogismus* (Paderborn, 1954).

PLOCHMANN, G. K. 'Nature and the Living Thing in Aristotle's Biology', *Journal of the History of Ideas*, XIV (1953), 167–90.

POHLENZ, M. (*1*). *Hippokrates und die Begründung der wissenschaftlichen Medizin* (Berlin, 1938).

POHLENZ, M. (*2*). 'Nomos und Physis', *Hermes*, LXXXI (1953), 418–38.

POPPER, K. R. (*1*). 'Back to the Presocratics', *Proceedings of the Aristotelian Society*, NS, LIX (1958–9), 1–24.

POPPER, K. R. (*2*). *The Logic of Scientific Discovery* (*Logik der Forschung*, Vienna, 1935, with later additions), trans. J. and L. Freed (London, 1959).

PRITCHARD, J. B. (ed.). *Ancient Near Eastern Texts*, 2nd ed. (Princeton, 1955).

RANULF, S. *Der eleatische Satz vom Widerspruch* (Copenhagen, 1924).

RAVEN, J. E. *Pythagoreans and Eleatics* (Cambridge, 1948).

READ, J. (*1*). *Prelude to Chemistry* (1st ed. 1936), 2nd ed. (London, 1939).

READ, J. (*2*). *Through Alchemy to Chemistry* (London, 1957).

REGENBOGEN, O. *Eine Forschungsmethode antiker Naturwissenschaft* (Quellen und Studien zur Geschichte der Mathematik, Astronomie und Physik, B 1, 2, Berlin, 1930–1), pp. 131–82.

REHM, A. 'Zur Rolle der Technik in der griechisch-römischen Antike', *Archiv für Kulturgeschichte*, XXVIII (1938), 135–62.

REINHARDT, K. (*1*). *Parmenides und die Geschichte der griechischen Philosophie* (Bonn, 1916).

REINHARDT, K. (*2*). *Kosmos und Sympathie* (Munich, 1926).

REY, A. *La Science dans l'antiquité*, 5 vols. (Paris, 1930–48).

REYMOND, A. *Histoire des sciences exactes et naturelles dans l'antiquité gréco-romaine* (1st ed. 1924), 2nd ed. (Paris, 1955).

RIEZLER, K. 'Das homerische Gleichnis und der Anfang der Philosophie', *die Antike*, XII (1936), 253–71.

RIVIER, A. *Un Emploi archaïque de l'analogie* (Lausanne, 1952).

ROBIN, L. *Greek Thought* (*La Pensée grecque*), trans. M. R. Dobie (London, 1928).

ROBINSON, R. (*1*). 'Plato's Consciousness of Fallacy', *Mind*, NS, LI (1942), 97–114.

ROBINSON, R. (*2*). *Plato's Earlier Dialectic* (1st ed. 1941), 2nd ed. (Oxford, 1953).

ROSCHER, W. H. *Die hippokratische Schrift von der Siebenzahl in ihrer vierfachen Überlieferung* (Paderborn, 1913).

ROSS, W. D. (*1*). *Aristotle, Metaphysics*, a revised text with introduction and commentary, 2 vols. (Oxford, 1924).

ROSS, W. D. (*2*). *Aristotle's Physics*, a revised text with introduction and commentary (Oxford, 1936).

ROSS, W. D. (*3*). 'The Discovery of the Syllogism', *Philosophical Review*, XLVIII (1939), 251–72.

ROSS, W. D. (*4*). *Aristotle's Prior and Posterior Analytics*, a revised text with introduction and commentary (Oxford, 1949).

ROSS, W. D. (*5*). *Aristotle, Parva Naturalia*, a revised text with introduction and commentary (Oxford, 1955).

ROSS, W. D. (*6*). *Aristotle, De Anima*, edited with introduction and commentary (Oxford, 1961).

ROTHSCHUH, K. E. 'Idee und Methode in ihrer Bedeutung für die geschichtliche Entwicklung der Physiologie', *Sudhoff's Archiv für Geschichte der Medizin und der Naturwissenschaften*, XLVI (1962), 97–119.

RUNCIMAN, W. G. (*1*). 'Plato's *Parmenides*', *Harvard Studies in Classical Philology*, LXIV (1959), 89–120.

RUNCIMAN, W. G. (*2*). *Plato's Later Epistemology* (Cambridge, 1962).

SAMBURSKY, S. (*1*). *The Physical World of the Greeks*, trans. M. Dagut (London, 1956).

SAMBURSKY, S. (*2*). *Physics of the Stoics* (London, 1959).

SAMBURSKY, S. (*3*). *The Physical World of Late Antiquity* (London, 1962).

SCHUHL, P. M. *Essai sur la formation de la pensée grecque* (1st ed. 1934), 2nd ed. (Paris, 1949).

SEGAL, C. P. 'Gorgias and the Psychology of the Logos', *Harvard Studies in Classical Philology*, LXVI (1962), 99–155.

SENN, G. (*1*). 'Über Herkunft und Stil der Beschreibungen von Experimenten im Corpus Hippocraticum', *Sudhoff's Archiv für Geschichte der Medizin*, XXII (1929), 217–89.

SENN, G. (*2*). *Die Entwicklung der biologischen Forschungsmethode in der Antike und ihre grundsätzliche Förderung durch Theophrast von Eresos* (Veröffentlichungen der Schweizerischen Gesellschaft für Geschichte der Medizin und der Naturwissenschaften, 8, Aarau–Leipzig, 1933).

SHOREY, P. (*1*). 'The Origin of the Syllogism', *Classical Philology*, XIX (1924), 1–19.

SHOREY, P. (*2*). 'The Origin of the Syllogism Again', *Classical Philology*, XXVIII (1933), 199–204.

SINGER, C. *Greek Biology and Greek Medicine* (Oxford, 1922).

SKEMP, J. B. (*1*). *The Theory of Motion in Plato's Later Dialogues* (Cambridge, 1942).

SKEMP, J. B. (*2*). *Plato's Statesman* (London, 1952).

SNELL, B. (*1*). *Die Ausdrücke für den Begriff des Wissens in der vorplatonischen Philosophie* (Philol. Untersuch. 29, Berlin, 1924).

SNELL, B. (*2*). 'Die Sprache Heraklits', *Hermes*, LXI (1926), 353–81.

SNELL, B. (*3*). *The Discovery of the Mind* (*Die Entdeckung des Geistes*, 2nd ed. Hamburg, 1948), trans. T. G. Rosenmeyer (Oxford, 1953).

SOLMSEN, F. (*1*). *Die Entwicklung der aristotelischen Logik und Rhetorik* (Neue Philol. Untersuch. 4, Berlin, 1929).

SOLMSEN, F. (*2*). 'The Discovery of the Syllogism', *Philosophical Review*, L (1941), 410–21.

SOLMSEN, F. (*3*). 'Aristotle's Syllogism and its Platonic Background', *Philosophical Review*, LX (1951), 563–71.

SOLMSEN, F. (*4*). 'Aristotle and Presocratic Cosmogony', *Harvard Studies in Classical Philology*, LXIII (1958), 265–82.

SOLMSEN, F. (*5*). *Aristotle's System of the Physical World* (Cornell, 1960).

SOUILHÉ, J. *Étude sur le terme* δύναμις *dans les dialogues de Platon* (Paris, 1919).

SPRAGUE, R. K. *Plato's Use of Fallacy* (London, 1962).

STEBBING, L. S. *A Modern Introduction to Logic* (1st ed. 1930), 2nd ed. (London, 1933).

STELLA, L. A. 'Importanza di Alcmeone nella storia del pensiero greco', *Reale Accademia dei Lincei*, Memorie, ser. 6, vol. VIII, 4 (1938–9), 233–87.

STENZEL, J. (*1*). 'Über den Einfluss der griechischen Sprache auf die philosophische Begriffsbildung', *Neue Jahrbücher für das klassische Altertum, Geschichte und deutsche Literatur*, XLVII (1921), 152–64.

STENZEL, J. (*2*). 'Speusippos', *Pauly–Wissowa Real-Encyclopädie der classischen Altertumswissenschaft*, Bd IIIA (Stuttgart, 1929), cols. 1636–69.

STENZEL, J. (*3*). *Plato's Method of Dialectic* (*Die Entwicklung der platonischen Dialektik*, Leipzig, 1931), trans. D. J. Allan (Oxford, 1940).

STOCKS, J. L. (*1*). *Aristotle, De Caelo*, Oxford trans. (1922).

STOCKS, J. L. (*2*). 'The Composition of Aristotle's Logical Works', *Classical Quarterly*, XXVII (1933), 115–24.

STOKES, M. C. (*1*). 'Hesiodic and Milesian Cosmogonies. I', *Phronesis*, VII (1962), 1–37.

STOKES, M. C. (*2*). 'Hesiodic and Milesian Cosmogonies. II', *Phronesis*, VIII (1963), 1–34.

STRYCKER, E. DE. 'Le Syllogisme chez Platon', *Revue néo-scolastique de philosophie*, XXXIV (1932), 42–56 and 218–39.

SULLIVAN, J. P. 'The Hedonism in Plato's *Protagoras*', *Phronesis*, VI (1961), 10–28.

SZABÓ, Á. (*1*). 'Beiträge zur Geschichte der griechischen Dialektik', *Acta Antiqua Academiae Scientiarum Hungaricae*, I (1951–2), 377–406.

SZABÓ, Á. (*2*). 'Zur Geschichte der Dialektik des Denkens', *Acta Antiqua Academiae Scientiarum Hungaricae*, II (1954), 17–57.

SZABÓ, Á. (*3*). 'Zum Verständnis der Eleaten', *Acta Antiqua Academiae Scientiarum Hungaricae*, II (1954), 243–86.

SZABÓ, Á. (*4*). 'Eleatica', *Acta Antiqua Academiae Scientiarum Hungaricae*, III (1955), 67–102.

TAILLARDAT, J. 'Le sens d' "amorgos" (Empédocle, Fr. 84 Diels) et les lanternes dans l'antiquité', *Revue des études grecques*, LXXII (1959), xi–xii.

TANNERY, P. *Pour l'histoire de la science hellène* (1st ed. 1887), 2nd ed. (Paris, 1930).

TARRANT, D. 'Greek Metaphors of Light', *Classical Quarterly*, NS, X (1960), 181–7.

TAYLOR, A. E. *A Commentary on Plato's Timaeus* (Oxford, 1928).

THOMPSON, D'A. W. (*1*). *Aristotle, Historia Animalium*, Oxford trans. (1910).

THOMPSON, D'A. W. (*2*). 'Aristotle the Naturalist', *Science and the Classics* (London, 1940), pp. 37–78.

THOMSON, J. A. *Heredity*, 1st ed. (London, 1908).

TIMPANARO CARDINI, M. 'Respirazione e Clessidra', *La Parola del Passato*, XII (1957), 250–70.

TREVASKIS, J. R. 'Classification in the *Philebus*', *Phronesis*, V (1960), 39–44.

UNTERSTEINER, M. *The Sophists* (*I sofisti*), trans. K. Freeman (Oxford, 1954).

USENER, M. *Epicurea* (Leipzig, 1887).

VANHOUTTE, M. *La Méthode ontologique de Platon* (Louvain–Paris, 1956).

VLASTOS, G. (*1*). 'The Disorderly Motion in the *Timaios*', *Classical Quarterly*, XXXIII (1939), 71–83.

VLASTOS, G. (*2*). 'Equality and Justice in Early Greek Cosmologies', *Classical Philology*, XLII (1947), 156–78.

VLASTOS, G. (*3*). 'The Physical Theory of Anaxagoras', *Philosophical Review*, LIX (1950), 31–57.

VLASTOS, G. (*4*). 'Theology and Philosophy in Early Greek Thought', *Philosophical Quarterly*, II (1952), 97–123.

VLASTOS, G. (*5*). 'Isonomia', *American Journal of Philology*, LXXIV (1953), 337–66.

VLASTOS, G. (*6*). 'On Heraclitus', *American Journal of Philology*, LXXVI (1955), 337–68.

VLASTOS, G. (*7*). Review of F. M. Cornford (*10*), *Gnomon*, XXVII (1955), 65–76.

WAERDEN, B. L. VAN DER. *Science Awakening*, trans. A. Dresden (Groningen, 1954).

WEBSTER, T. B. L. (*1*). 'Personification as a Mode of Greek Thought', *Journal of the Warburg and Courtauld Institutes*, XVII (1954), 10–21.

WEBSTER, T. B. L. (*2*). 'From Primitive to Modern Thought in Ancient Greece', *Acta Congressus Madvigiani*, II (Copenhagen, 1958), 29–43.

WEBSTER, T. B. L. (*3*). *Greek Art and Literature 700–530 B.C.* (London, 1959).

WEIL, E. 'La Place de la logique dans la pensée aristotélicienne', *Revue de métaphysique et de morale*, LVI (1951), 283–315.

WELLMANN, M. *Die Fragmente der sikelischen Ärzte Akron, Philistion und des Diokles von Karystos* (Berlin, 1901).

WIGHTMAN, W. P. D. *The Growth of Scientific Ideas* (Edinburgh–London, 1950).

WILAMOWITZ-MOELLENDORFF, U. VON. *Euripides, Herakles* (1st ed.), 2 vols. (Berlin, 1889).

WILSON, J. A. 'Egypt', *Before Philosophy* (H. Frankfort, *2*), pp. 39–133.

WOLFSON, H. A. 'The Plurality of Immovable Movers in Aristotle and Averroes', *Harvard Studies in Classical Philology*, LXIII (1958), 233–53.

ZELLER, E. and MONDOLFO, R. *La Filosofia dei Greci nel suo sviluppo storico* (*Die Philosophie der Griechen*, translated, edited and enlarged by R. Mondolfo), part I, vols. I, II, IV (Florence, 1932–61).

ZILSEL, E. 'The Genesis of the Concept of Physical Law', *Philosophical Review*, LI (1942), 245–79.

ZUBOV, V. P. 'Beobachtung und Experiment in der antiken Wissenschaft', *das Altertum*, V (1959), 223–32.

INDEX OF PASSAGES QUOTED
OR REFERRED TO

459

INDEX OF PASSAGES

ARIUS DIDYMUS
ap. Eus. *PE* xv (15, 817 d), 416 n.

CENSORINUS
de die nat. (4, 7), 323 n. 1; (6, 3), 324 n.

CHALCIDIUS
in Ti. (p. 256 Waszink), 323

CHRYSIPPUS
ap. D.L. vii (142–3), 416 n.

CICERO
de nat. deor. ii (15, 42), 259 n. 2; (16, 44), 259
Tusc. Disp. i (6, 13), 114 n. 2

CLEANTHES
Hymn to Zeus, 416 n.
ap. Hermias *Irris. Gent. Phil.* (14), 416 n.

DEMOCRITUS
fr. (11), 123 n. 2, 338 n. 2; (125), 18, 123 n. 2, 248; (148), 337 n. 1, 340 n. 2; (164), 250 n. 3, 270–1, 340; (167), 250 n. 1; (278), 250 n. 3

DIODORUS
i (7, 3), 57 n. 3

DIOGENES OF APOLLONIA
fr. (1), 231 n. 2; (3), 225, 292; (5), 18 n. 3, 219–20, 250 nn. 2–3, 251, 273–4, 291–2; (7), 251; (8), 219, 251

DIOGENES LAERTIUS
i (24), 239 n.
ii (1), 427 n. 1; (12), 267 n. 2
vii (134), 416 n.; (137), 416 n.; (142–3), 416 n.
viii (34), 49 n. 3; (63–7), 222; (72), 222
ix (6), 222; (9–10), 321–2; (31–2), 249 n. 2, 250 n. 1, 270 n. 2; (44), 250 n. 1

EMPEDOCLES
fr. (2), 337 n. 2; (3), 337 n. 2; (8), 241 n. 3, 243; (9), 241 n. 3, 243; (11), 106 n.; (12), 106 n., 423; (13) 106 n.; (14), 106 n.; (17), 217–18, 227–8, 241 n. 3, 242–3, 251, 275 and n. 2, 299–301; (21) 242 n. 2, 251, 426; (22), 242 n. 2; (23), 335 n. 1; (26), 16, 217 n., 241 n. 3; (27), 63 n., 211 n. 1; (27a), 63 n.; (28), 211 n. 1; (29), 211 n. 1, 255 n. 4; (30), 218 and n. 2, 224, 228, 300; (33), 189 n. 1, 335 n. 1; (34), 274, 278; (35), 275 n. 2; (53), 275 n. 2; (55), 334, 363, 403; (56), 275 n. 1; (59), 275 n. 2; (62), 270; (64), 242; (65), 17 n. 4, 58 n.; (67), 17 n. 4, 58 n.; (68), 335; (73), 274, 278, 301, 335 n. 1; (75), 275 n. 1, 301; (79), 335; (81), 335 n. 2; (82), 335–6, 365; (84), 325–7, 331, 333, 344, 403 n. 2; (86), 275 and nn. 1 and 2;

471

GENERAL INDEX

above/below, 52–3, 64

Academy, use of method of division in, 150, 153–5, 158, 160

acid, 70, 278 n. 2, 339–40, 355

acoustics, Pythagorean experiments in, 428 and n. 3

ἀήρ (air-mist), in Anaximander, 16, 44 n. 1, 309, 312; in Anaximenes, 233, 235–6, 239, 254 n. 2, 317–19; in Empedocles, 16, 217; in the Atomists, 248 n. 1; in Diogenes of Apollonia, 219, 225, 250 n. 2, 251, 292, 298; in *On Breaths*, 216 n. 1; hot and wet in *On Fleshes*, 19 n. 2; cold in Philistion, 19 n. 2; in Plato, 217, 360–1; hot and wet in Aristotle, 25; in Aristotle's account of rivers, 362

Aetius, as source for Anaximenes' theories, 235 and n. 3, 315 and n. 2, 317 n. 1; on Parmenides' *Way of Seeming*, 217, 322

a fortiori, arguments, 386 and n.

agriculture, ideas derived from, 278, 286

αἰθήρ, 19 n. 2, 47 n. 1, 57, 205; Aristotle's doctrine of, 259–60, 268–9

air, *see* ἀήρ, αἰθήρ, πνεῦμα

αἴτιον, senses of, 230–1

alchemical writings, theories of opposites in, 84–5

Alcmaeon, doctrine of opposites, 16, 36; pathology, 20; biological theories, 322–5; use of dissection, 323, 427

allegory, in Homer, 201 and n. 3

alternative questions, 93–4, 127–8, 134–7, 141, 157

ambidexterity, 55 n. 3

ambiguity: of hot and cold, 60; Heraclitus' exploitation of, 101–2; Aristotle on the detection of, 404 n. 3

Amboyna, 32–3

anamnesis, *see* recollection

Anaxagoras, 224 n., 267 n. 2, idea of logical impossibility in, 424
  biology: theory of differentiation of sexes, 17, 50
  cosmology and physics: opposites in, 16, 57, 81 n., 244 and n. 2; aither, earth and water in, 16, 57, 245 n. 2; seeds in, 243–7, 251, 300; doctrine of whirl, 250 and n. 1; like to like, 270; corporeality of air, 332 n. 1, 339; on the moon, 339, 381; on the rainbow, 339 n. 3
  doctrine of mind, 219–21, 225, 244, 246, 250–1, 298
  ὄψις ἀδήλων τὰ φαινόμενα, 338–9, 341, 343, 353

Anaximander, doctrine of the Boundless, 16, 212–13, 231 n. 2, 233, 234–5, 239, 273; opposites in, 16, 44 n. 1; on origin of living things, 57 n. 3, 323 n. 1; idea of justice and retribution in, 212–13; account of

476

Democritus (*cont.*)

    dictum, ὄψις ἀδήλων τὰ φαινόμενα, 338–41; on winds, 340; *see also* Atomists

design, element of, in cosmological theories, 276–7, 288–92, 416 and n.

dialectic: Plato's method of, 1, 432–3; Plato's distinction between controversy and dialectic, 141; Aristotle's distinction between dialectical and apodeictic reasoning, 410

diaphragm, 53 n. 1, 286 n. 6

Dicks, D. R., 233 n. 1, 308 n. 2

Diels, H., 253 n. 1, 313, 314 n. 1, 329

diet, analysed into opposites, 21–2, 58

δίκη, senses of, 215, 216 n. 2; *see also* justice

Diller, H., 306 n. 1

Diogenes of Apollonia, 224 n.; doctrine of air, 18 n. 3, 219–21, 225, 250 n. 2, 251, 292, 298; doctrine of soul, 250 n. 3; account of Nile, 337 n. 1

Dioscuri, 319 n.

diseases, Homeric description of origin of, 206–7; connected with Pandora, 42; personified in Hesiod, 207 n. 2, 298; Alcmaeon on, 20, 216 n. 1; Hippocratic theories of, 20–3, 69–70, 345–7, 350–1; Plato on, 24 n. 1; Aristotle on, 26

dissection, use of, 73–4, 323, 327, 333, 352 n., 427

divination, methods of, 47 n. 2, 181–2

division, method of, in Plato, 148–52, 432–3; in Academy, 153–5, 158; criticised by Aristotle, 154–6, 158–61; recommended by Aristotle in defining, 156–8

dreams, Aristotle on, 374–5; dreamlike, contrasted with waking, knowledge, by Plato, 399–400

dropsy, 350 n. 2

dry and wet, 28–30, 43–6; in Anaximander's account of the origin of living things, 323 n. 1, in Heraclitus, 44 n. 1, 98, 101 n. 1, 214; in Alcmaeon, 20, 216 n. 1; in Parmenides, 57; in Anaxagoras, 16, 57, 244; in Diogenes of Apollonia, 18 n. 3

    in *On the Nature of Man*, 19–20, 44, 71 n. 1, 74; in *On Fleshes*, 19 n. 2, 57 n. 3, 76; in *On Regimen* 1, 20, 57 n. 3, 58–9, 60 n. 1; in *On Ancient Medicine*, 20–1, 69–70, 82; in *On Affections*, 20–1; in Petron, 19 n. 2; in Philistion, 19 n. 2

    in Aristotle's physical theory, 25–6, 61–2, 64 and nn. 1–2, 76–8, 79 n., 85; Aristotle's definition of, 60

δύναμις: senses of, 230; in Aetius' description of Alcmaeon's pathological theory, 20, 216 n. 1; in Parmenides, 217; in *On Ancient Medicine*, 70, 355–6; in Philistion, 19 n. 2; in Aristotle, 230, 365

Durkheim, E., 4–5, 28, 29 n. 1, 36–8

dynamics, development of, 270–2

Earth
   antithesis between earth and sky in Greek religion, 41–2, 46, 48; in cosmogonical myths, 47 n. 1, 81, 85; in Hesiod's *Theogony*, 204–5, 205 n.; in Empedocles' *Purifications*, 63 n.; in Plato, 49
   earth as constituent substance: in Xenophanes, 81; in Heraclitus, 237; in Parmenides, according to Aristotle, 63 n.; in Empedocles, 16, 217, 243; question of the status of earth in Anaxagoras' physical theory, 16, 57, 245 and nn. 1–2; in *On Fleshes*, 19 n. 2; in Philistion, 19 n. 2; in Plato, 361; in Aristotle, 25, 61, 77, 371
   accounts of the earth's position in space: Thales, 306–9; Anaximander, 309–12; Anaximenes, 317–19; Empedocles, 334
   Aristotle's theory that the earth is subject to cycles of growth and decay, 263, 362–4
earthenware, 367 n.
earthquakes, attributed to Poseidon, in Homer, 203 and n. 3; Thales' account of, 308–9, 318; Aristotle on, 362
east/west, 40, 89; in Greek divination, 47 and n. 2
eclipses, Anaximander's account of, 314–15; Heraclitus' account of, 321–2
eddies, comparisons with, in Aristotle's account of redundant embryonic growths, 370–1; in Aristotle's account of sensation, 374–5
efficient, or moving, cause: idea of, emerges in Presocratic cosmology, 250–1, 275; Aristotle's doctrine of, 24, 291, 302
egg, Alcmaeon and Aristotle on which part of the egg serves as nutriment, 324, 404; investigation of the growth of a hen's egg, in *On the Nature of the Child*, 352 n.; in Aristotle, 379 n.; Aristotle on the growth of fishes' eggs, 368; on the reason why eggs go rotten, 371
Egyptian thought and mythology, 29 n. 3, 34 n. 4, 202 n. 2, 211, 272 n. 2, 307 and n. 1, 322 and n. 2; length of Egyptian year, 186 n. 2; Egyptian astronomy, 269 n. 2
embryology, 17, 50–1, 73–4, 310, 323–4, 346–8, 350–2, 368–70, 427
Empedocles, assessment of the value of the senses, 337; idea of impossibility in, 423–4
   biology: on differentiation of the sexes, 17 and n. 4, 58; on water-animals, 18, 71; on constitution of bone, flesh and blood, 243; on formation of living creatures and their parts, 274–5, 275 n. 2; theory of the functioning of the eye, 325–7; theory of respiration, 328–33; on the sterility of mules, 334–5; on milk, 335; comparisons between the parts of different species of animals and plants, 335–6, 365
   cosmology and physics: doctrine of four roots, 16, 217, 243, 301; doctrine of Love and Strife, 16, 63 n., 82, 213–14, 214 n. 1, 275 n. 2;

483

fig-juice, Aristotle's account of, 77; comparisons referring to, 189 n. 1, 335 n. 1, 346–7, 369–70

Finley, M. I., 195 nn. 1 and 3, 208 n.

fire, connected with Hephaestus, 199–200

as constituent substance, in Heraclitus, 100, 215, 236–7, 239, 273, 301; in Parmenides, 16, 57, 63 n.; in Empedocles, 16, 217, 243; in *On Regimen* 1, 19–20, 57 n. 3, 58–9, 60 n. 1, 252; in Plato, 361; in Aristotle, 25

Plato on the Form of, 132–3

referred to, in comparisons, in connection with physiological and psychological theories, in Aristotle, 372–3, 375

fish, in Anaximander's theory of the origin of men, 323 n. 1; in Aristotle's classification of animals, 62, 160 and n. 1; do not respire, according to Aristotle, 373

fish-trap, in Plato's account of respiration, 360 and n.

flesh, Empedocles on, 243, 274; Anaxagoras on, 244, 246–7; *On Diseases of Women* 1, on difference between men's and women's, 349; Plato on formation of, 278 n. 2; Plato, on the lack of, round the brain, 283 n. 1

Fraenkel, E., 189

Fränkel, H., 187

Frankfort, H., 201 n. 2

front/back, 52–3, 55 n. 2, 64

fruit, 59 n. 1, 335, 347–8

Furley, D. J., 328–32

Galen, 17 nn. 3–4, 50 n. 2

Geb, Egyptian myth of, 307 and n. 3

Gifford, E. W., 34

gifts, obligations created by giving and receiving, 196 and n. 2

Gigon, O., 118 n. 2

gnomon, 427

gods, 91, 92 n. 2; similes to describe, 187–8; Olympian gods as society, 194, 196–200, 209, 210; connected with natural phenomena, in Homer, 194, 199–200, 203; human characteristics of, 195 and nn. 1 and 4; relationship of other gods with Zeus, 197–9

in Greek philosophy: Thales, 233–4, 254 n. 1, Xenophanes, 92 n. 2, 219, 273 n. 3; Heraclitus, 96 n., 100, 215 n. 3, 273 n. 3; Diogenes of Apollonia, 250 n. 2, 251; Plato, 255 n. 2, 257 n., 276–9, 282–3; Aristotle, 259–61

see also mortal/immortal

Goldschmidt, V., 394 n. 2

Hippocratic Corpus (*cont.*)

350 and n. 2; theory of nutrition, 347; on the movement of the humours between the different sources of the body, 350–1

On the Diseases in Women I, on the difference in temperature between the sexes, 58; on the difference between men's flesh, and women's, 349

On the Eight Month Child, embryological theory, 347

Epidemics, theory of critical days, 22; puts forward no general pathological theory, 438

On Fleshes, heart as the source of the veins, 10 n. 2; element theory, 19 n. 2, 76; on connection between humidity and vital heat, 57 n. 3; on nutrition of the embryo, 324 n.; carries out tests with blood in connection with theory of formation of parts of the body, 352 n., 358 n. 3, 428

On Generation, on differentiation of the sexes, 17 n. 5, 350; embryological theories, 348

On the Heart, heart as the source of the veins, 10 n. 2; use of dissection and vivisection, 352 n.

On Humours, on the function of the stomach, 367 n.

On the Nature of the Child, on the development of the embryo, 346, 348 and n. 2; on respiration in the womb, 348 n. 2, 358; on the secretion of milk, 350; on growth, 351; investigation of the growth of a hen's egg, 352 n.

On the Nature of Man, cosmological theory based on opposites, 19, 252 n. 1; pathological theory, 20–1; analysis of seasons, 44; analysis of four humours, 71 n. 1, 74; uses tests with drugs to support theory of four humours, 74–5, 79, 347; microcosm and macrocosm analogy in, 252 n. 1

On the Places in Man, pathological theory, 20–1

Prognostic, right and left in, 23

On Regimen I–III, cosmological theory, 19–20; analysis of diet, 21; theory of generation, 57 n. 3; on differences between the two sexes, 58–9; on differences between the four ages of man, 60 n. 1; microcosm and macrocosm analogy in, 252; analogies between nature and art in, 353–4

On the Sacred Disease, theory of North and South winds, 22, 348 n. 2; right and left in, 22–3

On Sevens, microcosm and macrocosm analogy in, 253 and n. 2

On the Seventh Month Child, embryological theory, 347

On Superfetation, theory of differentiation of the sexes, 50

homeopathic magical practices, non-Greek, 178–9; Greek, 180–1

Homer, religious polarity in, 42–8, 62; scepticism about religious beliefs expressed in, 67–8; polar expressions used by, 90–4; terms for oppo-

Homer (*cont.*)

sites, 126 n. 2; as evidence for magical practices, 181; as evidence for methods of divination, 181–2; use of similes, 183–92; conception of fate, 192–3, 198 and n.; conception of gods, 193–209, 213, 225, 297–8; conception of sleep, 202; of lightning and thunder, 202; personification in, 202–3; conception of diseases, 206–7; interest in contemporary technology, 208; use of arguments from analogy, 384–8; notion of probability in, 424; appeals to evidence in, 425–6; refers to certain limitations to human knowledge, 425–6; criticised by Herodotus and Thucydides, 427 and n. 2

Homeric scholars, Aristotle on, 404

Homeric society, 194–8, 208–9, 223, 292

homology, principle of, 335–6, 365

Hopkins, A. J., 84 nn. 1 and 3

Hort, A., 311 n. 2

hot and cold, relevance of climate to theories based on, 28–30; origins of theories based on, in Greek philosophy, 43–6; disagreements about, 60–1; applicability of theory based on, to physical objects, 80–1

in Anaximander, 16, 44 n. 1, 57 n. 3, 235, 309; Anaximenes on, 68; in Heraclitus, 44 n. 1, 98, 101 n. 1, 214; in Alcmaeon, 20, 216 n. 1; in Parmenides, 57, 58; in Empedocles, 17, 58, 71; in Anaxagoras, 16, 57, 244; in Diogenes of Apollonia, 18 n. 3

in Hippocratic pathological theories, 20–2; criticised in *On Ancient Medicine*, 20–1, 69–70, 82, 354; in *On Fleshes*, 19 n. 2, 57 n. 3, 76, 352 n.; in *On the Nature of Man*, 19, 20, 44, 71 n. 1, 74; in *On Regimen* I, 20, 57 n. 3, 58–9, 60 n. 1; in Philolaus, 19 n. 2, 71, 238 n. 2; in Petron, 19 n. 2; in Philistion, 19 n. 2

in Aristotle's general physical theory, 25, 64, 76–8, 79 n., 85, 289; in Aristotle's biology, 25–6, 53 n. 3, 59, 60–1, 368–9, 371–4; Aristotle defines, 60; in Aristotle's classification of animals, 61–2

Hume, D., 172–3

humours, in theories of diseases, 20, 346–7, 350; debate on which are hot and which cold, 71; as constituent substances in the body, 74–5, 252 n. 1, 347, 350–1; Democritus derives from differences in the shapes of atoms, 339–40

ὑπόθεσις, *On Ancient Medicine* attacks theories based on ὑποθέσεις in medicine, 69–70, 79, 82, 438–40

impossibility, development of idea of logical, 423–4

inanimate objects, various attitudes towards, in early Greek literature, 200–2; distinction between animate and inanimate objects in Greek philosophy, 240, 250 and n. 3, 258, 263 and n. 3, 270–1, 299, 415

induction, and analogy, 172–5; and paradigm, in Aristotle, 406–8; Aristotle on complete or perfect induction, 408, 410–11

intermediates, between opposites, 87, 93, 95–6, 130, 147–8, 162–3

Jacobsen, T., 194 and n.
Java, 34
Jevons, W. S., 172
Joachim, H. H., 153 n. 3
Jones, W. H. S., 22 n. 1, 23
justice, notion of, in early Greek cosmologies, 212–19, 224–6; *see also* δίκη

Kahn, C. H., 236 n. 2
Kemmer, E., 90 n.
Kerferd, G. B., 114 n. 2, 117 n., 118 n. 1
kettle, comparisons referring to, in *On Breaths*, 345–6
Keynes, J. M., 173–5, 179 and n. 2, 357 n.
Khnum, creator-god in Egyptian mythology, 272 n. 2
kidneys, Aristotle on position of, 53 and n. 1
kinship, obligations created by, 196 and n. 2, 197
Kirk, G. S., 11, 96 n., 97 nn. 1–2, 98 n. 2, 99 n. 2, 100 n., 201 n. 1, 205 n., 212, 214, 231 n. 2, 233 n. 1, 234 and n. 2, 235 nn. 3–4, 236 n. 2, 237, 310 n. 1, 313 n., 314, 317 n. 1, 318, 323 n. 1
knowledge, opposed to supposition, in Gorgias, 120–1; based on reason or sensation, 122–3; opposed to true opinion, in Plato, 132–3; idea of limitations of human knowledge, in Greek philosophy, 337–8; distinguished from mere opinion, in Greek philosophy, 425
κόσμος, senses of, 215 and n. 2, 221, 226
Kranz, W., 253 n. 1, 306 n. 1
Kroef, J. M. van der, 32–4, 41

land-animals, division of animals into land and water-animals, 154 and n. 2, 155 n. 1
language, theories of, 124–5
lantern, in Empedocles' account of the eye, 325–7, 356–7
Laplace, 175 n. 2
law, idea of rule of, in early Greek cosmology, 212–13, 214–15, 221–2, 224; codification of laws, 223–4; use of evidence in, 429
leaves, 317–18, 348 n. 2, 371–2
Le Blond, J. M., 272 n. 1, 287 n. 3
legends, referred to in arguments from analogy, 385–7
Lémery, 361 n.
Leophanes, 50 n. 2, 73

man, considered as norm of living creature, 54–5, 296–7; exemplifies distinction between right and left, 55; Protagoras' doctrine of man as the measure, 123 n. 1, 394–5; definition of, reached by method of division, 154–9; Anaximander on origin of, 323 n. 1

many, *see* one/many

Maori beliefs, 42 n. 4, 47 n. 2

market, comparison with, in Democritus' account of winds, 340

marrow, 253, 278, 369 n. 1

matter or material cause, 264, 275, 279, 285–9, 291, 369

measurement of length, system of, 185 and n. 2, 186

Mechanics, On, analyses circular motion into two rectilinear motions, 269 n. 1

Meleager, story of, 386

Melissus, analyses apparent change partly in terms of opposites, 19; arguments against plurality, 109–10, 431–2; on the evidence of the senses, 122–3; idea of necessity in, 422–3; idea of impossibility in, 423

membrane, 249, 325–7, 346, 347

memory, Aristotle's account of, 374–5

Menon, a source of the account of Greek medical theories in *Anonymus Londinensis*, 19 n. 2

menses, 58, 59 and n. 2, 71, 349, 369 and n. 2, 370

Meru, 33, 41

Mesopotamia, religious beliefs, 194; attitude towards nature and society, 211

metallurgy, ideas derived from, 208, 274, 278, 334–5, 347, 354 n. 1, 376, 381, 382

metaphor, distinguished from literal use of term, 192–3; in Plato's cosmology, 225–7, 284; Aristotle on the use of, 404–5

meteorites, 339

μετεωρολογία, scope defined by Aristotle, 13 n.

microcosm and macrocosm analogies, 235–6, 252–3, 267, 295–6

milk, referred to in Alcmaeon's account of eggs, 324; Empedocles' account of, 335; account of secretion of, in *On the Nature of the Child*, 350; Aristotle's account of, 369 n. 2; *see also* curdling

Milky Way, 314

Mill, J. S., 173–4

Mimnermus, 322 n. 1

mind, in Xenophanes, 219, 273 n. 3; in Empedocles, 210; in Anaxagoras 219–21, 225, 244, 246, 250–1, 298

mist, *see* ἀήρ

Miwok, 34, 95

mixture, different illustrations of, in Empedocles, 335 n. 1; Aristotle on different modes of, 376–7, 382

modelling, ideas derived from, 277 and n. 3, 285–6, 366–7

μοῖρα, in Homer and Hesiod, 198 and n.; in Parmenides, 216; in Anaxagoras' physical theory, 244–7, 338

monstrosities, *see* deformities

moon, antithesis between sun and, 32, 40, 84, 88–9; Heraclitus on, 322; Anaxagoras on, 339

mortal/immortal, antithesis between, 42, 48; as polar expression, 91–2; in Heraclitus, 101 n. 1; in Plato, 23; as example of the use of division, 154, 156

moving cause, *see* efficient cause

myths, referred to in analogical arguments, 385–7; Plato's use of, 226, 400 n. 2

nature, and convention, 124–5, 211, 225–6; and society, distinguished, 211, 227 and n., 299, 415; Aristotle on nature, 264, 275 n. 2, 285–90, 292–3, 298, 366; Aristotle on natural motion, 259–60, 263–5, 268–9, 271 and n. 2

necessity, in Heraclitus, 214; in Parmenides' *Way of Truth*, 216–17; in Plato, 256, 283 n. 1; conditional, in Aristotle, 288; development of idea of logical necessity, 422–3

Needham, J., 35

Needham, R., 33, 38 n. 1, 39 n. 4, 41

Neugebauer, O., 269 n. 3

Newton, 269 and n. 1

night, symbolic associations in early Greek literature, 42–3; in Hesiod's *Theogony*, 43, 204–5; in Pythagoreans, 16, 49, 95; in Parmenides' cosmology, 16, 57, 63, 81, 216–17, 242

Nile, Diogenes' account of summer flooding of, 337 n. 1; Herodotus on course of, 342–5; Herodotus on summer flooding of, 344 n. 1, 429

Nimuendaju, C., 32, 89

North/South winds, 66; pathological theories referring to, 22 and n. 2, 348 n. 2, 358 n. 3; in Aristotle's theory of winds, 362

Nuer, 37 n. 2, 40, 42 n. 4, 272 n. 2

Nun, Egyptian myth of, 307 and n. 3

nutrition, growth and, Alcmaeon on, 324; *On Diseases* IV on, 347, 350–1; *On the Nature of the Child* on, 351; Aristotle on, 25–6, 26 n. 1, 367 n., 368

oar, in Anaximenes' account of lightning, 315–16

oath, in Empedocles, 218–19, 228–9, 300

odd/even, in Pythagoreans, 16, 49, 95–6; in Plato, 49 n. 4; as example of
correct division, 149, 158; in pathological theory of critical days, 22

Ogle, W., 53 n. 1, 153 n. 2

oil, Aristotle on, 77; test with hide soaked in, in *On the Nature of the Child*,
350; evaporated with water in test in *On Diseases* IV, 350

Olympian gods, 42, 46 and n., 48, 49 n. 4, 193–5, 199–200, 204; *see also*
gods

omens, *see* divination

ὅμοιος, use of Greek term, 109, 110 n., 129–31, 433 n. 2, 434 n. 2

one/many, in Pythagoreans, 16; in the arguments of Zeno, 107–8; in
Melissus, 109; dilemmas involving, 112–13; in Gorgias, 117–19,
120; Plato on, 112 and n. 2, 144, 433; in Aristotle, 64 n. 2, 230

Onians, R. B., 188 n. 1, 192, 198 n., 207 n. 3

opposites, Greek terms for, 126 n. 2; Aristotle's terms for, 164 n. 3

ὄψις ἀδήλων τὰ φαινόμενα, 338–41, 343, 353

order, notion of, in early Greek cosmologies, 212–13, 215, 224–6, 229–30,
256, 277, 283, 289 and n. 2, 297–9, 415–16

organism, living, as model for cosmos, 234–6, 238, 249, 252–3, 254–7, 295,
416; compared with state, 295 and n.

painter, mixing of four roots compared to work of, in Empedocles, 335
n. 1; Nature compared to, in Aristotle, 285

Pandora, myth of, 42, 208, 272, 293 n. 2, 298

paradigm, in Plato, 397–403; in Aristotle, 405–8, 411, 418–19

paradox, in Heraclitus, 101–2; in Gorgias, 118–19; arising from arguments concerning nature and convention, 125 n. 2

Parmenides

theory of differentiation of sexes, 17, 50 and n. 1; on difference in
temperature between the sexes, 58

Way of Seeming: cosmology based on light and night, 16, 19, 36, 81, 217;
other opposites in, 57 and n. 2, 63 n.; as third way, 104; idea of
justice in, 217; idea of Eros in, 242 and n. 1, 297; account of
heavenly bodies, 322

Way of Truth: it is and it is not as mutually exclusive and exhaustive
alternatives in, 103–6, 111, 431–2; rejects change, 105–6, 241–2;
opposes reason to senses, 122, 338; Fr. 7 criticised by Plato, 143;
idea of justice in, 216–17; idea of necessity in, 216–17, 422; idea of
fate in, 216–17, 422; idea of impossibility in, 423

pathology, *see* diseases

Peck, A. L., 142 n. 1, 245 n. 1, 370 n. 1

personification, in early Greek thought, 200–4

Petron of Aegina, 19 n. 2

Plato (*cont.*)

contradictory, 146–8; use of method of division, 149–52, 432–3; gives examples of correct divisions, 149, 157–8; distinguishes myths and images from demonstrations, 226, 300, 394–5, 400; use of arguments from analogy, 389–403; account of the use of paradigms, 397–400; points out the need to verify conclusions of certain analogies, 397, 400–1; use of myths, 400 n. 2; theory of collection, 402, 410, 432; idea of logical necessity, 423; distinguishes substance and attribute, 430; indicates that universal affirmative statements are not convertible, 430–1; on mistaking resemblance for identity, 433 n. 2

on his predecessors: on Parmenides' doctrine of what is not, 143; criticises empirical methods used in acoustics, 428

psychology: doctrine of soul, 254, 283–4, 391–2, 394, 397, 401; on the world-soul, 254–7; on bad souls, 256–7; on how the soul of the sun moves its body, 257

Platt, A., 59 n. 1, 366 n.

πνεῦμα, 77, 235–6, 348 n. 2, 351, 352 n., 358, 362

polar expressions, 90–4

pores, in Empedocles' theory of respiration, 328–9; in *On Breaths*, 346; Aristotle's criticism of theory of, 167–8

Poseidon, relationship with Zeus, 198–9; connected with sea, 199–200; connected with earthquakes, 203 and n. 3, 308–9

pottery, manufacture of, 77 n. 1; ideas derived from, 208, 272 n. 2, 278, 285, 354 n. 1

Praxagoras, 10 n. 2

precession of the equinoxes, discovery of, 269 n. 3

'pre-logical' mentality, Lévy-Bruhl's conception of, 3–6

πρηστήρ, 313 n., 314 n.

primitive thought, 32–41, 67, 88–90, 176–80, 208–9, 272 n. 2

probability, conception of, 424–5; distinguished from proof by Plato, 394–5

projectiles, 269, 272 n. 1, 364, 374–5

proportion, in Aristotle's theory of generation, 368–9; in his theory of colours and music, 377

proportional analogy, 175; in Aristotle, 409 and n. 2

proposition, distinguished from sentence by Aristotle, 161 n. 2

Protagoras, problem of false statement connected with, 114; on sense-perception, 123; doctrine of man the measure, 123 n. 1, 394–5

providence, 248 n. 2, 416 n.

psychology: concrete images for psychological phenomena in early Greek literature, 188–9; comparisons in Aristotle's psychological theories, 374–7, 379–80

Purum, 33 n.

putrefaction, 335 n. 2, 371

Pythagoreans, poverty of information about, 9, 294; theory of opposites, 16, 36, 48–9, 56, 63–4, 94–6; ἀκούσματα, 49 n. 3; identification of things with numbers, 95 and n. 2; unit as even-odd, 95 n. 1; notions of seed and inhalation in Pythagorean cosmology, 237–8; doctrine of transmigration of souls, 240, 254

rain, 47 n. 1, 82 n. 1, 371, 373–4

rainbow, Xenophanes on, 321; Anaxagoras on, 339 n. 3

Ranulf, S., 103 n. 1

rare/dense, 17, 82 and n. 1; in Anaximenes, 17 n. 1; in Parmenides, 57; in Anaxagoras, 57; in Aristotle, 64 and n. 2

Raven, J. E., 11, 108 n. 1, 181 n. 2, 218 n. 3, 238 nn. 1–2, 244 n. 1, 245 n. 2, 246 n. 1

Read, J., 84

reason, and sensation, controversies concerning, 122–4; and true opinion, in Plato, 132–3; cosmic, in Plato, 220–1, 255–6, 282–4, 297–8, 300, 401

recollection, Plato's theory of, 402 n. 1, 432

reductio ad impossibile arguments, in Aristotle, 165–6

Regenbogen, O., 306 n. 1

Reinhardt, K., 235 n. 3

religious polarity, Hertz's conception of, 37–41

rennet, 369–70

repletion and depletion, pathological theories based on ideas of, 20–1, 24 n. 1, 70, 345 n. 2

residues, Aristotle's theory of, 59, 363–4, 367, 369 n. 2, 371, 373–4

respiration, accounts of, in Empedocles, 328–33; in Plato, 360; in Aristotle, 26 and n. 2, 373 and n., 382; of embryo, in *On the Nature of the Child*, 348 n. 2

rest, and movement or change, antithesis between, in Pythagoreans, 16, 96; in Empedocles' *Purifications*, 63 n.; in Plato's *Sophist*, 142–5

Rey, A., 4

Reymond, A., 4

right and left, in primitive thought, 33, 37–41, 47 n. 2; in Chinese thought, 35, 39 n. 3, 51; symbolic associations for ancient Greeks, 42, 47 and n. 2

in Pythagoreans, 16, 48–9, 49 n. 3, 56, 95; in Parmenides, 17, 50, 56; in Anaxagoras, 17, 50, 56; in Hippocratic treatises, 22–3, 50 and n. 1; in Leophanes, 50 n. 2, 73; in Plato, 49, 55 n. 3; in Aristotle, 26, 51–5, 61, 64 and n. 1, 73–4, 261; in Galen, 50 n. 2

499

war, Heraclitus' notion of, 97, 100, 214–15, 219, 221–2, 297
water, antithesis between earth and, 89–90; in Thales, 57 n. 3, 306–9; in
    Xenophanes, 81; in Heraclitus, 236–7; one of Empedocles' four
    roots, 16, 217, 274; in Anaxagoras, 245 n. 2; in *On Regimen* I, 19–20,
    58–9, 60 n. 1, 252; a humour, in *On Diseases* IV, 346, 350; one of
    Philistion's elements, 19 n. 2; one of the simple bodies, in Plato, 278,
    360–1; in Aristotle, 25, 76–7
water-animals, Empedocles on, 18, 71–2; division of animals into land
    and water animals, 154 and n. 2, 155 n. 1
wax, 350, 352, 374
wax-modeller, 277, 293
Webster, T. B. L., 319 n.
wheels, in Anaximander's theory of heavenly bodies, 312–15
whirl, 250 and n. 1
white/black, symbolic associations of, 43, 46 and n., 49 and n. 3, 89; in
    Alcmaeon, 16; in Aristotle's theory of colours, 376–7
wickerwork, 286, 366
Wilamowitz-Moellendorff U. von, 90 n.
Wilson, J. A., 202 n. 2, 272 n. 2, 307 n. 1, 322 n. 2
winds, addressed in prayers in Homer, 203; in Hesiod's *Theogony*, 204;
    cause lightning and thunder, according to Anaximander and
    Anaximenes, 315–17; Democritus on, 340; Aristotle on, 263 n. 2,
    344, 362, 381; *see also* North/South
wine, 77, 335 n. 2, 348 n. 2, 350 n. 1, 358 n. 3, 371
wine-skins, used by Empedocles and Anaxagoras to show corporeality of
    air, 331–2, 339
winged/wingless, division between, in classifications of animals, 154 and
    n. 2, 155 n. 1, 158 n., 159
Winnebago, 31 n. 2
womb, theory that males and females conceived in different parts of, 17,
    50–1, 73–4; theory that size of, determines size of embryo, 348; *On
    Ancient Medicine* on, 355
women, belief in inferiority of, 42 and n. 3, 59 and n. 2; connected with
    evil, 42 and n. 4, 48–9; Plato's doctrine that women should have
    the same education as men, 140–1
'woody bodies', 335
wool, referred to in test in *On Diseases of Women* I, 349, 352

Xeniades, 113, 123
Xenophanes, earth and water as origin of living things, 81; on god,
    92 n. 2, 219, 273 n. 3; rejects anthropomorphism, 194, 210; astro-
    nomical and meteorological theories, 321 and n. 1; on limitations of

Xenophanes (*cont.*)
  human knowledge, 337; distinguishes knowledge from mere opinion, 425; uses evidence of fossils, 427

yawning, account of, in *On Breaths*, 345–6
yeast, referred to in Aristotle's account of growth of fishes' eggs, 368
Yin and Yang, 35, 39 and n. 3, 84
young/old, 45 and n. 4, 60 n. 1, 66 and n. 2, 91, 98, 100–1, 374–5

Zeno of Citium, 416 n.
Zeno of Elea, 18–19; arguments against plurality, 107–8, 118, 125; idea of necessity in, 422–3
Zeus, as supreme god in Homer, 196–200, 213, 218, 225, 291, 297–8; relationship with Poseidon and Hades, 198–9, 218; bound by oaths, 198–9; and fate, 198 n.; connection with sky and celestial phenomena, 199–200, 202, 208; Hesiod's account of how Zeus acquired power, 199; role of, in myth of Pandora, 208–9, 293 n. 2; law and justice the gifts of, in Hesiod, 227 n.
Zuñi, 34, 39 and n. 2